ANNUAL REVIEW OF
PUBLIC HEALTH

EDITORIAL COMMITTEE (1994)

ANNUAL REVIEW OF PUBLIC HEALTH

VOLUME 15, 1994

GILBERT S. OMENN, *Editor*

University of Washington

JONATHAN E. FIELDING, *Associate Editor*

University of California at Los Angeles

LESTER B. LAVE, *Associate Editor*

Carnegie Mellon University

ANNUAL REVIEWS INC.   4139 EL CAMINO WAY   P.O. BOX 10139   PALO ALTO, CALIFORNIA 94303-0897

ANNUAL REVIEWS INC.
Palo Alto, California, USA

International Standard Serial Number: 0163–7525
International Standard Book Number: 0–8243–2715-2

Typesetting by Kachina Typesetting Inc., Tempe, Arizona; John Olson, President; Jeannie Kaarle, Typesetting Coordinator; and by the Annual Reviews Inc. Editorial Staff

PRINTED AND BOUND IN THE UNITED STATES OF AMERICA

PREFACE

In the United States, we expect 1994 to be a watershed year in the development of medical care and public health policy and reform of health services throughout the country. The President and the Congress are finally ready to grapple with the need for universal access with a credible plan for cost containment *and* emphasis on prevention. Most key players recognize that prevention—or health promotion and disease prevention—requires a complementary investment in population-oriented, community-based programs (public health) and in office- or clinic-based-preventive services (preventive medicine). Implementation beginning in 1995, at least in vanguard states, would support the long-cycle theory of major advances in public policy—with Social Security in 1935, Medicare and Medicaid in 1965, and Health Care Reform in 1995!

This volume of the *Annual Review of Public Health* sustains our commitment to commission timely articles that embrace the multiple disciplines of public health and the interaction of academic public health and public health practice in the U.S. and internationally. We encourage the reader to explore topics throughout the five sections of the book—Epidemiology/Biostatistics, Public Health Practice, Behavioral Aspects of Health, Health Services, and Environmental/Occupational. Many articles could be listed in more than one section; the assignment reflects the orientation of the article and the disciplines of the authors. We recommend that readers note the many still-timely articles in previous volumes of the *Annual Review*; please note the cumulative table of contents at the end of the volume.

The breadth of public health creates a dilemma for the public health professional. Being expert often requires the sort of specialization common in medicine, biology, and toxicology. Yet, the public health professional must be reasonably knowledgeable about a full range of public health issues, and so should academics!

The *Annual Review of Public Health* is designed to address this dilemma. Our authors provide review articles across the breadth of public health. While no one annual can cover all topics, we manage to cover the range every few years. And for specialists, the chapters provide a thoughtful interpretation by other experts of the issues and latest research in that topic.

There is much excitement in public health about the maturing or changing paradigm of our practice and our educational and research missions. The section on Public Health Practice presents views from two schools of public health, as well as a local health department and CDC view of the path to realization of *Healthy People 2000* goals and objectives. Knowledge about health services for special populations must be incorporated into health care

(Continued)   v

reform decisions and especially into transition schemes for the implementation of universal access to private medical care. Articles here on Latino populations, veterans, Head Start, people with disabilities, victims of child abuse, underinsured Americans, and vulnerable populations underline the message that we cannot simply jump to vouchers that treat all Americans as equally able to utilize "the system". Environmental and behavioral influences impairing or capable of improving health status receive major attention here, too. Integration of these approaches with clinical services is essential to the common goals of complementary reform of medical care and public health programs.

GILBERT S. OMENN
JONATHAN E. FIELDING
LESTER B. LAVE

Annual Review of Public Health
Volume 15 (1994)

CONTENTS

(Continued)   vii

SOME RELATED ARTICLES IN OTHER *ANNUAL REVIEWS*

From the *Annual Review of Genetics*, Volume 27 (1993):

> *Imprinting the Genome: Imprinted Genes, Imprinting Genes, and a Hypothesis for their Interaction*, C. Sapienza and K. Paterson
>
> *Mapping Polygenes*, S. D. Tanksley
>
> *Genetic Epidemiology*, N. E. Morton

From the *Annual Review of Medicine*, Volume 45 (1994):

> *Metabolic Interactions of Diabetes and Pregnancy*, T. A. Buchanan and J. L. Kitzmiller
>
> *Pathogenesis and Host Response in* Pneumocystis carinii *Pneumonia*, T. H. Su and W. J. Martin
>
> *Malaria, The Red Cell, and the Endothelium*, B. L. Pasloske and R. J. Howard
>
> *Factors Affecting Outcome After Recovery from Myocardial Infarction*, K. S. Woo and H. D. White
>
> *Prostate Carcinoma*, G. L. Andriole and W. J. Catalona
>
> *Use and Abuse of Human Growth Hormone*, E. K. Neely and R. G. Rosenfeld
>
> *Male Sex Determination: Current Concepts of Male Sex Differentiation*, M. L. Gustafson and P. K. Donahoe

From the *Annual Review of Nutrition*, Volume 14 (1994):

> *Organic Substrate and Electrolyte Solutions for Oral Rehydration in Diarrhea*, J. F. Desjeux, S. K. Nath, and J. Taminiau
>
> *The Role of Iron-Binding Proteins in the Survival of Pathogenic Bacteria*, T. A. Mietzner and S. A. Morse
>
> *Nutritional Role of Resistant Starch: Chemical Structure vs Physiological Function*, G. Annison and D. L. Topping
>
> *Dietary Polyunsaturated Fatty Acid Regulation of Gene Transcription*, S. D. Clarke and D. B. Jump
>
> *Diet, Body Build, and Breast Cancer*, D. J. Hunter and W. C. Willett

From the *Annual Review of Psychology*, Volume 45 (1994):

> *Health Psychology: Why Do Some People Get Sick and Some Stay Well?* N. Adler and K. Matthews

From the *Annual Review of Sociology*, Volume 20 (1994):

Annu. Rev. Public Health. 1994. 15:1–18

SHARING STATISTICAL DATA IN THE BIOMEDICAL AND HEALTH SCIENCES: Ethical, Institutional, Legal, and Professional Dimensions

Stephen E. Fienberg

Department of Statistics, Carnegie Mellon University Pittsburgh, Pennsylvania 15213

KEY WORDS: archives, data access, journal data policies, ownership of data, research data as public good

INTRODUCTION

A 1992 report issued from the National Research Council observes: "The general norms of science emphasize the principle of openness. Scientists are generally expected to exchange research data as well as unique research materials that are essential to the replication or extension of reported findings." (34). While these norms have been acknowledged over centuries, the actual practice of sharing research data has varied widely even within individual disciplines, and until recently it has rarely been instantiated in the form of specific rules and formal mechanisms. Recent technological changes have given new meaning to access to research data, and scientists are questioning whether the principle of scientific openness actually requires providing access to their own research data. What has emerged is the notion of research data as a public good, irrespective of the source of funding for the research. In essence, there appears to be general agreement that research data become a public good when the research results enter into the public domain through publication or formal presentation in some scientific or public policy forum.

1

0163-7525/94/0510-0001$05.00

Over the past decade, there has been a shift in attitudes and practice regarding the sharing of data among health professionals and researchers and a growing recognition regarding its importance. This shift has been linked in part to allegations of scientific misconduct and data misrepresentation and in part to public pressure for greater accountability by universities and research institutions. In this paper, we review key elements of data sharing in the health sciences and focus on some unresolved issues. We begin by reviewing the benefits and costs that accrue from the sharing of research data originally outlined in a 1985 report prepared by the Committee on National Statistics, and then we turn to developments specific to data gathered and analyzed by health professionals and researchers, looking separately at the perspectives from government funding agencies, data archives, professional organizations and journals, institutions, and the courts. We conclude with a reminder that the modern infrastructure of computer networking, now so much taken for granted, and the availability of cheap mass storage have removed many major barriers to data sharing that existed only a decade ago.

BENEFITS AND COSTS OF DATA SHARING

In 1985, the Committee on National Statistics released a report on sharing research data, with a special focus on social science data (17). In the ensuing debate, there was widespread sentiment among reviewers that the recommendations and discussion are more broadly applicable, in particular to research data arising in the biomedical and health sciences. Indeed, several appendices to the report deal with examples from these areas.

The report highlighted many widely agreed upon benefits of sharing research data, noting that sharing data:

reinforces open scientific inquiry

encourages a diversity of analyses and conclusions

permits (a) reanalyses to verify or refute reported results, (b) alternative analyses to refine results, (c) analyses to check if the results are robust to varying assumptions

promotes new research and allows for the testing of new or alternative theories and methods

encourages appropriate use of empirical studies in public policy formulation and evaluation through independent critiques and reviews

serves to improve methods of data collection and measurement through the scrutiny of others

encourages alternative perspectives, especially those from other disciplines

avoids the expense of duplicative data collection by others, thereby reducing
   the burden of data collection on human subjects
respects the desires of respondents and other subjects to contribute to
   societal knowledge
serves to protect against faulty data, whether inadvertently distorted or
   willfully fabricated
provides a resource for training in research.

Balancing these benefits are various costs. In particular, the Committee's
report noted that those requesting access to data need to address the costs
involved in surmounting technical obstacles, such as incompatibilities of
data formats associated with different hardware and software systems;
providing adequate documentation and explanation so others may use data
in an informed manner; storing, reproducing, and transferring data.

In many ways the technological changes that have occurred in the
intervening years, especially those associated with networked computing,
have reduced most of the technical obstacles, but the issues of documentation
and explanation remain and they are often expensive, especially when
advanced provision has not been made.

There are also more problematic costs. The following charges must
ultimately be borne solely by the sharer who allows others access to his or
her data:

responding to discovery of errors by others
reacting to unwarranted criticism based on poorly done analyses by others
foregoing the exclusive right to future discoveries that others may make
   and/or for which they may receive credit
breaching confidentiality of responses or prior agreements regarding limiting
   of access to data.

In weighing these costs and benefits of data sharing, the Committee
arrived at a primary recommendation based on what it took to be the ethical
imperatives of researchers seeking to publish their results in the open
scientific literature: *Sharing data should be a regular practice.*

The Committee's remaining recommendations were organized according
to the different parties involved. In particular, the Committee recommended
that

Initial investigators should share their data by the time of the publication
   of initial major results of analyses of the data except in compelling
   circumstances, and they should share data relevant to public policy
   quickly and as widely as possible. Moreover, plans for data sharing
   should be an integral part of a research plan whenever data sharing is

feasible. Finally, investigators should keep data available for a reasonable period after the publication of results from analyses of the data.

Subsequent analysts who request data from others should bear the associated incremental costs and they should endeavor to keep the burdens of data sharing to a minimum. They should explicitly acknowledge the contribution of the initial investigators in all subsequent publications.

Funding organizations should encourage data sharing by careful consideration and review of plans to do so in applications for research funding. In particular, those organizations funding the collection of large-scale, general-purpose data sets should be alert to the need for data archives and consider encouraging them where a significant need is not being met.

Editors of scientific journals should require authors to provide access to data during the peer review process, should give more emphasis to reports of secondary analyses and to replications. These reports must give full credit and appropriate citations to original data collections. Finally, editors should strongly encourage authors to make detailed data accessible to other researchers.

Institutions and organizations through which scientists are rewarded should recognize the contributions of appropriate data-sharing practices.

THE RESPONSE TO DEMANDS FOR DATA ACCESS AND SHARING

The efforts of a number of scientists to establish the practice of sharing data as a scientific norm during the 1980s would likely have had limited results but for a number of celebrated cases of fraud and scientific misconduct that captured the attention of Congress, university officials, and the national media (24). Although few in number, these cases consumed a disproportionate amount of time and effort on the part of scientists, administrators, editors, reporters, members of Congress and their staffs, and revealed the inadequacies of policies and regulations related to scientific misconduct. As a result, federal funding agencies have begun to establish mechanisms to review allegations of misconduct (5, 19).

Since several celebrated scientific misconduct cases involved allegations of falsification or misrepresentation of data, the issues of data access and data sharing were keenly debated at conferences, workshops, and studies, and in these forums the data sharing recommendations of the Committee on National Statistics, outlined in the preceding section, received considerable attention. We report here on the responses of various parties responsible for setting standards for access to data or for responding to situations where access was a fundamental issue.

Government Funding Agencies

In 1990, the National Institutes of Health issued guidelines (29) for its intramural research programs that included the following statement:

> Research data, including primary experimental results, should be retained for a sufficient period to allow analysis and repetition by others of published material from those data. In some fields five or seven years are specified as the minimum period of retention but this may vary under different circumstances. ... [E]ach paper should contain all of the information that would be necessary for the scientific peers of the authors to repeat the experiments. This principle requires that any ... unpublished data ... that are essential for repetition of the published experiments be made available to other qualified scientists.

The NIH does not yet have an overarching policy regarding access to data from extramural grants and contracts, although Representative Ted Weiss did introduce a bill, the NIH Grants Research Integrity Amendments of 1991 (H.R. 1819), that had two notable data-sharing features. First, Section 3 would have required all data and materials relevant to an NIH-supported biomedical or behavioral research project to be made available to other researchers for a five-year period, beginning on the earlier of (*a*) the date on which the research findings are published in a scientific journal, (*b*) three years after the data when NIH financial assistance ends. Special exceptions relate to data confidentiality. The obligation here falls on the institutional recipient of the funds. Following the five-year period, the obligations for data sharing were to remain until the data are destroyed or otherwise leave the institution. Second, Section 4 would have required the Secretary of the Department of Health and Human Services to establish recommendations regarding the timely dissemination of any research results with any clinical application to a disease or disorder that is a significant threat to the public health, including the publication of such results in scientific journals.

This bill was referred to the House Committee on Energy and Commerce but was never reported out of Committee. While this specific bill may not necessarily be introduced again, others in Congress clearly support providing NIH with a specific mandate for scientific integrity that would include data sharing. In the meantime, individual institutes within the NIH have developed specific policies on the release of research data. For example, the National Institute on Aging cooperates with ICPSR in the preparation and maintenance of archival files as noted below.

A very different example, relating to constraints on data sharing, comes from the National Heart, Lung, and Blood Institute (NHLBI), which includes a clause in its contracts for multicenter clinical trials to the effect that:

> Written advance notice of at least 45 days will be provided to the Contracting Officer of the Contractor's intent to release findings of studies or research which have the possibility of adverse effects on the public or the Federal agency. If the Contracting Officer does not pose any objections in writing within the 45-day period, the contractor may proceed with disclosure.

The NHLBI claims that the intent of this clause is not so much to restrict publication of results and the release of data, but rather to assure that publication represents the collective judgment of all collaborators in the trial. Stanford University recently objected to the inclusion of this clause in the contract for a major clinical trail and lost the contract as a consequence. Stanford then filed a lawsuit against the NIH (13), and a Federal District Court Judge ordered the contract reinstated, noting that the degree of restriction in the clause was a violation of First Amendment rights and thus was unconstitutional (2).

In 1989, the Director of the National Science Foundation (NSF), Erich Bloch, issued a notice on the conduct of research (32) that included the following statement:

> The NSF advocates and encourages open scientific communication. The NSF expects ... investigators to share with other researchers, at no more than incremental cost and within a reasonable time, the primary data, samples, physical collections, and other supporting materials created or gathered in the course of the research.

Within the Social Science Directorate of NSF, this policy has led to a requirement for grantees to deliver data with adequate documentation to some designated archive within one year of project completion. (For a discussion of the NSF policy and other social science examples of requirements for data sharing, see ref. 40.)

The Development of Health-Related Research Archives

In the area of public health, there is a long tradition of public use files from national surveys, stimulated by the policy of the US National Center for Health Statistics (NCHS) to make available public use tapes from its major national surveys such as the National Health Interview Survey (NHIS). Recent data releases from the NHIS and other NCHS surveys are currently available from the Inter-university Consortium on Political and Social Research (ICPSR) at the University of Michigan, Ann Arbor. Many of the ICPSR health data files are available directly by network file transfers to scientists at member institutions, as well as on traditional media such as magnetic tape, diskette, and CD-ROM.

The ICPSR holdings in the area of public health are not restricted to public use files from government surveys. The National Archive of Computerized Data on Aging (NACDA), established in 1988, is located within

ICPSR and includes research data files specific to the study of aging, from both the public and private sectors. Hawthorne (21) describes this effort and illustrates its value by reference to the Tecumseh Community Health Study, 1959–1969, which has led to approximately 450 peer-reviewed scientific articles. He notes that

> the "owners" of data-sets like Tecumseh, the Lipids Clinical trials, MRFIT, Framingham, HDFP, and many more are reluctant to relinquish hold on what they have come to regard as their private property; yet each could benefit greatly from the activities of secondary analysts without any infringement on current and projected in-house studies.

Other health-related archives include the Data Archive on Adolescent Pregnancy and Pregnancy Prevention (8) established in 1982 by the US Office of Population Affairs.

The Response of Professional Organizations and Journals

Despite these formal archival efforts, the tradition of sharing health research data widely is still in its infancy. The Committee on Data Sharing of the Society for Epidemiologic Research, in an unpublished report (1992), has made a thoughtful attempt to weigh the concerns of epidemiologists concerned about data sharing and to provide positive guidance to epidemiologists regarding when and how to share their data (placing a special emphasis on confidentiality and individual identifiers).

The Committee on Radiation Epidemiological Programs at the National Research Council (10) has also addressed the special issues of confidentiality and privacy arising when an epidemiological study focuses on a rare condition, such as toxic shock syndrome or Reye's syndrome, where the release of seemingly innocuous background variables might be sufficient to allow the identification of specific individuals. The Committee was concerned with occupational exposure to ionized radiation and took special note of the fact that the reconstruction of exposure histories or the consideration of alternative outcome measurements can typically not be done without the identification of individuals. Thus, data sharing in such contexts must presume some trust in work of the original investigators to construct appropriate data on exposure for subsequent secondary analysis. Statistical techniques for preserving confidentiality (14, 16) are now in widespread use and are appropriate for application to such epidemiological data before they are shared.

The Committee discussion of data access was a backdrop to its own recommendation regarding the data from the Department of Energy's controversial epidemiological research program, which collected and analyzed occupational health data on the contractors' workers at the Department's production nuclear facilities who may have been exposed to low-dose irradiation. (The lawsuit brought to gain access to the data on approximately 270,000 workers is described below.) The Committee recommended that the formal archives being developed by the Department for these data be made accessible to interested parties, subsequent to modifications to preserve confidentiality. Further, the Committee recommended that all plans for further analyses of these data and proposals for [related] epidemiological studies should include a schedule for data access and effective data sharing (10). This particular initiative is of special interest because the data were originally collected for administrative monitoring rather than for research. Concurrent with the Committee's report the Department of Energy transferred oversight of its analytical studies involving these data to the Department of Health and Human Services, thereby reinforcing the separation of administrative and research uses of the data.

Among the professional organizations to have sponsored symposia and sessions on the topic of data sharing are the American Association for the Advancement of Science, the American Statistical Association, the Industrial Epidemiology Forum Conference on Ethics in Epidemiology, the US Public Health Service, and the Society for Clinical Trials. Various professional and scholarly associations have also adopted policies on data sharing. In addition to the position of the Committee of the Society for Epidemiologic Research described above, we take special note of the position of the American Sociological Association, whose 1982 Code of Ethics mandates data sharing, even though the implementation of this mandate in the association's own journals has proven to be problematic (4, 20).

Other journals have adopted policies on access to research data used in published analyses, e.g. *Accounting Review, American Economic Review, Journal of Business and Economic Statistics, Journal of Personality and Social Psychology* (1). A specialized journal dealing in part with issues of data access, *Accountability in Research: Policies and Quality Assurance*, began publication in the late 1980s. Finally, in the field of public health, *American Journal of Public Health* now explicitly requires that primary data be shared with editors and other researchers (11).

The Response of Institutions Carrying Out Research

While all American universities and research institutes are required, in effect, to have research policies in compliance with specifications set out by federal funding agencies such as the National Science Foundation and the National Institutes of Health, most institutional policies deal with issues of scientific misconduct and few explicitly address the issues associated with the ownership of and access to research data. Such issues are rarely addressed specifically in intellectual property policies either.

To give some notion of the issues that must be addressed in institutional policies, we ask a series of oft-recurring questions, drawn in part from (41), and we follow each question with a vignette illustrative of a data dispute.

Are data from funded research controlled by the investigator, by the research institution, or by the funder?   In 1989, at Michigan State University, a professor of microbiology in the Colleges of Veterinary and Osteopathic Medicine dismissed a Ph.D. student for insubordinate behavior. The student then removed tissue samples and data on which she had been working from the professor's laboratory. The professor considered these materials to be the common property of a project funded by NIH on which he and the student had been working. The professor actually persuaded the student to return some of the material, but not all. Somehow the university obtained the rest of the data but did not return them to the professor. The Professor sought the intervention of NIH's Office of Scientific Integrity (OSI), but it responded by referring him back to local law enforcement authorities and the university, which claimed that any data produced under contract with faculty members belong to the university (27). While this dispute was simmering, the student prepared a paper based on her analyses of the tissue samples and data and published it in *Tropical Medicine and Parasitology,* in June 1991, as the sole author. The professor then filed charges against the student and three faculty members who had helped her to publish the paper. In late 1992, an independent panel of inquiry reported that the student's actions deviated from accepted scientific practice and represented an act of scientific misconduct. The panel recommended that the university conduct a formal investigation of charges that the three faculty members assisted her in publishing the paper, and criticized the university for its handling of the entire matter (28).

Until quite recently the question Who owns the data? was typically not an issue and, if it was, the answer given was invariably "the researcher". As this case study suggests, the question does not necessarily have a clear-cut answer. Some university policies place ownership in the hands of the institution (12), but these policies are rarely designed to resolve disputes among colleagues or between faculty and students within institutions, let alone disputes that transcend institutional boundaries.

When should one obtain informed consent from subjects to share data they have provided? What if data were originally gathered for administrative purposes?   Sieber (39) provides the following instructive vignette: "An epidemiologist researched the effects of radiation-related symptoms in subjects and their offspring, under funding from the laboratory where the subjects were employed. She found a far higher than normal incidence of radiation-related disease. Two years later, administrators at the laboratory asked for the data, including the names of the subjects, ostensibly to carry out job-site research designed to increase occupational safety. The epidemiologist refused, explaining that she would not breach her promise of confidentiality to subjects. The laboratory administrators then proposed that employees be asked, individually, if they were willing for the employer to have their data. However, the epidemiologist was worried that the administrators might lay off employees who were identified in the data, on the grounds that subsequent illness would become costly to the laboratory."

When and in what form must data be released for sharing? In 1979, Herbert Needleman and colleagues at the Harvard Medical School published an article (31) showing that childhood exposure to environmental lead, as measured by lead levels in babies' teeth, was correlated with subsequent behavioral and intelligence deficits. The research findings were criticized by a number of authors, e.g. Ernhart, Landa & Schell (15), and some questioned the original statistical analysis. An examination of Needleman's work in 1984 by the Environmental Protection Agency (EPA) led to concerns about missing data and statistical methods, and the reviewers decided that the evidence was inconclusive. They also examined Ernhart's results and reached similar conclusions. Needleman responded to these reviews with further analyses. By the time the EPA panel reported its findings, it concurred with Needleman's original conclusions.

This might have been the end of the dispute over Needleman's data but for the fact that, in 1990, he testified about his findings in a lawsuit brought by the government against the former owners of a lead smelter. Ernhart and Sandra Scarr (who was one of the EPA reviewers especially critical of Needleman's methods) were scheduled to testify for the defendants and they asked for access to the data used in Needleman's 1979 study. Initially, he refused, but later allowed Ernhart and Scarr and the defense lawyers to examine six volumes of computer printout in his laboratory, but without any direct assistance from Needleman himself. In essence, data access, albeit briefly, was mandated because Needleman had become a party involved in the litigation.

When the case was settled, Ernhart and Scarr continued to battle for access to Needleman's data and filed a complaint with NIH's OSI (33). The University of Pittsburgh, where Needleman had subsequently moved, established a special review panel to examine the allegations of data and statistical improprieties and, at an open hearing in April, 1992, several experts testified about their reexamination of Needleman's analyses and their own reanalyses of his data. Their testimony was generally supportive, although they raised some questions about the appropriateness of his statistical methodology. By late 1992, the special panel appeared to have cleared Needleman of charges of scientific misconduct and he published his own account of the events (19). Before the NIH's OSI could report on the matter, however, Needleman filed suit to dismiss the entire matter (22).

Throughout this dispute, Needleman contended that the repeated requests for access to his raw data by Ernhart and Scarr were frivolous and a form of harassment. The public policy and legal implications of his research results, even though they are now 15 years old, are what makes the notion of data sharing in this example compelling. But it is not clear that any form of data sharing short of access to the raw data and computer printouts would have satisfied Ernhart and Scarr. And few researchers would want to turn over their raw materials and data to facilitate critics whose only goal appears to be embarrassing the original investigators. A compromise, even one in accord with the basic principals of data sharing outlined above, would not have satisfied either party in this instance.

In collaborative research with specialized scientific roles, who controls the data, who is responsible for their correctness, who orchestrates the sharing, and who is answerable to questions and criticism? In 1987, a group of researchers at the University of Pittsburgh published a paper in the *New England Journal of Medicine* (NEJM) on the efficacy of amoxicillin based on results from a randomized clinical trial (26). Prior to publication, the director of the research center carrying out the trial had criticized a draft of the manuscript prepared by the principal investigator and others working on the project. He ultimately withdrew his name from the manuscript and prepared an alternative analysis with two new coauthors, in which they reached a conclusion contradictory to the claim of efficacy in the original paper. They circulated this manuscript to the others involved in the trial and then they submitted this second paper for publication to the NEJM, making explicit reference to the original paper and to their disagreements with its authors. Officials from the University of Pittsburgh wrote to the NEJM stating that the authors of the second manuscript has acted without proper authority, at which point the editor of the NEJM returned the second manuscript to the authors without submitting it to peer review (7). A lengthy dispute extending over four years followed, involving allegations of conflict of interest and inappropriate scientific behavior. The dispute led to reviews by the NIH's OSI and by an appeals panel at the University of Pittsburgh. Ultimately, the second paper was published in the *Journal of the American Medical Association* (6) with an accompanying editorial explaining the actions of the Journal's editors (36):

In order to function coherently, institutions have to have commonly accepted modes of operation, and it is accepted that the principal investigator, for the pains of taking scientific, legal, and monetary responsibility, has first dibs on the data. But the problem with this is that the institution is unlikely to decide a dispute about the matter on the basis of the quality of the science, but on the basis of institutional hierarchy. Having the name of the principal author on a manuscript certainly does not guarantee that it is scientifically valid, or even that it is more valid than the studies that any of the other workers might publish . . .

Meetings arranged by OSI on data ownership and sharing over the last two years have shown that no one has a clear idea who owns data, let alone how to share them . . . If the principal investigator has had his or her chance, however, data should, after a reasonable time, become accessible to the public. In the present instance, plenty of time has passed. Moreover, Cantekin was not simply a member of the public, some outsider, but was research director at the [center] . . . Surely he has rights of publication too?

These basic questions about data access and the complex situations described in these case studies illustrate the need for careful institutional policies and regulations on data access. Such policies need: (a) to protect the rights of researchers and the institutions in which they work; (b) to provide clear guidance to researchers and students as to their responsibilities to share data in a timely fashion; (c) to be responsive to the requirements of funding agencies; and (d) to provide confidentiality protection for human subjects who provide data as study participants. Institutional Review Boards (IRBs) that have traditionally dealt with the prior review of studies involving human subjects may need to take a much greater interest in and responsibility for data sharing (39, 43).

The Response of the Courts

Throughout the 1980s the courts were, by and large, supportive of efforts to gain access to research data, and they have shown an increasing appreciation of the issue of data sharing as a scientific norm. We illustrate this trend with a brief description of four different lawsuits involving requests for data access. In general, such requests have typically involved attempts to use the Freedom of Information Act (FOIA) and standard legal requirements of expert witnesses involved in litigation to provide the bases for their expert opinion to opposing counsel.

In one of the early lawsuits (17a) brought under the FOIA, researchers sought access to data collected as part of a long-term study of the effectiveness of diabetes treatments, known as the University Group Diabetes Program (UDGP) and funded by the National Institute of Arthritis, Metabolism and Digestive Diseases. The data remained at all times in the control of UDGP scientists, whose publications from the studies indicated that certain drugs used to treat diabetes led to increased risk of death from cardiovascular disease. These results were challenged by a group of critics who sought to obtain access to the data under the FOIA. In 1980, the case ultimately reached the US Supreme Court, which denied these critics access to the UDGP data because it found that the FOIA did not confer any direct rights of public access to records developed by research grants. Cecil & Griffin (9) provide further details of this and other early attempts to use the FOIA for gaining access to research data. Several years later, when the pressures for data sharing had increased but actual interest in the UDGP results had diminished, the UDGP data were made generally available to other researchers.

Reye's syndrome is an extremely rare disease whose incidence was linked in the early 1980s with aspirin use by children suffering from chicken pox or flu. In 1984, the Centers for Disease Control provided funding for scientists at the Institute of Medicine to carry out a pilot study of 29 children with Reye's syndrome and 143 controls. This study found that children with chicken pox or flu who took aspirin had an increased risk of acquiring Reye's syndrome (with an observed odds ratio of 25). When the preliminary results were published (23), aspirin manufacturers sought access to the data with a FOIA request. Since the data were in the possession of a private contractor, by the earlier UDGP precedent, the data were not subject to disclosure under the Act. The manufacturers then sought the data directly from the Department of Health and Human Services (HHS) via subpoena. The private contractor who collected the data for the Institute of Medicine argued against their release because it could not guarantee its ability to maintain its promise of confidentiality to the subjects due to the rareness of the disease. The researchers had told the parents of the children in the study that no names, addresses, or other identifying information would be released. Ultimately the manufacturers, HHS, and the contractor entered into a court-approved protective order (4a) that allowed the manufacturers access to the data on condition that they would not contact study participants and that certain identifying information be removed (44).

A pair of studies coauthored by Selikoff of Mount Sinai Hospital in New York City (37, 38) claimed evidence for the multiplicative effect of smoking and asbestos exposure on the risk of developing cancer. Several years later, when the Selikoff studies were referred to by an expert witness in a lawsuit brought against several tobacco companies, the companies sought access to his raw research data and files. In 1987, a New York State Superior Court denied access on the grounds that the request was too sweeping and burdensome. In addition, the court noted that neither Selikoff nor his coauthors were witnesses in the litigation. Shortly thereafter, in connection with other lawsuits, the tobacco companies again sought access to Selikoff's data, but this time with a more specific request for only those data relied upon in the preparation of the articles, not the original research materials. This second request included a provision for the maintenance of confidentiality of the study participants, and with an offer to cover the costs of preparing the data to be shared. Mount Sinai Hospital and Selikoff argued that the process of redacting the data so as to ensure confidentiality would be burdensome (23b). This time a Federal Court ruled that Selikoff should release the data. The Court noted that it would not be necessary for Selikoff himself to do the redaction and that a scholar such as he should anticipate that others would wish to scrutinize the bases for his published work. This ruling was appealed by Selikoff and Mount Sinai Hospital, but the appellate court found no basis for reversal (23a).

The court's order to Selikoff could be thought of as being in accord with the principles and obligations of data sharing as articulated above, but such is not true for a more recent lawsuit. In 1991, Joseph DiFranza coauthored one of a trio of papers in the *Journal of the American Medical Association* on the response of children to advertisements for Camels brand cigarettes. In a suit brought in California against the maker of Camels, R.J. Reynolds Tobacco Co., alleging misleading advertising, the company subpoenaed the lead authors on all three studies to surrender all related research materials, including the names of the children interviewed in the studies. The authors, who were not involved in the lawsuit in any direct way, resisted and the basis for the subpoenas was reviewed in three separate jurisdictions by three different courts. Ultimately, DiFranza was the only one of the three researchers who was forced to turn over all of his research materials, but he was not required to reveal the subjects' names (3).

During the 1960s and 1970s, the US Atomic Energy Commission (AEC) supported a series of studies regarding the feasibility of using personnel, exposure, and health records to estimate a bound on the risk of cancer associated with exposure to low levels of radiation in AEC facilities and at facilities operated for it by private contractors. A data-base project was ultimately established at the University of Pittsburgh, under the supervision of T.F. Mancuso, and with support of staff at the Oak Ridge Associated Universities. In 1977, after a period of time during which no scientific findings were published, Mancuso, Stewart & Kneale (25) published an analysis of data from the AEC facility at Hanford, Washington, in which they found excess cancers at permitted exposure levels. There was an extended controversy over these findings and a series of published reanalyses, some carried out by the original authors. In 1977, the contract for the maintenance of the data was transferred to the Oak Ridge Associated Universities and the workers health studies were expanded to include many additional facilities and groups of workers (10). During the subsequent years the contractors published over 80 articles analyzing these data; however, the data were not generally shared with others.

In the late 1980s, the Three Mile Island Public Health Fund, established as part of the settlement for the reactor accident on Three Mile Island, Pennsylvania, sought, under the FOIA, to obtain access from the Department of Energy (the successor agency to the AEC) to the full data on these worker health studies. An out-of-court settlement in 1990 gave the Health Fund access to data on approximately 270,000 workers, but it did not provide for access to these data by others. This issue of selective access was later addressed by the Department of Energy in its decision to develop a publicly accessible Comprehensive Epidemiologic Data Resource for the data from the workers health studies (10). The Secretary of Energy, who supported these developments, repeatedly acknowledged the importance of treating these research data as a public good.

THE CHANGING COMPUTING ENVIRONMENT AS A FACILITATOR

As we have argued in the preceding sections, attitudes toward data sharing have clearly evolved over the past decade, driven in part by external forces linked to public controversies over scientific misconduct and changing legal requirements. But the actual extent of data sharing and its many implementations would not have taken place but for the rapidly changing computer environment in which researchers have found themselves. Two decades ago, when researchers sought access to the UDGP data, major computer facilities were required to mount the UDGP data tapes. Today, these data files can easily be stored on a typical personal computer. Further, most researchers in the health sciences now have direct access to computer networks, such as the Internet, that link them to their colleagues worldwide. Data can now be transferred through these networks, thus alleviating the need for tapes and more modern storage media and lowering access costs. Even when desktop machines cannot easily accommodate very large data files, the proliferation of rapid-access mass storage devices should soon give researchers easy local access to suitable file space for virtually any set of health sciences research data.

Greenberg (18) describes how this current computer environment is already transforming the conduct of analyses of multi-center clinical trials and he notes some of the problems that ensue:

> With the advent of personal computers and analysis programs written for the new generation of users, investigators could have a complete set of data from the trial in a format that they can use in the comforts of their offices or homes.

Once the trial sponsor, whether it be NIH or industry, receives its copy of the data tape, usually at the time of publication of the primary paper, the tape should be made available to any collaborating investigator who wants it. In trials in which primary data may be released sequentially, as in [the Cardiac Arrhythmia Suppression Trial], the release of data will be guided by the degree of unmasking at each step …

Such a proposal poses risks … With data less protected than they would be in a single, central data-processing unit, there is a risk that unauthorized investigators or competitor drug companies will gain access … Junior investigators with only peripheral involvement in the trial could publish material that may overlap the analyses of the senior principal investigators … Senior collaborators working in similar areas may produce nearly identical papers with predictable unpleasant results. As updated data tapes are produced by the coordinating center, it will be difficult to ensure that each investigator will update his or her version of the database. Discrepancies in published results can discredit important findings.

Greenberg goes on to propose greater control by the steering committee for the clinical trial and restricted access to the data. He then notes that this type of arrangement has actually worked in the Coronary Artery Risk Development in Young Adults trial (35).

The instantaneous access to data for those investigators with a clinical trial as described by Greenberg must at some point become more widespread. Researchers involved in a clinical trial cannot expect to control access to the data for extended periods of time after the publication of the paper with the primary results. Those who have worked on the trial have a competitive advantage over outside researchers as result of knowledge shared among trial investigators, but this advantage diminishes over time. Access to research data from clinical trials, as in other areas of science, must occur at a more rapid pace than original investigators would otherwise choose. The principle of scientific openness would seem to dictate an orderly approach to data sharing that serves both the private and the public interest.

Moving beyond clinical trials, we see an important role of President Clinton's proposed national data highway as a facilitator to data sharing for large public health databases. For many of us, that future is already now.

It is also time for the government and for universities to act positively in support of data sharing. All funding agencies need to require some form of data sharing as a condition for research support. Universities must begin to include statements on data sharing in their official policies, not just for funded projects but for all research. And medical and public health researchers should actively support such initiatives as a mechanism to help preserve the integrity of scientific research.

Most of the public health controversies involving access to research data are focused on issues of whether or not some substance or treatment is or is not a health risk. In such circumstances, the public's right to health must override a researcher's proprietary interest in the data from research studies. I therefore believe that the results of clinical trials and epidemiological studies must be made available to others for reanalysis. Only then can public health decision making be well-informed. Thus, I urge the government agencies, such as the FDA and the EPA, to adopt more formal rules to allow access by interested parties to research data for some reasonable period of time before studies can be accepted as the basis for government decisions and policies.

ACKNOWLEDGMENTS

The preparation of this paper was supported in part by a grant from the Natural Sciences and Engineering Research Council of Canada. Several colleagues have generously shared materials on data sharing with me over the years, most of which have found their way into this paper, either explicitly or implicitly. In particular, I thank R Boruch, R Chalk, W Cooper, J Greenhouse, R Hauser, W Kruskal, T McGuire, P Meier, and M Straf.

Any *Annual Review* chapter, as well as any article cited in an *Annual Review* chapter, may be purchased from the Annual Reviews Preprints and Reprints service. 1-800-347-8007; 415-259-5017; email: arpr@class.org

---

Literature Cited

1. Allison J, Cooper WW. 1991. *Data disclosure and data sharing in scientific research*. Presented at Conf. Res. Policies Qual. Assur., Rome, Italy, May 6–7

2. Barinaga M. 1991. Free speech and clinical trials. *Science* 254:23

3. Barinaga M. 1992. Who controls a researcher's files. *Science* 256:1620–21

4. Baron JN. 1988. Data sharing as a public good. *Am. Sociol. Rev.* 53:6–8

4a. Bunch v. Dow Chemical Co., Misc. Petition No. 6446 (Circuit Ct., Montgomery County, MD)

5. Buzelli DE. 1993. The definition of misconduct in science: a view from NSF. *Science* 259:584–85, 647–48

6. Cantekin EI, McGuire TW, Griffith TL. 1991. Antimicrobial therapy for otitis media with effusion ("secretory" otitis media). *J. Am. Med. Assoc.* 266:3309–17

7. Cantekin EI, McGuire TW, Potter RL. 1990. Biomedical information, peer review, and conflict of interest as they influence public health. *J. Am. Med. Assoc.* 263:1427–30

8. Card JJ. 1989. Facilitating data sharing. *Footnotes Am. Sociol. Assoc.* (Am. Sociol. Assoc.) (Jan.):8

9. Cecil JS, Griffin E. 1985. The role of legal policies in data sharing. In *Sharing Research Data*, ed. SE Fienberg, ME Martin, ML Straf, pp. 148–98. Washington, DC: Natl. Acad. Press

10. Comm. Radiat. Epidemiol. Res. Programs. 1990. *Providing Access to Epidemiological Data*. Washington, DC: Natl. Acad. Press

11. Cordray DS, Pion GM, Boruch RF. 1990. *Sharing research data: with whom, when, and how much*. Presented at Public Health Serv. Workshop, April, Chevy Chase, MD

12. Culliton BJ. 1988. Random audit of papers proposed. *Science* 242:657–58

13. Culliton BJ. 1990. Stanford, claiming censorship, sues NIH. *Science* 250:746

14. Duncan GT, Pearson RB. 1991. Enhancing access to microdata while protecting confidentiality: prospects for the future (with discussion). *Stat. Sci.* 6:219–39

15. Ernhart CB, Landa B, Schell NB.

1981. Subclinical levels of lead and developmental deficit: a multivariate follow-up reassessment. *Pediatrics* 67: 911–19

16. Fienberg SE. 1994. Conflict between the needs for access to statistical information and demands for confidentiality. *J. Off. Stat.* 10: In press

17. Fienberg SE, Martin ME, Straf ML. 1985. *Sharing Research Data.* Washington, DC: Natl. Acad. Press

17a. Forsham v. Harris, 445 U. S. 169. 1980

18. Greenberg H. 1992. Access to data: a contemporary direction for clinical trials. *Control. Clin. Trials* 13:93–96

19. Hamilton DP. 1992. OSI: Better the devil you know? *Science* 255:1344–47

20. Hauser RM. 1987. Sharing data: It's time for ASA Journals to follow the folkways of a scientific sociology. *Am. Sociol. Rev.* 52. Unnumbered pages

21. Hawthorne VM. 1992. Archiving epidemiologic data: benefits and challenges. *Inter-university Consortium on Political and Social Research Bulletin,* Feb., pp. 1–4. ICPSR: Ann Arbor, MI

22. Holden C. 1993. Random samples. Needleman case still simmers. *Science* 258:1302

23. Hurwitz ES, Barrett MJ, Bregman D, Gunn WJ, Schonber LB, et al. 1985. Public Health Service Study on Reye's syndrome and medications: report on the pilot phase. *N. England J. Med.* 313:849–57

23a. In re American Tobacco Co., 880 F. 2d 1520 (2nd Cir. 1989)

23b. In re R. J. Reynolds Tobacco Co., 136 Misc. 2d 282, 518 N. Y. S. 2d 729 (Sup. Ct. 1987)

24. LaFollette MC. 1992. *Stealing into Print. Fraud, Plagiarism, and Misconduct in Scientific Publishing.* Berkeley: Univ. Calif. Press

25. Mancuso, TA, Stewart A, Kneale G. 1977. Radiation exposure of Hanford workers dying from cancer and other causes. *Health Physics* 33:369–85

26. Mandel EM, Rockette HE, Bluestone CD, Paradise JL, Nozza RJ. 1987. Efficacy of amoxicillin with and without decongestant—antihistamine for otitis media with effusion in children. Results of a double-blind, randomized trial. *N. England J. Med.* 316:432–37

27. Marshall E. 1991. Fight over data disrupts Michigan State project. *Science* 251:23–24

28. Marshall E. 1993. MSU officials criticized for mishandling data dispute. *Science* 259:592–94

29. Natl. Inst. Health. 1990. *Guidelines for the Conduct of Research at the National Institutes of Health.* pp. 8–9. Bethesda, MD

30. Needleman HL. 1992. Salem comes to the National Institutes of Health: Notes from inside the crucible of scientific integrity. *Pediatrics* 90:977–81

31. Needleman HL, Gunnoe C, Leviton A, Reed R, Peresie H, et al. 1979. Deficits in psychologic and classroom performance of children with elevated dentine lead levels. *N. England J. Med.* 300:689–95

32. Natl. Sci. Found. 1989. *Responsibilities of Institutions and Investigators in the Conduct of Research.* No. 106. Washington, DC

33. Palca J. 1991. Get the lead-out guru challenged. *Science* 253:842–44

34. Panel Sci. Responsib. Conduct Res. 1992. *Responsible Science. Ensuring the Integrity of the Research Process.* Vol. I. Comm. Sci. Eng. Public Policy. Washington, DC: Natl. Acad. Press

35. Perkins LL, Cutter GR, Wagenknecht LE, Savage PJ, Dyer AR, Birch R. 1992. Distributed data analysis in a multicenter study: The CARDIA Study. *Controlled Clin. Trials* 13:80–90

36. Rennie D. 1991. The Cantekin affair. *J. Am. Med. Assoc.* 266:3333–37

37. Selikoff IJ, Seidman H. 1979. Asbestos exposure, cigarette smoking and death rates. *Ann. NY Acad. Sci.* 330: 473–90

38. Selikoff IJ, Seidman H, Hammond EC. 1980. Mortality effects of cigarette smoking among amosite asbestos factory workers. *J. Natl. Cancer Inst.* 65:507–13

39. Sieber JE. 1989. Sharing scientific data I: New problems for IRBs. *IRB: Rev. Hum. Subjects Res.* 11:4–7

40. Sieber JE, ed. 1991. *Sharing Social Science Data. Advantages and Challenges.* Newbury Park, CA: Sage

41. Sieber JE. 1991. Social scientists' concerns about sharing data. See Ref. 40, pp. 141–50

42. Deleted in proof

43. Weil V, Hollander, R. 1990. Sharing scientific data II: Normative issues. *IRB: Rev. Hum. Subjects Res.* 12:7–8

44. Yolles BY, Connors JC, and Grufferman S. 1986. Obtaining access to data from government-sponsored medical research. *N. England J. Med.* 315:1669–72

Annu. Rev. Public Health. 1994. 15:19–38
Copyright © 1994 by Annual Reviews. All rights reserved

SCIENTIFIC AND ETHICAL ISSUES IN THE USE OF PLACEBO CONTROLS IN CLINICAL TRIALS

Pamela I. Clark

Division of Community Health Sciences, Northeastern Ohio Universities College of Medicine, Rootstown, Ohio 44272

Paul E. Leaverton

Department of Epidemiology and Biostatistics, University of South Florida, College of Public Health, Tampa, Florida 33612

KEY WORDS: placebo effect, controlled clinical trial, research design, comparison group

The experience of being a subject in a clinical trial may include such activities as multiple clinic visits, research-subject interactions, the performance of diagnostic tests, the taking of test medications, and many other measurable and unmeasurable features. All of these aspects may contribute to improvement in the signs and symptoms of the disease process being studied. The object of a clinical trial is to estimate the true effect of a therapeutic intervention. To accomplish this, one must be able to distinguish the effectiveness of the test therapy from the effect of simply being in a trial. Placebos are used in randomized trials with the intention of providing a control group whose experience in the trial is as similar as possible to that of the investigational group, except for the presence of the active ingredient(s) being tested.

Placebos have long been used as therapeutic agents, generally without the knowledge and cooperation of the patient. The primary difference in the use of placebos in the context of a randomized trial is that both researcher and subject are aware that the subject has a chance of receiving a placebo instead of the test intervention. Much of our knowledge of placebos as

19

therapeutic interventions, however, is directly applicable to the case of placebos used as controls in clinical trials.

A DEFINITION AND BRIEF HISTORY OF PLACEBOS

Indirect evidence for the existence of a placebo effect might be found in the high honor and esteem in which healers have been held despite their history of "exotic, expensive and gory cures such as lizard's blood, crocodile dung, fly specks, ground Egyptian mummy, oil of frog sperm, usnea (moss scraped from inside the skull of a hanged criminal), bleeding, leeching, blistering, puncturing, the royal touch, etc." (22). While many of these "therapies" were used for hundreds of years, most have been discarded as useless with the advent of the scientific method. Yet patients often display marked improvement when given substances, or after undergoing procedures, that have no real medicinal properties.

As part of the considerable spectrum of individual variability in the natural course of most maladies, many of the afflicted simply get better on their own. If they happen to have taken an innocuous and ineffective substance, it is obviously easy to attribute the "getting better" to such a substance: a causal inference. Indeed, the prevalence of such occurrences is what maintains medical quackery today. And the science-based medical establishment is not above occasionally exploiting this phenomenon. The medical bromide "take two aspirins and call me in the morning" undoubtedly has lasted through the years largely for the same reason.

A biologically inert substance given with the intention of providing relief is known as a placebo. The resulting effect upon the patient or subject is called a placebo effect. With the advent of controlled clinical drug trials, placebos have been widely used to diminish, if not eliminate, investigator and subject bias (through blinding), and to estimate the magnitude of true pharmacologic effect.

Formal definitions of placebos have been much discussed (9, 35, 76), but for the purpose of this paper we use the straightforward definition proposed by Shapiro (76): a placebo is "any therapeutic procedure (or component of any therapeutic procedure) which is given deliberately to have an effect, or unknowingly has an effect on a patient, symptom, syndrome, or disease, but is objectively without specific activity for the condition being treated". We further expand this definition to the use of placebos as alternatives to active treatment controls in randomized clinical trials.

The purposive use of placebos is not a new phenomenon. Sir Thomas Percival discussed placebo use in his 1803 paper on "Medical Ethics"; Hooper's "Medical Dictionary" of 1811 described placebo as "an epithet given any medicine adopted more to please than to benefit the patient" (68).

And, as early as 1753, placebo controls were advocated by Dr. James Lind when he evaluated the effects of lime juice on scurvy (49).

A landmark paper on the placebo was published by Pepper in 1945 (59). In 1946, the role of placebo in controlled clinical trials was recognized when the Cornell Conference on Therapy focused on placebos and double-blind methodology (16). In 1955, Beecher published his systematic study of patients' subjective responses to placebo (5).

The Kefauver-Harris Amendment to the Food, Drugs, and Cosmetic Act of 1962 mandated that the FDA evaluate not only safety but also efficacy claims for any new experimental agent before approving it for general use (39). Prior to that time, there was a notable lack of interest in controlled research methodology by the pharmaceutical industry, perhaps because many drugs were of only marginal effectiveness (68). In 1970, the United States Food and Drug Administration (FDA) published its first rules for "Adequate and Well-Controlled Clinical Evaluations" (25). The federal regulations identified five types of controls that might be employed to meet the standard of "adequate and well-controlled" trials. However, the FDA acknowledged the variability in assumptions required for interpretation of trials utilizing the different control conditions (i.e. placebo, dose-comparison, active, historical, and no treatment), and identified the placebo control as an indispensable tool (45).

THE PSYCHO-PHARMACOLOGY OF PLACEBOS

The potency of placebo (or nonspecific) effects has been recognized in most physical and virtually all psychiatric disorders (64). Nonspecific effects include any measurable physiologic or psychologic change that is not drug-specific. These nonspecific effects may be secondary to fluctuations in the course of illness with the passage of time, the effect of clinician-patient interaction, expectations of drug effect by both investigator and subject, or other aspects of the care environment.

Placebos have been noted to be effective in the treatment of arthritis, angina pectoris, peptic ulcer, asthma, various tumors, diabetes, high blood pressure, multiple sclerosis, Parkinson's disease, radiation sickness, postoperative pain, insomnia, hay fever, common cold, cough, seasickness, anxiety, depression, varicose veins, dysmenorrhea, panic disorder, and schizophrenia (5, 7, 24, 36, 53, 71, 77, 78, 80).

The proportion of trial subjects responding positively to placebos and the magnitude of responses vary greatly among studies. Approximately 35 percent of subjects show satisfactory improvement on placebo, and placebo adverse reactions occur at approximately that same rate (6). Placebos may have marked physiologic effects, including such "objective" outcomes as the healing of wounds. A component of every successful treatment effect can be attributed to the placebo response (35). The object of controlled clinical trials is to determine whether active treatment has any benefit beyond the baseline placebo effect.

Nonspecific Treatment Effects

The treatment milieu is important in producing therapeutic responses, and contributes much to the placebo response. The attitudes of the research staff, perceived reputation of the doctor, contact with other patients, and many more subtle elements can profoundly affect outcomes. Interestingly, the efficacy of both active treatment and placebo may be enhanced if the physician has faith in the new treatment (35). The emergence of consumers educated by the popular press has resulted in more preconceived notions of treatment efficacy among potential study subjects.

A study of bleeding ulcers by Volgyesi (91) demonstrated the potential impact of nonspecific treatment effects. Doctors injected one group of patients with the medication, and nurses injected another group. The nurses explained to their group that they were subjects in an investigation. Both groups received only placebo. In the group injected by doctors, results were excellent in 70 percent of subjects over a year, with some complete cures verified through objective means. Only 25 percent showed improvement in the group injected by nurses.

Knowledge of potential assignment to a placebo group can change expectations of efficacy for the active treatment. In a review of antidepressant drug studies, Wechsler and associates (94) found that when drugs were evaluated against a placebo control they were less likely to produce positive responses, compared to those in active control trials. The authors interpreted the results as a tendency for staff to rate improvement more conservatively if they knew that not all patients were on active therapy.

Mechanisms of the Placebo Effect

Many explanations for the placebo effect have been offered, with particular emphasis on psychological effects (38, 71). Two popular explanations are that of classical conditioning, and the effect of placebo administration on neurohormones. Another theory is that mental imagery produces specific and measurable physiologic effects (41).

In a study of the relative roles of conditioning and verbal expectancy in the placebo response, Voudouris and coworkers (92) studied responses to pain stimulation with and without a placebo cream. A visual analog scale was used to test pain perception. The effect of expectancy was evaluated by informing the subjects that the placebo cream contained a powerful analgesic (expectancy) or that it was neutral (no expectancy). The role of conditioning was evaluated by reducing the level of pain stimulus following application of the cream (conditioning), or by maintaining the same level of pain (no conditioning). They divided subjects into four groups, one receiving a combined expectancy and conditioning manipulation, one expectancy alone, one conditioning alone, and the fourth group served as controls. Their results suggested that both conditioning and verbal expectancy were important mediators, but that conditioning was more powerful in eliciting a placebo response.

Several mediation channels have been suggested for placebo effects, including motor or autonomic nervous systems, hormone systems, and immune systems (41). Endogenous brain systems of opioid, antiopioid, and gamma-aminobutyric acid polypeptide transmitters, and neuronal receptors may be important in placebo mediation of pain, and other neurohumoral systems may be involved in mediation of other responses (57, 58). Lipman and co-workers (50) measured the level of an endogenous opioid in cerebrospinal fluid sampled from chronic pain patients. A significant 2.3-fold increase was measured in the peak beta endorphin level of the placebo reacting group. They concluded that the study provided direct evidence that an opioid is correlated with placebo pain relief in chronic pain patients.

Supporting the endorphin theory is the evidence for placebo antagonism found by Levine and coworkers (48). They showed that the opiate antagonist, naloxone, caused a significantly greater increase in dental pain among placebo responders compared to nonresponders. Similar indirect evidence for the endorphin theory has subsequently been reported (34, 47).

A model of mental imagery producing specific physiologic effects is attractive in that it may explain the connection between psychologic and physiologic components of the placebo response. Kojo has hypothesized that patients generate some kind of imagery about their syndromes and the effects of treatment (41). If the content of the imagery is appropriate, it will act on the relevant body system, producing a placebo effect. He stated that the results of the imagery would emerge each time it is repeated, accounting for the long-term effects of some placebo treatments. The subject may also modify imagery about the treatment several times over the course of a trial, producing varied physiologic effects.

Gradual improvement may be the result of spontaneous remission, rather than a placebo response. Gradual attenuation of response may reflect worsening of the underlying disease process. Abrupt improvement on placebo may actually be a manifestation of regression to the mean. As an example, if subjects are selected as suitable candidates for an antihypertensive trial because they exceed a threshold level of blood pressure, some may have regressed to their true mean blood pressure levels at the time of subsequent evaluations, mimicking a placebo response.

Temporal Patterns of the Placebo Effect

Responses in patients given placebos may be abrupt, or there may be continued improvement over time. Those responses may diminish over time. Just as in drug withdrawal, withdrawal of placebo can be associated with relapse (7, 43).

A pattern of continued improvement over the course of a trial was reported by Lasagna and coworkers (43). They told patients with tuberculosis that a yellow tablet, given daily for seven days, would improve appetite and energy. The pills, all of which were placebos, showed a gradually increasing effect on energy and appetite over the course of the week, with a residual effect for days afterward.

Placebo responses may attenuate over time. In a study of primary dysmenorrhea, for instance, Fedele and coworkers (24) found a large initial placebo improvement in a first cycle, which then diminished with subsequent cycles, with 84, 29, 16, and 10 percent of women improving in each of four consecutive cycles.

Lack of persistence of the response to placebo may be secondary to decreased susceptibility of motor or autonomic nervous systems, hormone systems, or immune systems to the placebo effect, or to deconditioning mechanisms. If mental imagery is an important component of placebo responses, imagery may be modified by monitoring of body reactions, or monitoring of behavior and attitudes of the research team, resulting in changes in placebo response over time (41).

The persistence of the response to placebo may be difficult to evaluate because the fear of exposing patients to placebo over long periods has often resulted in trial designs that limit placebo periods. However, relatively long placebo periods have been infrequently used. For instance, in a long-term trial of placebo as the only antianginal medication for a cohort of 35 patients, the number of angina attacks decreased by 48 percent during titration (eight weeks), and by 77 percent during the entire six-month period (8).

There is a large conflicting literature concerning patterns of placebo response, especially in psychiatric disorders. Abrupt improvement was characterized as more likely than gradual improvement to be transient in patients with depression (65). Dager at al (19) found persistent placebo effects in panic disorder, but Mellergard & Rosenberg (53) reported that many panic disorder patients demonstrated early but temporary remission on placebo.

The conflicting literature may be entirely expected considering the complex elements that make up the placebo response, including continued interaction between subjects and treatment team, monitoring of treatment effects by both subjects and researchers, and changes in disease processes over the course of the study.

Is There a Typical "Placebo Responder"?

The search for the characteristics of placebo-sensitive subjects is as muddled as the literature on patterns of placebo response. Gender (56), age (95), marital status (66), levels of neuroticism (37), and other personality traits (67) are among the elements that have been inconsistently implicated. There are no invariable or predictable placebo responders (10). The failure to find consistent characteristics is understandable considering the situation-specific nature of the placebo response (22).

Effects of Placebos on "Hard" Endpoints

It has been written that "when the response measured is a hard one, a placebo-controlled double-blind design is not essential." (70). Our increasing dependence on, and faith in, technology contributes to the belief that "hard", objective end-points are unlikely to be influenced by the placebo effect, which is not always the case.

Vayssairat and associates (88) used a double-blind, placebo-controlled crossover design to examine the effectiveness of the drug naftidrofuryl for severe limb ischemia, typical signs were rest, pain, and gangrene. They used transcutaneous measurement of delivery of oxygen to the tissues ($TcPO_2$) as an objective measure of improvement. In both naftidrofuryl and placebo-treated patients $TcPO_2$ increased significantly. Murali and colleagues (55) investigated the effect of single-blind oral "inotropic" placebo on exercise time, peak oxygen consumption, and oxygen consumption at anaerobic threshold in patients with chronic cardiac failure. They found significant improvement in some objective measures after placebo dosing.

The measurement of blood pressure is an "objective" measurement. Studies of placebo response in hypertension have been mixed, with some showing blood pressure reduction (33, 42), and some showing no effect (74, 90). In general, a response has been more likely with measurement processes that involve considerable operator input, such as sphygmomanometry, and less likely with more automatic devices, such as automatic oscillometric techniques (63) or intra-arterial monitoring (33).

The finding of placebo responsiveness despite the use of objective outcome measures provides insights into the complexity of "nonspecific effects". In the case of placebo improvement in severe limb ischemia (88), the authors noted an increase in blood pressure that may have increased perfusion pressure. Other explanations are also possible. The patients were hospitalized for the study, and hospitalization may have favorably affected warmth and rest of the extremities, and perhaps decreased the frequency of smoking.

In the case of the "inotropic" placebo (55), improvement may have occurred because of learning or training effects on exercise duration, or subtle communications between subjects and the research team (the researchers were aware of the nature of the single-blind study). In some disease processes, our incomplete understanding of pathophysiology may be evident in an apparent "placebo response". Thus, treatment of warts with an innocuous dye was reported to produce more loss of warts than occurred in untreated controls, implying a psychogenic component to the pathophysiology of warts (81).

Not all of the factors operating in any given study can be fully known and accounted for in the analysis of trial results. If the placebo effect were merely that of the taking of a pill, our faith in objective measures might be more justified. Objective measures certainly improve interpretability of studies (80), but placebo control groups are often still necessary to sort out the components of true drug effects from the myriad other potential influences on study outcomes.

SCIENTIFIC ISSUES IN THE CHOICE OF CONTROLS

> Placebo controls are our surest protection against fads and fashions that come and go in pharmacology, against reckless claims of therapeutic enthusiasts, and, most important, against our own mistaken beliefs and prejudices (45).

Clinical trials, to be of greatest benefit, must be valid, generalizable, and efficient.

Sackett (73) wrote that "... validity has become a nonnegotiable demand; hence the ascendancy of the randomized clinical trial." And hence the ascendancy of the placebo as control in clinical trials. The only direct test of the efficacy of a new treatment is a comparison of the treatment response between the new therapy and an indistinguishable inactive preparation, using the same or similar patients (60). To render the least ambiguous results, trials of new drugs require placebo controls. Exceptions occur when there are standard drugs available that are known to favorably affect survival or irreversible morbidity, or when there is no treatment known for a severe disease with a universally poor outcome. Under these circumstances, alternatives to placebos may be necessary, but trials lacking placebo controls must be interpreted with exceptional caution.

Uncontrolled Trials

While the placebo-controlled, randomized, double-blind clinical trial has become the gold standard for new drug evaluation, there are some diseases with such poor outcomes that placebo-controlled trials may be considered unethical. Byar and coworkers (12), in a discussion of design considerations in trials of AIDS, suggested five criteria that should be met to consider testing a new therapy in an uncontrolled trial: (a) there must be no other treatment available for use as a control; (b) there must be sufficient experience with the disease to know that the prognosis is universally poor without therapy; (c) the new therapy must not be expected to produce toxic side effects, such that adverse effects would outweigh potential benefits from the drug; (d) there must be an expectation of sufficient benefit from the drug, so that the trial can be interpreted unambiguously; and (e) the scientific grounds for the treatment must be strong enough for positive results of an uncontrolled trial to be widely accepted. Situations satisfying all of these requirements are exceedingly rare. HIV/AIDS certainly did not and still does not have a sufficiently predictable natural history to justify uncontrolled trials.

Untreated Controls

The placebo effect can be powerful, and its scope goes beyond the taking of a pill to the entire treatment environment. Therefore, no treatment is not the equivalent of placebo treatment.

One component of every efficacious treatment is its placebo effect (35). When evaluating the efficacy of a new drug, one must evaluate whether it has any utility beyond its baseline placebo effect. To determine if improvement in the treated group is due to drug effect, rather than the act of being treated, the investigator must treat both drug and control groups in an identical manner except for the presence of the active drug ingredients (61). An effective and essential method of protecting against treatment-related bias is the use of blinding. Another unacceptable feature of the no-treatment control model is that it does not permit blinding.

Nonconcurrent Controls

The interpretation of uncontrolled studies may be indistinguishable from historically controlled studies. That is, the outcomes of patients treated with the new agent are compared to outcomes prior to the availability of the agent.

Several authors have advocated the use of historical controls as a means of reducing the considerable expense of studies and to prevent any patients from being denied allegedly superior treatments (12, 18, 20, 26, 28, 29). Such was the situation with the introduction of antibiotics and with the adoption of many surgical procedures. "For example, although no controlled statistical trials have been done to demonstrate that surgeons can rejoin the parts of an arm or leg that was traumatically severed, the efficacy of the procedure has been made apparent by historical comparisons" (26).

Historical controls are superficially attractive to some investigators given the substantial costs of performing randomized clinical trials. However, the use of historical controls may result in ambiguous interpretations of otherwise scientifically rigorous studies (72).

Problems in comparisons arise because of changes in diagnostic criteria and techniques, evolution of definitions of successful outcomes, and differences in ancillary care (26). Historical data may be of different quality and completeness. The fact that the prospective group must undergo the process of informed consent may result in much different selection of participants/patients compared to the historical controls.

Even when the course of a frequently fatal disease would appear to be predictable by relatively recent clinical observations, patients selected for trials may differ in important ways from their historical controls. This is the case for trials in the acquired immune deficiency syndrome (AIDS). Patients currently diagnosed with AIDS may have a longer latency period than those diagnosed earlier in the epidemic (12). Treatment and prophylaxis for opportunistic infections have advanced so far as to create a radically different disease profile from that experienced by the control group.

Examples of the pitfalls inherent in the use of historical controls can be found in the insightful review by DuPont (21). Despite political pressure and economic constraints, concurrent controls are the only practical way to control for subtle, and often unmeasurable, differences in groups.

Dose-Ranging Studies

A dose-ranging study may, in fact, be a variation of a placebo-controlled trial. The lowest dose is assumed to be less effective than a larger dose; an even higher dose is expected to produce more side effects, with or without increasing efficacy. The lowest effective dose of most medications may well be equivalent to the effect of being treated (the placebo effect), rather than the therapeutic effect of the drug itself.

The problem with the dose-ranging trial without a placebo group is that placebos can also show a dose response. For instance, Rickels and coworkers (69) reported the results of a randomized double-blind study (drug vs placebo) in anxious or depressed outpatients. Among those given placebos in one clinical setting, 50 percent improved with one placebo pill and 87 percent improved with four pills. In another clinical setting, 33 percent improved with one pill and 50 percent improved with four, so that in both settings, more frequent "higher doses" produced greater effects. Other studies have shown dosage effects, with larger placebo pills being more efficacious than smaller ones, and two pills working better than one (22).

In addition, placebos may show dosage effects for adverse events (62). Dose-related responses may also be seen in proportion to the degree of compliance on placebo. For instance, in the Coronary Drug Project, mortality was 15.1 percent among subjects who adhered well to the placebo regimen and 28.3 percent among poor compliers (17).

Because patterns of placebo response cannot be predicted in the design stage, the finding of a dose-related response in a dose-ranging study that does not include a placebo group is difficult to interpret. In addition, if there is an ethical objection to withholding effective treatment from some participants (a placebo group), the same ethical issues are relevant in a dose-ranging trial. The lowest dose is usually a subtherapeutic dose, so that, in terms of ethical issues, the use of dose-ranging studies offers no improvement over placebo-controlled trials, and the results may be much more ambiguous.

Active (Positive) Controls

There is growing sentiment among Institutional Review Boards, and some investigators, to restrict the use of placebo controls if a standard therapy is available to serve as control treatment (30, 46, 51, 93). The ethical question is whether it is justifiable to expose patients to ineffective treatment (placebo) and possibly to discomfort or risk, when there is a generally effective treatment available. It is clear that a placebo cannot be used when existing treatment is known to favorably affect survival or morbidity. In the case of many chronic diseases, treatment does not alter survival or morbidity. Or, the course of a clinical trial may be of such short duration, representing a small segment of lifetime management of a disease, and brief use of placebo controls does not alter long-term outcome.

There is substantial experience with the use of a previously "proven" effective therapy for comparison against a new drug (51). One might ask, however, how "proven" the efficacy of a standard drug is. For instance, Burkhardt & Kienle (11), in reference to accepted current drugs such as morphine, digitalis, aspirin, insulin, penicillin, and corticosteroids, note that "it would be held as unethical to make controlled trials now". Yet, when some of these "proven" therapies, introduced without controlled clinical trials, are subjected to rigorous study, they perform poorly against placebo. Such is the case with the standard therapy of corticosteroids for the treatment of acute optic neuritis. The investigators (4) of the Optic Neuritis Treatment Trial found that outcomes for the group that received oral prednisone did not differ from those in the placebo group, except that the rate of new episodes of optic neuritis was actually higher in the oral prednisone group. If a new treatment for optic neuritis had been tested against the standard treatment, prednisone, and the drugs had been found to be equally efficacious, the results would not have been properly interpreted. Showing that a new drug is equal in efficacy to an old one does not establish that either is effective (45, 51, 86).

When a "standard" therapy has been shown to be effective in controlled trials, the interpretation of outcomes of trials in which it is used as a control may still be suspect. "To properly interpret an active control trial, one must have some assurance that the active control treatment is as efficacious under the new experimental conditions as it was in previous placebo-controlled trials...an implicit historical control assumption" (51).

Active (or positive) controls can lead to some other serious methodologic problems. When the aim of a study is to show the equivalence of two therapies, there is "no agreed upon test for statistically significant similarity" (86). This is an issue of the size of the beta-error, which reflects the magnitude of the difference one would want to detect (27, 51, 86). The question of adequacy of sample sizes, an issue of the alpha-error, is also neglected when the intention is to test equality. Statistical approaches to this atypically posed problem, based primarily on the use of confidence bounds, are addressed by Fleming (27) and Gould (31, 32).

The aim of showing that two drugs are equivalent may produce incentives to perform sloppy research. The endeavor of finding true differences between two drugs leads to a need for excellence in study performance. By poor design and execution of a study, however, the finding of "no difference" may result just because of a high level of "background noise" (45, 86).

Design Options Which Try to Minimize Placebo Treatment

Design options that include small "vestigial" placebo groups have been suggested for trials in which withholding of active therapy may be "medically inappropriate" (32). This approach is valid only if one accepts the unlikely notion that exposing a small group to potential harm is any more ethical than exposing a larger group to the same harm.

ETHICAL ISSUES IN THE CHOICE OF PLACEBO CONTROLS

> One has only to review the graveyard of discarded therapies to discover how many patients might have benefitted from being randomly assigned to a control group (13).

Independent of regulatory requirements, investigators must be satisfied that it is proper to expose patients to either the experimental or the control treatment (52). Testing of a new drug in humans is warranted only if there is a reasonable expectation that it will work, but a reasonable doubt about its efficacy.

Our honest doubts about the merits of any new therapy must therefore be considered in any discussion of the ethics of placebo-controlled trials. It would not be ethical to initiate a clinical trial about which the results are already certain (for instance that the new therapy is definitely superior to its control), and inferior trials are both unscientific and unethical (82).

Given the above admonitions, there are ethical issues specific to the use of placebo controls. The most often cited are: (*a*) the concept of placebo as a planned deception and (*b*) the withholding of effective therapy.

Placebos as Planned Deception

Kluge (40), writing about the ethics of placebo use, commented on the nature of the physician-patient relationship: "Considered purely materially, the overriding characteristic of the relationship is that it is therapeutic. The patient comes to the physician for treatment, whether it be curative or palliative." In the case of the physician-as-investigator the relationship is more complex. The physician may be said to be soliciting from the patient assistance in performing a clinical trial. Even when the treating physician is not the same individual as the investigator, the patient may have difficulty perceiving or assimilating such a disruption of the expected fiduciary relationship. The obligation of the clinician to protect the research subject from undue harm takes on an even higher priority because of the expectations of the patient that the clinical contact will be to his or her personal benefit. It is in this context that all informed consent procedures must proceed.

The issue of deception was raised before the era of informed consent as an integral part of clinical research (84). Patients were unknowingly switched between inactive and active medications, and thus were deceived. Institutional regulations now prohibit withholding the knowledge of a placebo phase in clinical trials. Double-blinding brings balance to the relationship in that both investigator and subject are theoretically blind to treatment. Thus, careful and explicit explanation of the "planned deception" of placebo brings the clinician and the patient into a joint partnership based on ignorance of treatment assignment (15).

The issue therefore becomes one of adequacy of informed consent. Stanley (83) reported that patients show a fair understanding of the nature of treatments, and their risks and benefits, but have difficulty understanding the process of clinical research. She noted that they particularly had trouble appreciating that research was conducted for the good of society, and not necessarily for their personal benefit. Park & Covi (58) found that some patients who were informed that they were receiving placebo refused to believe it. Appelbaum and coworkers (2) reported that 40 percent of subjects in psychopharmacologic trials failed to recognize that some patients seeking therapy would fail to receive it, and that nearly 70 percent had little or no understanding of the process of random treatment assignment. They noted that subjects "in medical settings expect that the physicians will focus on the subjects' needs in making decisions about their care" and "despite disclosures of randomization, placebos, double-blind procedures, and invariant treatment schedules, subjects often continue to believe that research procedures are intended primarily for their benefit" (1). Appelbaum and associates (2) coined the term "therapeutic misconception" for the tendency of subjects to distort information that contradicts the assumption that the clinician is dedicated to their best interests alone.

These findings, and others (85), indicate that aspects of experimental design, such as randomization and placebo controls may be the most difficult part of the consent process to convey to patients. Full understanding of these processes by the research subject is necessary to form a researcher-subject partnership in the planned deception of placebo controls; only with full understanding can placebo-controlled trials be performed with deception, but without unethical behavior.

Withholding of Effective Therapy

It has been proposed that it is unethical to expose patients to a study in which some patients are expected to do worse or less well than others (3). This argument is difficult to accept given the large number of drugs that have been promising enough to warrant the risk and expense of clinical trials, but which have been shown to have no real value, or even to be harmful. Application of controlled, randomized trials "give each patient a 50–50 chance not to get the new therapy" (82). According to Lasagna (44), "too often the placebo-treated patients turn out to be the lucky ones in a drug trial, deprived only of a toxic and ineffective chemical." If it is thought to be unethical to assign subjects to receive placebo, thereby delaying their access to a drug with known effectiveness, then it is also unacceptable to delay effective treatment while testing an investigational drug, which may be not only ineffective, but hazardous. If the criteria for choosing between placebo and active controls (above) have been satisfied, and there is doubt about the efficacy of the new treatment, exposure of some subjects to placebo in well-designed and executed clinical trials should not continue to pose ethical dilemmas.

The Conflict Between Science and Ethics in Trials of Treatment for AIDS

The Acquired Immune Deficiency Syndrome (AIDS) is a life-threatening infectious disease. The sense of urgency engendered by the rapid spread of this fatal disease is often in conflict with the need for carefully controlled trials of new therapies. The drug investigation process in AIDS may be compared to that of other frequently fatal diseases, such as certain cancers. AIDS research presents another difficulty, however, in that the disease is also chronic, and the slow process of gathering information on survival time is an important issue in AIDS trials (23). The need to develop more efficient trial methodologies, and attention to ethical issues concerning the choice of suitable control groups, have demanded the attention of AIDS trialists. Recent controversies surrounding drug trials in AIDS have resulted in unprecedented dialogue between scientists, regulatory agencies, and the public regarding trial methodology and ethics.

OTHER CONSIDERATIONS IN THE USE OF PLACEBO CONTROLS

The Safety of Placebo Controls

The safety of withholding active therapy and enrolling patients in trials of new drugs is not an issue if standard treatment is expected to prevent irreversible morbidity or to alter survival, thereby rendering the use of placebo controls unacceptable. This, however, is not the case in many studies of new drugs.

There have been few systematic evaluations of the safety of placebo controls. Experience with short-term placebo-controlled trials in peptic ulcer disease suggest that placebo-treated patients have not been subjected to undue risk (79). Schiller & Fordtran (75) reviewed 48 placebo-controlled trials of drugs for duodenal ulcer, and found that among almost 3500 patients (1560 receiving placebos), 9 percent of placebo patients and 7.5 percent of active drug patients were dropped from trials. Most dropouts were not related to ulcer disease, with 2.3 percent of placebo-treated patients, and 0.5 percent of drug-treated patients dropped because of ulcer problems. Serious ulcer complications occurred in 0.2 percent of placebo-treated patients and 0.3 percent of those who received active drug.

The placebo dropout rate because of pain in gastric ulcer studies has been estimated by Smith (79) to be between five percent and ten percent, with drug-treatment dropouts consistently less at three to five percent. Smith speculated that the reasons that placebo-treated patients improve in controlled trials may be related to the natural history of the disease, the criteria used for subject selection, the close observations that the patients receive, the inclusion of antacids in the protocols, or the expectations of improvement.

As is the case with peptic ulcer disease, the treatment of angina is directed at relief of symptoms, rather than at the underlying disease. While the use of β-adrenergic blocking agents has been found to affect survival favorably following acute myocardial infarction, no medical treatment has been shown to be effective in altering survival in the case of chronic stable angina. Yet there has been growing opposition from institutional review boards to the use of placebo controls in trials of new antianginal agents (30, 93). In response to that opposition, Glasser and associates (30) investigated the safety of exposing patients with chronic, stable, exertional angina to placebo periods in controlled clinical trials. All events leading to dropout were identified from trials of twelve antianginal drugs submitted in support of new drug applications to the FDA. Withdrawals from the trials were classified, without knowledge of group assignment, as either due to adverse cardiovascular events or due to other causes. There were 3161 subjects who entered any randomized, double-blind phase of placebo-controlled protocols; 197 (6.2 percent) withdrew because of cardiovascular events. There was no difference in risk of adverse events between drug and placebo groups. A prospectively defined subgroup analysis showed that groups who received calcium antagonists were at an increased risk of dropout compared with placebo groups (p = 0.04), primarily because of a disproportionate number of adverse events in one trial. The authors concluded that the withholding of active treatment does not increase the risk of serious cardiac events.

Boissel and co-workers (8) followed a group of angina patients for six months. Aside from nitroglycerine as needed, the 35 patients used only placebo as antianginal medication. No severe cardiac events occurred, although six subjects had "adverse effects" from the placebo.

Appropriate controlled trials of surgical interventions are difficult, resulting in many procedures becoming commonplace without any evidence of efficacy beyond the placebo effect. Beecher (6) commented that, in the past "... one could hear senior surgeons saying that to treat pelvic inflammatory disease, 'You just open up the belly and let in a little light and air'; not so long before that, many colectomies were done to cure epilepsy. One can wonder which of current operations will be placed in a similar classification by the next generation."

Of course, for those operative procedures to have been applied for as long as they were, some patients must have improved. The power of surgery as placebo was extensively reviewed by Beecher (6). He cited studies that showed no differences in outcome between internal mammary artery ligation and sham operations. The studies were flawed by their very small sample sizes, but some important observations were made regarding the influence of investigator enthusiasm for a procedure. It was noted that "enthusiastic" investigators got results that were better than those of "skeptics" (38 percent and 10 percent, respectively).

Surgical treatments are costly and not without potential for harm, and may result in no more than a placebo effect. Designing valid studies of surgical outcomes, especially when the anticipated benefits are principally subjective, remains a challenge for trialists.

CONCLUSIONS

Placebo effects are a varied collection of real and interesting human responses that are now well recognized. The degree of effect depends as much on the myriad components of the trial milieu as on the disease process itself. Research contributing to a better understanding of the psychological-physiological relationships underlying the phenomenon is certainly warranted. While there are occasional ethical concerns regarding their use in clinical drug trials, the necessity of using placebos in most such experiments has been documented beyond question.

Literature Cited

1. Appelbaum PS, Roth LH, Lidz CW. 1983. Ethics of the randomized clinical trial (Letter). *N. England J. Med.* 308:344
2. Appelbaum PS, Roth LH, Lidz CW, Benson P, Winslade W. 1987. False hopes and best data: consent to research and the therapeutic misconception. *Hastings Cent. Rep.* 17:20–24
3. Baringa M. 1988. Placebos prompt new protocols for AIDS drug tests. *Nature* 335:485
4. Beck RW, Cleary PA, Anderson MM, Keltner JL, Shults WT, et al. 1992. A randomized, controlled trial of corticosteroids in the treatment of acute optic neuritis. *N. England J. Med.* 326:581–88
5. Beecher HK. 1955. The powerful placebo. *J. Am. Med. Assoc.* 159:1602–6
6. Beecher HK. 1961. Surgery as placebo. *J. Am. Med. Assoc.* 176:1102–7
7. Berg AO. 1977. Placebos: a brief review for family physicians. *J. Fam. Pract.* 5:97–100
8. Boissel JP, Philippon, AM, Gauthier E, Schbath J, Destors JM. 1986. Time course of long-term placebo therapy effects in angina pectoris. *Eur. Heart J.* 7:1030–6
9. Brody H. 1980. *Placebos and the Philosophy of Medicine*, pp. 25–44. Chicago: Univ. Chicago Press
10. Brown WA, Dornseif BE, Wernicke JF. 1988. Placebo response in depression: a search for predictors. *Psychiatry Res.* 26:259–64
11. Burkhardt R, Kienle G. 1978. Controlled clinical trials and medical ethics. *Lancet* 2:1356–59
12. Byar DP, Schoenfeld DA, Green SB, Amato DA, et al. 1990. Design considerations for AIDS trials. *N. England J. Med.* 323:1343–47
13. Chalmers TC. 1968. Prophylactic treatment of Wilson's disease. *N. England J. Med.* 278:910–11
14. Chalmers TC. 1982. A potpourri of RCT topics. *Controlled Clin. Trials* 3:285–98
15. Controlled Trials: Planned Deceptions? (Editorial). 1979. *Lancet* i:534–35
16. Cornell Conf. Therapy. 1946. The use of placebo in therapy. *NY State J. Med.* 46
17. Coronary Drug Proj. Res. Group. 1980. Influence of adherence to treatment and response of cholesterol on mortality in the coronary drug project. *N. England J. Med.* 303:1038–41
18. Cranberg L. 1979. Do retrospective controls make clinical trials "inherently fallacious"? *Br. Med. J.* 2:1265–66
19. Dager SR, Kahn A, Cowley D, Avery DH, Elder J, et al. 1990. Characteristics of placebo response during long-term treatment of panic disorder. *Psychopharm. Bull.* 26:273–78
20. Dudley HAF. 1983. The controlled clinical trial and the advance of reliable

knowledge: an outsider looks in. *Br. Med. J.* 287:957–60

21. DuPont WD. 1985. Randomized vs. historical clinical trials. Are the benefits worth the cost? *Am. J. Epidemiol.* 122:940–46

22. Eastman CI. 1990. What the placebo literature can tell us about light therapy for SAD. *Psychopharm. Bull.* 26:495–504

23. Ellenberg SS, Finkelstein DM, Schoenfeld DA. 1992. Statistical issues arising in AIDS clinical trials. *J. Am. Stat. Assoc.* 87:562–71

24. Fedele L, Marchini M, Acaia B, Garagiola U, Tiengo M. 1989. Dynamics and significance of placebo response in primary dysmenorrhea. *Pain* 36:43–47

25. Federal Register. 1970. 35:7250

26. Feinstein AR. 1980. Should placebo-controlled trials be abolished? (Editorial). *Eur. J. Clin. Pharmacol.* 17:1–4

27. Fleming TR. 1987. Treatment evaluation in active control studies. *Cancer Treatment Rep.* 71:1061–65

28. Gehan EA. 1982. Progress of therapy in acute leukemia 1948–1981: randomized versus nonrandomized clinical trials. *Controlled Clin. Trials* 3:199–207

29. Gehan EA, Freireich EJ. 1974. Non-randomized controls in clinical trials. *N. England J. Med.* 290:198–203

30. Glasser SP, Clark PI, Lipicky RJ, Hubbard JM, Yusuf S. 1991. Exposing patients with chronic, stable, exertional angina to placebo periods in drug trials. *J. Am. Med. Assoc.* 265:1550–54

31. Gould AL. 1987. Placebo comparisons in active-controlled trials. *Proc. Am. Statist. Assoc.* (Biopharmaceut. Sect.) 255–65

32. Gould AL. 1991. Another view of active-controlled trials. *Controlled Clin. Trials* 12:474–85

33. Gould BA, Mann S, Davies AB, Altman DG, Raftery EB. 1981. Does placebo lower blood pressure? *Lancet* 2:1377–81

34. Gracely RH, Dubner R, Wolskee PJ, Deeter WR. 1983. Placebo and naloxone can alter post-surgical pain by separate mechanisms. *Nature* 306:264–65

35. Grünbaum A. 1986. The placebo concept in medicine and psychiatry. *Psychol. Med.* 16:19–38

36. Honigfeld G. 1964. Non-specific factors in treatment: I. Review of placebo reactions and placebo reactors. *Dis. Nerv. Syst.* 25:145–56

37. Janicki AG, Orzechowska-Juzwenko K, Swiderska-Blonska T. 1988. The methodological and clinical aspects of the placebo effect in angina pectoris. *Cor Vasa* 30:35–42

38. Jenson MP, Karoly P. 1985–86. Control theory and multiple placebo effect. *Int. J. Psychiatry Med.* 15:137–47

39. Kefauver-Harris Amendments of October 10, 1962 to the Food, Drugs and Cosmetic Act, *Code Fed. Regul.* Washington, DC: US GPO

40. Kluge E-H. 1990. Placebos: some ethical considerations. *Can. Med. Assoc. J.* 142:293–95

41. Kojo I. 1988. The mechanism of the psychophysiological effects of placebo. *Med. Hypotheses* 27:261–64

42. Krakoff LR, Dziedzic S, Man SJ, Felton K, Yeager K. 1985. Plasma epinephrine concentration in healthy men: correlation with systolic pressure and rate pressure product. *J. Am. Coll. Cardiol.* 5:352–56

43. Lasagna L, Laties VG, Dohan LL. 1958. Further studies on the "pharmacology" of placebo administration. *J. Clin. Inves.* 37:533–37

44. Lasagna L. 1970. Drug evaluation problems in academic and other contexts. *Ann. NY Acad. Sci.* 169:503–8

45. Leber P. 1986. The placebo control in clinical trials. (A view from the FDA). *Psychopharmacol. Bull.* 22:30–32

46. Levine JF. 1985. The use of placebos in randomized clinical trials. *IRB Rev. Hum. Subjects Res.* 7:1–4

47. Levine JD, Gordon NC. 1986. Method of administration determines the effect of naloxone on pain. *Brain Res.* 365:377–78

48. Levine JD, Gordon MC, Fields HL. 1978. The mechanism of placebo analgesia. *Lancet* 2:654–57

49. Lind JA. 1753. *A Treatise of the Scurvy.* Edinburgh

50. Lipman JL, Miller BE, Mays KS, Miller MN, North WC, Byrne WL. 1990. Peak B endorphin concentrations in cerebrospinal fluid: reduced in chronic pain patients and increased during the placebo response. *Psychopharmacology* 102:112–16

51. Makuch RW, Johnson MF. 1989. Dilemmas in the use of active control groups in clinical research. *IRB Rev. Hum. Subjects Res.* 11:1–5

52. Meinert CL, Tonascia S. 1986. *Clinical Trials: Design, Conduct, and Analysis,* p. 65. New York: Oxford Univ. Press

53. Mellergaård M, Rosenberg NK. 1990. Patterns of response during placebo treatment of panic disorder. *Acta Psychiatr. Scand.* 81:340–44

54. Meyers S, Janowitz HD. The "natural history" of ulcerative colitis: an analysis of the placebo response. *J. Clin. Gastroenterol.* 11:33–37

55. Murali S, Uretsky BF, Kolesar JA, Valdes AM, Reddy PS. 1988. The acute effect of an oral "inotropic" placebo on the exercise capacity of patients with chronic cardiac failure. *Chest* 94:262–66

56. Newlin DB. 1989. Placebo responding in the same direction as alcohol in women. *Alcoholism* 13:36–39

57. Oh WM. 1991. Magic or medicine? Clinical pharmacological basis of placebo medication. *Ann. Acad. Med. Singapore* 20:31–37

58. Park LC, Covi L. 1965. Nonblind placebo trial: an exploration of neurotic patients' responses to placebo when its inert content is disclosed. *Arch. Gen. Psychiatry* 12:336–45

59. Pepper OHP. 1945. A note on the placebo. *Am. J. Pharm.* 117:409–12

60. Pledger GW, Hall D. 1986. Active control trials: Do they address the efficacy issue? (with discussion). *Proc. Am. Statist. Assoc.* (Biopharmaceut. Sect.) 1–10

61. Pocock SJ. 1983. *Clinical Trials. A Practical Approach*, pp. 92–93. New York: Wiley

62. Pogge RC, Coats EA. 1962. The placebo as a source of side effects in normal people: influence of gradually increasing doses. *Nebraska S. Med. J.* 47:337–39

63. Portaluppi F, Strozzi C, degli Uberti E, Rambaldi R, Trasforini G, et al. 1988. Does placebo lower blood pressure in hypertensive patients. A noninvasive chronobiological study. *Jpn. Heart J.* 29:189–97

64. Prien RF. 1988. Methods and models for placebo use in pharmacotherapeutic trials. *Psychopharm. Bull.* 24:4–8

65. Quitkin FM, McGrath PJ, Rabkin JG, Stewart JW, Harrison W, et al. 1991. Different types of placebo response in patients receiving antidepressants. *Am. J. Psychiatry* 148:197–203

66. Rabkin JG, McGrath PJ, Quitkin FM, Tricamo E, Stewart JW, Klein DF. 1990. *Am. J. Psychiatry* 147:1622–26

67. Reich J. 1990. The effect of personality on placebo response in panic patients. *J. Nerv. Ment. Dis.* 178:699–702

68. Rickels K. 1986. Use of placebo in clinical trials. *Psychopharm. Bull.* 22:19–24

69. Rickels K, Hesbacher PT, Weise CC, Gray B, Feldman HS. 1970. Pills and improvement: a study of placebo response in psychoneurotic outpatients. *Arch. Gen. Psychiatry* 41:72–80

70. Ritter JM. 1980. Placebo-controlled, double-blind clinical trials can impede medical progress. *Lancet* 1:1126–27

71. Ross M, Olson JM. An expectancy-attribution model of the effects of placebos. 1981. *Psychol. Rev.* 88:408–37

72. Sachs H, Chalmers TC, Smith H. 1982. Randomized versus historical controls for clinical trials. *Am. J. Med.* 72:233–40

73. Sackett DL. 1980. The competing objectives of randomized trials. *N. England J. Med.* 303:1059–60

74. Sassano P, Chatellier G, Corvol P, Ménard J. 1987. Influence of observer's expectation on the placebo in blood pressure trials. *Curr. Ther. Res.* 41:305–12

75. Schiller LR, Fordtran JS. 1986. Ulcer complications during short-term therapy of duodenal ulcer with active agents and placebo. *Gastroenterology* 90:478–81

76. Shapiro AK. 1964. Factors contributing to the placebo effect. *Am. J. Psychother.* 18:73–88

77. Shapiro AK. 1971. Placebo effects in medicine, psychotherapy, and psychoanalysis. In *Handbook of Psychotherapy and Behavior Change: An Empirical Analysis*, ed. AI Bergin, SL Garfield, pp. 439–73. New York: Wiley

78. Shapiro AK, Morris LA. 1978. The placebo effect in medicine and psychological therapies. In *Handbook of Psychotherapy and Behavior Change: An Empirical Analysis*, ed. AI Bergin, SL Garfield, pp. 369–410. New York: Wiley

79. Smith JL. 1989. Placebos in clinical trials of peptic ulcer. *Am. J. Gastroenterol.* 84:469–74

80. Smith RP. 1987. Objective changes in intrauterine pressure during placebo treatment of dysmenorrhea. *Pain* 29:59–66

81. Spanos NP, Stenstrom RJ, Johnston JC. 1988. Hypnosis, placebo, and suggestion in the treatment of warts. *Psychosomatic Med.* 50:245–60

82. Spodick DH. 1983. Ethics of the randomized clinical trial (Letter). *N. England J. Med.* 308:343

83. Stanley B. 1987. Informed consent in treatment and research. In *Handbook of Forensic Psychology*, ed. JB Weiner, AK Hess, pp. 63–85. New York: Wiley

84. Stanley B. 1988. An integration of ethical and clinical considerations in

the use of placebos. *Psychopharm. Bull.* 24:18–20

85. Stanley B, Stanley M. 1987. Psychiatric patients' comprehension of consent information. *Psychopharm. Bull.* 23:375–78

86. Temple R. 1982. Government viewpoint of clinical trials. *Drug Inform. J.* 16:10–17

87. Deleted in proof

88. Vayssairat M, Baudot N, Sainte-Beuve C. 1988. Why does placebo improve severe limb ischaemia? (Letter) *Lancet* 1:356

89. Deleted in proof

90. Veterans Admin. Coop. Study on Antihypertensive Agents. 1967. Effects of treatment of morbidity in hypertension: results in patients with diastolic 119mmHg. *J. Am. Med. Assoc.* 202:116–22

91. Volgyesi JA. 1954. "School for patients," hypnosis-therapy and psychoprophylaxis. *Br. J. Med. Hypnotism* 5:8–17

92. Voudouris NJ, Peck CL, Coleman G. 1990. The role of conditioning and verbal expectancy in the placebo response. *Pain* 43:121–28

93. Way WL. 1984. Placebo controls (Letter). *N. England J. Med.* 311:413–14

94. Wechsler H, Grosser GH, Greenblatt M. 1965. Research evaluating antidepressant medications on hospitalized mental patients: a survey of published reports during a five-year period. *J. Nerv. Ment. Dis.* 141:231–39

95. Wilcox CS, Cohn JB, Linden RD, Heiser JF, Lucas PB, et al. 1992. Predictors of placebo response: a retrospective analysis. *Psychopharm. Bull.* 28:157–62

Annu. Rev. Public Health. 1994. 15:39–67
Copyright © 1994 by Annual Reviews Inc. All rights reserved

LATINO OUTLOOK: Good Health, Uncertain Prognosis

William A. Vega

School of Public Health, University of California, Berkeley, California 94720

Hortensia Amaro

School of Public Health, Boston University, Boston, Massachusetts 02118-2389

KEY WORDS;   health care in minority populations, sociodemographics, reproductive
              health, nutrition, morbidity and mortality patterns

INTRODUCTION

This article presents a profile of the health status of Hispanic (Latino) populations in the United States. The review is issue oriented and identifies those factors that have a continuing influence on Hispanic health. Heterogeneity is perhaps the most salient characteristic that defines Hispanic populations of the United States. Hispanic populations include native born, migrant, and immigrant peoples with distinctive national origins and regional settlement patterns (85). This multi-generational migratory and social adjustment process has produced important cultural variations within and among the respective Hispanic ethnic groups. Moreover, the demographic structure of Hispanic populations is also varied and complex (7). These historical, demographic, and sociocultural features shape the health and disease experience of Hispanics. Logically, respective Hispanic ethnic groups can be expected to vary in health status and to have differing needs for health services.

This review provides a demographic comparison of Hispanic ethnic groups in the United States, an assessment of health status for the largest Hispanic groups, a brief summary of services utilization issues, and a discussion of health promotion and disease prevention. Framing the overall presentation is a controversial issue that deserves careful consideration. Historically, the absence of comprehensive epidemiologic information on Hispanic morbidity

39

0163-7525/94/0510-0039$05.00

and mortality resulted in lumping Hispanics into a larger social category of "minorities." Presumably, since Hispanics were exposed to similar underclass social conditions as other minorities, especially African Americans, generalizations derived from minority health profiles could be extended to cover Hispanics as well. However, the advent of dedicated studies on Hispanic health has demonstrated that some Hispanic groups diverge very significantly from the classic minority morbidity or mortality profiles. The reasons for these differences are not well understood. However, a number of researchers and Hispanic health advocates have concluded that Hispanics have a more favorable health profile than would be expected from their socioeconomic and minority status, and attribute this to sociocultural characteristics of Hispanics that operate as protective factors, or to selective immigration patterns (47). Are Hispanics a super-healthy population with differing health promotion and services needs? One goal of this review is to provide a critical summary of information pertinent to this complex question.

DEMOGRAPHIC COMPOSITION OF HISPANIC ETHNIC GROUPS

There are approximately 21 million Hispanics in the United States according to the 1990 census (110), with an additional 3.5 million in Puerto Rico. Between 1980 and 1990, the Hispanic population increased by 53%, a rate of growth eight times higher than that of the white non-Hispanic population (112). It has been estimated that by the year 2020 Hispanics will constitute the largest minority group in the United States. The rapid rate of increase is attributable to two facts: a continuing large influx of documented and undocumented immigrants and high cumulative fertility among the largest Hispanic ethnic group—Mexican Americans.

The age-sex profile of the U.S. Hispanic population based on the 1990 census (111) demonstrates two outstanding features. First, a larger proportion of Hispanics than white non-Hispanics is under 30 years of age. Second, the large number of 20–29 year old males produces an asymmetry in gender by age with young adult males actually outnumbering females until age 40. This reflects, in part, the increased immigration from Mexico and Central America during the 1980s and the results of the Immigration Reform and Control Act of 1986, which granted legal residence to approximately 2.5 million formerly undocumented individuals. About 71.0% of Hispanics in the United States are native born, with 29% being immigrants, and about two of three Hispanics speak Spanish at home (90).

Sociodemographic differences between Hispanic ethnic groups are apparent in the 1990 census data. Mexican-origin Hispanics constitute the largest subgroup, 64.0%, and are the youngest with a median age of 24.1 years, and have the lowest education and income levels (median income = $12,527 for males and $8,874 for females). Only 44.1% of Mexican Americans have completed high school, and 69.6% of all Hispanics earning below poverty are Mexican origin. The most striking contrast is with Cuban-origin Hispanics. With a median age of 39.1, they are significantly older than either the Hispanic or non-Hispanic populations. Fully 14% of Cuban-origin Hispanics are 65 years of age or older, as contrasted with only 4.9% for the total Hispanic population. Cubans are also twice as likely to be college educated as the total Hispanic population, 20.2% compared to 9.2%, and Cubans are much less likely to have incomes (median = $19,336 for males and $12,880 for females) below the poverty level (15.2%). Puerto Ricans are a comparison group of considerable interest because they are US citizens and have never been immigrants. Nevertheless, their demographic characteristics most closely resemble Mexican Americans although they are more likely to have completed high school (55.5%) and to have a higher median income (median = $18,222 for males and $12,812 for females). However, a larger proportion of Puerto Ricans (33.0%) than Mexican Americans (28.4%) is living below the poverty line. The aggregated Central and South American origin group is older (median age = 28.0 years), better educated (58.5% high school graduates), and slightly less likely to live below poverty (18.5%) than the total Hispanic population. As a source of comparison, the following demographic profile of white non-Hispanics is provided: median age = 33.5 years; 79.6% are high school graduates; median income = $22,081 (males) and $11,885 (females); 11.6% live below the poverty level.

The variation in female-headed households among Hispanic ethnic groups is profound, with 38.9% of Puerto Rican households contrasting with 19.6% of Mexican and 18.9% of Cuban-origin households being female-headed. Hispanic families are larger than non-Hispanic families, with Mexican-origin families being the largest and Cubans being the smallest.

Unemployment among Hispanics is generally 40–60% higher than among white non-Hispanics and somewhat lower overall than among African Americans. Cubans have the lowest unemployment rate, 6.4%, whereas Puerto Rican and Mexican American levels are almost twice as high, 10.3% and 10.7%, respectively. Hispanic employment is concentrated in lower status occupations such as service workers/laborers, and least likely to be found among professionals and managers. About 73.5% of Hispanic men and 40.2% of Hispanic women, as compared with 51.4% of non-Hispanic men and 24.6% of non-Hispanic women, were employed in service, production and laborer occupations according to the 1990 Census.

Although Hispanics are in the process of becoming a national population, their regional distribution reflects historical migration and immigration patterns. Southwestern Hispanics are predominantly of Mexican origin; in the Northeast, Puerto Ricans are more numerous; and in South Florida, Cubans are the largest subgroup. However, immigration from the Caribbean Basin area, especially the Dominican Republic, Colombia, Guatemala, El Salvador, Honduras, and Nicaragua, has sharply increased the numbers of people immigrating from this region in the past decade into Miami, New York, Chicago, Washington D.C., Los Angeles, Houston, and other major urban centers of the United States. About nine of ten Hispanics live in urban areas, but there are proportionately and numerically more Mexican Americans than other Hispanics in rural areas, in part because of the farm-labor component of the Mexican-origin subgroup.

Gleaning the implications of this demographic profile of Hispanics is difficult because it is not a static population. Immigration from Latin America continues and the numbers of individuals from different sending nations, as well as their ultimate destinations, cannot be predicted with precision. It is very obvious that the past decade has decreased the educational level of foreign-born Hispanics, and by extension, their earning potential as well. Previous research has shown a consistent inverse relationship between socioeconomic status and morbidity or mortality in societies throughout the world (102). Therefore, the potential impact of low economic mobility on health among Hispanics is a serious concern. Continuing problems with communicable diseases among immigrant populations are to be expected. The disproportionate number of young males in the Hispanic population portends public health problems such as accidental death, alcohol and drug abuse, serious psychiatric disorders, sexually transmitted diseases, and increasing suicide rates. The high cumulative fertility of certain Hispanic ethnic groups has implications for reproductive health and nutrition, and the increasing size of the Hispanic population over 65 suggests that health issues associated with later life will receive increasing attention.

From a public health perspective, the most vexing issue is the marginal socioeconomic and educational position of the US Hispanic population. There are disturbing signs of increasing intergenerational poverty, reinforced by structural problems such as poor labor market conditions and a debilitated educational infrastructure. The critical question is whether, at this historical juncture, sufficient opportunity for social and economic mobility will be available to offset Hispanic population growth, and whether Hispanic cultural strengths can operate to mitigate the negative impact of structural factors on health and on the environments where Hispanics must live.

Mortality and Morbidity Indicators of Hispanic Populations

To reiterate, the health status of Hispanics arguably presents a paradox in public health (53, 77, 95, 123) because they have a health profile that is as good or better than that of white non-Hispanics (26, 47). The evidence to support this position is ambiguous, and so are the potential implications. Generally, the data suggest that Puerto Ricans in the continental United States have a more jeopardized health status than Mexican Americans. In turn, Mexican Americans have a more jeopardized health status than Cuban Americans. Further, variations in health status among Hispanics necessitate that health data be disaggregated by Hispanic group. Therefore, data on Hispanics as an aggregate group do not represent an accurate picture of the health status of all Hispanic ethnic groups and loose generalizations can lead to erroneous conclusions and faulty public health strategies.

Limitations of Existing Data

Before discussing the issues identified above, it is important to note some severe limitations of available data. The 1985 Secretary's Task Force on Black and Minority Health Report (114) was filled with apologies regarding the lack of Hispanic health data. Almost 10 years later, the Healthy People 2000 Report was not able to propose Hispanic-specific initiatives for the majority of measurable objectives due to the continued lack of baseline data. The failure of US health data systems to provide information on mortality and morbidity trends for Hispanic populations was noted in a 1992 report by the General Accounting Office (38). Health, United States, 1991, which provides systematic analysis of health data by race, provides extremely limited health data by Hispanic ethnicity. The most useful data on Hispanics have come from a one time cross-sectional study, the Hispanic Health and Nutrition Examination Survey, which is now ten years old. Improvement in the nation's health data systems has been slow and limited.

Most national health data systems do not provide adequate data on the health of Hispanics because (a) they do not collect appropriate and accurate data on Hispanic ethnicity; (b) they do not sample sufficiently large numbers of Hispanics; or (c) they fail to tabulate and report data separately for Hispanics. Moreover, the Council of Scientific Affairs of the American Medical Association concluded that: "Accurate estimates of Hispanic death rates are impossible to determine because, until 1988, the national model death certificates did not contain Hispanic identifiers. Although some states incorporated Hispanic origin on their death certificates, such reporting was not uniform and lacks precision" (25).

The most recent mortality statistics (73) present two additional limitations. First, 1990 mortality data that are based on Hispanic-origin population from 46 States and the District of Columbia, exclude Hispanics from New York City because more than 10% of death certificates had inadequate data for ethnicity (73). Although the exclusion of New York City does not seriously affect the data's coverage of the Mexican American population (99% covered), the Cuban American population (92% covered) or the Other Hispanic population (81% covered), the Puerto Rican population (58% covered) is grossly underrepresented. Further, since about half of the deaths attributed to Puerto Ricans are accounted for by New York City, the mortality rates for Hispanics overall and for Puerto Ricans in particular are underestimated (73). This is likely to introduce an underestimation of specific causes of death that are disproportionately found in the New York City Puerto Rican population (e.g. infant mortality, HIV/AIDS, tuberculosis). A second limitation of currently available death statistics is that, for Hispanics, they only provide absolute numbers of deaths and the ranking of the causes of death. Due to inadequate denominator data from the census (74), detailed cause-specific death rates for Hispanic subgroups have not been calculated for Hispanics since 1979–81. Death rates for 1987–89 have been calculated for selected causes of death and overall death rates for Hispanics (72).

In the following sections we present data on mortality and morbidity among Hispanics. When available, data are presented for the major Hispanic groups (i.e. Mexican Americans, Puerto Ricans, and Cubans). It has become increasingly important to also understand the health status and health care needs of other Hispanic populations (e.g. Central and South Americans) who represent a growing sector of the Hispanic population in the United States. These data are provided when available, but these groups are often not considered in the presentation of health data.

MORTALITY

Three commonly used mortality indicators are overall death rates, disease-specific death rates, and leading causes of death. For each of these, data are first presented for Hispanics overall; whenever data are available on specific Hispanic groups, such data are presented.

Death Rates for Hispanics

The most recently available overall death rates for Hispanics reflect 1988 deaths from 26 states and the District of Columbia (72). These data have been published only for Hispanics as a whole and do not provide Hispanic group breakdowns. Although these data provide relatively good coverage for the overall Hispanic population (82%), they provide poor coverage of the Cuban population (32%) (72, 74). Among 15–24-year olds (34, 72), the death rate for Hispanics (113 per 100,000) is greater than that for White non-Hispanics (95 per 100,000), but lower than for non-Hispanic Blacks (145 per 100,000). Similarly, among 25–44-year olds, the death rate for Hispanics (185 per 100,000), is greater than that for non-Hispanics (149 per 100,000) and lower than for non-Hispanic Blacks (367 per 100,000).

In the youngest age group (1–14 years), Hispanics have rates similar to white non-Hispanics (30 per 100,000). However, in the older age groups (45–65 and 65 years and older), Hispanics (609 per 100,000 and 3,482 per 100,000, respectively) have much lower death rates than white non-Hispanics (790 per 100,000 and 5106 per 100,000, respectively).

Death Rates for Specific Hispanic Groups

Mortality statistics that group all Hispanics together mask important differences in health conditions that affect specific groups. The most recent available data on overall death rates by Hispanic group come from 15 reporting States between 1979 and 1981, which included 45 percent of the Hispanic population (61). However, the accuracy of these data might also differ among the various Hispanic groups. The average annual age-adjusted death rates for Hispanic groups reflect significant within group variability. They are highest among Puerto Ricans (512.4 per 100,000) compared to other Hispanic groups (Mexican = 489.4; Cuban = 345.2; Other Hispanic = 341.3). Even among Puerto Ricans, however, the rate is lower than that for white non-Hispanics (529.5) and much lower than the rate for non-Hispanic Blacks (795.6).

Disease-Specific Mortality Rates

Data on specific causes of death for Hispanics as a group indicate that of 38 major categories representing 72 selected causes of death in 1979–80, Hispanics have higher rates for 20 major categories: tuberculosis, meningococcal infection, septicemia, viral hepatitis, syphilis, all other infectious and parasitic diseases, diabetes mellitus, nutritional deficiencies, meningitis, pneumonia and influenza, chronic liver disease and cirrhosis, cholelithiasis and other disorders of gallbladder, nephritis, nephrotic syndrome and nephrosis, complications of pregnancy-childbirth and the puerperium, certain conditions originating in the perinatal period, all other diseases, accidents and adverse effects, homicide and legal intervention and all other external causes (61). More recent data from 1987–89 (72), which provide information on Hispanic death rates for four major causes of death, show continued increasing rates among Hispanics that surpass the rate for white non-Hispanics for deaths due to accidents and adverse effects (especially among 15–44 year olds) and for homicide and suicide after age 14. Diseases of the heart and malignant neoplasms, the two leading causes of death by far, among Hispanics between 1987–89 continue to be much lower than for white non-Hispanics (72).

When disease-specific death rates are separated out by Hispanic group, it becomes clear that the above causes of death vary in importance across Hispanic groups (see Table 1). The average annual age-adjusted death rates

Table 1 Average annual age-adjusted death rates

| Cause of Death | Hispanic | | | | Non-Hispanic |
	Mexican	Puerto Rican	Cuban	Other Hispanic	White
All causes	489.4	512.4	345.2	341.3	795.6
Shigellosis and amebiasis	0.1	—	—	—	0.0
Certain other intestinal infections	0.1	0.0	—	0.1	0.2
Tuberculosis	1.5	1.1	0.4	0.5	0.4
Whooping cough	—	—	—	0.0	
Streptococcal sore throat, scarlatina, and erysipelas	0.0	—	—	—	0.0
Meningococcal infection	0.1	0.3	—	0.2	0.1
Septicemia	4.1	1.8	1.1	1.7	2.1
Acute poliomyelitis	—	—	—	—	0.0
Measles	—	—	—	—	0.0
Viral hepatitis	0.3	0.5	1.0	0.3	0.3
Syphilis	0.1	—	—	—	0.0
All other infectious and parasitic diseases	1.9	1.0	0.0	0.9	1.1
Malignant neoplasms	84.4	86.4	81.6	65.8	123.6
Benign neoplasms, carcinoma in situ, and neoplasms of uncertain behavior and of unspecified nature	1.3	1.9	0.9	1.0	1.7
Diabetes mellitus	18.6	16.8	6.1	7.7	8.8
Nutritional deficiencies	0.6	0.1	—	0.3	0.4
Anemias	0.6	0.6	—	0.7	0.7
Meningitis	0.5	0.5	0.0	0.4	0.4
Major cardiovascular diseases	186.9	202.6	141.1	130.8	240.6
Acute bronchitis and bronchiolitis	0.1	0.1	—	0.0	0.1
Pneumonia and influenza	11.4	18.1	7.5	9.0	11.3
Chronic obstructive pulmonary diseases and allied conditions	6.6	11.9	5.5	6.4	15.7
Ulcer of stomach and duodenum	1.1	1.6	1.0	1.3	1.6
Appendicitis	0.1	0.0	—	0.0	0.2
Hernia of abdominal cavity and intestinal obstruction without mention of hernia	1.4	0.5	0.6	0.7	1.2
Chronic liver disease and cirrhosis	14.7	34.2	9.2	12.8	9.4
Cholelithiasis and other disorders of gallbladder	1.6	0.7	0.2	0.8	0.7
Nephritis, nephrotic syndrome, and nephrosis	0.1	0.0	—	0.0	0.2
Infections of kidney	0.6	0.5	—	0.5	0.6
Hyperplasia of prostate	0.1	0.2	—	0.1	0.2
Complications of pregnancy, childbirth, and the puerperium	0.2	0.3	0.0	0.0	0.1
Congenital anomalies	5.0	5.0	1.6	5.0	5.4

Certain conditions orginating in the perinatal period				
All other diseases-residual	32.7	31.6	14.2	22.2	28.9
Accidents and adverse effects	46.9	25.5	19.5	27.9	36.8
Suicide	8.2	9.2	12.4	6.9	11.3
Homicide and legal intervention	24.7	35.3	20.9	18.8	5.2
All other external causes	1.1	6.4	3.0	2.9	1.6

for 1979–81 indicate that Puerto Ricans have the highest overall age-adjusted death rates among Hispanic groups, and Cubans and Other Hispanics have the lowest rates.

Data on infant mortality also demonstrate the pattern of higher death rates among Puerto Ricans (10.2) who have a higher infant mortality rate than Mexican Americans (7.7), Cubans (7.6), and white non-Hispanics (7.4) (73). Data from 1983–85, which did not exclude Puerto Ricans in New York City, showed a higher infant mortality rate among Puerto Ricans (12.3), which represents a 41% excess neonatal mortality and a 29% excess post-neonatal mortality compared to the rates for children of white non-Hispanic mothers (72). The reliability of these estimates for Mexican Americans has also been questioned due to under-reporting in the US-Mexico border region.

Leading Causes of Death

There are also important differences between Hispanics and white non-Hispanics in the leading causes of death. The ten leading causes of death among Hispanics are: diseases of the heart, malignant neoplasms, accidents and adverse effects, cerebrovascular diseases, homicide and legal intervention, diabetes mellitus, pneumonia and influenza, HIV infection, chronic liver disease and cirrhosis, and certain conditions generating in the perinatal period. Data from deaths in 1989 indicate that among Hispanics homicide and legal intervention, HIV infection, and certain conditions in the perinatal period rank in the ten leading causes of death, whereas among white non-Hispanics, these three categories are not found among the ten leading causes of death (71). Conversely, white non-Hispanics have three leading causes of death not found among the ten leading causes for Hispanics: chronic obstructive pulmonary disease and allied conditions, suicide, and atherosclerosis. Some of these differences are attributable to age differences between these groups. However, the following leading causes of death consistently rank higher among Hispanics within the same age categories: homicide and legal intervention (15–64 years of age), and HIV infection (1–64 years of age) (71). Among Hispanics aged 45 years and over, chronic liver disease also ranks higher than among white non-Hispanics. The 1990 data indicate that HIV changed from the 6th to the 8th leading cause of death, although this is surely an artifact of the exclusion of deaths from New York City.

Morbidity Among Hispanics

Indicators of health status, such as the incidence of chronic conditions and infectious diseases, other measures of illness such as bed-disability days, and health behaviors also vary across Hispanic groups.

Table 2 presents a summary of research studies documenting excess morbidity related to certain chronic conditions among Hispanics. Studies summarized in Table 2 show that much of the data on morbidity among Hispanics has been obtained in community-specific studies, many of which focus on Mexican Americans in San Antonio, Texas, or California, and on Puerto Ricans in New York City or Connecticut. The Hispanic Health and Nutrition Examination survey conducted between 1982–1984 is the only study that systematically provides data on all of the major Hispanic groups (Mexican Americans, Puerto Ricans, and Cuban Americans). In some cases, studies have compared data for Puerto Ricans living on the island. However, as shown in Table 2, there are few studies that provide such comparisons.

Table 2 shows diseases and conditions for Hispanic groups relative to non-Hispanic whites. For example, while the rates of diabetes among Cubans are similar to those of white non-Hispanics, Mexican Americans and Puerto Ricans have rates two to three times higher (35). Diabetes in Mexican Americans is also associated with a rate of complications, especially end-stage renal disease and retinopathy, that is six times higher than among white non-Hispanics (99). Higher prevalence of factors related to diabetes, such as obesity, proteinuria, and glucose intolerance, have also been documented among Mexican Americans and Puerto Ricans (35, 45, 78, 81, 100).

Rates of cardiovascular disease and related factors such as cholesterol levels among Hispanics have been reported to be similar or lower than among white non-Hispanics while other factors such as diabetes and obesity show higher rates in Hispanics (27). Some studies have reported that high blood pressure is more prevalent among Mexican Americans and Cubans than among white non-Hispanics (16, 31). However, other research indicates that Hispanics have similar or lower levels of high blood pressure compared to white non-Hispanics (65, 98). Most studies have consistently shown, however, that Hispanics have higher rates of untreated or unrecognized cases of high blood pressure (16, 27, 31, 65, 98).

Data from state cancer registries generally indicate lower overall rates of cancer among Hispanics, although for some cancers some Hispanic groups have higher rates. For example, studies of Hispanics in Connecticut and New York City (primarily Puerto Ricans) (83, 124) and California (majority Mexican Americans) (66) have documented increased incidence of stomach cancer in these groups, whereas data from Hispanics in Dade County, Florida (primarily Cubans) show lower rates than among white non-Hispanics (105). Disproportionately high cervical cancer rates (two times higher relative risk) have been found among Hispanic women in Connecticut, New York and California compared to white non-Hispanics (66, 83, 124). There is also evidence of increased rates of: gallbladder cancer among Hispanics in California (66) and male and female Hispanics in Dade County, Florida (105); cancer of the buccal cavity and pharynx among Hispanic men in New York City (124); cancer of the larynx and thyroid among Hispanic men and women in Dade County, Florida (105); cancer of the esophagus for Hispanic men and women, and cancer of the oral cavity among Hispanic men in Connecticut (83). There are higher rates of cancer of the liver and leukemia among Hispanic men than white non-Hispanics men in New York City and Connecticut (83, 124).

Infectious diseases disproportionately affect Hispanics (101). Increased rates of immunizable diseases, such as measles, rubella, congenital rubella, tetanus and pertussis, have been documented among Hispanics living in the Southwestern US and in the Northeast (101). Higher rates of bacterial gastrointestinal diseases, parasites, and other tropic-endemic diseases have been found among Hispanics living primarily in the Southwest and among Hispanic farmworkers in other geographic regions compared to white non-Hispanics (101).

The incidence of tuberculosis is two times higher among Hispanics (18.3 per 100,000) compared to white non-Hispanics (9.1 per 100,000) (115). The higher rates of tuberculosis have been documented among Hispanics living in New York City and in the Southwest (101). The rates (per 100,000) of primary and secondary syphilis are five times greater among Hispanic women (10.7) and men (22.8), compared to white non-Hispanics (1.8 and 2.9, respectively) (28). Other sexually transmitted diseases such as congenital syphilis, chancroid, chlamydia, and gonococcus have been demonstrated to affect Hispanics disproportionately and to be on the increase in this population. The increase in syphilis in Hispanics has been especially striking (24% increase) compared to that in Hispanic men (7% increase) and the minimal increase observed in white non-Hispanics (101).

The cumulative incidence rate for adults diagnosed with AIDS is 3.3 times higher among Hispanics; Puerto Ricans largely account for AIDS cases among Hispanics. They are seven times more likely than non-Hispanic whites to be diagnosed with AIDS (93, 94). Rates of AIDS cases among Hispanics in the Southwest are at levels similar to those in the white

Table 2 Summary of reported evidence of excess morbidity among Hispanic populations as compared to non-Hispanic whites (NHW)

Disease	Evidence	Geographic Area/Year of Data/Hispanic Group	Reference
CANCER			
overall rates	Lower overall incidence rates for Hispanics (RR = .88)	Dade County, FL, 1982–83 Hispanic (67% Cuban)	105
	Standardized incidence rates (SIR) for all invasive cancers higher for men (SIR = 1.16) and lower for women (SIR = .77) compared to NHW and higher than for Hispanics in Puerto Rico (males: SIR = 1.99; females: SIR = 1.39)	Connecticut, 1980–86 Puerto-Rican born CT, residents and residents of Puerto Rico	83
	Incidence lower (320/100,000) than for NHW (392) and higher than for those in Puerto Rico (245) for men and women	New York City, 1982–85 Hispanic (60% PR)	124
lung	Lower risk RR = .88	Dade County, FL, 1982–83 Hispanic (67% Cuban)	105
	SIR significantly reduced for females (SIR = .57) but not for males (SIR = .94)	Connecticut, 1980–86 (see above)	83
	Incidence rates for males and females lower than (51.5 vs. 73.2) and higher for NHW than for residents of Puerto Rico (22.9)	New York City, 1982–85 Hispanic (60% PR)	124
stomach	Increased incidence: SIR = 2.65 females, SIR = 2.91 males	Connecticut, 1980–86 (see above)	83
	Increased incidence: RR = 2.1 females, RR = 2.2 males	California, 1991 Mexican American	66

	Highest incidence rates per 100,000 in Puerto Rico (11.3/24.4), followed by Hispanics in NYC (10.3/18.7) and NHW (7/13.4) (female/male)	New York City, 1982–85 Hispanic (60% PR)	124
	Lower risk: RR = .61	Dade County, FL, 1982–83 Hispanic (67% Cuban)	105
reproductive system	Cervical cancer: higher incidence (SIR = 1.81; RR = 2.3) or rates (2.5 times) found in four regions	Studies in Florida, Connecticut, New York City, California, 1980s M-A, PR, C-A	66, 83, 105, 124
	Anglos get pap smears and mammograms more often	US, 1987–88 California, 1989 Hispanic (majority Puerto Rican)	15, 30
	Lower rate incidence in other reproductive organs: *breast cancer	New York City, 1982–85 Connecticut 1980–86 Hispanic (PR)	83, 124
	*corpus uteri and ovary	New York City, 1982–85 Connecticut 1980–86 Hispanic (PR)	83, 124
	*testicular (RR = .17)	Florida, 1982–83 Hispanic (67% Cuban)	105
gall bladder	Increased incidence for females: RR = 4.9	California, 1991 Mexican American	66
	Increased incidence among men and women (RR = 5.45)	Dade County, FL, 1982–83 Hispanic (67% Cuban)	105

Table 2 (*Continued*)

Disease	Evidence	Geographic Area/Year of Data/Hispanic Group	Reference
buccal cavity and pharynx	Higher rates than for NHW among males (23 vs 14.3)	New York City, 1982–85 Hispanic (60% PR)	124
oral cavity, larynx, thyroid and esophagus	Higher rates in larynx (RR = 1.58) and thyroid (RR = 3.12)	Dade County, FL, 1982–83 Hispanic (67% Cuban)	105
	Higher SIR* of esophageal cancer for males (RR = 2.76) and females, and of oral cavity for males (RR = 2.29)	Connecticut, 1980–86 Puerto-Rican born CT residents	83
	Lower rate of esophageal cancer	Dade County, FL, 1982–83 Hispanic (67% Cuban)	105
liver	Twice as prevalent for males	New York City, 1982–85 Hispanic (60% PR)	124
other sites	Higher rates of leukemia among males	Connecticut, 1980–86 (See above)	83
	Lower rates or relative risk in following sites: skin (melanoma), rectum, kidney, pancreas, colon, Kaposi's Sarcoma	Studies in California, New York City, Florida, Connecticut, 1980–86 M-A, PR, C-A	66, 83, 105, 124
CARDIO-VASCULAR DISEASE (including coronary artery disease)	Mortality declining more slowly among Hispanics than overall decline	Meta-analysis M-A, PR, C-A+	16
	Slightly lower age-adjusted prevalence rates of Rose angina for Mexican American women	Samples from 3 areas of USA, 1982–84 M-A, PR, C-A	53a
	Lower cardiovascular mortality for Mexican American men; no ethnic difference for women	San Antonio, 1979–88 Mexican American	64

Category	Finding	Population / Sample	Ref
risk factors cholesterol	Women had lower HDL cholesterol and higher triglycerides than NHW; no difference for total cholesterol or LDL; similar pattern for men but not significant	Florida Cuban	52a
hypertension	More prevalent, and higher rates of untreated or unrecognized cases	Meta-analysis M-A, PR, C-A	16
	Acculturation and age are stronger predictors of hypertension than poverty among older Mexican Americans	Samples from 3 areas of USA, 1982–84 M-A, PR, C-A	32
CHILDREN's ILLNESSES ASTHMA	Similar prevalence compared to NHW children; possibly higher morbidity related to poverty and limited insurance and health coverage	San Antonio, 1988–89 Mexican American	126
BIRTH OUTCOMES	Similar low birth weight (LBW) prevalence as compared to NHW (6.2% and 5.6%) with greater risk for Puerto Ricans (9.3%)	US sample and samples from 3 areas of USA, 1987 and 1982–84 M-A, PR, C-A	63
	Higher prevalence LBW babies among US-born Puerto Rican, Mexican and Cuban women than among foreign or island born women in all age groups	US sample and samples from 3 areas of USA, 1987 and 1982–84 M-A, PR, C-A	63
	Premature births more common among 3 Hispanic groups than among NHW women: highest for Puerto Ricans	US sample and samples from 3 areas of USA, 1987 and 1982–84 M-A, PR, C-A	63
CHRONIC MEDICAL CONDITIONS (CMC)	Puerto Rican children at greater risk for CMC than Mexican- or Cuban-American or NHW children	US sample and samples from 3 areas of USA, 1987 and 1982–84 M-A, PR, C-A	63
DIABETES	Rates of NIDDM* 3 times higher	San Antonio, 1979–82 Mexican American	45

Table 2 (*Continued*)

Disease	Evidence	Geographic Area/Year of Data/Hispanic Group	Reference
	Mexican American diabetics have higher levels of glycemia and clinical proteinuria (OR = 2.82)	San Antonio, 1979–82 Mexican American	45
	Prevalence 2–3 times greater for Puerto Ricans and Mexican-Americans	Sample 3 areas of USA, 1982–84 M-A, PR, C-A$^+$	35, 46
	Prevalence increases initially among migrant populations as they "modernize"; may then decline again for men and maybe women	San Antonio, 1989 Mexican-American	100
	Higher acculturation and, among women, higher SES associated with linear decline in obesity & diabetes	San Antonio, 1979–82 Mexican-American	49
related factors end-stage renal disease (ESRD)	Relative disparity for ESRD: 17% of diabetics and 22% of those seeking care for ESRD	Colorado, 1982–89 Hispanics in CO	21
	Increase in age-adjusted incidence rate (1982–89): Hispanics 770%, Blacks 440%, NHW 190%	Colorado, 1982–89 Hispanics in CO	21

obesity/ overweight	Higher prevalence; among Hispanics, highest for Mexican American; higher among women and low SES	Texas and US sample, 1982–84 Mexican American and other Hispanics	78
	Prevalence of obesity 31–34% for men and 38–42% for women among Hispanics	Sample 3 areas of, USA, 1982–84 M-A, PR, C-A[+]	81
	Body Mass Index (BMI) decreased for women as SES increased; high acculturation related to decrease in BMI	Texas, 1979–82 Mexican American	49, 100
glucose intolerance	Higher prevalence particularly among Mexican Americans and Puerto Ricans	Sample 3 areas of USA, 1982–84 M-A, PR, C-A[+]	35
	Higher prevalence of hyperinsulemia among nondiabetic Mexican Americans relative to nondiabetic NHW's	San Antonio, 1982–84 Mexican American	100

* NIDDM = non insulin-dependent diabetes mellitus
+ M-A: Mexican American; PR: Puerto Rican; C-A: Cuban-American

non-Hispanic population; rates for Hispanics in Florida fall between the two (18, 101). AIDS cases are especially disproportionately increased among Hispanic children (23% of pediatric AIDS cases) and women (20% of cases in women). Rates of HIV infection are also higher among Hispanics, especially in the Northeast, as demonstrated by higher rates of HIV antibody among US military service applicants, active duty military personnel, women attending family planning clinics, adolescents entering the Job Corps program, and blood donors (19, 20).

Rates of depression symptomatology and lifetime history of depression have been reported to be higher among Puerto Ricans when compared to rates obtained for the general population and for other Hispanic groups (67). Data on bed-disability days and activity limitation suggest that Puerto Rican children under 17 years of age have over two times the number of bed-disability days (43) and 50 percent more Puerto Rican children have some type of activity limitation due to an illness (6.2), compared to non-Hispanics whites (5.1; 4.0) or Black children (4.7; 3.7) (113).

Risk Behaviors

Certain behaviors or risk factors associated with negative health outcomes and impaired psychosocial development are also more prevalent among Hispanics compared to non-Hispanics. For example, pregnancy among girls age 17 and younger is more prevalent among Hispanics (158 per 1000) than white non-Hispanics (71.1 per 1000) and close to that of Blacks (186 per 1000) (121). Relatively little is known about family planning among Hispanic women. It remains inconclusive whether Hispanic women initiate intercourse at an older age and engage in sexual intercourse less often than other women. Paradoxically, relatively low rates of sexual intercourse among Mexican American teenage girls coincide with high fertility rates as a result of relatively low rates of use of contraceptives and low rates of abortion. Factors related to contraception decisions are not well understood, but Hispanic women may simply have more desire to have children than women in other ethnic groups. Similarly, little is known about sexual behavior among Hispanic women. In all of these areas considerably more comparative research is needed. Hispanic women (Mexican American = 39%; Puerto Rican = 37%; Cuban = 34%) are also more likely to be overweight than white non-Hispanics women (27%) (25, 78, 81).

Use of marijuana and cocaine varies greatly by Hispanic group and is more common among Puerto Ricans of both genders compared to women and men in other Hispanic groups (1). Puerto Rican women (30.3%) also have higher age-adjusted smoking rates than Mexican American (23.8%) and Cuban (24.4%) women (48).

In summary, the health status of Hispanics, as reflected in morbidity and mortality patterns, differs greatly among Hispanic subgroups. While patterns vary for specific diseases, Puerto Ricans in the continental US demonstrate a more unfavorable health profile than Mexican Americans. Although more sparse, the mortality and morbidity data on Cubans indicate that they are generally in better health than other Hispanics. The relatively low death rate among Mexican Americans, who share many of the economic disadvantages of Puerto Ricans and Blacks, has presented a public health paradox. This pattern runs counter to the well-documented gradient effect of socio-economic status on health (53, 77, 95, 123).

Health Status and Acculturation

There is evidence that the health habits and health status of Hispanic immigrants deteriorate with length of stay in the United States, as well as in succeeding generations, due to increased acculturation. The process of acculturation and the type of cultural contact experienced in migration among Hispanics is stressful because of the disruption of attachments to supportive networks, and the concomitant tasks of adapting to the economic and social systems in the host culture (86, 118). The work of Vega and colleagues (120) has provided evidence that the social support provided by networks of family and friends among immigrant Mexican women plays a critical role in adaptation to life in this country. The Hispanic migrant is also likely to experience discrimination, prejudice, and exclusion that frustrates expectations of improved social and economic status with increased adoption of the dominant culture's values. At the same time, the immigrant/migrant is faced with incorporating into his/her identity, a newly acquired "minority status". Berry (10) describes responses to these conditions and notes the vulnerability of the individual who, in the process of adaptation, abandons all or major parts of her/his cultural values and identification and assimilates into the dominant society. This assimilation may include the abandonment of culturally tied health beliefs and the loss of culturally tied resources and social support networks, which may place her/him at risk (52).

Other evidence indicates that some forms of cultural "adaptation" or acculturation are harmful to the health of Hispanics. The following health indicators worsen with increased acculturation: rates of infant mortality (8), low birth weight (8, 44, 63), overall cancer rates (30, 83, 124), high blood pressure (32), and adolescent pregnancy (121).

Certain behaviors also increase with acculturation. These include: decreased fiber consumption (30); decreased breast feeding (25); increased use of cigarettes (48); increased alcohol consumption—especially in younger women (14, 39, 58, 60, 76) and driving under the influence of alcohol (22); and increased use of illicit drugs (1, 75, 80, 82, 86, 92). Some studies have also documented that depressive symptomatology increases with acculturation (13, 42, 52, 67, 79, 96), although the relationship between depression and acculturation remains controversial (86).

The relationship between acculturation and risky behaviors or jeopardized health is often striking. For example, the rate of adolescent pregnancy is twice as high among Hispanics born in the U.S. compared to those born outside the continental U.S. (121). Furthermore, the rate of low birth weight infants born to second-generation Mexican American women is almost two times higher than that among comparable first-generation women (44). Use of illicit drugs increases with acculturation (1, 75, 80, 82, 92, 117). Data from the Hispanic HANES indicate that marijuana use is eight times higher among Mexican Americans and five times greater among Puerto Ricans who are highly acculturated compared to those who are not acculturated, even after socio-demographic factors are controlled (1). Also, use of cocaine is associated with acculturation among Mexican Americans and Puerto Ricans (1). Moreover, drug use and acculturation conflicts are related to increased suicide attempts among Hispanic adolescents (116). Use of cigarettes among Mexican American women is significantly lower among those with low levels of acculturation (19%) compared to those with high levels of acculturation (28%) (48).

There are, however, some exceptions to the trend toward worsening health and health habits with acculturation. Dietary habits (intake of total calories and fat), for example, improve with acculturation (30, 99). Body mass index (27), diabetes, and obesity (49, 100) also decrease with increased socioeconomic status and acculturation.

The acculturation process involves adaptation not only at the individual level, but also at the level of family and community. Szapocznik and colleagues (80, 92, 103) have described the effects of acculturation and its differential impact in generations within the family. Their work has demonstrated that gender and age mediate the experience of adaptation to a new culture. The effects of acculturation on the social character and group dynamics within communities and accompanying negative effects on health have been documented in other immigrant populations, such as the studies of the Roseto community (29). The Roseto Effect points to the need to understand the impact that community structure and organization have on the acculturative process and the health of Hispanics.

Research is needed to address a series of profound questions. First, we must understand the selective factors that operate in the migration process and how these shape immigrants' health status and risk behaviors. We also need to understand the nature of social networks, social support systems, and the organization and cohesion of the varied communities where Hispanics live and work (84, 86, 120). Finally, research is needed to better understand

Hispanic immigrants' experience of discrimination and its impact on social, environmental, and behavioral health risks.

HEALTH SERVICES UTILIZATION ISSUES

Key questions remain about Hispanic health services utilization patterns: Do Hispanics underutilize health services? If they do, which Hispanics are underutilizing and why? A cursory review of the literature on services utilization clearly suggests that Hispanics, as a composite population, use almost all forms of health care at a rate below that of white non-Hispanics. However, these differences are clearly attributable to the utilization behavior of Mexican Americans (11, 51, 55, 107), who have lower mortality rates for the leading chronic diseases.

Factors held responsible for Hispanic health use behaviors include: selective migration (12, 13); personal (47), cultural (23, 24, 37, 48, 51, 56, 88, 89, 97, 104, 108, 109, 122), and social characteristics (54); and structural barriers (9, 43, 91, 106). Although cultural beliefs affect the use of health services, very little empirical evidence supports the assertion that indigenous beliefs, cultural practices, or use of healers are offsetting use of orthodox medical providers in any significant way (3, 17). Similarly, no consistent relationship has been discerned between various indicators of acculturation and physician utilization (59).

Structural barriers to access include financial constraints and features of medical providers that deter or discourage potential or actual clients. Hispanics are less likely than other ethnic groups to have a regular medical provider or physician (9) or to have health insurance (106). The Mexican American population, with its large numbers of undocumented and seasonal workers, is much less likely to have public health insurance coverage and more likely to work for employers who do not provide private health insurance (106). In the absence of financial barriers, as among Hispanics who are eligible for medicaid, rates of use of health services are higher than for other populations (108). However, even when financial barriers are removed, provider characteristics (e.g. location, language, and cultural competence) mediate access to health services among Hispanics (3, 11, 40, 57).

Only a few (e.g. 2–5, 33) well-conceived theoretical models have been tested empirically with Hispanics to evaluate the relative contribution of explanatory factors to the use of health services. Analytical models of Hispanic services utilization need to be elaborated that supersede, and hopefully improve, traditional behavior models (2, 41, 62, 125), by including additional indicators that reflect the Hispanic cultural and social experiences (6). Another set of factors to be considered is contextual, occasioned by differences in provider characteristics that facilitate or act as barriers to care.

The advent of publicly assisted universal health coverage for large numbers of currently uninsured Hispanics will permit a direct test of whether intrinsic ethnic group factors (e.g. the notion that Mexican Americans are "super healthy") or structural factors (e.g. the low availability of public health insurance) are responsible for low utilization among Mexican Americans, and among other Hispanic ethnic groups, as well. Furthermore, it will be possible to assess the impact of unanticipated high level Hispanic enrollment on public and private health care providers, and how these providers change procedures and clinical practices to accommodate the needs of Spanish speaking clients. Indeed, bilingualism and multicultural competency may become much more highly valued and rewarded abilities among medical professionals as a result.

PREVENTION, HEALTH PROMOTION, AND PUBLIC HEALTH POLICY FOR HISPANICS

The fact that many Hispanics have no primary care provider of choice implies irregularity of preventive screening that, in turn, reduces prophylactic immunization or early detection and effective management of disease. To correct this situation, the National Institutes of Health are funding intramural and extramural projects to increase awareness of health issues, using various communication models. These initiatives emphasize the need for regular health screening for major diseases such as cancer, AIDS, and heart disease. There is increasing emphasis on health promotion and disease prevention projects to reduce smoking, alcohol consumption, risky sexual behaviors, and illicit drug use. More recently, these NIH initiatives have included the provision of technical assistance to design and implement community-based interventions, interaction with and use of social networks, design of media messages and campaigns, and the development of informational materials appropriate for interventions in multilingual or multicultural environments. Much remains to be learned in this area, but this earnest effort is a solid beginning. Continuing experimentation and dissemination of technical information is needed so that practitioners and researchers can keep abreast of the growing complexity of the US Hispanic population and the rapid pace of knowledge development.

The economic and educational gap between Hispanics and white non-Hispanics has direct consequences for Hispanic public health status by increasing community disintegration and risky behaviors. In Hispanic communities, lack of opportunity fosters conflicts among Hispanic youth that are directly related to acculturation. Unhealthy lifestyles and gang membership among urban adolescents and young adults proliferate in this environment. Regardless of improvements in access to care, medical care providers are unlikely to reduce the incidence of street violence, rising teen suicide, and sexual or physical abuse in families. Furthermore, the prevention of diseases such as AIDS depends on the primacy Hispanics assign to behavioral changes in the context of the harsh and debilitating inner city environment. Is it possible to prevent disease in communities where the basic requirements of physical survival are so burdensome, where public safety is questionable, and educational systems are in total disarray? Not in the long run, and certainly not in the short run.

The most fundamental and effective method to lower the incidence of morbidity and mortality among Hispanics may be through health promotion and prevention, but only if these activities can be linked to employment and improved economic opportunities. Prevention activities are frequently limited by their narrow scope, which restricts the number of individuals who can be reached, or are too costly to sustain. To overcome this limitation, health must become the business of the Hispanic community in direct and tangible ways. Increased training and employment opportunities as allied health professionals and as community health outreach workers are needed in Hispanic communities. Health media messages must be disseminated to communicate accurate information competently in homes, schools, community locations, and work sites. These activities could counteract among low income Hispanics the influences of alcohol and tobacco industry advertising and their high visibility financial support of Hispanic community cultural events. All intervention strategies, regardless of type, carry the burden of demonstrating that they are imparting something of local and personal value to community members. And these tactics must be implemented creatively, drawing on the aesthetic and spiritual qualities of Hispanic families and communities (47).

Despite a low prevalence for many health problems among some Hispanic groups, population growth will increase the magnitude of many common public health problems. For example, a recent epidemiologic study of perinatal substance use that used anonymous urine screening in California hospitals found that Hispanic women, who constitute about one quarter of all women in the state, had a 6.8% prevalence of alcohol-exposed infants (119). The prevalence for African American women was 11.6%, almost twice as high as Hispanic women. Nevertheless, because Hispanic women constitute a disproportionately large fraction of the birthing population, they were responsible for almost one half, as compared to one tenth for African Americans, of alcohol-exposed infants born in California in 1992. The implication of this finding is that health promotion and intervention are important public health activities within Hispanic communities, low prevalence rates notwithstanding. Current activities in this field are highly encouraging and, with persistence, may bring about fundamental changes in the way health is perceived and maintained among Hispanics in the United States. As Muñoz has forcefully argued, there is nothing intrinsic to Hispanic culture to suggest a lesser concern with health issues or innate resistance to interventions (68, 69).

Literature Cited

1. Amaro H, Whitaker R, Coffman J, Heeren T. 1990. Acculturation and marijuana and cocaine use: Finding from the HHANES 1982–84. *Am. J. Public Health* 80(Suppl.):54–60
2. Andersen R, Newman JF. 1973. Societal and individual determinants of medical care utilization in the United States. *Milbank Mem. Fund Q.* 51:95–124
3. Andersen RM. 1968. *A Behavioral Model of Families' Use of Health Services*. Chicago: Univ. Chicago Press
4. Andersen RM, Giachello AL, Aday LA. 1986. Access of Hispanics to health care and cuts in services: A state-of-the-art overview. *Public Health Rep.* 101:238–52
5. Andersen RM, Zelman, Lewis S, Giachello AL, Aday LA, Chiu G. 1981. Access to medical care among the Hispanic population of the Southwestern United States. *J. Health Soc. Behav.* 22:78–89
6. Angel R, Cleary PD. 1984. The effects of social structure and culture on reported health. *Soc. Sci. Q.* 65:814–28
7. Bean FD, Tienda M. 1987. *The Hispanic Population of the United States*. New York: Sage Found. 456 pp.
8. Becerra J, Hogue C, Atrash H, Perez N. 1991. Infant mortality among Hispanics. *J. Am. Med. Assoc.* 265:217–21
9. Berkanovic E, Telesky C. 1985. Mexican-American, Black-Americn and White-American differences in reporting illnesses, disability and physician visits for illness. *Soc. Sci. Med.* 20:567–77
10. Berry JW. 1980. Acculturation as varieties of adaptation. In *Acculturation: Theory, Models and Some New Findings,* ed. AM Padilla, pp. 9–25. Boulder, CO: Westview Press
11. Brown JP. 1992. Oral health of Hispanics: Epidemiology and risk factors. See Ref. 36a, pp. 132–43
12. Burnam MA, Hough RL, Escobar JI, Karno M, Timbers DM, et al. 1987. Six-months prevalence of specific psychiatric disorders among Mexican Americns and non-Hispanic whites in Los Angeles. *Arch. Gen. Psychiatry* 44:687–94
13. Burnam M, Hough R, Karno M, Escobar J, Telles C. 1987. Acculturation and lifetime prevalence of psychiatric disorders among Mexican Americans in Los Angeles. *J. Health Soc. Behav.* 28:89–102
14. Caetanno R. 1987. Acculturation and drinking patterns among U.S. Hispanics. *Br. J. Addict.* 82:789–99
15. Caplan LS, Wells BL, Haynes S. 1992. Breast cancer screening among older racial/ethnic minorities and whites: Barriers to early detection. *J. Gerontol.* 47):101–10
16. Caralis PV. 1990. Hypertension in the Hispanic-American population. *Am. J. Med.* 88(Suppl. 3B):3B–9S
17. Casas MM, Keefe SM. eds. 1978. *Family and Mental health in the Mexican American Community*. Los Angeles: Spanish Speaking Ment. Health Res. Cent.
18. Castro KG, Valdiserri RO, Curran JW. 1992. Perspectives on HIV/AIDS epidemiology and prevention from the 8th Int. Conf. AIDS. *Am. J. Public Health* 82:1465–70
19. Centers for Disease Control. 1987. Trends in immunodeficiency virus infection among civilian applicants for

military service—United States: Oct. 1985–Dec. 1986. *Morbid. Mortal. Wkly. Rep.* 36:273–76

20. Centers for Disease Control. 1988. Prevalence of human immunodeficiency virus antibody in US active-duty military personnel, April 1988. *Morbid. Mortal. Wkly. Rep.* 37:461–63

21. Centers for Disease Control. 1992. Incidence of treatment of end stage renal disease attributable to diabetes mellitus, by race/ethnicity—Colorado: 1982–89. *Morbid. Mortal. Wkly. Rep.* 41(44):845–48

22. Cherpitel CJ. 1992. Acculturation, alcohol consumption, and casualties among United States Hispanics in the emergency room. *Int. J. Addict.* 27:1067–77

23. Chesney AP, Chavira JA, Hall RP, Gary HE. 1982. Barriers to medical care of Mexican-Americans: The role of social class, acculturation and social isolation. *Med. Care* 20:883–91

24. Clark M. 1959. *Health in the Mexican-American Culture.* Berkeley: Univ. Calif. Press. 253 pp.

25. Counc. Sci. Aff. 1991. Hispanic health in the United States. *J. Am. Med. Assoc.* 265:248–52

26. Delgado M. 1990. Hispanic adolescents and substance abuse: Implications for research, treatment and prevention. In *Ethnic Issues in Adolescent Mental Health,* ed. AR Stiffman, LE Davis, pp. 303–20. Newbury Park, CA: Sage Found.

27. Derenowski J. 1990. Coronary artery disease in Hispanics. *J. Cardiovasc. Nurs.* 4:13–21

28. Div. STD/HIV Prev. 1991. Sexually transmitted disease surveilance, 1990. US DHHS. Atlanta: CDC

29. Egolf B, Lasker J, Wolf S, Potvin L. 1992. The Roseto effect: A 50-Year comparison of mortality rates. *Am. J. Public Health* 82:1089–92

30. Elder JP, Castro FG, deMoor C, Mayer J, Candelaria J, et al. 1991. Differences in cancer risk-related behaviors in Latino and Anglo adults. *Medicine* 20:751–63

31. Espino DV, Burge SK, Moreno CA. 1991. The prevalence of selected chronic diseases among the Mexican-American elderly: Data from the 1982–1984 Hispanic Health and Nutrition Examination Survey. *J. Am. Board Fam. Pract.* 4:217–22

32. Espino DV, Maldonado D. 1990. Hypertension and acculturation in elderly Mexican Americans: Results from

1982–84 Hispanic HANES. *J. Gerontol.* 45:M209–13

33. Estrada AL, Trevino FM, Ray LA. 1990. Health care utilization barriers among Mexican Americans: Evidence from HHANES 1982–84. *Am. J. Public Health* 80(Suppl.):27–31

34. Fingerhut LA, Makuc DM. 1992. Mortality among minority populations in the United States. *Am. J. Public Health* 82:1168–70

35. Flegal MK, Ezzatti TM, Harris MI, Haynes SG, Juarez RZ, et al. 1991. Prevalence of diabetes in Mexican Americans, Cubans, and Puerto Ricans from the Hispanic Health and Nutrition Examination Survey, 1982–1984. *Diabetes Care* 14(Suppl. 3):628–38

36. Fox SA, Stein JA. 1991. The effect of physician-patient communication on mammography utilization by different ethnic groups. *Med. Care* 29:1065–83

36a. Furino A, ed. 1992. *Health Policy and the Hispanic.* Boulder, CO: Westview Press. 240 pp.

37. Garrison V. 1975. Espiritismo: Implications for provisions of mental health services to Puerto Rican populations. In *Folktherapy,* ed. H Hodges, C Hudson. Miami: Univ. Miami Press

38. Gen. Account. Off. 1992. *Hispanic Access to Health Care: Significant Gaps Exist.* Washington, DC: US GPO

39. Gilbert M. 1989. Alcohol consumption pattern in immigrant and later generation Mexican American women. *Hisp. J. Behav. Sci.* 9:299–313

40. Ginzberg E. 1991. Access to health care for Hispanics. *J. Am. Med. Assoc.* 265:238–41

41. Goldsmith HF, Jackson DJ, Hough RL. 1988. Process model of seeking mental health services: Proposed framework for organizing the research literature on help-seeking. *NIMH, Ment. Health Serv. Syst. Rep., Ser. BN: Needs Assessment:Its Future,* No. 8: 49–64

42. Griffith J. 1983. Relationship between acculturation and psychological impairment in adult Mexican Americans. *Hisp. J. Behav. Sci.* 5:431–59

43. Guendelman S, Schwalbe J. 1986. Medical care utilization by Hispanic children: How does it differ from Black and White peers? *Med. Care* 24(10): 925–37

44. Guendelman SS, Gould J, Hudes M, Eskenazi B. 1990. Generational difference in perinatal health among the Mexican American population: Findings from HHANES, 1982–84. *Am. J. Public Health* 80:61–65

45. Haffner SM, Mitchell BD, Pugh JA, Stern MP, Kozlowski MK, Hazuda, HP, et al. 1989. Proteinuria in Mexican Americans and Non-Hispanic whites with non-insulin dependent diabetes mellitus. *J. Am. Med. Assoc.* 263:530–36

46. Harris MI. 1991. Epidemiological correlates of NIDDM in Hispanics, whites, and blacks in the US population. *Diabetes Care* 14(Suppl. 3):639–48

47. Hayes-Bautista D. 1992. Latino health indicators and the underclass model: from paradox to new policy models. See Ref. 36a, pp. 32–47

48. Haynes SG, Harvey C, Montes H, Nicken H, Cohen BH. 1990. Patterns of cigarette smoking among Hispanics in the United States: Results from the HHANES 1982–1984. *Am. J. Public Health* 80(Suppl.):47–53

49. Hazuda HP, Haffner SP, Stern MP, Eifler CW. 1988. Effects of acculturation and SES on obesity and diabetes in Mexican Americans: The San Antonio Heart Study. *Am. J. Epidemiol.* 128:1289–301

50. Higginbotham JC, Trevino FM, Ray LA. 1990. Utilization of curanderos by Mexican Americans: Prevalence and predictors. Findings from HHANES 1982–84. *Am. J. Public Health* 80(Suppl.):32–35

51. Hough RL, Landsverk J, Karno M, et al. 1987. Utilization of health and mental health services by Los Angeles Mexican Americans and non-Hispanic Whites. *Arch. Gen. Psychiatry* 44:702–9

52. Kaplan M, Marks G. 1990. Adverse effects of acculturation: Psychological distress among Mexican American young adults. *Soc. Sci. Med.* 31(12):1313–19

52a. Kato PM, Soto R, Goldberg RB, Sosenko JM. 1991. Comparison of the lipid profiles of Cubans and other Hispanics with non-Hispanics. *Arch. Int. Med.* 151:1613–16

53. Kehrer BH, Wollin CM. 1979. Impact of income maintenance on low birthweight. *J. Hum. Resour.* 12:434–62

53a. LaCroix AZ, Haynes SG, Savage DD, Havlik RJ. 1989. Rose questionnaire angina among US Black, white and Mexican American women and men. *Am. J. Epidemiol.* 131:423–33

54. Lewin-Epstein N. 1991. Determinants of regular source of health care in black, Mexican, Puerto Rican, and non-Hispanic white populations. *Med. Care* 29:543–57

55. Lopez, S. 1981. Mexican-American usage of mental health facilities: Underutilization reconsidered. In *Explorations in Chicano Psychology,* ed. A. Baron Jr, pp. 139–64. New York: Praeger

56. Madsen W. 1964. Value conflicts in folk psychiatry in South Texas. In *Magic, Faith and Healing,* ed. A. Kiev, pp. 420–40. New York: Free Press

57. Marin G, Marin BV, Padilla AM. 1982. Aspectos atribucionales de la utilización de servicios de salud. *Interam. J. Psychol.* 16:78–89

58. Markides KS, Levin JS, Ray LA. 1985. Determinants of physician utilization among Mexican Americans: A three generations study. *Med. Care* 23:226–46

59. Markides KS, Ray L, Stroup-Benham C, Trevino F. 1990. Acculturation and alcohol consumption in the Mexican American population of the Southwestern United States: Findings from the HHANES, 1982–84. *Am. J. Public Health* 80(Suppl.):42–46

60. Marks G, Garcia M, Solis J. 1990. Health risk behaviors of Hispanics in the United States: Findings from HHANES, 1982–84. *Am. J. Public Health* 80(Suppl.):20–26

61. Maurer JD, Rosenberg HM, Keemer JB. 1990. Deaths of Hispanic origin, 15 reporting States, 1979–1981. *Natl. Cent. Health Stat. Vital Health Stat.* 20(18):5–16

62. Mechanic D. 1979. Correlates of physician utilization: Why do major multivariate studies of physician utilization find trivial psychosocial and organizational effects? *J. Health Soc. Behav.* 20:387–96

63. Mendoza F, Ventura S, Valdez B, Castillo R, Saldivar L, et al. 1991. Selected measures of health status for Mexican-American, mainland Puerto Rican, and Cuban American children. *J. Am. Med. Assoc.* 265:227–32

64. Mitchell BD, Hazuda HP, Haffner SM, Patterson JK, Stein MP. 1991. Myocardial infarction in Mexican-Americans and non-Hispanic whites: The San Antonio Heart Study. *Circulation* 83:45–51

65. Mitchell BD, Stern MP, Haffner SM, Hazuda HP, Patterson JK. 1990. Risk factors for cardiovascular mortality in Mexican Americans and non-Hispanic whites: The San Antonio Heart Study. *Am. J. Epidemiol.* 131:423–33

66. Moran EM. 1992. Epidemiological fac-

tors of cancer in California. *J. Environ. Pathol. Toxicol.* Oncol.11:303–7
67. Mosciscki E, Locke B, Rae D, Boyd, JH. 1989. Depressive symptoms among Mexican Americans: The Hispanic Health and Nutrition Examination Survey. *Am. J. Epidemiol.* 130:348–60
68. Muñoz RF. 1980. A strategy for the prevention of psychological problems in Latinos: Emphasizing accessibility and effectiveness. In *Hispanic Natural Support Systems: Mental Health Promotion Perspectives,* ed. R Valle, W Vega, pp. 85–96
69. Muñoz RF, Ying YW, Armas R, Chan F, Gurza R. 1986. The San Francisco depression prevention research project: A randomized trial with medical outpatients. In *Depression Prevention: Research Directions,* ed. RF Muñoz, pp. 199–216. Washington: Hemisphere Publ. Corp. 301 pp.
70. Natl. Cent. Health Stat. 1991. *Advance Report of Final Mortality Statistics, 1988.* Mon. Vital Stat. Rep. 39(4), (Suppl. Health US)
71. Natl. Cent. Health Stat. 1992. *Advance Report of Final Mortality Statistics, 1989.* Mon. Vital Stat. Rep. 80 (8) (Suppl. 2)
72. Natl. Cent. Health Stat. 1992. *Health, United States, 1991.* Hyattsville, Maryland: PHS
73. Natl. Cent. Health Stat. 1993. *Advance Report of Final Mortality Statistics, 1990.* Mon. Vital Stat. Rep. 40(7) (Suppl.)
74. Natl. Cent. Health Stat. 1993. *Personal communication with Lois Fingerhut,* May 12, 1993
75. Natl. Inst. Drug Abuse. 1987. *Use of selected drugs among Hispanics: Mexican Americans, Puerto Ricans, and Cuban Americans. Findings from the HHANES.* Washington DC: US DHHS
76. Neff J. 1986. Alcohol consumption and psychological distress among U.S. Anglos, Hispanics, and Blacks. *Alcohol Alcoholism* 21:111–19
77. Nelson M. 1992. Socioeconomic status and childhood mortality in North Carolina. *Am. J. Public Health* 82:1133–36
78. Nichaman MZ, Garcia G. 1991. Obesity in Hispanic Americans. *Diabetes Care* 14(Suppl. 3):691–94
79. Padilla E, Olmedo E, Loya F. 1982. Acculturation and the MMPI performance of Chicano and Anglo college students. *Hisp. J. Behav. Sci.* 4:451–66
80. Page B. 1980. The children of exile: Relationships between the acculturation process and drug use among Cuban American youth. *Youth Soc.* 11:431–47
81. Pawson IG, Martorell R, Mendoza FE. 1991. Prevalence of overweight and obesity in U.S. Hispanic populations. *Am. J. Clin. Nutr.* 53:1522S–28S
82. Perez R, Padilla AM, Ramirez A, Ramirez R, Rodriquez M. 1980. Correlates and changes over time in drug and alcohol use within a barrio population. *Am. J. Commun. Psychol.* 6:621–36
83. Polednak AP. 1992. Cancer incidence in the Puerto Rican-born population of Connecticut. *Cancer* 70:1172–76
84. Portes A, Bach RL. 1985. *Latin Journey: Cuban and Mexican Immigrants in the United States.* Berkeley: Univ. Calif. Press. 387 pp.
85. Portes A, Rumbaut RG. 1990. *Immigrant America: A Portrait.* Berkeley: Univ. Calif. Press. 300 pp.
86. Rogler L, Cortes, D, Malagady R. 1991. Acculturation and mental health status among Hispanics. *Am. Psychol.* 46:585–97
87. Rubel A. 1960. Concepts of disease in Mexican-American culture. *Am. Anthropol.* 62:795–814
88. Ruiz P, Langrod J. 1976. The role of folk healers in community mental health services. *Commun. Ment. Health J.* 12:392–404
89. Sandoval MC. 1979. Santeria as a mental health care system: An historical overview. *Soc. Sci. Med.* 13B:137–51
90. Schick FL, Schick R. 1991. *Statistical Handbook on U.S. Hispanics.* New York: Oryx Press. 255 pp.
91. Schur CL, Bernstein AB, Berk ML. 1987. The importance of distinguishing Hispanic subpopulations in the use of medical care. *Med. Care* 25:627–41
92. Scopetta MA, King OE, Szapocznik J. 1977. Relationship of acculturation, incidence of drug abuse, and effective treatment for Cuban Americans. *Natl. Inst. Drug Abuse. Fin. Rep. Res. Contract No. 271-75-4136.* Bethesda, MD
93. Selik RM, Castro KG, Papaionnou M. 1988. Racial/ethnic differences in the risk of AIDS in the United States. *Am. J. Public Health* 78:1539–45
94. Selik RM, Castro KG, Papaionnou M, Ruehler JW. 1989. Birthplace and the risk of AIDS among Hispanics in the United States. *Am. J. Public Health* 79:836–39
95. Smith GD, Egger M. 1992. Socioeconomic differences in mortality in Britain and the United States. *Am. J. Public Health* 82:1079–81
96. Sorenson S, Golding J. 1988. Suicide ideation and attempts in Hispanics and

non-Hispanic whites: Demographic and psychiatric disorder issues. *Suicide Life-Threat. Behav.* 18:205–18

97. Stein SA, Fox SA, Maturata PJ. 1991. The influence of ethnicity, socioeconomic status, and psychological barriers on use of mammography. *J. Health Soc. Behav.* 32:101–13

98. Stern MP, Gaskell SP, Allen CR, Garza V, Gonzalez JL, Waldrop RH. 1982. Cardiovascular risk factors in Mexican Americans in Laredo, Texas: II. Prevalence and control of hypertension. *Am. J. Epidemiol.* 113:556–62

99. Stern MP, Haffner SM. 1992. Type II diabetes in Mexican Americans: A public health challenge. See Ref. 36a, pp. 57–75

100. Stern MP, Knapp JA, Hazuda HP, Haffner SM, Patterson JK, Mitchell BD. 1991. Genetic and environmental determinants of type II diabetes in Mexican Americans. *Diabetes Care* 14(Suppl. 3):649–54

101. Sumaya LV. 1991. Major infectious diseases causing excess morbidity in the Hispanic population. *Arch. Intern. Med.* 151:1513–20

102. Syme LS, Berkman LF. 1976. Social class, susceptibility and sickness. *Am. J. Epidemiol.* 104:1–8

103. Szapocznik J, Kurtines W. 1988. Acculturation, biculturalism and adjustment among Cuban Americans. In *Acculturation Theory, Model and Some New Findings,* ed. AM Padilla, pp. 139–59. Boulder, CO: Westview Press

104. Torrey EF. 1972. The irrelevancy of traditional mental health services for urban Mexican-Americans. In *On the Urban Scene,* ed. M Levitt, B Rubenstein, pp. 19–36. Detroit: Wayne State Univ. Press

105. Trapido EJ, McCoy CB, Strickman-Stein N, Engel S, Zavertnik JJ, Comerford M. 1990. Epidemiology of cancer among Hispanic males: The experience in Florida. *Cancer* 65:657–62

106. Trevino FM, Moyer ME, Valdez RB, Stroup-Benham CA. 1992. Health insurance coverage and utilization of health services by Mexican Americans, Puerto Ricans, and Cuban Americans. See Ref. 36a, pp. 158–70

107. Trevino RM, Moss AJ. 1984. Health indicators for Hispanic, Black and White Americans. *Vital Health Stat., Ser. 10, No. 148. Natl. Cent. Health Stat.* Hyattsville, MD

108. Trotter RT II. 1981. Remedios caseros: Mexican American home remedies and community health problems. *Soc. Sci. Med.* 15B:107–14

109. Trotter RT II, Chavira JA. 1981. *Curanderismo: Mexican American Folk Healing.* Athens: Univ. Georgia Press. 204 pp.

110. US Bur. Census, Curr. Popul. Rep. Ser. P-20, No. 449. 1991. *The Hispanic Population In the United States: March 1990.* Washington, DC: US GPO

111. US Bur. Census. 1991. *General, Social and Economic Data.* US Summary Table 152, PC80–1, no. 1

112. US Bur. Census. 1991. *Race and Hispanic Origin, 1990.* Census Profile No. 2. Washington, DC: US Dep. Commer.

113. US Dep. Health Hum. Serv. 1985. *Rep. Sec. Task Force on Black and Minority Health,* Vol. II. Crosscutting Issues in Minority Health. Washington, DC: US GPO

115. US Dep. Health Hum. Serv. 1986. *Rep. Sec. Task Force Black and Minority Health.* Vol. 8: Hispanic Health Issues. Washington, DC: US GPO

114. US Dep. Health Hum. Serv. 1990. *Healthy People 2000: Natl. Health Promotion and Disease Prevention Objectives.* Washington, DC: US GPO

116. Vega WA, Gil A, Warheit G, Apospori E, Zimmerman R. 1993. The relationship of drug use to suicide ideation and attempts among African American, Hispanic, and White Non-Hispanic male adolescents. *Suicide Life-Threat. Behav.* 23:110–19

117. Vega WA, Gil AG, Zimmerman RS. 1993. Patterns of drug use among Cuban-American, African-American, and white non-Hispanic boys. *Am. J. Public Health* 83:257–59

118. Vega WA, Hough RL, Miranda MR. 1985. Modeling cross-cultural research in Hispanic mental health. In *Stress and Hispanic Mental Health: Relating Research to Service Delivery,* ed. WA Vega, MR Miranda, pp. 1–29. DHHS Publ. No. (ADM) 85–1410. 289 pp.

119. Vega WA, Kolody B, Hwang J, Noble A. 1993. Prevalence and magnitude of perinatal substance exposures in California. *New England J. Med.*329:850–54

120. Vega WA, Kolody B, Valle R, Weir J. 1991. Social networks, social support, and their relationship to depression among immigrant Mexican women. *Hum. Organ.* 50:154–62

121. Ventura SJ, Tappel S.M. 1985 Childbearing characteristics of the US and foreign-born Hispanic mothers. *Public Health Rep.* 100:647–52

122. Wells IB, Hough RL, Golding JM, Burnam MA, Karno M. 1987. Which Mexican Americans underutilize health services? *Am. J Psychiatry* 144:918–22

123. Wilkinson RG. 1990. Income distribution and mortality: A "natural" experiment. *Sociol. Health Illness* 12:1082–84

124. Wolfgang PE, Semeiks PA, Burnett WS. 1991. Cancer incidence in New York City Hispanics, 1982–1985. *Ethn. Dis.* 1:263–72

125. Wolinsky FD. 1978. Assessing the effects of predisposing, enabling and illness-morbidity characteristics on health service utilization. *J. Health Soc. Behav.* 19:384–96

126. Wood PR, Hidalgo HA, Prihoda TJ, Kromer ME. 1993. Hispanic children with asthma: Morbidity. *Pediatrics* 265:227–32

Annu. Rev. Public Health. 1994. 15:69–90

THE EFFECTS OF MUSTARD GAS, IONIZING RADIATION, HERBICIDES, TRAUMA, AND OIL SMOKE ON US MILITARY PERSONNEL: The Results of Veteran Studies[1]

Tim A. Bullman and Han K. Kang

Department of Veterans Affairs, Environmental Epidemiology Service, Washington, DC 20036-3406

KEY WORDS: mortality, morbidity, exposure, environmental hazards, surveillance

INTRODUCTION

As an occupational group the men and women in the United States military perform a wide range of tasks in a wide variety of settings. One aspect of their duties that distinguishes them from most other occupational groups is the degree of risk to which they are exposed in time of war. Their service to their country is recognized not only by monetary rewards, but also by a commitment to their health and well-being. This commitment to the health of the military is related to both maintaining an efficient and ready force and to identifying health hazards they may encounter in the line of duty. The latter aspect of health surveillance is especially pertinent when discussing veterans or those who are no longer on active duty. The Department of Veterans Affairs (VA) was created in recognition of the national service performed by veterans.

Among the charges of VA are defining the veteran population and providing health care and other benefits, some of which may be compensation for health problems that are the direct result of their military service.

---

[1]The US Government has the right to retain a nonexclusive, royalty-free license in and to any copyright covering this paper.

Data and findings derived from surveys and epidemiological studies of veterans enable VA to better allocate resources and compensate for service connected health problems.

Veteran research is of value to both veterans and nonveterans. Findings from research on veteran groups may be generalizable to certain groups of the general population with similar exposures or experiences. For example, studies of veterans exposed to vaccines (yellow fever), environmental hazards (malaria), or occupational hazards (herbicides, ionizing radiation), or trauma may have implications for civilians likewise exposed.

Their unique characteristics make veterans a good target population for health research. Among those characteristics that both facilitate health surveillance and enhance their desirability as a study group is that they are a readily defined cohort. Cohort studies are one of the most valuable tools in testing hypotheses regarding causation of diseases. A cohort is defined by some shared characteristic(s) present prior to the disease under investigation. The cohort is observed over a period of time to determine, among other things, the frequency of disease. Thus, a veteran cohort, based on date of entering active duty, constitutes a readily defined group in terms of sex, race, age, and exposure, all important factors in any health study.

Veterans research is further enhanced by the availability of their active duty records and veterans records maintained by the Department of Defense (DOD) and VA. The ready availability of records not only facilitates development of a study cohort but also facilitates a high degree of follow-up without great expense.

An important characteristic unique to veterans is the "healthy veteran effect". The mortality of veterans after separation from service has been documented as lower than that of a similar age group of nonveterans (61, 63). The "healthy veteran effect" is related to the physical examination required at induction into military service, which screens those with health problems from entering the service. The military also provides physical health programs to increase both retention and readiness of its forces. Therefore, a comparison of a veteran cohort to general population may lead to a bias and should be viewed with caution.

This article aims to provide a current review of efforts both to define the veteran population and to identify specific health problems of selected veteran populations.

PROFILE OF US VETERANS

1987 Veteran Survey

The most recent and comprehensive accounting and analysis of the veteran population in the United States is based on the 1987 Survey of Veterans

Table 1   Selected military service characteristics by period of service among veteran population[a]

	Wartime			Peacetime	
				Post	Other
	WWII	Korea	Vietnam	Vietnam	Peace Time
Military Service	%	%	%	%	%
Type of Entry					
Drafted	52	32	23	1	27
Enlisted	47	67	76	98	72
Rank					
Commissioned officer	12	11	10	3	7
Warrant officer	1	1	1	1	.5
Enlisted	86	87	89	95	92
Length of Service					
<1 Yr.	5	1	3	5	9
1–2 Yrs.	37	34	31	22	46
3–5 Yrs.	46	37	41	65	40
6–10 Yrs.	4	7	10	7	3
11–+ Yrs.	7	19	15	.3	.5
Combat Exposure					
Exposed to combat	52	35	38	2	4
Served in combat zone	18	13	10	4	10
Not in combat or war zone	29	50	50	92	84

[a] Based on a sample of 26,143,000 veterans in 1987 survey (73)

Note: percentages may not add up to 100 as veterans may have served in more than one conflict and percentage of missing values not included in table.

conducted by the Census Bureau for VA (73). The survey was conducted between July and September, 1987, and provided information to evaluate current veteran programs and plan for the future.

Based on the US Bureau of Census counts taken between April 1986 and January 1987 there were 26,143,000 veterans residing in the United States, or approximately 15% of the total US population age 20 or older. Veterans in the survey were a weighted sample of that 1987 veteran population. Selected military service characteristics of the veterans surveyed in 1987 are presented in Table 1.

Additional data captured by the 1987 survey included health problems experienced by veterans. Due to the disparities in age composition of the different groups of veterans, WWII veterans had the highest percentage reporting health problems and disability (43%), followed by Korean veterans (30%), other peace time veterans (22%), Vietnam veterans (20%), and finally post-Vietnam veterans (11%).

Of the various veteran groups today, women veterans have been receiving increased attention by the media, health researchers, and Congress. During WWII 3% of all veterans were women compared to 7% of all post-Vietnam veterans. In 1972, the last year of the draft, approximately 45,000 women were on active duty, increasing to 120,000 in 1976, and to 200,000 in 1985, when women comprised 10% of the active forces. Commensurate with the increased number of women in the military has been change in their duties. Three out of four of the 12,600 women officers in the military in 1972 were nurses. By 1985, the largest segment of the female officer population held positions other than nursing. Finally, the recent decision by the Department of Defense to allow for women combat pilots is a further indication of the changing role of women in the military.

1984 Women Veterans Survey

The Veterans Administration sponsored a survey of women veterans in 1984 to aid in evaluating current programs and to plan for the increasing number of women veterans (72). Thirty-six percent of the 3000 women veterans surveyed were under 35, which is comparable to the 31% of all veterans and 36% of the total population under 35 in the 1987 survey. The racial composition of the women veterans, of which 87% were white, was similar to that reported for all veterans and the total US population in 1987 (86%).

Of the women in the 1984 survey, 15% reported a health problem, 8% reported mental or emotional problems, 14% of the 2130 who reported live births noted at least one birth defect among their children. Thirty percent of the women reported pregnancies that ended in miscarriage, stillbirth, or abortion. Comparing the specific health problems of the women veterans to a sample of women from another health survey, the only major difference between the two groups of women was a reported rate of cancer almost twice among women veterans as nonveteran women, 8.6% vs 4.8%. The most common cancers among the women veterans were cancer of the uterus, ovaries, or cervix (43%), and breast cancer (26%) (72).

1991 Annual Report of the Secretary of Veterans Affairs

Based on data from the 1991 Annual Report (74), as of September 30, 1991, there were 26.6 million veterans in the United States, of which 1.2 million were women. The median age of all veterans was 55.7 years, with those aged 45 to 64 comprising the largest age group (43%). The median age of women veterans was 49.2 years.

Additional data in the 1991 report included diagnostic data for any veteran discharged from a VA medical center during the fiscal year 1991 (Table 2). These diagnostic data were based on the computerized discharge records of all VA medical centers (Patient Treatment File). During the fiscal year

Table 2 Selected diagnoses[a] for veterans discharged from VA hospitals

Diagnostic Group[b]	Age Group						
	Under 35 %	35–44 %	45–54 %	55–64 %	65–74 %	75–84 %	85–+ %
Infectious diseases (000–139)	3	2	2	1	1	1	2
Neoplasms (140–23)	2	2	6	12	13	12	9
Blood and blood organ diseases (280–289)	.6	.5	.6	1	1	2	2
Mental disorders (291–319)	58	57	33	12	7	6	7
Nervous system diseases (320–389)	3	3	4	5	6	7	5
Circulatory diseases (390–458)	2	5	14	21	22	21	19
Respiratory diseases (460–519)	3	3	5	8	10	12	15
Injury and poisoning (E800–E999)	5	4	4	4	4	4	5

[a] Based on 944,162 principal diagnoses for veterans discharged from VA medical centers, fiscal year 1991, as recorded in the Patient Treatment File.
[b] Number in parentheses are *International Classification of Disease Code,* 9th Rev.

1991 there were 944,162 discharges of veterans from VA medical centers, with the largest percentage of hospital discharges accounted for by those aged 65–74 (31%), followed by those aged 55–64 (24%). The lowest number of hospital discharges was among those younger than 35 (6%) and 85 or older (1%). As expected, the percentage of veterans treated for diseases related to age, e.g. circulatory diseases, respiratory diseases, and cancer, increased with age. A large number of veterans age 44 or younger were treated for mental disorders (57%). The percentage of diagnoses related to mental disorders dropped significantly as age increased. The most common mental disorder diagnosis was alcohol and drug dependence. The surveys indicate that the composition of the veteran population is changing, and therefore veteran needs and issues are also changing. The survey data are limited by the self-reported nature of medical conditions, and the hospital data are subject to self-selection bias. However, the usefulness of these data in allocating VA resources is without question.

Specific veteran health issues vary according to the period of military service. The effects of mustard gas are of concern for WWI and WWII veterans, and the effects of ionizing radiation for post-WWII veterans who participated in atmospheric nuclear tests. Agent Orange exposure and Post Traumatic Stress

Disorder (PTSD) are the significant health issues for Vietnam veterans, whereas the effects of exposure to pollutants from oil fires and other chemicals are troubling to veterans who served in the Persian Gulf.

SPECIAL VETERAN POPULATIONS

WWII Veterans Exposed to Mustard Gas

Mustard gas, a chemical vesicant, was first used in warfare by the Germans in 1917, against British troops. During WWI as many as 28,000 of the American Expeditionary Forces suffered casualties from exposure on the battlefield. Soldiers were seldom exposed to lethal concentrations of mustard gas because of dispersion of the gas in the battlefield. During WWI, soldiers exposed to mustard gas first experienced irritation of the nose causing sneezing, followed a few hours later by signs of mustard gas poisoning: inflammation of the eyes and vomiting, followed by erythema of the skin and blistering. By the time the soldiers reached the casualty clearing stations they were virtually blind. Death within 24 hours usually resulted from chemical pneumonia, and after 24 hours from bacterial pneumonia. Most of the mustard gas casualties evacuated to England suffered from bronchitis, bronchopneumonia, burns, severe conjunctivitis, and various types of heart conditions. Sixty to 70 percent of all cases treated for mustard gas poisoning recovered within six weeks, and within two months all but a small number of severely affected persons had returned to duty.

Although mustard gas was not used in World War II, the Germans, Japanese, Americans, and British produced and stockpiled the chemical for possible use. At the beginning of the war, the US military initiated a secret research program to prepare against the threat of chemical attack by Germany or Japan. As no effective protection against the vesicant was known, top secret experiments of protective equipment, clothing, and antivesicant ointments were conducted at several sites, using military volunteers.

Three basic types of experiments were conducted with soldiers and sailors, of which the most common were patch or drop tests to assess the efficacy of protective ointments. A small amount of liquid mustard was applied on the forearm before or after application of some test ointments. At least 15,000 and perhaps as many as 60,000 WWII veterans were reported as having participated in these tests. In chamber tests, human volunteers wearing protective masks and clothing were each exposed to mustard gas in a gas chamber for an hour or more everyday or every other day until their skin showed evidence of moderate to intense chemical burns (erythema). The skin reaction would indicate that mustard gas was penetrating the protective mask or clothing.

Field tests required soldiers to traverse tropical or subtropical terrains where mustard gas was dropped to determine the value of masks, protective clothing, and ointments. Penetration of mustard gas through the protective equipment was also assessed by evidence of skin damage. At least 4000 US servicemen participated in the chamber tests or in field exercises over contaminated ground areas. No central roster was compiled of military personnel who volunteered for the testing programs, so the actual number and identity of all of the veterans exposed to vesicant are yet to be determined. Many WWII veterans have contacted the US Department of Veterans Affairs about health problems that they attribute to their exposure to mustard gas.

Late effects of exposure to mustard gas have been studied in British and US veterans of WWI and in workers involved with manufacture of mustard gas during WWII. A British study compared the mortality records from 1930 to 1952: 1267 war pensioners who suffered from mustard gas poisoning during WWI with those of two other groups: 1421 war pensioners who suffered from chronic bronchitis and 1114 war pensioners who were wounded but had not been poisoned by mustard gas (16). Mortality from cancer of the lung and pleura and chronic bronchitis was significantly higher among the mustard gas group and the chronic bronchitis group. A US study followed the mortality patterns from 1919 to 1955 (6) of 2718 veterans exposed to mustard gas, 1855 veterans who had pneumonia during the 1918 influenza epidemic but who had not been exposed to mustard gas, and 2578 wounded veterans with no history of mustard gas exposure or of pneumonia. The author concluded that the evidence was suggestive of increased lung cancer in veterans who had been subjected to mustard gas poisoning in 1918. An additional 10 years of follow-up of these veterans did not change the original conclusion (56).

A stronger association between mustard gas exposure and respiratory cancer is shown in the studies of workers exposed to mustard gas during the manufacture of the chemical. A mortality study of 3530 men and women employed in a British factory that manufactured mustard gas during WWII showed highly significant excesses of deaths from cancer of the larynx, pharynx, and other upper respiratory sites when compared to the national population. For lung cancer, the excess was also significant but moderate. Dose-response relationships, where dose was measured by duration of employment, were observed for cancers of the lung, pharynx, and larynx (26).

The literature suggests that the long-term effects of both WWI battlefield exposure (acute exposure) and occupational exposure (chronic exposure) to mustard gas may include the increased risk of respiratory cancer and nonmalignant respiratory diseases (pneumonia, bronchitis). However, there are few directly relevant data for evaluating the risk of the late effects of mustard gas associated with the specific exposure conditions experienced by the WWII test participants. Studies of WWI veterans are suggestive of an increased risk of respiratory cancer, but almost all men exposed to mustard gas also experienced acute pulmonary reactions. Whether long-term health effects of exposure to mustard gas can occur among WWII veterans in the absence of initial acute injury to the respiratory tract and skin needs to be studied. A significant number of WWII veterans were exposed to mustard gas during military experiments, and approximately two thirds of them should be still alive. Their exposure almost 50 years ago provides a sufficient latency period for chemically induced malignancy.

One of the most challenging aspects of studying the WWII veterans who volunteered for the testings is the identification of these veterans. Because of the secrecy surrounding the testing program, records of their participation are not readily available to the public. VA is working closely with the Defense Department to identify the test participants. Once the roster of participants is assembled and verified, mortality and morbidity studies can be undertaken to evaluate the long-term effects of mustard gas on these veterans.

Post-WWII Veterans Who Participated in Nuclear Weapon Testing

The United States conducted the first atomic bomb detonation on July 16, 1945, in New Mexico. From 1945 through 1962, the Manhattan Engineer District and its successor agency, the Atomic Energy Commission, conducted 235 atmospheric nuclear tests, primarily in Nevada and the Pacific Ocean. The Department of Defense estimated that approximately 250,000 military personnel participated in the tests. An additional 190,000 soldiers were potentially exposed to ionizing radiation as occupational forces within 10 miles of the city limits of either Hiroshima or Nagasaki, Japan, both sites of atomic bombing in August, 1945. Many American prisoners of war were also interned within 10 miles of the city limits at the time of the nuclear bomb detonation.

Some test participants were exposed to initial radiation emitted from the fireball and the cloud column during the first minute after the detonation. Others were exposed to residual radiation from military operations in a contaminated environment resulting in inhalation or ingestion of radioactive materials. When the first US occupation forces entered Hiroshima two months after the detonation, the intensity of induced radioactivity around the hypocenter was 0.03 milliroentgen per hour, which was reported to be a negligible level of radioactivity. About the same levels of induced radioactivity remained in Nagasaki when the main body of US troops arrived

45 days after the bombing (71). Many of the 250,000 test participants were exposed to low levels of radiation. The overall average radiation dose was estimated as 0.6 rem per year. Approximately 1700 personnel exceeded the current Federal Occupational radiation exposure guideline of 5 rem per year.

The biological effects resulting from exposure to ionizing radiation have been closely studied and are well documented. Examples of acute effects are erythema, blood changes, vomiting, loss of hair, and even death. Observable acute effects seldom occur at radiation doses below approximately 25 rem. Examples of delayed effects include cataracts and several forms of cancer. No threshold dose is required for induction of radiogenic cancer. Among atomic bomb survivors of the Hiroshima and Nagasaki attack leukemia, cancer of the thyroid, lung, stomach, colon, and esophagus were reported in excess (54).

In 1976, a claim relating acute myelocytic leukemia to radiation exposure from nuclear weapon testing received extensive publicity. This case prompted the Center for Disease Control (CDC) to study the incidence of leukemia among the veterans who participated in Shot Smoky (13), a 44-kiloton detonation that took place in August, 1957, as part of Operation Plumbob. Nine leukemia cases were identified among 3224 veterans, whereas 3.5 leukemia cases would be expected based on age- and sex-specific leukemia incidence rates in the general population. The CDC concluded that if the apparent excess of leukemia were not a chance occurrence, the Smoky participants may have received higher than anticipated radiation doses (perhaps from neutrons or inhaled radioactive material not detected by film badges), or radiation is more carcinogenic at low doses than previously assumed. This report generated considerable interest and prompted a follow-up study of the incidence as well as mortality rates of all forms of cancer (12). A total of 112 cancer cases were identified, which is below the expected number of 117.5 cases. Cancers of the digestive system, respiratory, genital, and urinary system occurred less often than expected. No cancers of the bone, soft tissue, endocrine system, or multiple myeloma were found. Leukemia cases were still significantly in excess among the Smoky participants. The authors concluded that the findings on leukemia were attributable to chance, to factors other than radiation, or to some combination of risk factors that might include radiation, in view of the lack of significant increase in either the incidence of or mortality from any other radiogenic cancers and the apparent lack of a dose effect by units.

The two CDC studies prompted another study by the National Academy of Science (NAS) Medical Follow-up Agency to determine whether the findings from the Smoky participants were unique to that test (59). Five test series were selected, three from the Pacific (Greenhouse, 1951; Castle, 1954; Redwing, 1956) and two from the Nevada Test Site (Upshot Knothole,

1953; Plumbob, 1957). Nearly 50,000 participants were identified by March, 1983. Radiation doses could be determined only for two thirds of the participants. The mean radiation dose was estimated to be 0.9 rem with about 2% of participants receiving more than 5 rem. The excess leukemia among Smoky participants was confirmed but no increase in mortality from other forms of cancer was discerned. No evidence was found of increased mortality from leukemia among participants at Plumbob tests or at four other test series. Combined data for the men in all test series showed no excess in deaths due to leukemia (56 observed, 56.4 expected) and a sizable deficit of deaths from all forms of cancer relative to overall mortality rates in the U.S.

The NAS study has been criticized for inappropriate statistical analysis that led to negative conclusions (8). The critics contended that the test participants should not have been compared to the general population because of "the healthy soldier bias". The military population consisted entirely of persons who were in apparently good health at the time of entry into the service, whereas the general population included those who were sick as well. Three other errors were listed: no analysis of a subgroup of veterans exposed to a higher level of radiation; no analysis of mortality data by latency period; and the combination of radiogenic and nonradiogenic cancers into one category. For example, the NAS analysis combined nonlymphatic leukemias, which are often radiogenic, with lymphatic leukemia, which is not. Correcting for the healthy soldier bias by comparing the standardized mortality ratios (SMR's) for cancer among Smoky participants with estimated exposure level above 300 mrem to those less than 300 mrem revealed a significant excess in respiratory cancer, leukemia, and all cancer (8). The authors of the NAS study, however, disagreed with the analytical steps suggested by the critics on the grounds that the data were being gerrymandered to make them appear to support preconceived ideas (42).

This much debated study will be repeated by the NAS Medical Follow-up Agency with a necessary modification. Further work by the Department of Defense indicated that about 15,000 of the original study cohort of 50,000 were not actually present at the test sites and that another group of about 28,000 participants was never considered. The updated study will make appropriate adjustments to reconstitute a study cohort and also create a veteran control group of equal size to that of the study cohort. The Medical Follow-up Agency is also conducting a study of the mortality experience of veterans who participated in Operation Crossroads, a nuclear weapon test conducted at Bikini Atoll in July 1946. This study was prompted by concerns on the part of Congress and veterans that participants may have been exposed to ionizing radiation in sufficient amounts to induce cancer. Approximately 46,000 veterans were identified as participants and an equal number of veterans who were in service at the time but did not participate in the test were selected for a comparison group (41a).

Several thousand "atomic veterans" have sought medical care and compensation from VA for medical conditions that they believe are related to the nuclear weapon testing or to their participation in military operations in or near Hiroshima and Nagasaki. The NAS Committee on the Biological Effects of Ionizing Radiation in 1990 (BEIR V report) (54) determined that lifetime risk of cancer attributable to a given dose of radiation appears somewhat larger than formerly estimated in 1980 (BEIR III report) (54a) for reasons including the following findings. Reassessment of atomic bomb dosimetry at Hiroshima and Nagasaki disclosed that the average dose equivalent in each city was smaller than previously estimated. Furthermore, continued follow-up of the A-Bomb survivors also indicated that the number of excess cancers per unit dose induced by radiation increases with age. The cancer risk estimates reported in the BEIR V report are about three times larger for solid cancers and about four times larger for leukemia than the risk estimates presented in the BEIR III report. The BEIR V report now projects that exposure to an acute whole-body dose of 0.1 sv (10 rem) to 100,000 males of all ages will result in an additional 500 to 1200 cancer deaths attributable to the exposure.

Further epidemiologic studies of veterans who participated in the nuclear weapon testing and in occupation of Hiroshima and Nagasaki are needed because of the large number of veterans with potential exposure to radiation and because of the uncertainty in how the exposure dose was reconstructed. If the studies show that the rates of cancer mortality in the veteran population in question are similar to those of other veterans who did not participate in the nuclear weapon tests, it may reassure the veterans that they are not at additional risk of cancer. Alternatively, if the studies find an excess in cancer deaths, it may indicate either that the exposure levels estimated by the military were erroneous or that the generally accepted estimates of cancer risk per unit exposure have been grossly underestimated.

Vietnam Veterans Exposed to Herbicides

Of the veteran groups whose service has raised questions concerning possible long-term adverse health consequences, those who served in Vietnam have perhaps generated the most controversy and intense scientific inquiry. Between January 1965 and March 1973, 2.5 to 3 million American military personnel were stationed in Southeast Asia, most of whom served in South Vietnam (75). Contained in the arsenal of US forces in Vietnam were a variety of herbicides used for strategic purposes to defoliate areas of dense jungle. From 1962 to 1971, 75 million liters of herbicides, including over 41 million liters of the phenoxy herbicide Agent Orange, were sprayed on almost 9% of Vietnam (22). US Air Force personnel sprayed hundreds of acres with Agent Orange, using fixed-wing aircraft as part of Operation Ranch Hand. Spraying on a smaller scale also occurred around American installations, such as base camps and air fields.

Agent Orange is a mixture of the chemical compounds, 2,4-D and 2,4,5-T. The compound 2,4,5-T was contaminated with small amounts of dioxin, a toxicant that is both teratogenic and carcinogenic in animals (45, 55, 58). Some studies of nonveteran groups who have been exposed to phenoxy herbicides in farming or manufacturing have reported increased risk of soft tissue sarcoma and non-Hodgkin's lymphoma (NHL) (29, 33, 37–39, 41).

The increased risk for some cancers associated with exposure to phenoxy herbicides that was documented in these occupational studies aroused widespread concern about the long-term health of Vietnam veterans. Responding to this concern, research was conducted to determine the effect(s), if any, of Vietnam service in general, or Agent Orange exposure in particular, on the health of Vietnam veterans. The mortality rate of various groups of Vietnam veterans was compared to that of veterans who served during the Vietnam War but not in Vietnam, or to the US general population. Several studies found no excess in either deaths due to all cancers or deaths due to any specific cancer among Vietnam veterans (2, 11, 21, 31, 49). In contrast, other mortality studies reported significant excesses in deaths due to soft-tissue sarcoma (STS) (46), laryngeal cancer (77), Hodgkin's disease, and testicular cancer (3) associated with Vietnam service. However, the mortality studies looked only at the effects of Vietnam service and not of exposure to Agent Orange.

Many case-control studies have been conducted to determine the association of various cancers with military service in Vietnam. No convincing evidence has been presented of an association between Vietnam service and STS (43, 66), Hodgkin's disease (67), liver cancer (67), or nasopharyngeal cancer (67). For NHL, the results were not consistent. The CDC reported an excess NHL risk among sea-based blue water Navy Vietnam veterans (65). The risk was not associated with surrogate measures of Agent Orange exposure such as dates of service, type of military unit, and place of employment. A VA study also failed to find an association between NHL and surrogate measures of Agent Orange exposure such as service in specific military branch, in certain areas within Vietnam, or in combat role (23). Although Vietnam veterans tend to report more health problems and symptoms than non-Vietnam veterans, medical examination revealed no significant difference in prevalence of a wide variety of medical conditions and laboratory values between two cohorts (18).

Several studies have directly addressed the issue of Agent Orange exposure. Two studies used potential biological markers to indicate Agent Orange exposure among two groups of Vietnam veterans as evidenced by elevated concentration of dioxin (20, 44). One study compared the dioxin concentration in the adipose tissue of Vietnam veterans to that of Vietnam era veterans and of a group of civilians (44). The other study compared the dioxin concentration in the blood serum of Vietnam veterans to that found in a group of Vietnam era veterans (20). In neither study was an association found between Vietnam service and amount of dioxin in the body. This finding suggests that heavy exposure to Agent Orange was unlikely for most troops. These studies also used surrogate measures of Agent Orange exposure, based on the location of each individual veteran's unit in relation to an area sprayed with Agent Orange and time lapsed since that area was sprayed. The information relating to areas sprayed with Agent Orange in Vietnam is stored on two computer tapes compiled by the Department of Defense and the US Army and Joint Services Environmental Support Group (69a). In neither study was the likelihood of Agent Orange exposure (as approximated by serving in a sprayed area) associated with elevated concentrations of dioxin.

Some studies have selected groups of veterans presumed to have increased potential for Agent Orange exposure. One such group was made up of Air Force veterans who participated in Operation Ranch Hand (50) and were exposed to the various herbicides used during flight operations as well as during maintenance of aircraft and spraying equipment. The study compared the health outcomes of approximately 1200 Ranch Hand Air Force veterans to those of 19,000 Air Force veterans involved in cargo flights in Southeast Asia. Another study compared the mortality of nearly 1000 veterans who served in the Army Chemical Corps in Vietnam to that of the total US population (68). Among the duties for veterans in this unit were the mixing and application of herbicides including Agent Orange. Neither study documented an excess of deaths due to cancer (50, 68).

Women veterans who served in Vietnam are also of interest. To date only one study has been published examining the mortality of women Vietnam veterans (69). The mortality of approximately 4600 women Vietnam veterans was compared to that of 5300 women veterans who did not serve in Vietnam. The only cause of death found to be significantly elevated among the women Vietnam veterans was death due to motor vehicle accidents. However, among nurses, cancers of the pancreas and uterine corpus were significantly elevated.

Although findings from the various mortality studies have been inconsistent regarding cancer outcomes, they have produced more consistent findings regarding external causes of death. Of those mortality studies previously discussed, six reported statistically significant excesses of deaths due to external causes (2, 11, 21, 31, 49, 77), which included accidental poison-ings, and motor vehicle accidents.

The possibility of fathering a child with birth defects as a result of exposure to Agent Orange has been one of the major concerns of Vietnam veterans. There have been numerous instances when Vietnam veterans reported fathering children with congenital malformations. However, little or no evidence supports an association between military service in Vietnam and the risk of fathering children with birth defects (19, 24, 28).

Vietnam Veterans and PTSD   Another area of concern regarding possible adverse health consequences of Vietnam service is related to mental/psy-chological health. Much of this research has centered on problems experi-enced by Vietnam veterans as they adjusted to civilian life (14, 27, 32, 78). Researchers and mental health clinicians have often associated adjust-ment problems with the occurrence of PTSD among Vietnam veterans. The diagnosis of PTSD is based on a variety of criteria as set forth by the American Psychiatric Association in the Diagnostic and Statistical Manual of Mental Disorders (DSM III-R) (1). One criterion for PTSD is exposure to a traumatic event. Studies of PTSD among Vietnam veterans have reported that seeing comrades killed, being fired upon, and being wounded are all risk factors for PTSD among Vietnam veterans (10, 15, 34, 36, 64). Other studies suggest that experiences prior to military service are responsible for the maladjustment problems of some Vietnam veterans (53, 79). However, these studies did not assess combat exposure nor was PTSD specifically examined as an outcome variable. Estimates of the prevalence rate of PTSD among Vietnam veterans range from 2% to 15% among all Vietnam veterans (17, 47) and 20% to 32% among wounded Vietnam veterans (40, 57).

The excess mortality due to external causes among Vietnam veterans and the high prevalence of PTSD among Vietnam veterans (2, 11, 21, 31, 40, 47, 49, 57, 77), while usually not associated with each other in their respective studies, may actually be related. Like PTSD, suicide has been associated with exposure to a traumatic event (5, 30, 52). Both PTSD and suicide also share certain emotional and behavioral characteristics including withdrawal, social isolation (1, 4, 7, 25, 60, 62), and alcohol and drug abuse (4, 7, 15, 17, 25, 60, 62). To date only one study has examined these two health outcomes for an association between PTSD and traumatic causes of death among Vietnam veterans (9). The findings from this study indicated that PTSD was a statistically significant risk factor for all external causes of death, including accidental deaths, all accidental poisonings, and suicides.

Reviewed collectively, findings from studies of Vietnam veterans do not indicate that Vietnam veterans are dying at a greater rate than other veterans or the general population except for traumatic deaths. A few studies have reported increased risks for certain types of cancer among Vietnam veterans, but the results are not conclusive. The prevalence rates of PTSD and psychological disorders are consistently high among Vietnam veterans, especially among combat veterans. The studies of reproductive outcomes among male veterans were not associated with the risk of fathering a child with birth defects, spontaneous abortions, still births, or neonatal deaths. Because maternal, not paternal, exposure to dioxin causes adverse reproductive events in animals, a study of women Vietnam veterans for adverse reproductive outcomes is warranted.

Persian Gulf War Veterans Exposed to Kuwaiti Oil-Well Fires

On February 15, 1991, the retreating Iraqi Army began destroying and setting fire to oil wells, storage tanks, and refineries in several oil fields in Kuwait. A total of 749 facilities were either set on fire or turned to oil gushers. According to Kuwaiti oil industry officials, up to 6 million barrels of oil were burned each day from 600 oil wells, creating one of the most extraordinary manmade environmental disasters in history. The 600,000 US troops deployed in the region were potentially exposed to smoke and other toxic combustion products. Air pollutants such as hydrogen sulfide, sulfur dioxide, hydrocarbons, particulate matters singularly or in combination can cause acute as well as chronic health problems. Therefore, immediate and long-term health risk to the troops has been of concern to individuals deployed in the region and to government agencies.

Soon after their return from deployment to the Persian Gulf region many soldiers started reporting a wide variety of nonspecific symptoms, including fatigue, joint pains, skin rashes, headaches, loss of memory, diarrhea, bleeding and painful gums, and loss of hair. These soldiers were evaluated by military medical teams without any unifying diagnosis (76). No evidence was reported of an outbreak or cluster of any unique disease process among these soldiers. Dental examination revealed gingivitis, periodontal diseases, caries, and other chronic oral conditions as likely causes for the dental symptoms. Results of specific testing indicated no role for leishmaniasis, brucellosis, and other infectious agents in causing the symptoms reported by this group of soldiers. As of May 1993, only 30 cases of leishmaniasis, a parasitic disease endemic in the Persian Gulf area, had been reported from the entire group of troops deployed in the Persian Gulf.

Stress associated with post-deployment adjustment to civilian life has been suggested as a plausible etiology for many of the symptoms reported (76). In one survey, 22% of 715 troops deployed to the Persian Gulf region reported at least mild levels of clinical depression, whereas 11% of 169 nondeployed troops had a similar level of depression. The prevalence of PTSD among Gulf veterans was about 10% using the DSM-R-derived PTSD Symptoms Checklist (35).

An alternate etiology proposed for the "mystery illnesses" among Gulf War veterans is multiple chemical sensitivity (MCS) (51). Multiple chemical sensitivity appears to involve two steps: induction or sensitization, and triggering. Induction or sensitization may have occurred among the Gulf veterans following a single, acute exposure or repeated low-level exposures to any of a wide variety of petrochemical combustion products while deployed in the Persian Gulf region. Once sensitized, exposure to extremely low levels of sensitizing agents or other chemicals could trigger a wide range of symptoms such as memory loss, headaches, weakness, fatigue, and mood changes.

The levels of air quality during the oil well fires have been investigated by a US Interagency Air Assessment Team (48). From March through May 1991 the team sampled air near the burning wells, flew instrumental airplanes into smoke plumes, and sampled the air at various locations in the path of the smoke, including population centers in Kuwait and Saudi Arabia. The air samples were analyzed for volatile organic compounds, polycyclic aromatic hydrocarbons, heavy metals, sulfur dioxide and inorganic acids, hydrogen sulfide, and total nuisance dust. Both hydrogen sulfide and sulfur dioxide were present in concentrations below the EPA limits near the sources of the fire and at locations sampled downwind. The only elevated levels observed in the population areas were for particulate matter. A very high level of fine particulate (PM-10), 8 to 10 times the EPA limit of 50 mg/M^3, was observed in Kuwait city and Dhahran, Saudi Arabia. These high readings were considered not unusual for the area, probably due to a combination of blowing dust and sand.

Department of Defense also dispatched its own environmental monitoring team to the area (70). A team of industrial hygienists from the US Army Environmental Hygiene Agency monitored the area from May 5, 1991, until December 3, 1991. At the start of monitoring, 558 wells were still on fire. Data collection continued until all fires were extinguished. Air monitoring stations were set up at four locations in Saudi Arabia and six locations in Kuwait, where large numbers of US troops were stationed. Soil samples were also taken to evaluate alternate exposure pathways. The DOD team reported that air sample measurements collected during this period did not suggest the oil fires were significantly contributing to air quality at ground-level sampling sites. Mean concentrations of organic compounds measured in Kuwaiti and Saudi sampling sites were comparable to levels observed in US cities (Houston, Philadelphia). In most cases concentrations of polycyclic aromatic hydrocarbons were below the detection levels. High concentrations of particulate matter were measured at all sampling locations as reported by the interagency team.

VA has initiated a health registry in response to health concerns expressed by the Persian Gulf War veterans. All Persian Gulf veterans with medical concerns that they believe are related to their deployment in the Persian Gulf region, are encouraged to come to a VA medical center for a free physical examination. Their demographic and medical data are included in the registry.

Demographic characteristics from the Registry for the first 1404 registry participants nearly approximate the characteristics of troops deployed in the area. Symptoms reported by the registry participants were nonspecific and were similar to complaints reported by other groups of Persian Gulf veterans. The common complaints were fatigue, skin rash, headache, loss of memory, muscle/joint pain, shortness of breath, cough, diarrhea, and chest pain. A wide range of medical conditions were diagnosed among the participants. About 20% of participants did not have a medical diagnosis. Prevalence of chronic respiratory diseases did not seem to be unusually high among these veterans: chronic bronchitis (1.2%), asthma (3.7%), chronic airway obstruction (1.9%). Prevalence of chronic PTSD was lower than reported in other groups of Persian Gulf veterans (2.6% observed vs 10% reported in another survey). Veterans with symptoms or with medical diagnoses were more likely to report having been in the contaminated area, in a smoky area, enveloped in smoke, or eating/drinking contaminated foodstuff than veterans without symptoms or medical diagnoses (74a).

Veterans in the Persian Gulf Registry, like those in the Agent Orange Registry, are self-selected for their concern about the possible adverse health effects from environmental conditions experienced during the deployment and are also willing to visit VA medical facilities for physical examination. Therefore, they may not be representative of the general Persian Gulf veteran population. A valid comparison of health outcomes from this group to another population is difficult to make due to this self-selection bias.

Hospital discharge diagnoses of 4514 Persian Gulf veterans and 4325 era veteran patients in VA medical centers showed no significant difference in distribution of major categories of diagnoses except in the category of adjustment disorders, including PTSD. More than 25,000 Persian Gulf veterans have visited VA's readjustment counseling centers. While there was considerable variation among counseling centers, aggregated data suggest that 9 percent of returning Persian Gulf veterans may have been suffering from significant symptoms of clinical PTSD shortly after their return from the Persian Gulf region.

The study of Persian Gulf War veterans has benefitted from earlier veteran studies, in particular those related to Vietnam. Two major difficulties in research concerning health effects of Agent Orange have been the inability to identify a large number of Vietnam veterans who were exposed to Agent Orange and the uncertainty in assessing the magnitude of their exposure. Reconstructing the Vietnam data related to Agent Orange after the fact is extremely difficult. To avoid similar problems in studying Persian Gulf Veterans, the Department of Veterans Affairs and the Department of Defense are collaborating to establish the following databases: (*a*) a roster of troops assigned to each military unit that served in the Persian Gulf area; (*b*) a file of unit location for the period January 15, 1991, through the date of unit withdrawal from the area; and (*c*) data on air pollution levels from a number of locations where troops were deployed. Once the roster of Persian Gulf-deployed troops is established, a sample of troops on the roster can be selected to conduct a morbidity or mortality study to test specific hypotheses about exposure and outcome association.

SUMMARY

Late effects of exposure to certain environmental hazards as a consequence of their active military service have become an issue of particular concern to veterans and the public at large. Approximately one out of four Americans is a veteran or a family member of a veteran. The US military develops and uses increasingly complex and sophisticated weaponry. As the military technology changes, so do the kinds of health issues to be addressed. The changing composition of military personnel, most notably the increasing number of women veterans and their expanding role into combat-related activities, will affect both the health issues to be addressed and the kind of health care to be provided. The emerging role of the military as peace-keepers in hostile but nonwar zones and as disaster-relief workers, often in developing countries, may subject soldiers to infectious diseases endemic to the area and to psychological stressors unrelated to combat.

The formation of a registry of military personnel exposed to potentially serious long-term health hazards would be highly advisable, whenever feasible. Such an exposure registry could serve as the basis for future medical surveillance and response to affected veterans and help avoid the kind of difficulty experienced in addressing health concerns of WWII veterans exposed to mustard gas and Vietnam veterans exposed to Agent Orange. Close cooperation between the Department of Veterans Affairs and the Department of Defense is essential in the identification of potential hazards and follow-up of affected individuals. Growing public awareness of potential occupational and environmental hazards, publicity surrounding such suspected health risks, and the limited scientific knowledge about low-level exposure to toxic substances may all lead to misunderstanding, unwarranted fear, and suspicion of government coverup. Establishment of an exposure registry of veterans may be seen as a government commitment to address the future effects of potential hazards.

Any *Annual Review* chapter, as well as any article cited in an *Annual Review* chapter, may be purchased from the Annual Reviews Preprints and Reprints service. 1-800-347-8007; 415-259-5017; email: arpr@class.org

Literature Cited

1. Am. Psychiatr. Assoc. 1980. *Diagnostic and Statistical Manual of Mental Disorders.* Washington, DC: Am. Psychiatr. Assoc. 3rd ed. rev.

2. Anderson HA, Hanrahan LP, Jensen M, Laurin D, Yick WY, et al. 1986. *Wisconsin Vietnam Mortality Study, Final Report.* State Wis. Dep. Health Soc. Serv., Div. Health

3. Bailey C, Baron R, Bosanac E, Brough J, Conroy C, et al. 1986. *West Virginia Vietnam Era Veteran Mortality Study, West Virginia Residents 1968–1983, Preliminary Rep.* W. VA Health Dep.

4. Barraclough B, Bunch J, Nelson B, Sainsbury P. 1974. A hundred cases of suicide: Clinical aspects. *Br. J. Psychiatry* 125:355–73

5. Beck AT, Lester D. 1976. Components of suicidal intent in completed and attempted. *J. Psychol.* 92:35–38

6. Beebe G. 1960. Lung cancer in World War I veterans: Possible relation to mustard gas injury and 1918 influenza epidemic. *J. Natl. Cancer Inst.* 5:1231–52

7. Borg SE, Stahl M. 1982. A prospective study of suicides among psychiatric patients. *Acta Psychiatr. Scand.* 65:221–32

8. Bross ID, Bross NS. 1987. Do atomic veterans have excess cancer? New results correcting for the healthy soldier bias. *Am. J. Epidemiol.* 126:1042–50

9. Bullman TA, Kang HK. 1993. *Post-traumatic stress disorders and the risk of suicide among Vietnam veterans on the Agent Orange Registry.* Presented at Annu. Meet. Soc. Epidemiol. Res., 26th, Keystone, CO

10. Bullman TA, Kang HK, Thomas TL. 1991. Posttraumatic Stress Disorder among Vietnam veterans on the Agent Orange Registry: A case-control analysis. *Ann. Epidemiol.* 1(6):506–12

11. Bullman TA, Kang H, Watanabe K. 1991. Proportionate mortality among US Army Vietnam veterans who served in military region. I. *Am. J. Epidemiol.* 132:670–74

12. Caldwell GG, Kelley D, Zack M, Falk H, Heath CW. 1983. Mortality and cancer frequency among military nuclear test (SMOKY) participants, 1957 through 1979. *J. Am. Med. Assoc.* 250:620–24

13. Caldwell GG, Kelley DB, Heath CW. 1980. Leukemia among participants in military maneuvers at a nuclear bomb test: A preliminary report. *J. Am. Med. Assoc.* 244:1575–78

14. Card JJ. 1983. *Lives after Vietnam: The Personal Impact of Military Service,* pp. 93–114. Lexington, MA: Health

15. Card JJ. 1987. Epidemiology of PTSD in a national cohort of Vietnam veterans. *J. Clin. Psychol.* 43:6–17

16. Case RM, Lea J. 1955. Mustard gas poisoning, chronic bronchitis, and lung cancer. *Br. J. Prev. Soc. Med.* 9:62–72

17. Cent. Dis. Control. 1988. Health status of Vietnam veterans. II. physical health. *J. Am. Med. Assoc.* 259:2708–14

18. Cent. Dis. Control. 1988. Health status of Vietnam veterans. I. Psychosocial characteristics. *J. Am. Med. Assoc.* 259:2701–7

19. Cent. Dis. Control. 1988. Health status of Vietnam veterans. III. Reproductive outcomes and child health. *J. Am. Med. Assoc.* 259:2715–19

20. Cent. Dis. Control. 1988. Serum 2,3,7,8-tetrachlorodibenzo-*p*-dioxin levels in U.S. Army Vietnam-Era veterans. *J. Am. Med. Assoc.* 260:1249–54

21. Cent. Dis. Control Vietnam Experience Study. 1987. Postservice mortality among Vietnam veterans. *J. Am. Med. Assoc.* 257:790–95

22. Comm. on the Effects of Herbicides in Vietnam. 1974. *The effects of her-*

bicides in South Vietnam. Part A-Summary and conclusions. Washington, DC: Natl. Acad. Sci.

23. Dalager NA, Kang HK, Burt VL. 1991. Non-Hodgkin's lymphoma among Vietnam Veterans. *J. Occup. Med.* 33:774–79

24. Donovan JW, MacLennan R, Adena M. 1984. Vietnam service and the risk of congential anomalies. *Med. J. Aust.* 140:394–97

25. Dorpat TL, Ripley HS. 1960. A study of suicide in the Seattle area. *Compr. Psychiatry* 1:349–59

26. Easton D, Peto J, Doll R. 1988. Cancers of the respiratory tract in mustard gas workers. *Br. J. Ind. Med.* 45:652–59

27. Egendorg A, Kaduschin C, Laufer RS, Rothbart G, Sloan L. 1981. *Legacies in Vietnam comparative adjustment of veterans and their peers,* Publ. No. 101:134–630. Washington, DC: US GPO

28. Erickson JD, Mulinare J, McClain PW, Fitch TG, James LM, et al. 1984. Vietnam veterans' risks for fathering babies with birth defect. *J. Am. Med. Assoc.* 252:903–12

29. Eriksson M, Hardell L, Berg N, Moller T, Axelson O. 1981. Soft tissue sarcomas and exposure to chemical substances: A case-reference study. *Br. J. Ind. Med.* 38:27–33

30. Farberow NL, Shneidman ES, eds. 1981. *Cry for Help.* New York: McGraw-Hill

31. Fett MJ, Nairn JR, Cobbin DM, Adena M. 1987. Mortality among Australian conscripts of the Vietnam conflict era. II. causes of death. *Am. J. Epidemiol.* 125:878–84

32. Figley CR. 1977. *The American Legion study of psychological adjustment among Vietnam veterans.* Lafayette, IN: Purdue Univ.

33. Fingerhut MA, Halperin WE, Marlow DA, Piacitelli LA, Honchar PA, et al. 1991. Cancer mortality in workers exposed to *2,3,7,8*-tetrachlorodibenzo-*p*-dioxin. *N. England J. Med.* 324:212–18

34. Foy DW, Siprelle RC, Rueger DB, Carroll EM. 1984. Etiology of Posttraumatic Stress Disorder in Vietnam veterans: Analysis of premilitary, military, and combat exposure influences. *J. Consult. Clin. Psychol.* 52:82–84

35. Freidman MJ. 1993. *Preliminary data on three VA ODS Follow-up Surveys.* Presented at Meet. Dep. Veterans Aff. Persian Gulf Expert Sci. Panel, May 7, Washington, DC. Unpublished

36. Frye JS, Stockton RA. 1982. Discriminate analysis of Posttraumatic Stress Disorder among a group of Vietnam veterans. *Am. J. Psychiatry* 139:25–56

37. Hardell L. 1981. Relation of soft tissue sarcoma, malignant lymphoma and colon cancer to phenoxy acids, chlorophenols and other agents. *Scand. J. Work Environ. Health* 7:119–30

38. Hardell L, Eriksson M, Lenner P, Lundgren E. 1981. Malignant lymphoma and exposure to chemicals, especially organic solvents, chlorophenols and phenoxy acids: a case-control study. *Br. J. Cancer* 43:169–76

39. Hardell L, Sandstrom A. 1979. A case-control study: soft tissue sarcoma and exposure to phenoxyacetic acids or chlorophenols. *Br. J. Cancer* 39: 711–17

40. Helzer JE, Robins LN, McEvoy L. 1987. Posttraumatic stress disorder in the general population. *N. England J. Med.* 319:1630–34

41. Hoar SK, Blair A, Holmes F, Boysen CD, Robel RJ, et al. 1986. Agricultural herbicide use and risk of lymphoma and soft tissue sarcoma. *J. Am. Med. Assoc.* 256:1141–47

41a. Howson CP, Page WF. 1992. *Mortality of Crossroads Nuclear Test Participants.* Natl. Acad. Sci. Follow-up Agency, Washington, DC

42. Jablon S. 1987. Do atomic veterans have excess cancer? New results correcting for the healthy soldier bias. Letter to the Editor. *Am. J. Epidemiol.* 126:1214

43. Kang H, Enziger F, Breslin P, Feil M, Lee Y, Shepard B. 1987. Soft tissue sarcoma and military service in Vietnam: A Case-Control study. *J. Natl. Cancer Inst.* 79:693–99

44. Kang HK, Watanabe KK, Breen J, Remmers J, Conomos M, et al. 1991. Dioxins and dibenzofurans in adipose tissue of US Vietnam veterans and controls. *Am. J. Public Health* 81:344–49

45. Kociba RJ, Keyes DG, Beyes JE, Carreon RM, Wade CE, et al. 1978. Results of a two-year chronic toxicity and oncogenicity study of *2,3,7,8*-tetrachlorodibenzo-*p*-dioxin (TCDD) in rats. *Toxicol. Appl. Pharmacol.* 46: 279–303

46. Kogan MD, Clapp RW. 1988. Soft tissue sarcoma mortality among Vietnam veterans in Massachusetts, 1972–1983. *Int. J. Epidemiol.* 17:39–43

47. Kulka RA, Schlenger WE, Fairbank JA, Hough RL, Jordan BK, et al. 1990. *Trauma and the Vietnam War*

Generation, p. 266. New York: Brunner/Mazel

48. Kuwait Oil Fires. Interagency Interim Rep. April 3, 1991. Washington, DC

49. Lawrence CE, Reilly AA, Quickenton P, Greenwald P, Page WF, et al. 1985. Mortality Patterns of New York State Vietnam veterans. *Am. J. Public Health* 75:277–79

50. Michalek JE, Wolfe WH, Miner JC. 1990. Health status of Air Force veterans occupationally exposed to herbicides in Vietnam. II. Mortality. *J. Am. Med. Assoc.* 264:1832–36

51. Miller CS. 1992. Possible models for multiple chemical sensitivity: Conceptual issues and role of the limbic system. *Toxicol. Ind. Health* 8:181–202

52. Moss LM, Hamilton DM. 1957. Psychotherapy of the suicidal patient. In *Clues to Suicide,* eds. ES Shneidman, NL Farberow, pp. 99–103. New York: McGraw-Hill

53. Nance EP, Obrien CP, Mintz J, Ream N, Meyers AL, et al. 1978. Adjustment among Vietnam veteran drug abusers two years post-service. In *Stress Disorders Among Vietnam Veterans: Theory, Research, and Treatment,* ed. CR Figley, pp. 71–83. New York: Brunner/Mazel

54. Natl. Res. Counc., Natl. Acad. Sci. 1990. *Health Effects of Exposure to Low Levels of Ionizing Radiation, BEIR V. Committee on the Biological Effects of Ionizing Radiations.* Washington, DC: Natl. Acad. Press

54a. Natl. Res. Counc., Natl. Acad. Sci. 1980. *The Effects on Populations of Exposure to Low Levels of Ionizing Radiation, BIER III.* Comm. Biol. Effects Ionizing Rad. Washington, DC: Natl. Acad. Press

55. Natl. Toxicol. Progr. 1982. *Carcinogenesis Bioassay of 2,3,7,8-tetrachlorodibenzo-p-dioxin (CAS no. 1746–01–6) in Osborne-Mendel Rats and B6C3F Mice (Gavage study).* Washington, DC: US GPO/US DHHS Publ. NIH 82–1765

56. Norman JE. 1975. Lung cancer mortality in World War I veterans with mustard gas injury, 1919–1965. *J. Natl. Cancer Inst.* 54:311–18

57. Pitman RK, Altman B, Macklin ML. 1989. Prevalence of Posttraumatic Stress Disorder in wounded Vietnam veterans. *Am. J. Psychiatry* 146:667–69

58. Poland A, Knutson JC. 1981. *2,3,7,8-*Tetrachlorodibenzo-*p*-dioxin and related halogenated aromatic hydrocarbons: examination of the mechanism of toxicity. *Annu. Rev. Pharmacol. Toxicol.* 22:517–54

59. Robinette CD, Jalon S, Preston TL. 1985. *Mortality of nuclear weapons test participants.* Medical Follow-up Agency. Washington, DC: Natl. Acad. Press

60. Robins E. 1981. *The Final Months,* pp. 221–320. New York: Oxford Univ. Press

61. Rothberg JM, Bartone PT, Holloway HC, Marlowe DH. 1990. Life and death in the U.S. Army: In Corpore Sano. *J. Am. Med. Assoc.* 264:2241–44

62. Sainsbury P. 1986. The epidemiology of suicide. In *Suicide,* ed. R Johnston. Baltimore: Wilkins

63. Seltzer CC, Jablon S. 1974. Effects of selection on mortality. *Am. J. Epidemiol.* 100:367–72

64. Solkoff N, Gray P, Keill S. 1986. Which Vietnam veterans develop Posttraumatic Stress Disorder. *J. Clin. Psychol.* 42(5):687–98

65. The Selected Cancers Cooperative Study Group. 1990. The association of selected cancers with service in the US military in Vietnam. I: non-Hodgkin's lymphoma. *Arch. Intern. Med.* 150:2473–83

66. The Selected Cancers Cooperative Study Group. 1990. The association of selected cancers with service in the US military in Vietnam. II: soft-tissue and other sarcomas. *Arch. Intern. Med.* 150:2485–92

67. The Selected Cancers Cooperative Study Group. 1990. The association of selected cancers with service in the US military in Vietnam. IV: Hodgkin's disease, nasal cancer, nasopharyngeal cancer, and primary liver cancer. *Arch. Intern. Med.* 150:2495–505

68. Thomas TL, Kang HK. 1990. Mortality and morbidity among Army chemical corps Vietnam veterans: A preliminary report. *Am. J. Ind. Med.* 18:665–73

69. Thomas TL, Kang HK, Dalager NA. 1991. Mortality among women Vietnam veterans, 1973–1987. *Am. J. Epidemiol.* 134:973–80

69a. US Army Joint Serv. Environ. Support Group. 1985. *Services Herbs Tape.* Washington, DC: US Army

70. US Army Environ. Hygiene Agency. 1992. Interim Kuwait oil fire health risk assessment No. 39–26–2192–91. Aberdeen Proving Ground, MD, June

71. US Defense Nuclear Agency. 1986. *For the Record. A History of the Nuclear Test Personnel Review Program.* DNA Tech. Rep. 6041F. Washington, DC: US Def. Nucl. Agency

72. US Dep. Veterans Aff. 1985. *Survey of Female Veterans: A Study of the Needs, Attitudes and Experiences of Women Veterans.* Washington, DC: US Dep. VA

73. US Dep. Veterans Aff. 1989. *1987 Survey of Veterans.* Washington, DC: US Dep. VA

74. US Dep. Veterans Aff. 1991. *Annual Report of the Secretary of Veterans Affairs.* Washington, DC: US Dep. VA

74a. US Dep. Veterans Aff. Persian Gulf Expert Panel. 1993. *Conference on Persian Gulf Veterans.* Washington, DC: US VA

75. US Veterans Adm. Off. Control. Rep. Stat. Serv. 1980. *Data on Vietnam era veterans.* Washington, DC: US VA

76. Walter Reed Army Inst. Res. 1992. *Investigation of a suspected outbreak of an unknown disease among veterans of Operation Desert Shield/Storm.* 123 Army Reserved Command. Fort Benjamin Harrison, Ind., April. Epidemiol. Consult. Serv. Div. Prev. Med., Washington, DC, June

77. Watanabe KK, Kang HK, Thomas TL. 1991. Mortality among Vietnam veterans: With methodological considerations. *J. Occup. Med.* 33:780–85

78. Wilson JP. 1980. Conflict, stress, and growth: The effects of war on psychosocial development among Vietnam veterans. In *Strangers at Home: Vietnam Veterans Since the War,* ed. CR Figley, S Leventman, pp. 123–65. New York: Prager

79. Worthington ER. 1978. Demographic and pre-service variables as predictors of post-military service adjustment. In *Stress Disorders Among Vietnam Veterans: Theory, Research, and Treatment,* ed. CR Figley, pp. 173–87. New York: Brunner/Mazel

Annu. Rev. Public Health. 1994. 15:91–105
Copyright © 1994 by Annual Reviews. All rights reserved

THE IMPACT OF THE AMERICANS WITH DISABILITIES ACT ON EMPLOYMENT OPPORTUNITY FOR PEOPLE WITH DISABILITIES

Mary Richardson

Graduate Program in Health Services Administration, Department of Health Services, School of Public Health and Community Medicine, University of Washington, Seattle, Washington 98195

KEY WORDS: disability, ADA, employment, disability policy, disability management

"segregation and isolation by others will no longer be tolerated."
US Senator Tom Harkin, Chief Senate Sponsor
of the ADA (27)

INTRODUCTION

The newly enacted Americans with Disabilities Act (ADA) is designed to protect the civil rights of individuals with disabilities. It takes aim at discrimination and articulates goals for equal opportunity, full participation, independent living, and economic self-sufficiency. It documents that people with disabilities, as a group, occupy an inferior status in our society, and are severely disadvantaged socially, vocationally, economically, and educationally. It calls for a "clear and comprehensive national mandate for the elimination of discrimination against individuals with disabilities" and provides enforceable standards for doing so (23).

The ADA defines disability as "a physical or mental impairment that substantially limits one or more of the major life activities of such individ-

91

uals, a record of such impairment, or being regarded as having such an impairment" (23). It is broad in its reach and prohibits discrimination on the basis of disability in the areas of employment, public accommodations, services provided by state and local governments, telecommunications, and transportation. Title I, which addresses employment, is perhaps the most far-reaching of the ADA provisions.

The ADA has the potential to affect the lives of substantial numbers of people. One estimate places the number of people with disabilities at 43 million (13), while another based on category or type of impairment suggests there are approximately 33 million people with sensory, motor, or cognitive disabilities severe enough to interfere with work or otherwise constitute a serious disability (6). These studies also cite 14 million adults (about 7% of the population) who have fourth grade or lower reading skills, which seriously impairs their capability for doing many kinds of jobs, especially those in information occupations.

The past two decades brought about a heightened awareness of the importance of work and the right of individuals with disabilities to equal opportunity in the workplace, while advancing technology offered new and creative approaches for overcoming functional limitations. Yet the employment picture for persons with disabilities worsened over the same period (16, 33), and disability remains a major cause of unemployment and poverty. While the overall labor force participation rate increased 10%, the labor force participation rate for working-age persons with disabilities fell by 4% (34) and their wages were generally lower (3, 14, 19). Half to two thirds of Americans with disabilities between the ages of 16 and 64 are not working at all (6, 13); sixty percent of those not working say they would like to (13) if the opportunity were made available.

The potential impact of the ADA on employers has been the subject of some consternation and considerable debate, although federal protection against discrimination based on disability is not new. The ADA is the second significant statute that prohibits employment discrimination against individuals with disabilities. The first, section 504 of the Rehabilitation Act of 1973, was more limited in scope. Its prohibitions on employment discrimination based on disability extended only to the federal government, federal contractors, and recipients of federal financial assistance. The ADA extends these prohibitions to virtually all employers, including state and local governments, with 25 or more employees. Beginning in July 1994, all employers with 15 or more employees are covered.

The essence and spirit of the ADA, as envisioned by its sponsors, is perhaps more eloquently expressed in the reauthorization of the Rehabilitation Act. Its statement of Findings, Purpose, Policy declares:

Disability is a natural part of the human experience and in no way diminishes the right of individuals to: A) live independently; B) enjoy self determination; C) make choices; D) contribute to society; E) pursue meaningful careers; and F) enjoy full inclusion and integration in the economic, political, social, cultural, and educational mainstream of American society... " (24)

Subtitle B of the Rehabilitation Act Amendments of 1993 goes on to state:

Congress finds that A) work is a valued activity, both for individuals and society, and fulfills the need of an individual to be productive, promote independence, enhances self-esteem, and allows for participation in the mainstream of life in America; and B) as a group, individuals with disabilities experience staggering levels of unemployment and poverty... (24)

The ADA does not give preference to persons with a disability in the employment setting. It does, however, prohibit an employer from discriminating "against a qualified individual with a disability" in the application, hiring, advancement, and discharge processes, or anything else related to that person's employment. A "qualified individual with a disability" is someone who is able to perform, with or without reasonable accommodation, "the essential functions of the employment position that such individual holds or desires."

The ADA specifically prohibits an employer from using screening methods and selection criteria that do not pertain to the requirements of the job and/or are meant to deny opportunity to a candidate because of his or her disability. Further, the employer is expected to articulate the skill demands of the position and the performance expectations. If a person can meet these demands and expectations, he or she must be considered equally with other candidates, regardless of disability. The ADA simply says that people with a disability deserve equal opportunity in the workplace.

Opponents to the legislation point to the potential costs of the structural components of the legislation, which require reasonable accommodation to a disability through the physical modification of buildings and work-sites, and express concerns about the cost of compliance. Supporters emphasize the untapped pool of eager workers who are willing to work hard and loyally in order to prove their capability and make a contribution to the workplace. They emphasize the cost of excluding a significant portion of the population from the mainstream of American life, and point to the costs of not working. Social Security Disability Insurance (SSDI) and Supplemental Security Income (SSI) are the governmental income security programs for people with a disability. SSDI experienced a twofold increase in enrollment during the 1970s, to 2.9 million people, while the cost of the program increased from $2.8 to $14.9 billion per year (33). Costs continued to rise despite efforts by two previous administrations to manage them by severely limiting enrollment. At the end of 1992 approximately 8.8 million people received SSDI and/or SSI benefits based on their own or a family member's disability for a total benefit cost of $52 billion.

Enlightened employers recognize the value not only of hiring talented persons who may have a disability but also the importance of establishing workplace programs aimed at preventing disabilities in the first place, and intervening early once they occur in order to maintain employment. In 1980, American employers paid over $70 billion in health and disability insurance premiums for their employees (25). More recent estimates of workers compensation costs to employers are in excess of $30 billion, with an aggregate cost of work place injuries including rehabilitation and partial wage replacement exceeding $100 billion (30).

This review examines the potential for full implementation of the employment provisions of the ADA. Implementation of both the spirit and letter of the law extends beyond the immediate provisions of the Act. First, it requires an expanded view of the nature of disability and work. Within this broader context, the impact of discrimination on the opportunity for work must be considered, along with the related effect of current federal programs that provide support for persons who have been determined unable to work. Comprehensive disability management, which includes the prevention of disabilities, intervention at the initial signs of disease or injury that may lead to a disability, and the promotion of flexible work environments for workers who do have a disability, will be presented as an important model for the successful implementation of the goals of the ADA.

THE NATURE OF DISABILITY

Disability is defined by the World Health Organization as the "restriction or lack of ability to perform an activity in the manner or within the range considered normal for a human being" (32). It is the consequence of physical and/or mental impairments that may begin very early in life (e.g. developmental disabilities), occur as a result of injury, or develop later in life (e.g. chronic conditions). Verbrugge (29) expands the concept to include social disability, which refers to the relationship between a person's capability and the demands of the environment as the individual carries out social roles.

Applying Verbrugge's model to disability and employment, disability creates a gap between the individual's ability to perform and the demands of the employer. Accommodation requires an effort by the individual to offset the impact of the limitation through rehabilitation, the application of technology, or learning another way of doing the same thing. The employer may need to reduce the demands of the workplace, or provide physical accommodation in response to the disability.

The concept of social disability would suggest that it is not enough to simply remove social barriers, such as discrimination, to accomplish the goals of the ADA. Changing the attitudes and educating employers may also not be enough. Rather, full implementation of the ADA requires the combined efforts of the individual with the disability, health care and rehabilitation providers who assist in the management of the disability, and the employer.

THE IMPACT OF DISCRIMINATION ON EMPLOYMENT OPPORTUNITY FOR PEOPLE WITH DISABILITIES

Work experience is different between men and women with disabilities, suggesting that discrimination may be based on gender as well as disability. Discrimination is not considered a problem by 80% of men who are employed. Although employed women with disabilities have not been similarly studied, it must be noted that less than 33% of women with disabilities are employed, and only 13% are employed full time. In addition, wage discrimination is reported between nondisabled women and women with disabilities (M Baldwin & WG Johnson, unpublished data). It should also be noted that employed women with disabilities earn less than men whether nondisabled or disabled, suggesting that determinants of employment and wage discrimination may be related to occupational segregation more than to disability (1). Both disabled and nondisabled women are over-represented in traditionally female clerical and service occupations and underrepresented in traditionally male skilled production.

Previous work experience may affect the degree to which a worker with a disability experiences discrimination and is related to gender in so far as women generally have less work experience than men. The wage differential between men with disabilities and their nondisabled counterparts is small because employed men with disabilities generally have many years of work experience. Working men with disabilities are likely to be experienced, older workers with chronic, degenerative diseases such as arthritis and cardiovascular conditions, which occur most frequently in middle age. Most of these men were likely to have been employed at the onset of their disabling condition and have skills that are recognized by their employer and viewed as compensating for any negative effect of the disability (17). Women may have less work experience than men, in general, and employers have limited incentives to invest in job accommodations and rehabilitation when a woman becomes impaired in middle age by an injury or illness (1).

Type of impairment or visibility of impairment may affect the intensity of prejudice (12, 36). Attitudes toward individuals with mental disorders, cognitive impairments, or impairments that affect appearance or behavior are substantially more negative. Prejudice towards these individuals is more likely to result in a substantial limitation of work opportunities.

Discrimination exists within the perception of the individual with a disability as well as through actual workplace experience. Perception of discrimination by persons who are disabled, along with self-defined disability, was examined by the International Center for the Disabled (ICD) in 1986 using a telephone survey (18). Among persons with work experience, 25% reported job discrimination; 47% of those working less than full time or not working at all stated that employers would not recognize their capacity for working full time. Other reasons cited for lack of full employment included poor education, lack of transportation, and lack of assistive equipment. However, most persons with activity limitation felt that their limitation rather than employer's attitudes was the greater barrier (18). Of those unemployed and looking for work, or unable to work, 77% felt limitation was a greater barrier than discrimination.

SOCIAL INSURANCE FOR INDIVIDUALS WITH DISABILITIES WHO ARE DETERMINED TO BE UNABLE TO WORK

Social Security Disability Insurance (SSDI) is the federal program that restores income lost when wage earners can no longer support themselves or dependents because of a physical or mental disability. Authorized as Title II under the Social Security Act in 1956, the SSDI program originally applied to workers age 50 and over. Later amendments included the dependents of eligible workers (1958) and added persons under the age of 50 (1960). In 1972, Social Security Insurance (SSI) was added as Title XVI to provide a minimum level of income for persons who are aged, blind, and disabled, and whose countable income does not exceed the Federal maximum SSI benefit.

Applicants who receive SSDI must demonstrate inability to engage in any substantial gainful activity by reason of medically determinable physical or mental impairment that can be expected to result in death or has lasted, or can be expected to last, for a continuous period of not less than 12 months. Physicians assess when a person cannot work or when a person is able to return to work. An earnings test is used to assess substantial gainful activity. In addition to limited earnings and a disability, the eligible individual must have been previously employed and achieved insured status through contribution to the Federal Insurance Contributions Act (FICA) tax. Eligibility is reevaluated approximately every three years.

Eligibility for SSDI is directly linked to the Medicare program although beneficiaries must wait an additional two years, after SSDI eligibility has been determined, for Medicare coverage to become available, unless they have end-stage renal disease. Medicaid coverage is available for those individuals who qualify.

Eligibility to the SSI program is also based on ability to work but the individual need have no prior work experience. (Note: SSI determination for children is different and is based on a categorical definition of disability). SSI payments are made to individuals under uniform, nationwide rules with respect to income and assets, and definitions of blindness and disability. In 1987 an estimated 4.4 million individuals received SSI payments, including 1.5 million older Americans, and 2.9 million persons who were blind or disabled (21). SSI eligibility is also linked to Medicaid.

FEDERAL POLICY, MEDICAL PRACTICE, AND THE GOALS OF THE ADA

Overall, federal policy has been poorly focused. On the one hand, the ADA places a strong emphasis on recognizing what people can do and providing equal opportunity. Yet removing discrimination as a barrier only addresses one element of the relationship between the individual and the employer. On the other hand, SSDI and SSI require people to demonstrate what they cannot do, and that they cannot work, in order to become eligible for benefits and retain their eligibility. Originally intended to reduce the impact of disability, such policies communicate to the individual as well as to society the image of being *un*able rather than able to work, thereby promoting dependence upon a federal income stream.

The SSDI and SSI programs have become part of the larger policy debate about the societal impact of entitlement programs. This concern led Congress and the Social Security Administration to enact work incentives such as trial work periods, the extension of eligibility beyond the trial period, continuation of Medicare coverage, and deduction of impairment-related work expenses from the earnings base used to calculate eligibility (9). Despite these efforts, a recent GAO study of ten state programs (8) found that only 1% of beneficiaries left the rolls after three years because they were employed. Rather, beneficiaries tended to remain on the rolls for fear they might lose disability payments and health insurance coverage.

Determining SSDI eligibility based on health status and capacity to work is subjective at best, although efforts have been undertaken to create more objective criteria. After sponsoring a study that found variable quality and limited reliability of physician rating of respiratory impairment (e.g. occupational asthma), the Washington State Department of Labor and Industries organized a team of physicians to develop more objective criteria. Using these new criteria, the Department will modify statewide policy and practice (Washington State Department of Labor and Industries, unpublished data).

If the policies of the SSDI and SSI programs inadvertently work towards the detriment of the goals of the ADA, medical practitioners may be the unwitting instrument. The medical practitioner establishes eligibility by declaring a person unable to work, and has done so with little empirical justification. Predicting who will stop working is impossible (10, 20, 35), and certifying who can work is equally difficult (2, 26).

Unfortunately, the diverse health care needs of persons with disabilities are poorly understood (5), and the goals of medical care are often too limited. Traditionally, health care practice has addressed the biological determinants of disability and concentrated on the physical consequences of such disability. Disability and health status are confused, and health care providers see the disability as the pathology, despite the fact that persons with disabilities may have functional limitations but not be "sick" (5). Determining cause and attending only to the restoration of function falls short of the potential for mediating the effect of disability on a person's opportunity to maintain a meaningful life, including employment, through effective education, prevention, and early intervention.

MANAGING DISABILITY

Reversing the negative impact of income security programs by changing medical care practice may potentially affect employment opportunities for persons with disabilities as much as the implementation of the ADA. Instead of simply determining when a person cannot work, medical care providers in concert with other health care specialists have an opportunity to determine the conditions under which individuals *can* work and assist them in managing the effect of their disability so that they may return to work, or continue working, after a disability occurs. To do so, medical care providers must move beyond identifying the cause and subsequent limitations created by the disability, and begin systematically to develop innovative prevention and health promotion strategies. Accomplishing this goal requires a broad framework for considering disability-related health care practice and an interdisciplinary approach that incorporates health care and social services providers, employers, and—most importantly—the individual with the disability.

Recently the Committee on a National Agenda for the Prevention of Disabilities, organized by the Institute of Medicine, developed a model for

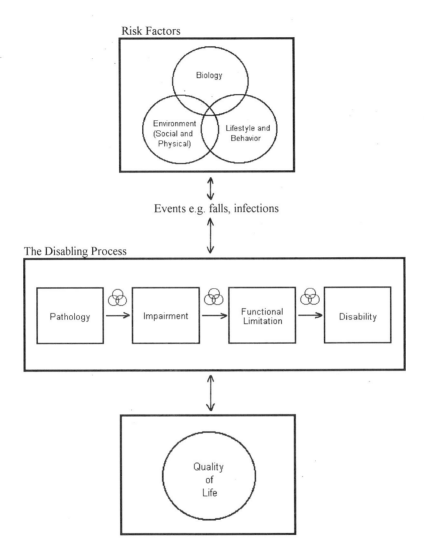

Figure 1   Model of disability [From (22)]

disability and disability prevention (22). This is a useful framework for considering an expanded approach to disability. It places disability within the context of health and social issues, and depicts the interactive effect of biological, environmental (physical and social), and life-style and behavioral risk factors that influence each stage of the disability process, the relationship of the disabling process to quality of life, and the stages of the disabling process that often precede disability (Figure 1; 22).

LEVEL I: RISK FACTORS   The three types of risk factors include biological, environmental (social and physical), and life-style or behavioral characteristics that are causally associated with health-related conditions. Identifying such factors can be a first step toward determining a mechanism of action in the disabling process.

LEVEL II: DISABLING PROCESS   The disabling process depicts the progression that most often occurs, but recognizes that an individual with a disability may skip over components of the model. The Committee cites an example in which a disfiguring condition may not result in functional limitations, but produces such negative societal response that the individual is restricted in carrying out normal activities. Thus, disability is the product of a complex interactive process involving biological, behavioral, and environmental risk factors. The progression can be influenced at each stage by personal, societal, and environmental factors in a manner that affects the degree of resulting disability that the individual experiences. Specific interventions may alter the limitation experienced by the individual and/or prevent secondary conditions.

LEVEL III: QUALITY OF LIFE   Quality of life is the value attached by the person with a disability to his or her position in life in the context of a particular culture and value system and in relation to personal goals, expectations, standards, and concerns.

The strategy preferred by many would be to prevent the occurrence of disability by addressing risk factors (Level I). However, this strategy has been accorded a lower priority in national policy than medical intervention once the disability has occurred: far more resources have been allocated to medical care interventions than to the prevention of disability. Medical interventions focus primarily on the disabling process itself (Level II), and interventions are aimed at stages one, two, and three of the process through identification of the disease or injury, assessment of the impairment, and determination of the impact on functional ability.

Researchers at the Center for Disability Policy and Research (CDPR), located at the School of Public Health and Community Medicine at the University of Washington in Seattle, with support from the Centers for Disease Control and Prevention, are developing strategies for health promotion for persons who have a disability, and for the prevention of secondary conditions resulting from the disability (DL Patrick, M Richardson, HE Starks & MA Rose, unpublished data). Using the IOM model, CDPR research focuses on interventions aimed at decreasing functional limitation and disability (steps three and four), reducing activity restriction, and promoting the performance of social roles.

The CDPR approach recognizes that a person is not always disabled or disadvantaged by an impairment, but may be restricted in activity by the way he or she receives health care and/or is treated by others. For example, a person who experiences a severe injury on the job will receive tertiary and rehabilitative services, most likely in a comprehensive medical center. After discharge the individual may be deemed unable to work and continue to receive subspecialty treatment, primarily disability-related, from the tertiary care center. Return to work, however, may depend on receiving effective health education and learning good self-care management, appropriate primary care, job retraining, access to group support activities, and the involvement of an employer willing to modify work demands and create an employment-related support network. Success in this program may require collaboration between primary and tertiary health care providers, social service providers, and employers. Moreover, the program places considerable responsibility on the individual with the disability to manage the care network.

Following the approach developed by the US Preventive Services Task Force (10), CDPR researchers are developing health promotion and prevention protocols that propose interventions to address disability throughout the lifespan (developmental disabilities, injury, and chronic conditions). We have identified specific topics, using interdisciplinary research teams composed of medical care providers, rehabilitation and other health care specialists, social service providers, and consumers. For example, teams working on developmental and injury-related disabilities selected contractures caused by limited motion. Another selection was social isolation, of interest to teams working in all three categories of disability. Protocols briefly describe the strategy or intervention, current health and/or social service practice related to the intervention, relevant research findings, a plan for implementing and evaluating the protocol, and make recommendations for future research.

The Center is developing two types of protocols that recognize the complex interaction between functional limitation, disability, and quality of life. One focuses on interventions that prevent the disablement from progressing (i.e. preventing contractures). The other focuses on offsetting the disadvantage created by the disability (i.e. preventing social isolation). Protocols are designed for use in clinical settings, or community-based settings such as work-sites, school, or home. Implementation of protocols may be undertaken by clinical providers, community service providers, the individual with the disability, family members, or some combination of involved persons.

WORKPLACE APPLICATIONS

Interdiscipinary team approaches using health care, rehabilitation, and human resource professionals are the basis for disability management programs springing up in many work-sites. Programs are based on the fundamental principles of prevention of the disability or related conditions, and early intervention and prevention of deterioration. Employers, too, have selected interventions aimed at steps three and four of the disabling process as described in Figure 1. Their goals are to restore an individual's working or functional capacity to prevent deterioration. Successful work-site disability management programs include measures aimed at developing an individual's own resources or removing obstacles imposed by the environment (15). Contact with employees is made early in the disablement process, both the employee and the supervisor become involved, and a flexible work environment is provided as part of an effective return-to-work policy (27).

Early efforts at disability management included employee assistance programs (EAP), attempts to reduce the financial losses caused by alcoholism and related behavioral problems (4). Work-site health promotion programs, another corporate effort aimed at maintaining productive workers and containing health care costs, have been adopted by nearly 66% of private sector work-sites (31), although no research exists on the impact of such programs on the health of persons with disabilities (7). More recently, disability management programs have been expanded to address a wider array of disabilities. A pilot program at Burlington Industries in North Carolina (K Mitchell & J Winfield, unpublished data) served as the prototype for programs now adopted by Xerox, Control Data Corporation, Kodak, 3M Corporation, Herman Miller, Inc., Steelcase, Inc., and General Motors in the private sector, as well as such public sector organizations as the Social Security Administration, Tennessee Valley Authority, and the US Postal Service (27).

Work-site disability management programs focus primarily on individuals who are already employed and develop disabilities resulting from injuries and chronic conditions. However, growing numbers of persons with developmental (early onset) disabilities are reaching adulthood in community settings. Many are actively seeking opportunities for work. These same approaches can be used to bring them into the workplace. Currently, some programs target older workers, reflecting the anticipated increase in older workers in the work force (25), and are designed to support the efforts of individual workers to maintain their employment by creating a receptive, less demanding work environment.

Workplace disability management programs potentially provide an opportunity for implementing the IOM model, using approaches such as those under development by CDPR researchers. Collaboration between health care practitioners and employers in developing innovative health care practices in the context of disability management programs may lead, in part, to reversing the perverse incentives currently created in governmental income security programs. This approach does not address concerns of many who fear loss of Medicare or Medicaid insurance coverage if they leave SSI and SSDI roles, but that issue may be resolved through proposed health care reform initiatives. Systematic development of intervention protocols, similar to those under development by CDPR researchers, allows implementation within a work-site or across work-sites, and provides the opportunity for evaluation. This adds a new and important dimension to existing management approaches, since little evaluation or follow-up research is currently being conducted on work-site programs.

SUMMARY

The impact of the American with Disabilities Act (ADA) on employers and the workplace extends well beyond the provisions of the Act. Besides demanding an end to discrimination in the workplace against persons with disabilities, both the ADA and the Rehabilitation Act articulate the goals of equal opportunity, full participation, independent living, and economic self-sufficiency. They state clearly the right of each person to a full and meaningful life regardless of disability. Promoting those goals through employment requires thinking more broadly about the interaction between the individual with the disability, the workplace, and society. The employer is not the only participant. The individual with the disability plays an important role, as do the health care providers. An opportunity to align the goals of SSI and SSDI more closely with the ADA may lie in efforts to expand health care approaches to disability, based on the IOM Model of Disability, and link such practice with disability management efforts in the workplace.

ACKNOWLEDGMENTS

The author would like to express her appreciation for the advice and support of Robert Silverstein, Staff Director, Senate Subcommittee on Disability Policy.

Literature Cited

1. Baldwin M. 1991. Evidence on the occupational segregation of women with disabilities. *J. Disabil. Policy Stud.* 2:31–47
2. Berkowitz E. 1987. *Disabled Policy: America's Programs for the Handicapped.* New York: Cambridge Univ. Press
3. Berkowitz E, Johnson WG, Murphy EH. 1976. *Public Policy Towards Disability.* New York: Praeger
4. Brody BE. 1988. Employee assistance programs: An historical and literature review. *Am. J. Health Prom.* Winter:13–18
5. DeJong G, Batavia A, Griss R. 1989. America's neglected health minority: Working age persons with disabilities. *Milbank Mem. Fund Q.* 67:311–51 (Part 2)
6. Elkind J. 1990. The incidence of disabilities in the United States. *Hum. Factors* 32:397–405
7. Galvin DE, Tate DG, Schwartz G. 1986. Disability management research: Current status, needs and implications for study. *J. Appl. Rehab. Couns.* 17:41–48
8. Gen. Account. Off. 1987. *Social Security: Little Success Achieved in Rehabilitating Beneficiaries*
9. Griss G. 1990. *Income and health benefits for the disabled—A look at social security disability insurance and its links to medicare.* Washington, DC: Natl. Health Policy Forum
10. Deleted in proof
11. Haber L. 1971. Disabling effects of chronic disease and impairments. *J. Chronic Dis.* 24:469–87
12. Hahn H. 1987. Advertising the acceptable employable image: Disability and capitalism. *Policy Stud. J.* 15:551–70
13. Harris L, and Associates. 1986. *Disabled Americans' Self Perceptions: Bringing Disabled Americans into the Mainstream.* New York: Harris & Assoc.
14. Haveman R, Wolfe B. 1990. The economic well-being of the disabled, 1962–1984. *J. Hum. Resour.* 25:32–54
15. Jarvikoski A, Lahelma E. 1980. *Early Rehabilitation at the Workplace,* Monogr. 6. New York: World Rehabil. Fund Inc.
16. Johnson G, Baldwin M. 1993. The Americans with Disabilities Act: Will it make a difference? In *Disability Policy as an Emerging Field of Public Policy Research,* ed. S Watson, D Pfieffer. In press
17. Johnson G, Lambrinos J. 1986. Wage discrimination against handicapped men and women. *J. Hum. Resour.* 20:264–77
18. LaPlante MP. 1991. The demographics of disability. The Americans with Disabilities Act—From policy to practice. *Milbank Mem. Fund Q.* 69(Suppl. 1, 2):55–77
19. Levitan SA, Taggert R. 1977. *Jobs for the Disabled.* Baltimore, MD: Johns Hopkins Press
20. Nagi S. 1976. An epidemiology of disability among adults in the United States. *Milbank Mem. Fund Q.* 54:439–68
21. O'Shaughnessy C, Price R. 1988. Financing and delivery of long-term care services for the elderly. *Congr. Res. Serv. Rep.,* pp. 55–58
22. Pope AM, Alvin R. 1991. *Disability in America,* pp. 7–10. Washington, DC: Natl. Acad. Press
23. Public Law. *Americans with Disabilities Act of 1990,* pp. 101–336
24. Senate Comm. Labor, Health, Educ. Rel. Agencies, pp. 102–973 [Sec. 2(a) and 121 (a)(2)]. 1993
25. Shrey DE, Mitchell DK. 1986. Disability management among private and public employers: Models and strategies for rehabilitation intervention. *J. Appl. Rehabil. Couns.* 17:13–19
26. Stone D. 1984. *The Disabled State.* Philadelphia: Temple Univ. Press
27. Tate D, Habeck RV, Galvin DE. 1986. Disability management: Concepts and principles for practice. *J. Appl. Rehabil. Couns.* 17:5–12
27a. US Prevent. Serv. Task Force. 1989. *Guide to Clinical Preventive Services: An Assessment of the Effectiveness of 169 Intervention.* Baltimore, MD: Williams & Wilbur
28. US Senate. 1989. *Congr. Rec.,* Sept. 7
29. Verbrugge LM. 1990. The iceberg of disability. In *Legacy of Longevity,* ed. S Stahl, pp. 55–75. Newbury Park, CA: Sage
30. Victor R. 1985. Trends in work place safety. *Bus. Health* 2:7–10
31. Walsh DC. 1988. Toward a sociology of worksite health promotion: A few reactions and reflections. *Soc. Sci. Med.* 26:569–75
32. WHO. 1980. *International Classification of Impairments, Disabilities, and Handicaps.* Geneva: WHO

33. Yelin, E. 1989. Displaced concern: The social context of the work disability problem. *Milbank Mem. Fund Q.* 67(Suppl. 2, Part 1):114–66

34. Yelin EH. Undated. *The recent history and immediate future of employment among persons with disabilities*. San Francisco: Univ. Calif. Rosalind Russell Arthritis Cent. Inst. Health Policy Stud.

35. Yelin E, Nevitt M, Epstein W. 1980. Toward an epidemiology of work disability. *Milbank Mem. Fund Q.* 58: 386–415

36. Yuker HE. 1987. *The Disability Hierarchies: Comparative Reactions to Various Types of Physical and Mental Disabilities*. Hempstead, NY: Hofstra Univ. Press

Annu. Rev. Public Health. 1994. 15:107–32

ACUTE RESPIRATORY EFFECTS OF PARTICULATE AIR POLLUTION

D. W. Dockery and C. A. Pope III

Environmental Epidemiology Program, Harvard School of Public Health, Boston, Massachusetts 02115-6096

KEY WORDS: particulate air pollution, adverse health effects

INTRODUCTION

In the 1930s, 40s, and 50s, several episodes of extreme air pollution focused attention on the potential for adverse health effects of air pollution. These included an episode in the Meuse Valley, Belgium, in December 1930 (15), an episode in Donora, Pennsylvania in 1948 (36), and several episodes in London, England (23, 44). The sudden large increases in sickness and death that accompanied such episodes demonstrated that air pollution can adversely affect human health. The increased mortality associated with such episodes provided the first quantitative measure of the adverse effects of air pollution.

By the 1970s, a link had been well established between respiratory disease and particulate and/or sulfur-oxide air pollution, but still there remained disagreement as to the level of pollution that would significantly affect human health. In reviewing research published between 1968 and 1977, Holland and several other prominent British scientists (19) concluded that particulate and related air pollution at high levels pose hazards to human health, but that health effects of particulate pollution at lower concentrations could not be "disentangled" from health effects of other factors. Shy (45) responded by asserting that the review by Holland et al systematically discounted evidence of pollution-related health effects at contemporary pollution levels. Shy, and other reviewers (1, 12, 45, 54), contended that the cumulative weight of evidence provided sound reasons to believe that

107

0163-7525/94/0510-0107$05.00

human health may be adversely affected by particulate pollution, even at relatively low concentrations.

Epidemiologic studies since the 1970s have provided more quantification of the health effects associated with particulate pollution at levels common in contemporary urban areas of the developed world. Recent epidemiological research has been based on more specific definitions and more precise measures both of pollution exposures and health endpoints. Advances in biostatistical and econometric analytic techniques for time-series data have expanded the opportunities to evaluate the acute health effects of particulate pollution and have increased the analytical rigor of these studies. In particular, advances in autoregressive Poisson and logistic regression analysis have permitted the evaluation of pollution associations in panels of patients or other small populations, which would not have been possible in the early 1970s. Most notable has been a series of studies showing that daily mortality is associated with particulate pollution at concentrations much lower than those experienced in the extreme episodes of the first half of this century.

Bates (3) has recently pointed out that the observation of increased mortality associated with air pollution exposures implies that measures of morbidity also must necessarily be increased—for example, hospital admissions, hospital emergency room visits, and outpatient or doctor's visits. Among potentially responsive subjects such as asthma patients, we expect to observe increased symptoms, lower lung function, increased medication use, and, ultimately, higher use of hospital services. A similar cascade of associations also may be detected among less sensitive individuals, i.e. among members of the general population. Bates (3) has described this as *coherence* of effects, i.e. the adverse effects of air pollution should be observable across a range of related health outcomes. Adverse effects of air pollution also should be reproducibly observed by different investigators in different settings, i.e. there should be *consistency* of effects across independent analytic studies.

This review presents a comparison of such recent studies of the acute effects of particulate air pollution and shows evidence for increased mortality and morbidity associated with particulate pollution, even at moderate concentrations. We evaluate both the coherency and consistency of recent epidemiologic data regarding adverse health effects of particulate air pollution. Our purpose is to stimulate a new look at these studies rather than to provide a comprehensive, detailed, or complete review.

SOURCES AND EXPOSURES

Particulate air pollution refers to an air-suspended mixture of solid and liquid particles that vary in size, composition, origin, and effects. The term 'aerosols' refers to a stable mixture of suspended particles and gases and therefore implies smaller-sized particles. Particulate air pollution is formed by condensation of gases or vapors, or by direct generation through mechanical processes. The different processes of formation lead to characteristic differences in size and composition of particles.

Particle Size and Chemical Characteristics

Particle size is expressed in terms of its aerodynamic diameter, defined as the diameter of a unit-density sphere that has the same settling velocity as the particle in question. The size distribution of suspended particles in the atmosphere is bimodal. Large particles (sometimes called "the coarse mode") are 2.5 to 30 μm aerodynamic diameter and most often have a basic pH. These large particles are derived from uncontrolled combustion and mechanical breakup of soil and other crustal materials. Biological particles such as pollens and spores are also found in this large-particle range. Smaller particles ("the fine mode") are < 2.5 μm aerodynamic diameter and are often acidic. These fine particles include soot and acid-condensates derived from vehicle emissions, manufacturing, power generation, and agricultural burning. Sulfate and nitrate aerosols generally make up the largest fraction of small particles by mass.

Deposition, Clearance, and Toxicity

Particle size is the most important characteristic influencing deposition in the respiratory system (2). Models of inhaled particle deposition relate aerodynamic particle diameter to the site of deposition. Most inhaled particles of greater than 5μm aerodynamic diameter deposit in the upper airways or larger lower airways. Particles smaller than 5μm aerodynamic diameter are more likely to deposit in the smaller airways, e.g. the bronchioles and the alveoli.

Particle clearance is achieved by several mechanisms. Particles deposited in the trachea and bronchioles rise on the mucociliary ladder to be expelled by coughing or to be swallowed. Particles deposited beyond the terminal bronchioles are cleared largely by lung macrophages that, in turn, transport the ingested particles onto the mucociliary ladder or into the lymphatic system. A small fraction of these distally deposited particles migrate through alveolar tissue directly into the lymphatic circulation.

Biologic effects of a particle are determined by the physical and chemical nature of the particle itself (particularly its solubility), the physics of deposition and distribution in the respiratory tract, and the physiologic events that occur in response to the particle's presence. Controlled human studies have focused on airway effects of single agents or simple mixtures. Toxicological studies have generally focused on chronic effects and single agents (e.g. silica, asbestos) (55), and on the effects on sites of deposition or distribution (airways, alveoli).

Measures of in vitro macrophage cytotoxicity demonstrate the high toxicity of certain urban particle complexes relative to the classic toxic dusts, e.g. silica and asbestos. Toxicity of urban particles and diesel particulate emissions depend in part on the type of metal compounds they contain, as well as their combustion-derived organic content (16).

REVIEW METHODS

Definition of Exposure

In 1987, the US Environmental Protection Agency redefined the National Ambient Air Quality Standard (NAAQS) for particles based on particulate matter smaller than $10\mu m$ aerodynamic diameter (PM_{10}) (13). This $10\mu m$-size cutoff focused monitoring and regulatory efforts on particles of a size that would be deposited in, and damaging to, the lower airways and the gas-exchanging portions of the lung. Recent epidemiologic studies have used PM_{10} measurements as the basis of exposure estimation. Earlier studies, however, used a variety of measures of particle concentration to define exposure. These alternative measures are discussed below to compare results with PM_{10}-based measures.

The EPA's initial standard reference measure for particles was Total Suspended Particulates (TSP), measured by high-volume samplers. This sampling method has an ill-defined upper size limit between $25\mu m$ and $45\mu m$ that is dependent on wind speed and direction (22). In addition, TSP measurements are subject to artifactual conversion of SO_2 to sulfate on the filters or to volatilization of nitrate aerosols from sampler filters. Many epidemiologic studies of air pollution in the 1960s and 1970s in the United States used TSP measurements as the indicator of particle exposures. The EPA (26) determined that the PM_{10}-to-TSP ratio was generally between 50% and 60% for US sampling sites.

In the late 1970s and early 1980s, the EPA established a network of particulate matter samplers with an upper-size cutoff of $15\mu m$ aerodynamic diameter (PM_{15}) to measure "inhalable particulates." This cutoff was recommended to define the fraction of particles that would deposit primarily in the conducting airways and the gas-exchange areas of the respiratory system during mouth breathing (24). Only very limited data are available comparing the PM_{15} to PM_{10} concentrations, but concentrations measured by these two methods appear to be similar.

In addition to the total inhalable particle concentration, particles smaller than $2.5\mu m$ aerodynamic diameter ($PM_{2.5}$) were measured based on consideration of their characteristic chemical composition and the predominant penetration into the gas-exchange regions of the respiratory tract (24). Spengler & Thurston (47) have presented data for $PM_{2.5}$ and PM_{10} from six US cities. The mean $PM_{2.5}$-to-mean PM_{10} ratio was approximately 60%.

In most parts of the United States, fine particle ($PM_{2.5}$) concentrations are highly correlated with sulfate (SO_4) concentrations. For example, in the Six Cities Study (47), city-specific correlations were all greater than 0.70, and in four cities, greater than 0.84. In these data, the mean ratio of SO_4 to PM_{10} was approximately 25%.

Studies from Great Britain and other European countries have often used a pseudomeasure of particle mass called British Smoke (BS). This is a measure of the darkness of particles collected on a filter and determined by reflectance. Mass concentration is estimated based on the reflectance of a standard particle mass. Calibration of reflectance depends on the specific chemical composition of the particles (22). The upper size limit of the sampler is nominally $4.5 \mu m$ aerodynamic diameter, although the penetration of particles through the sampler inlet does not define a sharp size cut-point (22). Generally, particles in the fine mode tend to be dark while those in the coarse mode tend to be lighter in color (1!). British Smoke, therefore, is thought of as a measure of fine particle mass concentrations. The EPA (26) concluded that British Smoke was equal to PM_{10} as a lower bound and equal to TSP as an upper bound.

In the United States, a similar method was used in which particles were deposited on a filter tape and the concentration was estimated by light transmission through the sample, measured in Coefficient of Haze (CoH) units. A comparison of CoH and PM_{10} measurements in Santa Clara County, California, indicated that the CoH-to-PM_{10} ratio equals 55% (14).

Thus for this discussion we will use the following guidelines for estimating PM_{10} exposures in epidemiologic studies where other measures of particle concentration were reported:

$$PM_{10} \approx PM_{15} \qquad\qquad PM_{10} \approx PM_{2.5}/0.60$$

$$PM_{10} \approx TSP * 0.55 \qquad\qquad PM_{10} \approx BS$$

$$PM_{10} \approx CoH/0.55 \qquad\qquad PM_{10} \approx SO_4 * 4$$

Criteria of Study Selection

In this review, we have included studies that provide the following information: (*a*) exposure to particulates reported as PM_{10} concentrations or a measure that allowed conversion to PM_{10}; (b) health effects measured as change in mortality or indicators of respiratory disease with time scales of days up to weeks or months; and (c) reported measures of association and their variance, which would allow calculation of the relative increase in effect compared to particle exposures and the confidence that can be ascribed to the effect estimate.

We have separated epidemiologic studies by comparable health endpoints (for example, mortality or exacerbation of asthma). Within each of these health endpoints, we have expressed reported results as the estimated relative percent change in the health measure associated with a 10 $\mu g/m^3$ increase in daily mean PM_{10} concentrations. For many recent studies that used logistic or Poisson regression and PM_{10}, this is a simple calculation based on reported regression coefficients and their standard errors. Many earlier studies, in which particle concentrations were not measured as PM_{10}, required converting from the reported measure of particle concentrations to PM_{10} concentrations, conversions based on relationships described above.

In some studies, particularly those with continuous health endpoints such as pulmonary function, associations are reported as a linear rather than a proportional (or logarithmic) change associated with particulate pollution. For these studies, we re-estimated the effect as percent change from the mean response associated with 10 $\mu g/m^3$ increase in PM_{10} above the mean exposure. This is a reasonable assumption for estimates close to the mean but will break down far from the mean.

For a few studies, particle concentrations had been transformed before including them in the analysis, e.g. effects reported as a function of the logarithm of the particle mass concentrations. For these studies, we estimated the effect of a 10 $\mu g/m^3$ increase in PM_{10} above the mean exposure. Again, this is appropriate close to the mean but should not be extrapolated to concentrations far from the mean.

Ninety-five-percent confidence intervals were calculated for each exposure estimate. In most cases, reports included standard errors of the estimates or confidence intervals. In a few early studies, however, only p-values were given. In these studies we estimated the standard error, assuming a normal distribution. When p-values were reported as less than some arbitrary cut-off (e.g. $p < 0.05$), the standard errors were calculated, based on the upper limit of the cut-off probability (e.g. $z = 1.96$ for $p < 0.05$).

To provide a combined estimate of the effect of 10 $\mu g/m^3$ increase in PM_{10} concentration for each health endpoint, a weighted average effect estimate was calculated where the study-specific effect was weighted by its inverse variance (one over the standard error squared).

HEALTH EFFECT STUDIES

Mortality

In the past few years, a series of papers has been published describing the association between daily mortality and suspended particulate concentrations in various communities across the United States. In 1990, an association between particle concentrations and daily mortality was reported for residents of Santa Clara County, California, for the period 1980–1986 (14). Associations were observed at relatively low concentrations of particles and sulfur dioxide.

This report was followed by analyses of similar data for Steubenville, Ohio (40) and for Philadelphia, Pennsylvania, (39). Both analyses suggested increased daily mortality associated with increased particle concentrations, even after adjusting for sulfur dioxide exposures. A quantitatively similar association was reported for Utah Valley, Utah, for the period 1985–89 (33). This study was notable because these associations with particle exposures are observed in the absence of substantial sulfur dioxide or ozone pollution. In analysis of data from St. Louis, Missouri, and Kingston, Tennessee (9), daily mortality was associated with several measures of particle exposures, but not with aerosol acidity, sulfur dioxide, ozone, or nitrogen dioxide concentrations.

In large communities (with a population of several million), the mean number of deaths/day is far enough from zero that the distribution is reasonably symmetric and Gaussian statistics can be applied. In most communities, however, the mean number of deaths/day is small and the distribution is skewed towards higher values. In both cases, because daily death counts can be modeled as following a Poisson process, regression analysis using the Poisson rather than the Gaussian distribution is appropriate. Associations are typically fitted to the logarithm (ln) of the number of deaths/day, that is, on a proportional rather than a linear scale. Specifically, the Poisson regression estimates the (ln) relative risk of mortality associated with a given exposure, which can be re-expressed as a percent increase in risk. All of the recent analyses of daily mortality and air pollution have used Poisson regression methods.

Use of the same endpoint (nonaccidental daily mortality), particulate exposure measures, which can be converted into a common metric (PM_{10}), and common analytic methods (Poisson regression) make it possible to tabulate approximately comparable effect estimates: the percent increase in daily mortality for each 10 $\mu g/m^3$ increase in PM_{10} concentrations (see Table 1).

Table 1 Studies of acute effects of particles on daily mortality

Location and period	Particulate measure	Mean PM_{10} ($\mu g/m^3$)	% Change in daily mortality for each 10 $\mu g/m^3$ increase in PM_{10} (95% Cl)	Reference
Total mortality				
St. Louis, MO 1985–86	PM_{10} (previous day)	28	1.5% (0.1%, 2.9%)	9
Kingston, TN 1985–86	PM_{10} (Previous day)	30	1.6% (−1.3%, 4.6%)	
Santa Clara, CA 1980–82, 84–86	Coefficient of haze	35	0.8% (0.2%, 1.5%)	14
Philadelphia, PA 1973–80	TSP (2-Day mean)	40	1.2% (0.7%, 1.7%)	39
Birmingham, AL 1985–88	PM_{10} (3-Day mean)	48	1.0% (0.2%, 1.9%)	38
Utah Valley, UT 1985–89	PM_{10} (5-Day mean)	47	1.5% (0.9%, 2.1%)	33
Detriot, MI 1973–82	TSP	48	1.0% (0.5%, 1.6%)	37
Steubenville, OH 1974–84	TSP (previous day)	61	0.7% (0.4%, 1.0%)	40
Combined			1.0%	
Respiratory				
Santa Clara, CA 1980–82, 84–86	Coefficient of haze	35	3.5% (1.5%, 5.6%)	14
Philadelphia, PA 1973–80	TSP (2-Day mean)	40	3.3% (0.1%, 6.6%)	39
Utah Valley, UT 1985–89	PM_{10} (5-Day mean)	47	3.7% (0.7%, 6.7%)	33
Birmingham, AL 1985–88	PM_{10} (3-Day mean)	48	1.5% (−5.8%, 9.4%)	38
Combined			3.4%	
Cardiovascular				
Santa Clara, CA 1980–82, 84–86	Coefficient of haze	35	0.8% (0.1%, 1.6%)	14
Philadelphia, PA 1973–80	TSP (2-Day mean)	40	1.7% (1.0%, 2.4%)	39
Utah Valley, UT 1985–89	PM_{10} (5-day mean)	47	1.8% (0.4%, 3.3%)	33
Birmingham, AL 1985–88	PM_{10} (3-Day mean)	48	1.6% (−0.5%, 3.7%)	38
Combined			1.4%	

There is good consistency in the estimated effect of PM_{10} across these studies. Effect estimates range between 0.7% and 1.6% increase in daily mortality for each 10 $\mu g/m^3$ increase in PM_{10} concentration with a weighted mean of 1.0%. Ostro (26a) has recently estimated a similar combined effect (0.96% per $10\mu/m^3$ PM_{10}) in a review of time-series and cross-sectional mortality studies.

Four of the daily mortality studies (14, 33, 38, 39) also provided a breakdown of mortality by broad cause-of-death categories. Cardiovascular deaths, which were about 45% of all deaths in these three studies, had effect estimates between 0.8% and 1.8% (weighted mean, 1.4%) increase for each $10\mu g/m^3$ PM_{10}. Respiratory deaths, which were 2% to 8% of the total, had effect estimates between 1.5% and 3.7% (weighted mean, 3.5%) increase for each 10 $\mu g/m^3$ PM_{10}. In all four studies, no associations were found with cancer mortality or with other causes.

Epidemiologic studies suffer from the weakness that observed associations with a specific exposure may result from an unmeasured association with an unknown or uncontrolled factor correlated with *both* exposure and disease, i.e. from a confounder. These time-series studies have the advantage that many major causes of increased mortality (such as smoking, hypertension, or even age) cannot confound the observed associations with particulate air pollution because these factors do not vary with daily pollution exposures. This is not to say that response may not differ by these factors. Indeed, the mortality effects of particulate air pollution are most strongly seen in the elderly in all those studies in which age is considered as an effect modifier.

Other factors such as weather conditions, which can vary with daily pollution exposures, are potential confounders in these analyses. All of the recent studies have attempted to control for weather factors (such as temperature) in the analysis. Residual confounding due to inadequate modeling or an unmeasured weather factor is removed by modeling the covariance of the residuals as autoregressive in these analyses. Similar associations are observed in areas with high winter particulate concentrations, characterized by trapping of direct industrial emissions—Utah Valley (33) and Steubenville (40)—and in areas of high summer particulate concentrations characterized by photochemical production of secondary particles such as sulfates and nitrates—Philadelphia (39) and Birmingham (38). The consistency of the effect estimate across different communities—in warm versus cold climates, in dry versus moist climates—suggests that climatic factors are in fact not important confounders.

If we accept the association between daily mortality and particulate air pollution shown in these studies, the possibility still remains that the true association is with some other pollutant correlated with PM_{10} or with a specific component of the mixture of particles that makes up PM_{10}. The study of St. Louis and Kingston (9) considered a variety of pollutants and found the strongest associations with PM_{15} concentrations. Several studies (9, 39) evaluated sulfur dioxide as a possible confounder; no such confounding was shown. More importantly, associations between daily mortality and particulate air pollution in communities with low sulfur dioxide concentrations—Santa Clara (14) and Utah Valley (33)—were comparable to associations in communities with high sulfur dioxide concentrations—Steubenville (40). Kinney & Özkaynak (20) reported associations between daily mortality and ozone in Los Angeles. They emphasize the association with ozone, but strong associations were also observed with KM, a measure of light scattering by particles similar to Coefficient of Haze. The consistency of results across communities suggests an important if not dominant role of particle mass concentration in producing the observed associations with daily mortality.

Another interesting feature of these studies is the consistent finding of lagged associations between particle exposure and increased mortality. Most of the results presented have reported associations of increased mortality with particle concentrations on the previous day. It would violate a basic tenet of causality if the observed effect were not either concurrent with or lagged behind the exposure. In their analysis of Utah Valley deaths, Pope et al (33) considered longer lag structures up to seven days and found the strongest associations with the five-day moving average, i.e. with the mean PM_{10} of the current day and the four previous days. Thus, these data suggest that mortality effects of particulate air pollution may be lagged by several days.

In summary, a series of time-series analyses of the associations of daily mortality with particulate air pollution has shown a ~1.0% increase in total deaths/day associated with each 10 $\mu g/m^3$ increase in PM_{10} concentration. Stronger associations were observed with cardiovascular disease (1.4% per 10 $\mu g/m^3$ PM_{10}) and respiratory disease (3.4% per 10 $\mu g/m^3$ PM_{10}). The consistency of these estimates across communities suggests that these results are not due to confounding with an unknown or uncontrolled factor and that the mass concentration of the particle mix common to many urban areas, rather than specific chemical species within the mix, may be responsible for the observed associations.

Hospital Usage

If daily mortality is associated with daily particulate pollution levels, then associations with increased hospital admissions and emergency department visits should also be expected. In a unique natural experiment, Pope (28,

29) observed hospital admissions of children for respiratory disease in Utah Valley dropped by over 50 percent during the winter of 1986–87 compared to adjacent years. During this winter, a strike at the local steel mill led to much lower PM_{10} concentrations—a mean of 51 $\mu g/m^3$ and maximum of 113 $\mu g/m^3$ compared to a mean of 90 $\mu g/m^3$ and a maximum of 365 $\mu g/m^3$ in the previous year. Regression analyses estimated a 4.2% decrease in asthma and bronchitis admissions of children and a 7.1% decrease in all respiratory admissions of children associated with a 10 $\mu g/m^3$ decrease in the two-month mean PM_{10} concentration.

Increased rates of respiratory admissions, including asthma, for the years 1974 to 1983 in Southern Ontario have been associated with increased sulfate and ozone concentrations (4). A more recent analysis of hospital admissions for respiratory disorders in Southern Ontario for the summers of 1983 to 1988 (7) found an association with increased sulfate concentrations that was independent of associations with ozone exposures. Both studies have been interpreted as suggesting an association between hospital respiratory admissions and an unmeasured air pollutant correlated with sulfates and ozone. Specifically, the authors have suggested a link to acid aerosol concentrations. Alternatively, these associations may be attributable to particle mass concentrations, another air pollutant not considered in the analyses.

Recently, Thurston and colleagues have reported analyses of hospital admissions for respiratory complaints for Toronto, Ontario (50) and for several cities in New York state (51). Although the focus of these studies is the effects of acid aerosols, effect estimates are reported for various measures of particle exposure (Table 2). Taken together, these studies found an increase in hospital admissions for all respiratory diagnoses ranging from 0.8% to 3.4% (weighted mean, 0.8%) for each 10 $\mu g/m^3$ increase in daily mean PM_{10}. A slightly greater effect was seen in hospital admissions for asthma, ranging from 1.9% to 2.1% (weighted mean, 1.9%) for each 10 $\mu g/m^3$ increase in daily mean PM_{10}.

Emergency department visits also have been analyzed by many investigators, and three studies provided quantitative effect estimates of the effects of particles (see Table 2). An analysis of emergency department visits for asthma in Seattle (42) found an increase of 3.4% associated with a 10 $\mu g/m^3$ increase in PM_{10}. Emergency department visits for chronic obstructive pulmonary disease in Barcelona (48, 49) increased by 1.7% associated with a 10 $\mu g/m^3$ increase in PM_{10}. Emergency department visits in Steubenville (35) increased by 0.5% associated with a 10 $\mu g/m^3$ increase in PM_{10}. The weighted mean of these combined effect estimates was a 1.0% increase in emergency department visits associated with each 10 $\mu g/m^3$ increase in PM_{10}.

Table 2 Acute effects of particles on hospital usage

Measure of hospital usage	Location and period	Particulate measure	% Change in hospital usage for each 10 $\mu g/m^3$ increase in PM_{10}	Reference
Hospital Admissions				
Asthma	New York City Buffalo, NY	Daily mean SO_4	1.9% (0.4%, 3.4%) 2.1% ($-$0.6%, 5.0%)	51
	Toronto, ONT Summer 86–88	Daily mean $PM_{2.5}$	2.1% ($-$0.8%, 5.1%)	50
	Combined		1.9%	
All respiratory	New York City Buffalo, NY	Daily mean SO_4	1.0% (0.2%, 1.8%) 2.2% (0.6%, 3.8%)	51
	Toronto, ONT Summer 86–88	Daily mean $PM_{2.5}$	3.4% (0.4%, 6.4%)	50
	Southern Ontario Summer 83–88	Daily mean SO_4	0.8% (0.4%, 1.1%)	7
	Combined		0.8%	
Emergency Department Visits				
Asthma (<65 yr)	Seattle, WA 1989–90	Daily mean PM_{10}	3.4% (0.9%, 6.0%)	42
Respiratory disease	Steubenville, OH	Daily mean TSP	0.5% (0.0%, 1.0%)	35
Chronic obstructive pulmonary disease	Barcelona, Spain Winter 85–89	British Smoke	2.3% (1.4%, 3.2%)	49
	Combined		1.0%	

Asthma

Evidence from hospital admissions and emergency department visits presented above suggests that particle exposures may be directly associated with asthma attacks. Several investigators have considered less severe asthmatic attacks reported by panels of asthma patients. Winter studies of asthmatic children with chronic respiratory symptoms in The Netherlands (34) and of asthmatic adults in Denver, Colorado, (27) both found substantial increases in reported asthmatic attacks associated with particle exposures. An earlier study of sixteen asthma panels in the Los Angeles area (56) reported increased attacks associated with particle exposures but the effect was much lower than in the more recent studies (see Table 3). In part this lower effect estimate may reflect over-control of lagged effects of particles by including the previous day's asthma status in the model. The weighted mean of these three studies, however, gives an effect estimate of 3% increase in asthmatic attacks associated with 10 $\mu g/m^3$ PM_{10}.

The use of bronchodilators also has been evaluated as a measure of exacerbation of asthma in a panel of asthmatics in The Netherlands (34) and in panels of symptomatic children and asthmatic patients in the Utah Valley (31; see Table 3). The weighted mean of these studies gives an estimated effect of a 2.9% increase in bronchodilator use associated with 10 $\mu g/m^3$ PM_{10}.

Lung Function

Lung function is a sensitive indicator of acute response to ozone in controlled exposure and chamber studies (21). Repeated measures of lung function in panels of children also have been used to evaluate the effect of particulate air pollution episodes on children.

Panels of elementary school children in Steubenville had their lung function measured weekly before, during, and after particulate and sulfur dioxide episodes during four periods in 1978 through 1980 (10). Forced Expired Volume in three-quarters of a second ($FEV_{.75}$) was reported to decline following these episodes. There was a suggestion that $FEV_{.75}$ remained depressed for up to two weeks following the episode. A study of weekly lung function measurement of school children in The Netherlands (7a) following a sulfur dioxide and particulate episode in January 1985 reported decreases in Forced Expired Volume in one second (FEV_1), which were similar in magnitude and in lag structure to those observed in Steubenville. Subsequent studies of panels of school children with weekly lung function measurements (17, 18) have also shown decreased FEV_1 associated with daily PM_{10} concentrations.

Analysis of longer lags in The Netherlands panel (17) found a significant association between decreased FEV_1 and mean PM_{10} over the previous seven days. Similarly, in a re-analysis of the Steubenville data, Brunekreef (6) found the strongest association with the mean TSP over the previous five days.

Recently, Pope & Kanner (32) analyzed repeated FEV_1 measurements in a panel of chronic obstructive pulmonary disease patients participating in the Lung Health Study. Measurements were taken 10 to 90 days apart. FEV_1 level was reported to be associated with a 0.2% decrease in FEV_1 for each 10 $\mu g/m^3$ increase in daily PM_{10}.

Taken together, these studies found a decrease of between 0.05% and

Table 3   STudies of acute effects of particles on exacerbation of asthma

Measure of asthmatic response	Location and period	Particulate measure	Subjects	% Change in daily asthma response for each 10 $\mu g/M^3$ increase in PM_{10}	Reference
Bronchodilator use	Utah Valley, UT Winter 1989–90	Daily mean PM_{10}	School panel Asthma panel	11.2% (2.4%, 20.7%) 12.0% (4.7%, 19.7%)	31
	2 Dutch Cities Winter 1990–91	Daily mean PM_{10}	School panel	2.3% (0.7%, 3.8%)	34
	Combined			2.9%	
Asthmatic attacks	2 Dutch Cities Winter 1990–91	Daily mean PM_{10}	School panel	1.1% (−3.5%, 5.9%)	34
	Los Angeles, CA 1972–75	TSP	Asthma panels	1.4% (0.3%, 2.6%)	56
	Denver, CO 1987–88	$PM_{2.5}$	Asthma panel	11.5% (8.9%, 14.3%)	27
	Combined			3.0%	

0.35% or a weighted average of 0.15% decrease in FEV_1 associated with each 10 $\mu g/m^3$ increase in daily mean PM_{10} (see Table 4).

Peak flow measurements have been widely used as a simple, inexpensive indicator of acute changes in lung function among asthmatic patients. Weekly peak flow measurements were made in the spirometric studies of school children in The Netherlands (17, 18). In these two studies, peak flow declined approximately 0.16% for each 10 $\mu g/m^3$ increase in PM_{10}.

Daily peak flow measurements have been gathered in a series of recent

Table 4 Studies of acute effects of particles on lung function

Measure of lung function	Location and period	Particulate measure	% Decrease in daily lung function for each 10 $\mu g/$ m^3 increase in PM_{10}	Reference
Forced Expired Volume				
$FEV_{.75}$	Steubenville, OH 1978–80	Daily Mean TSP	0.05% (0.00%, 0.10%)	10
FEV_1	4 Cities, NL Winter 1987–90	Daily Mean PM_{10}	0.06% (−0.01%, 0.14%)	18
	Wageningen, NL Winter 1990–91	Daily Mean PM_{10}	0.35% (0.23%, 0.48%)	17
	Salt Lake City, UT 1987–89	Daily Mean PM_{10}	0.21% (0.05%, 0.37%)	32
	Combined		0.15%	
Peak Expiratory Flow				
Daily (evening)	Utah Valley, UT 1989–90	Daily Mean PM_{10}	0.25% (0.10%, 0.39%)	31
	Utah Valley, UT 1990–91	Daily Mean PM_{10}	0.06% (−0.00%, 0.12%) 0.04% (−0.02%, 0.09%)	30
	Wageningen, NL 1990–91	Daily Mean PM_{10}	0.09% (−0.01%, 0.20%)	34
	Uniontown, PA Summer 1990	Daily Mean PM_{10}	0.19% (0.01%, 0.37%)	25
(> = weekly)	4 Cities, NL Winter 1987–90	Daily Mean PM_{10}	0.16% (0.05%, 0.28%)	18
	Wageningen, NL Winter 1990–91	Daily Mean PM_{10}	0.16% (−0.03%, 0.36%)	17
	Combined		0.08%	

studies. In two separate panel studies in the winters of 1989–90 and 1990–91 in Utah Valley (30, 31), panels of school children measured their peak flow daily before going to bed. In both cases, small but significant reductions in peak flow were found associated with mean PM_{10} concentrations that day. In both studies there appeared to be associations between lower peak flow and PM_{10} concentrations for up to five days prior, and stronger associations were found when these lag structures were included in the models. In the second study (30), the estimated effect was about twice as large with the five-day lagged mean compared to the one-day mean PM_{10}.

Similar winter panel studies of school children have been conducted in The Netherlands (34). Effects were observed between evening peak flow and daily mean PM_{10} concentrations, and seven-day mean PM_{10} concentration, which were similar to those observed in Utah.

A panel study of children was conducted in the summer of 1992 in Uniontown, Pennsylvania, (25) to evaluate peak flow changes in an area of high aerosol acidity. Although the strongest associations were found with aerosol acidity, there also was an association between evening peak flow and daily mean PM_{10} that was very consistent with the estimates from other studies.

Comparing the results from these studies of repeated peak flow measurements, there was a decrease of between 0.04% and 0.25% in peak flow (weighted mean of 0.08%) associated with each 10 $\mu g/m^3$ increase in daily mean PM_{10} concentration (Table 4).

In summary, studies of repeated measure of lung function consistently show a small decrement in FEV_1 (weighted mean 0.15%) and peak flow (weighted mean 0.08%) associated with each 10 $\mu g/m^3$ in PM_{10} daily mean concentration. There is a strong suggestion in these data that changes in lung function may reflect the cumulative exposure of several (5–7) days prior to the measurement.

Respiratory Symptoms

Daily diaries of respiratory symptoms, an inexpensive method of evaluating acute changes in respiratory health status, have been widely used in evaluating acute effects of particulate air pollution. In a commonly applied study design, panels of school children recorded the presence of specific respiratory symptoms daily on weekly or monthly calendars. These symptom reports are often aggregated into *upper respiratory symptoms* (including such symptoms as runny or stuffy nose, sinusitis, sore throat, wet cough, head cold, hayfever, and burning or red eyes) and *lower respiratory symptoms* (including wheezing, dry cough, phlegm, shortness of breath, and chest discomfort or pain). In addition, *cough,* the most frequently reported symptom, is often analyzed separately. In this review, symptom reports are presented separately for each of these symptom groups.

The frequency of reported respiratory symptoms was generally taken as their prevalence on any given day, that is, the fraction of participating children reporting a symptom complex on each day. In some cases (41), however, incident cases were reported, where "incidence" required that the child be symptom-free for two days prior to the incident symptom report.

Studies of upper and lower respiratory symptoms have been conducted in Utah Valley (30, 31), The Netherlands (17, 18), in a study of six US cities (41), and Southern California (27a; Table 5).

The combined weighted average from these studies gives an estimated effect of 3.0% increase in lower respiratory symptoms with each 10 $\mu g/m^3$ increase in daily mean PM_{10} concentrations. For upper respiratory symptom reports, the weighted average effect estimate was only a 0.7% increase in upper respiratory symptoms with each 10 $\mu g/m^3$ increase in daily mean PM_{10} (Table 5).

Cough reports were analyzed in three of these studies as well as in a winter diary study in The Netherlands (34), a study of two Swiss cities (5), and the summer diary study in Uniontown (25; Table 5). The weighted mean effect estimate from these studies was a 1.2% increase in cough associated with each 10 $\mu g/m^3$ increase in daily mean PM_{10}.

SUMMARY

Evidence from the selected epidemiologic studies presented in this review suggests a *coherence* of effects across a range of related health outcomes and a *consistency* of effects across independent studies with different investigators in different settings. This compilation also provides insights into the relative magnitude of effects being observed in various studies (Table 6).

Total mortality is observed to increase by approximately 1% per 10 $\mu g/m^3$ increase in PM_{10}. Somewhat stronger associations are observed for cardiovascular mortality (approximately 1.4% per 10 $\mu g/m^3$ PM_{10}), and considerably stronger associations are observed for respiratory mortality (approximately 3.4% per 10 $\mu g/m^3$ PM_{10}). No acute effects are detected with cancer and other nonpulmonary and noncardiovascular causes of mortality. These relative differences in cause-specific mortality are plausible, given the respiratory route of particle exposures.

If respiratory mortality is associated with particulate pollution, then health care visits for respiratory illness would also be expected to be associated with particulate pollution. Respiratory hospital admissions and emergency department visits increase by approximately 0.8% and 1.0% per 10 $\mu g/m^3$

Table 5 Studies of acute effects of particles on respiratory symptom reports

Measure of respiratory symptoms	Location and period	Particulate measure	Sample	% Change in daily symptom reporting for each 10 $\mu g/m^3$ increase in PM_{10}		Reference
Lower respiratory	Utah Valley, UT Winter 1989–90	Daily mean PM_{10}	Children Asthmatics	5.1% (1.1%, 0.2% (−4.2%,	9.3%) 4.8%)	31
	Utah Valley, UT Winter 1990–91	Daily mean PM_{10}	Symptomatic children Asymptomatic children	4.8% (1.5%, 2.4% (−1.8%,	8.3%) 6.8%)	30
	6 US cities Summer 1984–88	Daily mean PM_{15}	School children	15.2% (6.3%,	24.9%)	41
	Wageningen, NL Winter 1990–91	Daily mean PM_{10}	School children	1.2% (−3.1%,	5.7%)	17
	4 Dutch cities Winters 87–90	Previous day PM_{10}	School children	1.5% (−1.1%,	4.2%)	18
	Southern CA Winter 1978–79	Daily mean CoH	Nonsmoking adults	5.9% (−1.9%, 14.3%)		27a
	Combined			3.0%		
Upper respiratory symptoms	Utah Valley, UT Winter 1989–90	Daily mean PM_{10}	Children Asthmatics	3.7% (0.7%, −0.2% (−4.2%,	6.8%) 4.0%)	31
	Utah Valley, UT Winter 1990–91	Daily mean PM_{10}	Symptomatic children Asymptomatic children	3.7% (0.6%, −0.2% (−4.9%,	6.9%) 4.7%)	30

6 US cities Summer 1984–88	Daily mean PM_{15}	School children	6.9% (−0.7%, 15.0%)	41
Wageningen, NL Winter 1990–91	Daily mean PM_{10}	School children	2.6% (0.1%, 5.3%)	17
4 Dutch cities Winters 1987–90	Previous day PM_{10}	School children	−0.2% (−1.2%, 0.8%)	18
Southern CA Winter 1978–79	Daily mean CoH	Nonsmoking adults	2.7% (−2.5%, 8.2%)	27a
Combined			0.7%	
Cough symptoms				
Utah Valley, UT Winter 1990–91	Daily mean PM_{10}	Symptomatic children Asymptomatic children	5.2% (2.3%, 8.2%) 3.4% (−0.1%, 7.0%)	30
6 US cities Summer 1984–88	Daily mean PM_{15}	School children	8.6% (2.2%, 15.4%)	41
2 Dutch cities Winter 1990–91	Previous day PM_{10}	Symptomatic children	0.1% (−0.8%, 1.1%)	34
4 Dutch cities Winters 1987–90	Previous day $PM_{1)}$	School children	1.3% (−0.1%, 2.7%)	18
2 Swiss cities	Previous day TSP	Children	8.6% (2.1%, 15.6%)	5
Uniontown, PA Summer 1990	Daytime mean $PM_{2.5}$	Children	28.1% (4.5%, 57.1%)	25
Combined			1.2%	

Table 6 Combined effect estimates of daily mean particulate pollution

	% Change in health indicator per each $10\mu g/m^3$ increase in PM_{10}
Increase in daily mortality	
Total deaths	1.0
Respiratory deaths	3.4
Cardiovascular deaths	1.4
Increase in hospital usage (all respiratory)	
Admissions	0.8
Emergency department visits	1.0
Exacerbation of asthma	
Asthmatic attacks	3.0
Bronchodilator	2.9
Emergency department visits*	3.4
Hospital admissions	1.9
Increase in respiratory systems reports	
Lower respiratory	3.0
Upper respiratory	0.7
Cough	1.2
Decrease in lung function	
Forced expired volume	0.15
Peak expiratory flow	0.08

*One study only

PM_{10} respectively. Emergency department visits for asthmatics (3.4% increase per 10 $\mu g/m^3$ PM_{10}) and hospital admissions for asthmatic attacks (1.9% increase per 10 $\mu g/m^3$ PM_{10}) are more strongly associated. Asthmatic subjects also report substantial increases in asthma attacks (an approximate 3% increase per 10 $\mu g/m^3$ PM_{10}) and in bronchodilator use (an approximate 3% increase per 10 $\mu g/m^3$ PM_{10}).

Less severe measures of respiratory health also are associated with particle exposures. Lower respiratory symptom reporting increases by approximately 3.0% per 10 $\mu g/m^3$ PM_{10} and cough by 2.5% per 10 $\mu g/m^3$ PM_{10}. Weaker effects are observed with upper respiratory symptoms (approximately 0.7% per 10 $\mu g/m^3$ PM_{10}). While lung function provides accurate objective measures, the observed mean effects are fairly modest: approximately 0.15% decrease for FEV_1 or $FEV_{.75}$ and 0.08% decrease for peak flow per 10 mg/m³ PM_{10}. Despite the relatively small size of these lung-function effect estimates, they consistently achieve statistical significance. Moreover, mean changes in lung function may not reflect substantial changes in sensitive individuals.

In this review, changes in health measures are reported for only small changes in daily particulate pollution: 10 $\mu g/m^3$ increase in PM_{10} concentrations. Because daily concentrations of PM_{10} in some US cities average over 50 $\mu g/m^3$ and often exceed 100 or 150 $\mu g/m^3$, the effects of particulate pollution can be substantial for realistic acute exposures. For example, a 1% effect estimate per each 10 $\mu g/m^3$ increase would produce a 5% increase in the health measure for a 50 $\mu g/m^3$ increase in PM_{10} concentrations, and a 3% effect estimate would produce a 16% increase. Thus the estimated increase in attacks of asthma (3.0% per 10 $\mu g/m^3$ PM_{10}) would be 16% for a 50 $\mu g/m^3$ increase in PM_{10} concentrations.

LIMITATIONS

Mass concentration of inhalable particles is only one measure of a complex mixture of gaseous and particulate air pollution to which people are exposed. In this review the possible contribution of gaseous co-pollutants has been ignored. The mass concentration of PM_{10} includes a wide array of potentially toxic chemical species. It is, therefore, presumptuous to assign these observed health effects solely to the mass concentration of particulates. On the other hand, the consistency of these observed effects across so many communities suggests that, lacking an explicit hypothesis, these associations should be assigned to a nonspecific definition of inhalable or fine particle concentrations common to urban areas.

The physical and chemical characteristics of ambient particles are generally not known and so are impossible to duplicate in controlled animal- or human-exposure studies. Many health effects of particles are thought to reflect the combined action of the diverse components in the pollutant mix. Until controlled animal- and human-exposure studies identify the active component(s) of these complex mixtures and can characterize their underlying mechanisms of toxicity, it is prudent to ascribe health effects observed by epidemiologists to the undifferentiated particle mass rather than to any specific component.

Conversion of various measures of particle concentration to PM_{10} mass concentrations are approximations only, based on results presented in published reports. These conversions are certainly correct within a factor of two and are probably within 20% of the true relationship. Thus, while other reviewers may legitimately argue about specific relationships between the particle measures used in the various studies, the estimated effects would remain remarkably comparable, even assuming other reasonable conversions to PM_{10} mass concentrations.

The results of epidemiologic studies of acute effects of particulate air pollution, particularly those describing associations with cardiovascular mortality, have been called into question because of the lack of a biologically plausible mechanism (52, 53). The linkage between air pollution exposure and acute cardiovascular mortality is not clear. Many authors have suggested that air pollution episodes, like episodes of extreme temperature, high or low, are an additional environmental stress that may cause death in otherwise-compromised patients. Bates (3) has suggested three additional mechanisms by which respiratory and cardiovascular mortality might increase in air pollution episodes: (a) acute bronchitis and bronchiolitis may be misdiagnosed as pulmonary edema; (b) air pollutants may increase lung permeability and precipitate pulmonary edema in people with myocardial damage and increased left atrial pressure; (c) bronchiolitis or pneumonia induced by air pollution, in the presence of pre-existing heart disease, might precipitate congestive heart failure. An alternative explanation is that respiratory causes of death, either primary or contributing, are erroneously reported as cardiovascular. In a summary of a workshop of chronic obstructive pulmonary disease mortality, Speizer (46) observed that chronic obstructive pulmonary disease is considerably underdiagnosed on death certificates. While the specific biologic mechanism for these acute increases in mortality is not clear, the internal consistency of the mortality studies and the external consistency with evidence of acute increases in morbidity measures suggest that these results are not artifacts.

RECOMMENDATIONS

Mortality has always been a key health endpoint in epidemiologic studies, i.e. it serves as a leading indicator for hypothesis generation. It is a well-defined health outcome and mortality data are routinely collected and are readily available for epidemiologic analysis. When the numerous time-series studies of the association of mortality with particulate air pollution are compiled, using comparable measures of effect (% increase) and exposure (PM_{10}) as in Table 1, the consistency of estimated effects becomes clear. When estimated effects of particulate air pollution are similarly combined for other health indicators, the consistency and coherence of results also becomes apparent. These findings highlight the importance of using equivalent exposure metrics and health endpoints in air pollution studies.

Thus, we recommend that researchers report results such that they can be readily compared with previous (and future) investigations. The groupings of health endpoints considered here present some guidance. Likewise, the reporting of associations with PM_{10} concentrations is important. This recommendation should not be interpreted as a request for regimentation or an attempt to limit innovation. Rather, it is recommended that the associations with common endpoints and PM_{10} exposures be reported in addition to other, potentially more sensitive or specific, indicators of health effect or exposure.

A quantitative effect estimate and its estimated standard error should be reported in all cases. Reports of statistical significance without effect estimates are not very informative. Likewise, correlation coefficients and other unscaled measures of association fail to provide useful information.

Epidemiologic research regarding the health effects of particulate air pollution has been impeded by the lack of daily (or more frequent) particle measurements (8). In communities that are not likely to violate (or that clearly exceed) the NAAQS for particles, PM_{10} measurements are made only once every six days, as required by the EPA (13). Fortunately for epidemiologists, the EPA has required daily monitoring in communities likely to violate the NAAQS for particles. These regulations have had the unanticipated (but beneficial) effect of making feasible new epidemiologic studies of the acute effects of particles. Inasmuch as associations are being observed between daily particle exposures and adverse health effects down to the lowest measureable concentrations, it is recommended that daily PM_{10} concentrations be measured whenever possible. When alternative measures of particle concentrations are used, then a description of the relationship to PM_{10} concentrations should be provided.

Research into mechanisms of the adverse health effects of PM_{10} mass concentrations observed in recent epidemiologic studies needs to be undertaken in controlled exposure studies of humans and animals. It is only through integration of the complementary evidence from laboratory animal and controlled human exposure studies with the results from epidemiologic studies that the risk of particle exposures can be fully evaluated. Nevertheless, these recent epidemiologic studies implicate particulate air pollution as contributing to respiratory morbidity and mortality even at exposure levels below the current NAAQS in the United States.

ACKNOWLEDGMENTS

This review was supported in part by National Institute of Environmental Health Sciences grants ES-00002, ES-01108, ES-04595, and ES-06239; by the Environmental Protection Agency Cooperative Agreement CR816071 and CR 818090; and by the Electric Power Research Institute contract RP-1001. The authors particularly want to thank Gail Fleischaker for her thoughtful and meticulous editing of this manuscript. This review was written while CA Pope was a Visiting Scientist in the Interdisciplinary Programs in Health, Department of Environmental Health, Harvard School of Public Health.

Literature Cited

1. Bates DV. 1980. The health effects of air pollution. *J. Respir. Dis.* 1:29–37
2. Bates DV. 1989. *Respiratory Function in Disease.* Philadelphia, PA: Saunders. 3rd ed.
3. Bates DV. 1992. Health indices of the adverse effects of air pollution: The question of coherence. *Environ. Res.* 59:336–49
4. Bates DV, Sizto R. 1987. Air pollution and hospital admissions in Southern Ontario: The acid summer haze effect. *Environ. Res.* 43:317–31
5. Braun-Fahrländer C, Ackermann-Liebrich U, Schwartz J, Gnehm HP, Rutishauser M, Wanner HU. 1992. Air pollution and respiratory symptoms in preschool children. *Am. Rev. Respir. Dis.* 145:42–47
6. Brunekreef B, Kinney PL, Ware JL, Dockery DW, Speizer FE, et al. 1991. Sensitive subgroups and normal variation in pulmonary function response to air pollution episodes. *Environ. Health Perspect.* 90:189–93
7. Burnett RT, Dales RE, Raizenne ME, Krewski D, Summers PW, et al. 1993. Effects of low ambient levels of ozone and sulphates on the frequency of respiratory admissions to Ontario hospitals. *Environ. Res.* In press
7a. Dassen W, Brunekreef B, Hoek G, Hofschreuder P, Staatsen B, et al. 1986. Decline in children's pulmonary function during an air pollution episode. *J. Air Pollut. Control Assoc.* 36:1223–27
8. Dockery DW, Schwartz J. 1992. The authors' response to Waller and Swan. *Am. J. Epidemiol.* 135:23–25
9. Dockery DW, Schwartz J, Spengler JD. 1992. Air pollution and daily mortality: Associations with particulates and acid aerosols. *Environ. Res.* 59:362–73
10. Dockery DW, Ware JH, Ferris BG Jr, Speizer FE, Cook NR. 1982. Change in pulmonary function in children associated with air pollution episodes. *J. Air Pollut. Control Assoc.* 32:937–42
11. Dzubay TG, Stevens RK. 1975. Ambient air analysis with dichotomous sampler and x-ray fluorescence spectrometer. *Environ. Sci. Technol.* 9:663–68
12. Ellison JM, Waller RE. 1978. A review of sulphur oxides and particulate matter as air pollutants with particular reference to effects on health in the United Kingdom. *Environ. Res.* 16:302–25
13. Environ. Prot. Agency. 1987. 40 CFR Part 50. Revisions to the national ambient air quality standards for particulate matter: Final rules. *Fed. Regist.* 52(126):24634–69
14. Fairley D. 1990. The relationship of daily mortality to suspended particulates in Santa Clara County, 1980–1986. *Environ. Health Perspect.* 89: 159–68
15. Firket J. 1936. Fog along the Meuse Valley. *Trans. Faraday Soc.* 32:1192–97
16. Hatch GE, Boykin E, Graham JA, Lewtas J, Pott F, et al. 1985. Inhalable particles and pulmonary host defense: In vitro and in vivo effects of ambient air and combustion particles. *Environ. Res.* 36:67–80
17. Hoek G, Brunekreef B. 1993. Acute effects of a winter air pollution episode on pulmonary function and respiratory symptoms of children. *Arch. Environ. Health.* 48:328–35
18. Hoek G, Brunekreef B. 1993. Effects of low level winter air pollution concentrations on respiratory health of Dutch children. *Environ. Res.* In press
19. Holland WW, Bennett AE, Cameron IR, Florey CDV, Leeder SR, Schilling RSF, et al. 1979. Health effects of particulate pollution: Reappraising the evidence. *Am. J. Epidemiol.* 110:525–659

20. Kinney PL, Özkaynak H. 1991. Associations of daily mortality and air pollution in Los Angeles County. *Environ. Res.* 54:99–120

21. Lippmann M. 1989. Health effects of ozone—A critical review. *J. Air Pollut. Control Assoc.* 39:672–95

22. Lippmann M, Lioy PJ. 1985. Critical issues in air pollution epidemiology. *Environ. Health Perspect.* 62:243–58

23. Logan WPD. 1953. Mortality in London fog incident, 1952. *Lancet* 264(1):336–38

24. Miller FJ, Gardner DE, Graham JA, Lee RE Jr, Wilson WE, Bachmann JD. 1979. Size considerations for establishing a standard for inhalable particles. *J. Air Pollut. Control Assoc.* 29:610–15

25. Neas LM, Dockery DW, Spengler JD, Speizer FE, Tollerud DJ. 1992. The association of ambient air pollution with twice daily peak expiratory flow measurements in children. *Am. Rev. Respir. Dis.* 145(4):A429

26. Off. Air Qual. Plan. Standards. 1982. *Review of the national ambient air quality standards for particulate matter: Assessment of scientific and technical information.* Publ. Number EPA-450/5-82-001. Research Triangle Park, NC: US EPA

26a. Ostro BD. 1993. The association of air pollution and mortality. Examining the case for inference. *Arch. Environ. Health* 48:336–42

27. Ostro BD, Lipsett MJ, Wiener MB, Selner JC. 1991. Asthmatic response to airborne acid aerosols. *Am. J. Public Health* 81:694–702

27a. Ostro BD, Lipsett MJ, Mann JK, Krupnick A, Harrington W. 1993. Air pollution and respiratory morbidity among adults in Southern California. *Am. J. Epidemiol.* 137:691–700

28. Pope CA III. 1989. Respiratory disease associated with community air pollution and a steel mill, Utah Valley. *Am. J. Public Health* 79:623–28

29. Pope CA III. 1991. Respiratory hospital admissions associated with PM$_{10}$ pollution in Utah, Salt Lake, and Cache Valleys. *Arch. Environ. Health* 46:90–97

30. Pope CA III, Dockery DW. 1992. Acute health effects of PM$_{10}$ pollution on symptomatic and asymptomatic children. *Am. Rev. Respir. Dis.* 145:1123–28

31. Pope CA III, Dockery DW, Spengler JD, Raizenne ME. 1991. Respiratory health and PM$_{10}$ pollution. *Am. Rev. Respir. Dis.* 144:668–74

32. Pope CA III, Kanner RE. 1993. Acute effects of PM$_{10}$ pollution on pulmonary function of smokers with mild to moderate chronic obstructive pulmonary disease. *Am. Rev. Respir. Dis.* 147:1336–40

33. Pope CA III, Schwartz J, Ransom MR. 1992. Daily mortality and PM$_{10}$ pollution in Utah Valley. *Arch. Environ. Health* 47:211–17

34. Roemer W, Hoek G, Brunekreef B. 1993. Effect of ambient winter air pollution on respiratory health of children with chronic respiratory symptoms. *Am. Rev. Respir. Dis.* 147:118–24

35. Samet JM, Speizer FE, Bishop Y, Spengler JD, Ferris BG Jr. 1981. The relationship between air pollution and emergency room visits in an industrial community. *J. Air Pollut. Control Assoc.* 31:236–40

36. Shrenk HH, Heimann H, Clayton GD, Gafafer WM, Wexler H. 1949. *Air pollution in Donora, PA: Epidemiology of the unusual smog episode of October 1948,* Prelim. Rep. Public Health Bull. No. 306. Public Health Serv., Washington, DC

37. Schwartz J. 1991. Particulate air pollution and daily mortality in Detroit. *Environ. Res.* 56:204–13

38. Schwartz J. 1993. Air pollution and daily mortality in Birmingham, Alabama. *Am. J. Epidemiol.* 137:1136–47

39. Schwartz J, Dockery DW. 1992. Increased mortality in Philadelphia associated with daily air pollution concentrations. *Am. Rev. Respir. Dis.* 145:600–04

40. Schwartz J, Dockery DW. 1992. Particulate air pollution and daily mortality in Steubenville, Ohio. *Am. J. Epidemiol.* 135:12–19

41. Schwartz J, Dockery DW, Neas LM, Wypij D, Ware JW, et al. 1993. Acute effects of summer air pollution on respiratory symptom reporting in children. *Am. Rev. Respir. Dis.* In press

42. Schwartz J, Slater D, Larson TV, Pierson WE, Koenig JQ. 1993. Particulate air pollution and hospital emergency room visits for asthma in Seattle. *Am. Rev. Respir. Dis.* 147:826–31

43. Deleted in press

44. Scott JA. 1963. The London fog of December, 1962. *Med. Off.* 109:250–52

45. Shy CM. 1979. Epidemiologic evidence and the United States air quality

standards. *Am. J. Epidemiol.* 110:661–71

46. Speizer FE. 1989. The rise in chronic obstructive pulmonary disease mortality. Overview and summary. *Am. Rev. Respir. Dis.* 140:S106–7

47. Spengler JD, Thurston GD. 1983. Mass and elemental composition of fine and coarse particles in six U. S. cities. *J. Air Pollut. Control Assoc.* 33:1162–71

48. Sunyer J, Antó JM, Murillo C, Sáez M. 1991. Effects of urban pollution on emergency room admissions for chronic obstructive pulmonary disease. *Am. J. Epidemiol.* 134:277–89

49. Sunyer J, Sáez M, Murillo C, Castellsague J, Martinez F, Antó JM. 1993. Air pollution and emergency room admissions for chronic obstructive pulmonary disease: A 5-year study. *Am. J. Epidemiol.* 137:701–5

50. Thurston GD, Ito K, Lippmann M. 1993. *The role of particulate mass vs. acidity in the sulfate-respiratory hospital admissions association.* Preprint #93-11.03. Presented at Annu. Meet. Air Waste Manage. Assoc., 86th, June 13–18. Denver, CO

51. Thurston GD, Ito K, Kinney PL, Lippmann M. 1992. A multi-year study of air pollution and respiratory hospital admissions in three New York state metropolitan area: Results for 1988 and 1989 summers. *J. Expos. Anal. Environ. Epidemiol.* 2:429–50

52. Utell MJ, Samet JM. 1993. Particulate air pollution and health. New evidence on an old problem. *Am. Rev. Respir. Dis.* 147:1334–35

53. Waller RE, Swan AV. 1992. Invited commentary: Particulate air pollution and daily mortality. *Am. J. Epidemiol.* 135:20–22

54. Ware JH, Thibodeau LA, Speizer FE, Colome S, Ferris BG Jr. 1981. Assessment of the health effects of atmospheric sulfur oxides and particulate matter: evidence from observational studies. *Environ. Health Perspect.* 41:255–76

55. Warheit DB. 1989. Interspecies comparisons of lung responses to inhaled particles and gases. *Crit. Rev. Toxicol.* 20:1–29

56. Whittemore AS, Korn EL. 1980. Asthma and air pollution in the Los Angeles area. *Am. J. Public Health* 70:687–96

Annu. Rev. Public Health. 1994. 15:133–56

WOOD SMOKE: EMISSIONS AND NONCANCER RESPIRATORY EFFECTS

Timothy V. Larson and Jane Q. Koenig

Departments of Civil Engineering and Environmental Health, University of
Washington, Seattle, Washington 98195

KEY WORDS: respiratory effects, chemical composition, air emissions, air quality,
             young children

INTRODUCTION

During the past twenty years, the use of wood has become popular as an
alternative to conventional home heating fuels. Part of this movement has
been due to uncertainty about the availability of fossil fuels. About ten
percent of space heating in urbanized areas of the northern United States
is from wood burning, with up to fifty percent in some smaller, rural towns
(42, 63, 75, 85). Wood is obviously a renewable resource. This attraction
is offset, however, by the increased air pollution emissions from wood
heating devices compared with devices fueled with oil or gas. As noted
initially by Cooper (20), particle and organic carbon emission rates can be
as much as one to two orders of magnitude larger in wood heating devices
than in oil or gas heating units. Legislation restricting the sale of conventional
wood stoves first appeared in Oregon in 1984, followed by nationwide
restrictions in 1988. Although rapid progress has reduced emissions in some
types of modern wood heaters, older "conventional" wood stoves and
fireplace inserts are still the predominant appliance in use today. As discussed
later in this document, a number of communities continue to experience
elevated levels of wood smoke during the winter heating season. In addition,
elevated indoor air pollution levels have been observed in homes with
non-airtight or improperly operated wood stoves. As a result, there has been
an ongoing interest in the potential health effects of exposure to wood
smoke. Several reviews of the health effects of wood smoke have been

133

0163-7525/94/0510-0133$05.00

prepared (2, 3, 28, 53, 66, 75). The present review attempts to summarize the information available on the chemical composition of wood smoke, concentrations of wood smoke in both indoor and outdoor environments, emission data, and the adverse respiratory responses in animal toxicity studies and epidemiological studies of human populations. A more detailed discussion of the emissions and the chemical and physical properties of wood smoke can be found in Larson & Koenig (58).

WOOD COMBUSTION AND WOOD SMOKE

Most wood burned for heat is cordwood with some increasing use of wood pellets. Cordwood heaters burn wood with a deficit of oxygen and readily generate products of incomplete combustion, including carbon monoxide and numerous organic compounds. If these vapors are not immediately oxidized, they cool as they are exhausted to the atmosphere with subsequent formation of fine particles rich in relatively high molecular weight organic compounds. A "conventional" wood stove fits this description. To reduce emissions from cordwood heaters, these vapors are oxidized directly downstream of the combustion zone either by using a noble metal catalyst to more completely combust vapors at the lower exhaust temperatures, or by using an insulated secondary combustion chamber to maintain a high exhaust temperature while mixing the gases with a separate stream of additional combustion air. The former method is employed in "catalytic" stoves, the latter in "non-catalytic" or "high technology" stoves. In contrast to cordwood heaters, pellet stoves take advantage of the larger wood surface area per unit mass of wood. Consequently, the higher heat transfer rates from the combustion gases to adjacent wood result in efficient vaporization of the wood prior to combustion. Mixing these vapors with excess combustion air at the top of a pellet bed results in much more complete combustion than that in conventional stoves.

Wood consists of approximately 50 to 70 weight percent cellulose, which are polysaccharides, and about 30 weight percent lignin, which is a skeletal network of branch-chain polymers that provide structural integrity. In addition, there are small amounts of resinous materials and inorganic salts. The lignin polymer consists of two main monomers, a guaiacyclopropane structure and a syringylpropane structure. Upon heating, these structures break apart producing a large variety of smaller molecules, many of which are part of the general class of oxygenated monoaromatics (89). Included in this class are methoxy phenols and methoxy benzenes, as well as phenols and catechols. This decomposition also produces benzene and alkyl benzenes. The presence of guaiacol, syringol and their derivatives as a group are unique to the burning of wood because they are a direct consequence of the destruction of the unique lignin structure. In contrast, phenols, catechols, benzene, and alkyl benzenes are not unique to wood combustion and have been found in the exhaust gases of other combustion sources. Table 1 summarizes the reported constituents in wood smoke and provides quantitative information on their emission rates.

Of the trace elements, potassium is found at relatively high concentrations in wood smoke. Combustion of hardwoods produces more ash (and thus higher concentrations of trace elements) than does combustion of softwoods. The particulate elemental carbon concentrations reported in wood smoke are somewhat controversial. Some researchers claim that up to 95 weight percent of the total particle mass is extractable in dichloromethane and/or methanol (88), while others claim that up to 50 percent of the total particulate carbon is elemental carbon as measured by optical and thermal methods (78). It seems reasonable to conclude that 5 to 20 percent of the total particulate mass is unextractable and that this unextractable fraction contains elemental carbon.

The size distribution of wood smoke particles has been measured by several investigators (23, 47, 49). The particle volume peaks at between 0.15 and 0.4 μm, with essentially no particles greater than 1 μm. This is consistent with the fact that the majority of the mass is formed by condensation processes in the exhaust. Owing to their relatively small size, they are very efficient at reducing visibility and are not readily removed by inertial and gravitational processes.

Upon release to the environment, many compounds in wood smoke are expected to undergo some degree of chemical transformation in the atmosphere. However, there have been relatively few studies of these transformations (see ref. 58 for a more complete discussion).

ATMOSPHERIC CONCENTRATIONS OF WOOD SMOKE

In the past ten years, a number of studies have documented the outdoor concentrations of airborne particles resulting from wood burning. These studies are summarized in Table 2. We have included only those studies in this table that quantified the levels of airborne particles using one of several chemical tracer methods. These studies document that wood smoke has been identified in airsheds in many areas throughout the United States.

Numerous other studies have documented elevated levels of particulate matter in residential communities where wood burning is prevalent, but have not employed receptor models to estimate the wood burning fraction. Perhaps the most notable of these are the measurements taken in Klamath Falls, Oregon, that have exceeded 600 μg/m^3 on a 24-hr basis during the winter (43). Based upon inventories of fuel use, wood smoke may account

Table 1 Chemical composition of wood smoke

Specie[1]	g/kg wood[2]	Physical state[3]	Reference
Carbon monoxide	80–370	V	25, 74
Methane	14–25	V	74
VOCs (C_2–C_7)	7–27	V	74
Aldehydes	0.6–5.4	V	25, 62
Formaldehyde	0.1–0.7	V	25, 62
Acrolein	0.02–0.1	V	62
Propionaldehyde	0.1–0.3	V	25, 62
Butryaldehyde	0.01–1.7	V	25, 62
Acetaldehyde	0.03–0.6	V	25, 62
Furfural	0.2–1.6	V	30, 34
Substituted furans	0.15–1.7	V	30, 34
Benzene	0.6–4.0	V	74
Alkyl benzenes	1–6	V	89
Toluene	0.15–1.0	V	89
Acetic acid	1.8–2.4	V	30
Formic acid	0.06–0.08	V	30
Nitrogen oxides (NO,NO_2)	0.2–0.9	V	25, 74
Sulfur dioxide	0.16–0.24	V	25
Methyl chloride	0.01–0.04		48
Napthalene	0.24–1.6	V	89
Substituted napthalenes	0.3–2.1	V/P	89
Oxygenated monoaromatics	1–7	V/P	89
Guaiacol (and derivatives)	0.4–1.6	V/P	35
Phenol (and derivatives)	0.2–0.8	V/P	35
Syringol (and derivatives)	0.7–2.7	V/P	35
Catechol (and derivatives)	0.2–0.8	V/P	35
Total particle mass	7–30	P	74
Particulate organic carbon	2–20	P	21
Oxygenated PAHs	0.15–1	V/P	89
PAHs			
Fluorene	4×10^{-5}–1.7×10^{-2}	V/P	1, 19, 21, 46, 92, 99
Phenanthrene	2×10^{-5}–3.4×10^{-2}	V/P	1, 19, 21, 46, 92, 99
Anthracene	5×10^{-5}–2.1×10^{-2}	V/P	1, 19, 21, 46, 92, 99
Methylanthracenes	7×10^{-5}–8×10^{-3}	V/P	1, 19, 21, 92, 99
Fluoranthene	7×10^{-4}–4.2×10^{-2}	V/P	1, 19, 21, 92, 99
Pyrene	8×10^{-4}–3.1×10^{-2}	V/P	1, 19, 21, 92, 99
Benzo(a)anthracene	4×10^{-4}–2×10^{-3}	V/P	1, 19, 21, 92, 99
Chrysene	5×10^{-4}–1×10^{-2}	V/P	1, 19, 21, 92, 99
Benzofluoranthenes	6×10^{-4}–5×10^{-3}	V/P	1, 19, 21, 92, 99
Benzo(e)pyrene	2×10^{-4}–4×10^{-3}	V/P	1, 19, 21, 92, 99
Benzo(a)pyrene	3×10^{-4}–5×10^{-3}	V/P	1, 19, 21, 92, 99
Perylene	5×10^{-5}–$3 - 10^{-3}$	V/P	1, 19, 21, 92, 99
Ideno(1,2,3-cd)pyrene	2×10^{-4}–1.3×10^{-2}	V/P	1, 19, 21, 92, 99
Benz(ghi)perylene	3×10^{-5}–1.1×10^{-2}	V/P	1, 19, 21, 92, 99
Coronene	8×10^{-4}–3×10^{-3}	V/P	1, 19, 21, 92, 99

Table 1 *(Continued)*

Specie[1]	g/kg wood[2]	Physical state[3]	Reference
Dibenzo(a,h)pyrene	$3 \times 10^{-4} - 1 \times 10^{-3}$	V/P	1, 19, 21, 92, 99
Retene	$7 \times 10^{-3} - 3 \times 10^{-2}$	V/P	21, 46
Dibenz(a,h)anthracene	$2 \times 10^{-5} - 2 \times 10^{-3}$	V/P	19, 21, 46, 92, 99
Trace elements			
Na	$3 \times 10^{-3} - 1.8 \times 10^{-2}$	P	21, 46, 96
Mg	$2 \times 10^{-4} - 3 \times 10^{-3}$	P	21, 46, 96
Al	$1 \times 10^{-4} - 2.4 \times 10^{-2}$	P	21, 46, 96
Si	$3 \times 10^{-4} - 3.1 \times 10^{-2}$	P	21, 46, 96
S	$1 \times 10^{-3} - 2.9 \times 10^{-2}$	P	21, 46, 96
Cl	$7 \times 10^{-4} - 2.1 \times 10^{-1}$	P	21, 46, 96
K	$3 \times 10^{-3} - 8.6 \times 10^{-2}$	P	21, 46, 96
Ca	$9 \times 10^{-4} - 1.8 \times 10^{-2}$	P	21, 46, 96
Ti	$4 \times 10^{-5} - 3 \times 10^{-3}$	P	21, 46, 96
V	$2 \times 10^{-5} - 4 \times 10^{-3}$	P	21, 46, 96
Cr	$2 \times 10^{-5} - 3 \times 10^{-3}$	P	21, 46, 96
Mn	$7 \times 10^{-5} - 4 \times 10^{-3}$	P	21, 46, 96
Fe	$3 \times 10^{-4} - 5 \times 10^{-3}$	P	21, 46, 96
Ni	$1 \times 10^{-6} - 1 \times 10^{-3}$	P	21, 46, 96
Cu	$2 \times 10^{-4} - 9 \times 10^{-4}$	P	21, 46, 96
Zn	$7 \times 10^{-4} - 8 \times 10^{-3}$	P	21, 46, 96
Br	$7 \times 10^{-5} - 9 \times 10^{-4}$	P	21, 46, 96
Pb	$1 \times 10^{-4} - 3 \times 10^{-3}$	P	21, 46, 96
Particulate elemental carbon	0.3 – 5	P	21, 78
Normal alkanes ($C_{24} - C_{30}$)	$1 \times 10^{-3} - 6 \times 10^{-3}$	P	21
Cyclic di- and triterpenoids			
Dehydroabietic acid	0.01 – 0.05	P	87
Isopimaric acid	0.02 – 0.10	P	87
Lupenone	$2 \times 10^{-3} - 8 \times 10^{-3}$	P	87
Friedelin	$4 \times 10^{-6} - 2 \times 10^{-5}$	P	87
Chlorinated dioxins	$1 \times 10^{-5} - 4 \times 10^{-5}$	P	72
Particulate acidity	$7 \times 10^{-3} - 7 \times 10^{-2}$	P	72

[1]Some species are grouped into general classes as indicated by italics.
[2]To estimate the weight percentage in the exhaust, divide the g/kg value by 80. This assumes that there are 7.3 kg combustion air per kg of wood. Major species not listed here include carbon dioxide and water vapor (about 12 and 7 weight percent, respectively, under the assumed conditions).
[3]At ambient conditions; V = vapor, P = particulate, and V/P = vapor and/or particulate (i.e. semivolatile).

for as much as 80 percent of the airborne particle concentrations during the winter (36). The Klamath Falls studies emphasize another important point— the location of the air monitoring device. There is up to a fourfold difference between various parts of town, with the highest readings in the residential area (36). This same spatial variability was observed by Larson et al (56) using a mobile nephelometer. They found that the nighttime drainage flow tended to concentrate the wood smoke at valley floors, with a consistent factor of two to three difference between ridge line and valley smoke levels. With this caveat in mind, we can see from Table 2 that the average nighttime concentrations of fine particle wood smoke vary from location to location. As expected, concentrations are higher in residential areas than in downtown urban or industrial areas and generally higher at night than during the day. The agreement between different source apportionment methods, when compared, is good.

Several studies are of interest to later discussions of the health effects of wood smoke. In addition to the Klamath Falls studies discussed above, the limited measurements by Carlson (15) in Missoula, Montana, indicated that most of the fine particle mass was due to wood burning. The measurements taken in Boise, Idaho, also found that most of the extractable organic material found in fine particles was from wood burning, with the remainder due to mobile sources (50, 61). Finally, the measurements taken in Seattle, Washington, (56, 57) indicate not only that there are elevated concentrations of wood smoke particles during winter evening periods at a residential location, but also that most of the fine particle mass at this location is due to wood burning all weeks of the year. The fine particle mass concentrations at this site are low in the summer, and therefore the absolute concentrations due to wood burning are about an order of magnitude less in summer than in winter. Open burning restrictions did not go into effect in this area until September, 1992. Thus some wood burning is expected in the summer from burning of yard waste and land-clearing fires.

Although smoke levels in outdoor air are important, most people spend a majority of their time indoors, especially at night in residential areas. Indoor exposure can occur not only from infiltration of outdoor air, but also from emissions into the home from a wood burning appliance. Table 3 summarizes current knowledge of the effects of wood burning appliances on indoor air quality. The table is arranged by pollutants. Emissions occur into the home during fueling of the stove and may also occur during stove operation. More modern, airtight stoves generate fewer emissions directly into the home than older, nonairtight stoves or improperly operated and/or maintained stoves. To put the emission rates listed in Table 3 into perspective, consider a 100 cubic meter room (approximately 20 by 20 feet). If seven tenths of the volume of air in the room is exchanged with outside air every hour, and if 70 percent of the fine particles from the outside air penetrate into the home, then for a typical outdoor concentration of 20 $\mu g/m^3$ of wood smoke particles there is an effective infiltration rate of $20 \times 0.7 \times 0.7 \times 100 = 1$ mg per hour of fine particle mass. This value is comparable to estimated emission rates of fine particles into the home due to leakage from "airtight" stoves (2.3–3.6 mg/hr; see Table 3). Higher

Table 2 Summary of measured wood burning effects on airborne particle concentrations

Investigator[a]	Location	Measurement[b]	Concentration ($\mu g/m^3$) Mean	Range	Wood smoke (wt %)	Method[c]	Comments
Cooper (20)	Portland, OR	$PM_{2.5}$	68	—	36	[14]C	Single sample at residential location in winter
		total carbon	31.3	—	51		
Wolff et al (97)	Denver, CO	$PM_{2.5}$	39.5	—	12	K/Fe	Five samples during winter
		total carbon	27	7–43	33	[14]C	Average of winter samples
Carlson (15)	Missoula, MT	$PM_{3.5}$	—	—	68	CMB	Seven residential samples in winter
Imhoff (44)	Petersville, AL	$PM_{2.5}$	45	13–86	85	CMB	Sixty-one 24-hr samples in autumn and winter from 8 sites in WA, 1 site in ID and 1 site in OR
Core et al (22)	Spokane, WA; Seattle, WA; Tacoma, WA; Portland, OR; Boise, ID	$PM_{2.5}$	57	—	71	CMB	
	Medford, OR	$PM_{2.5}$	17.5	8.8–30.2	55		Annual average values for 3 sites
	Portland, OR		3.0	1.5–3.9	14		Annual average values for 4 sites
Ramdahl et al (76)	Elverum, Norway	total carbon (<3 μm)	20	5–50	65	[14]C	Ten 24-hr winter samples; avg PM_{10} = 51 $\mu g/m^3$ (range 31–101)
Naylor (71)	Las Vegas, NV	total carbon	36	25–46	47	[14]C	Four 12-hr winter samples (day and night)
Lewis et al (60)	Denver, CO	$PM_{2.5}$	19	?–47	8	MLR	Seventeen 12-hr daytime samples in winter
		$PM_{2.5}$	12	?–41	17		Nineteen 12-hr nighttime samples in winter
Klouda et al (51)	Raleigh, NC	total carbon	—	23–80	95	[14]C	Four 12-hr daytime samples in winter
		elemental carbon	3.2	—	68		One 12-hr daytime sample in winter
	Albuquerque, NM	total carbon	—	11–71	75	[14]C	Six 12-hr samples (day & night) at residential site in winter
		elemental carbon	4.6	—	41		Four 12-hr samples (day & night) at residential site in winter

Table 2 (Continued)

Investigator[a]	Location	Measurement[b]	Concentration (μg/m³) Mean	Range	Wood smoke (wt %)	Method[c]	Comments
Lewis et al (59)	Albuquerque, NM	total carbon	—	—	67	MLR ×^{14}C	Six 12-hr samples (day or night) in winter
			—	—	68		
		EOM	18.9	—	78	MLR	Forty-four 12-hr samples (day & night) in winter
Chow et al (16)	Sparks, NV	PM$_{10}$	41	?–154	30[d]	CMB	Fifty seven 24-hr samples every 6th day for one year at a residential site
			76		44[d]		Subset of above samples from Oct–Dec period (n = 15)
	Reno, NV		30	?–99	3[d]		Fifty six 24-hr samples every 6th day for one year at an urban site
			46		9[d]		Subset of above samples from Oct–Dec period (n = 15)
Benedict & Naylor (8)	Las Vegas, NV	PM$_{2.5}$	12.5	—	27	CMB	One 24-hr sample during winter
Magliano (65)	Bakersfield, CA	PM$_{10}$	8.7	—	12.9	CMB	Nine month average of every 6th day 24-hr samples (March–Dec)
		PM$_{2.5}$	13.8	—	62.8		
	Fresno, CA	PM$_{10}$	7.1	—	16.8		
		PM$_{2.5}$	5.3	—	35.5		
Dresser & Baird (29)	Telluride, CO	PM$_{10}$	—	—	33	CMB	Four 24-hr average spring samples
			205	—	58		Two 24-hr holiday winter samples
Larson et al (56)	Seattle, WA	PM$_{10}$	39	9–123	6	CMB	Seven 12-hr daytime samples at industrial site in winter of 1987–88
			30	8–61	11		The corresponding seven 12-hr nighttime samples at above site

							Comments
			45	12–104	54		Ten 12-hr daytime samples at residential site in winter of 1987–88
			75	5–144	82		The corresponding ten 12-hr nighttime samples at above site
			116	75–139	82		The sixteen highest 12-hr nighttime samples at the same residential site in the winter of 1988–89
Klouda et al (50)	Boise, ID	EOM	—	—	72–89	14C	Reported range of values (average not reported) for nine 12-hr daytime samples at a residential site in winter
		EOM	—	—	52–83		Range of values (average not reported) for nine 12-hr nighttime samples at residential site in winter
Lewis et al (61)	Boise, ID	EOM	22	—	67[d]	MLR	Forty 12-hr samples (day & night)
Larson et al (57)	Seattle, WA	PM2.5	14.8	6.0–32.9	71	CMB	Forty eight one-week average composite samples (Jan–Nov) at a residential site. The composite consisted of sampling for 15 min every 2 hr for the entire study period. Wood burning was the dominant source all seasons of the year, ranging from 60% in summer to 90% in winter

[a] Other investigators have measured elevated concentrations of particulate matter in wood burning communities, but did not use one of the methods cited above to quantify the fraction attributable to wood burning. Methods not listed above include emission inventory/atmospheric dispersion modeling (13, 42, 44, 55, 69, 71, 76, 80, 84), gaseous methyl chloride tracer measurement (47), time series of particle light scattering coefficient (54, 55) and thermography (54).

[b] PM_x = mass concentration of particles ≤ x μm in aerodynamic diameter; EOM = mass concentration of extractable organic matter from particles with aerodynamic diameters ≤ 2.5 μm; total carbon = total organic and elemental carbon mass concentration in particles ≤ 2.5 μm in aerodynamic diameter unless otherwise noted.

[c] 14C = isotopic carbon measurement to determine biogenic carbon concentration, i.e., contemporary carbon from biogenic material ~ 40 years or less old; CMB = chemical mass balance regression model; K/Fe = tracer enrichment method based upon the mass ratio of potassium to iron; MLR = multiple linear regression of individual tracer elements (e.g. potassium for wood and lead for motor vehicles) against mass concentration of relevant measurement listed above.

[d] Estimated from reported average concentration of wood smoke divided by average concentration of total mass

outdoor concentrations or more rapid air exchange rates would give larger infiltration rates. For most studies of fine particle mass in homes with airtight stoves, the indoor outdoor ratios are at or below 1.0, implying that infiltration is important even in homes with stoves. As also shown in Table 3, the indoor/outdoor ratios are much higher for carbon monoxide and formaldehyde, two species that have a number of indoor sources in addition to wood stoves. The data for formaldehyde are particularly striking, implying that although wood stoves emit formaldehyde, their emissions are not a major determinant of overall exposure to this specie.

HEALTH EFFECTS

Many of the constituents of wood smoke described earlier aggravate respiratory disease and irritate mucous membranes. Knowledge of the toxicity of a compound usually depends on data from three sources: animal toxicology, controlled human studies, and epidemiology. In this section, we review the available information on wood smoke exposures, with emphasis on studies of human subjects.

Animal Toxicology

We restrict our discussion of animal toxicology to those studies employing whole wood smoke; we do not discuss data on individual compounds found in wood smoke. Unfortunately few data are available on acute effects and none on chronic effects of inhalation of wood smoke in animals. One study found an overall depression in macrophage activity, increases in albumin and lactose dehydogenase (LDH) levels (both indicating damage to cellular membranes), and a large increase in red blood cell numbers (7). A morphological study of injury from inhalation of white pine wood smoke in rabbits showed a reproducible, necrotizing tracheobronchial epithelial cell injury (90). Another pathological result from wood smoke exposure comes from an investigation of smoke from burning pine wood delivered to the lungs of dogs (10). Significant increases in angiotensin-1-converting enzyme, a substance that regulates vasomotor activity in endothelial cells, was measured immediately after exposure and was even higher 30 min. post exposure. This pathological change could be an initial step toward pulmonary hypertension which is a suggested risk factor for a myocardial infarction. Fick and co-workers (32), in a study of young adult New Zealand white rabbits, reported significant changes in the numbers and functions of the macrophages after exposure to wood smoke from Douglas fir compared with control. Wong and co-workers (98) demonstrated a blunted respiratory response to CO in guinea pigs exposed to wood smoke, which may indicate disruption of respiratory neural control. Clark and co-workers (17) studied the distribution of extravascular lung water after acute smoke inhalation in

Table 3 Effects of wood burning appliances on indoor air quality[1]

Specie	Source[2]	Indoor concentration ($\mu g/m^3$) with source	without source	Average indoor:Outdoor ratio with	without	Estimated indoor source strength (mg/hr)[3]	Reference
PM$_{2.5}$	a	7–40	8–32	<1	<1	—	37, 38
	a,i	50–80	10–30	1.3	0.4	—1	37, 38
	a	3–27	—	0.3	—	—	22
	a,i	18	—	0.8	—	—	22
	a	28–38	—	1.1	—	2.3–3.6	52
	n	44–91	—	2.1	—	5.5–11.1	52
PM$_{3.5}$	—	13–15	8–32	>1	>1	—	18
	—	25 (19)	24 (22)	1.7	1.4	—	84
Total suspended particles	a	24–71	—	3.1	—	2.5–8.7	91
	n	28–1500	—	33.5	—	16–230	91
	b	19–24	—	1.3	—	1.1–1.6	91
Total suspended particles	a	52–65	—	1.2	—	4.1–7.5	52
	n	119–166	—	2.6	—	12–21	52
Carbon monoxide	a	1100–1960	—	2.4	—	55–182	52
	n	2450–4410	—	6.8	—	210–530	52
	a	490–3430	—	2.2	—	12–170	91
	n	2200–17,000	—	24.5	—	270–2200	91
	a	1100–2700	—	1.0	—	—	22

Table 3 (Continued)

Specie	Source[2]	Indoor concentration ($\mu g/m^3$) with source	Indoor concentration ($\mu g/m^3$) without source	Average indoor:Outdoor ratio with	Average indoor:Outdoor ratio without	Estimated indoor source strength (mg/hr)[3]	Reference
Nitric oxide	a	27–47	—	1.6	—	0.4–3.2	52
	n	26–67	—	4.4	—	2.0–9.4	52
Nitrogen dioxide	a	12–25	—	0.05	—	<0–2.4	52
	n	18–26	—	0.7	—	2.1–3.6	52
Formaldehyde	a	12–51	18–25	8	5	—	100
	a,i	15–33	17–34	3	4	—	37, 100
Benzo(a)pyrene	a	3×1^{-4}–3.5×10^{-3}	—	1.6	—	2×10^{-5}–7.6×10^{-4}	91
	n	2×10^{-3}–4.9×10^{-1}	—	84	—	2×10^{-3}–5.7×10^{-2}	91
	b	4×10^{-5}–1.6×10^{-3}	—	0.2	—	1×10^{-5}	91
Extractable organic matter *particulate phase*	a	1.4–2.3	—	0.6	—	—	22
	a,i	2.0	—	0.6	—	—	22
	a	12–20	16–20	3.0	3.5	—	67
vapor phase (semi volatile)	a	14.4–14.5	—	2.1	—	—	22
	a,i	29.1	—	2.6	—	—	22
	a	268–308	296–308	3.0	3.5	—	67

[a]Studies listed here include simultaneous measurements of indoor and outdoor concentrations. Other studies of note not listed include (4, 9, 73, 95). These latter studies document the impacts on indoor air quality of wood burning devices by comparison with "no-burn" periods, but do not specifically control for outdoor pollution variability.

[2]a = airtight wood stove; i = improperly operated wood stove; n = non-airtight wood stove; f = fireplace; b = background test (no stove present).

[3]Reported estimates via mass balance from indoor and outdoor levels as well as air exchange rates.

mongrel dogs. The exposures were for two hours. Extravascular lung water, determined by using Evans dye, which binds quickly to plasma albumin, was increased in the smoke-exposed dogs compared with controls. Wood smoke was generated by burning a standard mixture of fir plywood sawdust and kerosene. Whether the plywood contained epoxys and the contribution of toxicity from kerosene were not discussed.

Extrapolation of the results of these animal studies to human populations living in areas with elevated wood smoke concentrations is very difficult. Instillation of material directly into the lung certainly is different from inhalation. Also, inhalation from a smoke stream would result in breathing considerably higher concentrations of smoke than seen in neighborhoods in the human breathing zone. None of the animal studies evaluated pulmonary function or symptoms of respiratory illness, the endpoints assessed in epidemiological studies. Some individual components of wood smoke, such as formaldehyde (5) and various products of incomplete combustion (25a), have been studied more extensively in animals.

Controlled Laboratory Studies

No controlled laboratory studies of human subjects exposed to wood smoke per se have been reported. There are some related studies with formaldehyde and environmental tobacco smoke but these are not discussed here.

Studies in Developing Countries

The health effects of inhalation of wood smoke have been documented in developing countries where women spend many hours close to an open unvented indoor fire used for cooking (2, 66). Increased respiratory symptoms, decreased pulmonary function, and large increases in the prevalence of chronic bronchitis have been reported in New Guinea, India, and Nepal. However, measurements of particulate matter have not been reported in most of these studies. Other studies, such as one in Nepal, compared concentrations of indoor particulate matter in huts where traditional cooking methods were practised to those where an improved cookstove was used (79). Concentrations of total suspended particulate matter in the former averaged 2.7 mg/m^3; a similar average concentration associated with the improved cook stove was 1.0 mg/m^3, still much higher than concentrations of particulate matter to which US populations currently are exposed. A recent report of indoor air pollution in a similar situation in China (indoor use of an open cooking fire) measured concentrations up to 25 mg/m^3 PM$_{10}$ (33).

A recent clinical report describes a group of 30 nonsmoking patients whose lung disease may be due to wood smoke exposure (81). These individuals were seen in Mexico City and all had a history of living in the countryside away from urban air pollution. The smoke exposure was the result of the use of wood and biomass for home cooking. These patients had abnormal chest X-ray scans showing a diffuse, bilateral, reticulonodular pattern, and evidence of pulmonary arterial hypertension. Their pulmonary function tests were consistent with a mixed restrictive-obstructive disease diagnosis. The authors suggest that this group of patients was suffering from wood-smoke inhalation-associated lung disease (WSIALD) (81).

Epidemiology

Reports of lung function decreases in children associated with fine particulate matter in the early 1980s (24, 27) inspired investigations of one source of those fine particles, wood smoke. Epidemiological investigations of adverse respiratory effects of wood smoke emissions in the US have centered on either symptomatology or pulmonary function. The symptoms measured have been the traditional respiratory disease outcomes; cough, wheeze, upper or lower respiratory infection. Pulmonary functions measured have been FEV_1, a measure of air flow limitation caused by obstruction in the airways, or FVC, a measure of the total amount of air that can be forcibly exhaled from the lungs. All but one of the available studies have been carried out in children, most likely on the assumption that children are most at risk for adverse effects from inhaled irritants due to the small size of their lungs and also due to the immature nature of their immune system. Other advantages of children as subjects in studies of respiratory effects of air pollution are the relative lack of confounders such as years of cigarette smoking or occupational exposure. There is good precedence from the numerous studies of the effects of environmental tobacco smoke on children's respiratory health for suspecting that young children are vulnerable to inhaled agents. Eight reports have been published of associations between lung function and wood smoke in children studied in the field and one study of responses in adult subjects, summarized in Table 4. An additional study of the association between visits to emergency departments for asthma and fine particulate matter (82) is included since this study was conducted in Seattle where a considerable percentage of fine particles are produced by residential wood burning.

The earliest report of adverse health effects from exposure to wood smoke in the US came from Michigan. Honicky and co-workers studied 31 young children who lived in homes with wood stoves and compared them to 31 children who lived in homes with other sources of home heating (41). They recorded respiratory symptoms over the telephone using a modified Epidemiology Standardization Project Children's Questionnaire (31). The occurrence of cough and wheeze was much greater in children from the homes with stoves and, in general, both moderate and especially severe symptoms

Table 4 Summary of studies of respiratory effects of exposure to wood smoke

Reference	Age (yr)	Number of subjects	Endpoints measured	Results
41	1–7 yr	34 w/stoves 34 without	Symptoms	More symptoms in children with stoves p < 0.001
93	5–11*	258 w/stoves 141 without	Symptoms	Risk ratio = 1.1, showing no significant effect
11	1 and older	455 high smoke** 368 low smoke	Symptoms disease prevalance	No significant effects. Trend in children aged 1–5
54	8–11	296 healthy*** 30 asthmatic	Spirometry	Significant association between fine particles and lung function in asthmatics, p = 0.05
14	1–5 ½	59	Symptoms	Significant correlation between wood-stove use and wheeze and cough frequency p = 0.01
68	<24 mo	58 pairs	Respiratory disease	Woodstove significant risk factor for lower resp infection
36	8–11	410***	Spirometry	Significant decrease in PFTs with elevated wood smoke
45	8–11	495	Spirometry	Significant relation of functional decrease with elevated wood smoke
64	$\bar{X}$ = 46	182	Symptoms	Significant association
82	all ages	2955, asthma 3810, gastro-enteritis	Emergency	Significant association between room visits asthma visits fine particles

*Described as kindergarten through grade 6.
**Geographical areas with high or low wood smoke pollution.
***Grades 3 through 6.

of respiratory diseases were significantly greater in the wood smoke-exposed children (p < 0.001). No measurements of wood smoke were reported.

Previously, Tuthill reported the results of an investigation of symptoms of respiratory illness and respiratory disease prevalence associated with wood smoke and formaldehyde exposure (93). Symptoms were collected using a questionnaire; chronic respiratory illness was defined as physician-diagnosed chronic bronchitis, asthma, or allergies. The subjects were 399 children from kindergarten through the sixth grade. Two hundred fifty eight lived in homes with wood stoves and 141 lived in homes without stoves. Although he found increased risk ratio = 2.4 (confidence intervals 1.7–3.4) for exposure to formaldehyde (from off-gassing of building materials after new construction or remodeling, from foam insulation, or from wood burning), the risk ratio for exposure to wood smoke of 1.1 (0.76–1.7) was not significant. The difficulty assigning formaldehyde exposure to sources other than wood burning was not discussed, although it is consistent with data from studies reviewed in Table 3.

The effects of wood stoves on general respiratory health in preschool age children was studied by Butterfield and others (14). Ten symptoms of respiratory disease were tracked in 59 children during the 1985–86 winter heating season in the Boise, Idaho, area. The children ranged in age from 1 to 5 1/2 years. Symptoms significantly associated with living in a home with a wood stove in use were frequency of wheeze, severity of wheeze, frequency of cough, and waking up at night with cough. An independent study of sources of extractable organic material in ambient particles in Boise during the 1986–87 heating season showed an average of 67% due to wood burning (61).

Another study compared the incidence of lower respiratory tract infection in Native American children with presence of a wood stove in the home (68). The children lived on the Navajo reservation in Arizona. Cases were children less than 24 months of age with lower respiratory tract infection (bronchiolitis or pneumonia) who were matched with a control case visiting the clinic as part of a well-child program. Fifty-eight age and gender matched pairs participated in the study. Forty-nine percent of the cases lived in homes using wood-burning for heat, whereas only 33 percent of the control children lived in such homes. In this study, living in a home with a wood burning source of heat was a risk factor for lower respiratory tract infection (odds ratio = 4.2, $p < 0.001$).

Heumann and co-workers (36) studied pulmonary function in a group of elementary school children in Klamath Falls, Oregon, using standard spirometric values. Pulmonary function test data were collected on 410 children in grades 3 through 6 at three time periods during the 1990 heating season. There was a significant decrease in average FEV_1 and FVC among children who had the highest exposure to wood smoke. A preliminary report of this study was presented (35); analysis is still ongoing.

The 1977 Montana legislature funded an extensive Montana Air Pollution Study (45), designed to evaluate whether air pollution was associated with adverse health effects in urban centers. The study involved third, fourth, and fifth grade children in five Montana cities. It measured lung function both within and between communities. Thus, lung function of school children living in communities with different levels of air pollution was ascertained. Also, comparisons of lung function changes of school children and air quality within a single community were evaluated. Each child served as his or her own control and analysis of covariance was used to test for statistical significance in the acute study within a single community. In the multicity study, linear regressions and principal components techniques were used and appropriate adjustments were made for factors such as altitude, which varied from city to city. Three-day averages of the pollutants were used. Both studies detected significant lung function effects associated with total suspended particulate matter (TSP) and both fine and coarse respirable particulate matter. Pulmonary function decrements ranged from 1% to 10%, 24-hr average TSP ranged from 24 to 128 $\mu g/m^3$ during the study period. Sources of the particulate matter were not identified, however the authors state that the particulate matter essentially was from wood burning and entrained dust. Measurements of fine particles ($PM_{3.5}$) during this period found 68% by weight attributable to wood smoke in Missoula, Montana (15).

One study in Denver, Colorado, of a panel of adult subjects with asthma was conducted evaluating the presence of a wood stove or fireplace in the home and symptoms of respiratory disease and shortness of breath (64). Using logistic regression analysis, the presence of a wood stove in the home was associated with shortness of breath in females and both shortness of breath and moderate or severe cough in males ($p < 0.01$ in all cases).

Two studies of the health effects of wood smoke have been conducted at the University of Washington. The first was a questionnaire study of respiratory health in areas of high and low ambient wood smoke pollution (11). The communities were chosen based on extensive air monitoring of wood smoke distributions in the greater Seattle area (56). Six hundred residences in each community were sent questionnaires and asked to answer for one adult and one children at each address. The initial questionnaire asked about chronic symptoms of respiratory disease, in mild, moderate, and severe categories (31). Two follow-up mailings asked about acute symptoms over the past two weeks. During the study period, PM_{10} concentrations in the low wood smoke area averaged 33 $\mu g/m^3$; in the high wood smoke area, the average for the three months of the study was 55 $\mu g/m^3$. Questionnaire responses were stratified by age; 1–5; 6–14; 14–44; 45–64; and >65. No statistically significant differences emerged between residents of the high and low wood smoke communities, however there was a pattern of increased symptoms and chronic illness in children aged 1–5 in the area with high wood smoke.

These suggestive data stimulated another study in the same air shed. In this second study, pulmonary function was measured in third through sixth grade children in two elementary schools in the area characterized as being affected by wood smoke (54). FEV_1 and FVC were measured before, during, and after the heating season in 326 children during 1988–89 and in just 26 children with asthma in 1989–90. Wood smoke was assessed using an integrating nephelometer, a light scattering device. In this airshed there is a high correlation between light scattering coefficient and PM_{10}. Analyses show that greater than 80% of particles in residential neighborhoods are from wood burning during winter months (57). Random and mixed effects models of statistical association were used to evaluate the relationships between lung function and wood smoke concentrations. Lung function measurements were compared with wood smoke concentrations for the previous 12 hr period from 7 p.m. to 7 a.m. Statistically significant decrements in both FEV_1 and FVC were seen in young children with asthma, both at the $p < 0.05$ level. FEV_1 and FVC dropped an average of 34 ml and 37 ml, respectively, for each unit of light scattering coefficient (1×10^{-4} m^{-1}). During the study period the PM_{10} levels were over 90 µg/m^3 on four nights in 1988–89 but not above 110; the highest value during 1989–90 was 103 µg/m^3. Thus, the National Ambient Air Quality Standard for PM_{10} was not violated during either heating season. It was concluded that wood smoke is significantly associated with respiratory function decrements in young children with asthma.

A study of the relationship between fine particulate matter and emergency room visits for asthma in the metropolitan Seattle area was designed to help determine whether air pollution is a risk factor for asthma (82). Using Poisson regressions controlling for weather, season, time trends, age, hospital, and day of the week, a significant association ($p < 0.005$) was found between fine particles measured at the residential monitoring station used in the studies described above and visits to emergency departments in eight participating hospitals. Analyses show that between 60 and 90% of particles in residential neighborhoods measured either gravimetrically or by nephelometers are from wood burning year round (57).

Suspended particulate air pollution is associated with decreased lung function and increased prevalence of respiratory disease symptoms in young children under 12 years of age (27). In this two-year study of the relationship between pulmonary function changes in third and fourth grade children and air pollutant alerts in Steubenville, Ohio, researchers found a decline in pulmonary function tests associated with increasing 24-hr concentrations of total suspended particulate matter (TSP). Peak values of TSP ranged from 27 µg/m^3 to 422 µg/m^3. The pulmonary function declines were small but persisted for up to two weeks. The elimination of children with reported prevalence of coughs, colds, and other respiratory symptoms did not change the estimated mean effect. Similar findings were reported from the Netherlands (24) in a study of children aged 6–11 years before and during an air stagnation episode, although the effects of allergy and chronic respiratory disease were not evaluated. More recently, Dockery and co-workers (26) have reported increased rates of cough, bronchitis, and chest illness in children exposed to inhaled particulate pollution.

It certainly is biologically plausible that wood smoke could cause adverse respiratory effects. The average size of the particles (< 1 µm) is such that these will travel deep into the lower respiratory tract (2). Some chemical species in wood smoke are chemically reactive and thus present a risk to respiratory tissues. The complex mixture of wood smoke allows deposition of reactive chemical onto particles that then can be carried into the alveolar region of the lung. As stated by Ammann (2), "irritants such as phenols, aldehydes, and quinones, as well as nitrogen oxides and sulfur oxides, in smoke may also contribute to both acute and chronic health problems. Generally irritants interfere with ciliary activity ... and hence the flow of the particle-trapping mucous stream. Inflammation, with all of its sequelae, also results."

In the earlier Six City Study report of children in Steubenville (27), a group median estimate of the slope between FVC and total suspended particulate was -0.081 mL/μg/m^3 for all children. When the estimate of a similar relationship (FVC/measure of fine particle concentration) is made using the Seattle data (54), the estimated mean FVC decrease per unit increase of PM$_{2.5}$ is -1.8 mL/μg/m^3 and $+0.34$ mL/μg/m^3 for asthmatic and nonasthmatic children, respectively. The FVC change per unit increase in PM$_{2.5}$ for the asthmatic children in our study is sufficiently pronounced as to suggest that fine particulate matter measured with a nephelometer may be more irritating than general industrial TSP. However, the difference between the two studies may be due solely to a increased sensitivity to airborne irritants in children with asthma. Based on prior work by Larson (56), the fine particulate matter measured on winter nights in this Seattle residential area is almost exclusively the result of residential wood-burning.

SUMMARY

In conclusion, this review reveals much about the constituents and fate of wood smoke but not enough about the health effects. Animal toxicological studies show that wood smoke exposure can disrupt cellular membranes, depress macrophage activity, destroy ciliated and secretory respiratory epithelial cells, and cause aberrations in biochemical enzyme levels. With respect to the human epidemiological data, the literature summarized in Table 4 shows a coherence of the data from young children, with 7/8 studies especially in children with asthma, reporting increased respiratory symptoms, lower respiratory infection, and decreased pulmonary function as a result of exposure to wood smoke. As Bates (6) has discussed, coherence of the data, although not amenable to statistical tests, carries the weight of linkage and plausibility. These adverse respiratory effects associated with wood smoke exposure also comply with many of Brandon Hill's aspects of association necessary to establish causation (40). There is strength of association, consistency (7/8 studies showing positive associations), temporality, plausibility, coherence, and analogy (using ETS exposure; 70, 94). A biological gradient has not been shown, although one is suggested in the study of pulmonary function in wildfire fighters. We conclude that the preponderance of the data suggest a causal relationship between elevated wood smoke levels and adverse respiratory health outcomes in young children.

Literature Cited

1. Alfheim I, Becker G, Hongslo JK, Ramdahl T. 1984. Mutagenicity testing of high performance liquid chromatography fraction from wood stove emission samples using a modified salmonella assay requiring smaller sample volumes. *Environ. Mut.* 6:91–102
2. Ammann H. 1986. Health implications of wood smoke. *Int. Congr. Resid. Wood Energy; Conf. Inst., Reno,* WSU WWREC, pp. 331–48
3. Anderson N. 1989. *Risk assessment document for residential wood combustion emissions.* Maine Dep. Hum. Serv.
4. Baechler MC. 1986. The compatibility of house tightening and residential wood burning: A case study of Bonneville power administration's analyses and programs. *Proc. Int. Conf. Resid. Wood Energy, Reno,* WSU WWREC, pp. 423–30
5. Bardana EJ Jr, Montanaro A. 1991. Formaldehyde: an analysis of its respiratory, cutaneous, and immunolgic effects. *Ann. Allergy* 66:441–52
6. Bates DV. 1992. Health indices of the adverse effects of air pollution: The question of coherence. *Environ. Res.* 59:336–49
7. Beck BD, Brain JD. 1982. Prediction of the pulmonary toxicity of respirable combustion products from residential wood and coal stoves. *Proc. Resid. Wood Coal Combust. Spec. Conf. (SP 45) Air Pollut. Control Assoc., Pittsburgh*
8. Benedict R, Naylor M. 1988. Fine particulate receptor modeling in Las Vegas using combined gaseous and particulate source profiles. See Ref. 66a, pp. 518–30
9. Benton G, Miller DP, Reimold M, Sisson R. 1982. A study of occupant exposure to particulates and gases from

woodstoves in homes. See Ref. 20a, pp. 539–50
10. Brizio-Molteni L, Piano G, Rice PL, Warpeha R, Fresco R, et al. 1984. Effect of wood combustion smoke inhalation on angiotensin-1-converting enzyme in the dog. *Ann. Clin. Lab. Sci.* 14:381–89
11. Browning KG, Koenig JQ, Checkoway H, Larson TV, Pierson WE. 1990. A questionnaire study of respiratory health in areas of high and low ambient wood smoke pollution. *Pediatr. Asthma All. Immunol.* 4:183–91
12. Burnet P, Edmisten NG, Tiegs PE, Houck JE, Yoder RA. 1986. Particulate, carbon monoxide, and acid emission factors for residential wood burning stoves. *J. Air Pollut. Control Assoc.* 36:1012–18
13. Butcher SS, Sorenson EM. 1979. A study of wood stove particulate emissions. *J. Air Pollut. Control Assoc.* 29:724–28
14. Butterfield P, LaCava G, Edmundson E, Penner J. 1989. Woodstoves and indoor air: The effects on preschoolers' upper respiratory systems. *J. Environ. Health* 52:172–73
15. Carlson JH. 1982. Residential wood combustion in Missoula, Montana: An overview of its air pollution contributions, health effects, and proposed regulatory solutions. See Ref. 20a, pp. 539–50
16. Chow JC, Watson JG, Frazier CA, Egami RT, Goodrich A, Ralph C. 1988. Spatial and temporal source contributions to PM_{10} and $PM_{2.5}$ in Reno, NV. See Ref. 66a, pp. 438–57
17. Clark WR, Nieman G, Hakim TS. 1990. Distribution of extravascular lung water after acute smoke inhalation. *J. Appl. Physiol.* 68:2394–402
18. Colome SD, Spengler JD. 1982. Res-

idential indoor and matched outdoor pollutant measurements with special consideration of wood-burning homes. See Ref. 20a, pp. 455–55

19. Cooke WM, Allen JM. 1982. Characterization of emission from residential wood combustion sources. See Ref. 20a, pp. 139–63

20. Cooper JA, Currie LA, Klouda GA. 1981. Assessment of contemporary carbon combustion sources to urban air particulate levels using carbon-14 measurements. *Environ. Sci. Technol.* 15: 1045–50

20a. Cooper JA, Malek D, eds. 1982. *Residential Solid Fuels: Environmental Impacts and Solutions.* Beaverton: Oregon Grad. Cent.

21. Core JE. 1989. Receptor modeling source profile development for the Pacific Northwest States: The Pacific Northwest source profile library. *EPA Region X, States of Oregon, Washington, Idaho, Puget Sound Air Pollut. Control Agency and Lane Reg. Air Pollut. Control Auth.*

22. Core JE, Cooper JA, Neulicht RM. 1984. Current and projected impacts of residential wood combustion on Pacific Northwest air quality. *J. Air Pollut. Control Assoc.* 34:138–43

23. Dasch JM. 1982. Particulate and gaseous emissions from wood-burning fireplaces. *Environ. Sci. Technol.* 16: 639–45

24. Dassen W, Brunekreef B, Hoek G, Hofschreuder P, Staatson B, et al. 1986. Decline in children's pulmonary function during an air pollution episode. *J. Air Pollut. Control. Assoc.* 36:1223–27

25. DeAngelis DG, Ruffin DS, Reznik RB. 1980. Preliminary characterization of emissions from wood-fired residential combustion equipment. *EPA-600/7–80–040.* Research Triangle Park: US EPA

25a. Dep. Health, Educ. Welf. 1979. *Smoking and health. Report of the Surgeon General.* DHEW Publ. No 79–50066

26. Dockery DW, Speizer FE, Stram DO, Ware JH, Spengler JD, Ferris BG Jr. 1989. Effects of inhalable particles on respiratory health of children. *Am. Rev. Respir. Dis.* 139:587–94

27. Dockery DW, Ware JH, Ferris BG Jr, Speizer FE, Cook NK, Herman SM. 1982. Change in pulmonary function in children associated with air pollution episodes. *J. Air Pollut. Control Assoc.* 32:937–42

28. Dost FN. 1991. Acute toxicology of components of vegetation smoke. *Rev. Environ. Contam. Toxicol.* 119:1–46

29. Dresser AL, Baird BK. 1988. A dispersion and receptor model analysis of the wintertime PM_{10} problem in Telluride, Colorado. See Ref. 66a, pp. 458–71

30. Edye LA, Richards GN. 1991. Analysis of condensates from wood smoke: Components derived from polysaccharides and lignins. *Environ. Sci. Technol.* 25:1133–37

31. Ferris BG. 1978. Epidemiology standardization project. *Am. Rev. Respir. Dis.* 118:1–53

32. Fick RB, Paul ES, Merrill WW, Reynolds HY, Loke JSO. 1984. Alterations in the antibacterial properties of rabbit pulmonary macrophages exposed to wood smoke. *Am. Rev. Respir. Dis.* 129:76–81

33. Harris BB, Chapman RS, Mumford JL. 1992. *Battery powered PM_{10} indoor air samplers applied to unvented Third World residential sources.* Presented at 85th Annu. Meet. Air Waste Manage. Assoc., Kansas City

34. Hawthorne SB, Krieger MS, Miller DJ, Mathiason MB. 1989. Collection and quantitation of methoxylated phenol tracers for atmospheric pollution from residential wood stoves. *Environ. Sci. Technol.* 23:470–75

35. Hawthorne SB, Miller DJ, Barkley RM, Krieger MS. 1988. Identification of methoxylated phenols as candidate tracers for atmospheric wood smoke pollution. *Environ. Sci. Technol.* 22: 1191–96

36. Heumann MA, Foster LR, Johnson L, Kelly LE. 1991. *Woodsmoke air pollution and changes in pulmonary function among elementary school children.* Presented at 84th Annu. Meet. Air Waste Manage. Assoc., Vancouver, BC

37. Highsmith VR, Merrill RG, Zweidinger RB. 1988. Characterization of the indoor and outdoor air associated with residences using woodstoves in Raleigh. *Environ. Int.* 14:213–19

38. Highsmith VR, Rodes C, Zweidinger RB, Lewtas J. 1988. Influence of residential wood combustion on indoor air quality of Boise, ID, residences. *Proc. EPA/Air Pollut. Control Assoc. Sym. Measure. Toxic Related Air Pollut. APCA Publ. VIP-10 (EPA 600/9–88–015),* pp. 804–13

39. Highsmith VR, Rodes CE, Zweidinger RB, Merrill RG. 1987. The collection of neighborhood air samples impacted by residential wood combustion in

Raleigh, NC and Albuquerque, NM. *Proc. EPA/Air Pollut. Control Assoc. Symp. Measure. Toxic Related Air Pollut. APCA Publ. VIP-8 (EPA 600/9–87–010)*, pp. 562–72

40. Hill AB. 1965. The environment and disease: association or causation? *Proc. R. Soc. Med.* 58:295–300

41. Honicky RE, Osborne JS III, Akpom CA. 1985. Symptoms of respiratory illness in young children and the use of wood-burning stoves for indoor heating. *Pediatrics* 75:587–93

42. Hornig JF, Soderberg RH, Larsen D, Parravano C. 1982. Ambient air assessment in rural village and small town locations in New Hampshire where wood is an important fuel. See Ref. 20a, pp. 506–19

43. Hough M. 1988. Oregon's approach to reducing residential woodsmoke as part of the PM$_{10}$ strategy. In *Trans. PM$_{10}$ Implementation and Standards*, pp. 646–53. Air Pollut. Control Assoc. Spec. Conf., San Francisco

44. Imhoff RE. 1982. Final report on a study of the ambient impact of residential wood combustion in Petersville, Alabama. In *Residential Wood and Coal Combustion Air Pollut. Control Assoc. Spec. Conf. Proc. SP-45*, pp 161–88

45. Johnson KG, Gideon RA, Loftsgaarden DO. 1990. Montana air pollution study: Children's health effects. *J. Official Stat.* 5:391–407

46. Kalman D, Larson TV. 1987. *Puget Sound receptor modeling feasibility study final report*. Rep. submitted to the Puget Sound Air Pollut. Control Agency

47. Kamens RM, Rives GD, Perry JM, Bell DA, Paylor RF Jr, et al. 1984. Mutagenic changes in dilute wood smoke as it ages and reacts with ozone and nitrogen dioxide: An outdoor chamber study. *Environ. Sci. Technol.* 18: 523–30

48. Khalil MAK, Edgerton SA, Rasmussen RA. 1983. A gaseous tracer model for air pollution from residential wood burning. *Environ. Sci. Technol.* 17: 555–59

49. Kleindienst TE, Shepson PB, Edney EO, Claxton LD, Cupitt LT. 1986. Wood smoke: measurement of the mutagenic activities of its gas- and particle-phase photooxidation products. *En-, viron. Sci. Technol.* 20:493–501

50. Klouda GA, Barraclough D, Currie LA, Zweidinger RB, Lewis CW, Stevens RK. 1991. *Source apportionment of wintertime organic aerosols in Boise,*

ID by chemical and isotopic (^{14}C) methods. Presented at 84th Annu. Meet. Air Waste Manage. Assoc., Vancouver, BC

51. Klouda GA, Currie LA, Sheffield AE, Wise SA, Benner BA, et al. 1987. *The source apportionment of carbonaceous combustion products by microradiocarbon measurements for the integrated air cancer project. Proc. EPA/Air Pollut. Control Assoc. Sym. Measure. Toxic Related Air Pollut., APCA Publ. VIP-8 (EPA 600/9–87–010)*, pp. 573–78

52. Knight CV, Humphreys MP, Kuberg DW. 1985. Summary of three-year study related to wood heater impacts on indoor air quality. *Proc. Int. Conf. Residential Wood Energy*, pp. 409–22. Reno

53. Koenig JQ, Covert DS, Larson TV, Maykut N, Jenkins P, Pierson WE. 1988. Wood smoke: Health effects and legislation. *Northwest. Environ. J.* 4: 41–54

54. Koenig JQ, Larson TV, Hanley QS, Rebolledo V, Dumler K, et al. 1993. Pulmonary function changes in children associated with fine particulate matter. *Environ. Res.* 63:26–38

55. Kowalczyk JF, Greene WT. 1982. New techniques for identifying ambient air impacts from residential wood heating. See Ref. 20a, pp. 469–94

56. Larson TV, Kalman D, Wang S, Nothstein G. 1990. *Urban air toxics mitigation study*. Rep. submitted to Puget Sound Air Pollut. Control Agency, June

57. Larson TV, Koenig JQ. 1993. A summary of the chemistry, emissions, and non cancer respiratory effects of wood smoke. *EPA 453/R-93–008*

58. Larson TV, Yuen PF, Maykut N. 1992. Weekly composite sampling of PM$_{2.5}$ for total mass and trace elemental analysis. In *Proc. Air Waste Manage. Assoc. Spec. Conf. Fugitive Emissions and PM$_{10}$ Control Strategies*, Scottsdale

59. Lewis CW, Baumgardner R, Stevens RK, Claxton L, Lewtas J. 1983. The contribution of wood smoke and motor vehicle emissions to ambient aerosol mutagenicity. *Environ. Sci. Technol.* 22:968–71

60. Lewis CW, Baumgardner RE, Stevens RK, Rosswurm GM. 1986. Receptor modeling of Denver winter haze. *Environ. Sci. Technol.* 20:1126–36

61. Lewis CW, Stevens RK, Zweidinger RB, Claxton LD, Barraclough D, Klouda, GA. 1991. *Source apportion-*

ment of mutagenic activity of fine particle organics in Boise, Idaho. Presented at 84th Annu. Meet. Air Waste Manage. Assoc., Vancouver, BC

62. Lipari F, Dasch JM, Scruggs WF. 1984. Aldehyde emissions from woodburning fireplaces. Environ. Sci. Technol. 18:326–30

63. Lipfert FW, Dungan JL. 1983. Residential firewood use in the United States. Science 219:1425–27

64. Lipsett M, Ostro B, Mann J, Wiener M, Selner J. 1991. Effects of exposures to indoor combustion sources on asthmatic symptoms. Presented at 84th Annu. Meet. Air Waste Manage. Assoc., Vancouver, BC

65. Magliano KL. 1988. Level 1 PM$_{10}$ assessment in a California air basin. See Ref. 66a, pp. 508–17

66. Marbury MC. 1991. Wood smoke. In Indoor Air Pollution, ed. JM Samet, JD Spengler, pp. 209–22. Baltimore: Johns Hopkins Press

66a. Mathai CV, Stonefield DH, eds. 1988. Transactions, PM10 Implementation and Standards. Pittsburgh: Air Pollut. Control Assoc.

67. Merrill R, Zweidinger R, Martz R, Koinis R. 1988. Semivolatile and condensible organic materials distribution in ambient and woodstove emissions. Proc. EPA/ Air Pollut. Control Assoc. Sym. Measure. Toxic Related Air Pollut., APCA Publ. VIP-10 (EPA 600/9–88–015), pp. 828–34

68. Morris K, Morganlander M, Coulehan JL, Gahagen S, Arena VC. 1990. Wood-burning stoves and lower respiratory tract infection in American Indian children. Am. J. Dis. Child 144: 105–8

69. Murphy D, Buchan RM, Fox DG. 1982. Ambient particulate and benzo(a)pyrene concentrations from residential wood combustion, in a mountain resort community. See Ref. 20a, pp. 495–505

70. Natl. Acad. Sci. 1986. Environmental tobacco smoke; Measuring exposures and assessing health effects. Natl. Res. Counc., Washington, DC

71. Naylor MN. 1985. Air pollution from fireplaces in Las Vegas, Nevada. Presented at 78th Annu. Meet. Air Pollut. Control Assoc., Detroit

72. Nestrick TJ, Larparski LL. 1982. Isomer-specific determination of chlorinated dioxins for assessment of formation and potential environmental emission from wood combustion. Anal. Chem. 54:2292–99

73. Neulicht RM, Core J. 1982. Impact of residential wood combustion appliances on indoor air quality. In Residential Wood and Coal Combustion. Air Pollut. Control Assoc. Spec. Conf. Proc. SP-45, pp. 240–52

74. OMNI Environ. Serv. 1988. Environmental impacts of advanced residential and institutional (woody) biomass combustion systems. Final Rep. US DOE Pac. Northwest. and Alaska Reg. Biomass Energy Progr. Contract: DE AC79–86 BP61196

75. Pierson WE, Koenig JQ, Bardana EJ Jr. 1989. Potential adverse health effects of wood smoke. West. J. Med. 151:339–42

76. Ramdahl T. 1983. Retinue—a molecular marker of wood combustion in ambient air. Nature 306:580–82

77. Ramdahl T, Schjoldager J, Currie LA, Hanssen JE, Moller M, et al. 1985. Ambient impact of residential wood combustion in Elverum, Norway. Sci. Total Environ. 36:81–90

78. Rau JA. 1989. Composition and size distribution of residential wood smoke particles. Aerosol Sci. Technol. 10: 181–92

79. Reid HF, Smith KR, Sherchand B. 1986. Indoor smoke exposures from traditional and improved cookstoves: Comparisons among rural Nepali women. Mountain Res. Dev. 6:293–304

80. Romero AE, Buchman RM, Fox DG. 1978. A study of air pollution from fireplace emissions at Vail Ski Resort. Environ. Health 41:117–19

81. Sandoval J, Salas J, Martinez-Garcia M, Gomez A, Martinez C, et al. 1992 Pulmonary arterial hypertension and cor pulmonale associated with chronic domestic woodsmoke inhalation. Chest 103:12–20

82. Schwartz J, Slater D, Larson TV, Pierson WE, Koenig JQ. 1993. Particulate air pollution and hospital emergency visits for asthma. Am. Rev. Respir. Dis. 147:826 31

83. Sexton K, Spengler JD, Treitman RD. 1984. Effects of residential wood combustion on indoor air quality: A case study of Waterbury, VT. Atmos. Environ. 18:1371–83

84. Sexton K, Spengler JD, Treitman RD, Turner WA. 1984. Winter air quality in a wood-burning community: A case study in Waterbury, Vermont. Atmos. Environ. 18:1357–70

85. Skog EK, Wattersen IA. 1983. Survey completion report, residential fuel wood use in the United States: 1980-81. US Dep. Agric., Forest Serv. Rep.

86. Deleted in proof
87. Standley LJ, Simoneit BRT. 1990. Preliminary correlation of organic molecular tracers in residential wood smoke with the source of the fuel. *Atmos. Environ. B* 24:67–73
88. Steiber RS, Dorsey J. 1988. GC/MS analysis of stove emissions and ambient samples from a woodsmoke impacted area. *Proc. EPA/APCA Sym. Measure. Toxic Related Air Pollut., Air Pollut. Control Assoc. Publ. VIP-10 (EPA 600/9–88–015)*, pp. 828–34
89. Steiber RS, McCrillis RC, Dorsey JA, Merrill RG Jr. 1992. *Characterization of condensable and semivolatile organic materials from Boise woodstove samples.* Presented at 85th Annu. Meet. Air Waste Manage. Assoc., Kansas City
90. Thorning DR, Howard ML, Hudson LD, Schumacher RL. 1982. Pulmonary responses to smoke inhalation: Morphological changes in rabbits exposed to pine wood smoke. *Hum. Pathol.* 13:355–64
91. Traynor GW, Apte MG, Carruthers AR, Dillworth JF, Grimsrud DT, Gundel LA. 1987. Indoor air pollution due to emissions from wood-burning stoves. *Environ. Sci. Technol.* 21:691–97
92. Truesdale RS. 1984. *Characterization of emissions from a fluidized bed wood chip home heating furnace.* NTIS #PB84–179878
93. Tuthill RW. 1984. Woodstoves, formaldehyde, and respiratory diseases. *Am. J. Epidemiol.* 120:952–55
94. US Environ. Prot. Agency. 1992. *Respiratory health effects of passive smoking: Lung cancer and other disorders.* 600/6–90/006F
95. van Houdt JJ, Daenen CMJ, Boleij JSM, Alink GM. 1986. Contribution of wood stoves and fire places to mutagenic activity of airborne particulate matter inside homes. *Mut. Res.* 171:91–98
96. Watson JG. 1979. *Chemical element balance receptor-model methodology of assessing the sources of fine and total suspended particulate matter in Portland, Oregon.* PhD thesis. Environ. Sci., Oregon Grad. Cent., Portland
97. Wolff GT, Countess RJ, Groblicki PJ, Ferman MA, Cadle SH, Muhlbaier JL. 1981. Visibility-reducing species in the Denver "Brown Cloud"-II. sources and temporal patterns. *Atmos. Environ.* 15:2485–502
98. Wong KL, Stock MF, Malek DE, Alarie Y. 1984. Evaluation of the pulmonary effect of wood smoke in guinea pigs by repeated CO_2 challenges. *Toxicol. Appl. Pharmacol.* 75:69–80
99. Zeedijk IH. 1986. Polycyclic aromatic hydrocarbon concentrations in smoke aerosol of domestic stoves burning wood and coal. *J. Aerosol Sci.* 17:635–38
100. Zweidinger RB, Tejada S, Highsmith VR, Westburg H, Gage L. 1988. Volatile organic hydrocarbon and aldehyde distribution for the IACP Boise, ID, Residential study. *Proc. EPA/ Air Pollut. Control Assoc. Sym. Measure. Toxic Related Air Pollut., APCA Publ. VIP-10 (EPA 600/9–88–015)*, pp. 814–20

Annu. Rev. Public Health. 1994. 15:157–78
Copyright © 1994 by Annual Reviews Inc. All rights reserved

PUBLIC HEALTH RISKS FROM MOTOR VEHICLE EMISSIONS

Mark J. Utell

Departments of Medicine and Environmental Medicine, University of Rochester Medical Center, Rochester, New York 14642

Jane Warren[1]

Health Effects Institute, 141 Portland Street, Suite 7300, Cambridge, Massachusetts 02139

Robert F. Sawyer

Department of Mechanical Engineering, University of California, Berkeley, California 94720

KEY WORDS: air pollution, carbon monoxide, health effects, motor vehicles, ozone

INTRODUCTION

The automobile was first identified as a major contributor to urban air pollution in Los Angeles, California, in the 1940s. With continued growth in the number of motor vehicles and the total number of miles driven, every major urban area worldwide now experiences air pollution problems traceable to its automobiles. Johnson (29) reviews current automotive emissions issues.

Motor vehicle emissions, and their atmospheric derivatives, include *regulated* or criteria pollutants, for which National Ambient Air Quality Standards (NAAQS) are set, and *unregulated* pollutants, the myriad of pollutants for which no standards exist. The contribution of motor vehicles to regulated

---

[1]Views expressed in this article have not been evaluated in HEI's review process and are not intended to represent the views of HEI.

0163-7525/94/0510-0157$05.00

pollutants is controlled through emissions standards. Section 202(a)(1) of the Clean Air Act (CAA) gives the EPA Administrator authority to prescribe (and from time to time revise) ... standards applicable to the emission of any air pollutant from ... new motor vehicles or motor vehicle engines, which may ... cause, or contribute to, air pollution which may reasonably be anticipated to endanger public health or welfare. Section 202(a)(4) states that no new technologies designed to decrease exposure to certain pollutants should result in increased health risk.

There are large numbers of compounds in the ambient air derived from motor vehicle emissions that at some concentration are toxic. Because motor vehicle pollutants do not have unique effects and, for the most part, are present at low concentrations in ambient air, it is difficult to determine their contribution to health effects. However, the fact that effects are hard to quantify does not mean that they may not be of public health significance. Adverse effects in a small percent of the population could result in large numbers being affected. In particular, some individuals may be sensitive because of genetic factors, pre-existing disease, age, lifestyle, or other conditions that affect dose retained, metabolism, or response.

This paper addresses the issue of outdoor air pollution in the context of motor vehicle emissions and consequent health effects. First, it reviews the characteristics of motor vehicle emissions and introduces the concept of emission controls. Next, the health effects and possible mechanisms of the principal outdoor air pollutants are addressed. Finally, it focuses on two criteria pollutants for which important new health data exist: ozone, a direct toxicant to the respiratory tract, and carbon monoxide (CO) for which the lungs merely act as a conduit.

EXPOSURE CHARACTERIZATION

Motor Vehicles, Engines, and Fuels

In US cities, passenger cars, light duty trucks and vans, primarily powered by gasoline engines, dominate motor vehicle emissions. Heavy duty trucks and buses are primarily powered by diesel engines. Both gasoline and diesel engines power medium duty trucks.

BEFORE CONTROLS   The uncontrolled gasoline engine operated fuel rich, and emitted high levels of CO. The gasoline that it burned contained a lead additive to control engine knocking and produced lead oxide emissions. Hydrocarbons, ranging from methane to raw fuel components, were emitted uncontrolled from the engine exhaust and crankcase ventilation, and evaporated from the fuel system. Additional hydrocarbon vapors freely flowed from the fuel tank during refueling. Oxides of nitrogen (NO_x), primarily nitric oxide (NO), were produced in the high-temperature combustion environment and emitted unabated from the exhaust.

Diesel engines were inherently low emitters of CO and hydrocarbons. They shared the gasoline engine's NO_x emission problem and also emitted a carbonaceous particulate, the often visible black smoke associated with diesel trucks and buses.

GASOLINE ENGINES   The gasoline engine mixes and evaporates its liquid fuel into air before the spark-ignited combustion process begins. Ideally, a homogeneous, fully vaporized mixture is obtained before combustion. A volatile fuel helps this process, which is particularly difficult during cold starting, but high fuel volatility increases evaporative emissions. Maintaining the proper, uniform, fully vaporized, fuel-air mixture in each cylinder and over all operating conditions is essential to low emissions.

DIESEL ENGINES   In a diesel engine, liquid fuel is injected at high pressure directly into the cylinder, which contains compressed air at sufficiently high temperature to ignite the fuel, which burns as it evaporates. This fuel-rich combustion zone leads to fuel pyrolysis and the formation of soot. The diesel operates overall with an excess of air so that later in the combustion process CO and hydrocarbons burn to low concentrations. The soot burns more slowly and can survive to be emitted in the exhaust. NO_x is formed in high-temperature regions as in the gasoline engine.

MOTOR VEHICLE FUELS AND ADDITIVES   Practically all fuel used in motor vehicles is derived from petroleum. Modern refineries produce fuels tailored to specific engines, with an overall objective of maximizing the yield of high-value gasoline and diesel fuels. Interest in alternate motor fuels, such as natural gas, methanol, ethanol, and mixtures, relates to potential air quality benefits and to reducing dependence upon petroleum. The CAA Amendments of 1990 and California Air Resources Board regulations require introduction of reformulated gasoline to reduce emissions. Reducing vapor pressure, sulfur, heavy molecular weight compounds, olefins, and aromatics and adding oxygenates in reformulated gasoline reduces emissions (see Table 1).

The CAA amendments require use of oxygenates in gasoline in 39 areas of the U.S. that exceed the NAAQS for CO. In the winter of 1992, several cities started using methyl-tertiary butyl ether (MTBE) at levels up to 15% in fuel. MTBE had previously been used, at concentrations up to 4%, as an octane booster in the late 1970s, when lead was being phased out, and in the 1980s at concentrations up to 8% to reduce CO levels in some areas.

Table 1 ARCO EC-X reformulated gasoline emissions reductions in light duty passenger cars and trucks with three-way catalysts (13)

Species	Percent change
Total hydrocarbons (THC)	−31
Nonmethane organic gases (NMOG)	−36
NO_x	−26
CO	−26
Toxics, total	−46
Benzene	−52
1,3-butadiene	−32
Formaldehyde	+18
Acetaldehyde	−31
Evaporative hydrocarbons	−35
Reactivity, MIR, THC	−14
Reactivity, MIR, NMOG	−8

Emissions and Their Control

The first motor vehicle emissions regulations were imposed in California during the 1960s and subsequently in the remainder of the U.S. and in most other industrialized countries. Regulatory requirements are based on emissions standards and specification of standard test procedures. Tailpipe emissions standards currently represent tailpipe emission reductions of 96% of hydrocarbons, 96% of CO, and 76% of NO_x compared to precontrol light duty vehicles. The comparable numbers for heavy duty vehicles are 90%, 90%, and 50%, respectively. The CAA amendments of 1990 call for even lower levels (see Table 2), and the State of California has adopted still more stringent reductions, including the production and sale of some "zero emission vehicles," which generally are interpreted to be electric.

The 1990 CAA amendments require regulation of vehicles or fuels (or both) to control hazardous air pollutants. These regulations are to apply at a minimum to benzene and formaldehyde and are to be based on a study by EPA (59) that focuses "on those categories of emissions which pose the greatest risk to human health or about which significant uncertainties remain, including . . . benzene, formaldehyde, and 1,3-butadiene." Mobile source toxic air pollutants are defined in the CAA amendments as benzene, 1,3-butadiene, polycyclic organic matter, acetaldehyde, and formaldehyde.

Table 3 provides comparative information on emissions of NAAQS pollutants or precursors (volatile organic compounds, VOCs) in 1981 and 1990. Although lead emissions have decreased dramatically and emissions

Table 2   United States passenger car emission standards, to be met at 80,000 km, Federal Test Procedure. Requirements in 1994 and subsequent years established by the Clean Air Act amendments of 1990

Species	1960[a]	1981–1993	1994–1996	2004[b]
HC (g/km)	6.6	.26	.16[c]	.078
NO_x (g/km)	2.6	.62	.25	.125
CO (g/km)	52.5	2.12	2.12	1.1
Evap HC (g/test)	46.6	2.0	2.0[d]	2.0[d]

[a] precontrol
[b] 160,000 km, to be reviewed by the Administrator of the EPA
[c] nonmethane hydrocarbons
[d] new test procedure

of CO and VOCs significantly, emissions from motor vehicles have fallen less than might be suggested by the emissions standards. The number of motor vehicles, miles traveled, and fuel consumed have eroded the reductions in tailpipe and evaporative emissions. Standards are for new vehicles but the in-use fleet has a distribution of vehicle years. Test methods do not adequately mimic the range of actual vehicle usage and environmental conditions. Also, vehicles do not emit over their lifetimes at the standards to which they were certified, due to poor maintenance, component failures, misfueling, and other causes.

Regulations on pollutant emissions have brought major changes in gasoline engine design. Crankcases and fuel systems are now sealed to reduce hydrocarbon vapor release. In the fuel system a canister containing activated charcoal collects and stores hydrocarbon vapors that are then burned in the engine. The critical emissions control component is the exhaust catalyst that originally was added to assist in the oxidation of hydrocarbons and CO. Extending catalyst control to include NO_x required constraining the engine air-fuel ratio to precisely stoichiometrically correct conditions, which led to the introduction of computer-control of the engine. The computer has revolutionized engine design and operation, allowing emissions reductions and also improving fuel economy and vehicle drivability. Emissions from new cars in good operating condition are greatly reduced from precontrol levels.

However, the efficiency of catalysts is low until the engine is warmed up. In modern vehicles, most CO emissions occur during cold start, particularly on cold days and in cold climates. Catalyst oxidation of CO requires precise fuel-air ratio control. Enrichment for increasing power at conditions outside of the certification test increases CO emissions.

Hundreds of different hydrocarbon compounds have been identified in engine exhaust, but there are probably thousands more. These compounds vary

Table 3 National emissions estimates for NAAQS pollutants for transportation and other source (58)

Emission source	Year	National emissions estimates (million metric tons/yr)					
		VOC[a]	CO[b]	NO$_x$[c]	SO$_x$[d]	PM$_{10}$[e]	Lead
Transportation	1981	8.9	55.4	9.9	0.9	1.3 (1985)	46.5
	1990	6.4	37.6	7.5	0.9	1.5	2.2
Total	1981	21.3	77.5	20.9	22.5	6.0	56.0
	1990	18.7	60.1	19.6	21.2	6.4	7.1

[a] Volatile organic compounds
[b] Carbon monoxide
[c] Nitrogen oxides
[d] Sulfur oxides
[e] Particulate matter less than 10 μm in diameter

in molecular weight from methane to heavy unburned fuel components to traces of polycyclic aromatic hydrocarbons. Partially oxygenated compounds, such as aldehydes, alcohols, and ketones, are also formed in the engine.

Control of emissions of hydrocarbons follows the same approaches, and faces the same problems, as for CO. A second important source of hydrocarbons is evaporation from the fuel system. The problem is worsened by high ambient and engine-operating temperatures and by high fuel volatilities. New evaporative emission test procedures will impose higher temperature requirements and catch emissions missed by the current test. Until vehicles are introduced that meet the new test requirements, current automobiles have greater hydrocarbon emissions than regulations would suggest. The lowering of fuel vapor pressure is required in many areas and will immediately reduce evaporative hydrocarbons.

NO is the dominant oxide of nitrogen. Nitrogen dioxide (NO_2), nitrous oxide (N_2O), and nitrous acid (HONO) also can be present. The three-way catalyst (oxidizes CO and hydrocarbons and reduces NO_x) is an effective control for NO_x. Another approach used on many vehicles is exhaust gas recirculation to reduce peak cylinder temperatures.

Tetra alkyl lead compounds as fuel additives to reduce engine knock produce lead oxide particulates. An unequivocal success in motor vehicle emissions control has been the near elimination of these emissions. Unleaded gasoline was essential to the introduction of catalyst control technology. The use of tetra alkyl lead compounds in motor fuel ended completely in 1993. Another antiknock additive, an organic manganese compound, is banned in the U.S. but used in Canada.

The soluble organic fraction of diesel particulate contains polycyclic aromatic hydrocarbons and nitroaromatics. A combination of technologies

Table 4 Urban air pollution and air quality standards

Pollutant	Sensitive population	Effects	Averaging time	Primary US NAAQS	Ca Std	Peak ambient concentrations (45) Los Angeles 1991	Peak ambient concentrations (45) Mexico City 1986–89
Ozone (ppm)	Exercising children and young adults	Respiratory symptoms, lung function decrements, decreased exercise capacity, lung inflammation	1 hr[a]	0.12	0.09	0.32	0.44
CO (ppm)	Individuals with coronary artery disease	Myocardial ischemia (including angina) during exercise	1 hr	35	20	30	—
			8 hr	9.5	9 (6[b])	17.4	24
NO_2 (ppm)	Children, asthmatics	Respiratory symptoms, lung function decrements, increased airway reactivity	1 hr	—	0.25	0.38	0.32
			1 yr	.053	—	—	—
SO_2 (ppm)	Asthmatics	Respiratory symptoms, decrements in lung function	1 hr	—	0.25	—	—
			24 hr	0.14	0.04	0.019	0.14
			1 yr	0.03[d]	—	—	—
PM_{10}[c] ($\mu g/m^3$)	Individuals with respiratory disease	Increased mortality, respiratory symptoms, decrements in lung function	24 hr	150	50	340	—
			1 yr	50[d]	30[e]	—	—
Lead ($\mu g/m^3$)	Fetuses and young children	Impairment of neural development	30 day	—	1.5	—	—
			3 mo	1.5	—	0.014	1.9

[a] Allowed once in one year averaged over the preceding three years
[b] Lake Tahoe Air Basin only
[c] Particulate matter less than 10 μm in diameter
[d] Arithmetic mean
[e] Geometric mean

is proving successful in meeting the difficult problem of lowering particulate emissions from diesel engines. Higher pressure, computer-controlled fuel injection systems improve fuel evaporation and mixing with the air and thereby reduce soot formation and improve soot oxidation in the combustion chamber. Further soot reduction can be obtained with a continuously operating catalyzed trap or a trap that stores particulate, which is periodically burned off.

Sulfur oxides, a consequence of sulfur in motor fuels, are being reduced by lowering sulfur in diesel fuel to less than 0.05%. Levels in gasoline are generally less than 0.03% and will be reduced to about 0.003% in reformulated gasoline.

Atmospheric Transport and Transformation

Dispersion processes affect the concentrations of pollutants to which people are exposed. The highest concentrations of primary pollutants (emitted directly from motor vehicles) occur near their source. The highest concentrations of secondary pollutants (formed in atmospheric reactions, such as ozone, nitrogen dioxide, and photochemical aerosols) often occur away from the sources of their precursors. Outdoor and indoor concentrations can vary greatly.

Concentrations of the primary pollutants, CO, NO, diesel particulate, and lead particulate are greatest on or near highly trafficked freeways, in congested streets, and in confined regions such as tunnels and parking garages. Dilution occurs through atmospheric mixing. Highest concentrations are experienced in enclosed, or partially enclosed, environments, for example, inside automobiles.

Ozone, the most important component of photochemical smog, results from a complex reaction of hydrocarbon and NO_x precursors in the presence of sunlight. Other oxidant compounds, such as NO_2, SO_2, aldehydes, nitrates, and organic and inorganic acids are also important components of photochemical smog, and account for perhaps half of the total oxidizing power. Monitoring and control measures focus on ozone on the reasonable presumption that it is generally a good surrogate for total photochemical smog. Both gas and aerosol phase pollutants are present in urban atmospheres.

Ozone concentrations are highly variable throughout the day, peaking in the late afternoon and falling to near zero at night. Levels are lower indoors than outdoors, with the ratio depending upon ventilation. Peak levels depend on the photochemical reactivity of the hydrocarbon precursors, which vary greatly among compounds, hydrocarbon to NO_x ratios, and previous day conditions. Historically, control of ozone has focused on the control of hydrocarbons. Recently, the importance of NO_x, especially in nonurban regions, has been recognized.

Atmospheric Concentrations and Exposure

Personal exposure to air pollution represents the time-weighted average of pollutant concentrations in microenvironments with relatively homogeneous air quality. Thus, for an office worker, relevant microenvironments might include home, office, car, outdoors at home, outdoors at work, and a movie theater. For some pollutants (e.g. ozone or acid aerosols), outdoor environments may make the predominant contribution to total personal exposure; for others (e.g. NO_2 and formaldehyde), indoor locations are most important. Assessment of the exposure of individuals requires combining environmental levels with activity patterns.

Ambient pollutant levels in cities are monitored at a few arbitrarily located outdoor sites. Averaging times range from hours (for ozone and CO) to months (for particulates). Such measurements cannot adequately reflect the exposure of those who do not live near the monitoring stations, those who spend time indoors, or those who are mobile.

The Los Angeles basin has the worst air quality of US urban areas. In 1989 one or more of the federal air quality standards was exceeded on 219 days (51). Ozone, the most serious problem, reaches concentrations almost three times the NAAQS. Table 4 summarizes recent peak ambient concentrations for criteria pollutants in Los Angeles and Mexico City and lists the

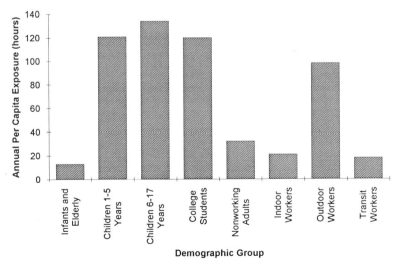

Figure 1   Distribution of annual exposure in the Los Angeles air basin to ozone levels above the NAAQS according to population group (62).

standards for comparison. An assessment of microenvironmental pollutant concentrations and activity patterns in the Los Angeles basin showed that children spend four hours and adults one hour outdoors per day (62). Outdoor/indoor/in-vehicle concentration ratios were estimated to be 1/0.5/0.2 for ozone and 1/0.7/1 for PM_{10}. There was a large range in exposure to ozone among different groups (Figure 1). Infants and the elderly are exposed for 18 hr per year to ozone levels above the NAAQS compared to 134 hr for children aged 6 to 17.

HEALTH EFFECTS

Overview

The development of air quality standards or assignment of risk for acute and chronic inhalation of low-level environmental pollutants is complex. Typically, the database for risk assessment arises from three investigational approaches: epidemiology, animal toxicology, and human inhalation studies. Each possesses both advantages and limitations. For example, epidemiologic studies examine exposures in the "real world" but struggle with confounding factors like cigarette smoking, socioeconomic status, and occupational exposures, as well as difficulties in characterizing complex exposures. In contrast, inhalation studies in animals allow precision in quantifying exposure duration and concentration, measurement of a wide variety of physiological, biochemical, and histological endpoints, and examination of extremes of the exposure-response relationship. Interpretation of animal studies is often constrained by difficulty in extrapolating findings to humans. Human clinical studies use relevant atmospheric conditions in laboratory settings and document health-related effects from breathing the atmospheres. These studies can characterize dose-response relationships as well as examine interaction between pollutants per se or with other variables such as exercise, humidity, or temperature. Susceptible populations can be studied. For practical and ethical reasons, studies must be limited to small groups, to short durations of exposure, and to pollutant concentrations that are expected to produce only mild and transient responses. Endpoints that can be used are also limited.

Table 4 presents the health basis for the regulation of criteria pollutants and groups identified as sensitive to these pollutants. The standards are based on effects in humans, often in sensitive groups, at the lowest concentrations of exposure. Animal data are generally used to provide supportive evidence and to suggest a margin of safety. Lead exposure, while still of major concern in children, for example from eating paint that contains lead, is no longer a problem related to motor vehicle emissions in the U.S., although it is in other countries.

Many diseases or conditions involving various organ systems are affected by pollutants derived from motor vehicle emissions. While many inhaled pollutants have direct respiratory consequences, others affect the heart or nervous system (Table 4). Furthermore, pollutant exposure may alter normal activities and life-style. Within the respiratory tract itself, pollutants derived from motor vehicle emissions have the potential to induce bronchoconstriction, reduce pulmonary function, increase susceptibility to respiratory infections, and contribute to tumor formation. Several air pollutants are regulated on the basis of pulmonary function effects (Table 4). For example, acute ozone and NO_2 exposures can cause respiratory symptoms or decrements in lung function at concentrations in ambient air. The health significance of these short-term effects is not well understood, and the contribution of repeated, reversible acute effects to chronic damage is not known. Low-level exposures may initiate an inflammatory process leading, for example, to production of excess connective tissue and ultimately to the development of chronic pulmonary disease.

Inhaled pollutants react with biological macromolecules. For CO, the predominant reaction is with hemoglobin, which provides a good marker for inhaled dose as well as a mechanism for the effects of CO, i.e. decreasing delivery of oxygen to tissues. For many pollutants like ozone, which reacts with a large number of molecules, it is difficult to determine which reactions are on the pathway to disease. Animal models are useful for investigating the mechanisms of disease and in identifying markers of exposure or effects that may prove useful in human studies.

Ambient compounds derived from motor vehicle emissions may cause mutations, result in DNA-adduct formation, and may ultimately be carcinogenic. The mobile air toxics specified in the CAA amendments (acetaldehyde, benzene, butadiene, formaldehyde, and polycyclic organic matter) are of concern mainly because of their potential carcinogenicity. However, there is a great deal of uncertainty both about the human unit risk estimates and the exposures (24, 59). In addition, for some compounds, noncancer effects may be of concern, even under ambient exposure conditions. Particles emitted by diesel engines consist of carbonaceous cores to which organic compounds are adsorbed. Many of these compounds are highly mutagenic and some are carcinogenic. Several studies in rats at exposure concentrations of 2 to 7 mg/m^3, about 1000 or more times higher than ambient concentrations, reported that diesel particles produce lung tumors (reviewed in 36). Studies in mice showed evidence of carcinogenicity in females but not in males, and all studies in Syrian hamsters have been negative (36). A key question in extrapolating the results from rats to humans, in addition to questions about species differences, is how to extrapolate from the high doses used in these studies to the lower concentrations experienced by humans. There is a question of whether high-level exposures to particles, as used in rat studies that demonstrated carcinogenicity of diesel particles, and which lead to accumulation of particles in the lung, may cause tumors by a different mechanism than levels to which humans are exposed since particles of various types, by themselves, have been shown to be carcinogenic (42). Particles cause inflammation, increased rates of cell proliferation, and sequestering of macrophages that contain particles. Recent studies in which rats were exposed to particles lacking adsorbed organic compounds, as well as to diesel particles, suggested that they are similar, at these high concentrations, in their carcinogenic effects (25, 26, 37). An IARC monograph (28) concluded that there was sufficient evidence of carcinogenicity in experimental animals of whole diesel exhaust and of extracts of diesel exhaust particles, but limited evidence for the carcinogenicity of diesel engine exhaust in humans. Overall diesel engine exhaust was classified as probably carcinogenic to humans. Epidemiological studies have provided weak support that diesel exhaust is carcinogenic, but even the strongest studies of occupationally exposed workers have provided small increases in relative risks for lung cancer from diesel exposure (reviewed in 36). A serious problem in epidemiologic studies is the absence of good information on exposure to diesel exhaust.

The mixture of pollutants derived from motor vehicle emissions is not only complex, but ever-changing, because fuels, engine technology, and emission-control devices are continually being modified to decrease emissions of toxic compounds. Since these modifications aim to decrease deleterious effects of exposure to motor vehicle emissions, it is important to ensure that in decreasing some emissions, others are not increased or new, more harmful emissions introduced. For example, use of methanol as an alternative fuel is expected to decrease emissions of CO, nitrogen dioxide, and particles and may have a beneficial effect on ambient ozone levels, but it would expose the public to methanol, and probably to greater amounts of formaldehyde, which is already present in motor vehicle emissions. Exposure to low concentrations of methanol would occur through inhalation, dermally from spilling, and even possibly by ingestion. High-level exposure to methanol is toxic to the nervous system and may cause blindness, coma, and death. Although projections of population exposures to methanol from its use as a motor vehicle fuel are relatively low, more research is needed to determine whether any effects, particularly to the visual or nervous system, are predicted from protracted or repeated low-level exposure (12, 23, 24, 30).

In response to the CAA amendments of 1990, use of MTBE has been increased in fuels to decrease CO emissions. This action was initiated in the absence of much toxicity information outside of rodent studies. Pharmacokinetic data on the disposition and metabolism of MTBE in primates would be helpful in extrapolating potential effects to humans (12). Potential health effects of exposure to MTBE could be compared to those from elevated CO exposure, discussed below, as part of the assessment of relative risk from alternative fuel choices.

Health Effects of Low-level CO Exposure

When inhaled into the lungs, CO diffuses across the alveolar-capillary barrier into the plasma and through the red blood cell membrane. Inside the red blood cell, CO reacts rapidly with hemoglobin, forming carboxyhemoglobin (COHb). The affinity of CO for hemoglobin is about 240 times that of oxygen. Reaction of CO with hemoglobin not only decreases the amount of hemoglobin combined with oxygen (oxyhemoglobin) in the blood, but also shifts the oxyhemoglobin dissociation curve, causing oxygen to be less readily released from hemoglobin, thereby reducing oxygen delivery to peripheral tissues and producing a state of relative hypoxia in the tissues (44). CO can also bind to myoglobin, and with lower affinity to other respiratory proteins, but COHb is thought to be the main mediator of CO toxicity at low exposures to CO.

While high levels of COHb are lethal, because of deprivation of oxygen to tissues, low levels resulting from ambient exposures are generally not associated with adverse effects in normal individuals. However, conditions that limit oxygen delivery to tissues may make individuals more susceptible to the adverse effects of CO exposure. These include anemia, which decreases the oxygen-carrying capacity of the blood, chronic lung disease, which causes hypoxemia because of gas-exchange deficiencies, coronary artery disease, in which blood flow to the myocardium is limited, and exposure at high altitude, where ambient oxygen tension is reduced. Effects have been seen in individuals with coronary artery disease at the lowest COHb levels (2%) (2–4). There is some evidence for effects on behavior at COHb levels as low as 5% in normal individuals (57). Effects on vigilance or coordination could be of particular concern with respect to safety during driving in dense traffic, where CO concentrations in the air may be high. Effects on the nervous system might be found at lower COHb levels if sensitive groups such as those with impaired cerebral blood flow were studied. Because of their elevated COHb levels (about 4% compared to 1% or less (43)) and high incidence of coronary artery disease, smokers may be sensitive to the effects of CO exposure.

Coronary artery disease limits the ability to increase coronary blood flow in response to increased myocardial oxygen consumption during exercise. When myocardial blood flow is insufficient to meet oxygen demand, the myocardium becomes ischemic, resulting in the development of chest pain (angina pectoris) or electrocardiographic changes or both. Symptoms of myocardial ischemia occur in individuals with coronary artery disease at specific levels of exercise and limit their exercise capacity. Several recent studies conducted at differing COHb levels investigated the effect of CO exposure on exercise capacity and on the occurrence of myocardial ischemia (2–4, 31, 32, 49). These studies were undertaken to confirm the validity of earlier studies (5–7) using small numbers of subjects, which provided justification for the CO NAAQS. These early studies reported a decrease in the time to the onset of angina pectoris during exercise in subjects with coronary artery disease after CO exposures producing about 2–3% COHb. The recent studies (2–4, 31, 32, 49) all reported a decrease, or were consistent with a decrease, in the time to the occurrence of myocardial ischemia in people with coronary artery disease during exercise after CO exposure. The lowest CO dose at which a decrease in time to the onset of angina has been observed is 2% COHb (2–4). In this study a mean 5.1% decrease was observed in the time to electrocardiographic changes indicative of myocardial ischemia and a mean 4.2% decrease in the time to angina at 2% COHb compared to control (air exposure) days and greater effects at 3.9% COHb. With a mean exercise time of about 9 minutes before the onset of angina, there was a mean decrease of 25 seconds in the time to onset of angina and a mean decrease of 30 seconds in the time to the occurrence of electrocardiographic changes at 2% COHb (3). These increments in time should be interpreted in terms of level of exercise since different studies use different types of exercise tests. The exercise test used in this study is graded, with the workload increasing every two minutes, and the time at which myocardial ischemia is noted can be roughly associated with a level of exercise of five to six METs (a unit of oxygen consumption). One MET represents light to moderate activity, such as climbing two flights of stairs or walking on level ground at a pace of two to three miles per hour for a distance of one half to one mile (3). The data demonstrate a significant dose-response relationship for the individual differences in time to the onset of electrocardiographic changes at the three COHb levels. In animal studies, adverse effects were not observed at carboxyhemoglobin levels as low as those for which effects were observed in humans.

Physiological variations affecting breathing rate and lung diffusing capacity cause individuals to take up CO into the blood at different rates when exposed to the same air concentrations of CO. The best way to assess individual exposures is by measuring the amount of CO bound to hemoglobin in blood. Exposures to CO allowed by the NAAQS are projected to produce blood carboxyhemoglobin levels of 1.4 to 2% under conditions of moderate exercise (55). These slight elevations above the endogenous level, about 0.7–1.0% in nonsmoking individuals, have measurable effects in subjects with cardiovascular disease. To interpret the health significance of exposure to ambient levels of CO, it is important to know how many people, particularly those sensitive to CO, have COHb levels as high as 2%.

Ambient CO concentrations in urban areas vary greatly depending on proximity to traffic and other sources of CO. Not surprisingly, therefore, Wallace & Ziegenfus (60) found that CO levels at monitoring stations in 20 US cities did not correlate well with COHb levels measured in blood of residents. In four of 20 cities, individuals with COHb levels in the top 5% had mean levels greater than or equal to 2.0% COHb. Although many individuals had COHb levels greater than 2%, only one of the 36 monitoring stations reported a mean level above the 8-hr standard of 9 ppm. Using personal exposure monitors and diaries, 24-hr exposure profiles were determined for 450 people in Denver and 800 in Washington, D.C. (1). These data showed that 10% of residents in Denver and 4% in Washington, D.C. were exposed to 8-hr average CO levels above 9 ppm. In a Washington, D.C. study, the average CO exposure levels for commuters in automobiles ranged from 9–14 ppm, while fixed-site monitors gave averages of 2.7 to 3.1 ppm for the same rush-hour periods (16). Better information on the concentration of CO in various microenvironments and on personal activity patterns, particularly for people who might be sensitive, such as those with coronary artery disease, would facilitate assessment of the potential health risk from CO outdoors. Alternatively, COHb levels could be measured in sensitive individuals.

Health Effects of Ozone Exposure

Ozone is a highly reactive, poorly soluble gas. When inhaled into the respiratory tract by resting subjects, approximately 90% of the ozone is taken up, with substantial uptake occurring in the upper and proximal lower airways (18). Uptake of $^{18}O_3$ in humans exposed during exercise (2 hr at 0.4 ppm) shows excess $^{18}O_3$ in the cell and soluble protein fractions as well as the surfactant-containing fraction in the supernatant of bronchoalveolar lavage fluid (20). Thus, inspired ozone does reach the distal alveolar regions of the lung. These experimental data are generally consistent with dosimetric models (40) indicating that the highest tissue dose per unit of surface area is in the region of the terminal airways.

Health effects in the general community from ozone exposure were first reported among high-school athletes in California, who experienced reduced performance on high-exposure days (61). The initial NAAQS in 1971 was 0.80 ppm of total oxidant. In 1979, the standard was revised to 0.12 ppm based on clinical studies by DeLucia & Adams (14) showing that exercising asthmatic adults exposed for 1 hr to 0.15 ppm in an environmental chamber had increased dyspnea, cough, and wheezing, along with a small but nonsignificant reduction in pulmonary function (56). The current NAAQS for ozone remains at 0.12 ppm and is a one-hour maximum not to be exceeded more than once per year. Since more than half of the US population lives in communities exceeding the NAAQS (57), the appropriate level of the standard continues to be debated.

Over the past 15 years, acute responses to ozone identified in humans include reductions in lung function and increases in respiratory symptoms, airway reactivity, airway permeability, and airway inflammation. These observations were derived from studies in which human volunteers are exposed to ozone in a laboratory setting or from field studies of children. Children and young adults are more susceptible to acute ozone exposure and progressively develop pain on deep inspiration, irritative cough, and a reduced vital capacity and FEV_1. Recent controlled studies of acute responses have used exposure protocols of 6–8 hr duration, concentrations of 0.08 to 0.12 ppm, and intermittent exercise throughout the exposure period. Statistically significant, progressive decrements in mean FEV_1 have been found in healthy, young men exposed for 6.6 hr to as little as 0.08 ppm ozone while exercising to achieve a minute ventilation of approximately 40 L/min for 5 hr (27). However, even within these carefully controlled homogeneous populations of healthy volunteers, there has been a wide range of inter-subject responsiveness. McDonnell and coworkers (38) demonstrated that as the ozone concentration is increased from 0 to 0.4 ppm, the percent of responders increases. Furthermore, despite the wide inter-subject susceptibility, intra-subject responses were relatively reproducible (39).

Complementing the chamber studies, studies of children in summer camp (52, 53) associated daily exposures to ozone levels at or near the NAAQS with decrements of lung function, including vital capacity and FEV_1. Exposure-response relationships were steeper in some camp studies than in the controlled laboratory studies, perhaps reflecting longer exposures, potentiation by particles, more vigorous and persistent exercise, or carryover effect from the previous day. Recovery of function was usually complete by 24 hr. Evidence from these field studies in children, together with findings from the 6–8 hr low-level controlled ozone exposures, has raised the issue of whether the ozone standard should be modified to account for the temporal profile of ambient ozone levels (35).

The mechanism of the ozone-induced reduction in FVC and FEV_1 has received attention recently. Changes in lung function appear to be largely due to involuntary inhibition of inspiration (21) rather than to changes in respiratory mechanical properties, and may be related to activation of C fibers in the large airways. Pretreatment with cyclooxygenase inhibitors, indomethacin and ibuprofen, diminishes the spirometric responses to ozone (22, 46) and reduces the potential C-fiber activator PGE_2 in postexposure bronchoalveolar lavage fluid (22). Vagal afferent stimulation may be responsible for the pattern of decreased tidal volume and increased respiratory rate observed in response to ozone. The inability of ozone-exposed subjects to take a deep breath does not result from changes in lung elastic recoil, reductions in inspiratory muscle force, or increased lung water (21).

Acute ozone exposure also induces upper and lower airway inflammatory responses that do not correlate closely with spirometric responses. Bronchoalveolar lavage studies, which sample fluid and cells within the alveolar space, have shown that exposure to ozone causes inflammation in the lung. Exposure to 0.4 ppm ozone for two hours with exercise resulted in an eightfold increase in polymorphonuclear leukocytes (PMN) recovered by lavage, accompanied by increased recovery in lavage fluid of inflammatory mediators, including fibronectin, elastase, plasminogen activator, and prostaglandin E_2 (33, 34). Time-course studies following single exposures to ozone suggest that the peak inflammatory response occurs approximately 6 hr after exposure and does not correlate with symptoms or changes in airway function (47). The largest percentage of PMN appear in the first lavage aliquot, suggesting that ozone exposure results in an acute bronchiolitis. Seven-hour exposures to concentrations of ozone as low as 0.1 ppm, which is below the NAAQS of 0.12 ppm, resulted in a fivefold increase in PMN in lavage fluid (33, 34).

Ozone exposure has the potential to irritate airways throughout the respiratory tract, from the nose to alveoli, because of its physical properties of high reactivity and relative insolubility. Nasal inflammation in response to exposure can be assessed by nasal lavage, with quantification of inflammatory cells in the fluid returned, similar to bronchoalveolar lavage. Graham & Koren (19) found that exposure to 0.4 ppm ozone for 2 hr resulted in a sixfold increase in PMN recovered by nasal lavage 18 hr after exposure, but no significant correlation was noted between nasal lavage and bronchoalveolar lavage recovery of PMN after ozone exposure among the 10 subjects ($r = 0.4$, $p = 0.24$).

Surprisingly, controlled human studies have not demonstrated dramatic effects of ozone on lung function in asthmatic subjects, atopic nonasthmatic subjects, or subjects with chronic obstructive pulmonary disease (11). Several possible explanations exist. In contrast to studies with healthy volunteers, studies of asthmatic subjects have not been performed using many-hour exposures or repeated daily exposures. Furthermore, few studies with asthmatic subjects have incorporated multiple periods of exercise, an essential factor in provoking changes in airway function with low-level ozone exposure in healthy volunteers.

Several recent clinical studies provide evidence that asthmatics may ultimately prove to be hyperresponsive to ozone. Aris and coworkers (8)

observed a relationship between baseline airway hyperreactivity to metha-
choline and responsiveness to ozone, a finding of considerable interest but
not in agreement with earlier studies. Their observation suggested that airway
hyperresponsiveness may be a risk factor for ozone sensitivity even among
healthy, asymptomatic athletes. Using a different approach to study environmental interactions, Molfino et al (41) investigated whether inhalation
of 0.12 ppm ozone for one hour potentiates the airway allergic response in
asthmatics with seasonal symptoms. Although ozone did not significantly
alter baseline function, reactivity to inhaled allergen was significantly
enhanced by prior ozone inhalation. Ozone has been shown to increase
airway permeability using a variety of markers; prior ozone exposure may
thus increase access of allergen to subepithelial mediator secreting cells.
Furthermore, studies by Bates & Sizto (9, 10) have implicated ozone as a
contributing cause of hospital admissions in Southern Ontario. For the period
between 1974–1983, the maximum one-hour ozone average concentration
was significantly associated with daily admissions for asthma, as were
temperature and sulfates. However, the study design could not distinguish
the ozone effect from the concomitant effect of acidic aerosols and sulfur
dioxide.

The findings of Bates & Sizto (9, 10) and Molfino et al (41) emphasize
the potential for interactions between ozone and other environmental pollutants. Frampton et al (17) have examined whether prior exposure to low-level
sulfuric acid aerosol sensitizes human airways to ozone. Exposure-response
relationships were examined using three levels of ozone (0.08, 0.12, and
0.18 ppm ozone), with pre-exposure 24 hr earlier to 100 $\mu g/m^3$ H_2SO_4 or
sodium chloride aerosol. The findings revealed an interactive relationship
between the level of ozone exposure and pre-exposure to sulfuric acid or
sodium chloride aerosols in asthmatic subjects, but not in normal volunteers.
The effect was enhanced with increasing ozone exposure concentrations.
Although these findings await confirmation, they lend support to the concept
of increased responsiveness in individuals with underlying airway dysfunction.

Although the short-term effects following single or several day exposures to
ozone have been well documented, knowledge about chronic effects of ozone
is much less complete. Epidemiologic studies in Southern California suggest
that chronic oxidant exposures affect baseline respiratory function; however,
methodological problems including lack of detail on exposure, potential
selection bias, and potential confounding factors have limited interpretation of
these data sets. In the most recent Southern California study (15), children and
adults living in Glendora (a high-oxidant community) and in Lancaster (a
lower-oxidant community) were evaluated on two occasions five years apart.
Although there was substantial subject dropout over time, analysis showed

significant mean decrements in FEV_1 and nitrogen washout across all groups in the Glendora community with higher levels of ozone, sulfates, and particulate matter. Impaired nitrogen washout was present in the youngest age group, 7–10 years, and worsened with age. The suggestion of small airway dysfunction is consistent with observations in animals. In support of a chronic effect, a recent autopsy study of accident victims in Southern California (50) revealed evidence of bronchiolitis not expected for such young subjects although complete data on smoking and drug abuse were not available. Finally, Schwartz (48) also provided evidence for chronic effects of ozone based on an analysis of data on pulmonary function from the National Health and Nutrition Examination Survey from 1976–1980. Using ambient ozone data from nearby monitoring sites, he reported a highly significant ozone-associated reduction in lung function for people living in areas where the average ozone concentration exceeded 40 ppb. Thus, there are some indications of chronic ozone effects but the data are sketchy and difficult to interpret. This is an area where further research is needed.

CONCLUSIONS

Determining the health effects of exposure to air pollutants derived from motor vehicle emissions is a complex task because of the number and variety of pollutants, their relatively low concentration in ambient air, and the changing picture of emissions due to changes in technology and fuels. Questions about the health effects of motor vehicle emissions are important to resolve to determine which new directions in fuels and technology will be the most beneficial to health. Methanol, MTBE, and reformulated gasoline are examples of new fuels that might alleviate some emissions problems, but for which toxicity information is needed before risks can be weighed against benefits. Despite substantial decreases in motor vehicle emissions in recent years, concerns about the possibility of significant effects of exposures due to motor vehicles remain. Perhaps the most important and challenging issue is whether there are chronic effects of exposure to ozone at the levels that exist in many urban areas in the United States.

ACKNOWLEDGMENTS

MJU's work was supported in part by grant nos. ESO2679 and KO7 ES00220 from the National Institute of Environmental Health Sciences; contract no. 88-8 from the Health Effects Institute, an organization jointly funded by the U.S EPA (assistance agreement X-812059) and motor vehicle manufacturers; contract 3009-01 from the Electric Power Research Institute; and grant no. RR00044 from the Division of Resources of the National Institutes of Health.

Literature Cited

1. Akland GG, Hartwell TD, Johnson TR, Whitmore RW. 1987. Measuring human exposure to carbon monoxide in Washington, D.C. and Denver, Colorado, during the winter of 1982–1983. *Environ. Sci. Technol.* 19: 911–18

2. Allred EN, Bleecker ER, Chaitman BR, Dahms TE, Gottlieb SO, et al. 1989. Short-term effects of carbon monoxide exposure on the exercise performance of subjects with coronary artery disease. *N. England J. Med.* 321:1426–32

3. Allred EN, Bleecker ER, Chaitman BR, Dahms TE, Gottlieb SO, et al. 1989. *Acute Effects of Carbon Monoxide Exposure on Individuals with Coronary Artery Disease.* Res. Rep. No. 25, Health Effects Inst.

4. Allred EN, Bleecker ER, Chaitman BR, Dahms TE, Gottlieb SO, et al. 1991. Effect of carbon monoxide on myocardial ischemia. *Environ. Health. Perspect.* 91:89–152

5. Anderson EW, Anderson RJ, Strauch JM, Fortuin NJ, Knelson JH. 1973. Effect of low-level carbon monoxide exposure on onset and duration of angina pectoris. *Ann. Intern. Med.* 79:46–50

6. Aronow WS. 1981. Aggravation of angina pectoris by two percent carboxyhemoglobin. *Am. Heart J.* 101: 154–57

7. Aronow WS, Isbell MW. 1973. Carbon monoxide effect on exercise-induced angina pectoris. *Ann. Intern. Med.* 79:392–95

8. Aris R, Christian C, Sheppard D, Balmes JR. 1991. The effects of sequential exposure to acidic fog and ozone on pulmonary function in exercising subjects. *Am. Rev. Respir. Dis.* 143:85–91

10. Bates DV, Sizto R. 1987. Air pollution and hospital admissions in southern Ontario: The acid summer haze effect. *Environ. Res.* 43:317–31

11. Bates DV, Sizto R. 1989. The Ontario air pollution study:Identification of the causative agent. *Environ. Health Perspect.* 79:69–72

12. Bromberg PA. 1988. Asthma and automotive emissions. See Ref. 60a, pp. 465–98

12. Costantini MG. 1993. Health effects of oxygenated fuels. *Environ. Health Perspect.* 101(Suppl. 6) In press

13. DeJovine JM, McHugh KJ, Paulsen DA, Rapp LA, Segal JS, et al. 1991. *EC-X Reformulated Gasoline Test Program Emissions Data. ARCO Products Co., Clean Fuels Rep. 91.06*

14. DeLucia AJ, Adams WC. 1977. Effects of O₃ inhalation during exercise on pulmonary function and blood biochemistry. *J. Appl. Physiol.* 43:75–81

17. Detels R, Tashkin DP, Sayre JW, Rokaw SN, Massey FJ, et al. 1991. The UCLA population studies of CORD: X. A cohort study of changes in respiratory function associated with chronic exposure to SOx, NOx, and hydrocarbons. *Am. J. Public Health* 81:350–59

16. Flachsbart PG, Mack GA, Howes JE, Rodes CE. 1987. Carbon monoxide exposures of Washington commuters. *J. Air Pollut. Control Assoc.* 37:135–42

17. Frampton MW, Morrow PE, Cox C, Levy PC, Speers DM, et al. 1992. Does pre-exposure to acidic aerosols alter airway response to ozone in humans? *Am. Rev. Respir. Dis.* 145: A428

18. Gerrity TR, Weaver RA, Berntsen J, House DE, O'Neil JJ. 1988. Extrathoracic and intrathoracic removal of ozone in tidal breathing humans. *J. Appl. Physiol.* 65:393–400

19. Graham DE, Koren HS. 1990. Biomarkers of inflammation in ozone-exposed humans. *Am. Rev. Respir. Dis.* 142:152–56

20. Hatch GE, Costa DL, Koren H, Devlin RB, McDonnell WF, et al. 1992. Measurement of the dose of ozone (O₃) to the human lung through oxygen-18 (¹⁸O) labeling: comparison with rats. *Am. Rev. Respir. Dis.* 145:A96

21. Hazucha MJ, Bates DV, Bromberg PA. 1989. Mechanism of action of ozone on the human lung. *J. Appl. Physiol.* 67:1535–41

22. Hazucha, MJ, Pape G, Madden M, Koren H, Kehrl H, et al. 1991. Effects of cyclooxygenase inhibition on ozone-

induced respiratory inflammation and lung function changes. *Am. Rev. Respir. Dis.* 143:A701

23. Health Effects Institute. 1987. *Automotive Methanol Vapors and Human Health: An Evaluation of Existing Scientific Information and Issues for Future Research.* Cambridge, MA: Health Effects Inst.

24. Health Effects Institute. 1993. *Research Priorities for Mobile Air Toxics.* Cambridge, MA: Health Effects Inst. HEI Commun. 2, 130 pp.

25. Heinrich U. 1993. Carcinogenic effects of solid particles. See Ref. 40a, pp.

26. Heinrich U, Peters L, Creutzenberg O, Dasenbrock C, Hoymann H-G. 1993. Inhalation exposure of rats to tar/pitch condensation aerosol or carbon black alone or in combination with irritant gases. See Ref. 40a, pp.

27. Horstman DH, Folinsbee LJ, Ives PJ, Abdul-Salaam S, McDonnell WF. 1990. Ozone concentration and pulmonary response relationships for 6.6 hr exposures with 5 hr of moderate exercise to 0.08, 0.10 and 0.12 ppm. *Am. Rev. Respir. Dis.* 142: 1158–63

28. International Agency for Research on Cancer. 1989. *IARC Monographs on the Evaluation of Carcinogenic Risks to Humans: Diesel and Gasoline Engine Exhaust and Some Nitroarenes,* Vol. 46. Lyons, France: Int. Agency Res. Cancer

29. Johnson JH. 1988. Automotive emissions. See Ref. 60a, pp. 39–75

30. Kavet R, Nauss KM. 1990. The toxicity of inhaled methanol vapors. *CRC Crit. Rev. Toxicol.* 21:21–50

31. Kleinman MT, Whittenberger JL. 1985. *Effects of short-term exposure to carbon monoxide in subjects with coronary artery disease.* Final Rep. Calif. Air Resour. Board. South. Occup. Center, Univ. Calif., Irvine, CA, Nov.

32. Kleinman MT, Davidson DM, Vandagriff RB, Caiozzo VJ, Whittenberger JL. 1989. Effects of short-term exposure to carbon monoxide in subjects with coronary artery disease. *Arch. Environ. Health* 44:361–69

33. Koren HS, Devlin RB, Graham DE, Mann R, McDonnell WF. 1989. The inflammatory response in human lung exposed to ambient levels of ozone. In *Atmospheric Ozone Research and Its Policy Implications,* ed. T Schneider, SD Lee, GJR Wolters, LD Grant, pp. 745–53. Amsterdam: Elsevier

34. Koren HS, Devlin RB, Graham DE,

Mann R, McGee MP, et al. 1989. Ozone-induced inflammation in the lower airways of human subjects. *Am. Rev. Respir. Dis.* 139:407–15

35. Lippmann M. 1989. Health effects of ozone: A critical review. *J. Air Pollut. Control Assoc.* 39:672–95

36. Mauderly JL. 1992. Diesel exhaust. In *Environmental Toxicants. Human Exposures and Their Health Effects,* ed. M Lippmann, pp. 119–62. New York: Van Nostrand Reinhold

37. Mauderly JL, Snipes MB, Barr EB, Belinsky SA, Bechtold WE et al. 1993. Influence of particle-associated organic compounds on carcinogenicity of diesel exhaust. In *Annu. Health Effects Inst. Conf. Progr., Abstr. Posters, 9th,* p. 19

38. McDonnell WF, Horstman DH, Hazucha MJ, Seale E, Haaked ED, et al. 1983. Pulmonary effects of ozone exposure during exercise: dose-response characteristics. *J. Appl. Physiol.* 45: 1345–52

39. McDonnell WF, Chapman RS, Leigh MW, Strope GL, Collier AM. 1985. Respiratory responses of vigorously exercising children to 0.12 ppm ozone exposure. *Am. Rev. Respir Dis.* 132: 875–79

40. Miller FJ, Overton JH, Jaskot RH, Menzel DB. 1985. A model of the regional uptake of gaseous pollutants in the lung. I. The sensitivity of the uptake of ozone in the human lung to lower respiratory tract reactions and exercise. *Toxicol. Appl. Pharmacol.* 79:11–27

40a. Mohr U, Dungworth DL, Mauderly JL, Oberdorster G, eds. 1993. *Toxic and Carcinogenic Effects of Solid Particles in the Respiratory Tract. Proc. Int. Inhalation Symp., 4th, Hanover, Germany.* Washington, DC:ILSI Press. In press

41. Molfino NA, Wright SC, Katz I, Tario S, Silverman F, et al. 1991. Effect of low concentration of ozone on inhaled allergen responses in asthmatic subjects. *Lancet* 338:199–203

42. Morrow PE. 1988. Possible mechnisms to explain dust overloading of the lungs. *Fundam. Appl. Toxicol.* 10:369–84

43. Radford EP, Dridz TA. 1982. *Blood Carbon Monoxide Levels in Persons 3–74 Years of Age: United States 1976–80.* Hyattsville, MD: US Dep. Health Hum. Serv., Natl. Cent. Health Stat. PHS 82–1250

44. Roughton FJ, Darling RC. 1944. The effect of carbon monoxide on the

oxyhemoglobin dissociation curve. *Am. J. Physiol.* 141:17–31

45. Sawyer RF. 1993. Reformulated gasoline for automotive emissions reduction. *Int. Symp. Combustion, 24th*, pp. 1423–32. Pittsburgh: Combustion Inst.

46. Schelegle ES, Adams WC, Siefkin AD. 1987. Indomethacin pretreatment reduces ozone-induced pulmonary function decrements in human subjects. *Am. Rev. Respir. Dis.* 136:1350–54

47. Schelegle ES, Siefkin AD, McDonald RJ. 1991. Time course of ozone-induced neutrophilia in normal humans. *Am. Rev. Respir. Dis.* 143:1353–58

48. Schwartz J. 1989. Lung function and chronic exposure to air pollution: A cross-sectional analysis of NHANES II. *Environ. Res.* 50:309–21

49. Sheps DS, Adams KF Jr, Bromberg PA, Goldstein GM, O'Neil JJ, et al. 1987. Lack of effect of low levels of carboxyhemoglobin on cardiovascular function in patients with ischemic heart disease. *Arch. Environ. Health* 42:108–16

50. Sherwin RP, Richters V. 1991. Centriacinar region (CAR) disease in the lungs of young adults: A preliminary report. In *Tropospheric Ozone and the Environment (TR-19)*, ed. RL Berglund, DR Lawson, DJ McKee. Pittsburgh: Air Waste Manage. Assoc. 178 pp.

51. South Coast Air Qual. Manage. District and South. Calif. Assoc. Gov. 1990. *Draft Air Quality Management Plan, South Coast Air Basin, December 1990*

52. Spektor DM, Lippmann M, Lioy PJ, Thurston GD, Citak K, et al. 1988. Effects of ambient ozone on respiratory function in active normal children. *Am. Rev. Respir. Dis.* 137:313–20

53. Spektor DM, Thurston GD, Mao J, Hayes C, Lippmann M. 1991. Effects of single- and multi-day ozone exposures on respiratory function in active normal children. *Environ. Res.* 55:107–22

54. US Environ. Prot. Agency. 1984. *Review of the NAAQS for Carbon Monoxide: Reassessment of Scientific and Technical Information. EPA-450/5–84–004*. Off. Air Qual. Plan. Stand., Research Triangle Park, NC: US EPA

55. US Environ. Prot. Agency. 1986. *Air quality criteria for ozone and other photochemical oxidants, Vol. 2. EPA/600/8–84/0206F*. ECAO, Research Triangle Park, NC: US EPA

56. US Environ. Prot. Agency. 1988. *Review of the National Ambient Air Quality Standards for Ozone—Preliminary Assessment of Scientific and Technical Information*. Off. Air Qual. Plan. Stand., Draft Staff Pap.

57. US Environ. Prot. Agency. 1991. *Air Quality Criteria for Carbon Monoxide. EPA 600/8–90\045F, ECAO*. Research Triangle Park, NC: US EPA

58. US Environ. Prot. Agency. 1991. *National Air Quality and Emissions Trends Report, 1990. EPA-450/4–91–023*. Off. Air Qual. Plan. Stand., Research Triangle Park, NC; US EPA

59. US Environ. Prot. Agency. 1993. *Motor Vehicle-Related Air Toxics Study, EPA 420-R-93–005*. Off. Mob. Sources. Ann Arbor, MI: US EPA

60. Wallace LA, Ziegenfus RC. 1985. Comparison of carboxyhemoglobin concentrations in adult nonsmokers with ambient carbon monoxide levels. *J. Air Pollut. Control Assoc.* 35:944–47

60a. Watson AY, Bates RR, Kennedy D, eds. 1988. *Air Pollution, the Automobile, and Public Health*. Washington, DC: Natl. Acad. Press

61. Wayne WS, Welihle PF, Carroll RE. 1967. Oxidant air pollution and athletic performance. *J. Am. Med. Assoc.* 199:901–4

62. Winer AM, Lurmann FW, Coyner LA, Colome SD, Poe M. 1989. *Characterization of Air Pollutant Exposures in the South Coast Air Basin: Application of a New Regional Human Exposure (REHEX) Model*. South Coast Air Qual. Manage. District, El Monte, Calif., June 1989

Annu. Rev. Public Health. 1994. 15:179–201
Copyright © 1994 by Annual Reviews Inc. All rights reserved

INTERPRETATION OF LOW TO MODERATE RELATIVE RISKS IN ENVIRONMENTAL EPIDEMIOLOGIC STUDIES

John F. Acquavella, Barry R. Friedlander, and Belinda K. Ireland

Monsanto Company/A2SL, Department of Medical and Health Sciences 800 North Lindbergh Boulevard, St Louis, Missouri 63167

KEYWORDS: cancer, precision, reproductive effects, validity

INTRODUCTION

This paper addresses health effects of involuntary exposures from ambient and occupational environments. Studies of diet, smoking, and other personal habits that are often lumped in the environmental (i.e. nongenetic) category are expressly excluded from the scope of this review, although these factors often must be evaluated as potential confounders. Some exposures skirt the boundaries of our definition. For example, ultra violet (UV) radiation from sun exposure during vacation would be voluntary, while UV exposure during farming is largely involuntary. Nonetheless, we consider studies of malignant melanoma rates related to UV exposure environmental in the present context. Effects of environmental tobacco smoke (ETS) for nonsmokers are largely involuntary, though admittedly most adults (but not children) choose their spouses and/or associates with knowledge of their smoking status.

A prevailing, though unsubstantiated, view is that most current and future studies that are "positive" will provide evidence only of small environmental risks. This view reflects a belief that decades of research have identified almost all of the strong risk factors for cancers, reproductive disorders, and other diseases. This viewpoint includes a burgeoning number of scientists

179

0163-7525/94/0510-0179$05.00

who believe some low level exposures may exert small protective effects and actually lower disease rates (i.e. hormesis) (9), as well as those scientists who believe there is no safe level for most environmental exposures. Resolution of a potentially fractious debate requires an unbiased framework for evaluating research findings. Accordingly, more emphasis may need to be placed on scientific interpretion of studies that find small to moderate differences in disease rates for exposed versus unexposed populations, by which we mean a relative risk (RR) of 1.5 or less. We work within the presumption that such relative risks are more difficult to interpret than large relative risks, though we do not feel bound by it. In practice, as we illustrate later, the inferential process proceeds similarly for exposures with strong or weak exposure-disease associations.

BASIC PARADIGM

How do we know when an association is causal? This question, often taken for granted in everyday scientific practice, is a matter of considerable discussion in the epidemiologic community (52a) and is at the heart of the interpretation of "low-risk" environmental epidemiologic studies. A widely used approach for causal inference involves applying the criteria for causality proposed by Sir A. Bradford Hill to the available scientific evidence (26; see Table 1). The Surgeon General (56) made extensive use of these criteria in concluding that smoking causes lung cancer and, more recently, the Environmental Protection Agency (58) applied a slight variation of Hill's criteria to support their position that ETS is related to lung cancer. In the smoking-lung cancer debate, application of Hill's criteria helped consolidate scientific opinion against an initial backdrop of considerable skepticism. In retrospect, we see that the smoking-lung cancer relationship satisfied most of Hill's criteria with the notable exception of specificity—an irrelevant

Table 1 Hill's criteria for causality

	Everyday usage
Strength of the association	size of the relative risk
Consistency	findings are replicated, particularly by other researchers
Dose response	relative effect increases with increasing exposure
Temporality	cause precedes the effect
Biological plausibility	consistent with experimental or other research
Coherence	consistent with temporal patterns of disease
Specificity	related to one disease (frequently violated)

Reference (26)

criterion. It remains to be seen whether causal criteria will consolidate scientific opinion regarding ETS and lung cancer.

Hill's criteria emphasize the necessary precedence of exposure before disease, the size of the RR, and whether the RR increases or decreases with increasing exposure. Emphasis is also given to biological plausibility, though this criterion is inherently judgmental and limited by our current knowledge of basic disease processes. Hill's criteria work well for strong risk factors, but moderate relative risks are unlikely to satisfy the strength-of-association criterion or embody a clear trend of RRs with increasing environmental exposure. In addition, the biological responses to environmental exposures are seldom well understood. Therefore, Hill's criteria are unlikely to be satisfied in evaluating many moderate relative risks from environmental exposures.

A second method commonly used to assess causality is by scientific consensus. Such consensus is often sought by governmental and other organizations, which use Hill's criteria as a point of reference, but place more emphasis on the opinions of committee members. These opinions may or may not be reflective of a broader scientific consensus, and such committee categorizations may subsequently influence scientific consensus. For example, the categorization by the International Agency for Research on Cancer of strong acid mists containing sulfuric acid as a known human carcinogen (28) was probably a surprise to most occupational epidemiologists familiar with the literature. It remains to be seen whether this categorization will be influential with interested scientists and whether subsequent research will support this categorization.

There have been many worthy criticisms of Hill's causal criteria and the workings of consensus committees (53). In fact, it has been argued for some time that there are disturbing cracks in the logic of scientific induction—the logic most frequently applied to determine causal associations—and that we can never really know whether an association is causal (33). These criticisms have led to an alternate logic for interpreting scientific research and, in some ways, provide a practical solution to the issue of whether we can ever know whether an association is causal.

This alternate viewpoint, championed by Karl Popper, is popular among epidemiologists who have written on causal inference (8, 33). According to Popper, a theory is strengthened by its ability to withstand falsification (46). Viewed in this context, scientists believe strongly that cigarette smoking causes lung cancer because this theory has withstood repeated efforts at falsification, not because the results of studies adhere to Hill's causal criteria (33). Likewise, theories about environmental effects become more believable as a theory is proposed and competing theories are tested and rejected. Moderate relative risks would be interpreted to support a causal association to the extent that a particular finding and the resulting theory have been challenged and could not be falsified. We should recognize, however, that we may be fairly certain of our belief today only to be reversed in the future by additional knowledge and a better theory. But that is true of all scientific endeavors.

Statistical significance—i.e. a p value, by convention, less than 0.05 for the probability, assuming the null hypothesis is true, of obtaining findings as extreme or more extreme than those observed in a given study—is not mentioned as a criterion by Hill or included in the alternate framework for evaluating scientific research. There are two reasons for this intentional omission. First, significance testing relates only to random variability at an arbitrary level of significance and neglects systematic error(s) (e.g. confounding and other biases), which is a more important consideration in epidemiologic studies. P values mix the size of the RR and the precision with which the RR is measured, when these quantities can be expressed unambiguously by the RR and the confidence interval (CI) (50). These latter quantities and the evaluation of validity concerns are key to determining whether an association is causal. Second, as Land (32) has pointed out for radiation exposure, rejection of the null hypothesis for low-level risks and rare outcomes like cancer can require impractically large study sizes. Nonetheless, the magnitude of the RR and the related CI, if unbiased, can provide evidence of the presence or absence of a relationship between exposure and disease regardless of whether the finding is statistically significant. Such a finding can provide the basis for evaluating competing theories to explain apparent associations between exposure and disease.

METHODOLOGIC CONSIDERATIONS

Methodologic considerations, in large part, govern whether a specific exposure disease association is estimated validly. Therefore, a brief review of some major methodologic considerations relating to environmental epidemiology studies is appropriate.

Goal of the Study

The goal of environmental epidemiologic studies, like any epidemiologic study, is to compare the rate of disease in an exposed population to the rate that would have occurred in that same population without the exposure. Operationally, this usually involves comparing disease rates for an exposed population with rates for a separate unexposed population. An exception to this rule might be studies of transient, reversible effects that could be studied in one population at various times corresponding to the presence or absence of exposure. In the more usual situation with separate exposed and unexposed populations, the key assumption is that the rate among the unexposed is the same as would have occurred among the exposed in the absence of exposure. The rate among the unexposed population, however, is not necessarily the expected rate among the exposed population because of differences that may be related to confounding factors, other biases, genetic differences, and biological variability (i.e. chance). Study designs can address all these factors, except genetic differences (unless twin studies are done), and thereby improve the credibility of a particular result. Evaluations of a particular exposure-disease association must consider confounding, other biases, and chance.

Study Design Issues

Most environmental epidemiologic studies use the basic study designs that collect exposure and disease information at the individual level: cohort, case control, and cross-sectional studies. The strengths and weaknesses of these study designs are well known and much is known about the types of bias and effects of bias in these research designs (13, 31, 52).

An ecologic study design is also frequently used in environmental studies. The strengths and weaknesses of this study design are also well known, though the types of bias and consequences of misclassification are less well appreciated. Ecologic designs differ from individual level studies in that disease and/or exposure information is not known at the individual level, but instead at the group level. Therefore, ecologic designs can be considered to be "incomplete" compared with studies that collect exposure and disease information for individuals (39).

For example, studies that correlated cancer rates with county characteristics, such as the percent of the population employed in various industries (6), would be hampered by not knowing whether diseased individuals in the county might have worked in a specific industry to a greater or lesser extent than the county average. In fact, it is possible that all or none of the diseased individuals in an ecologic study had the relevant exposure. Bias in ecologic studies reflects the failure of the ecologic design to measure the true effect at the individual level (39), which is the basis for the so-called ecologic fallacy. More importantly, the magnitude of ecologic bias is likely to be greater and less predictable than the bias from individual level studies.

Morgenstern & Thomas (39) detail the unpredictability of bias in ecologic studies. For example, in individual level studies a confounding factor must be associated with exposure at the individual level for it to have a confounding effect. In ecologic studies, confounding can occur if the factor is associated with exposure across regions, but not at the individual level. Furthermore, adjustment for confounding factors removes bias in individual level studies, but in ecologic studies adjustment at the group level may control only a portion of the bias and may even increase bias. Exposure misclassification also tends to manifest differently in individual and ecologic studies. In individual level studies, nondifferential exposure misclassification (i.e. exposure misclassification independent of disease status) usually results in bias toward the null RR of 1.0 (15, 17, 31). However, in ecologic studies nondifferential exposure misclassification usually results in overestimation of the RR, which can be severe (7)! The conditions for valid estimation of the RR from ecologic studies are still not well understood and wholly ecologic studies serve as a very weak basis for inference. However, useful information from these studies can be gained more confidently by incorporation of substudies to determine the distribution of factors on an individual level (39).

Characteristics of the Disease

Characteristics of the disease being studied affect the design, execution, and interpretation of environmental studies. Knowledge of disease development, its clinical presentation, and resulting diagnostic accuracy are necessary for valid evaluations of exposure-disease relationships.

Paramount among these characteristics are the induction and latent periods of disease. The induction period concerns the time during which sufficient exposure and related necessary events accumulate until disease onset. The latent period starts at the end of the induction period and continues until detection of disease (51). Exposures during the induction period are causal factors for disease, so study designs need to focus on relating diseases to exposures during the induction period. This partitioning of the induction and latent periods differs from the more common usage of latent period as the combined induction and latent periods.

The induction and latent periods determine the time lapse between exposure and disease detection. The longer the time lapse, the more difficulties can arise with enumeration of the exposed population, population migration, exposure assessment, assessment of potential confounding factors, etc. Therefore, all other things being equal, diseases with short induction-latent periods (e.g. adverse reproductive outcomes) offer a more favorable opportunity for research and interpretation than diseases with long induction-latent periods (e.g. lung cancer).

Included within the discussion of latency is the concept of sufficient exposure and related necessary events. A given disease rarely develops in all individuals experiencing the same type and amount of exposure. Instead, disease occurrence will vary with the presence or absence of other interacting factors in the individual, many of which are unknown. This is commonly referred to as differences in susceptibility. Factors affecting susceptibility include age and genetics as well as other environmental factors. For instance, children under one year of age who consume honey or corn syrup are at risk of developing botulism, whereas older children and adults are not. Their susceptibility to colonization by the toxin-producing bacteria, *Clostridium botulinum,* which may contaminate honey and corn syrup, is believed to be due to the lack of competing microorganisms among their intestinal microflora (4). Another example is mental retardation resulting from phenylalanine in the diet, which occurs only among phenylketonurics who are unable to metabolize phenylalanine normally because of their inherited deficiency of the enzyme phenylalanine hydroxylase (4).

For many diseases, the presence of an underlying condition or other disease will affect the susceptibility, progression, and lethality of the disease being studied. These conditions are commonly labeled as risk factors or predisposing conditions for the development of disease and modifiers for the expression and progression of disease. For example, in family groups with genetic predisposition to allergy and atopy, the exposure to environmental agents like dust mites and animal dander may produce respiratory symptomatology that would not develop in persons lacking the allergic predisposition. For these groups the superimposition of environmental irritants may trigger respiratory symptomatology such as coughing, wheezing, and shortness of breath at much lower threshold doses than would be experienced in a population without underlying allergic and atopic disposition (55). Research design and analysis must therefore be developed with sufficient understanding of the predisposing and underlying conditions that affect how a disease is manifested.

A second important consideration is the clinical presentation of a disease and the resulting limitations on diagnostic accuracy. Rarely is a disease manifested the same in each patient. Individual factors such as age, severity of disease, and pain perception affect the presentation of illness. In actual clinical practice, diagnoses are rarely established at the first clinic visit and require ongoing interaction between physician and patient to fully characterize the disease process. Even a disease such as rheumatoid arthritis, for which established clinical criteria exist, requires long-standing presence of symptoms and repeated observations of joint involvement by a physician for positive diagnosis (2). Thus, studies that rely on data collected at clinical centers as part of routine medical care would be expected to be more accurate than data collected cross-sectionally. However, even in clinical samples, the problems of different manifestations of disease are compounded by the lack of exact diagnostic criteria for many diseases. One such example is asthma, for which there exists no pathognomonic feature nor definitive diagnostic exam (34, 62). Asthma and other diseases may move through a continuum from normal to abnormal with no clear demarcation to indicate when disease begins.

Some diagnostic categories relate more to treatment and prognostic factors than to etiology and are therefore less useful for epidemiologic study. The diagnosis chronic obstructive pulmonary disease is a category that includes pathology resulting from chronic bronchitis or emphysema. The apparent diagnostic obscurity is unimportant in clinical practice since therapy remains the same for the patient with either chronic bronchitis or emphysema (47), but this limits the usefulness of the diagnostic category in studies seeking etiologic understanding. Soft tissue sarcoma (STS)—a generic term for sarcomas of 100 or more types (23)—provides another good example. Much of the controversy about occupational exposures and STS resulted from studies reporting elevated STS rates for exposed workers, with heterogeneity of numerous subtypes of STS across the individual studies (19, 24, 25). While it is possible that a single exposure operates in a similar way for many different tissues, it is considered less likely than would be a specific relationship with a single sarcoma type.

Changes in diagnostic categories over time, spurred by advances in medical information and technology, further complicate diagnostic comparability. A current example is the ongoing increase in information on acquired immunodeficiency syndrome (AIDS) and the resulting revisions by the Centers for Disease Control (CDC) (11) in surveillance case definition criteria for the reporting of AIDS.

A lack of comparability of diagnoses across time and across sources greatly limits large environmental studies. Lack of comparability exists even for diseases that are assumed to have standard reporting requirements within the United States, such as communicable diseases, for which Sacks (54) found substantial variation between states, including differences in requirements of laboratory confirmation. A secondary finding was that for each of twelve selected reportable diseases, less than half the states had a case definition of the disease. This underscores the importance of research into the quality and limitations of any data source for disease-outcome measures.

Death certificates are frequently used to determine diagnoses in epidemiologic studies. In many instances this practice is satisfactory, although in others it imparts diagnostic inaccuracy that can differ across study populations. For some diseases, such as multiple myeloma, death certificate diagnoses are exceptionally accurate. Based on data from the Surveillance Epidemiology and End Results Program, Percy et al (45) found that 97% of multiple myeloma death certificate diagnoses could be confirmed. Many other cancer sites showed similar good agreement, but some did not. For leukemias overall the agreement was 94%, but agreement was less for the individual leukemia types: 81% for lymphocytic (ICD code 204), 86% for myeloid (ICD code 205), and 50% for monocytic (ICD code 206).

Percy et al (45) also followed incident cancer cases diagnosed in 1974 and 1975 to the individual's death to determine the detection rate of hospital-diagnosed cancers as the underlying cause on death certificates. Multiple myeloma showed almost complete detection at 97%. However, for subtypes of leukemias, detection rates were 77% for lymphocytic, 77% for myeloid, and 49% for monocytic. Incomplete detection for specific diseases offers the opportunity for diseases to be diagnosed more or less completely for exposed or unexposed study populations, raising validity concerns for RRs calculated on the assumption of equal detection across study populations. It is important that research designs recognize the limitations of diagnostic accuracy and underreporting for some types of cancer deaths.

For noncancer deaths, especially when the underlying disease is one lacking rigid diagnostic criteria, death certificate diagnoses may be accurate but incomplete. For example, when Hunt et al (27) reviewed complete medical records for all decedents in Rochester, Minnesota, who had pulmonary diagnoses in patient care charts, they found death certificate recording of asthma to be fairly accurate for those listed on death certificates, but over half of the deaths that should have been attributed to asthma did not have asthma as a death certificate diagnosis. Death certificates identified only 22 of the 53 asthma deaths that were verified by expert panel review of patient care charts. Infant deaths may be even more susceptible to inaccuracies in death certificate diagnoses. The CDC (10) reported substantial misclassification of infant deaths in Alaska for the years 1990–1991, with 5 of the 9 deaths listed on death certificates judged inaccurate on chart review. Cole compared the death certificates for 343 infant deaths occurring in Scotland in 1986 to a national neonatal mortality survey that places neonatal deaths into one of seven general categories. Even with such broad criteria to match on, she still found 10% disagreement, with the majority resulting from inadequate or inaccurate information provided by the certifying doctor on the death certificate (14). Clearly, procedures are needed to insure diagnostic accuracy and complete disease ascertainment for both the exposed and unexposed populations.

In some environmental studies, outcome is assessed at the time of the study by a cross-sectional examination of disease status. To accurately determine disease status in a study population, it is important to use standardized diagnostic criteria developed prior to the study that are rigidly applied to all study subjects without knowledge of exposure status. For some diseases, standardized criteria exist, often developed to create uniform reporting requirements or to provide for comparability among study populations. Unfortunately, as in the example of diagnostic criteria for rheumatoid arthritis, it is uncommon for the criteria to be a single clinical sign or laboratory marker that is always present in all diseased subjects. Instead, balance must be achieved in selecting disease criteria that identify only persons with the disease (specificity) and that identify all the persons with the disease (sensitivity). In most instances, if the misdiagnosis rate is the same for exposed and nonexposed persons (i.e. nondifferential with respect to exposure), there will be no bias—only a loss of precision in estimating the RR. However, opportunity for differential disease misclassification between exposed and referent populations is increased if concern about the effects of a specific exposure sensitizes the exposed population and their clinicians to look especially hard for indications of a specific illness. Reporting bias may also increase with the uncertainty of the diagnosis.

An example of this point comes from a study by the Agency for Toxic Substances Disease Registry (1) of residents near an "apparent" toxic waste site and residents of a nearby control community. Extensive environmental measurements failed to detect exposure to toxic chemicals for residents in the exposed county, but the health investigation was conducted anyway because of public concern. Residents in the exposed community had higher rates of self-reported "physician-diagnosed" cancer than residents in the control county after adjusting for demographic factors. However, when the investigators sought validation for all cancer cases and when the analysis was restricted to validated cancer cases, there was no difference in cancer rates between the communities. Thus, even for a disease like cancer, a disease that people recognize and that should be well communicated to patients by physicians, there was overreporting due, in some measure, to concern about the presumed toxic waste site. Likewise, interpretations of self-reported symptom data in this study, even symptoms requiring physician attention, were necessarily tempered by the lack of a validation source and the prospect for overreporting in the "exposed" area.

Occupational studies frequently offer an opportunity for increased diagnostic scrutiny being applied to workers compared to the general population group. This may be because workers at most large manufacturing facilities have comprehensive health insurance benefits and may be concerned about work-related health effects. Therefore, these workers may receive a more thorough evaluation and more accurate diagnosis than persons who would comprise the comparison population in an epidemiologic study. This might be especially true in geographic areas where there is widespread public concern about occupational or environmental health issues, which may sensitize physicians to be particularly thorough and to order additional diagnostic tests for workers in specific industries. An example of such a bias was postulated in a study of brain tumors in the photographic manufacturing industry (22).

Neutra et al (42) looked into various explanations for overreporting in the vicinity of perceived environmental hazards using health evaluations of five waste sites conducted by the California Department of Health Services

(CDHS). In all but one of these studies, symptoms were excessive only in those who complained of odors. In one study, Baker et al (3) found an approximate twofold overreporting of skin cancer by residents near a waste site (compared with a control community) and attributed the overreporting to increased recall that a skin lesion had been removed and evaluated for cancer. Roth et al (49) evaluated public opinions as part of a health study of waste sites in Louisiana. The authors found symptom rates were only elevated among those who believed that hazardous waste was dangerous. Reviewing the results of this study and the CDHS studies, Neutra et al (42) hypothesized that symptom complaints and reporting bias may result from stress and behavioral sensitization. Since these factors apparently act as effect modifiers in environmental studies, more attention needs to be devoted to measuring these variables correctly and evaluating effect modification in the analysis. More research may also be warranted to evaluate physiologic responses among the apparent overreporters in these and similar studies.

Exposure Assessment

Exposure determination is usually the most difficult component of environmental epidemiologic studies. Both occupational and nonoccupational studies can be plagued by exposure misclassification, especially when studies are retrospective.

Occupational exposure assessment is somewhat less complex than exposure assessment outside the workplace. Occupational studies can frequently use extensive records on plant design, inventories, process modifications, and information on worker job and work locations (e.g. personnel records, union records, medical records). More recently, a substantial investment has been made in biological monitoring in many industries, which helps transform ambient exposure measures into assessments of actual dose. Occupational exposures are usually at much greater concentrations than community exposures, are usually limited in number, and are usually dominated by a primary route of exposure. In contrast to occupational situations, rarely is there historical information to allow retrospective reconstruction of community exposures.

Community environmental exposures are usually orders of magnitude lower than those found in workplace settings, even when concentrations of contaminants in certain media (e.g. soil, sediments) may be quite high. For example, Table 2 gives our comparison of methylene chloride exposure via occupational sources and via exposure from a landfill. In this case, occupational exposures were hundreds or thousands of times greater than those sustained by residents near landfills. Environmental exposures may not vary as much as occupational exposures over a fixed time period.

Default exposure scenarios have been developed by some regulatory

Table 2 Estimated annual air exposure of individuals to methylene chloride (mg/adult/year)

		Percentile range	
Source	Estimated average	10%	90%
U.S. ambient	10	1	125
Vicinity of landfills	20	0	100
Urban U.S.	50	10	110
Occupational	43,500	750	4,100,000

agencies to estimate population exposures. However, substantial variability within populations and over time limits the epidemiological value of these approaches.

Environmental exposures may be via inhalation, dermal contact, or ingestion. Assessment from different media pathways is frequently required to determine the most important pathway (Table 3). One route may not always predominate nor be predictive of total exposure. In an example given (Table 3), the greatest percentage of adult exposure was derived from outdoor

Table 3 Potential exposure routes and hypothetical percent distribution of total adult exposure for air particulate emissions

	Route of Exposure		
Contaminated matrix	Dermal contact	Ingestion	Inhalation
Ground water	0%	2%	0%
Surface water	0%	0%	0%
Sediment	0%	0%	0%
Soil/Dust	5%	2%	1%
Air: Vapor phase			
Indoor	0%	0%	0%
Outdoors	0%	0%	0%
Air: Particulates			
Indoor	1%	1%	3%
Outdoors	2%	2%	59%
Food			
Fish and shellfish	0%	1%	0%
Meat and game	0%	4%	0%
Dairy	0%	1%	0%
Eggs	—	—	—
Vegetables	0%	10%	0%
TOTALS = 100%	9%	28%	63%

Example adapted to EPA matrix of potential exposure routes (57)

inhalation of emitted, respirable air particles and from consumption of locally farmed vegetables. But widely different scenarios could exist, making individualized assessments necessary. These types of assessments are necessary to target interventions to pathways of greatest public health impact.

Community epidemiologic studies are often undertaken after publicity about adverse health effects. This publicity can increase the difficulty in assessing histories of recreational activities, site use, gardening patterns, and other personal influences on exposure potential and create the opportunity for recall bias. Indeed, studies are needed to validate information that has been recorded in diary-type studies (5). Thus determinations of general environmental exposures are distinctly more complex, less precise, and more open to bias than occupational exposure assessments.

Ideally, exposure assessments for epidemiologic studies could be aided by contributions from experts in analytic and environmental sciences. The goal would be to relate the frequency and degree of contact with environmental exposure sources to an absorbed dose. However, translation of concentrations in sediment, soil, air, water, and food into exposure indices may not be good predictors of absorbed dose (41). Rarely are adequate data available to accomplish assessment of delivered dose.

Prospective studies offer the potential to capture estimates of key exposure potential for study populations. Time/activity studies can help determine where exposure measurements should be concentrated. While it is difficult to characterize human activity patterns for long periods of time, patterns can be characterized over shorter time intervals as a basis for estimating exposure potential.

Classifications of human activity (Table 4) can be cataloged (35) to detail environmental contact with chemicals, physical, or biological agents. Selected measurements coupled with activity assessments and personal dosim-

Table 4   Basic categories of human activity*

1. Working time and time associated with work
2. Domestic work
3. Leisure activities, sports, travel
4. Passive leisure activities
5. Private needs (meals, sleep, etc.)
6. Education and professional training
7. Civic and group activities
8. Child care and related activities
9. Purchasing of goods and services
10. Social life and entertainment

*Adapted from (35)

etry can lead to valid exposure estimates. Further validation can be accomplished through biomonitoring, provided the metabolism of the parent compound is known.

There have been few attempts to apply integrated exposure estimates in environmental epidemiology studies. It is simply too expensive to be done regularly. In most cases, it is more efficient to limit exposure assessment to key exposures with toxic potential and to characterize exposures both from indoor and outdoor sources. The indoor environment should not be neglected because it is often the more important source of exposure.

For example, the EPA has developed the Total Exposure Assessment Methodology (TEAM) to estimate community exposure to a defined set of chemical agents (43, 44, 59, 61). These exposure assessments are based on population probability samples from communities with urban, rural, industrial, and nonindustrial characteristics. A characteristic finding of the TEAM studies has been higher indoor than outdoor exposures to most chemicals resulting from household sources (e.g. smoking, cooking, fuel emissions from attached garages, waxes, cleaning solvents, perfumes, deodorants). Table 5 displays the actual indoor air concentrations and the ratio of indoor to outdoor concentrations for eighteen volatile organic chemicals (VOCs) as measured in Los Angeles during both winter and summer months (60). Most concentrations are several times higher indoors than outdoors and vary with the personal activities of the household members. Clearly, indoor exposures must be considered in nonoccupational environmental epidemiologic studies for both exposed and comparison populations. For some populations, time in transit vehicles (cars, buses, airplanes, boats) may also contribute substantially to total exposure and should be considered.

The pathway of exposures in communities is often complex, and can easily be misrepresented (40). Simplistic models, such as concentric rings around a point air emission source, are usually inadequate. Consideration must be given to the chemical characteristics of specific exposures: whether they are gaseous, vapor, or particulate; whether they form droplets, coalesce, or remain distinct; what proportion of their size distribution is of respirable size; whether they are likely to be deposited and recirculated in houses via dust on shoes or clothing (48); or whether households are likely to form barriers to exposure.

Topographic, geologic, meteorologic, and man-made features of the geographic area must also be considered. Exposure variations over relatively small geographic areas mean that often a series of measurements of personal exposure are necessary to predict patterns of population exposure. Reconstruction of historical patterns is rarely possible since man-made alterations of the environment can vastly change exposure patterns.

Multidisciplinary teams are usually needed to assess air, water, soil, and

Table 5   Average 24-hr air concentrations (μg/m3) indoor and percent of outdoor measurements
TEAM Study, Los Angeles, 1987*

Chemical	February (45 homes)		July (40 homes)	
	Indoor	% of Outdoor	Indoor	% of Outdoor
Benzene	13.0	180	6.0	160
Carbon tetrachloride	0.7	100	0.7	100
Chloroform	1.4	300	1.2	130
Decane	7.0	390	3.8	590
p-Dichlorobenzene	30.0	1500	7.2	1240
Dodecane	3.1	520	3.8	590
Ethylbenzene	5.8	180	2.8	160
Limonene	37.0	2300	7.9	—†
Nonane	5.7	290	3.1	350
Octane	5.4	230	3.3	330
a-Pinene	5.1	750	2.5	—†
Styrene	2.9	170	2.4	560
Tetrachloroethylene	6.8	160	2.2	120
1,1,1-Trichloroethane	19.0	170	16.0	590
Trichloroethylene	1.2	550	1.0	—†
Undecane	7.8	560	4.5	980
o-Xylene	12.0	180	4.3	150
m,p-Xylene	30.0	170	12.0	160

*Adapted from (60)
†Not available

other community exposure pathways. Testing of models by actual environmental and biologic measurements increases the faith in their applicability for the circumstance considered. Exposure modeling and verification in environmental epidemiologic studies are emerging disciplines that need further development to improve the validity of studies of environmental risks.

A COMPREHENSIVE EXAMPLE

The preceding sections have outlined a myriad of considerations in evaluating findings from specific studies. Most of these considerations are generic and can be used widely to evaluate studies. Next, we apply these considerations to a recent study that provides a good example of some of the tradeoffs inherent in environmental studies and the validity implications of those tradeoffs. Then we discuss whether the best available interpretation of this study is a causal association and the modifications that can be made to be more supportive of a causal inference.

Congenital Malformations around Toxic Waste Sites

Geschwind et al (20) conducted a case control study to determine whether rates of congenital malformations were elevated for residents exposed to chemicals from toxic waste sites. They selected 9313 cases in 1983 and 1984 from the New York State Congenital Malformations Registry (CMR). The CMR registers malformations diagnosed in liveborn children up to two years of age. Controls were selected from among the 506,183 live births in New York State in 1983 and 1984. Exclusion criteria for cases and controls were residence in New York City, births in counties without census mapping coordinates, multiple births, and malformations included on the CDC's "Exclusion List" (cases only). The latter were characterized by the authors as being either benign or frequently misclassified.

The possible sources of exposure included 917 waste sites. Sites in New York City were excluded, as were sites located in relatively rural counties, sites not assigned to census tracts, or sites with incomplete address information. Also excluded were 49 sites that were investigated by New York State inspectors and found to have no waste. The remaining 590 sites in 20 New York counties were considered to be potential exposure sources in the study. Exposure to chemicals from waste sites was assumed if the mother's address at the time of the child's birth was within a one-mile radius of a waste site.

The major finding from this study was an estimated 12% elevation in the congenital malformation rate (i.e. RR = 1.12, 95% CI 1.06–1.18) for residents living within a one-mile radius of a waste site. From this finding, the authors inferred that maternal proximity to hazardous waste sites may confer a small increased risk of congenital malformations.

Goal of the Study

In evaluating any study it helps to be clear about the goals and inherent assumptions. In this case, the goal was to compare the rate of congenital malformations among women with exposures from toxic waste sites with the rate that would have occurred had these women not had exposures from waste sites. It bears recognizing that the rates in question are interpreted as prevalence rates, since calculating incidence rates would require knowing the number of adverse outcomes among the underlying population of embryos and fetuses, many of whom have early embryonic (unnoticed) or early fetal death (52).

To accomplish this goal, the authors used a case control design whereby they ascertained all the cases in New York State (with certain exclusions) and sampled the population at risk from around the state (with exclusions similar to those used in case selection). The odds ratio from this study represents the ratio of malformation rates for children of exposed women versus children of unexposed women (i.e. the RR).

Study Design Issues

An inherent assumption in this study design is that women who live near the exposure sources are similar with regard to risk factors to women who live more distant from waste sites, with the exception of factors that can be ascertained and controlled in the analysis. A second assumption is that diagnostic scrutiny is uniform across the study area or at least not correlated with proximity to waste sites. These assumptions are especially important because the choice of a statewide data source for cases and controls ensured large numbers of cases and controls, maximizing statistical power and the precision of the RR, but precluded the collection of information on important potential confounding factors and on reporting biases—two important validity concerns. Thus, the major issue in evaluating this study is uncontrolled bias; that is, the weak but very precise finding could have resulted from failing to account for a (weak) confounding factor(s) or other biases (e.g. reporting bias, differential exposure misclassification). In evaluating whether causal inference is warranted from this study, these issues form the alternative hypotheses that will be contrasted with the hypothesis that proximity to waste sites is related to congenital malformations.

Characteristics of the Disease

Adverse reproductive outcomes occur with relatively short induction and latent periods and therefore can be studied with much less uncertainty about exposures than chronic diseases with longer induction and latent periods. Exposure information can therefore be collected without many of the assumptions necessary in retrospective studies.

The authors focused in their analysis on broad categories of reproductive outcomes described in the International Classification of Disease ninth revision (ICD9). These included all malformations (ICD9 740–759): nervous system (ICD9 740–742); musculoskeletal system (ICD9 754–756); integument system (ICD9 757); oral clefts (ICD9 749); digestive system (ICD9 750–751); chromosome anomalies (ICD9 758); and other (ICD 743–748, 752–753, 759). Our review of the ICD9 codes included in the analysis and the exclusion criteria referred to by the authors indicates that these categories mix malformations with deformations and potentially teratogenic malformations with genetic disorders. It would seem preferable to have restricted the study to focus on teratogenic effects—the only effects that seem likely from chemical exposures. This would have reduced the study size considerably and reduced the statistical power as well, but if there is a true association between waste site exposure and teratogenic events, a higher RR would be expected by limiting the analysis to the relevant health outcomes.

It would be important to distinguish between malformations and deformations to discriminate probable teratogenic events from events that are more likely to be a consequence of intrauterine malposition and pressure. The latter are less likely to be related to environmental exposures and are far more commonly associated with maternal factors that result in uterine constraint (e.g. first pregnancy, small uterus) (16). Reliance on ICD9 categories, which are grouped with regard to clinical assessment of adverse outcomes by organ system rather than by developmental category, blurred the distinction between malformations and deformations. This would have the greatest consequences for the musculoskeletal system category, where a high proportion of the cases would be in categories that include common nonteratogenic deformations like congenital hip dislocations and club foot (when not accompanied by other anomalies) and the integument system, which includes inherited (i.e. nonenvironmental) skin disorders such as ichthyosis, congenital epidermolysis bullosa, and ectodermal dysplasia. Therefore, a more specific subcategory analysis would seem to be necessary to determine whether the reported findings really concern teratogenic events or were unrelated to exposure from waste sites.

The issue of reporting bias near to waste sites (more or less complete reporting) can sometimes be addressed by conducting distinct analyses for major and minor malformations. Major malformations would be expected to be reported uniformly throughout New York State, while minor malformations might be reported less completely in areas of low population density. Reanalysis of the study with respect to the degree of the malformations (as a surrogate for adequacy of reporting) would provide insight into reporting bias. For example, Goldberg et al (21) focused their study of birth defect risk associated with advancing age on ICD subcategories believed to represent major malformations that were adequately ascertained throughout the United States.

Exposure Assessment

Focus on teratogenic events should place the emphasis regarding exposure assessment on the first trimester. However, in this study, exposure to chemicals from waste sites was assumed if the mother's address at the time of the child's birth was within a one-mile radius of a waste site. Address at birth, therefore, is only relevant to the extent that it is a surrogate for address during the first trimester. This is not a trivial concern as the authors cited an estimate in another study that 20% of women change residences between the time of conception and birth (30). A slight differential trend toward waste sites for mothers of cases could have produced the low RR of 1.12 in the presence of no true effect. Likewise, a differential trend away from waste sites would have resulted in an underestimate of the RR.

Residence during the first trimester is one component of an accurate assessment of exposure in this study. The other component involves how well the study's exposure criterion—residence within a one-mile radius of a waste site—serves as a surrogate for exposure. It seems likely that some (or many) of the 590 sites were not sources of sufficient exposure to influence malformation rates and that a one-mile radius around true exposure waste sites would not adequately describe exposure potential. Thus, there is the potential for substantial exposure misclassification. In light of the exposure misclassification there will be bias in the RR to the extent that misclassification is differential with respect to disease status or correlated with other risk factors that are related to teratogenic events.

Confounding Factors

Several confounding factors were considered in the analysis including age, race, education, previous pregnancy complications, sex of the offspring, and previous live births (living and deceased). Information on these factors was available from the CMR. Data on a number of other potentially important confounding factors—nutritional factors, alcohol consumption, smoking, drug usage, and occupational exposures—were not available from the CMR and could not be collected easily given the large number of study subjects. Differences between cases and controls for these factors could have confounded the analysis of malformation rates near waste sites. The authors acknowledged this limitation for alcohol, but argued against the possibility of bias by smoking or occupational exposures, citing studies that found no association between maternal smoking and malformations (37) or environmental pollution and malformations (36). Nutritional factors were not mentioned, although recent research indicates that folic acid deficiency is associated with neural tube defects (38), and these findings were persuasive enough for CDC to recommend that all women contemplating pregnancy take supplemental folic acid (12). It is possible that nutritional status is worse with proximity to waste sites as a consequence of lower social class.

The lack of data on maternal alcohol consumption is a special concern because characteristics associated with fetal alcohol syndrome (e.g. facial abnormalities, severe malformations of the heart and genital system) (29) would be included as malformations in this study. Smoking and drug usage may be important for several reasons related to prematurity and the increased diagnostic scrutiny typically afforded to very low birth weight infants. Smoking has also been associated with neural tube defects, facial clefts, and congenital heart defects (29). Occupational exposures comprise an exposure source to chemicals that seems more direct and presumably at much higher concentrations than residing within one mile of a waste site. The possibility of confounding remains an important consideration in evaluating this study.

Evaluation of Causality

This study was obviously a logistically difficult endeavor on an important issue. To complete the study with available resources, tradeoffs had to be made balancing precision and validity concerns. The findings from this study suggest a weak association between residence near waste sites and congenital malformations. However, our evaluation is that a causal interpretation is only one of several hypotheses for the findings of this study. Inference from this study or other studies on this topic will be improved to the extent that the focus is on teratogenic effects and that alternate hypotheses (confounding, misclassification, etc) are evaluated.

Further analyses of this study could possibly clear up some of these issues. An analysis might be done that focuses on teratogenic events overall or within specific subcategories. Also, taking a lesson from ecologic studies, a small substudy focusing on residential histories and confounding factors would enable analyses to evaluate alternative hypotheses for the reported findings. Regarding assessment of exposure, estimation of misclassification rates for a sample of cases and controls would be useful in determining whether misclassification of exposure was nondifferential. Resolution of these validity concerns would strengthen inferences from this study.

CONCLUSIONS

The previous study offered a good example of many decisions made in designing an environmental study and how these decisions affect the interpretation of the results of environmental studies. Statistical power (a precision consideration) seems often to be an overriding concern in the design of environmental studies. This emphasis is linked to the notion that a study should have sufficient power to detect a certain level of RR with a high probability (by convention usually 80%); otherwise its results may be considered difficult or impossible to interpret (and publish). Emphasis on statistical power in study design almost always shortchanges considerations of validity, which require detailed data on both exposure and outcome measures for individual study participants. In our opinion, causal inference always hinges on validity concerns. Thus, validity concerns should be given higher priority than power considerations in the development and evaluation of environmental studies.

Literature Cited

1. Agency Toxic Subst. Dis. Regist. 1990. *Studies of disease and symptom prevalence in residents of Yukon and Cokeburg, Pennsylvania.* ATSDR/HS-90/10

2. Arneh FC, Edworthy SM, Bloch DA, McShane DJ, Fries JF, et al. 1988. The American Rheumatism Association 1987 revised criteria for the classification of rheumatoid arthritis. *Arthritis Rheum.* 31:315–24

3. Baker D, Greenland S, Mendlein J, Harmon P. 1988. A health study of two communities near the Stringfellow waste site. *Arch. Environ. Health* 43:325–34

4. Behrman RE, ed. 1992. *Nelson Textbook of Pediatrics.* Philadelphia: Saunders

5. Blancata J, Hulebak K. 1992. Exposure assessment as applied to risk characterization. *J. Exp. Anal. Environ. Epidemiol.* 2:151–53

6. Blot WJ, Brinton LA, Fraumeni JF, Stone BJ. 1977. Cancer mortality in U.S. counties with petroleum industries. *Science* 198:51–53

7. Brenner H, Savitz DA, Jockel KH, Greenland S. 1992. The effects of nondifferential exposure misclassification in ecologic studies. *Am. J. Epidemiol.* 135:85–95

8. Buck C. 1975. Popper's philosophy for epidemiologists. *Int. J. Epidemiol.* 4:159–68

9. Calabrese EJ, McCarthy ME, Keynon E. 1987. The occurrence of chemically induced hormesis. *Health Phys.* 52:531–42

10. Cent. Dis. Control. 1992. Misclassification of infant deaths—Alaska 1990–1991. *Morbid. Mortal. Wkly. Rep.* 41:584–91

11. Cent. Dis. Control. 1992. 1993 Revised classification system for HIV infection and expanded surveillance case definition for AIDS among adolescents and adults. *Morbid. Mortal. Wkly. Rep.* 41:961–62

12. Cent. Dis. Control. 1992. Recommendations for the use of folic acid to reduce the number of cases of spina bifida and other neural tube defects. *Morbid. Mortal. Wkly. Rep.* 41(RR-14):1–7

13. Checkoway H, Pierce N, Crawford-Brown D. 1989. *Research Methods in Occupational Epidemiology.* New York: Oxford Univ. Press

14. Cole SK. 1989. Accuracy of death certificates in neonatal deaths. *Commun. Med.* 11:1–8

15. Copeland KT, Checkoway H, McMichael AJ. 1977. Bias due to misclassification in the estimation of relative risk. *Am. J. Epidemiol.* 105:488–95

16. Cotran R, Kumar V, Robbins S, eds. 1989. Diseases of infancy and childhood. In *Robbins Pathologic Basis of Disease.* Philadelphia, PA: Saunders, 4th ed.

17. Dosemeci M, Wacholder S, Lubin J. 1990. Does nondifferential misclassification of exposure always bias a true effect toward the null value? *Am. J. Epidemiol.* 132:746–48

18. Deleted in proof

19. Fingerhut MA, Halperin WE, Marlow DA, Picatelli LA, Honchar PA, et al. 1991. Cancer mortality in workers exposed to 2,3,7,8-tetrochlorodibenzo-p-dioxin. *N. Engl. J. Med.* 324:212–18

20. Geschwind SA, Stolwijk JA, Bracken M, Fitzgerald E, Stark A, et al. 1992. Risk of congenital malformations associated with proximity to hazardous waste sites. *Am. J. Epidemiol.* 135:1197–207

21. Goldberg MF, Edmonds LD, Oakley GP. 1979. Advancing birth defect risk in advanced maternal age. *J. Am. Med. Assoc.* 242:2292–94

22. Greenwald P, Friedlander BR, Lawrence CE, Hearne T, Earle K. 1981. Diagnostic sensitivity bias—an epidemiologic explanation for an apparent brain tumor excess. *J. Occup. Med.* 23:690–95

23. Hajou SI. 1981. Soft tissue sarcomas: Classification and natural history. *CA Cancer J. Clin.* 31:271–80

24. Hardell L, Eriksson M. 1988. The association between soft tissue sarcomas and exposure to phenoxyacetic

acids: a new case control study. *Cancer* 62:652–56

25. Hardell L, Sandstrom A. 1979. Case control study: soft tissue sarcomas and exposure to phenoxyacetic acids or chlorophenols. *Br. J. Cancer* 39:711–17

26. Hill AB. 1965. The environment and disease: association or causation. *Proc. R. Soc. Med.* 58:295–300

27. Hunt L, Silverstein M, Reed C, O'Connell E, O'Fallon W, Yunginger J. 1993. Accuracy of the death certificate in a population-based study of asthmatic patients. *J. Am. Med. Assoc.* 269:1947–52

28. IARC Monogr. Eval. Carcinogen. Risks Hum. 1992. Vol. 54. *Occupational exposures to mists and vapours from strong inorganic acids and other industrial chemicals.* Lyon, France

29. Kallen B. 1988. *Epidemiology of Human Reproduction.* Boca Raton, FL: CRC Press

30. Khoury M, Stewart W, Weinstein A, Panky S, Lindsay P, Eisenberg M. 1988. Residential mobility during pregnancy: implications for environmental teratogenesis. *J. Clin. Epidemiol.* 41:15–20

31. Kleinbaum D, Kupper L, Morgenstern H. 1982. *Epidemiologic Research: Principles and Quantitative Methods.* Belmont, CA: Lifetime Learning Publ.

32. Land CE. 1980. Estimating cancer risk from low doses of ionizing radiation. *Science* 209:1197–203

33. Lanes SJ. 1988. The logic of causal inference in medicine. See Ref. 52a, pp. 59–75

34. Leatherman J, Ingram RH. 1992. Asthma. *Sci. Am. Med.* 14:1–19

35. Lioy PJ. 1991. Human exposure assessment: A graduate level course. *J. Exp. Anal. Environ. Epidemiol.* 1:271–81

36. Longo L. 1980. Environmental pollution and pregnancy: risks and uncertainties for the fetus and infant. *Am. J. Obstet Gynecol.* 137:162–73

37. Malloy MH, Kleinman JC, Bakewell JM, Schramm WF, Land H. 1989. Maternal smoking during pregnancy: no association with congenital malformations in Missouri 1980–83. *Am. J. Public Health* 79:1243–46

38. Milunsky A, Hick H, Jick SS, Bruell CL, MacLaughlin DS, et al. 1989. Multivitamin/folic acid supplementation in early pregnancy reduces the prevalence of neural tube defects. *J. Am. Med. Assoc.* 262:2847–52

39. Morgenstern H, Thomas D. 1993. Principles of study design in environmental epidemiology. *Environ. Health Perspect.* In press

40. Natl. Res. Counc. Rep. 1991. *Environmental epidemiology: Public health and hazardous wastes,* 1:101–53. Washington, DC: Natl. Acad. Press

41. Needham LL, Pirkle JL, Burse VW, Patterson DG, Holler JS. 1992. Case studies of relationship between external dose and internal dose. *J. Exp. Anal. Environ. Epidemiol.* 1(Suppl.): 209–21

42. Neutra R, Lipscomb J, Satin K, Shusterman D. 1991. Hypotheses to explain the higher symptom rates observed around hazardous waste sites. *Environ. Health Perspect.* 94:31–38

43. Pellizzari ED, Perritt K, Hartwell TD, Michael LC, Whitmore R, et al. 1987. *Total Exposure Assessment Methodology (TEAM) Study: Elizabeth and Bayonne, New Jersey; Devils Lake, North Dakota; and Greensboro, North Carolina,* Vol. 2. EPA/600/6–87/002b

44. Pellizzari ED, Perritt K, Hartwell TD, Michael LC, Whitmore R, et al. 1987. *Total Exposure Assessment Methodology (TEAM) Study: Selected Communities in Northern and Southern California,* Vol. 3. EPA/600/6–87/002c

45. Percy CL, Miller BA, Ries LAG. 1990. Effect of changes in cancer classification and the accuracy of cancer death certificates on trends in cancer mortality. *Ann. NY Acad. Sci.* 609:87–99

46. Popper KR. 1968. *The Logic of Scientific Discovery.* New York: Harper & Row

47. Pritchard JG, Tierney LM. 1990. Pulmonary medicine. In *Textbook of Family Practice,* ed. RE Rakel. Philadelphia: Saunders

48. Roberts JW, Budd WT, Ruby MG, Camann DE, Fortmann RC, et al. 1992. Human exposure to pollutants in the floor dust of homes and offices. *J. Exp. Anal. Environ. Epidemiol.* 1(Suppl.):127–46

49. Roth LH, Vernon SW, Weir FW, Peir SM, Sullivan P, Lindsey RJ. 1985. Community exposure to hazardous waste sites: assessing reporting bias. *Am. J. Epidemiol.* 122:418–33

50. Rothman KJ. 1978. A show of confidence. *New Engl. J. Med.* 299:1362–63

51. Rothman KJ. 1981. Induction and latent periods. *Am. J. Epidemiol.* 114:253–59

52. Rothman KJ. 1986. *Modern Epidemiology.* Boston: Little, Brown & Co.

52a. Rothman KJ, ed. 1988. *Causal Infer-*

ence. Chestnut Hill, MA: Epidemiol. Resourc. Inc.

53. Rothman KJ. 1988. Inferring causal connections—habit, faith, or logic. See Ref. 52a, pp. 3–12

54. Sacks J. 1985. Utilization of case definitions and laboratory reporting in the surveillance of notifiable communicable diseases in the United States. *Am. J. Public Health* 75:1420–22

55. Soto-Aguilar MC, Salvaggio JE. 1991. Immunologic aspects of occupational asthma. *Sem. Respir. Med.* 12:185–95

56. US Dep. Health Hum. Serv. 1982. *The Health Consequences of Smoking: Cancer*. Rockville, MD. Public Health Serv. Publ. 82–50179

57. US Environ. Prot. Agency. 1989. *Risk Assessment Guidelines for Superfund. Vol. 1. Health Evaluation Manual, Part A*. EPA/540/1–89/002. Washington, DC

58. US Environ. Prot. Agency. 1992. *Respiratory Health Effects of Passive Smoking: Lung Cancer and Other Disorders*. EPA/600/6–90/006F. Washington, DC

59. Wallace LA. 1987. *Total Exposure Assessment Methodology (TEAM) Study: Summary and Analysis*, Vol. 1. EPA/600/6–87/0021

60. Wallace LA. 1991. Personal exposure to 25 volatile organic compounds. EPA's 1987 Team study in Los Angeles, California. *Toxicol. Ind. Health* 7:203–8

61. Wallace LA. 1993. A decade of studies of human exposure: What have we learned? *Risk Anal.* 13:135–39

62. Weiss KB, Gergen PJ, Wagener DK. 1993. Breathing better or wheezing worse? The changing epidemiology of asthma morbidity and mortality. *Annu. Rev. Public Health* 14:491–513

Annu. Rev. Public Health. 1994. 15:203–21

EPIDEMIOLOGIC RESEARCH ON THE ETIOLOGY OF INJURIES AT WORK

M. A. Veazie, D. D. Landen, T. R. Bender, H. E. Amandus

Division of Safety Research, National Institute for Occupational Safety and Health, Morgantown, West Virginia 26505

KEY WORDS: analytical epidemiology, occupational injury, occupational safety, injuries, accidents

INTRODUCTION

During the past half century, traumatic injuries have emerged as a pre-eminent public health challenge. Injury is the leading cause of hospitalization and death in persons younger than 45 years of age; results in more years of potential life lost than cancer or heart disease; and is second only to respiratory conditions as a reason for contact with physicians (3). One third of all nonfatal injuries and one sixth of all injury fatalities among adults aged 20 to 64 occur on the job (3).

The public health response to a broad spectrum of occupational health and safety problems has embraced three traditional applications of epidemiology: surveillance; etiologic research (i.e. studies to identify risk factors); and evaluation of the effect of interventions. With the increased recognition of injury as a serious public health problem, it is logical that efforts to prevent and control occupational injury should rely on the same epidemiological approach used to attack other public health problems (9, 13).

In industry and government, the role of surveillance in identifying the most important occupational injury problems, targeting high-risk populations, and monitoring trends has been recognized for a long time (16, 26, 28, 48). The application of epidemiological methods to the study of the etiology of occupational injury is far less common.

This review is intended to summarize etiologic studies of occupational injuries, identify their methodological strengths and limitations, point out needs for methodological improvement in such studies, and suggest a research agenda. In order to limit the scope of this broad topic, studies focusing exclusively on musculoskeletal injuries and intentional injuries have been excluded from this review. The epidemiological research literature on back injuries has been reviewed elsewhere (16a, 18a, 37). Intentional injuries have only been recognized as a serious public health problem (outside and within the workplace) within the past decade (2a, 34, 52a, 58) and the preponderance of causality studies to date have appeared in criminology and sociology literature, rather than in the public health literature.

BACKGROUND

We reviewed studies of occupational injuries or mishaps with the potential to result in injury that were published in peer-reviewed journals after 1969 and which evaluated hypotheses by comparing risk of injury among workers of varying characteristics. Surveillance studies, case-series, intervention evaluations, and studies that exclusively focus on musculoskeletal and intentional injuries were excluded from review. Abstracts of studies of work-related injury published in eight selected journals or identified by a key-word literature search of multiple databases were reviewed to determine whether they met the above inclusion criteria. A description of the key-word criteria, multiple databases, and journals included in this search as well as the complete reference list will be provided upon request.

Few studies of occupational injuries have been published that use the methods of analytical epidemiology. Our search of multiple databases and journals over the 22-year period from 1970 through 1992 found only 117 studies, including studies of work-related transportation injuries. The studies we reviewed were published in 42 different journals representing a variety of fields including medicine, safety, public health, and psychology. Sixty-five (55 percent) of the 117 articles reviewed were published in *Accident Analysis and Prevention* (21 articles), *Journal of Occupational Accidents/ Safety Sciences* (20 articles), *The Journal of Occupational Medicine* (12 articles), or *The Journal of Safety Research* (12 articles). Various study designs were used: 67 cohort studies (any longitudinal study comparing rates); 21 cross-sectional studies; 17 case-control studies; 4 quasi-experi-mental study designs; and 8 other designs, or designs that could not be determined.

THE FOCUS OF EPIDEMIOLOGICAL STUDIES

Worker Populations

Among the papers reviewed, manufacturing, with 29 studies, has been the most commonly studied industry group. There were eighteen studies in the transportation industry, particularly of bus and truck drivers. The mining industry and the military each had thirteen studies. There were only eight studies in health care, seven in farming, four in public administration, three in logging, two in construction, and one in utilities. Nineteen studies failed to specify if any particular industry was under study or considered risk factors common to many industries.

The emphasis on manufacturing may reflect the large proportion (24 percent) of the working population in the manufacturing sector (8) and the relative ease with which studies can be conducted in the fixed, measured, resource-rich, and organized environment of manufacturing facilities. The relative emphasis on mining and transportation seems appropriate, given that they have the first and third highest rates of traumatic fatalities among industry divisions (33). Although the greatest number of work-related fatalities occurs in the transportation industry, many studies in the transportation environment failed to distinguish between occupational injuries, injuries to nonworkers, and property damage crashes. Studies that isolated actual injuries to working drivers were rare. More research on occupational injuries in the transportation environment is needed.

That few studies have addressed agriculture and logging is a noteworthy gap given the high-risk nature of these industries (33, 52). Although there have been some surveillance studies (38, 61) and at least one series of mishap investigations (70), not even one study in our review targeted the fishing industry. That only two very limited studies targeted construction is inconsistent with the public health importance of injuries in this industry. The construction industry is second only to mining in fatality rates (33) and reports the highest rate of lost workday injuries to the Bureau of Labor Statistics (8). However, these higher-risk industry groups, particularly agriculture, logging, fishing, and construction, are difficult candidates for rigorous etiologic research due to the transient and independent nature of their workers.

Outcomes

While in some studies the case-definition included mishaps not resulting in injury, most studies excluded noninjury incidents. In many studies the case-definitions were not more detailed than the word "accident," making it difficult to determine injury involvement and interpret the results. Most studies examined injuries of all external causes (e.g. falls, motor-vehicle crashes) combined. Many studies that did restrict their case-definition or stratified their analysis by external cause, focused on mishaps involving buses or trucks. A few studies on slips, trips, or falls; needle-sticks and sharps exposure; diving injuries; and other miscellaneous classifications were noted. Except for one study on ambulance crashes (1) and another on automobile crashes among police officers (64), there were no studies of motor-vehicle injuries in industries other than transportation. This is inconsistent with the importance of motor-vehicle injuries, which are among the leading causes of occupational injury fatalities in many industries, not just in transportation (2a, 33).

Many studies included all injuries, however minor. Analytical studies that focused on severe injuries and fatalities were rare. Only four studies conducted analyses specific to fatalities and four studies focused on traumatic injuries severe enough to require hospitalization. Studies to identify risk factors unique to severe injuries are clearly needed since research has shown that external causes of minor injuries, the majority of injuries in employer reports, differ from those of severe occupational trauma and fatalities (60, 63).

In the occupational injury field studies are needed to examine risk factors that affect the severity of injury, given the occurrence of a mishap. Only fifteen studies in our review examined the severity of injury, usually measured using lost workdays as the dependent variable.

Risk Factors

Risk factors for occupational injury can be grouped into three broad categories: human, job content, and environment. The human category includes variables such as demographics, job title, experience, physical attributes and impairments, stress reactions, knowledge, and attitudes. Job content refers to the design of tasks, how tasks are organized into jobs, and how jobs are scheduled. The environment includes social and organizational factors, physical stressors (e.g. noise, heat), and physical hazards.

Risk factors for 32 better quality studies that did not appear to have shortcomings due to confounding, misclassification, or selection bias, are listed in Tables 1, 2, and 3. It is evident from these tables that many potential risk factors have been examined and found to be significantly associated with injury. However, with the exception of age, job title, experience, and number of hours worked, only a few risk factors have been examined by multiple studies.

In 79 of the 117 studies (68%), at least one human variable was evaluated. Often demographics or job title were included as potential confounders when studying other factors. Physical attributes or impairments (e.g. visual impairment, hearing loss, or prior back pain) were commonly studied risk factors. One particularly noteworthy example of a well-controlled study of physical attributes examined the risk of injury in shipyard workers as a function of noise exposure, hearing loss, alcohol use, and other factors influencing perceptual acuity (46). Another methodologically sound longi-

Table 1   Demographic and human factors examined in higher quality studies[a]

Risk factor	Reference	Risk factor	Reference
Ethnic group	2	Cardiovascular disease	30
Age	2[b], 6[b], 25, 27, 30[b], 31, 35[b], 36[b], 44, 47[b], 57[b], 66[b],	Medication use	30
		Fatigue	25[b]
Marital status	30, 31, 47	Job satisfaction	27, 44[b]
Years education	30, 47	Confidence in co-workers	27
Height	47	Mechanical aptitude	25
Weight	47, 66[b]	Perceived safety risk	17[b]
Gender	31[b], 40, 57[b]	Sleep pattern	30[b]
Number of children	25	Year of hire	2[b]
Job title/tasks	2[b], 6[b], 19[b], 27[b], 31[b], 43, 46, 47, 57[b]	Supervisory position	6[b]
		Safety high priority	17[b]
Experience	5, 6, 27[b], 29[b], 30, 36[b], 47[b]	Feel accidents preventable	17[b]
Unaccustomed to job	27	Lack of time	17[b]
Worked other jobs	27	Low value on safety	17[b]
Years worked	5, 6[b], 25	Morale	17[b]
Hearing loss	30, 46[b]	PPE not available	30
Left-handed	46	PPE not used	30[b]
Sports in leisure	30, 46	PPE thought inadequate	30
Somatic complaints	44	Glove type	19
Prior injury	30, 27[b], 45	Helmet use	15[b]
Reaction time	25	Ear plugs	46[b]
Simple motor speed	25	SCBA use	27[b]
Hand-eye coordination	25[b]	Glasses used	46, 66[b]
Body sway test	25[b]	Alcohol consumption	27, 30, 31, 46[b]
Coordination	25[b]	Drugs	31, 46
Involuntary control	25[b]	Smoking	30, 46

Table 1 (*Continued*)

Risk factor	Reference	Risk factor	Reference
Blood loss	19[b]	Previous traffic accident	46
Duration of surgery	19[b]	Intelligence	25
Vascular procedures	19[b]	Expectancy reaction	25[b]
Abdominal procedures	19[b]	Personality inventory	25
Perceived HIV/HBV risk	19	Attention level	25[b]
Previous laminectomy	73	Stable behavior	25[b]
Vision poor	30	Hand performance test	25[b]
Acute illness	30	Impeded movement	66[b]
Chronic illness	30		

[a] 32 studies without marked potential for confounding, misclassification bias, or selection bias
[b] P-value less than .05

Table 2 Job content variables examined in higher quality studies[a]

Risk Factor	Reference	Risk Factor	Reference
Job change during week	30	Lack of lunch break	30
Unusual task	30[b]	Resting/napping	46, 55[b]
Unusual material used	30	Time off before shift	27, 36[b]
Department	2	Slept during shift	27
Number job changes/year	47[b]	Volume of work	27, 57[b]
Shift	40[b], 56	Absent previous day	22
Hour start shift	41, 56	Driving pattern	36[b]
Hour of day	40[b], 41[b], 56	Location of job	5[b], 29[b], 35[b], 62
Hours worked	6, 25, 35[b], 36[b], 40, 41[b], 57[b]	Mining method	6
Alternating shift	30, 41, 55	Change in job location	27, 47[b]
Number days in shift tour	41[b]	Prior training	27[b]
Rapid change in shift	41	Flexibility in work schedule	25[b]

[a] 32 studies without marked potential for confounding, misclassification bias, or selection bias
[b] P-value less than .05

Table 3 Work environment variables examined in higher quality studies[a]

Risk Factor	Reference	Risk Factor	Reference
Seniority, pay grade	51	Stairway design factors	66[b]
Manager age	17	Season	57[b]
Manager experience	17[b]	Power equipment	5
On/off duty	29[b]	Geographic area	5[b]
Overtime	17	Road type	54[b]
Safety incentives	17[b]	Truck type	54[b]
Lack of training material	17[b]	Vehicle weight	54[b]
Cooperative Supervisor	17[b]	Equipment failure	35[b]
Cooperative Staff	17[b]	Load of truck	35
Management style: Discipline	17[b]	Truck carrier type	35[b]
Management style: Supervision	17[b]	Power steering	35[b]
Management style: Criticism	17[b]	Steering violation	35[b]
Management style: Enforcement	17[b]	Deceleration during crash	62[b]
Replacement crew members	22[b]	Parachute type	4
Work group size	23[b]	Circumstances of injury	5[b], 6[b], 21[b]
Ergonomic stress level	44[b]	Number of vehicles	21[b]
Survivability of accident	62	Poisson process	67
Noise	46[b]	Defective material used	30[b]
Slippery surface	30	Environmental annoyance	44[b]
Improper equipment used	30[b]		

[a] 32 studies without marked potential for confounding, misclassification bias, or selection bias
[b] P-value less than .05

tudinal study examined the risk of non-back occupational injuries associated with prior lumbar laminectomy for degenerative disc disease (73).

Another frequently studied human variable was experience in job or task experience, which was included in 33 studies. Other human variables examined included psychological traits (7 studies), knowledge and attitudes (11 studies), the use of personal protective equipment (10 studies), substance use and abuse (8 studies), and other work and nonwork-related practices and behaviors (8 studies). Only five studies examined psychological, physiological, or behavioral reactions to stress at work (e.g. job satisfaction) as risk factors for injury.

In a well-controlled study, Mohr & Clemmer showed that injury repeaters accounted for only a small proportion of injuries occurring among oil rig drillers (45). That this was the only study to address "accident proneness" suggests that the search for the "accident prone" individual as the primary research agenda typical of previous decades has finally diminished.

While 68 percent of the studies we reviewed included at least one human variable, 36 percent included a variable measuring some characteristic of job content. Difficulty in measuring these variables may partly explain why only 42 studies have evaluated how the risk of injury may be affected by job content. Existing personnel records and injury reports are not likely to include this type of situational and ergonomic information. Most of the cohort studies cited in this review are based on such records.

Among the job content variables examined, shiftwork and scheduling alone were the subject of 22 studies. Thus, shiftwork as a risk factor for injury may have followed lack of experience as the second most frequently evaluated hypothesis in epidemiologic causality studies of occupational injury. Other job-content variables examined as risk factors represented diverse dimensions of job design and layout. These included variables such as organization and planning of work, scheduling, frequency and number of tasks, job difficulty, workload, job rotation, level of mechanization, amount of walking, and, in studies of workers who drive, the nature of the trip (e.g. intercity, interstate).

Environmental factors were the least studied. Most environmental factors studied were design features such as stairway design (66) or recognized material hazards such as equipment defects (35). Some studies examined environmental factors that would affect human performance. For example, 16 studies examined the potential effect of variables describing the organizational and social environment such as firm size, method of payment, management commitment and style, work group size, peer and supervisor relations, and safety incentives. Only six studies evaluated physical stressors such as heat and noise exposure.

Risk Factors for Future Research

To identify which risk factors should be the subject of future research, it is first necessary to define (*a*) what types of risk factors for injury require the use of analytical epidemiology, and (*b*) what types of research questions are likely to lead to effective interventions. On the first point, epidemiological research is needed to do what a series of mishap investigations cannot do—evaluate the impact of risk factors whose contribution to injury can be measured only by a controlled study. The impact of many direct causes of injury (e.g. lack of machine guarding, equipment failure) can be measured by systematic mishap investigation techniques such as those described by Ferry (18). Examples of less direct risk factors that require controlled population studies to quantify their effects include physical stressors such as heat and noise, psychosocial variables such as decision latitude and psychological demands of the job, and ergonomic factors.

Having suggested that the less obvious, underlying risk factors require the use of analytical epidemiology for evaluation, which types of research questions would lead to effective interventions? Passive engineering controls that automatically protect the worker rather than rely on changing worker behavior have long been recognized as valuable in injury control (13a, 24, 57a, 71). The role of etiologic research in this approach is limited since the need for engineering controls is usually established by examining the direct and obvious causes of injury using surveillance and mishap investigation.

The greatest need for etiologic research may be to evaluate risk factors for injury that are identified by two emerging trends in occupational health. The first is the increasing role of ergonomics and human factors. The second related trend is the initiative to redesign the job and reorganize the workplace to reduce occupational stress. The epidemiological evaluation of risk factors for injury predicted by human factors, ergonomics, and occupational stress research would lead to injury-prevention measures based on redesigning jobs, improving physical and social work environments, and restructuring organizations.

Studies to date only begin to test the related hypotheses predicted by ergonomics, human factors, and occupational stress research. Although many studies have been conducted on shiftwork, much greater emphasis on other job content and environmental variables is needed. Even the human variables that should be examined to understand the relationships between workplace stressors and injury risk have not been adequately addressed in the literature. Outside of alcohol and substance use, only five studies examined the effects on injury risk of psychological, physiological, or behavioral responses to workplace conditions. Fatigue, hostility, depression, anxiety, sleep disorders, and impaired concentration are examples of the documented effects of workplace stress that may lead to increased injury risk, but for which there are very few studies.

Finnish researchers have examined hypotheses regarding the interaction between job design and human limitations in information processing (59). These hypotheses are promising candidates for more rigorous epidemiological evaluation. With respect to environmental variables, the few studies on the relationship of noise exposure and injuries underscore the importance of future research that may lead to changes in how noise is assessed and controlled in the workplace (46).

Behavioral and management approaches to occupational injury control are currently popular with industry, have demonstrated some effectiveness (53), and are often considered progressive (11). Assumptions underlying behavioral approaches to occupational injury control, such as the assumption that positive safety attitudes contribute to a reduction of risk, need to be evaluated. Etiologic studies of how injury risk is affected by such factors as knowledge, attitudes, beliefs, and intentions may improve the usefulness of evaluation research strategies that use these factors as indicators of safety performance. However, even more important than etiologic research is the need for properly controlled intervention studies to evaluate the effectiveness of behavioral and management approaches.

METHODOLOGICAL CHALLENGES

Rare Events and Situational Exposures

Researchers and commentators in the safety literature have observed that injuries, especially severe injuries, are too rare to be used as reliable outcomes in safety research and evaluation. This view is understandable from the perspective of injury reduction in a single plant, company, or production system. There are simply not enough severe trauma cases and fatalities to provide sufficient sample sizes for quantitative research. In the practice of epidemiology, however, studies of entire regions, states, and nations are commonplace, and sample size is usually less of a problem in these settings. If the events to be studied are rare, such as severe trauma and fatalities, hospital-based case-control studies can be used. Cohen & colleagues (12), for example, ascertained injuries from ladder falls that were treated in hospital emergency rooms throughout the entire United States and were reported to the Consumer Product Safety Commission. Workers from the same work site were selected as controls and exposures were measured by field investigations and interviews.

Another challenge in occupational injury epidemiology is the measurement of situational exposures (i.e. factors that change over time). Exposure to variables such as familiarity with tasks, the routineness of tasks, ambient temperature, and the presence of hazards right before the occurrence of injury is of interest. Jones & Stein (35) provide one example of how this problem is handled. They examined tractor-trailers involved in crashes (cases) for violations of safety standards, and then selected and stopped control vehicles traveling down the same road. These controls were inspected for the same violations. Thus, cases at time of injury were compared to controls at a time that did not result in injury.

Recurrent Events

Longitudinal studies of occupational injury require different statistical methods than classical occupational cohort studies where the endpoint is death or chronic disease. Injuries may occur to the same individual multiple times. The application of classical statistical methods violates the assumption of independence and may result in biased variance estimates (71a).

Greater use should be made of newly developed methods to analyze correlated, categorical data in longitudinal studies. To adjust variance estimates for correlated observations in a study of slips, trips, and falls among painters, Hunting (32) used generalized estimating equations in a longitudinal data analysis. This new method accommodates logistic and Poisson regression, which are popular in epidemiological studies (72). While this approach is functional for cohort studies, no straightforward methods have been developed to account for correlations between an individual's multiple events in case-control studies.

Homogeneous Exposures

Certain potential risk factors for occupational injury may affect entire worker populations, leaving little variation in exposure to permit the assessment of differences in risk. Examples of exposures that all employees in a firm may experience include management styles of an organization, worker-participation in safety, organizational stress indicators, measures of safety climate, shiftwork schedules, and mechanization. One potentially promising approach to this problem is to conduct large studies (e.g. national longitudinal surveys, population-based case-control studies) that compare individual workers from different firms. This approach is complicated by the need to measure and control for a large number of potential confounding variables.

Another option is to compare firms rather than individuals. Many studies comparing firms, however, are difficult to interpret because the measurements of exposures and confounders are incomplete or imprecise, and because they are vulnerable to "ecologic fallacy," i.e. the observation that the correlation between two variables observed in multiple populations is often very different from the corresponding correlation between individuals within any given population.

More longitudinal, quasi-experimental study designs such as time series comparisons are also needed. This approach can be an effective method of evaluating the injury effects of exposures that are homogeneous at one point in time but heterogeneous over time, even within a single company.

Confounding

One of the most difficult challenges in epidemiology is the measurement of, and control for, confounding. In this review, 60 percent of the studies only analyzed associations between injury and one other variable at a time without any effort to adjust for the effects of potentially confounding variables. Seventy percent were judged likely to have been biased by confounding.

In occupational injury epidemiology, many human, environment and job content variables are correlated to varying degrees with exposure to risk, i.e. the physical danger of the job tasks, work intensity, and hours of work. In some studies, it is particularly important to control for exposure to risk using very specific measures. Variables like shiftwork and piece-rate pay, for example, can conceivably be tightly correlated with work intensity. In studies of needle-stick injuries among nurses, it would be important to control for the number of procedures performed per shift when assessing the effect of shiftwork on injury rates. Some physical stressors, such as noise, can be strongly correlated with sources of hazardous energy.

Data on confounders are not routinely collected in employer records or injury reports. Thus, studies that collect original data are more likely to control successfully for confounding. Techniques that measure the exposure to risk associated with specific jobs and tasks are in common use in epidemiological studies of occupational illnesses (10). Similar techniques can be applied to the epidemiology of occupational injuries. One study, for example, validated an observational assessment of the job called the "ergonomic stress level" based on body motion and posture, physical effort, active hazards, and environmental stressors (44). The ergonomic stress level then served as an effective measure of exposure to risk in an analysis that also examined job satisfaction as a risk factor.

Other Biases

Selection and misclassification bias (i.e. measurement error) are common concerns in most of occupational epidemiology, including studies of injury at work. The use of existing records is an important source of measurement error because data were collected for other purposes and not collected in a scientifically rigorous manner. Only 40 percent of the studies we reviewed collected original data to measure exposures using interviews, questionnaires, or direct observation. More occupational injury studies that collect original data with valid instruments are needed.

Another form of misclassification noted in the literature stems from the use of one-year or longer recall periods in cross-sectional studies. Some studies even used three-year and five-year recall periods for relatively minor injuries (49, 50). A recent evaluation of recall bias in the National Health Interview Survey showed that a one-year recall period resulted in substantial underreporting of all injuries at work (39). Studies of self-reported injuries may be more valid when recall periods are confined or adjusted to less than six months.

Another form of misclassification bias in the current literature is the widespread use of "all accidents" (otherwise undefined) as the study outcome. This practice may mask the effect of risk factors that are concentrated on very specific external causes of injury such as "slips, trips, and falls." Although many risk factors are postulated to have effects on a broad spectrum of injuries, future research will need to study the effects of some risk factors that are unique to specific groups of injuries. A study of risk factors for injury to firefighters, for example, provides an example of segregating analyses by meaningful injury outcomes (e.g. falls from elevations, smoke inhalation, and burns) (27).

Measurement error is also likely when the classification of the study outcome requires an investigator or respondent to subjectively assign cause or responsibility to an injury event. The investigators in one study asked nurses to recall "accidents" they felt were caused by sleepiness (20). Thus, misclassification of outcome may have occurred if nurses who were exposed to the hypothesized risk factor, rotating shiftwork, were more likely to attribute their "accidents" to sleepiness even though they may suffer from the same injury rate as day-shift workers. Other examples of this problem are the studies of "pilot error" mishaps in aviation (7) or the studies of industrial injuries comparing actively and passively involved victims (68, 69). The use of panels, which assign cause or responsibility based on specific criteria and are blinded to exposure status, could reduce this bias.

Selection bias was considered likely or possible in 31 percent of the studies and was suspected in 25 percent of the studies reviewed. Many of the cross-sectional studies were based on low response rates (e.g. 30 to 40 percent). In cohort studies, we suspect a form of survivor bias, or "safe worker effect". Some studies restricted their analyses to employees who were at risk throughout the entire study period and excluded those who left the company. If the probability of dropping out varied by both injury risk and level of the risk factor studied, the results of the study would be biased. Another problem noted in some epidemiological causality studies was the selection of noncomparable controls or comparison groups.

Selection bias is a definite concern when reports required by the Occupational Safety and Health Administration (OSHA) or workers' compensation systems are used to ascertain injuries. A report by the National Research Council documents concern regarding underreporting of injuries on the OSHA log that employers are required to keep (51). Studies of occupational deaths reported from multiple sources have shown that workers' compensation systems have a problem with underreporting (65). Cohort and case-control studies using workers' compensation records to ascertain cases may suffer from severe selection biases if the probability of reporting an injury to workers' compensation varies by exposure status.

Measurement of Severity

The 16 studies we reviewed that did analyze injury severity usually used lost workdays as a measure of severity. Although this measure is an indication for cost of injury, it is less suitable as a measure of injury severity because it is not only a function of severity, but also of job demands, workplace policies, and disability qualification criteria that partly determine whether an injury results in lost work time. The development and evaluation of more accurate and interpretable measures of severity would be useful in studies of occupational injury.

The Abbreviated Injury Score (AIS) (42), the Injury Severity Score (ISS) (42), and the Anatomic Profile (AP) (14) are validated measures of severity that predict survival based on the degree of damage to the body, and to a lesser degree on other severity consequences. These measures should be incorporated more frequently into studies of acute, life-threatening occupational trauma in order to examine risk factors that affect the severity of injury. Unfortunately, AIS, ISS, and AP cannot precisely discriminate between severity levels among the relatively less severe occupational injuries on which etiologic research most commonly focuses. Mitchell and colleagues, for example, examined the severity of injuries treated in an industrial plant's medical department and found that most injuries fell within a narrow range of AIS scores (44a). More sensitive scales are required that can discriminate between different levels of anatomical damage among occupational injuries.

SUMMARY OF FINDINGS AND RECOMMENDATIONS

Relatively few (only 117) analytical epidemiological studies of occupational injury causality were published during 1970–1992 in the peer-reviewed literature that we surveyed. Some very high-risk industries have been the subject of few or no studies at all.

Evidence from the literature indicates that a large number of risk factors have been evaluated by epidemiologic research. Although most risk factors have been evaluated by only a few studies that appeared to be of higher quality (Tables 1, 2, 3), the contribution to injury risk of many factors was found to be significant.

The paucity of well-controlled analytical studies suggests that much still remains to be done in occupational injury epidemiology. Future research should encompass the following: (a) targeting of high-risk industries, including construction, agriculture, fishing, and logging; (b) employment of precise and appropriately restricted definitions of injury; (c) a focus on severe trauma, perhaps by greater reliance on hospital-based studies; (d) identification of the predictors of injury severity; (e) verification of some assumptions of behavioral strategies typically used in safety management; and (f) evaluation of job content, environmental and human variables that may alter the risk of injury as predicted by research in human factors, ergonomics, occupational stress, and organizational behavior.

Important job content variables for future injury research include the design and scheduling of tasks and jobs, and how tasks are integrated into jobs. Environmental variables to be examined include psychosocial factors (e.g. worker control, social support, psychological demands) and organizational structure and change (e.g. continuous quality improvement, management commitment). Stressors in the physical environment (e.g. noise, lighting, heat) are also in need of investigation. Behavioral, psychological, and physiological responses to stressors on the job are categories of human variables that merit future consideration.

Significant methodological problems were found in 85 of the 117 studies reviewed. Future improvements in injury research methodology include: (a) use of appropriate study designs for rare events; (b) collection of situational data for workers at risk at the time workers were injured, and during injury-free reference periods; (c) development of appropriate methods to estimate the contribution of injury risk factors when some workers have recurrent injuries; (d) development of methods to estimate and control for exposure to safety hazards; (e) estimation of, and control for, recall bias in studies of self-reported injuries and exposures; (f) use of longitudinal study designs or multi-firm national surveys to evaluate exposures that are homogeneous at one point in time, but change over time; and (g) development of severity measures for occupational injuries.

CONCLUSIONS

While widespread application and evaluation of known strategies for occupational injury control should not be delayed, further advances are possible with a better understanding of how job design and the physical, psychosocial, and organizational environments influence the risk of injury. This will require tools to estimate the relative contribution of causal factors that cannot be ascertained from injury surveillance or mishap investigations alone. In conjunction with methodologies from other fields such as human factors, behavioral sciences, stress research, organizational behavior, and systems safety engineering, analytical epidemiology provides an important tool. Future etiologic research on occupational injuries must be multifactorial, which requires a multidisciplinary approach, and must begin to make wide use of advanced epidemiological methods.

While the public health model is well established in preventing disease through the application of descriptive epidemiology or surveillance, etiologic research, and experimental trials or intervention studies, the model needs to be applied more frequently to occupational injury. The success of future occupational injury research and the possibility of improved injury prevention efforts may lie in the ability of safety and public health disciplines to come together to more fully implement this model.

Literature Cited

1. Auerbach PS, Morris JA, Phillips JB, Redliner SR, Vaughn WK. 1987. An analysis of ambulance accidents in Tennessee. *J. Am. Med. Assoc.* 258: 1487–90
2. Baker CC. 1987. Ethnic differences in accident rates at work. *Br. J. Ind. Med.* 44:206–11
2a. Baker SP, Samkoff JS, Fisher RS, Van Buren CB. 1982. Fatal occupational injuries. *J. Am. Med. Assoc.* 248:692–97
3. Baker SP, O'Neill B, Ginsburg MJ, Li G. 1992. *The Injury Fact Book*, pp. 8–16. New York: Univ. Press
4. Baldwin CC. 1988. Parachuting injuries and type of parachute in a reserve rescue unit. *Aviat. Space Environ. Med.* 59:780–82
5. Bennett JD, Passmore DL. 1985. Multinomial logit analysis of injury severity in US underground bituminous coal mines. *Accid. Anal. Prev.* 17:399–408
6. Bennett JD, Passmore DL. 1984. Probability of death, disability, and restricted work activity in United States underground bituminous coal mines, 1975–1981. *J. Saf. Res.* 15:69–76
7. Borowsky MS, Gaynor J, Barrett G, Beck A. 1981. Relationships between US Navy carrier landing accidents and flight experience parameters. *Aviat. Space Environ. Med.*52:109–11
8. Bur. Labor Stat. 1993. *Occupational Injuries and Illness in the United States by Industry, 1990.* US GPO Bull. 2399
9. Cent. Dis. Control. 1992. *Setting the National Agenda for Injury Control in the 1990's.* Natl. Injury Cont. Conf. 3rd, April 22–25, 1991, pp. 327–74. Denver, CO. US GPO 634–666
10. Checkoway H, Pearce NE, Brown DJC. 1989. *Research Methods in Occupational Epidemiology*, pp. 29–34. New York: Oxford Univ. Press
11. Cohen A. 1977. Factors in successful occupational safety programs. *J. Saf. Res.* 9:168–78
12. Cohen HH, Lin L. 1991. A retrospective case-control study of ladder fall accidents. *J. Saf. Res.* 22:21–30
13. Comm. Trauma Res. 1985. *Injury in America. A Continuing Public Health Problem*, pp. 6, 25. Washington, DC: Natl. Acad. Press
13a. Comm. Trauma Res. 1985. See Ref. 13, pp. 37–41
14. Copes WS, Champion HR, Sacco WJ, Lawnmick MM, Gann DS, et al. 1990. Progress in characterizing anatomic injury. *J. Trauma* 30:1200–7
15. Crowley JS. 1991. Should helicopter frequent flyers wear head protection? A study of helmet effectiveness. *J. Occup. Med.* 33:766–69
16. DeReamer R. 1980. *Modern Safety and Health Technology*, pp. 269–334. New York: Wiley
16a. Deyo RA, Cherkin D, Conrad D, Volinn E. 1991. Cost, controversy, crisis: Low back pain and the health of the public. *Annu. Rev. Public Health.* 12:141–56
17. Eyssen GM, Hoffman JE. 1980. Managers' attitudes and the occurrence of accidents in a telephone company. *J. Occup. Accid.* 2:291–304
18. Ferry TS. 1988. *Modern Accident Investigation and Analysis,* pp. 141–224. New York: Wiley
18a. Garg A, Moore JS. 1992. The epidemiology of low back pain in industry. *Occup. Med.* 7:593–608
19. Gerberding JL, Littell C, Tarkington A, Brown A, Schecter WP. 1990. Risk of exposure of surgical personnel to patients' blood during surgery at San Francisco General Hospital. *N Engl. J. Med.* 322:1788–93
20. Gold DR, Rogacz S, Bock N, Tosteson TD, Baum TM, Speizer FE. 1992. Rotating shift work, sleep, and accidents related to sleepiness in hospital nurses. *Am. J. Public Health.* 82:1011–14
21. Golob TF, Recker WW, Leonard JD. 1987. An analysis of the severity and incident duration of truck-involved freeway accidents. *Accid. Anal. Prev.* 19: 375–95
22. Goodman PS, Garber S. 1988. Absenteeism and accidents in a dangerous environment: Empirical analysis of underground coal mines. *J. Appl. Psychol.* 73:81–86

23. Guastello DD, Guastello SJ. 1987. The relationship between work group size and occupational accidents. *J. Occup. Accid.* 9:1–9

24. Haddon W. 1974. Strategy in preventive medicine: Passive vs. active approaches to reducing human wastage. *J. Trauma* 14:353–54

25. Hakkinen S. 1979. Traffic accidents and professional driver characteristics: A follow-up study. *Accid. Anal. Prev.* 11:7–18

26. Hanrahan LP, Moll MBV III. 1989. Injury surveillance. *Am. J. Public Health.* 79:38–45

27. Heineman EF, Shy CM, Checkoway H. 1989. Injuries on the fireground: Risk factors for traumatic injuries among professional fire fighters. *Am. J. Ind. Med.* 15:267–82

28. Heinrich HW. 1959. *Industrial Accident Prevention,* pp. 92–107. New York: McGraw-Hill

29. Helmkamp JC, Bone CM. 1987. The effect of time in a new job on hospitalization rates for accidents and injuries in the US Navy, 1977 through 1983. *J. Occup. Med.* 29:653–59

30. Hertz RP, Emmett EA. 1986. Risk factors for occupational hand injury. *J. Occup. Med.* 28:36–41

31. Hingson RW, Lederman RI, Walsh DC. 1985. Employee drinking patterns and accidental injury: Study of four New England States. *J. Stud. Alcohol.* 46:298–303

32. Hunting KL, Matanoski GM, Larson M, Wolford R. 1991. Solvent exposure and the risk of slips, trips, and falls among painters. *Am. J. Ind. Med.* 20:353–70

33. Jenkins EL, Kisner SM, Fosbroke DE, Stout NA, Layne LA, Castillo DN, et al. 1993. Fatal injuries to workers in the United States, 1980–1989: A decade of surveillance, National Profile. *DHHS (NIOSH)* Publ. No. 93–108

34. Jenkins EL, Layne LA, Kisner SM. 1992. Homicide in the workplace. *Am. Assoc. Occup. Health Nurses J.* 40: 215–18

35. Jones IS, Stein HS. 1989. Defective equipment and tractor-trailer crash involvement. *Accid. Anal. Prev.* 21:469–81

36. Kaneko T, Jovanis PP. 1992. Multiday driving patterns and motor carrier accident risk: A disaggregate analysis. *Accid. Anal. Prev.* 24:437–56

37. Kelsey JL, Golden AL. 1988. Occupational and workplace factors associated with low back pain. *Occup. Med.* 3:7–17

38. Kennedy R, Helmkamp J, Conway G, Myers M, Klatt M. 1993. Commerical fishing fatalities in Alaska, January 1991–December 1992. *Morbid. Mortal. Wkly. Rep.* In press

39. Landen DL, Hendricks SA. 1992. Estimates from the National Health Interview Survey on occupational injury among older workers in the United States. *Scand. J. Work Environ. Health* 18:18–20

40. Laundry BR, Lees REM. 1991. Industrial accident experience of one company on 8- and 12-hour shift systems. *J. Occup. Med.* 33:903–6

41. Laursiden O, Tonnesen T. 1990. Injuries related to the aspects of shift working. *J. Occup. Accid.* 12: 167–76

42. Mackenzie EJ. 1984. Injury severity scales: Overview and directions for future research. *J. Emerg. Med.* 2:537–49

43. McKenas DK, Jackson WG. 1987. Retrospective cohort analysis of class A mishaps in aviators evaluated at USAFSAM: 1957–1984. *Aviat. Space Environ. Med.* 58:735–41

44. Melamed S, Luz J, Najenson LT, Jucha E, Green M. 1989. Ergonomic stress levels, personal characteristics, accident occurrence and sickness absence among factory workers. *Ergonomics* 32:1101–10

44a. Mitchell CS, Cloeren M, Schwartz BS. 1993. Application of an injury surveillance system to injuries at an industrial facility. *Accid. Anal. Prev.* 25:453–58

45. Mohr DL, Clemmer DI. 1988. The "accident prone" worker: An example from heavy industry. *Accid. Anal. Prev.* 20:123–27

46. Moll van Charante AW, Mulder PGH. 1990. Perceptual acuity and the risk of industrial accidents. *Am. J. Epidemiol.* 131:652–63

47. Mueller BA, Mohr DL, Rice JC, Clemmer DI. 1987. Factors affecting individual injury experience among petroleum drilling workers. *J. Occup. Med.* 29:126–31

48. Muldoon JT, Wintermeyer LA, Eure JA, Fuortes L, Merchant JA, et al. 1985. State activities for surveillance of occupational disease and injury. *Morbid. Mortal. Wkly. Rep.* 1987, 36(SS-2):7–13

49. Murphy DJ. 1981. Farm safety attitude and accident involvement. *Accid. Anal. Prev.* 13:331–37

50. Napier TL, Goe WR, Pugh AR. 1985. Incidence and predictive factors associated with farm accidents in Ohio.

Res. Circ. Ohio Agric. Res. Dev. Cent. 287:1–15

51. Natl. Res. Counc. Pollack ES, Keimig DG, eds. 1987. *Counting Injuries and Illnesses in the Workplace: Proposals for a Better System*, pp. 53–62, 67–68. Washington, DC: Natl. Acad. Press

52. Natl. Saf. Counc. 1992. *Accident Facts*. Chicago

52a. Omenn GS. 1982. Preventing injuries, disability and death at work (Starting with vehicles and guns!). *J. Am. Med. Assoc.* 248:723–24

53. Peters RH. 1991. Strategies for encouraging self-protective employee behavior. *J. Saf. Res.* 22:53–70

54. Philipson LL. 1981. Statistical analyses of highway commercial vehicle accidents. *Accid. Anal. Prev.* 13:289–306

55. Pokorny MLI, Blom DHJ, van Leeuwen P, van Nooten WN. 1987. Shift sequences, duration of rest periods, and accident risk of bus drivers. *Hum. Factors* 29:73–81

56. Pokorny MLI, Blom DHJ, van Leeuwen P. 1987. Shifts, duration of work and accident risk of bus drivers. *Ergonomics* 30:61–88

57. Pratt DS, Marvel LH, Darrow D, Stallones L, May JJ, Jenkins P. 1992. The dangers of dairy farming: The injury experience of 600 workers followed for two years. *Am. J. Ind. Med.* 21:637–50

57a. Robertson LS. 1983. *Injuries: Causes, Control Strategies, and Public Policy.* Lexington, MA: Lexington Books. 219 pp.

58. Rosenberg ML, Fenley MA, eds. 1991. *Violence in America: A Public Health Approach*. New York: Oxford Univ. Press

59. Saari J, Lahtela J. 1981. Work conditions and accidents in three industries. *Scand. J. Work Environ. Health.* 7:97–105

60. Salmilnen S, Saari J, Saarela KL, Rasanen T. 1992. Fatal and non-fatal occupational accidents: identical versus differential causation. *Saf. Sci.* 15:109–18

61. Schnitzer PG, Landen DD, Russell JC. 1993. Occupational injury deaths in Alaska's fishing industry,1980–1988. *Am. J. Public Health* 83:685–88

62. Shanahan DF, Mastroianni GR. 1984. Spinal injury in a US Army light observation helicopter. *Aviat. Space Environ. Med.* 55:32–40

63. Shannon HS, Manning DP. 1980. Differences between lost-time and non-lost-time industrial accidents. *J. Occup. Accid.* 2:265–72

64. Stotland E, Pendleton M. 1989. Workload, stress, and strain among police officers. *Behav. Med.* 15:5–17

65. Stout N, Bell C. 1991. Effectiveness of source documents for identifying fatal occupational injuries: A synthesis of studies. *Am. J. Public Health* 81:725–28

66. Templer J, Archea J, Cohen HH. 1985. Study of factors associated with risk of work-related stairway falls. *J. Saf. Res.* 16:183–96

67. Van Nooten WM, Blom DHJ, Pokorny MLI, van Leeuwen P. 1991. Time intervals between bus drivers' accidents. *J. Saf. Res.* 22:41–47

68. Verhaegen P, Strubbe J, Vonck R, Van Den Abelle J. 1985. Absenteeism, accidents and risk-taking. *J. Occup. Accid.* 7:177–86

69. Verhaegen P, Vanhalst B, Derijcke H, Hoecke M. 1976. The value of some psychological theories on industrial accidents. *J. Occup. Accid.* 1:39–45

70. Wagenaar WA, Groeneweg J. 1987. Accidents at sea: Multiple causes and impossible consequences. *Int. J. Man-Machine Studies* 27:587–98

71. Weeks JL, Levy BS, Wagner GR, eds. 1991. *Preventing Occupational Disease and Injury,* p. 55. Washington, DC: Am. Public Health Assoc.

71a. Zeger SL, Liang KY. 1992. An overview of methods for the analysis of longitudinal data. *Stat. Med.* 11:1825–39

72. Zeger SL, Liang KY, Albert PS. 1988. Models for longitudinal data: A generalized estimating equation approach. *Biometrics* 44:1049–60

73. Zwerling C, Ryan J. 1991. Risk and severity of non-back occupational injuries after lumbar laminectomy for degenerative disc disease. *Am. J. Ind. Med.* 19:531–38

Annu. Rev. Public Health 1994. 15:223–35

THE MATURING PARADIGM
OF PUBLIC HEALTH

Abdelmonem A. Afifi and Lester Breslow

School of Public Health, University of California, Los Angeles, California 90024

KEY WORDS: community medicine, public health practice, core disciplines of public health, health professions, scientific basis of public health

INTRODUCTION

Evolution of Public Health

Modern public health emerged as social action to control communicable diseases during nascent industrialization. In the early 1800s people flocked into urban slums around burgeoning industrial plants. The undernutrition, crowding, filth and excessive work, which characterized life for early factory workers and their families, induced severe disease outbreaks. The 1842 Chadwick Report in England (7) and the 1850 Shattuck Report in the United States (14) aroused a sanitary awakening and social reform that constituted the public health of that time.

Scientific advances, especially in microbiology, during the latter part of the nineteenth and early twentieth centuries created a new and remarkably effective dimension in the field. The potential of organized action against communicable diseases, along with growing related knowledge, led to formation of governmental public health departments. These agencies participated prominently not only in communicable disease control, but also in improving maternal and child health and in paving the way to other health successes.

Meanwhile, however, a whole new set of health problems has arisen, and public health has not rapidly adapted itself to them while still dealing with formerly dominant and still existing challenges.

223

0163-7525/94/0510-0223$05.00

The Dynamic Nature of Public Health

The fact that health problems emerge mainly in response to conditions of life requires that public health remain highly adaptive, especially when living conditions are changing rapidly. Nowadays, in developing as well as in developed nations, technological innovations are vastly altering how people live.

Thus, industrialization and its spread around the world during the nineteenth and twentieth centuries stimulated first the problems of communicable disease, and then the epidemics of chronic disease—coronary heart disease, cancer, diabetes, and chronic obstructive lung disease. Public health geared up initially in response to the first set of problems and is now moving to control the second. A third large group is already upon us: HIV/AIDS, domestic and street violence, and substance abuse.

Adjustment of the majority of Euro-American public health workers to different cultures and alteration of practice to meet the special needs of other ethnic groups, who constitute a growing proportion of the population, remain high priorities for public health in this country.

How to manage the nuclear power that has been released in the twentieth century has attracted much public health attention. That new feature of life poses many health risks: international violence; exposure of uranium miners and nuclear plant workers to harmful radiation; nuclear plant disasters; disposal of nuclear waste; and exposure of patients to potentially harmful medical radiation procedures. All of these issues have arisen during the past half-century; confronting them has entailed substantial commitment of a variety of public health workers.

The striking growth of the elderly population in recent decades is both a tribute to the successes of past public health endeavor and an inspiration to further work. It is necessary now to seek and apply ways of maintaining health into the later years. Beyond this preventive approach to the problem, public health must also develop efficient and effective services to help older people cope with the frailties that so often plague them—just as public health has developed services for those starting life.

Health problems that have accompanied the growth of industrialization, racial-ethnic tensions, nuclear power, and an aging population illustrate the dynamic nature of public health and why its core disciplines must always remain "on the ready." Consequences of public health rigidity may be seen in the recent health history of the Russian and East European people. During the early days of the Soviet regime public health took the form of "epidemic stations" to abate typhus and other communicable diseases with the modalities then available. Failure to cultivate the public health disciplines, especially epidemiology, left inadequate resources to cope with the subsequent epidemics of coronary heart disease and lung cancer. The result was not learning from Western experience, or their own, about the origin of such conditions. That failure led to shortening millions of lives after other developed nations had begun to bring those pandemics under control. Now, the situation is being corrected.

Meanwhile, in this country, according to the Institute of Medicine report (3), "This nation has lost sight of its public health goals and has allowed the system of public health activities to fall into disarray." The field is now responding to that challenge.

It therefore seems timely to consider the paradigm of public health as it exists today. Its mission has been well stated as "fulfilling society's interest in assuring conditions in which people can be healthy" (3). Providing opportunity, the conditions, for health as a basic human right thus constitutes the public health goal. Although this mission statement has been criticized for unrealistically encompassing responsibility for broad factors underlying health such as education, jobs and housing, which lie outside of public health agencies (12), the latter must attend to the public's health-specific aspects. Furthermore, public health carries primary responsibility, for example, for minimizing exposure to toxic agents, guaranteeing access for all to good medical care, eliminating inducements to harmful behavior such as promotion of cigarette smoking, and fostering empowerment of the socially disadvantaged.

Carrying out that mission requires both social commitment and appropriate expertise. Hence, public health now draws substantially upon several scientific disciplines and related professions. From these sources public health has developed its own core disciplines and integrated them into a profession with its own distinctive paradigm. Our intent in this review is to elucidate that paradigm. In an accompanying article, Fineberg et al also discuss the public health paradigm in the context of professional education in schools and programs of public health (6).

Scientific Disciplines and Professions Underlying Public Health

A paradigm is a fundamental unit that cannot be reduced to smaller components and serves as the basis for abstracting laws, theories, and points of views that enrich the scientific and professional activity in a given field (8). Some scientific disciplines and professions, such as physics and medicine, are sufficiently mature that it is relatively easy to describe their unique focus and draw their boundaries. Quite to the contrary, and by its very nature, the field of public health is multidisciplinary. This characteristic leads to difficulty in understanding it as a whole and defining its operations. To be able to do that, we must note the underlying scientific disciplines and professions feeding into public health. The scientific disciplines include biomedical sciences, statistics, physical sciences, economics, and socio-behavioral sciences.

It is also essential that workers in the several disciplines of public health understand and serve the practice of public health. Commitment to that principle characterizes the *profession* of public health which, in turn, draws upon several other professions.

Medicine's concern with health makes it perhaps the most obvious relative of public health. As the dominant healing arm of Euro-American society, medicine has evolved largely as a mechanistic approach to people and the diseases that affect them. Beyond simply observing what seems to preserve and, when necessary, restore the health of individuals, physicians and their medical scientist allies have delineated the parts of the body (anatomy), how they function (physiology), their disorders (pathology), and the agents of disease (etiology). With these and related kinds of knowledge, practitioners have developed means of combatting disease with a focus on repairing breakdown of the "machinery". Diagnosis and treatment of *individuals,* with the primary professional branches—medicine and surgery—constitute the core of clinical medicine. Prevention receives some attention, but the more dramatic appeal of cure typically overwhelms it. Over the years, some physicians have recognized the roles of social and environmental as well as biological factors in the origin and progress of disease. Often these same physicians have seen disease as it affects populations not just individuals, and they have moved toward public health (15).

In former times, applying the *engineering* profession's paradigm, solving machine-system problems, to the circumstances of human life made it a highly visible ally of public health; now its role seems to be growing again in relation to new technologies and their impact on health. A third profession, *education,* contributes heavily to the human base upon which public health builds. Finally, the *management* profession is playing an increasingly important role in improving the organization and services of health care institutions.

THE CHANGING CONCEPT OF HEALTH

As early humans began to consider more and more consciously the nature of their existence, the concept of health must have emerged. Until the past few decades, however, health meant essentially the absence of disease and disability. The latter were such dominant factors in existence that merely not being affected by them appeared to be ultimate good health. Meanwhile, undernutrition, epidemic and endemic communicable diseases, and injuries cut life short and/or seriously detracted from it for the vast majority of people.

As recently as the start of the twentieth century in the United States the average length of life was only 47 years. Myocardial infarction as the principal manifestation of coronary heart disease had not even been described. Asked what good health meant, a typical person might then have responded: avoiding injury and epidemic disease, escaping tuberculosis and pneumonia, and living to age 65. By 1990 longevity had increased to 75 years; people feared guns and the AIDS epidemic, but generally expected to live well beyond 65 years and increasingly in good health.

In this evolving situation the founders of the World Health Organization put forward a new definition of health: "complete physical, mental and social well-being and not merely the absence of disease or infirmity." That idea reflected a switch from a purely negative to a positive view of health. Health was not just something to be achieved by minimizing harm to the organism. Such damage had been viewed variously: disease and injury or pathology, as judged by the physician; illness, personal misery as judged by the individual; and sickness, with excuse from one's social role, as judged by society. The patient called it illness, the physician named it a disease, and the employer recorded it as sickness.

Rather, health now has a more positive meaning: strength for living. Every living person possesses a certain degree of health, some potential, which can be expanded, for remaining alive and pursuing life's fruits. Maintaining health as a resource for enjoying the later years has become highly relevant. Thus, health is taking on a new meaning, i.e. the capacity to live fully. That entails keeping up the physical, mental and social reserves for coping with the circumstances of life in a way that brings satisfaction.

Both the Hippocratic tradition of Western medicine and Chinese traditional medicine emphasize balance, a dynamic equilibrium between organism and environment, as the essence of health. Closely related to that health concept of equilibrium is the notion of an organism's reserve or potential for maintaining the balance. Thus, Noack speaks of health balance and health potential (11).

Moving toward the measurement of health, one can regard health (or better, health status, the extent of balance with the environment at any one time) as a spectrum. Every living person occupies some place on such a health spectrum, with three dimensions; physical, mental and social (2). Antonovsky has proposed the term salutogenesis—the opposite of pathogenesis—to express the idea of a health continuum from ease to dis-ease (1).

The idea of health risks is also receiving more attention today. Risks can occur in the environment, ranging from toxic materials to racism. Certain personal behaviors in response to the environment, for example, using alcohol to excess, likewise constitute health risks. Moreover, limitation of the bodily reserves, as in hypertension or high blood sugar level, may be regarded as health risks.

The aim of those concerned with health, either of individuals or of populations, must be movement toward the health end of the spectrum, or at least restraining movement toward the invalid position thereon. Thus, public health workers seek to optimize weight and cholesterol levels, to maintain immunity to measles and influenza, to avoid tobacco consumption—using both medical and educational measures—and to minimize chemical, physical, and infectious risks to health from the environment.

Public health must adapt to this changing concept of health. It should concern itself with the measurement and advancement of health in the positive sense, not just the negative, i.e. the control of physical and mental diseases, illness, and sickness.

THE CORE DISCIPLINES OF PUBLIC HEALTH

To assess health problems, determine their origins, test means for dealing with them, and measure progress against them, two analytical disciplines have evolved: epidemiology and biostatistics. These comprise the "diagnostic tools" of public health, to use a medical analogy. To prevent disease and promote the health of populations, public health professionals employ three types of intervention: fostering healthful behaviors, providing environmental health services, and facilitating effective personal health services. These comprise the "treatment tools." Thus five component disciplines—epidemiology, biostatistics, health behavior, environmental health, and personal health services—constitute the core of public health. The underlying paradigms for each of these disciplines will be discussed in this section. They each obviously relate to other fields, and together they do not encompass the whole of public health; nutrition, for example, embracing both dietary behavior and an adequate food supply, is also crucial.

Epidemiology

Epidemiology has been described as "the basic science of public health" (3). Indeed, the population-based approach of epidemiology is fundamental to the whole field. This paradigm notes that the probability of a disease, or of being at a particular point in the spectrum of health, is a function of many factors: (a) biological, including heredity; (b) environmental, both physical and social; (c) nutrition; and (d) behavior.

To understand a given disease or health state, we must examine the distribution of the disease or state together with the distributions of these several factors in the whole population. A modern epidemiologist needs to comprehend thoroughly not only the biology of the situation, but also all of these other factors in order to perform adequately the assessment function of public health (9). A sophisticated mathematical ability is also becoming a requirement.

To determine which risk factors are responsible, and to what degree, for a given outcome, the epidemiologist must examine the strength of the observed association, its consistency, its specificity, its coherence, the chronology of events (exposure preceding outcome), and the plausibility of an underlying biological mechanism (17). Understanding the relationship between risk factors and outcome draws heavily on statistics, biology, physics, chemistry, and the social sciences. Once the risk factors and their consequences have been sorted out, the question of policy development becomes easier to handle since policies directed at specific risk factors can then be formulated. Only then can society fully reap the benefits of the "second epidemiologic revolution," i.e. expansion of the domain of epidemiology from only infectious diseases to all diseases and health states (16).

Biostatistics

The collection, organization, storage, and display of vital statistics constituted one of the earliest activities in public health and, as such, can be considered to be the original nucleus of biostatistics. Today, however, data *analysis* is much more on the minds of biostatisticians than data description.

Practically every part of statistics contributes to modern biostatistics. The dominant paradigms for statistics are, therefore, the same for biostatistics; namely, the translation of scientific method into statistical terms, with emphasis on public health and life-sciences applications. Relying on the philosophy of science advanced by Popper (13), the main task of the statistician (or biostatistician) is to formulate theories (hypotheses) to explain observed phenomena and proceed to test them based on carefully collected data. When repeated, this process helps the scientist understand the world better.

The advent of modern computers has greatly enhanced statistical data analysis. Today, statisticians can perform very complicated multivariate techniques that were developed in the 1930s but lay largely dormant until the 1960s. Computers also subtly motivated the consolidation of various statistical models, previously considered independent, into unified classes. For example, the so-called generalized linear models now include the general linear model, the log linear model for categorical data, and logistic regression (17). In addition, the computer has facilitated simulation of theoretical and applied models. Statistical simulation is a tool that has yet to achieve its full potential in pretesting alternative public health policies for meeting specified goals.

Personal Health Services

Effective medical practice blossomed in the complaint-response model in which the physician elicits the individual patient's complaint, diagnoses the immediate problem and responds with therapy. Unfortunately, however, grossly inadequate arrangements for socio-economically disadvantaged groups in rural and inner-city areas became evident when those population groups achieved greater prominence and providing free service to the poor had fallen out of fashion in American medicine. Fee-for-service patterns and the middle-class desire for higher incomes took physicians away from care for those who could not pay. Government increasingly filled the medical service void, but what it offered to the poor tended to be second-class. In response, providing medical services equitably and efficiently through appropriate, socially organized arrangements became a goal of public health leaders.

Some physicians sought to bring the benefits of modern medicine to entire communities, especially to disadvantaged segments of the population (5). Adapting medical practice to the needs of all persons in the population in an organized fashion meant assuring access to services and sensitivity to the previously neglected populations, particularly regarding their health attitudes, knowledge, and beliefs; cultural heritages; and transportation difficulties. That effort, called community medicine, linked naturally to public health. For those who could afford it, obtaining standard medical care posed no great difficulty; if anything, excessive procedures constituted more of a problem than deficient services. For those who could not afford it, however, the lack of adequate care became a substantial health problem, aggravated by their greater disease burden.

Insofar as "assuring conditions in which people can be healthy" involved the availability of adequate medical services, public health and community medicine joined forces. Both recognized the need for attention to the circumstances of people's lives as well as their biological problem. Local departments of health, as providers of last resort for personal health services, found themselves burdened with overwhelming and severely underfunded primary medical care roles.

Health Behavior

An integral part of public health from the outset, health-related behavior has recently become an even more important concern. When microbial diseases constituted the major public health problem, personal hygiene played a well-recognized role in overcoming health threats. Now the relationship of larger aspects of lifestyle to the occurrence of heart disease, cancer, diabetes, and other diseases causing widespread mortality and morbidity has been clearly established.

People's behavior with respect to tobacco, alcohol, illicit drugs, calories, and other nutrients, exercise, sexual practices, and other aspects of daily life determine in large part the diseases that will affect them. Although the underlying mechanisms are not yet completely understood, habits regarding these things, that are now generally available to Americans, grow out of human biological nature interacting with the social milieu of life.

Psychology and sociology as well as related fields of behavioral science offer clues concerning how to grapple with such problems from a public health perspective. Those disciplines derive knowledge from studies of how behavior evolves and what influences it. For example, it is now realized that young people responding to the biological urge to explore their surroundings encounter social encouragement to smoke cigarettes. Trial leads subtly into addiction. Subsequently, most smokers try to quit. Cessation also proceeds through stages: pre-contemplation, contemplation, action, maintenance—a psycho-social process that may be facilitated by a synthetic substitute for the nicotine obtained from tobacco. Thus, psycho-biological processes are closely intertwined, both in the development of behavior and in modifying it.

Elucidating the mechanisms and external stimuli of behavior and determining how to influence them so as to favor health comprise the paradigm of behavioral sciences as they relate to public health.

Environmental Health

René Dubos wrote: "Man is in general more the product of his environment than his genetic endowment. The health of the people is determined not by their race but by the conditions of their life." (4). Without dwelling upon the "nature vs nurture" argument, one can note virtually universal agreement that understanding the relationship between environment and health is fundamental to advancing public health. As a core discipline of public health, environmental health is concerned with the delineation of environmental factors and their relationship to human health. These factors include air, food, water, radiation, toxic chemicals, wastes, disease vectors, safety hazards, and habitat.

In addition to their historical contribution to basic sanitation, environmental sciences help assess environmental risks and their possible effects on human health, set policies and regulations for protecting the environment as well as for protecting the health of the public from harmful elements in the environment, and devise ways for communicating their findings to the population in general. Having succeeded in bringing the grosser environmental hazards largely under control, environmental health scientists have turned attention to less obvious risks such as exposure to low levels of chemical pollutants and radiation. This often involves delineating subtle but important health effects and then struggling to control extensive, but previously unrecognized, pollution—as in the case of lead in gasoline, paint and other materials. Industrial hygiene, one part of environmental health, deals with the adverse effects of workplaces on health.

Environmental health is thus a microcosm of public health with a similar paradigm and, as for the whole of public health, with an emphasis on prevention. It draws upon all the professions and disciplines contributing to public health.

PUBLIC HEALTH PRACTICE

Public health practice embraces all those actions that are directed to the assessment of health and disease problems in the population; the formulation of policies for dealing with such problems; and the assurance of environmental, behavioral, and medical services designed to accelerate favorable health trends and reduce the unfavorable.

The assessment function depends primarily upon public health professionals in the epidemiological and biostatistical fields. They develop and operate the essential databases, such as vital statistics, disease registries, and health surveys; and they use these sources to maintain surveillance over population health trends and factors responsible for them. Further, they analyze the data and trends both to guide known actions for health improvement and to delineate relationships between poor health and possibly responsible factors that may indicate new actions. While those specifically trained in epidemiology and biostatistics are mainly responsible for the public health assessment function, they often must be joined in this endeavor by other public health experts, for example, in the effectiveness of medical procedures or the toxic effects of air pollutants.

Many governmental and other agencies determine policies affecting the public's health. Practitioners of public health participate in that process by formulating, advocating and implementing such policies. Their effectiveness in that role depends upon their grasp of the problems, competence in proceeding from assessment to the design of appropriate action, and skill in communication and other aspects of advocacy. Within certain limits, of course, public health practitioners have authority to determine and implement policies. For the larger issues, however, they comprise one group of players in a complex process. Others involved come from several fields such as economics, industry, public interest groups and political leadership. Working successfully in that milieu to advance policies on issues that are favorable to the public's health—for example, reducing fat in school lunches, moderating prices of pharmaceuticals, devoting inner-city space to opportunities for physical fitness, curtailing chemical pollution of water—constitutes a major challenge to public health professionals. In this essentially political realm, forming alliances with commonly related groups such as those in education, welfare, medicine, and urban planning can be very useful. Policies affecting public health are adopted in local, state, national and international areas of social action. With an eye to the populations involved, public health professionals therefore must and do operate at all these levels. Often the adoption of policies occurs at one level, but the equally important implementation is carried out at another, for example, in the case of state legislatures and local health departments. Dynamic interchange among the various entities is the ideal relationship.

Assuring the conditions in which people can be healthy constitutes the third fundamental function of public health. After assessment and within the limits of relevant public policy, public health practice proceeds along three avenues.

One consists of influences on health-related behavior. Thus, for example, stopping tobacco advertisements, especially to young people; making tobacco purchase more difficult, both in physical availability and price; reducing the places where smoking is permitted; educating people about its harm to health; and offering aid in cessation through help in overcoming nicotine addiction, all contribute to a milieu unfavorable to tobacco use. Behavioral sciences, applied to population groups as well as in approaches to individuals, have substantially advanced public health effectiveness in that regard. Access to conditions for healthful behavior, however, is at least as important as influences on what people choose to do; for example, to use seat belts they first must be available in automobiles. Inner city youngsters can engage in health sports only with appropriate facilities and leadership.

Environmental influences comprise a second avenue toward health. Industrialized societies have created a host of impediments to health with which public health is now seriously beginning to grapple. Clearing the path to health from the physical and chemical as well as the biological agents of disease has become prominent on the public health agenda. Expert judgment along with scientific studies of the adverse health consequences of specific forms of environmental pollution is ever more important to public health. Practitioners must steadfastly seek expansion of knowledge concerning environmental factors in health and its full application toward protection of the public's health while also avoiding pressures for action not well-founded in science.

Environmental health action often takes the form of adopting regulations and enforcing them. Public attitudes about such matters and the lag in public health departments' aggressive movement on the environmental front have led to the development of separate new agencies for control of adverse environmental circumstances. Improving the relationship of these agencies to public health, if not integrating them, has become an important matter.

Access of all people to appropriate, high-quality personal health services is the third condition for assuring health. Usually directed or performed by physicians, those services can contribute substantially to the prevention, cure or amelioration of disease. Although historically aimed at responding to complaints of ill health by diagnosing and treating the underlying disease, physicians are increasingly adopting as their aim health maintenance during various periods of life, for example, in pregnancy and early childhood. Public health's concern with personal health services derives from their potential for both prevention and effective treatment of disease, and the promotion of health. Thus public health practice includes assuring the availability of necessary medical services and particularly overcoming cost, distance, cultural and other impediments to using them; educating people about their appropriate use, for example, in prenatal care, immunization, and cancer detection; and ensuring that the services meet a standard of quality. The first of these tasks has in 1993 been elevated to the national political arena; public health practitioners around the country are active in the struggle to assure access. Health educators and public health nurses have long been engaged in the second task. The third, dealing with the quality issue, has thus far attracted attention mainly from academics in public health. Extending further into the realm of personal health service from experience with overseeing the quality of laboratory service offers one approach to the practice of public health.

The entry of terms like ozone, LDL, genetic counseling, radon, PSA, and violence into the public health lexicon indicates the expanding scope of public health practice. As the conditions of life change, and science reveals more about their relationship to health, society's expectation of public health advances. That is the challenge to public health practice.

CONCLUDING THOUGHTS

The paradigm of public health practice is based on the assumption that the provision of well-planned services produces favorable results for the health of the population. Such a paradigm is shared by other human-service-oriented professions including, for example, social welfare and urban planning. Also the public health profession as a whole is similar to many other professions, including health professions, in that it draws upon a number of scientific and professional disciplines. However, the feature of public health that distinguishes it from other health professions is that it is founded on the population-based paradigm of epidemiology.

Taken together, the particular combination of principles, methodologies and practices of public health described in this paper define a unique profession that is not simply the sum of its separate components.

ACKNOWLEDGMENTS

We would like to express our deep appreciation to Stella Grosser for her very able research assistance at various stages of the writing of this paper. Our thanks also go to Carol Aneshensel, Clifford Brunk, William Hinds, Thomas Rice, Leonard Sagan and Judith Siegel for their very helpful discussions.

Literature Cited

1. Antonovsky A. 1981. *Health, Stress and Coping.* London: Jossey-Bass
2. Breslow L. 1972. A quantitative approach to the World Health Organization definition of health: Physical, mental and social well-being. *Int. J. Epidemiol.* 1:347–55
3. Comm. Study of the Future of Public Health, Inst. Med. 1988. *The Future of Public Health.* Washington, DC: Natl. Acad. Press
4. Dubos R. 1966. *Man and His Environment.* Washington, DC: Pan Am. Health Organ., Sci. Publ. No. 131
5. Deuschle KW, Fulmer H, McNamara MJ, et al. 1966. The Kentucky experiment in community medicine. *Milbank Med. Q.* 44:9–22
6. Fineberg, HV, Green GM, Ware JH, Anderson BL. 1994. Changing public health training needs: Professional education and the paradigm of public health. *Annu. Rev. Public Health* 15: 237–57
7. Flinn MW, ed. 1965. *Report on the Sanitary Conditions of the Labouring Population of Great Britain by Edwin Chadwick, 1842.* Edinburgh: Edinburgh Univ. Press
8. Kuhn TS. 1962. *The Structure of Scientific Revolutions.* Chicago: Univ. Chicago Press

9. Lilienfeld AM, Lilienfeld DE. 1980. *Foundations of Epidemiology.* New York: Oxford Univ. Press
10. McCullagh P, Nelder JA. 1988. *Generalized Linear Models.* New York: Chapman & Hall. 2nd ed.
11. Noack H. 1987. Concepts of health and health promotion. In *Measurement in Health Promotion and Protection,* ed. T Abilin, ZJ Brzezinski, VDL Carstairs. Geneva: WHO Reg. Publ., Eur. Ser. No. 22
12. Omenn G.S. 1988. Review of "The Future of Public Health". *Issues Sci. Technol.* Winter: 105–6
13. Popper KR. 1959. *The Logic of Scientific Discovery.* London: Anchor
14. Shattuck L. 1850. *Report on a General Plan for the Promotion of Public and Personal Health.* Boston: Dutton & Wentworth
15. Sigerist HE. 1933. *The Great Doctors.* New York: Norton
16. Terris M. 1985. The changing relationship of epidemiology and society: The Robert Cruikshank Lecture. *J. Public Health Policy* 6:15–36
17. US Dep. Health Educa. Welfare. 1964. *Smoking and Health, Report of the Advisory Committee to the Surgeon General of the Public Health Service.* Washington, DC: US Public Health Serv., Publ. No. 1103

Annu. Rev. Public Health. 1994. 15:237–57

CHANGING PUBLIC HEALTH TRAINING NEEDS: Professional Education and the Paradigm of Public Health

Harvey V. Fineberg, Gareth M. Green, James H. Ware, and Bernita L. Anderson

Harvard School of Public Health, Boston, Massachusetts 02115

KEY WORDS: public health education, schools of public health, educational reform, professional competency, public health practice

---

During a century of unprecedented advances in life expectancy and quality of life in this country, a succession of reports have called for improvements in public health training. This fact leads to the inescapable conclusion that public health, despite enormous success, has yet to fulfill certain expectations fundamental to its mission. In this paper, we review the recommendations for public health education made over the past eight decades, examine the state of contemporary public health education, and outline some ideas we feel would benefit the training of public health professionals.

While we have limited the scope of this paper to professional education programs in public health, schools of public health also prepare scientists and researchers whose careers are devoted to seeking new discoveries that will advance the public's health. The efforts of these laboratory scientists, social and policy scientists, environmental health scientists, and others serve as a tie to the larger world of biomedical and biobehavioral sciences. Since the early decades of this century, the advancement of knowledge has been recognized as an important function of a school of public health. However, the most distinctive role of public health education lies in the preparation of public health professionals, and we have chosen in this paper to focus on this critical mission.

0163-7525/94/0510-0237$05.00

EIGHT DECADES OF RECOMMENDATIONS

Public health, especially in the United States, has always been a multidisciplinary field with shifting contributory disciplines to match newly emerging problems. The great public health movement of nineteenth-century England and America was stimulated by unhealthy social conditions in both industrialized urban and rural areas, and public health workers at that time were as likely to be engineers as physicians. In the United States, public health positions tended to be part-time or voluntary, and public health training—not to mention public health organization itself—was left to local government. This began to change in the early twentieth century when the Rockefeller Foundation took an interest in developing a national training system intended to professionalize the practice of public health (2).

This interest was a result of the foundation's establishment, in 1909, of the Rockefeller Sanitary Commission for the Eradication of Hookworm Disease, then a major health problem in southern states. The program was directed by Wickliffe Rose, who, unable to find full-time, competent health officers for the program, determined that a new profession of public health must be created and that it should include professionals at three levels: leaders, specialists, and field workers. While several institutions—notably Harvard, Yale, Columbia, Michigan, and Pennsylvania (which had been educating medical students in hygiene since the 1870s)—were already offering programs in public health (16), participants in a 1914 conference sponsored by the Rockefeller Foundation worked on a proposal to create from scratch the ideal public health training system. The resulting report, known as the Welch-Rose report after its coauthors, came to be "the central reference point for emerging schools of public health" (2).

A public health institute, according to the Welch-Rose report (17), should focus on the education of future public health officials: prospective local and state health officers and commissioners; technical experts, including statisticians, sanitary engineers, chemists, bacteriologists, and epidemiologists; inspectors of schools, sanitation, food, factories, and so forth; public health nurses; and those preparing to enter the US Public Health Service. The institute would provide training in both public health (i.e. administration) and hygiene (science) and would offer a range of subjects reflecting the scope of knowledge required by public health professionals, including epidemiology and infectious diseases; sanitary parasitology, chemistry, and engineering; hospital construction and administration; heredity and eugenics; diet and nutrition; hygiene of air, soil, water, and climate; rural, farm, and dairy hygiene; quarantine and immigration; and industrial hygiene, to name but a few of the topics cited by Welch and Rose. While some of these topics are not of general interest today, many are still of fundamental relevance to a well-rounded education in public health.

The proposal for this new institute leaned toward the model of the physician as public health leader, suggesting that the majority of candidates for admission would be graduates in medicine. At the same time, allowances were made for the admission of others "with a satisfactory preliminary education," and the recommendation was given for a program of sufficient flexibility to meet a variety of needs.

In 1916, the Rockefeller Foundation allocated funds for the creation of a new "school of hygiene and public health" at the Johns Hopkins University, and in the years following, the number of public health schools in the United States quickly grew. When the Rockefeller Foundation conducted an evaluation of public health training in 1938, ten universities were offering graduate degrees in public health, another fourteen taught graduate courses in public health, and a number of others provided training in public health nursing or engineering (2). Despite this expansion in educational opportunities, the Rockefeller-sponsored Parran-Farrand report (1938) found that a majority of health department personnel had no formal public health training. At the same time, the report projected the imminent expansion of public health services for which hundreds more professionals would have to be educated. Parran and Farrand therefore recommended that the Rockefeller Foundation increase its financial support for three schools—Johns Hopkins, Harvard, and Toronto—judged to be of national and international importance, and that three additional schools be selected and supported to serve as regional training centers in the western, midwestern, and southern United States (3).

The next major report on the status of public health education came more than three decades later. In 1972, the Milbank Memorial Fund's Commission for the Study of Higher Education for Public Health undertook an evaluation of the relations between professional education and professional practice in public health, in the context of the changing values, expectations, and needs of society (9). The Milbank report of 1976, in defining the fundamental subjects in the study of public health, essentially updated and summarized the lengthy list generated by Welch and Rose sixty years before, recommending that programs be built around the three elements central and generic to public health: the measurement and analytic sciences of epidemiology and biostatistics; social policy and the history and philosophy of public health; and management and organization of public health. Relevant content from fields such as medicine, economics, political science, sociology, biology, and the physical sciences should also be integrated into the program.

The Milbank report recommended that schools of public health focus their attention on educating future leaders, here defined as people who would function as executives, planners, and policymakers. Others to be appropriately trained in a public health school were identified as technical specialists such as epidemiologists and biostatisticians, and research scientists and educators. Admission requirements should acknowledge several types of background: first, those with a professional degree in a health field; second, those with a graduate degree in a relevant field; and third, those with a bachelor's degree and several years of work experience in some aspect of public health. The preparation of those who would work at the operating level in public health fields should not, according to Milbank, be the concern of a school of public health; this should take place in other parts of the university with the public health school's assistance. Citing statistics predicting the doubling of public health manpower needs during the 1970s, Milbank assigned to the federal government the responsibility of monitoring these needs and of building a cadre of trained public health personnel by providing financial support to schools responding to national needs.

The Institute of Medicine (IOM) report, *The Future of Public Health,* appeared in 1988, at a time when the public health system was perceived as having fallen "into disarray" (6). Unlike the Welch-Rose and Milbank reports, which focused primarily on the organization of schools of public health, the IOM report directed most of its recommendations toward governmental roles, at various levels, in advancing public health. A smaller number of recommendations related to aspects of education for the practice of public health.

Like its predecessors, the IOM report suggested that while most public health workers lack formal training in the field, schools of public health are not equipped to train large numbers of personnel and should focus on the training of leaders, bearing in mind current employment opportunities and needs. Schools should provide training in the full scope of subjects relevant to public health practice, including environmental, educational, and personal health approaches to the solution of public health problems; the basic epidemiological and biostatistical techniques for analysis of those problems; and the political and management skills needed for leadership in public health. In admissions, the report advises, "appropriate" weight should be given to prior public health experience as well as to academic qualifications, which in a sense ascribes a greater importance to experience than did the previous reports.

Perhaps the single most influential recommendation of the IOM report is its insistence that professional education be grounded in "real world" public health. Schools of public health were criticized in the document for their isolation from current community health issues and for their failure to link theory with applied problem solving. The IOM report recommended the addition of practicum experiences to the curriculum, the establishment of formal linkages between schools of public health and public health agencies, and the exchange of faculty and agency professionals, giving students the opportunity to learn from instructors with hands-on experience.

In response to the IOM report's broad mandate for public health and professional education, a collaborative study was undertaken in 1989 by the Johns Hopkins School of Hygiene and Public Health and the Association of Schools of Public Health to define more precisely the essential elements of the public health profession. The study was sponsored by the US Bureau of Health Professions of the Health Resources and Services Administration and the Public Health Practice Program Office of the Centers for Disease Control. Participants included representatives from health departments, foundations, and every US school of public health. Known as "The Public Health Faculty/Agency Forum," this initiative worked through a consensus document that was debated at professional meetings, modified, and codified in a published report (15).

The report's recommendations present two organizing principles for the improvement of public health education: First, the public health curriculum should be structured around competencies universally required of public health practitioners; the report included a list of such competencies (Table 1). Second, schools of public health should establish and nurture broad cooperative agreements with major local, regional, and state agencies. Perhaps the most important benefit of developing such relationships would be the organization of supervised practica for students. While not pretending to be comprehensive of all areas of public health, the report of the Faculty/Agency Forum goes a long way toward defining a competency-based profession.

Professional competencies and practical experience were also emphasized in the October, 1991, report issued by the Pew Health Professions Commission (14). Echoing many of the concerns about the state of American health and health systems discussed in the IOM report, the Pew report, entitled *Healthy America: Practitioners for 2005,* aimed to explore the attitudes and skills that health practitioners—physicians, public health professionals, dentists, nurses, pharmacists, and others—ought to possess to be most responsive to the health needs of the public, and to recommend ways that health professional schools might work toward instilling these attitudes and skills in their students. This can best be achieved, according to the Pew Commission, by training health professionals in community-based settings where they can learn as part of a team composed of various providers and managers. The Pew report recognizes that sweeping changes will be required, particularly because of the need to reconsider the educational core "in light of the evolving needs of the public" (14). The Pew Commission's

Table 1 Professional competencies in public health, adapted from the report of the Faculty/ Agency Forum (15)

Universal competencies	Behavioral sciences
Analytical skills	Awareness and ability to implement be-
Communication skills	havior change strategies for primary,
Policy development/program planning	secondary, and tertiary health promotion/
skills	disease prevention activities in the public
Cultural skills	health setting
Basic public health sciences skills	Ability to disseminate knowledge of be-
Financial planning and management skills	havior and social concepts and methods
	Cultural sensitivity and understanding of
Public health administration	how culture affects behavior and health
Policy analysis/strategic planning	status
Communication skills	Ability to conduct an ongoing community
Team leadership	mental and medical needs assessment, in-
Financial management	dividually or as part of a team
Human resources management	Knowledge of the public health system
Program planning and administration	and policy and regulation development
Organizational management/positioning	Evaluation skills
Cultural competence	Leadership skills
Basic health sciences	Communication skills
Political analysis	
Epidemiology and biostatistics	Environmental public health
Individual competencies in epidemiology:	Risk assessment skills
Situation analysis	Risk management skills
Study design	Risk communication skills
Study implementation	Epidemiology of acute and chronic dis-
Data management and analysis	eases associated with environmental
Presentation of health information	stresses
	Biostatistics
Individual competencies in biostatistics:	Basic sciences
Data requirements	Communicable/chronic disease
Database management	Economic considerations in environmental
Descriptive statistics	public health
Statistical inference	Environmental law
Statistical reporting	

1993 report, *Health Professions Education for the Future: Schools in Service to the Nation,* supplements these initial recommendations with a discussion of the need for strategic planning in public health education and the importance of collaboration among schools, between schools and health departments, and between schools and the community (11).

A summary of the recommendations from the major reports of the past eight decades reveals several consistent themes (Table 2). First, the basic content of the public health curriculum should be broad in scope and should include the fundamental public health disciplines, epidemiology and biostatistics, as well as the relevant methodologies and content from the biological, behavioral, social, and environmental sciences. Over time, increasing emphasis has been given to the importance of acquiring key skills, as well as knowledge. Second, public health training should prepare students, who come to the schools with a variety of educational and employment backgrounds, for careers as leaders and specialists rather than field workers.

Third, there are many routes to public health training. These alternative paths would benefit from the assistance of the schools of public health. Several reports expressed the view that the technical expertise found in schools of public health should be shared with programs in other parts of the university, including undergraduate programs, and even with other institutions of higher education in the geographic region. The Welch-Rose report, for example, proposed an institute of hygiene that would cooperate with engineering and nursing schools in the training of sanitary engineers and public health nurses, as well as with schools of medicine and social work (17).

A fourth common thread relates to the importance of field experience. In 1915, Welch and Rose quaintly expressed the opinion that "hygienic excursions . . . constitute a valuable part of practical sanitary training" (17); they also recognized the enormous educational value of working relations with the US Public Health Service and with local and state health departments. The belief that field experience is a critical component of public health training has gained strength throughout the century, receiving particular emphasis in the most recent IOM, Pew, and Faculty/Agency Forum reports.

Finally, the reports agree that schools of public health must provide for the lifelong educational needs of practicing public health professionals. Through continuing education programs, public health schools can contribute to elevating the competence of the vast number of public health workers who lack formal public health training. These programs can fill gaps in basic knowledge and help keep professionals abreast of the latest advances, many of which emerge from the research programs of the schools of public health themselves.

PUBLIC HEALTH EDUCATION TODAY

The growing demand for professionals with formal education in public health has led to a substantial expansion in training programs during the latter half of the twentieth century. In 1958, the earliest year for which complete data are available, there were eleven schools of public health in the United States with a total enrollment of fewer than 1,200 students. The typical student

Table 2 Summary of the recommendations of four important reports

	WELCH-ROSE (1915)	MILBANK (1976)	IOM (1988)	PEW (1991)
Purpose of report	To develop a proposal for a new institute of public health and hygiene that would help meet the country's need for trained public health personnel.	To develop unity of purpose and direction among public health schools and to help them respond to changes in the needs of society.	To respond to the perception that the U.S. has lost sight of public health goals and allowed the system to fall into disarray.	To explore attitudes and skills practitioners must have to be most responsive to health needs, and to recommend changes to meet these needs.
Organization	The institute should be part of a university, housed in its own building with the requisite laboratories and facilities and its own staff of full-time teachers and researchers. It should be organized into divisions: chemical, biological, engineering, statistical, and preventive medicine.	Universities should have a high-level administrative focus on public health to ensure representation of key knowledge bases and optimum resource use. The school should have a clear statement of mission and respond to short-term training needs without altering long-term plans.	The health professional school should be an integral part of the university's academic mission. The university should provide a flexible administrative policy to allow the changing environment and to the needs of the public.	Schools should develop missions and organizational structures responsive to the changing needs of the health care system and of the community. In a time of declining government support, schools should reconsider traditional sources of income and the productivity of the educational process.
Educational goals	To educate prospective health officers and commissioners; technical experts (e.g. statisticians, sanitary engineers, bacteriologists, and epidemiologists); sanitary inspectors; public health nurses; members of the US Public Health Service.	To prepare people who will function as executives, planners, and policy-makers; epidemiologists and biostatisticians; and research scientists and educators. Other schools should prepare those who will function at the operating level in public health fields.	Education programs for public health professionals should be informed by comprehensive and current data on public health personnel and their employment opportunities and needs.	Programs should provide the competencies that will be demanded of their graduates. All dimensions of the professional education program, including natural, behavioral, and population sciences, should be reviewed within the context of this core. The teaching-learning process should promote inquiry skills and the ability to manage large volumes of information.

		Programs should offer greater flexibility to allow earlier access to professional training, inter-professional training, and multi-competency training, as well as opportunities to explore professional career options more fully.	Training of health professionals should occur increasingly in community-based centers. Schools should assume responsibility for understanding and addressing health care needs of particular populations, especially those in the school's immediate vicinity.
Curriculum	Should include administrative and scientific aspects of public health (e.g. vital statistics, epidemiology, infectious diseases, industrial hygiene, sanitary parasitology and engineering, hospital construction and administration, genetics, social and personal hygiene, quarantine).	Should include the quantitative and analytic sciences of epidemiology and biostatistics, social policy, the history and philosophy of public health, and management and organization of public health, and content from medicine, economics, political science, sociology, biology, and the physical sciences.	Schools should provide students an opportunity to learn the entire scope of public health practice, including environmental, educational, and personal health approaches to the solution of public health problems; epidemiological and biostatistical techniques for problem analysis; and political and management skills.
Practice links	Hygienic excursions are a valuable part of practical training. The institute should establish working relations with state and local departments of health and with the US Public Health Service.	Field training is an integral part of education. Schools should have reciprocal relationships with health agencies, and faculty should participate in community health services and serve as advocates of policies and programs.	Schools should establish firm practice links with public health agencies so that significantly more faculty members may undertake professional responsibilities in these agencies, conduct research there, and train students in such practice situations.

Table 2 (*Continued*)

	WELCH-ROSE (1915)	MILBANK (1976)	IOM (1988)	PEW (1991)
Students	While most students would be graduates of medical schools, admission should be open to all with satisfactory preliminary education.	Should have a health professional degree, relevant graduate degree, or 3 years experience. Training of minorities and foreign nationals should be a priority.	Admission of students should give appropriate weight to prior public health experience as well as to academic qualifications.	
Research	A main function of the institute should be the development of the spirit of investigation and the advancement of knowledge.	A sustained research effort is needed in all graduate programs in public health, with schools specializing in different areas of expertise.	Should emphasize real public health problems. Should include basic research, applied research and development, and program evaluation and implementation research.	Schools' research missions should include inquiry into health services and education issues.
Continuing education	The institute should provide the opportunity for those engaged in health work to pursue short courses or advanced work.	Continuing education should occupy a distinct and prominent role in all institutions providing higher education for public health.	Schools should undertake an expanded program of short courses to help upgrade the competence of current public health personnel.	Schools should help develop programs designed to assess and assure continued competency throughout health professionals' careers.
Relation to medical school	While the institute should be independent of the university's medical school, the two schools should be closely related, and facilities of each should be open to students from both schools. Medical students should be trained in the principles of hygiene.	The medical and public health schools in a university should share resources for teaching and research. Public health should be emphasized in medical training. Medical schools should review the status of the teaching of community health and should form links with preventive medicine programs.		

Relation to other schools

The institute should provide training to students in schools of engineering, nursing, and social work.

Schools of public health should assist other programs that train health manpower (e.g., nursing, pharmacy, dentistry).

Schools should take advantage of training resources elsewhere in the university and should seek and maintain links with parent disciplines. Schools of public health should serve as regional resources for graduate programs in higher education for public health within specified geographic areas.

Universities should encourage programmatic efforts in health professional education across disciplines. Public health schools should extend their expertise to advise and assist with these programs and should make a special effort to expose undergraduates to public health.

Role of government

There should be a national effort to build a qualified cadre of public health personnel and a program to monitor manpower needs and supply. The government should support public health training programs.

Should explore ways to ensure access to care and encourage policies consistent with desired practitioner skills and values.

Should explore innovative approaches to manpower utilization, support educational innovation, and encourage accreditation policies that promote outcome standards of performance. Licensure regulations should address issues of continued competency.

Role of professional associations

Should help develop professional identity, position schools as providers of life-long learning, and encourage licensing and accrediting bodies to work closely with schools.

at that time was a white male, about 35 years old, enrolled in a one-year master's degree program (12). Over the next twenty years, total enrollment grew rapidly, due in large part to an influx of younger students, including an increasing number of women, with little prior health experience and no prior graduate study. In the 1980s, enrollment growth slowed, and the student body saw a resurgence of older, more experienced students (12). Today, the 27 graduate schools of public health (including one seeking accreditation) have a combined enrollment of over 13,000 students, more than a tenfold increase over the past 35 years.

While this paper is concerned only with degree programs offered by the accredited schools of public health, it is worth noting that professional education in public health is widely dispersed, encompassing another seven accredited health education programs, eleven community medicine programs, an estimated 69 nonaccredited programs offering master's degrees in public health, and over 300 nonaccredited programs offering related degrees.

In the fall of 1992, almost half (46 percent) of the students in accredited schools of public health were enrolled in Master of Public Health (MPH) programs (the leading professional degree in public health), another 24 percent were enrolled in other master's degree programs, 23 percent were pursuing doctoral degrees, and 7 percent were nondegree students. These percentages have remained stable during the past two decades. One significant change has been the substantial increase in part-time students and students enrolled in nontraditional degree programs: 35 percent of students were enrolled part time in the fall of 1992, and more than 900 students were enrolled in nontraditional programs. Coinciding with the growth of part-time and nontraditional degree programs has been an increase in the number of physicians graduating with public health degrees. The percentage of graduates who are physicians has fluctuated over time, dropping from a high of 26 percent in 1962 to a low of 10 percent in 1982–83, and rising again to 21 percent in 1990–91.

Looking at schools as a group, the subject areas in which students choose to specialize have also remained stable during the past 20 years. More than half (54 percent) of students concentrate in health services administration, epidemiology, or environmental science. Behavioral science, public health practice, and biostatistics form the second most frequently cited set of specializations. While the areas of study emphasized in schools of public health have changed slowly, the content of courses in those areas has evolved more rapidly to reflect new epidemiologic and statistical methods, new discoveries in the laboratory, and new ways of thinking about social and policy problems.

The aggregate data about student body composition and subject concentrations may falsely suggest a high degree of homogeneity among the programs that simply does not exist. In fact, the loose definition of public health training under which these programs are subsumed presents a barrier to standardization of the product of the educational system (11). In contrast to graduate programs leading to professional degrees such as MD or JD, MPH programs are minimally standardized. The Council on Education in Public Health requires that every accredited MPH program include education in five areas: behavioral science, biostatistics, environmental health, epidemiology, and health services administration/management. However, neither the content nor the extent of coursework in these areas is specified, and no postgraduate examination is required for certification in public health. As a result, schools of public health vary in their MPH curricula and in their expectations about the competencies of their graduates.

Requirements for admission also allow great diversity in the prior experience of MPH students. For example, a number of schools admit both students with a bachelor's degree and students with a prior MD or other health-related doctoral degree to their MPH programs. Some of these schools allow students with an MD or comparable degree to complete the MPH program in one year, while two years of study are normally required for those having only a bachelor's degree at enrollment. This means that many schools are using the same degree program—the difference being one year more or less of coursework—to provide both specialized secondary training to individuals with prior preparation in a health profession and primary training for pre-professionals who may be straight out of college. This tradeoff between prior education or experience and the length of the graduate program in public health assumes some overlap between the competencies of the public health professional and those of the physician, but typically fails to make those competencies explicit.

THE PUBLIC HEALTH APPROACH

Contemporary health challenges—including chronic disease, teenage pregnancy, AIDS, drug abuse, injury, drug-resistant tuberculosis, violence, environmental hazards, the effects of industrial and natural disasters, and the organization and management of effective health care systems—demand prodigious professional skills and depend on the active engagement of the very populations who are subjected to the afflictions. While public health problems have assumed increasing complexity during this century, today's health challenges continue to require advances in public health sciences and the application of the public health approach for their solution.

The public health approach begins by understanding health problems in the context of defined populations. These populations range in scope and attribute, encompassing members of a local community or of a broad region, workers at a particular site or in an entire industry, or groups of individuals of the same age, ethnic background, economic position, sexual preference, or other unifying characteristic. Health goals for populations in the broadest sense have in recent decades been established by the World Health Organization ("Health for All by the Year 2000") (8) and by the US Public Health Service ("Healthy People 2000") (1). The discipline that defines events in populations is the field of epidemiology, the cornerstone of public health. Epidemiology strives to detect associations between possible causative factors and health effects, or between interventions and changes in health status. Epidemiology, together with the quantitative tools of biostatistics and sensitive measures of biological, chemical, and physical events, is the stethoscope of the public health professional, serving in diagnosis, surveillance, and evaluation of preventive interventions.

A second characteristic of the public health approach is the recognition that many problems of public health are deeply rooted in the behavior of individuals and in their social context. While human behavior (for example, personal hygiene) has always played an integral role in public health problems and their solution, today's issues involve behaviors that seem to be more difficult to alter. The public health professional must have a firm grasp of the behavioral and social sciences in order to understand causation and remedy with the same clarity that microbiology, for example, gives to epidemic contagion. A major difference between these fields, however, is the direct involvement of moral and ethical values in the behavioral patterns that underpin modern social epidemics and the demands made on those value systems by prescribed intervention (such as safer sexual practices for prevention of AIDS). Few other professions depend so heavily on applied socio-behavioral science, and schools of public health need strong emphasis in these disciplines.

Third, the public health problems of the late twentieth century are rooted in the technologies of economic development: industrialization, super-urbanization, agricultural mechanization, rapid and mass transportation, communication and information management, and massive exploitation of natural resources. Each of these necessary technologies of the modern world has byproducts that contribute to environmental pollution and degradation, with the attendant effects on natural habitat, ecological integrity, and human health. From the outset, public health has incorporated environmental and ecological analysis into its portfolio to control vector-borne disease and to achieve the health objectives of the great sanitary revolution. Public health today, in collaboration with government and industry, is coping with new environmental threats to health posed by chemical and physical hazards of the industrial era and by poorly defined potential risks of high technologies.

Fourth, public health problems continue to require the engagement of the body politic, in the form of government participation, for their solution. Therefore, the public health professional must be trained to be efficient, at ease, and effective in the public decision-making process. He or she must be skilled in the leadership, financing, and administration of small and large organizations in the private as well as the public sector. Because the public will is expressed through the laws of the legislatures and the regulations of enforcing agencies, the public health professional must be knowledgeable in these requirements, even while constrained by insufficient resources to meet all needs adequately.

No other profession combines these essential characteristics of knowledge, attitudes, skills, and resources. The prospects for a workable definition of what constitutes public health and public health education have never been better as practicing professionals team up with employers, academicians, professional associations, and government financing agencies in an exceptional partnership to specify requirements for recognized competencies, educational criteria, and participation of practitioners in the preparation of professionals-in-training. However, there remains much work to be done to transfer the criteria identified through these partnerships into the curricula of the schools of public health.

Signs of progress include the efforts of the Council on Education for Public Health to revise its accreditation criteria to give further specification to the curricular requirements for attaining and evaluating professional competencies. Granting agencies (notably the Health Resources and Services Administration) have established a "special projects" grant series to foster change in schools' curricula to implement the recommendations of the IOM report and to achieve the educational objectives of the Faculty/Agency Forum. At this writing, the Clinton administration is in the late stages of preparing legislation for health care reform that will reportedly include a number of specific proposals to renew the public health infrastructure and strengthen public health education. Many schools of public health are already innovating in organizational structure and in curriculum to provide greater opportunity for professional skill development through field application of classroom theory. The University of Washington, for example, has established the Northwest Center for Public Health Practice and initiated a summer institute for practical training (10).

CASE STUDY OF EDUCATIONAL REFORM

To illustrate the nature of reform in professional education for public health, we describe in more detail the setting with which the authors are most familiar. At the Harvard School of Public Health, a 1987 student survey set off a three-year planning process to reform the school's flagship professional program, the Master of Public Health (7). The initiative culminated in its transformation from a collection of discipline-oriented, departmentally based curricula (plus a vaguely focused general program) to a centrally coordinated set of five career-oriented concentrations, as follows:

Health Care Organization and Management educates students to evaluate medical practices and to manage large health care institutions, primarily in the private sector. The curriculum emphasizes the management of patient care services and large data systems, and advances students' understanding of issues related to quality of care, new technologies, financing and reimbursement systems, malpractice, and risk.

Public Management and Community Health prepares students to manage state and local public-sector health services and community primary care settings by providing them with skills in community epidemiology, needs assessment, governmental financial mechanisms, legislative processes, management of large public systems of care, negotiation, leadership, and health law.

Environmental and Occupational Health is geared toward the management of public- and private-sector organizations requiring knowledge of toxicology, epidemiology, industrial hygiene and safety, occupational and environmental law, standard setting and regulation, exposure assessment, surveillance and monitoring, and risk characterization, management, and reduction.

Quantitative Methods prepares students for careers in governmental agencies, industry, and health care institutions in roles requiring a high level of skill in epidemiology, biostatistics, decision science, demography, forecasting, needs assessment, and evaluation.

International Health focuses on the management skills required to work in developing countries, preparing students for positions with governmental and independently funded organizations, stressing community health and management of health services, primary health care, priority-setting with limited resources, health worker training and utilization, population-based preventive strategies, regional and national health system development, international health politics, population nutrition, and infectious disease.

Each concentration was equipped with a faculty leader, an advisory committee, and specified educational objectives. A new Office for Professional Education was established at the dean's office level and a defined budget committed to manage and nourish the innovations.

Reflecting the recommendations of the key historical reports outlined earlier in this paper, the revamped MPH curriculum incorporates three elements: first, the theory and content of epidemiology, biostatistics, environmental and biologic science, and the social and behavioral sciences; second, the acquisition of applied skills in program design and implementation (including assessment, strategic planning, and decision-making), management (including personnel systems, organizational strategies, and fiscal management), consultation and technical assistance, and evaluation; and, third, the history, philosophy, and ethics of public health. Six new courses were developed and a number of existing courses revised to emphasize the integration of theory and application in the discussion of public health problems. A practice-based course is required in each concentration. The aim is to combine, as expressed by Frenk (4), a balance between "the academic excellence of programs and their relevance to decision making."

Accompanying this curricular reformation is an educational capacity-building initiative focused on strengthening faculty teaching skills and encouraging creative innovation and research in the classroom. A seminal grant from Harvard's president supported a variety of early activities, including a faculty seminar in the philosophy and skills of group discussion leadership and the development of an active-learning pedagogy emphasizing the mobilization of technical knowledge for problem solving. The use of case material drawn from professional experience, so useful in business and legal education, is gaining new prominence in public health education, and a small grants program funds the production of public health cases characterized by a population perspective, integration of health sciences, inclusion of personal and societal values in health, complex technical content, and a relationship to governmental regulation and finance. Finally, new ideas about teaching are being supported by minigrants that enable faculty to test new strategies and techniques to enliven their classrooms and draw the students into active participation in the learning process.

IMPRESSIONS AND CONCLUSIONS

Influential policy documents on public health education appear to emerge at major turning points in public health: during the fight against infectious disease in the early 1900s (Welch-Rose), in the effort to organize health care delivery in the 1970s (Milbank), and as we recognized the importance of communities and of influencing behaviors and life-styles in the 1980s and 1990s (IOM, Pew, Faculty/Agency Forum). In each case, the major impetus behind these policy-setting documents on education for public health seems to have been the magnitude of the emergent public health problems of that time, the required expansion in the number of public health workers to address the problems, and the perceived lack of training of the then-current workforce.

The basic content areas of public health education in schools of public health have, with notable exceptions, remained remarkably stable over the eight decades since their formulation in the Welch-Rose report of 1915. These include studies in quantitative methods, behavioral and social sciences, biological and environmental sciences, health policy and management, and the content of public health problems. Reports prior to 1970 had recommended that schools of public health train a broad range of public health officials, technical experts, inspectors, nurses, and candidates for the US Public Health Service with a strong emphasis in the natural sciences and technologies. The Milbank report in 1972 recommended a focus on executives, planners, policymakers, and specialists—leaders, not operational workers—and emphasized social and managerial sciences in addition to the quantitative disciplines. The more recent documents from the IOM, Pew Foundation, and Faculty/Agency Forum stress the need for acquisition of practice skills and professional competencies learned through the association of schools with public health agencies. These reports seem to be in reaction to a perceived isolation of public health education from public health problem solving in practice and echo the more encompassing views of the original Welch-Rose model.

Clearly, Welch and Rose exhibited prescience in their design in that subsequent evaluations of public health education have not yielded proposals that deviate dramatically in structure, content, or mission. The continual reappearance of similar recommendations does suggest, however, that public health schools persist in their failure to execute them. What is preventing these schools from completely fulfilling their mission to train public health leaders and professionals? This question can be looked at in three ways.

The problem may be one of magnitude. While the twentieth century has been an era of real health progress, the intrinsic difficulty of public health problems has not diminished. Infectious diseases vanquished early in the century have been replaced by new diseases, such as AIDS, and by a surge in cancer and other chronic diseases; other problems, such as violence and injury, not formerly considered public health problems, are now within the purview of public health professionals. In the past decade, problems relating to health and health care have become issues of paramount interest in America, and public expectation for the solution of these problems has escalated. Yet the social and institutional response to the broadening scope of public health problems—especially through the training of public health professionals—has been meager indeed. There are still only 27 schools of public health in the United States and even if they followed every recommendation about training to the letter, they could account for only a fraction of the response demanded by the public health problems of today.

A second perspective would view the problem as a deficiency in implementation. Public health programs as currently constructed simply may be unable to prepare their students adequately for public health practice and leadership. In particular, programs of one year or less may be too constrained to do equal justice to all of the goals of the MPH. Though past recommendations make sense, perhaps the programs have not sufficiently hewed to them or succeeded in converting them to reality. This problem of execution has been the focus of most reform efforts at Harvard and other schools of public health.

Finally, the problem may be one of concept. As demonstrated in the key reports of the twentieth century, the concept of who should be trained for what kind of work, and how, has shifted over the years. This shift has occurred in parallel with an evolution in the intellectual domains and practices that constitute public health. Yet, the field of public health has never attained the status of a recognized, single independent profession and thus endures an ongoing crisis of identity. Professional training in public health has traditionally been seen as a period of reorientation, as brief as nine months, for professionals previously trained in other fields, notably medicine. Should this view continue, or is it time to create a new paradigm of leadership whose primary orientation and commitment would be to public health? If so, how would these new leaders fit into the realities of career paths in public health, today and in the foreseeable future? What role can certification or licensure of public health professionals play in defining both the field of public health and the knowledge and skills required for a new leadership?

The creation of a new paradigm for the public health leader requires an acknowledgment that the acquisition of the knowledge and skills in the breadth and depth necessary to become a fully competent professional on graduation from a school of public health may well be an overly ambitious undertaking for a master's-level program. Even students with a great deal of prior professional training and experience feel inadequately prepared for the complex demands on a public health professional, and public health agencies are increasingly demanding opportunities for continuing professional education in public health. One wonders, if strict national competency examinations were required of all graduating public health students, whether the current reliance on master's-level education would prove adequate to the demands of the skilled practice of public health.

A few voices have called for the introduction of doctoral preparation for senior professionals in public health, particularly for those who lack prior professional training at the doctoral level. The conclusions of the IOM report, while not calling explicitly for doctoral degrees, provide clear support for the principles of doctoral education in their emphasis on high-level professional training in collaboration with local health agencies, and on interdisciplinary and team approaches to problem solving. Green (5) recognized this need in environmental health and established a doctoral training program at Johns Hopkins leading to the Doctor of Public Health degree. Students complete the MPH requirements, take additional coursework in their respective areas of interest in environmental health, participate in field practica, and undertake an interdisciplinary problem-solving thesis as a dissertation. Supported by the W.K. Kellogg Foundation, this program is a working model of the professional doctorate in public health.

Roemer (13) is another early advocate of the professional doctorate. He calls for a five-year curriculum leading to the Doctor of Public Health degree in which students would enter from undergraduate programs in the social sciences and humanities as well as the natural sciences, with preference given for some experience in a population-based health program. The curriculum would comprise the basic tools of social analysis, health and disease in populations, protection of health and prevention of disease, and health care systems and their management. While he does not specify internships or practica per se, he describes 38 prototype courses and clearly recognizes the need for field study in relevant health care settings. The same principles might well be used to strengthen training programs at the master's level.

The shortcomings in public health education resulting from problems of magnitude, implementation, and concept may each be balanced by new and expanding opportunities. For example, the growing magnitude of today's public health problems is countered by rapid growth in new knowledge, by the continuing diversification of this knowledge, from molecular biology to macroeconomics, and by an explosion in information technology. Recognized failures in implementation are prompting schools to find ways to bridge the gap between the academy and the practitioner by establishing mutually beneficial relationships with the community of public health practice and by developing innovative methods for public health teaching. Problems of concept are stimulating a deeper inquiry into the variety and depth of competencies required of public health professionals and into the challenge of integrating increasingly specialized knowledge with general problem-solving capacities.

These challenges require that schools of public health be ready to undertake a major revamping of professional education; politically and socially the climate is right. The end of the Cold War has led to a shift in how the United States is deploying its national energies, and health reform has surged on the national agenda. Public health provides the theoretical base for prevention and the practical tools for population-based care. It is now up to the public health schools to reconceptualize the role and competency of the graduating professional, to advocate for expansion of educational opportunity in public health science and practice, and to participate in the design of population-based health care and the implementation of national health care goals. Taking account of the missions, traditions, and resources of different public health institutions, the time is ripe to realize a new vision of public health education.

Any *Annual Review* chapter, as well as any article cited in an *Annual Review* chapter, may be purchased from the Annual Reviews Preprints and Reprints service. 1-800-347-8007; 415-259-5017; email: arpr@class.org

---

Literature Cited

1. Breslow L. 1987. Setting objectives for public health. *Annu. Rev. Public Health* 8:289–307
2. Fee E. 1991. Designing schools of public health for the United States. In *A History of Education in Public Health: Health that Mocks the Doctors' Rules*, ed. E Fee, RM Acheson, pp. 155–94. Oxford: Oxford Univ. Press
3. Fee E. 1987. Extending the Hopkins model. In *Disease and Discovery: A History of the Johns Hopkins School of Hygiene and Public Health, 1916–1939.* Baltimore/London: Johns Hopkins Univ. Press
4. Frenk J. 1993. The new public health. *Annu. Rev. Public Health* 14:469–90
5. Green GM. 1987. Development and environmental health: criteria for professional education. *Asia-Pac. J. Public Health* 1:19–22
6. Inst. Med. (US). 1988. Committee for the Study of the Future of Public Health. *The Future of Public Health.* Washington, DC: Natl. Acad.
7. Kahn K, Tollman SM. 1992. Planning professional education at schools of public health. *Am. J. Public Health* 82:1653–57
8. Mahler H. 1988. Present status of WHO's initiative "Health for all by the year 2000." *Annu Rev. Public Health* 9:71–97
9. Milbank Mem. Fund Commission. 1976. *Higher Education for Public Health.* New York: Prodist
10. Omenn GS, Oberle M, Gale J, Hoover JJ, Sandlin D, Tapp J. 1993. Notes

from the field: the Northwest Center for Public Health Practice. *Am. J. Public Health.* In press
11. O'Neil EH. 1993. *Health Professions Education for the Future: Schools in Service to the Nation.* San Francisco, CA: Pew Health Prof. Comm.
12. Parlette N, Brand R, Gentry D, Gemmell M. 1992. *Longitudinal Study of Graduates, Schools of Public Health, 1956–1985.* Washington, DC: Assoc. Schools Public Health
13. Roemer MI. 1986. Need for professional doctors of public health. *Public Health Rep.* 101:21–29
14. Shugars DA, O'Neil EH, Bader JD, eds. 1991. *Healthy America: Practitioners for 2005, An Agenda for Action for U.S. Health Professional Schools.* Durham, NC: Pew Health Prof. Comm.
15. Sorensen A, Bialek R, eds. 1993. *The Public Health Faculty/Agency Forum: Final Report.* Gainesville, FL: Florida Univ. Press.
16. Viseltear A. 1991. The emergence of pioneering public health education programmes in the United States. See Ref. 2, pp. 155–94
17. Welch WH, Rose W. 1915. Institute of hygiene: being a report by Dr. William H. Welch and Wickliffe Rose to the General Education Board, Rockefeller Foundation. In *The Welch-Rose report: a public health classic; a publication by the Delta Omega Alpha Chapter to mark the 75th anniversary of the founding of the Johns Hopkins Univ. School of Hygiene and Public Health.* 1992

Annu. Rev. Public Health. 1994. 15:259–75

HEALTHY PEOPLE 2000 AND COMMUNITY HEALTH PLANNING

Mark W. Oberle and Edward L. Baker

Public Health Practice Program Office, Centers for Disease Control and Prevention, Atlanta, Georgia 30333

Mark J. Magenheim

Sarasota County Public Health Unit, Sarasota, Florida 34230

KEY WORDS;   health objectives, public health practice, health reform, assessment, administration, health planning

Categorical public health programs have always set process and outcome objectives for specific diseases and health promotion efforts (5), but *Healthy People 2000* (64) and its predecessor report *Promoting Health/Preventing Disease: Objectives for the Nation for 1990* (63) were the first to set detailed objectives for the entire public health system in the United States. Efforts at establishing and achieving the national public health objectives have been well documented by researchers, the lead Public Health Service agencies, and their state counterparts (65–67). However, implementing the objectives at the local level is a complicated task that has not been as well documented. As part of a growing interest in community health planning, *Healthy People 2000* and other planning tools have been increasingly used to mobilize communities for health. In this review we will summarize the relevance of national health objectives for community use, other health planning tools available to implement these objectives, and the formation of partnerships between health agencies and community groups.

PROGRESS TOWARD THE 1990 OBJECTIVES

By the end of the 1980s the United States had met or exceeded its target goal for mortality reductions in infants, children, and adults, but had not met its goal for mortality reduction in youth and adolescents (15–24 years of age) or the target goal for morbidity reduction in older adults (32). Of the 226 health objectives for 1990, 32% were achieved or exceeded, 30% showed partial progress (1% to 99% of target), and 15% had no progress (32). Data were inadequate to assess progress for the remaining 23% of objectives. Trends were actually worsening for some objectives in the areas of teenage pregnancy, unintended pregnancy, sexually transmitted diseases, measles, and suicide (32, 42).

NATIONAL OBJECTIVES FOR THE YEAR 2000

The underlying principle of the national health objectives is that they should be measurable and achievable with the application of current technology (30, 31). Additional considerations are that the objectives should be understandable to a broad audience, balanced between outcome and process objectives, linked to the 1990 Objectives where possible, and able to engender active participation by professional groups, consumers, advocates, and health agencies at all levels (31). Public Health Service agencies developed detailed projection models for possible objectives to reduce mortality, morbidity and disability, improve quality of life, and address special concerns of minority groups (55).

The Institute of Medicine coordinated regional hearings in Birmingham, Los Angeles, San Antonio, Houston, Seattle, Denver, Detroit, and New York at which over 750 people provided testimony on proposed objectives. A working draft was distributed to 13,000 individuals and groups for review (32) before the final publication in 1990 (30). As a result of this process, *Healthy People 2000* sets out three broad goals to help the nation reach its full potential:

1. Increase the span of healthy life for Americans
2. Reduce health disparities among Americans
3. Achieve access to preventive services for all Americans.

To reach these goals, the report establishes 300 objectives and 223 sub-objectives for the year 2000. These are arranged in 22 priority areas (Table 1).

As of 1992, 3% of the Year 2000 objectives had been met, and clear progress had been made on reaching 28% of the objectives (42). Data sources have been identified for all objectives, and baseline data have been obtained for 90% of objectives.

To provide a broad indication of the general health status of a community

Table 1 *Healthy People 2000* priority areas

Health promotion
  1. Physical activity and fitness
  2. Nutrition
  3. Tobacco
  4. Alcohol and other drugs
  5. Family planning
  6. Mental health and mental disorders
  7. Violent and abusive behavior
  8. Educational and community-based programs
Health protection
  9. Unintentional injuries
 10. Occupational safety and health
 11. Environmental health
 12. Food and drug safety
 13. Oral health
Preventive services
 14. Maternal and infant health
 15. Heart disease and stroke
 16. Cancer
 17. Diabetes and chronic disabling conditions
 18. HIV infection
 19. Sexually transmitted diseases
 20. Immunization and infectious diseases
 21. Clinical preventive services
Surveillance and data systems
 22. Surveillance and data systems
Age-related objectives
    Children
    Adolescents and young adults
    Adults
    Older adults

Source: Ref. 64

(10, 25, 58, 64), a committee of public health professionals developed a consensus set of 18 health status indicators (*Healthy People 2000*, Objective 22.1) (Table 2). These 18 indicators are designed to enable comparison of available data for federal, state, and local health agencies (17, 28, 75). Some of the 18 indicators are relevant for small local health departments, e.g. "Births to adolescents (females 10–17 years) as a percentage of total number of live births." Other consensus indicators may reflect events too rare to calculate stable rates for small jurisdictions, e.g. "Race/ethnicity-specific infant mortality, as measured by the rate (per 1000 live births) of deaths among infants <1 year of age."

Table 2 Consensus set of indicators* for assessing community health status and monitoring progress toward the year 2000 objectives: United States, July 1991

Indicators of health status outcome
1. Race/ethnicity-specific infant mortality, as measured by the rate (per 1000 live births) of deaths among infants <1 year of age

Death rates+ (per 100,000 population) for:
2. Motor vehicle crashes
3. Work-related injury
4. Suicide
5. Lung cancer
6. Breast cancer
7. Cardiovascular disease
8. Homicide
9. All causes

Reported incidence (per 100,000 population) of:
10. Acquired immunodeficiency syndrome
11. Measles
12. Tuberculosis
13. Primary and secondary syphilis

Indicators of risk factors
14. Incidence of low birth weight, as measured by percentage of total number of live-born infants weighing <2500 g at birth
15. Births to adolescents (females aged 10–17 years) as a percentage of total live births
16. Prenatal care, as measured by the percentage of mothers delivering live infants who did not receive prenatal care during first trimester
17. Childhood poverty, as measured by the proportion of children <15 years of age living in families at or below the poverty level
18. Proportion of persons living in counties exceeding US Environmental Protection Agency standards for air quality during previous year.

---

*Position or number of the indicator does not imply priority.
+Age-adjusted to the 1940 standard population.
Source: Ref. 10

STATE OBJECTIVES

The national health objectives are intended to be adapted, modified, and prioritized by the States. As of July 1993, 27 states had completed their own health objectives plans, with most using the year 2000 as a target date. All but two of the remaining States have statewide objective-setting processes in progress. Priority areas vary among those State plans that have been completed (67), with Maternal and Infant Health, and Immunization and Infectious Disease the two priority areas most often selected (Figure 1).

Processes for prioritizing health objectives varied considerably among the States (67). For example, Oregon developed a 20-member "Health Team 2000 to develop its objectives, with professional facilitators leading the

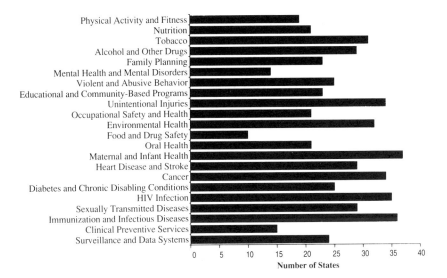

Physical Activity and Fitness
Nutrition
Tobacco
Alcohol and Other Drugs
Family Planning
Mental Health and Mental Disorders
Violent and Abusive Behavior
Educational and Community-Based Programs
Unintentional Injuries
Occupational Safety and Health
Environmental Health
Food and Drug Safety
Oral Health
Maternal and Infant Health
Heart Disease and Stroke
Cancer
Diabetes and Chronic Disabling Conditions
HIV Infection
Sexually Transmitted Diseases
Immunization and Infectious Diseases
Clinical Preventive Services
Surveillance and Data Systems

Number of States

* Includes all States that had determined priority areas as of December 1, 1991

Figure 1   Priority areas in state objectives. Source: Ref. 67

strategic planning process. Specific public and private groups were identified to implement action steps.

Another example is Florida's "Healthy Communities, Healthy People Plan." This framework for community-based health promotion was mandated by Florida's Health Care Reform Act of 1992. Florida's plan documents the value of effective prevention strategies to reduce public expenditures which were almost half of total health expenditures in 1992. Through this new legislation, Florida expects to decrease the need for resources to treat the effects of ill health and to move toward the healthy communities goals of Florida's State Comprehensive Plan.

The US Public Health Service Office of Disease Prevention and Health Promotion will publish a detailed analysis and overview of state plans in 1994.

HEALTH PLANNING TOOLS FOR LOCAL HEALTH DEPARTMENTS

Just as the distribution of disease in a population is uneven—-occurring in focal outbreaks, clusters, or high-risk groups—-national progress in health will evolve with shifting foci of local effort in communities across the nation. Selecting local priority health objectives requires a balancing of cultural and political forces (73). Priority rating schemes that work well for professionals may emphasize morbidity and mortality, rather than issues related to quality of life that may be of more immediate concern to a specific community, e.g. prevention of automobile injury or teenage pregnancy (68).

To adapt broad objectives to local needs, states often impose or negotiate public health program standards (51, 52, 59, 71). Although local governments in our federal system are subservient to state governments, many State health officials have found that local health departments are more likely to enthusiastically embrace those standards that are adapted through negotiation rather than imposed with threat of penalties (53).

To facilitate the adaptation of the national health objectives, the American Public Health Association has developed the third edition of *Healthy Communities 2000: Model Standards,* a guidebook to meld the national objectives with local efforts (2, 3). The Model Standards approach is an eleven-step process that selects outcome and process objectives compatible with both local priorities and the national health objectives. The work book provides a template of objectives that can be adapted locally. For example: "By ____(2000) reverse the rise in cancer deaths to achieve a rate of no more than ____(130) per 100,000 people. (Age-adjusted baseline: 133 per 100,000 in 1987)." In this example, the local health department would fill in the target year and the target rate based on their own best judgment of a locally achievable objective.

To establish and achieve these community objectives, two other planning tools are commonly used: APEX/PH and PATCH (Figure 2).

The Assessment Protocol for Excellence in Public Health (APEX/PH) is a community process for setting health status goals and programmatic objectives (40). The APEX process was designed to assist local health departments in assessing and improving their own organizations, and in working with the local community to assess and improve community health status. APEX was a collaborative project of the Centers for Disease Control and Prevention (CDC), the National Association of County Health Officials (NACHO), the American Public Health Association (APHA), the Association of Schools of Public Health, the Association of State and Territorial Health Officials, and the United States Conference of Local Health Officers. The manual consists of three sections: Part I, Organizational Capacity Assessment; Part II, The Community Process; and Part III, Completing the Cycle. The APEX manual and process were developed for self-assessment by individual local health departments. The organizational capacity assessment requires health department staff to assess both

Targeting the Year 2000

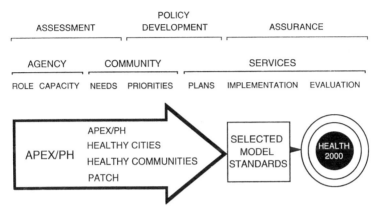

Figure 2 Relationship between planning tools and year 2000 objectives. Source: William Dyal, unpublished.

the importance and current status of indicators in nine broad functional areas: legal authority, community assessment, community relations, policy development, assurance of services, financial management, personnel management, program management, and interaction with a policy board. Part II, the community process, analyzes community health status data and community perception of health issues, and engages a health committee in a community health planning process. Part III entails policy development and assurance activities to ensure that an organizational action plan is effectively implemented. The APEX/PH tool was designed for individual local health department use, but some states such as Michigan, Washington, Kansas, and Illinois are experimenting with collaborative or statewide usage. Kansas' 96 local health departments are using APEX/PH Part I as part of its Primary Care Project (3).

The Planned Approach to Community Health (PATCH) model has been developed by CDC as a community health promotion tool (13, 24, 48). PATCH consists of five phases: mobilizing the community, collecting and organizing data, choosing health priorities and target groups, choosing and conducting health promotion interventions, and evaluating the process and interventions. While APEX/PH focuses on a public health agency's potential role in all aspects of public health practice, PATCH originally focused on identifying chronic disease prevention and health promotion efforts that might be coordinated with or without a locality's formal public health agency.

The Model Standards Project, coordinated by the American Public Health Association, provides an integrated overview of the use of these tools (3).

An example of how these tools can be integrated is the Healthy Sarasota 2000 Initiative in Florida. This model community health development program is underway in Sarasota County, a community of over 300,000 on the Gulf Coast. Sarasota County was the first in Florida (1986) to utilize the PATCH program, and the PATCH process now involves over 250 individuals and over 130 public and private agencies working in concert to deal with nine key community health problems identified through broad community participation. The effort is coordinated by the local public health department and integrates PATCH, APEX/PH, *Healthy Communities 2000,* and *Healthy People 2000.*

The main purpose of integrating these tools instead of using them separately was to strengthen the community's health development process. By promoting interest, awareness, and understanding of how problems and activities at the local level reflect national and state community health problems, the local public health agency anticipated that the local community would be better able to formulate a coherent vision and specific action plans if these were coordinated with other efforts at state, regional, and national levels. In addition, the community's integration of these planning tools improves efficient use of local resources and fosters increased cooperation among agencies and citizens around a common and shared vision of a healthy community future. In Sarasota this integrated approach led to increased community awareness and understanding of the community's health problems and their precursors, specific reorganization of local public health resources to rebuild the core infrastructure, reinfusion of financial commitment to address community health problems, and linkages among complementary resources.

To date, sixteen target objectives from *Healthy People 2000* have been identified for action in Sarasota County and comprehensive assessment by the local community using Part II of APEX/PH has been completed for six: maternal and infant health, HIV infection, immunization and infectious diseases, cancer, family planning, and sexually transmitted diseases. Analyses include years of potential life lost (YPLLs) for these six health problems for all ages and subpopulations in the county, and direct and indirect economic costs of excess morbidity and mortality from these conditions. Detailed community health improvement action steps have been organized for eight problem areas, and implementation thus far is in place for four of these (50). In 1993, the elected governing bodies of Sarasota County Government and of the sole publicly funded independent hospital addressed the problem of access to affordable health care by creating a Sarasota County Health Care Coordination Council. This program was a direct outgrowth of the PATCH and APEX/PH coalition activity.

DIVERSE LOCAL HEALTH DEPARTMENT PERSPECTIVES ON OBJECTIVES

Opportunities

Objective setting processes such as *Healthy People 2000* and *Healthy Communities 2000* offer local health departments a number of opportunities. These include: offering a comparative perspective to communities and boards of health to argue for budget or resource prioritization; highlighting extreme health problem areas; rallying professional groups around specific targets in their specialty area (47); trumpeting successes; learning from failures; and identifying gaps in surveillance data (8, 32).

A former President of APHA has challenged all local health departments to adapt the objectives set out in *Healthy People 2000* (1), but how widely used are these tools? In 1992, Miller et al conducted a survey of 14 local health departments that had been selected for an earlier study because of high levels of performance (33–36). The health directors were asked about their use of *Healthy People 2000* and *Healthy Communities 2000*. All of these selected respondents reported that the tools were useful and could help them argue for budget and program expansion and assist in priority setting. NACHO and CDC are completing a national survey of local health departments to examine a nationally representative sample (57). Preliminary results indicate that 71% of local health departments reported using *Healthy People 2000* for program or organizational planning, 48% reported using Healthy Communities 2000, 32% reported using APEX/PH, and 11% reported using PATCH. This study should provide useful data on the characteristics of health departments that are likely to adapt objective-setting processes using these tools.

Obstacles to Comprehensive Community Health Planning

Many local health departments can only focus on a few health objectives because of restrictions and pressures unique to the local level of government. Many local health departments lack maneuvering room with categorical funds and have a limited funding base from general funds (4, 34, 70). In many states, more than 70% of local health department funding derives from state or federal sources that restrict local flexibility in programming

(38, 39). Many local departments are organized in health districts that have to respond to multiple elected oversight boards. Local health departments usually compete with highways, education, and police departments for a slim general revenue base (8, 22, 45, 58), and each of these other agencies proffers parallel arguments based on prevention and unique opportunities that society cannot afford to miss. A disadvantage that public health agencies have is the perception by some local boards of health that health departments are part of a larger health care system whose costs are out of control and with multiple sources of easily available external revenue, such as Medicaid and insurance. Many local boards of health also focus on immediate problems, such as personnel matters or septic system variances, rather than major goal-setting.

Local health officers must present potential objectives carefully when rallying support to address a specific health area. Success in meeting a prevention objective may result in a perception that support for the relevant program can be curtailed. For example, if a local area has achieved an objective in foodborne disease control, why not eliminate the food protection program (26)? On the other hand, focusing on a problem often leads to better surveillance and a spurious increase in disease incidence, suggesting that the department may be doing a bad job. Small health departments often face a problem of lack of expertise in certain fields (23, 39), especially since many public health workers lack general public health training (23, 25) and have entered the field because of a particular interest in one specific public health area. Small departments also face a problem in interpreting rates of rare events because of unstable numerators, e.g. annual rates of race-specific infant mortality. Finally, elected officials may feel national measures are irrelevant because "all politics is local."

THE NEED FOR COALITIONS

Community health promotion efforts will be important tools for achieving health objectives for noninfectious diseases (18, 21, 58). Large-scale community intervention trials have demonstrated reductions in disease risk for cardiovascular disease and other health problems through community rather than individual interventions (16, 27, 29, 62, 69). The extent of involvement of the formal health agency in these trials has varied. Beyond well-financed research demonstrations, local public health leaders face formidable problems in obtaining the resources, training, and political collaboration necessary to implement similar community interventions (7). Financial constraints on government at all levels in the 1990s require health departments to catalyze the creation of coalitions to achieve objectives wherever possible, rather than rely on hierarchical, bureaucratic approaches that may work in times of generous budgets. The coalitions developed to date for achieving health objectives, however, may be only scratching the surface of possibilities. One ambitious initiative is the 1992 W.K. Kellogg Foundation's $16 million Community-based Public Health Initiative with seven consortia in California, Georgia, Maryland, Massachusetts, Michigan, North Carolina, and Washington. Each consortium consists of health departments, community-based organizations, and a school of public health. The focus is on community-based needs assessments of public health problems to address local priorities.

A GOVERNMENTAL PRESENCE AT THE LOCAL LEVEL—AGPALL

Anecdotes of successful refocusing of health departments on emerging public health issues should not lull us into the trap of an ascertainment bias. With almost three thousand local health agencies in the United States, we are still not certain whether the American people are adequately served by local health agencies, because we do not fully understand the current range of public health functioning at the local level (9, 11). At the moment a simple description of the characteristics of local health agencies is just emerging. *Healthy People 2000* Objective 8.14 aims to "increase to at least 90 percent the proportion of people who are served by a local health department that is effectively carrying out the core functions of public health. Local health department refers to any local component of the public health system, defined as an administrative and service unit of local or State government concerned with health and carrying some responsibility for the health of a jurisdiction smaller that a State (64)." A governmental presence at the local level (AGPALL) is difficult to ascertain because of the variegated division of authority throughout the nation (44, 59), as well as our evolving definition of public health practice.

Wissell approached the question of public health coverage from the perspective of services. He examined the 14 most prevalent public health services reported by 2363 local health departments in a 1989 NACHO survey, and found that departments with a population base of greater than 65,800 and those located in the Southern US were likely to offer a larger number of these services (74). However, departments that responded to the survey differed significantly from nonresponders, making interpretation difficult.

The Washington State Association of Local Health Officials analyzed the use of Part I of APEX/PH, the organizational self-assessment, in 24 of the state's 32 health departments and districts (46). They found that most local departments rated as strengths their program management and direct provision of services, whereas most felt lacking in the assessment function, and the utilization of data to guide community and program planning and policy. This self-analysis through the APEX/PH process prepared the local health departments in Washington for a particularly important role in formulating the State's 1993 health reform legislation, which embraces both medical and public health reform.

Several attempts are underway to characterize public health practice so that the coverage of public health services can be measured. CDC convened a series of focus groups with representatives from professional organizations to develop a taxonomy of public health practices within the framework of the three functions of public health: assessment, policy development, and assurance (8, 15, 49; Table 3). Individual categorical programs can be examined within the context of these ten core public health practices, and the ten practices can be further subdivided into more detailed functions. Miller (35, 36) used these functional areas in a pilot survey to examine whether health departments or other agencies provided these core public health practices in each jurisdiction. Illinois has developed 2–5 organizational practice measures for each of the ten practices, and is evaluating their use in a surveillance system to monitor local public health departments' ability to carry out the core functions of public health (60, 61). President Clinton's Health Security Plan delineates eight public health functions (72; Table 4). These and similar classifications of public health activity (56) need to be applied to current practice to determine how extensive public health coverage is in this nation and to estimate costs of expanded coverage.

Table 3   Core practices of public health

I. *Health assessment*
  Assess the health needs of the community
  Investigate the occurrence of health effects and health hazards in the community
  Analyze the determinants of identified health needs
II. *Health policy development*
  Advocate for public health, build constituencies, and identify resources in the community
  Set priorities among health needs
  Develop plans and policies to address priority health needs
III. *Assurance of available, quality health services*
  Manage resources and develop organizational structures
  Implement programs
  Evaluate programs and provide quality assurance
  Inform and educate the public

Source: Ref. 15, 49

Table 4   Core public health functions in President Clinton's Health Security Plan

Health-related data collection, surveillance, and outcomes monitoring
Protection of environment, housing, food, and water
Investigation and control of diseases and injuries
Public information and education
Accountability and quality assurance
Laboratory services
Training and education
Leadership, policy development, and administration

Source: Ref. 72

THE ROLE OF HEALTH DEPARTMENTS UNDER HEALTH REFORM

Under a reformed US health system, health departments may expand their assessment role and decrease their role in direct service provision (6, 54, 72). Just as practice guidelines and outcomes research may alter the way clinical medicine is practiced in a reformed health care system, accountability—as measured by progress toward long-term objectives—will probably play an increasingly important role in public health. Currently, only 3% of national health care dollars are spent on prevention (12). To increase prevention efforts, President Clinton's proposed Health Security Plan includes a public health core functions grant (72). These funds would be used for strengthening the core functions of public health, with accountability monitored through progress in achieving a common set of health outcomes derived from *Healthy People 2000*. Electronic access to health databases is facilitating the ability of local health departments to track these indicators (19, 20).

Most state "health" reform efforts to date have focused on illness care and insurance reform. As of this writing only Washington State has enacted health care reform legislation that provides universal access to clinical services and redefines public health in terms of functions as well as services (41, 43). The Washington Health Services Act of 1993 authorizes the development of a Public Health Improvement Plan consisting of:

1. A definition of minimum standards for public health protection, defined as assessment, policy development, and assurance
2. A list of communities not meeting those standards
3. Budget and staffing plans to remedy deficiencies
4. Reduction of personal health services from public health agency responsibility, and increasing public health funding—tied to specific objectives—with a dedicated revenue stream from motor vehicle excise taxes and a portion of statewide health care insurance revenue.

The Washington Public Health Improvement Plan is due in late 1994. The Washington State Department of Health and the Independent Health Services Commission are coordinating input on the Plan with assistance from citizens, advocates, other state and local agencies, the Indian Health Service, CDC, and other federal agencies. This approach may be a useful model for the national health and health care reform effort.

CONCLUSION

Public health officials require community planning tools and objectives for their "community-as-patient" just as a clinician requires a treatment plan and clinical objectives in managing an individual patient. However, the time scale varies for feedback on accomplishing objectives. The emergency physician receives feedback in a matter of minutes, the pediatrician in a matter of days, the rehabilitation specialist in a matter of months, but the public health official often requires years to measure progress toward most health objectives for communities (14).

To reach the *Healthy People 2000* goal of delivering preventive services to all Americans by the year 2000, access to primary care, clinical preventive medicine, and community-oriented public health services will be necessary. To achieve this goal, health departments will need to establish partnerships, using the tools described here, to adapt and implement objectives at the community level.

Literature Cited

1. Allukian M Jr. 1990 President's Address: forging the future: the public health imperative. *Am. J. Public Health* 83:655–60
2. Am. Public Health Assoc. 1991. *Healthy Communities 2000: Model Standard*. Washington, DC: Am. Public Health Assoc. 3rd ed.
3. Am. Public Health Assoc. 1993. *The Guide to Implementing Model Standards: Eleven Steps toward a Healthy Community*. Washington, DC: Am. Public Health Assoc.
4. Axnick NW, Katz M. 1986. Survey of city/county public health agencies to determine the development, use and effect of program performance standards. *Am. J. Public Health* 76:692–94
5. Breslow L. 1987. Setting objectives

for public health. *Annu. Rev. Public Health* 8:289–307
6. Brooks EF, Miller CA. 1987. Recent changes in selected local health departments: implications for their capacity to guarantee basic medical services. *Am. J. Prev. Med.* 3:134–41
7. Brownson R, Smith C, Jorge N, Dean C, DePrima L. 1992. Controlling cardiovascular disease: the role of the local health department. *Am. J. Public Health* 82:1414–16
8. Buttery CMG. 1991. *Handbook for Health Directors*. New York: Oxford Univ. Press. 200 pp.
9. Cent. Dis. Control Prevent. 1991. *Characteristics of Local Health Departments: A Selected Bibliography*. Public Health Serv., US DHHS
10. Cent. Dis. Control Prevent. 1991. Con-

sensus set of indicators for assessing community health status and monitoring progress toward the Year 2000 objectives. *Morbid. Mortal. Wkly. Rep.* 40: 450–51

11. Cent. Dis. Control Prevent. 1991. *Profile of State and Territorial Public Health Systems: United States, 1990*. Public Health Serv. US DHHS. 473 pp.

12. Cent. Dis. Control Prevent. 1992. Estimated national spending on prevention—United States, 1988. *Morbid. Mortal. Wkly. Rep.* 41:529–31

13. Cent. Dis. Control Prevent. 1992. *Planned Approach to Community Health (PATCH): Program Descriptions*. Public Health Serv., US DHHS, Atlanta, GA

14. Duffy J. 1990. *The Sanitarians: A History of American Public Health*. Chicago: Univ. Illinois Press. 330 pp.

15. Dyal WW. 1991. *Public Health Infrastructure and Organizational Practice Definitions*. Atlanta: Div. Public Health Syst., Public Health Practice Progr. Off., CDC

16. Farquhar JW. Fortmann SP, Flora JA, Taylor CB, Haskell WL, et al. 1990. Effects of community wide education on cardiovascular disease risk factors: the Stanford five-city project. *J. Am. Med. Assoc.* 264:359–65

17. Freedman MA. 1991. Health status indicators for the year 2000. *Healthy People 2000 Statistical Notes. US DHHS, Natl. Cent. Health Stat.* 1(1):1–4

18. Frenk J. 1993. The new public health. *Annu. Rev. Public Health* 14:469–89

19. Friede A, Freedman MA, Paul JE, Rizzo NP, Powate VI, Turczyn. 1993. DATA2000: an information system within CDC WONDER that links Healthy People 2000 objectives to data sets. *Am. J. Prevent. Med.* In press

20. Friede A, Reid JA, Ory HW. 1993. CDC WONDER: A comprehensive on-line public health information system of the Centers for Disease Control and Prevention. *Am. J. Public Health* 83: 1289–94

21. Green L, Kreuter M. 1990. Health promotion as a public health strategy for the 1990s. *Annu. Rev. Public Health* 11:319–34

22. Hanlon JJ, Pickett GE. 1984. *Public Health Administration and Practice*, pp. 176–78. St. Louis: Mosby. 8th ed.

23. Health Resourc. Serv. Admin. *Health Personnel In The United States Eighth Report To Congress 1991*. DHHS Publ. No. HRS-P-OD-92-1

24. Hustell CA, Meltzer CR, Lindsay GB, McClain R. 1992. Creating an effective infrastructure within a state health department for community health promotion: the Indiana PATCH experience. *J. Health Educ.* 23:164–66

25. Inst. Med. 1988. *The Future of Public Health*. Washington, DC: Natl. Acad. Press. 225 pp.

26. Irwin K, Ballard J, Grendon J, Kobayashi J. 1989. Results of routine restaurant inspections can predict outbreaks of foodborne illness: The Seattle-King County experience. *Am. J. Public Health* 79:586–90

27. Jacobs DR Jr, Luepker RV, Mittlemark MB, Folsom AR, Pirie PL, et al. 1986. Community-wide prevention strategies: evaluation design of the Minnesota Heart Health Program. *J. Chron. Dis.* 39:775–88

28. Klein RJ, Hawk SA. 1992. Health status indicators: definitions and national data. *Healthy People 2000 Statistical Notes* 1(3):1–8. Hyattsville, MD:Natl. Cent. Health Stat.

29. Kottke TE, Puska P, Salonen JT, Tuomilehto J, Nissinen A. 1984. Changes in perceived heart disease risk and health during a community-based heart disease prevention program: the North Karelia project. *Am. J. Public Health* 74:1404–5

30. Mason JO, McGinnis JM. 1990. Healthy People 2000: An overview of the national health promotion and disease prevention objectives. *Public Health Rep.*, pp. 105:441–46

31. McGinnis JM. 1990. Setting objectives for public health in the 1990s: experience and prospects. *Annu. Rev. Public Health* 11:231–49

32. McGinnis JM, Richmond JB, Brandt EN Jr, Windom RE, Mason JO. 1992. Health progress in the United States. Results of the 1990 objectives for the nation. *J. Am. Med. Assoc.* 268:2545–52

33. Miller CA, Brooks EF, DeFriese GH, Gilbert B, Jain SC, Kavaler F. 1977. A survey of local public health departments and their directors. *Am. J. Public Health* 67:931–39

34. Miller CA, Moore KS, Richards TB. 1993. The impact of critical events of the 1980s on core functions for a selected group of local health departments. *Public Health Rep.* 108:695–700

35. Miller CA, Moore KS, Richards TB, Kotelchuck M, Kaluzny AD. 1993. Longitudinal observations on a selected group of local health departments—a

preliminary report. *J. Public Health Policy* 14:34–50

36. Miller CA, Moore KS, Richards TB, Monk JD. 1993. A proposed method for assessing local public health performance. *Am. J. Public Health.* In press

37. Miller CA, Moos M-K. 1981. *Local Health Departments. Fifteen Case Studies.* Washington, DC: Am. Public Health Assoc.

38. Mullan F, Smith J. 1988. *Characteristics of State and Local Health Agencies.* Baltimore, MD: Johns Hopkins Sch. Hygiene Public Health

39. Natl. Assoc. County Health Officials. 1990. *National Profile of Local Health Departments.* Washington, DC: NACHO. 61 pp.

40. Natl. Assoc. County Health Officials. 1991. *Assessment Protocol for Excellence in Public Health (APEX/PH).* Washington, DC: NACHO

41. Natl. Assoc. County Health Officials. 1993. *Core Public Health Functions.* Washington, DC: NACHO. 16 pp.

42. Natl. Cent. Health Stat. 1993. *Healthy People 2000 Review.* Hyattsville, MD: Public Health Serv.

43. Omenn GS. 1993. Challenges facing public health policy. *J. Am. Diet. Assoc.* 93:643

44. Pickett G. 1980. The future of health departments: The government presence. *Annu. Rev. Public Health* 1: 297–321

45. Pickett G. 1989. Local public health and the state. *Am. J. Public Health* 79:967–68

46. Pratt M, Oberle M, McDonald S, Libbey P. 1993. *The Washington APEX public health project.* Presented at Prevention 93, St. Louis, MO

47. Rigau PJG. 1987. El tabaquismo y la salud en Puerto Rico: Progreso hacia los objectivos nacionales de salud para 1990 (XII). *Bol. Asoc. Med. Puerto Rico* 79:108–14

48. Rivo ML, Gray K. 1992. Health corners: reducing chronic disease risks among black public housing residents in the Nation's Capital. *Am. J. Public Health* 82:611–12

49. Roper WL, Baker EL, Dyal WW, Nicola RM. 1992. Strengthening the Public Health System. *Public Health Rep.* 107:609–15

50. Sarasota County Public Health Unit. 1993. *Healthy Sarasota 2000: The community action plan.* Sarasota, FL

51. Shaefer M. 1985. Moving the standards movement. *Am. J. Public Health* 75: 645–47

52. Shaefer M, Alexandre A. 1985. Standards for local public health services: Where stand the states? *Am. J. Public Health* 75:649–50

53. Spain C, Eastman E, Kizer K. 1989. Model standards impact on local health department performance in California. *Am. J. Public Health* 79:969–74

54. Stoto MA. 1992. Public health assessment in the 1990s. *Annu. Rev. Public Health* 13:59–78

55. Stoto MA, Durch JS. 1991. National health objectives for the year 2000: demographic impact of health promotion and disease prevention. *Am. J. Public Health* 81:1456–65

56. Studnicki J, Steverson B, Blais HN, Goley E, Richards TB, Thornton JN. 1993. An analysis of organizational practices: a methodology to describe the work activities of the local health department. *Public Health Rep.* In press

57. Suen J, Aberle-Grasse J, Cooper A, Elwell R, Gatewood D, et al. 1993. *A national profile of local health departments—descriptive data for 1993 health reform.* Presented at Annu. Meet. Am. Public Health Assoc., 121st, San Francisco

58. Terris M. 1990. Public health policy for the 1990s. *Annu. Rev. Public Health* 11:39–51

59. Tilson HH. 1982. Standards—a model for the nation. *Am. J. Public Health* 72:1223–24

60. Turnock B, Handler A. 1992. *Surveillance of effective public health practice: preliminary and draft set of performance standards and performance indicators.* Chicago: Sch. Public Health, Univ. Illinois

61. Turnock BJ, Handler A, Dyal WW, Christenson G, Vaughn EH, et al. 1993. Building public health capacity through organizational practices. *Public Health Rep.* In press

62. US Dep. Health Hum. Serv., Natl. Cancer Inst. 1991. *Strategies to control tobacco use in the USA: a blueprint for public health action in the 1990's.* Washington, DC: US DHHS 92–3316

63. US Public Health Serv. 1980. *Promoting health, preventing disease. Objectives for the nation.* Washington, DC: US DHHS

64. US Public Health Serv. 1991. *Promoting health/preventing disease: Year 2000 health objectives for the nation.* Washington, DC: US DHHS 91–50212

65. US Dep. Health Hum. Serv. 1992. *Healthy People 2000 Action Series:*

Consortium Action. Washington, DC: DHHS

66. US Dep. Health Hum. Serv. 1992. *Healthy People 2000 Action Series: Public Health Service Action.* Washington, DC: DHHS

67. US Dep. Health Hum. Serv. 1992. *Healthy People 2000 Action Series: State Action.* Washington, DC: DHHS

68. Vilnius D, Dandoy S. 1990. A priority rating system for public health programs. *Public Health Rep.* 105: 463–70

69. Wagner EH, Koepsell D, Anderman C, Cheadle A, Curry SG, et al. 1991. The evaluation of the Kaiser Family Foundation health promotion grants program: overall design. *J. Clin. Epidemiol.* 44:685–99

70. Wasserman MP, Rawding N, Aberle-Grasse JM. 1992. A survey of local health officials' view on current resources for public health services. *J. Public Health Policy* 13: 261–66

71. Weiler P, Boggess J, Eastman E, Pomer B. 1982. The implementation of model standards in local health departments. *Am. J. Public Health* 72:1230–37

72. White House Dom. Policy Counc. 1993. *The President's Health Security Plan,* pp. 161–69. New York: Random House. 284 pp.

73. Wiesner PJ. 1993. Four diseases of disarray in public health. *Ann. Epidemiol.* 3:196–98

74. Wissell RA. 1993. *Factors influencing the provision of services by local health departments.* DrPH thesis. Univ. Mich., Ann Arbor. 179 pp.

75. Zucconi SL, Carson CA, Holsinger GL and the Project Team. 1993. *Assessing community health needs: implications for health reform.* HPI Policy Ser. No. 19. Pittsburgh, PA: Health Policy Inst., Univ. Pittsburgh

Annu. Rev. Public Health. 1994. 15:277–301

PROGRAMS AGAINST MICRONUTRIENT MALNUTRITION: Ending Hidden Hunger*

G. F. Maberly[1], F. L. Trowbridge[2], R. Yip[2], K. M. Sullivan[1], and C. E. West[1&3]

[1]Center for International Health, Emory School of Public Health, Atlanta, Georgia 30329; [2]Division of Nutrition, National Center for Chronic Disease Prevention and Health Promotion, Centers for Disease Control and Prevention, Atlanta, Georgia 30333; [3]Department of Human Nutrition, Wageningen Agricultural University, Wageningen, The Netherlands

KEY WORDS: micronutrient malnutrition, cognitive function, infant mortality, productivity, food

INTRODUCTION

An adequate intake of the micronutrients iodine, vitamin A, and iron is of immense importance to global development. Prevention of these nutrient deficiencies is potentially the most important achievable international health goal of the decade, conceivably exceeding the impact of the global eradication of smallpox in the 1970s (69). While prevention of micronutrient malnutrition (MM) is no panacea for such ills of the Third World as famine, AIDS, political strife, and poverty, the normal intellectual functioning and well-being associated with micronutrient sufficiency may be essential to long-term resolution of these national and regional problems.

Programs to eliminate MM cannot be separated from other national nutrition programs such as food production, food security, and the elimination of protein-energy malnutrition, or isolated from other major public

---

health or development issues. Success requires the combined efforts of technical experts, food producers, and marketers of improved products, and the policy makers for decisions regarding public health interventions. The relative simplicity and low cost of the interventions, and their enormous potential benefit to nations may capture the imagination of policy makers and help raise other nutrition and health issues on the scale of national development priorities.

This article reviews the nature and magnitude of the problem of MM and discusses possible strategies for agencies and countries who are committed to its sustained elimination.

NATURE OF THE PROBLEM

Iodine Deficiency

Endemic goiter and cretinism associated with iodine deficiency have been depicted in paintings and statues since earliest times (55). Only during the past decade, however, have iodine deficiency disorders (IDD) been recognized as the leading cause worldwide of intellectual impairment (36, 69). Development of the central nervous system for normal intellectual functioning depends on an adequate supply of thyroid hormones which require iodine for biosynthesis (21).

Endemic cretinism is the most severe manifestation of the lack of maternal and fetal thyroid hormone arising from severe dietary iodine deficiency (63). Hallmarks include mental retardation, pyramidal neurological signs in an upper limb distribution, extrapyramidal signs, and a characteristic gait related to the neurological disorder, as well as joint laxity and deformity. Squinting of the eyes, deafness, and persistence of primitive brain reflexes are frequently noted (33). In some populations, there are additional manifestations of endemic cretinism resulting from continuing postnatal thyroid hormone deficiency: severe stunting of growth, skeletal retardation, and sexual immaturity (14). A prevalence of cretinism as high as 3 to 15 % may be found in severely affected rural populations, imposing a major social and economic burden on the community (14, 33, 62).

Mild iodine deficiency has been reported to reduce intelligence quotients (I.Q.) by 10–15% (15, 25, 81) and cause increased rates of stillbirths, perinatal mortality, and infant mortality (36, 54). There is good evidence from community-based assessments and iodine intervention trials that IDD can leave entire populations with below average intelligence and impaired motor functions. Iodine prophylaxis given before or during pregnancy has resulted in improved cognitive functioning in offspring in Ecuador (25–27, 81). Iodine supplementation given to school-age children can improve performance on tests of intellectual functioning (5, 21).

Vitamin A Deficiency

The most widely known vitamin A deficiency problems are related to the eye, collectively referred to as xerophthalmia, Greek for "dry eyes"; night blindness, caused by a reversible lack of retinol in the retina; conjunctival xerosis; Bitot's spot, an accumulation of cell debris on the conjunctival surface; corneal xerosis; corneal ulceration; and keratomalacia, which results in irreversible blindness. Vitamin A deficiency is the most preventable cause of blindness worldwide (87). These conditions are typically accompanied by serum retinol levels below 0.35 μmol/l, well below the normal lower limit of 0.70 μmol/l. Corneal xerophthalmia constitutes a medical emergency, because it progresses to irreversible blindness and is associated with increased mortality related to overwhelming infection and malnutrition (87).

The impact of vitamin A deficiency, however, is more extensive than the ocular effects. Xerophthalmia and low vitamin A levels are associated with increased mortality and severity of morbidity from respiratory and gastrointestinal disease (30, 56, 77, 78, 79). Thus, the extent of vitamin A deficiency is often not noticed in affected communities, either by the people themselves or by researchers carrying out cross-sectional studies, because of the high mortality (82, 85). Vitamin A deficiency impairs the body's defenses against infections (88, 64, 70) by breakdown of resistant barriers at epithelial and mucosal surfaces and impairment of both humoral and cellular immunity. The effect of vitamin A may be more likely to be related to inadequate response to infection rather than impaired resistance to becoming infected, based on meta-analysis in which vitamin A supplementation trials were shown not to affect incidence and duration of disease, but to reduce both severity and mortality rates associated with diarrheal and respiratory infections and with measles (9, 76). One meta-analyses of six randomized controlled trials reported a reduction in mortality of 30% (32) while another of eight trials found a reduction in mortality of 23% in children from 6 months to 5 years (9).

Iron Deficiency

Iron deficiency is most severely manifest in younger children and in women, especially during pregnancy (1, 52). The deficiency in children is due to an increase in demand for iron during their growth period, and in women due to monthly menstrual losses, an increased demand for iron during pregnancy and losses associated with childbirth (13). The main function of iron in the body is to produce hemoglobin, which circulates in the red blood cells. Hemoglobin is the essential gas transport mechanism for respiration— transport of oxygen from the lungs to tissues, and transport of carbon dioxide from the tissues back to the lungs. Anemia, reduced hemoglobin level or red cell mass, is a well-known consequence of significant iron deficiency. In extreme cases, anemia is associated with tissue hypoxia and heart failure leading to death in young children and pregnant women. Maternal anemia aggravated by hemorrhage and sepsis at child birth is a key factor worldwide for maternal mortality (90); 20% of all maternal deaths may be attributed to iron deficiency anemia during pregnancy (47). The morbidity and mortality of severe anemia in African children has been increasing because of HIV infection related to the common practice of using transfusion as the main form of treatment for children with severe anemia.

In the less extreme range, reduced aerobic capacity related to anemia significantly reduces the physical performance and work productivity of adults. This is particularly evident when the concentration of hemoglobin falls below 10g/dl, which is 2–4 g/dl below the lower limit of normal for adults. Iron supplementation to plantation workers in Indonesia has resulted in a quantifiable 50% increase in work productivity of males (4), 24% increase in women after four months (38), and 20% after just one month in Sri Lanka (22, 23). In countries where there is a large proportion of anemic adults, the reduced work translates into a significant loss of economic output. Worldwide, almost half the women and 20% of the men in developing countries suffer from some degree of iron deficiency (69).

Beyond anemia, numerous enzymes and cellular functions are iron-dependent and, hence, affected in iron deficiency. Well-characterized consequences of iron deficiency affecting the functions of various organ systems are summarized below:

Neuropsychological disturbances   Iron deficiency clearly contributes to developmental delay, behavioral disturbances, and attention deficits among infants and younger children (16, 22, 65).

Enhanced heavy metal absorption   The compensatory mechanism for iron deficiency is an enhanced gastrointestinal absorption capacity for iron. Unfortunately, this mechanism is not specific for iron, so other heavy metals, including toxic metals such as lead, cobalt, and cadmium, are absorbed more effectively. High blood levels of lead are more common in children with iron deficiency (20, 49, 86, 92, 93).

Altered immunity   Iron deficiency has a profound effect on the immune response, in fact, cell-mediated immunity is often impaired before anemia can be detected and overt clinical signs are observed (65). Decreased resistance to infection has been documented in both humans and experimental animals (3, 66). Clinical studies indicate that iron-deficient infants have increased susceptibility to childhood respiratory and intestinal infections (32, 52). Oral dosing with iron stimulates intestinal infection with *Entamoeba histolytica* (60), and parenteral dosing may increase infections such as respiratory infections, malaria and gram-negative sepsis neonatorum. This suggests that iron supplementation must be accompanied by appropriate treatment of infection.

Adverse birth outcomes   Recently there has been increased evidence that iron-deficiency anemia is associated with greater rate of fetal mortality, low birth weight and pre-term births (71); the impact of this problem must be substantial on a global basis.

Reduced cold resistance   An impaired capacity to maintain body temperature in a cold environment is characteristic of iron-deficiency anemia (6–8), due to decreased secretion of thyroid-stimulating hormone and thyroid hormone.

Iodine, vitamin A, and iron deficiencies have cumulative and multiplicative detrimental effects on human populations. Taken together, these micronutrient deficiencies result in impairment of physical growth; impairment and loss of sight and hearing; irreversible damage to brain function and cognitive ability; decreased well-being and survival of infants and young children; reduced physical and intellectual performance of school-age children; reduced work ability, performance, and productivity of adults; and diminished survival and reproductive performance of women. By denying human beings their developmental and performance potential, these micronutrient deficiencies may impede attempts by policy makers to make meaningful improvements in the areas of education, productivity, and economic and social development.

Other Important Micronutrients

Folic acid deficiency is the most common of all vitamin deficiencies in the United States (37). Symptoms may include pallor, weakness, forgetfulness, sleeplessness, and bouts of euphoria (19, 32). It is estimated that up to one third of all pregnant women worldwide suffer from folic acid deficiency of varying severity (72). The CDC recommends consumption of 400 μg folate daily prior to conception and during pregnancy to substantially reduce the risk of spina bifida and other neural tube defects (NTD) that occur in the United States and worldwide (18).

Zinc is a component of over 70 enzymes necessary for many metabolic processes. Zinc deficiency was first noted in young men in Iran and Egypt who exhibited the most salient features of the syndrome, dwarfism and delay of sexual maturity (67). Zinc-deficient dwarfs have been observed in Turkey, Portugal, Morocco, and other countries where phytate-containing cereal products, which inhibit absorption of zinc, make up a substantial portion of the diet (68). Zinc deficiency is also a public health problem in the United States (73). Other features of zinc deficiency include fetal malformations, difficult births, reduced appetite, poor growth rates, mental lethargy, skin changes, and slow wound healing (34, 57).

Selenium, like iodine, is found in the soil. Thus, the selenium content of foods and the prevalence of human selenium deficiency varies by geographic location. Selenium defeciency in humans has been related to Keshan cardiomyopathy and to the Kaschin-Beck "large-joint disease" (44–46).

Selenium is essential for functioning of the enzyme glutathione peroxidase. This enzyme metabolizes lipid and other peroxides, which are destructive by-products of oxidative metabolism. Because of their similar antioxidant roles, selenium and vitamin E may interact additively. Selenium is a constituent of type 1 iodothyronine 5-deiodinase, which catalyzes the conversion of thyroxine to tri-iodothyronine (2, 10, 11). Studies in Zaire suggest that selenium deficiency in iodine-deficient areas can contribute to the myxedematous form of cretinism (84), but the proportion of myxedematous forms of cretinism is lower in regions of China where selenium deficiency is severe.

Insufficient exposure to sunlight is an etiological factor in vitamin D deficiency. Even in the tropics, many women and young children are so wrapped up in their clothing when they go outside that vitamin D synthesis in the skin is insufficient to meet their needs. Often it is easier to modify behavior than increase intake.

MAGNITUDE OF THE PROBLEM

Accurate assessments of the extent of MM worldwide are not currently available and are subject to change on a yearly basis. The reasons are severalfold. First, many of the most severely affected countries have only recently recognized the importance of MM. Second, the problem is often not overtly evident in the affected populations. Hence, the term "hidden hunger" has been coined by UNICEF and WHO (83). Countries frequently have not invested the resources to attain the technical capacity to undertake surveys, process the samples, and interpret the data. Third, we lack clear criteria for judging the severity and public health significance of MM problems. Clinical criteria for cretinism, goiter in school children, xerophthalmia in preschool-age children and anemia in women and children are highly subjective. When tested against more objective measures such as thyroid ultrasound, or biochemical parameters from populations, these clinical methods frequently have been shown to greatly underestimate the extent and severity of the problem. Existing information on MM prevalence is based on out-dated, small, selective studies in limited geographic areas.

More data are needed from a number of affected countries with varying levels of severity of MM to establish clear public health criteria for severity to enable effective surveillance and comparative evaluation of interventions.

In 1992, WHO (89–91), using the best available data from many sources including member states and other international and bilateral organizations, estimated that 1 billion people (20% of humanity) in 95 countries live in areas at risk for iodine deficiency (90), the vast majority in developing countries. In March 1992, 300 leading scientists and public health policy makers met in Brussels, Belgium, to examine clinical and biochemical data related to iodine deficiency in Europe. The meeting concluded with a declaration that both Western and Eastern Europe had an increasingly serious iodine-deficiency problem (61).

Forty million pre-school children are estimated to be vitamin A deficient, with 13 million of these having some eye damage. Each year, half a million of these children go blind (79). Approximately 190 million school children are at potential risk of vitamin A deficiency (90). Globally, the total population at risk, including women of childbearing age, infants, preschool and school children, has been estimated at 800 million (90).

Close to 50% of humanity, approximately 2.2 billion people, are anemic (91). The reasons for anemia are multifactorial and interrelated, but iron deficiency is the most significant contributing factor. The populations most at risk are pregnant women, school-age children, and low-birth-weight infants. Although iron deficiency is a greater problem in developing countries, it is still a considerable public health problem in the industrialized world, with prevalence of anemia as high as 10% in pregnant women.

The composite table of the population at risk of MM by region, compiled for the executive board of WHO, December 1991 (90), indicates that many of those affected are the same underprivileged persons, so that the total number of subjects at risk is around 2 billion, most of whom live in developing nations. About three fifths of the world's people live in countries with low to middle incomes, where nutritional problems are generally related to poverty associated with a young and fast-growing population, the absence of a social security system, and minimal economic development. A reliable, affordable food supply cannot be taken for granted, nor can clean drinking water. Infections are an additional burden. In 1945, 60% of the world's population lived in developing nations; by 2000 this figure is projected to rise to 80%, and by 2025 to 95%. If MM persists globally or increases in incidence, as expected, socioeconomic development of the Third World will be further imperilled: increasing economic and environmental interdependence. Failure to achieve a substantial decrease in MM will have profound implications in today's increasingly interdependent global economy.

THE GLOBAL INITIATIVE

Eliminating MM is on the global agenda. Seventy-one heads of state and senior policy-makers from 80 other countries attended The World Summit for Children in September, 1990 and endorsed The World Declaration and 1990–2000 Plan of Action on the Survival, Protection and Development of Children (83). The plan stated that the world is in a position to "overcome the worst forms of malnutrition ... to halve protein-energy malnutrition, virtually eliminate iodine-deficiency disorders, virtually eliminate vitamin A deficiency and its consequences including blindness, and to reduce by one third the 1990 levels of iron deficiency anemia among women of child-bearing age". Recognizing the possibilities created by this global movement, a historic conference, "Ending Hidden Hunger: a Policy Conference on Micronutrient Malnutrition," was convened by WHO and UNICEF in Montreal in October 1991. The meeting was supported by the international development agencies of the USA and Canada, the World Bank, UNICEF, UNDP, FAO and WHO. In attendance were three hundred ministers, policy leaders, and scientists from 55 countries. Representatives attended from over 50 intergovernment, bilateral, and nongovernment organizations interested in collaborating to overcome micronutrient malnutrition. One outcome of the conference has been the inclusion of micronutrient malnutrition elimination as a key element of national development plans.

Agreement is now closer than ever before on ways to meet this challenge. At the International Conference on Nutrition held in Rome in 1992, governments again confirmed their commitment to summit goals, this time to specific policies and timetables for implementation. Fortification, supplementation, dietary diversification, and other public health measures are feasible methods of preventing MM. Newly emerging laboratory and information technologies are simpler, more accurate, more acceptable and less costly than previous technologies, so countries will be able to readily determine where interventions are needed, and to monitor program activities.

A FRAMEWORK FOR ACTION AT THE NATIONAL LEVEL

The basic objective of all national micronutrient programs is to ensure that needed micronutrients are available and consumed by vulnerable populations. Programs directed towards the sustained elimination of MM need to be broadly based so that interventions become accepted community practices. Hence, program tactics need to be synchronous with this objective and based upon empowering people and communities so that they will be capable of arranging for and sustaining an adequate intake of micronutrients, inde-

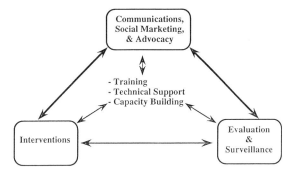

Figure 1   Components of a micronutrient malnutrition control program. The linkage among these components are as important as the components themselves.

pendent of outside aid. Achieving and sustaining this status requires a commitment from a network of people from both the local community and various organizations.

Strategic planning for the elimination of MM at the global, national, provincial, county, or community level is critical to the success of the process. In levering momentum for implementation, the planning process needs to involve key change agents and be adaptable to the situation where the interventions will be introduced. Any such plan can be broken down to its components; however, all components are tightly linked and their relationships to each other are as important as the elements themselves.

Figure 1 provides a useful framework around which all MM programs can be built. The key elements include (*a*) communications and social marketing; (*b*) interventions, and (*c*) evaluation and surveillance. These components are closely linked and require the support and perspectives of advocates, policy makers, and managers. The program benefits from an ongoing process of applied research and development.

Integration of iodine, vitamin A, and iron-deficiency control is more effective and efficient than isolated and potentially competitive control of each micronutrient individually. Multiple micronutrient deficiencies, the required technical skills, facilities, and information resources frequently overlap, and interventions to address several deficiencies can often be delivered through the same system. The schema in Figure 2 demonstrates some of the benefits of an overlapping matrix of activities for iodine, iron, and vitamin A deficiencies. A more detailed report discussing the benefits of coordinated strategies was the outcome of a conference in 1991 sponsored by the International Life Sciences Institute (ILSI) and the Program Against Micronutrient Malnutrition (PAMM) (80).

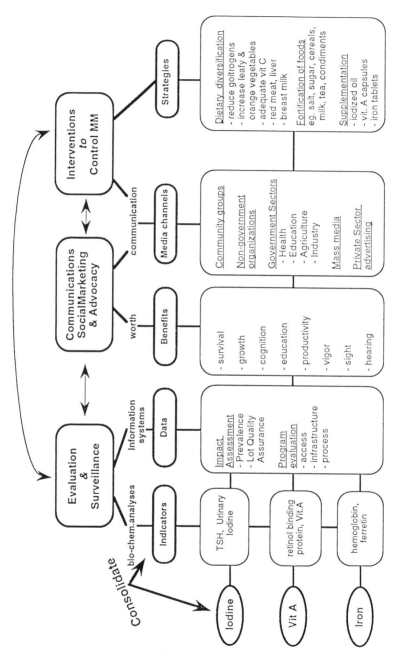

Figure 2   Examples of opportunities for consolidation of effort in programs against micronutrient.malnutrion

Communications, Social Marketing, and Advocacy

Advertising has long been used for social purposes, but traditionally did not consider social causes in terms of product, price, and place. It was defined in simple terms, as the application of marketing practices to nonprofit/social purposes (50). In this article we use the broader concept of social marketing that integrates aspects of the traditional approach with modern communication and educational technologies, leading to more systematic development of strategy. Defining and promoting acceptable concepts, behaviors, or products, and in the case of products, distributing and pricing them for the market are the key components of a social-marketing plan. A complete social-marketing strategy not only develops and promotes a good "product" but also achieves and maintains political support, and trains and motivates program implementers. Well-designed social marketing programs invite the participation of program beneficiaries to designate feasible interventions, and take a comprehensive and systematic approach to the analysis and solution of problems (24).

In the social marketing approach to communications, activities to achieve objectives are based on formative research to uncover the facts related to the intervention, implementation, and testing of messages and behaviors with the target groups themselves, and evaluation to determine the success of the intervention. Research is conducted to understand the cultural, attitudinal, economic, and logistical resistances that prevent people from carrying out the desirable behaviors. Such data provide critical information to formulate better targeted and more effective messages, which eventually lead to better reception by the public—the ultimate beneficiaries.

Well-designed communications are creative. They do not merely convey information in a conventional, factual manner, but deliver a message based upon the knowledge, attitudes, and perceptions of the target group. Based on formative research, an attractive "image" of fortified foods or supplements is portrayed and supported via mass and interpersonal communication. Messages contain effective appeals or motivational statements. What is of greatest concern to mothers? Is it their own health, the health of their babies, the difficulty of adopting a certain behavior, or religious or cultural beliefs about certain behaviors? Messages must address and respect these concerns, and at the same time appeal for behavior change. Many creative approaches and methodologies of social marketing are similar to the manner in which commercial advertisers approach product promotion.

Advocacy, a component of social marketing, involves raising the consciousness of decision makers at any number of levels—from officials of UN agencies to national political leaders and technocrats, from provincial leaders to village chiefs—regarding health-supportive laws, inter sectorial cooperation, alliances with various nongovernment institutions and private agencies, basic communication strategies, importance of the problem, and the potential effectiveness of current or potential solutions.

Interventions

Though the quantity of micronutrients needed for good health is very small, the requirement may not be met for a variety of reasons. Population groups may be deficient because their access to micronutrient-rich foods is limited by poverty, climatic conditions, or geographic isolation; because their dietary habits do not include adequate consumption of these foods; or because the absorption and utilization of the micronutrients is impaired once the foods are consumed. The interventions to overcome these constraints include the following:

DIETARY DIVERSIFICATION   Many micronutrient deficiencies would disappear if enough food were available to all members of the population to allow them to eat sufficient food in a balanced diet. The diets may be imbalanced not only because of a general shortage of food, but also for other reasons that may be difficult to identify and modify. Sometimes, technological intervention has replaced a food item that contains a micronutrient with one that does not; other times the condition is longstanding. In any case, the use of existing foods to solve micronutrient deficiencies requires the provision of foods acceptable to those expected to eat them, and education to promote their use.

Desirable foods are obtained by direct purchase at a free market or subsidized rate (including through food-for-work programs), through direct efforts of household members such as the growing of vegetables, the catching of fish or the collection of salt that contains sufficient natural iodine, or by gift from a donor agency. It may well be that there is an absolute shortage of a nutrient which requires intervention in some way other than the use of normal foods. Iodine deficiency, for example, arises from iodine-deficient soil. Under many circumstances, it is necessary to provide people in such areas with iodine in some form other than foods in their natural state.

FORTIFICATION AND ENRICHMENT   These two approaches involving the addition of nutrients to foods are very similar. Fortification is the addition to a food of one or more nutrients absent or present only in minimal amounts. The amount added is designed to contribute substantially to the nutrient status with respect to that nutrient. Enrichment is the addition to a food of one or more nutrients that are already present in the food, but in insufficient amounts for optimal nutrition. Fortification and enrichment have been used widely throughout the world. Examples include vitamin A added to sugar in Central America and to monosodium glutamate in the Philippines, iron added to milk in Chile, and iodine added to salt in many countries (40, 58, 59).

The decision on which food to use as the dietary vehicle for a specific nutrient should be based on a number of factors. The dietary vehicle should be consumed by essentially all the population with little day-to-day variation in per capita consumption, thus providing an adequate intake with a low risk of overdosing. Fortification or enrichment of the dietary vehicle by the nutrient should be possible at a level sufficient to contribute to prevention of the deficiency in the population for which the program is designed, and the end product should not cost significantly more than the unfortified or unenriched product. In addition, there should be no technological constraints to fortification or enrichment. For example, a fortified or enriched product should be stable and a premix should mix well with the dietary vehicle and not separate from it. The fortified or enriched product should be indistinguishable by taste, smell and, if possible, color from the unfortified or unenriched product and should have the same physical characteristics. Finally, the dietary vehicle should be produced by a limited number of manufacturers, thus allowing the fortification or enrichment process to be supervised.

Certain legal provisions related to fortification of food should be considered for addition to a country's food-control law. A general fortification approach is preferred as it is more efficient and flexible for a government to develop and propose one piece of legislation covering various fortification activities instead of multiple legislation dealing with each fortification activity. The law should encourage input from interested parties—the government, industry, educational, scientific, and community representatives in an advisory role for planning, consultation, and coordination. The law should clearly state what is required or prohibited so that people understand what is required of them and government officials can tell when the provisions are violated, and should include quality control in terms of definite fortification procedures and standards. Provisions that reflect the interests of the population and the inclusion of incentives and penalties would ensure compliance and allow effective enforcement.

MASSIVE TREATMENT   Massive dosing involves either giving a nutrient by mouth or by injection to provide sufficient stores of that nutrient long term. For example, oral doses or injections of iodated oil have been used to provide sufficient iodine for a period of 1–2 years, while vitamin A capsules provide sufficient vitamin A for four to six months. Three separate approaches are used in massive dosing programs:

1. Medical therapeutic dosing. Acute medical problems related to a nutrient deficiency are treated in such a way as to produce immediate results. In developing countries, for example, a malnourished child presenting with measles is often given a massive dose of vitamin A to prevent blindness produced by corneal ulceration. A person presenting with tetany produced by low serum calcium is routinely given an injection of calcium gluconate.
2. Universal prophylactic dosing. Massive dosing is sometimes extended to the whole population when a nutrient deficiency is widespread.
3. Targeted prophylactic dosing. Massive dosing is targeted only at vulnerable groups. The targeting can be aimed at specific groups based on age, gender, income, or geographic location, to name a few, e.g. to provide iodated oil to women aged 15 to 45 years in areas with iodine deficiency, and to provide oral doses of vitamin A to children under 5 years of age in refugee camps.

A variation on massive dosing is supplementation, in which a specific nutrient, in liquid or solid form, is provided at a level adequate to cover short-term requirements. Thus, supplementation usually involves daily or weekly provision of the supplement. Iron has been provided both in a liquid and tablet form in many countries. However, successful and sustainable supplementation requires close supervision and organization.

INDIRECT METHODS   Because some micronutrient deficiencies are secondary to other nutritional deficiencies, illnesses, or social conditions, eliminating the underlying problem causing the malnutrition is essential to the sustained elimination of the deficiency. For example, improvements in sanitation resulting in decreased hookworm infection may lead to improvements in iron status, malaria control may lead to improved folic acid status, vaccination against measles may lead to improved vitamin A status, and birth control may make food more available generally and also help to prevent iron and iodine deficiency in both women and children (9, 39).

Often, a combination of the methods outlined above is used to combat deficiency of a micronutrient. For example, massive dosing may be used to solve an immediate problem of vitamin A deficiency/corneal blindness, fortification of sugar may be used for the intermediate term, while a food-based approach may provide a long-term solution. Long-term solutions at the expense of immediate needs should be avoided. One cannot advise the mother of a vitamin A-deficient child to go home and grow dark green leafy vegetables for her child. In several years, the prevalence of corneal blindness may diminish in the population, but unfortunately her child may go blind within several days.

Monitoring and Surveillance

The surveillance of MM may serve a variety of distinct purposes, including the assessment and tracking of the prevalence of MM, the identification of high-risk populations, and evaluation of the activities of control programs.

ASSESSING THE PREVALENCE OF MM   A fundamental purpose of MM surveillance is to determine the magnitude and distribution of MM within a population. This information can serve as a basis for advocacy to highlight the extent of MM problems and stimulate action, including the allocation of resources required for MM elimination. Assessment of prevalence can also provide an essential, quantitative baseline for long-term monitoring of MM problems. Two key objectives are involved in assessing the prevalence of MM: first, to collect the minimal amount of data that are representative of the target population; and, second, to provide a stable prevalence estimate within a desired level of precision. The survey method to be used depends upon many factors, including the target group, the survey site, and the size of the geographic area of interest. In large countries, it may be desirable to perform prevalence surveys at a provincial level. For practical purposes, the number of geographic units to be studied should be kept to a minimum. It is usually neither feasible nor cost effective to estimate prevalence levels in units smaller than large counties.

IDENTIFICATION OF HIGH-RISK POPULATIONS   Surveillance of MM may also be concerned with the identification of priority areas for intervention to maximize the use of resources. However, at the level of areas smaller than a province or county technical and resource constraints generally do not permit regular estimates of prevalence. Moreover, at the small area or community level the information required is actually not to assess prevalence so much as to address certain key operational questions such as: "Is there a MM problem in the community?", "Is there an appropriate intervention?", and "Is the intervention working and, if not, why not?". These operational questions relate to decisions about whether action is required to intervene in a particular population.

MONITORING PROGRAM IMPLEMENTATION   Although surveillance is often aimed at the assessment of micronutrient status, the same concepts should equally be applied to the assessment of the process of program implementation. While the goal is to improve micronutrient status, achievement of that goal will be through the successful implementation of intervention programs. Surveillance of the process of program implementation is basically concerned with documenting the effective access of deficient populations to micronutrient supplies. In regard to IDD, process surveillance often takes the form of assessing the distribution of iodized salt and monitoring the adequacy of salt iodine content at the level of the marketplace and the household.

SELECTION OF TARGET GROUPS FOR SURVEILLANCE   An important issue in prevalence surveys for MM is the selection of appropriate target groups for assessment. Target groups may include newborns, infants, preschool or school-aged children, and adults. The selection of the optimal target group or groups depends on factors such as vulnerability of the target group to MM, the representativeness of the group as an indicator of prevalence within the population, and the accessibility of the group. Another factor may be the usefulness of the target group for surveillance of other health problems. Of course, final selection depends upon local conditions and practices.

SELECTION OF APPROPRIATE INDICATORS   Once the target population(s) for assessment are defined, the next step is to select the specific indicators to be used. In some situations the selection of an indicator may guide the choice of a target population. The list of possible indicators is now quite extensive and several new approaches are under research and development. A full discussion of the nature, advantages, limitations and interpretation of these indicators is beyond the scope of this article. This topic has been the focus of several recent technical advisory meetings at WHO, Geneva, and papers summarizing these meetings are expected shortly (91a).

A number of criteria need to be considered when selecting indicators including acceptability, technical feasibility, performance and cost. Each of these factors is considered below.

Acceptability   The acceptability of an indicator depends upon the beliefs and cultural background of the population. Some measures, such as clinical examination of the thyroid gland or eyes, may be acceptable. The drawing of venous blood samples may be unacceptable in some populations, while the collection of small capillary blood samples or of blood spots onto filter paper may be more acceptable.

Technical feasibility   Technical feasibility involves such factors as ease of sample or data collection, sample storage and transport requirements, transportability and ruggedness of field equipment, and the availability of trained personnel to obtain and analyze the specimens. The use of blood spots on filter paper is convenient for storage and transportation for measurement of TSH in the assessment of iodine deficiency and for hemoglobin for iron deficiency. Promising initial results have been found in adapting the measurement of vitamin A and retinol-binding protein (RBP) from blood spots for the assessment of vitamin A deficiency in populations.

Performance   The performance of indicators in identifying MM status in terms of sensitivity, specificity, and reliability is important. Judging by these criteria, the performance of indicators based on examination for clinical signs of MM (such as goiter or xerophthalmia) may be limited. The poor performance of clinical indicators is often related to the variability in findings by different observers and because clinical signs are frequently nonspecific. As progress is made towards eliminating MM clinical indicators become less useful. The reporting of a low prevalence of clinical signs of MM in a population does not exclude the possibility of a significant public health problem related to these deficiencies. In general, it is recommended that biochemical indicators be included in surveillance systems designed to track the sustained elimination of these disorders.

Cost   Costs associated with the use of certain indicators include the costs associated with collection of the sample, capital and maintenance costs for facilities/equipment, recurring costs for supplies/reagents, and the cost of training. The costs for establishing national or provincial laboratories have been decreasing as the equipment becomes more readily available. International and bilateral donor agencies, such as UNICEF, can now provide national governments with a list of laboratory equipment known to be appropriate and a procurement mechanism that uses local currency rather than foreign exchange. The equipment cost for establishing an MM laboratory and supply of reagents for national monitoring can usually be equated with the costs of obtaining and running two motor vehicles in government service.

Availability of reference data   Interpretation of MM status depends on the availability of reference data for use in establishing cut-off values and prevalence levels to determine whether a public health problem exists. Use of standardized reference data greatly enhances the interpretation of results across different populations.

SAMPLING STRATEGIES   Sampling strategies for MM surveillance vary according to the specific purposes at hand. Several different sampling strategies are described below, along with an indication of the specific circumstances when they are most appropriately applied.

Probability proportionate to size cluster sampling   When the objective is to assess prevalence, a common approach for immunization and anthropometric household-based surveys is the "probability proportionate to size" (PPS) cluster method. This method is useful when census data are inadequate. In general, all villages and cities are listed and a systematic sampling scheme is used on the cumulative population. This sampling scheme assures that larger villages and cities are more likely to be selected than smaller ones. Thirty villages or cities ("clusters") are selected, and within each cluster, seven children are selected in immunization surveys, and thirty children in anthropometry surveys. Thirty clusters are selected to assure a valid estimate of the prevalence; collecting substantially fewer can lead to estimates that differ dramatically from the true prevalence (12). The number of individuals to sample within each cluster depends upon the prevalence of the condition, the degree of precision desired (based on the type and width of the confidence interval), and the design effect (a measure of the variability of the prevalence between clusters).

Surveys designed to assess the prevalence of MM in schools or health clinics could use either a PPS cluster sampling method or a two-stage cluster sample approach (75). In the latter, the schools or clinics are generally selected at random (not by PPS) from a listing, and then individuals are selected at random from within selected schools or clinics. Either a fixed number of individuals from each school or clinic or a proportion of the population is selected. A two-stage cluster survey, unlike a PPS survey, requires an accurate count of the population under study in each cluster. The population counts are used to weight the results in proportion to cluster size.

Lot quality assurance sampling (LQAS)   This method is recommended for community level assessments as an efficient method for screening multiple sites. The method was developed by industry to ensure that each "lot" of a product on a production line maintains certain essential qualities. LQAS methods have been adapted to public health activities such as immunization programs (43), but may also have great potential in MM control programs. For example, LQAS would be useful in a situation where school children were the target group for surveillance for identifying areas with a high prevalence of goiter. To find the high prevalence areas, every school within a geographic area would be surveyed, and within each school a sample of school children would be examined. If a large number of children had goiter, then the area would be identified as "high prevalence."

To continue the example, imagine that the estimated prevalence of goiter among school children in a region is estimated to be 10%, and the provincial authorities are interested in identifying schools with a prevalence greater than 30%. How many children would need to be palpated in each school, and at what point should they classify a school as having a severe IDD problem? Using published tables (43) and assuming a significance level of 5% and power of 90%, 33 children in each school would need to be palpated. If five or more children had goiter, the school would be classified as having an IDD problem (analogous to a "rejected" lot); if fewer than five had goiter, the school would be classified as not having a problem (i.e. an "accepted" lot). In order to minimize the number of schools to be screened, the area under surveillance could be limited to include only areas at higher risk of having IDD, such as rural mountainous areas. If all schools in an area are included in an LQAS survey, there are ways in which this information can be used to derive a prevalence estimate for the area.

Similar approaches using LQAS can be developed for other indicators to identify high risk populations for other micronutrient deficiencies. These approaches are also useful for assessing the effectiveness and coverage of the interventions in populations. For example, LQAS can be used to assess the number and types of foods available in the market or the home garden, micronutrient levels in a fortified food vehicle at different points along the distribution chain, or the number of doses of supplement dispensed via a primary health care system.

Interpretation and presentation of results   In the past, assessing deficiencies in individual subjects was often emphasized. Various indicators for each deficiency were therefore required for individual diagnosis and treatment. In the assessment of populations, on the other hand, the overall distribution of the results is more important than those for individuals. Even though indicators of micronutrient status may not correlate on an individual basis, the indicators may be useful for population assessments.

Many indicators of MM measured on a continuous scale are not normally distributed. The use of means and standard deviations in describing such data is likely to be inappropriate, although in some situations it may be possible to transform the data or, alternatively, use nonparametric statistics. If possible, the full distribution of results should be presented, in addition to a measure of the central tendency (mean or median, whichever is appropriate) and cut-off points to describe the upper and/or lower tails of the distribution. The prevalence of individuals at the extremes of a distribution can be characterized by using standard cut-off points and tabulating the prevalence of values below or above cut-off values. Several cut-off points may be used to provide a more adequate impression of the magnitude of the problem. For example, lower cut-off points may be selected to highlight the most extreme cases, while less extreme cut-off points may be useful to describe the proportion of the population that may be at-risk of a micronutrient deficiency, but is not necessarily severely deficient.

Combined Strategies for MM Surveillance

Much of the cost and work involved in the surveillance of MM status is incurred in obtaining access to the target groups. Moreover, considerable overlap exists in the appropriate target groups for assessment of iodine, iron, and vitamin A status. Given these realities, it is likely to be cost effective to undertake coordinated surveillance of micronutrient problems. For example, preschool children seen in clinics or in household surveys may be assessed simultaneously for iron deficiency by hemoglobin measurement as well as for IDD using a blood spot TSH. As simplified tests are further developed, it may be feasible to measure vitamin A status from a blood spot. A single investment in reaching a target population may thus yield valuable information to assesst multiple micronutrient problems.

Support to National Programs

Successful elimination of MM depends ultimately on the political will within individual countries to place the sustained elimination of these disorders as a national development priority and commit resources commensurate with the magnitude of the problem. This response needs to go beyond the limited activities normally relegated to nutrition departments within the ministries of health or agriculture. It must be recognized that people eat food, not micronutrients. National strategies for MM elimination must involve all those concerned with the production, distribution, and consumption of food, including the private and public sectors and individual consumers.

The support of the international donor community can do much to catalyze and facilitate the implementation of these national programs. Also required is construction of a supportive infrastructure that includes capacity in such key program components as communication and behavioral change, interventions, evaluation, and surveillance. These linkages are as important as the components themselves. Training and technical support from donor agencies are crucial in assisting countries to build national and local capacity to implement sustainable MM control programs. The training should include the development of teams of personnel skilled in management, advocacy, policy, legislation, food-based interventions, communications, social marketing, epidemiology, assessment, quality assurance, and laboratory testing. The training needs to emphasize the devolution and transfer of these skills from the center down to the provinces, and from the provinces to smaller community units where the consumer can be engaged.

CONCLUSION

Iodine, iron, and vitamin A deficiencies are among the oldest known maladies. Descriptions of goiter, cretinism, intellectual dullness, infant blindness in children, and night blindness have been recorded in literature, art, and sculpture through the ages. In 1990 at the World Summit for Children, 70 heads of state agreed to the virtual elimination of these disorders within ten years. Subsequently, numerous international, multinational, bilateral and nongovernment agencies have provided support to countries working toward these goals. The International Conference on Nutrition in Rome, in December 1992, further affirmed this commitment and called for the development of more detailed national strategies by member states. These are remarkable commitments that, if fulfilled, will result in a public health achievement of truly historic proportions.

ACKNOWLEDGMENTS

We thank others within the Program Against Micronutrient Malnutrition (PAMM) in Atlanta for their valuable technical input. These included Susan Burger, Robin Houston, Warwick May, Sandra May, and Dale Nordenberg. A special thanks to graduate MPH students Rachel Friday and Maneesha Mehra for editorial contributions.

This paper was produced with support from the US Agency for International Development, Office of Nutrition, under a cooperative agreement no. HRN-5110-A-00-2048-00.

Literature Cited

1. Andelman MB, Sered BR. 1966. Utilization of dietary iron by term infants. A study of 1,048 infants from a low socio-economic population. *Am. J. Dis. Child.* 111:45–55
2. Arthur JR, Nicol F, Beckett GJ. 1990. Hepatic iodothyronine 5'-deiodinase. The role of selenium. *Biochem. J.* 272:537–40
3. Baggs RB, Miller SA. 1973. Nutritional iron deficiency as a determinant of host resistance in rats. *J. Nutr.* 103:1554–60
4. Basta SS, Soekirman KD, Scrimshaw NS. 1979. Iron deficiency anemia and the productivity of adult males in Indonesia. *Am. J. Clin. Nutr.* 32:916–25
5. Bautista SA, Barker PA, Dunn JT, Sanchez M, Kaiser DL. 1982. The effects of oral iodized oil on intelli-
gence, thyroid status, and somatic growth in school age children from an area of endemic goiter. *Am. J. Clin. Nutr.* 35:127–34
6. Beard JL, Borel ML. 1988. Thermogenesis and iron deficiency anemia. *Nutr. Today* 23:41–45
7. Beard JL, Borel ML. April 1989. *Thermoregulation in tissue iron deficient nonanemic females.* FASEB meet., New Orleans, LA (Abstr.)
8. Beard JL, Green W, Finch CA. 1984. Effects of anemia and iron deficiency on thyroid hormone levels and thermoregulation during acute cold exposure. *Am. J. Physiol.* 247:R114–19
9. Beaton GH, Martorell R, L'Abbe KA, Edmonston B, McCabe G, et al. 1992. Effectiveness of vitamin A supplementation in the control of young child morbidity and mortality in developing

countries. *Rep. Can. Int. Dev. Agency, Contract 8714, RC:871/11109*

10. Beckett GJ, Fergus N, Rae PWH, Beech S, Guo Y, Arthur JR. 1993. Effects of combined iodine and selenium deficiency on thyroid hormone metabolism in rats. *Am. J. Clin. Nutr.* 57:240–43 (Suppl.)

11. Behne D, Kyriakopoulos A, Meinhold H, Kohrle J. 1990. Identification of type I iodothyronine 5'-deiodinase as a selenocysteine. *Biochem. Biophys. Res. Commun.* 173:1143–49

12. Binkin N, Sullivan MK, Stachling N, Nieburg P. 1992. Rapid nutrition surveys: how any clusters are enough? *Disasters* 16(2):97–103

13. Bothwell TH, Charlton RW. 1981. *Iron Deficiency in Women.* Washington, DC: Nutrition Found.

14. Boyages SC, Halpern J-P, Maberly GF, Eastman CJ, Morris JG, et al. 1988. A comparative study of neurological and myxedematous endemic cretinism in Western China. *J. Clin. Endocrinol. Metab.* 67:1262–66

15. Boyages SC, Collins JK, Maberly GF, Jupp JJ, Morris JG, Eastman CJ. 1989. Iodine deficiency impairs intellectual and neuromotor development in apparently normal persons. A study of rural inhabitants of north-central China. *Med. J. Aust.* 150:676–82

16. Brown CV, Brown GW, Bonrhill B. 1967. Iron deficiency and its functional consequences. *Alaska Med.* 9:93–99

17. Deleted in proof

18. Cent. Dis. Control Prev. 1991. Use of folic acid for prevention of spina bifida and other neural tube defects— 1983–1991. *Morbid. Mortal. Wkly. Rep.* 40:513–16

19. Chanarin I. 1979. Folic acid. In *The Importance of Vitamins to Human Health,* ed. TG Taylor 1:49–51. Lancaster, England: MTP Press. 173 pp.

20. Clark M, Royal J, Seeler R. 1988. Interaction of iron deficiency and lead and the hematologic findings in children with severe lead poisoning. *Pediatrics* 81:247–54

21. Dodge PR, Palkes H, Fierro-Benitez R, Ramirez I. 1969. Effect on intelligence of iodine in oil administered to young Andean children—a preliminary report. In *Endemic Goiter,* ed. JB Stanbury. Washington DC: *Pan Am. Health Organ.* 193:378–80

22. Edgerton VR, Ohira Y, Gardner GW, Senewiratne B. 1982. Effects of iron deficiency anemia and voluntary activities in rats and humans. In *Iron*

Deficiency: Brain Biochemistry and Behavior, pp. 141–60. New York: Raven

23. Edgerton VR, Ohira Y, Hettiaraachi J, Senewiratne B, Gardner GW, Barnard RJ. 1981. Elevation of hemoglobin and work performance in iron deficient subjects. *J. Nutr. Sci.* 27:77–86

24. Favin M, Griffiths M. 1991. *Social Marketing of Micronutrients in Developing Countries.* Rep. Popul. Hum. Res. Dep. World Bank, pp. 1–47. Washington, DC: Manoff Group, Inc.

25. Fierro-Benitez R, Ramirez I, Suarez J. 1972. Effect of iodine correction early in fetal life in intelligence quotient: a preliminary report. See Ref. 79b, pp. 239–47

26. Fierro-Benitez R, Ramirez I, Estrella E, Stanbury JB. 1974. The role of iodine in intellectual development in an area of endemic goiter. In *Endemic Goiter and Cretinism: Continuing Threats to World Health. Pan Am. Health Organ.* 292:135–42, ed. JT Dunn, GA Madiero-Netos. Washington, DC

27. Fierro-Benitez R, Cazar R, Stanbury JB, Rodriguez P, Garces F, et al. 1988. Effects on school children of prophylaxis of mothers with iodized oil in an area of iodine eficiency. *J. Endocrinol. Invest.* 11:327–35

28. Fortuine R. 1966. Acute purulent meningitis in Alaska natives: Epidemiology, diagnosis and prognosis. *Can. Med. Assoc.* 94:19–23

29. Foster AO. 1936. On a probable relationship between anemia and susceptibility to hookworm infection. *Am. J. Hyg.* 24:109

30. Foster AO, Sommer A. 1987. Corneal ulceration, measles and childhood blindness in Tanzania. *Br. J. Opthalmol.* 71:331–43

31. Giles C, Brown JA. 1962. Urinary infection and anemia in pregnancy. *Br. Med. J.* 11:10–13

32. Glasizou PP, Mackerras DEM. 1993. Vitamin A supplementation in infectious diseases: meta-analysis. *Br. Med. J.* 306:366–70

33. Halpern J-P, Boyages SC, Maberly GF, Collins JK, Eastman CJ, Morris JG. 1991. The neurology of endemic cretinism. A study of two endemias. *Brain* 114:825–41

34. Hambridge KM, Hambridge C, Jacobs M, Baum JD. 1972. Low levels of zinc in hair, anorexia, poor growth and hypogeusia in children. *Pediatr. Res.* 6:868–74

35. Herbert V. 1962. Experimental nutri-

tional folate deficiency in man. *Trans. Assoc. Am. Physicians* 75:307–20

36. Hetzel BS, Maberly GF. 1986. Iodine. In *Trace Elements in Human and Animal Nutrition*, ed. W. Mertz, 2: 139–208. New York: Academic. 499 pp.

37. Hunt SM, Groff JL. 1990. *Advanced Nutrition and Human Metabolism*, pp. 208–9. St. Paul: West Publ. Co. 518 pp.

38. Husain KHD, Gunadi H. 1981. Evaluation of nutritional anemia intervention among anemic female workers on a tea-plantation. In *Iron Deficiency and Work Performance*. Washington, DC: Nutrition Found. 73 pp.

39. Hussein MA, Hassan HA, Abdel-Chaffar, Samem S. 1989. Effect of iron supplements on the occurrence of diarrhoea among children in rural Egypt. *Food Nutr. Bull.* 10:35

40. INACG. 1990. *Combating Iron Deficiency Anemia Through Food Fortification Technology*. Work. Group Present. INACG Meeting, 12th. PAHO, Washington, DC

41. Kim I, Hungerford DW, Yip R, Kuester AS, Zyrkowski C, Trowbridge FL. 1992. Pregnancy nutrition surveillance system—United States, 1979–1990. *Morbid. Mortal. Wkly. Rep.* 41:25–41 (Suppl.7)

42. Lemeshaw S, Robinson D. 1985. Surveys to measure program coverage and impact: a review of the methodology used by the Expanded Program on Immunizations. *World Health Stat. Q.* 38(1):65–75

43. Lemeshaw S, Stroh G Jr. 1988. *Sampling Techniques for Evaluating Health Parameters in Developing Countries*. Washington, DC: Natl. Acad. Press

44. Levander OA, Cheng L. 1980. *Ann. NY Acad. Sci.* 355:1–372

45. Levander OA. 1986. Selenium. In *Trace Elements in Human and Animal Nutrition*, ed. W Mertz, pp. 223–25. New York: Academic. 499 pp.

46. Levander OA. 1988. In *Modern Nutrition in Health and Disease*, ed. ME Shils, R Young, pp. 266–67. Philadelphia: Lea & Febiger, 1694 pp.

47. Levin HE, Pollitt E, Galloway R, McGuire JM. 1990. Micronutrient Deficiency Disorders. Draft monogr. *World Bank Health Sect. Prior. Rev.* Washington, DC

48. Lin-Fu JS. 1973. Vulnerability of children to lead exposure and toxicity (first part). *New England J. Med.* 289:1229–33

49. Lin-Fu JS. 1973. Vulnerability of children to lead exposure and toxicity (second part). *New Engl. J. Med.* 289:1289–93

50. Ling JC, Franklin BAK, Lindsteadt JF, Gearon SA. 1992. Social marketing: Its place in public health. *Annu. Rev. Publ. Health.* 13:341–62

51. Lukaski HC, Hall CB. 1988. *Effect of iron status on thermogenic response of females to acute cold exposure*. FASEB Meet. Las Vegas, NV

52. Mackay H. 1928. Anemia in infancy: its prevalence and prevention. *Am. J. Dis. Child.* 111:45–55

53. Mahaferry KR. 1981. Nutritional factors in lead poisoning. *Nutr. Rev.* 39:353–62

54. McMichael AJ, Potter JD, Hetzel BS. 1980. Iodine deficiency, thyroid function, and reproductive failure. See Ref. 79a, pp. 445–60

55. Merke F. 1984. *The History and Ichnography of Endemic Goiter and Cretinism*. Lancaster: MTP Press

56. Menon K, Vijayraghavan K. 1980. Sequelae of severe xerophthalmia: a follow-up study. *Am. J. Clin. Nutr.* 33:218–20

57. Mertz W. 1983. The significance of trace elements for health. *Nutr. Today* Sept./Oct:26–31

58. Muhilal MA, Azis I, Saidin S, Jahari AB, et al. 1988. Vitamin A fortified mono-sodium glutamate and Vitamin A status: A controlled field trial. *Am. J. Clin. Nutr.* 48:1265–70

59. Muhilal PD, Idjradinata YR, Muherdiqantiningsih KD. 1988. Vitamin A fortified monosodium glutamate and health, growth, and survival of children: A controlled field trial. *Am. J. Clin. Nutr.* 48:1271–76

60. Murray MJ, Murray A, Murray CJ. 1980. The salutary effect of milk on amoebiasis and its reversal by iron. *Br. J. Med.* 1:1351–52

61. Nordenberg FD, Sullivan MK, Wiley V, Wilkins B, Bamforth F, et al. 1992. Congenital hypothyroid screening programs and the sensitive thyrotropin assay: strategies in the surveillance of iodine deficiency disorders. In *Iodine Deficiency in Europe: A Continuing Concern*, ed. F Delange, J Dunn, D Glinoer. New York: Plenum

62. Pandav CS, Kochupillai N. 1982. Endemic goiter in India: Prevalence, etiology, attendant disabilities and control measures. *Ind. J. Pediatr.* 50: 259

63. Pharoah POD, Delange F, Fierro-

300   MABERLY ET AL

Benitez R, Stanbury JB. 1980. Endemic cretinism. See Ref. 79a, pp. 395–421

64. Pinnock CB, Douglas RM, Badcock NR. 1986. Vitamin A status in children who are prone to respiratory tract infections. *Aust. Pediatr. J.* 22: 95–99

65. Pollitt E, Pollitt SC, Leibel R, Viteri FE. 1986. Iron deficiency and behavioral evelopment in infants and preschool children. *Am. J. Clin. Nutr.* 43:555–65

66. Porter DA. 1935. Studies on the effect of milk diet on the resistance of rats to *Nipostrongylus muris*. *Am. J. Hyg.* 22:467

67. Prasad AS, Halstead JA, Nadimi M. 1961. Syndrome of iron deficiency anemia, epatosplenomegaly, hypogonadism, dwarfism, and geophagis. *Am. J. Med.* 31:532–46

68. Prasad AS. 1981. Nutritional zinc today. *Nutr. Today.* March/April:4–11

69. Ramalingaswami V. 1992. Challenges and opportunities—one vitamin, two minerals. *World Health Forum* 13:222–31

70. Rep. Joint WHO/USAID/NEI Consultation of Principal Investigators of Vitamin Mortality and Morbidity Studies. Geneva, 1992

71. Roszkowski I, Wojcicka J, Zaleska K. 1966. Serum iron deficiency during the third trimester of pregnancy: maternal complications and fate of the neonate. *Obstet. Gynaecol.* 28: 810–15

72. Rothman D. 1970. Folic acid in pregnancy. *Am. J. Obstet. Gynecol.* 108: 149–75

73. Sandstead HH. 1973. Zinc nutrition in the United States. *Am. J. Clin. Nutr.* 26:1251-80

74. Sandstead HH, Prasad AS, Schulert AR, Farid Z, Miale A, et al. 1967. Human zinc eficiency, endocrine manifestations and response to treatment. *Am. J. Clin. Nutr.* 20:422–42

75. Schaeffer RL, Mendenhall W. 1990. *Elementary Survey Sampling.* Belmont, CA: Duxbury Press. 4th ed.

76. Shenai JP, Kennedy KA, Chytil F, Stahlman MT. 1987. Clinical trial of vitamin A supplementation in infants susceptible to bronchopulmonary dysplasia. *J. Pediatr.* 111:269–77

77. Sommer A. 1983. Mortality associated with mild, untreated xerophthalmia. *Trans. Am. Ophthalmol. Soc.* 81:825–53

78. Sommer A, Tarwotjo I, Djunaedi E,

West KP Jr, Loeden AA, et al. 1986. Impact of vitamin A supplementation on childhood mortality: A randomized controlled community trial. *Lancet* 1: 1169–73

79. Sommer A, Tarwotjo I, Hussaini G, Susanto D, Soeglharto T. 1981. Incidence, prevalence and scale of blinding malnutrition. *Lancet* 1:1407–8

79a. Stanbury JB, Hetzel BS, eds. 1980. *Endemic Goiter and Endemic Cretinism.* New York/Chichester/Brisbane/Toronto: Wiley. 597 pp.

79b. Stanbury JB, Kroc RL, eds. 1972. *Human Development and the Thyroid Gland. Relation to Endemic Cretinism.* New York: Plenum. 513 pp.

80. Trowbridge FL, Harris SS, Cook J, Dunn JT, Florentino RF, et al. 1993. Coordinated strategies for controlling micronutrient malnutrition: a technical workshop. *J. Nutr.* 123:775–87

81. Trowbridge FL. 1972. Intellectual assessment in primitive societies, with a preliminary report of a study of the effects of early iodine supplementation on intelligence. See Ref. 79b, pp. 137–49

82. Underwood BA. 1991. Eliminating vitamin A deficiencies as a public health problem. Implementing the Bellagio Declaration: Ending half the world hunger by the year 2000. *Rep. 4th Annu. Hunger Res. Briefing Exch.* Providence, RI: Brown Univ.

83. UNICEF. 1990. First call for children. *World Declaration and 1990–2000 Plan of Action on the Survival, Protection and Development of Children.* New York: UNICEF

84. Vanderpas JB, Contemp're B, Duale NL, Goossens W, Bebe N, et al. 1990. Iodine and selenium deficiency associated with cretinism in northern Zaire. *Am. J. Clin. Nutr.* 36:579–83

85. Venkataswamy G, Cobby M, Pirie A. 1979. Rehabilitation of xerophthalmic children. *Trop. Geogr. Med.* 31:149–54

86. Watson WS, Hume R, Moore MR. 1980. Oral absorption of lead and iron. *Lancet* 2:236-37

87. West KP, Howard JR, Sommer A. 1989. Vitamin A and infection: Public health implications. *Annu. Rev. Nutr.* 9:63–86

88. West KP, Pokhrel JRP, Katz J, LeClerq SC, Khatry SK, et al. 1991. Efficacy of vitamin in reducing preschool child mortality in Nepal. *Lancet* 338:67–71

89. World Health Org. 1992. *The Prevalence of Anemia in Women: A Tabu-*

lation of Available Information. Geneva: WHO. 2nd ed.

90. World Health Org. 1991. *National strategies for overcoming micronutrient malnutrition. EB 89/27*

91. World Health Org. 1992. *National strategies for overcoming micronutrient malnutrition. A45/17*

91a. World Health Org. 1994. *Indications for assessing iodine deficiency disorders and their control programs.* Rep.

joint WHO/UNICEF/ICCIDD consultation, Nov. 3-5, 1992, pp. 1–33. WHO/NUT/93.1

92. Yip R, Norris TN, Anderson AS. 1981. Iron status of children with elevated blood-lead concentration. *J. Pediatr.* 98:922–25

93. Yip R. 1989. The interaction of lead and iron. In *Dietary Iron: Birth to Two Years,* ed. LJ Filer Jr. New York: Raven

Annu. Rev. Public Health. 1994. 15:303–23

THE RE-EMERGENCE OF TUBERCULOSIS

John D. H. Porter and Keith P. W. J. McAdam

London School of Hygiene and Tropical Medicine, University of London, London WC1E 7HT, United Kingdom

KEY WORDS: multidrug resistance, diagnostics, vaccines, control programs, dual infection

INTRODUCTION

Tuberculosis is a disease of poverty and its major impact worldwide is therefore in developing countries and in centers of urban decay in the industrialized world. The disease spreads readily in crowded conditions and among the malnourished. Underfinancing and poor management of the health care infrastructures needed to support teams of health care workers to identify and treat people with tuberculosis are also important factors.

An estimated 1.7 billion people, a third of the world's population, are infected with *Mycobacterium tuberculosis* (TB). Tuberculosis is the leading cause of death from infectious disease in adults (3); between six to eight million people develop tuberculosis annually and between two to three million die of the disease each year (64). Tuberculosis accounts for 7% of all deaths in the developing world, 18% of all deaths in adults aged 15 to 59, and 26% of avoidable adult deaths (58).

This review discusses three themes about the resurgence of TB in the 1990s: first, that the incidence and severity of tuberculosis are increasing internationally, compounded by the interaction between TB and human immunodeficiency virus (HIV) infection and the emergence of multidrug resistance; second, that urgent research is needed on diagnostics, new drugs, vaccines, and control program strategy; and third, that considerably higher investment is required in existing cost-effective methods for control (66). These messages emerged from a 1993 public health conference entitled "Tuberculosis—back to the future," at the London School of Hygiene and Tropical Medicine attended by immunologists, epidemiologists, economists,

303

0163-7525/94/0510-0303$05.00

clinicians, policy makers, and directors of TB control programs, particularly from developing countries (66). The ultimate success of any strategy will depend on the close collaboration of research scientists and staff working in national tuberculosis control programs.

THERE IS AN INCREASING TUBERCULOSIS PROBLEM COMPOUNDED BY THE INTERACTION BETWEEN TUBERCULOSIS AND HIV INFECTION AND THE EMERGENCE OF MULTIDRUG RESISTANCE

Historical Aspects

Human tuberculosis is an ancient disease that may have evolved during the Neolithic period (ca 6000 BC) at a time of population increases and cattle domestication in Europe and the Near East (55). Tuberculosis was certainly present in Egypt from early dynastic times (51). The recorded study of tuberculosis dates from the sixteenth century, but it was Pasteur who began experimenting with airborne transmission in 1862. He succeeded in isolating *Mycobacterium tuberculosis* in 1882. Not until the 1930s, however, was William Wells able to prove airborne spread by droplet nuclei (69). Meanwhile, the death rate from tuberculosis in industrialized countries declined markedly *before* the introduction of effective chemotherapy, mainly due to improved socioeconomic conditions (26).

Before the discovery of streptomycin in 1944 (71), treatment of tuberculosis consisted of bed rest and a dry climate with fresh air, and surgical therapies like pulmonary resection and thoracoplasty (35). This new antituberculosis medication heralded a new era, but resistance to streptomycin soon developed, prompting the British Medical Research Council (BMRC) to undertake a successful trial of combined therapies and, later, of intermittent therapies (6, 25). The next major advance in treatment was the development of short-course therapy in the 1970s, the precursor of effective strategies for global tuberculosis control (25).

When tuberculosis is introduced into a susceptible population, morbidity and mortality rates follow an epidemic wave, with a sharp rise to a peak followed by a more gradual descent (38). While this curve is measured in weeks or months in many infectious diseases, the tuberculosis epidemic appears to spread by natural selection of susceptible persons and runs its course over decades and centuries. The present epidemic in England began in the sixteenth century and reached its peak around 1780 at a time of rapid industrialization. The wave has yet to peak in the developing countries of Asia and Africa. Thus, the epidemic is declining in one geographical area while still rising or just reaching its peak in another (64).

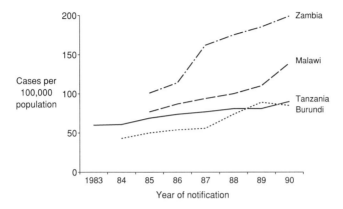

Figure 1   Annual tuberculosis notification rates in selected African countries (all cases), 1983–1990 (58a).

DEVELOPING COUNTRIES   The risk of infection in most developing countries is currently comparable to the size of the tuberculosis problem in industrialized countries in the late 1930s. Thus, in developing countries, tuberculosis is the most important public health problem caused by a single pathogen (57).

In the pre-HIV era, the risk of infection in most developing countries declined by 1–5%/year, although the decline was outweighed by overall population increases of 3%/year. Since the mid-1980s, however, this falling trend has been reversed by the HIV epidemic. National tuberculosis control programs are now documenting increasing rates of all forms of tuberculosis (Figure 1).

INDUSTRIALIZED COUNTRIES   In industrialized countries, reported tuberculosis deaths have been declining from the middle of the past century. In England and Wales, for example, notifications have declined steadily since they were first recorded in 1913, attributable largely to improved socioeconomic conditions (64).

However, this falling rate has been halted and reversed in many industrialized countries. The changing pattern was first observed in the United States in New York City in 1986, and was ascribed to the following causes: increased immigration from countries where tuberculosis is prevalent; the interaction between tuberculosis and HIV infection; and decay in the health care infrastructure that supports tuberculosis control programs.

The Effects of HIV on Rates of Tuberculosis

The effects of HIV on rates of tuberculosis will be greatest where the two infections most frequently occur together, i.e. in developing countries. Eighty percent of those presently infected with both HIV and *M. tuberculosis* reside in Africa (22). Cases of "dual infection" will increasingly be seen as the epidemic of HIV spreads to and within Asia (22).

Three mechanisms have been identified in the development of HIV-associated tuberculosis: reactivation, progression from recent infection, and reinfection. Reactivation appears to be the most important contributor. Studies have shown that the risk of active tuberculosis in persons with dual infection is 3–8% per year, with a lifetime risk of ~50% or higher (73).

DEVELOPING COUNTRIES   An estimated 305,000 excess cases of tuberculosis attributable to HIV occurred globally in 1990, of which 230,000 were in Africa (81). Although these HIV-associated cases represent only ~4% of the total worldwide, for Africa this figure represents a 20% increase in case rates. Excess mortality due to HIV-associated tuberculosis worldwide has been estimated between 120,000 and 150,000 in 1990, of which 100,000–120,000 occurred in Africa.

A review (72) of TB and HIV described HIV seroprevalence rates of 20–67% among tuberculosis cases in different sub-Saharan African countries, the highest in countries where seroprevalence rates were highest in the general population. The annual incidence of tuberculosis for Kampala, Uganda, where the prevalence of HIV infection in young adults currently exceeds 30%, is predicted to reach 2% by the end of the century, representing an excess burden of tuberculosis of ~800% over the incidence forecast in the absence of HIV (72). In African cities where the adult HIV seroprevalence is 10%, the excess tuberculosis incidence may be ~300%.

Furthermore, HIV has affected the clinical character of the disease. In dual infection there is an increased frequency of extrapulmonary involvement, often concomitant with pulmonary tuberculosis (62, 82, 83). The most frequent forms of extrapulmonary disease are lymphadenitis and miliary disease. Involvement of the bone marrow, genitourinary tract, and central nervous system are also common (2). Diagnosis of TB has become more difficult because of the increase in HIV-infected persons of false-negative tuberculin skin tests (43), of sputum smear-negative disease (pulmonary and extrapulmonary) (30), and of atypical radiological manifestations (43, 63).

Studies on therapy of people with tuberculosis and HIV infection have shown that standard treatment regimens are associated with increased relapse rates, increased mortality, and increased rates of side effects from drugs (2, 23, 40). In Nairobi, Kenya, the probability of death after six months of treatment for HIV-positive and HIV-negative persons was 21% and 6%, respectively (59). Similar rates have been reported from Abidjan, Ivory Coast (45). In Nairobi the increased mortality was not due to tuberculosis as much as to other HIV-associated complications, particularly nontuberculous bacterial septicemia (59).

Side effects from drugs have increased, with thiacetazone causing the most frequent side effects in developing countries. One fifth of HIV-positive patients who receive the drug suffer from reactions that produce severe or even fatal cutaneous hypersensitivity (59).

INDUSTRIALIZED COUNTRIES   Annual reports of tuberculosis cases in the United States declined steadily until 1984 when surveillance data showed a reduction in the rate of decline, and subsequently an increase in cases (76; Figure 2).

The groups with the greatest increases, blacks and Hispanics aged 22–24 years, also have highest rates of HIV infection and AIDS. HIV seroprevalence in patients attending tuberculosis clinics ranged from 0–46% (60). As in developing countries, the rates of relapse, death, and side effects from drugs have all increased.

In San Francisco, a relapse rate of 3.6 per 100 person years was documented in HIV-infected patients following treatment, which may not be different from that seen in HIV-negative persons in that city (74). The median survival in HIV-positive patients treated for tuberculosis was 16 months after diagnosis, and 6% of the deaths were considered attributable to tuberculosis. Adverse effects required 18% of patients to have their therapy changed (74). Side effects were attributed, in descending order, to rifampicin, pyrazinamide, isoniazid, and ethambutol.

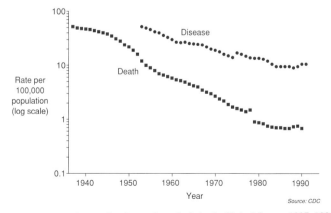

Figure 2   Morbidity and mortality from tuberculosis in the United States, 1937–1991.

Table 1 Primary drug resistance rates based on random sampling

Region/ Country	Period	No. of Subjects	Percent resistant			
			INH	SM	RIF	Total
America[1]	1985–86	550	2.7	8.7	0	14.4
America[2]	1985–86	274	8.4	13.1	1.8	20.4
Africa[3]	1988–89	239	13.0	8.4	3.3	31.0
Tanzania	1988–90	921	7.5	2.0	0.1	11.0
Korea	1985	161	13.7	3.7	2.5	17.4

[1] Chile, Cuba, Colombia, Mexico, Peru
[2] Argentina, Bolivia, Paraguay, Brazil
[3] Mali, Mauritania, Rwanda, Gambia
Source: WHO

Multidrug Resistance

In addition to the increase in tuberculosis cases from dual TB/HIV infection, multidrug resistance (MDR) has increased.

Drug resistance has been a problem since streptomycin was first introduced as a single therapeutic agent in the 1940s and was found to induce resistance. Drug resistance and treatment failure occur because of erratic selective medication—taking antituberculosis drugs irregularly or taking only one agent to which the organisms are susceptible. For these reasons, resistance to isoniazid is particularly prevalent in many developing countries (47: Table 1). For example, in Tanzania, resistance to isoniazid at the time of initial diagnosis remained stable between 1968 and 1988 at between 5 and 8%, whereas acquired resistance was 41% in treatment failures and 59% in relapses (16).

DEVELOPING COUNTRIES   Data from well-organized national tuberculosis control programs in Algeria (4), Korea (46), and South Africa (88) provide direction on how to address the constant threat of drug resistance. In these programs both initial and acquired drug resistance rates have decreased in recent years. In Korea, the rate of initial resistance to any single drug has declined from 31% in 1980 to 15% in 1990; acquired resistance has declined over the same period from 75% to 47%, multidrug resistance (>3 drugs) was found in 4.7% of initial cases and 12.9% in treated cases. The high priority given to the problem and improved drug compliance are responsible for this achievement. A similar improvement has been seen in Algeria (4).

The effect of HIV on the rate of acquisition of drug resistance has been studied in Zaire. In Kinshasa, in 349 samples of consecutive tuberculosis cases, the rate of initial resistance to isoniazid was 20%; to isoniazid and rifampicin 0.9%; to one drug 22%; to two drugs 1.8%; and to three drugs 0.9% (JH Perriens, M St Louis, Y Mukadi, C Brown, J Prignot, manuscript submitted). No difference in resistance was recorded between the 218 seronegative and the 131 seropositive patients. These results suggest that the development of drug resistance in industrialized countries such as the United States is unlikely to be directly related to HIV, but rather is linked to poor compliance produced by decaying tuberculosis control infrastructures.

INDUSTRIALIZED COUNTRIES   The incidence of tuberculosis cases caused by multidrug-resistant strains of *Mycobacterium tuberculosis* is reported to be rising in the United States. Increased initial resistance to one or several drugs has been observed, mainly in New York City where it rose from 10% in 1982–1984 to 23% in 1991 (34), though a steady decrease had been noted nationwide between 1975 and 1982 (9).

With an overall incidence of resistance (initial and acquired) of 33%, the case fatality rate of tuberculosis is alarming, reaching 27% after 9 months of follow-up in patients in New York City (34). For the U.S. as a whole, nearly 90% of resistance appears in HIV-positive patients, with a case fatality rate of 70–90% four to sixteen weeks after diagnosis (77).

Since 1990, the Centers for Disease Control (CDC) have investigated several outbreaks of multidrug-resistant tuberculosis (MDR-TB). The outbreaks have involved hospitals, prisons, and substance abuse treatment facilities (11, 12, 14, 28, 31), all with features in common: people with HIV infection living in restricted environments such as hospitals and prisons; delay in the diagnosis of tuberculosis, which allowed dissemination of the infection; and, frequently, inadequate facilities to isolate infectious patients. Characterization of strains of tuberculosis using restriction fragment length polymorphism (RFLP) demonstrated identical strains of the bacterium in outbreaks. In some outbreaks the mortality rate exceeded 80% (31). Most isolates were resistant to rifampicin and isoniazid but some were resistant to as many as seven or more antibiotics (14, 28, 31).

Resistance was acquired mostly from treatment failures or relapses due to disorganized treatment programs. Some researchers hold that the problem reflects inadequate provision of medical care to those people most at risk from HIV infection and tuberculosis (7). The resultant poor compliance increases the prevalence of acquired resistance.

A National Action Plan to combat MDR-TB has been published (13). The report includes recommendations to limit nosocomial transmission, conduct surveillance to determine patterns of drug susceptibility, and improve compliance through directly observed therapy (DOT).

RESEARCH NEEDS: DIAGNOSTICS, DRUGS, VACCINES, AND CONTROL PROGRAM STRATEGIES

At the TB meeting in London, Young proposed two general perspectives on research needs in tuberculosis (91). First, since tuberculosis is a disease for which an effective treatment is available, the role of research should be to provide tools to facilitate delivery of that treatment. Alternatively, since tuberculosis has not been controlled in most of the developing world despite the availability of effective treatment for over 30 years, the broader goal should be identifying radical new approaches to disease control (91). We believe that both perspectives must be included in the design of a tuberculosis research strategy. Basic scientific research must be harnessed to the pursuit of these goals.

Tuberculosis research must be structured to ensure that it is useful and appropriate for both developing and developed countries. Research programs should be targeted to tuberculosis questions relevant to the developing countries where most tuberculosis cases occur, not just to industrialized countries, which have the financial resources to plan, develop, and implement tuberculosis research. Experience gained in the developing world will assist tuberculosis control in the industrialized world.

Diagnostics

Tuberculosis is diagnosed on clinical examination, microscopy, culture, and radiological tests. However, these techniques present many problems, especially negative sputum smears in patients with both TB and HIV infection.

CLINICAL EVALUATION   The first phase of diagnosis comes with the clinical examination of the patient. This evaluation is an important part of diagnosis, particularly in countries with a high prevalence of HIV infection because the frequency of positive sputum smears is lower in people with HIV infection (2, 30, 59). Since tuberculosis is likely to be the diagnosis in HIV-infected persons with respiratory symptoms in developing countries (20, 44), patients with respiratory symptoms and who are thought to be HIV-infected should be candidates for antituberculosis chemotherapy.

One important tool used in evaluation, the tuberculin skin test, is becoming less useful because it does not distinguish between BCG and TB infection and, therefore, is difficult to interpret. BCG vaccination has been widely employed in developing countries though not in the U.S. (see below). New scientific initiatives are now underway to improve the tuberculin test. The present test, which is difficult to standardize from batch to batch, could be improved in three ways: use of one or more defined antigens to elicit a response with similar sensitivity; a skin test reagent to discriminate between

BCG vaccination and exposure to *M. tuberculosis;* and a reagent to discriminate between the immune response resulting from exposure or subclinical infection with *M. tuberculosis* from the response associated with the onset of clinical disease (91).

MICROSCOPY   After clinical examination, a sputum specimen is taken. The sensitivity of microscopy for identifying acid-fast bacilli (AFB) in the sputum of patients with pulmonary tuberculosis depends on the skill of the microscopist, the number of specimens examined, and the concentration of the organisms in the sputum. Under operational conditions positive smears have been found in 50–70% of patients who subsequently have a positive culture (84). The sensitivity is increased if a second specimen is obtained. Based on these assessments, the use of AFB smears alone to diagnose tuberculosis for treatment will find as many as 70% of active cases and will therefore identify the most infectious people who present the greatest risk to others. These steps are the present World Health Organization (WHO) recommendations (90).

However, waiting until the disease has progressed to produce positive sputum before beginning treatment means that more new people will have been infected than if the case were found at an earlier, less infectious stage. Several studies have examined the role of presumptive treatment of patients who have negative sputum smears and cultures but have radiographic abnormalities suggestive of tuberculosis. These studies showed that presumptive treatment based on radiographic findings decreased the number of potentially infectious cases of tuberculosis (27, 37, 39).

Thus, we recommend treatment of "presumed" tuberculosis in persons with negative sputum smears but with chest radiographic findings compatible with TB. The identification of patients for treatment should involve both microbiologic and radiographic services, which many programs cannot afford. The expenditure of limited resources must be balanced against the gains provided by more expensive but sensitive diagnostic studies (41).

CULTURE   The definite diagnosis of *Mycobacterium tuberculosis* can be established only by isolating the organism from the patient. However, most cases of tuberculosis worldwide are diagnosed not by cultures but by microscopic examination of sputum alone (or other specimens) and, in certain situations, by clinical and radiographic findings. Culture of specimens requires an appropriately equipped laboratory and the results are not available for four to six weeks. The interaction between tuberculosis and HIV infection is making diagnosis more difficult and new diagnostic tools are needed.

The application of DNA amplification techniques (polymerase chain reactions, PCR) is making enormous strides in the early detection of mycobacteria (5, 29). However, contamination remains a major problem.

Since minute quantities of DNA can be amplified, rigorous laboratory safeguards must be maintained to detect false positives and avoid contamination. Urgently needed are single sealed tube PCR tests to reduce the chances of contamination, as well as detection methods for the applied product that use nonradioactive, preferably color or luminescent, systems.

DNA fingerprinting uses repetitive DNA elements randomly inserted within the genome of *M. tuberculosis* in 8–10 copies (36a). Each isolate exhibits a different banding pattern detectable by radioactivity, luminescence, or color reaction. Fingerprinting can address the epidemiology of the disease: it can identify an infection source, distinguish relapse from reinfection, and potentially differentiate reinfection from reactivation.

Another recent innovation is the use of a bioluminescent reporter mycobacteriophage that infects mycobacteria and emits light if the mycobacteria are alive. This system can be used to detect the presence of not only mycobacteria but also their viability and drug sensitivity profile.

RADIOGRAPHIC EXAMINATION   Chest X rays have historically been used to assess pulmonary involvement in tuberculosis, progression, or resolution of disease over time. Targeted populations have been screened for suspicious "shadows" that might indicate tuberculosis infection. Measurement of the number of zones involved, presence of cavitation, collapse, enlarged lymph nodes, scarring, calcification, and pleural/pericardial involvement have been used to quantify pulmonary involvement. However, these systems are relatively subjective and depend on skilled observers. Moreover, the HIV epidemic has brought atypical presentations of pulmonary tuberculosis (43, 63). Furthermore, bacterial pneumonias are often difficult to differentiate by chest X ray and a trial of a broad-spectrum antibiotic may be required initially.

The increased incidence of tuberculosis calls for reassessment of mass chest X ray screening in different situations, including developing countries, though the problems of supplies, servicing, and costs are often likely to be prohibitive. Quantitative schemes for evaluation of chest X rays need to be revisited in the context of HIV, particularly in children, who are notoriously difficult to diagnose radiologically. Especially helpful would be guidelines for excluding active tuberculosis in those HIV positives who are being considered for monodrug tuberculosis prophylaxis. Clearly, use of a single agent would be unwise in sputum smear-negative individuals with active tuberculosis because of the likelihood of inducing drug-resistant organisms.

Drugs

Drugs to treat tuberculosis have been available since the 1940s but they have not been applied appropriately. New drugs are needed to assist with improving patient compliance; for example, drugs that reduce the duration of treatment, formulations containing several drugs in appropriate fixed dosage ratios, and depot preparations would all potentially improve the problem of compliance and improve cure rates while reducing the problem of multidrug resistance.

In the past decade an increasing number of fixed combinations have been marketed (rifampicin-isoniazid, thiacetazone-isoniazid, and triple combinations of rifampicin, isoniazid, and pyrazinamide). Tuberculosis control programs encourage the use of these combined preparations to improve the ease of administration, to reduce the risk of the development of drug resistance, and to discourage diversion of drugs for other uses (49). However, fixed combinations preclude flexibility in dosage and timing of constituents with differing half lives, and incur major problems of absorption of some combination formulations. New formulations require evidence of bioavailability of each constituent.

Current research on the tubercle bacillus by microbiologists and molecular biologists is directed to the discovery of the mechanism of virulence, to identify at a molecular level the properties of *M. tuberculosis* responsible for causing disease and to understand mycobacterial persistence.

The nature of tuberculosis as a reactivation disease and the requirement for extended chemotherapy both suggest an ability of *M. tuberculosis* to persist in some "dormant" form in infected tissues. Understanding the molecular basis of this persistence could have enormous implications for tuberculosis control. Interventions to activate dormant TB could contribute to shortening of treatment schedules, with the reverse strategy used to prevent reactivation of the disease. Unraveling of the mechanism of virulence will help in the development of new drugs and methods of treatment (91).

Commercial drug development programs are attempting to devise screens based on defined enzymes or metabolic pathways from *M. tuberculosis*, since such systems would provide a feasible starting point for future therapeutic interventions. There is renewed interest in elucidating the mechanisms involved in the action of established drugs and in determining the genetic basis of drug resistance. The development of techniques for genetic manipulation of mycobacteria opens new research possibilities, and mechanisms of susceptibility and resistance to all major antituberculosis drugs are likely to be elucidated within the next few years. Development of rapid tests for drug resistance will also have a high priority.

Operations researchers are looking at the rational use of drugs, a neglected aspect of drug management (32), and an International Network for the Rational Use of Drugs has been established (48). Rational drug use depends on the ability to make the correct diagnosis, prescribe and dispense appropriate drugs, and foster patient compliance.

Vaccines

An attenuated strain of *Mycobacterium bovis* was produced by Calmette and Guerin (BCG) after 231 passages through media containing glycerin and oxbile (50). The vaccine was safely administered to a child in 1921 and its use spread quickly across Europe. Numerous controlled studies of BCG have been conducted, with a wide variation in protective efficacy, ranging from 0 to 80%.

The emerging consensus about the vaccine is that it does not prevent infection, and that, when it is protective, BCG reduces the risk of extrapulmonary forms of the disease, e.g. miliary disease and meningitis, more than pulmonary forms. It does little to reduce the actual number of infectious tuberculosis cases (79). BCG is the most widely used immunization worldwide, with an estimated global coverage of 80% (85), yet its effectiveness in different environments remains uncertain (18, 70). Because the vaccine is given at birth in many countries and there is little or no evidence of protection after 15 years, BCG has had minimal effect on the epidemiological trend of tuberculosis (79).

The concept of reinforcing the body's natural ability to cope with infection has obvious attraction as a means of tuberculosis control. To understand protective immunity to *M. tuberculosis* at a cellular and molecular level is perhaps the most important research goal for the 1990s, with direct implications not only for vaccine development but also for diagnosis, treatment, and epidemiology (91). An adequate animal model is still needed to assist with the evaluation of vaccine candidates.

TUBERCULOSIS CONTROL PROGRAMS AND OPERATIONAL ISSUES

The philosophy of a tuberculosis control program should be that successful completion of therapy is the responsibility of the provider or program that undertakes to treat patients with tuberculosis. The benefits of effective treatment should be viewed as accruing not only to the patient but to society as well. Thus, providing "the cure" for tuberculosis is a societal imperative both in industrialized and developing countries (41). An effective tuberculosis control program requires an organized network of primary and referral services, with cooperation between public and private providers and among the various components of the health care system (41).

The prerequisite for the management of tuberculosis is an efficiently organized and adequately funded control program, which will depend on political and government commitment. Unfortunately, in the United States public attitudes toward the disease were shaped by the success of chemotherapy, translated into progressively reduced public health attention (68) and a seriously deteriorated infrastructure (41). Data published in the late 1980s and early 1990s associated the increase in tuberculosis cases with the breakdown of effective delivery systems in the United States and the consequent increase in MDR-TB (7).

Tuberculosis Control

The four methods currently available to control and prevent tuberculosis infection are: improvement of socioeconomic conditions; case finding and treatment; chemoprophylaxis; and vaccination. Since improvement of socio-economic conditions is a long-term strategy and present BCG vaccination is ineffective, good case finding and effective chemotherapy are the pre-eminent methods of control at present (19).

CASE FINDING AND TREATMENT   Three principles are basic to the treatment and social management of patients and their contacts: the use of at least two agents to which the organisms are susceptible; maintenance of treatment over an extended period of time (6–8 months even with short course chemotherapy), and regular administration of medication (41).

CHEMOPROPHYLAXIS   Preventive therapy for tuberculosis involves the treatment of asymptomatic persons infected by *M. tuberculosis* to prevent the development of active disease. The intervention is therefore not prophylaxis but the treatment of latent tuberculosis. Preventive therapy has been most extensively applied in North America, and detailed recommendations have been issued by the American Thoracic Society (1, 10). These recommendations also apply to other countries with well-functioning tuberculosis control programs and adequate resources to undertake preventive therapy. Preventive therapy has not been considered for resource-poor countries because of the high prevalence of tuberculosis. However, isoniazid (INH) preventive therapy is recommended for children under five years of age living in a household with infectious cases (90).

HIV infection is the strongest risk factor identified in promoting the development of active tuberculosis in persons with HIV infection and tuberculosis co-infection (73). Preventive therapy with isoniazid is the only practical control measure that is available to reduce the occurrence of HIV-associated tuberculosis. An observational study of intravenous drug users in New York City suggested substantial protection from INH against the development of tuberculosis (73). A placebo controlled study in Zambia found protection from administration of isoniazid daily for six months (86). A study in Haiti demonstrated the protective effect of isoniazid and also found decreased mortality and fewer HIV-related illnesses among those receiving the drug (61). Current trials of prophylaxis are testing isoniazid alone daily or intermittently, rifampicin/pyrazinamide intermittently, and rifampicin/isoniazid/pyrazinamide combinations.

BCG   BCG is the most widely used immunization worldwide, with an estimated global coverage of 80% (72). Despite being the most popular form of immunization, its effectiveness remains uncertain (73, 74). Because BCG is given at birth in many countries and because there is little or no evidence of its being effective after 15 years, BCG has had little effect on the epidemiological trend of tuberculosis. As already stated, a new vaccine is urgently needed.

Operational Research Issues

Internationally, the major operational issue in tuberculosis control is compliance. In developing countries, poor compliance among tuberculosis patients is the major barrier to implementation of a successful chemotherapy program (15, 42). The problem is compounded by the erratic supplies of drugs and of supplies for diagnosis and by variable job performance and commitment by health care workers. Three areas of compliance need to be addressed within programs: treatment regimens; supervision; and drug supply.

Treatment Regimens

Treatment regimens of shorter duration with combination preparations will enhance patients adherence, although close supervision and an effective administration/management system remain essential (41).

Supervision

Successful national tuberculosis control programs emphasize close supervision, ideally directly observed swallowing of the medications, to ensure a high completion rate in treatment. Unsuccessful programs, e.g. in New York City, are characterized by a virtual absence of supervision (3). Supervision may require a community-based approach, with widespread community endorsement and participation (78). In a project among homeless people in San Francisco, supervision of preventive therapy is provided by "peer health advisors"—persons largely self-selected from among the residents of homeless shelters (41). Direct observed treatment is costly and labor intensive but is balanced by improved rates of cure and decreased frequency of drug resistance. In developing countries innovative approaches to supervision are also being studied.

At the start of treatment, patients should be evaluated to determine the likelihood of completion of therapy. Although these assessments are known to be inaccurate, certain patient characteristics are predictive of difficulty. These include the use of alcohol, young age, and single status (21). Other variables have been identified in studies in urban tuberculosis clinics in the United States (41).

Drug Supply

Four objectives must be followed for a control program to ensure an appropriate drug supply: accurate forecasting of drug needs; adequate financing for drug supply; efficient procurement of drugs of good quality; and full distribution of drugs to TB patients. WHO is investigating the problem of drug supply for tuberculosis control programs to develop strategies to ensure a safe and adequate supply of drugs (87).

In the future, the highest priority must be given to avoiding the development of drug resistance within national tuberculosis control programs (67). This can be achieved by a regular supply of drugs (36), tight control of the use of rifampicin, strict observation of its administration and the use of combination tablets, and the prohibition of sales of the drug in the private sector in conjunction with the use of an adequate retreatment regime. The high cure rates attainable in initial chemotherapy (17) are critical to the prevention and reduction of resistance. Depot preparations are being evaluated, as are sustained release oral formulations.

COST-EFFECTIVE METHODS FOR CONTROL ARE AVAILABLE BUT ARE UNDERAPPLIED AND ARE USED TO INVEST MORE IN CONTROL METHODS THAT ARE KNOWN AND UNDERSTOOD.

Tuberculosis accounts for more than 3% of the total global burden of disease (56). The potential increase can be averted through the different interventions of case treatment, chemoprophylaxis, and BCG, tools already known and understood. WHO has established targets for developing countries to detect 70% of smear-positive cases and to treat effectively 80% of those detected. However, to achieve these targets requires resources. Is tuberculosis cost-effective to control?

Of the control measures available, chemoprophylaxis is not used in developing countries because of the high prevalence of tuberculosis, and BCG, despite widespread use, has had little effect on the epidemiological trend of the disease (79); neither measure is cost-effective for national control programs. However, evaluations of short course chemotherapy programs have demonstrated that, for both pulmonary smear-positive and -negative patients, these short course regimens are extremely cost-effective (24, 56, 57).

The World Development report from the World Bank, *Investing in Health,* is an important fresh statement about international public health (54, 58). It approaches public health in developing countries from an economic viewpoint. The concept of the disability-adjusted life-year (DALY)—the present value of the future years of disability-free life lost because of

Increase in DALYs (log scale)

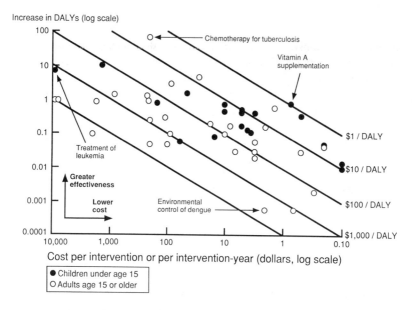

Cost per intervention or per intervention-year (dollars, log scale)

● Children under age 15
○ Adults age 15 or older

Figure 3   Benefits and costs of forty-seven health interventions. (With permission, World Bank and Oxford University Press.)

premature death or disability in a given year (89)—will help certain countries target resources more appropriately at certain diseases (Figure 3). In low-income countries, diseases that can be controlled for under $100/DALY are considered cost-effective. Tuberculosis is one of these diseases: TB treatment costing $100,000 will directly save ~500 patients and gain ~35,000 DALYs by preventing infection of others. The cost-effectiveness studies and the World Development Report all point to high priority for treatment of TB as an appropriate cost-effective health intervention.

With the economic information now available, Ministries of Health should act to combat tuberculosis. Such interventions are cost-effective and are already available: they must be implemented appropriately. Future research will assist in making the interventions easier to introduce and ultimately more appropriate and more cost-effective.

THE WAY FORWARD

The rising tide of tuberculosis has accentuated the divisions and inequalities between the industrialized and developing world, as well as the problem of fragmentation of communities within societies. The attention of the international health community must focus on combating poverty, as improvement in socioeconomic conditions reduces the incidence of tuberculosis and other diseases (53).

Obviously this prescription will be slow. In the meantime, national tuberculosis control programs should concentrate on case finding and treatment, ensuring that tuberculosis patients receive and take the appropriate medication, and that drug resistance is avoided. Meanwhile research scientists must work closely with the health care workers who run the programs so that field needs can drive research. The best field workers ultimately are those who are seeking better answers, and the best researchers are those who see their ideas implemented. Research and implementation should be interconnected (33).

The pharmaceutical industry is a critical player in the control of tuberculosis. As with the development of the first generations of drugs against *M. tuberculosis,* the pharmaceutical industry and smaller biotechnology companies will again play a key role in translating research efforts into new tools for disease control. WHO and federal agencies in the U.S. have cooperated in bringing together the pharmaceutical industry and researchers to discuss strategies for the development of new antituberculosis drugs. Additional government funds for research, tax incentives for product development, and the possible designation of anti-tuberculosis drugs as orphan products covered by the Orphan Drug Act may facilitate action in this field (75).

Since the incidence of tuberculosis is highest in the developing world, most research should be focused in that arena. However, support from the industrialized world for infrastructure building and research in developing countries will bring dividends of improved tuberculosis control at home. In the United States, for example, the increase in tuberculosis cases is mainly attributable to immigrants from countries where tuberculosis is prevalent.

With the ever-increasing pace of international contact between peoples and continents, greater commitment, collaboration, and generosity are vital if we are to find solutions to the tuberculosis problem within the framework of the North/South divide and the fragmentation of communities within society. Communication and cooperation between public health practitioners, scientists, the pharmaceutical industry, and politicians are integral to the formulation of a cohesive plan to deal with this latest international public health challenge.

Literature Cited

1. Am. Thorac. Soc./Cent. Dis. Control. 1986. Treatment of tuberculosis and tuberculosis infection in adults and children. *Am. Rev. Respir. Dis.* 134: 355–63
2. Barnes PF, Bloch AB, Davidson PT, Snider DE. 1991. Tuberculosis in patients with human immunodeficiency virus infection. *New Engl. J. Med.* 324:1645–50
3. Bloom BR, Murray CJL. 1992. Tuberculosis—commentary on a reemergent killer. *Science* 257:1055–64
4. Boulahbal F, Khaled S, Tazir M. 1989. Intérêt de la surveillance de la résistance du bacille tuberculeux pour l'évaluation d'un programme. *Bull. Union Int. Tuberc. Mal. Respir.* 64:23–25
5. Brisson-Noel A, Aznar C, Churea C, Nguyen S, Pierre C, et al. 1991. Diagnosis of tuberculosis by DNA amplification in clinial practice evaluation. *Lancet* 338:364–66
6. Br. Med. Res. Counc. 1950. Treatment of pulmonary tuberculosis with streptomycin and para-amino-salicylic acid. A Medical Research Council Investigation. *Br. Med. J.* 2:1073–85
7. Brudney K, Dobkin J. 1991. Resurgent tuberculosis in New York City: Human immunodeficiency virus, homelessness, and the decline of tuberculosis control programs. *Am. Rev. Respir. Dis.* 144: 745–49
8. Deleted in proof
9. Cent. Dis. Control. 1983. Primary resistance to antituberculosis drugs United States. *Morbid. Mortal. Wkly. Rep.* 32:521–23
10. Cent. Dis. Control. 1990. The use of preventive therapy for tuberulous infection in the United States. Recommendations of the Advisory Committee for the Elimination of Tuberculosis. *Morbid. Mortal. Wkly. Rep.* 39:9–12
11. Cent. Dis. Control. 1991. Transmission of multidrug resistant tuberculosis from an HIV-positive client in a residential substance-abuse treatment facility—Michigan. *Morbid. Mortal. Wkly. Rep.* 40:129–31
12. Cent. Dis. Control. 1991. Nosocomial transmission of multidrug resistant tuberculosis among HIV-infected persons—Florida and New York 1988–1991. *Morbid. Mortal. Wkly. Rep.* 40: 585–91
13. Cent. Dis. Control. 1992. National action plan to combat multidrug resistant tuberculosis. *Morbid. Mortal. Wkly. Rep.* 41:1–48
14. Cent. Dis. Control. 1992. Transmission of multidrug resistant tuberculosis among immunocompromised persons in a correctional system—New York 1991. *Morbid. Mortal. Wkly. Rep.* 41: 507–9
15. Chaulet P. 1987. Compliance with antituberculosis chemotherapy in developing countries. *Tubercule* 68(Suppl.): 19–24
16. Chonde TM. 1989. Le rôle des services bactériologiques dans le programme national contre la tuberculose et la lèpre en Tanzanie. *Bull. Union Int. Tuberc. Mal. Respir.* 64/3:37–40
17. Chum HJ. 1989. Dix ans de contionnement du programme national contre la tuberculose et la lèpre en Tanzanie. *Bull. Union Int. Tuberc. Mal. Respir.* 64:34–40
18. Clemens JD, Chuong JJH, Feinstein AR. 1983. The BCG controversy: a methodological and statistical reappraisal. *J. Am. Med. Assoc.* 249:2362–69
19. Crofton J. 1962. The contribution of treatment to the prevention of tuberculosis. *Bull. Int. Union Tuberc.* 32: 643–53
20. Daley CL, Chen LL, Small PM, Mugusi F, Aris E, et al 1992. Pulmonary complications of HIV infection in Tanzania. *Am. Rev. Respir. Dis.* 145: A821
21. Darbyshire JH, Aber VR, Nunn AJ. 1984. Predicting a successful outcome in short-course chemotherapy. *Bull. Int. Union Tuberc.* 59:22–23
22. De Cock KM. 1994. The interaction of tuberculosis and HIV infection. See Ref. 65, pp. 35–42
23. De Cock KM, Soro B, Coulibaly I-M, Lucas SB. 1992. Tuberculosis and HIV infection in sub-Saharan Africa. *J. Am. Med. Assoc.* 268:1581–87
24. De Jonghe E, Murray CJL, Chum HG, Nyangulu DS, Salamao A, Styblo K. 1993. *Int. J. Health Policy Manage.* In press
25. D'Esopo ND. 1982. Clinical trials in pulmonary tuberculosis. *Am. Rev. Respir. Dis.* 125:85–93
26. Dubos R, Dubos J. 1952. *The White Plague: Tuberculosis, Man and Sociey.* Boston: Little Brown
27. Dutt AK, Moens D, Stead WW. 1989. Smear and culture-negative pulmonary tuberculosis: Four month short course

chemotherapy. *Am. Rev. Respir. Dis.* 139:867–70

28. Edlin BR, Tokars JI, Grieco MH, Crawford JT, Williams J, et al. 1992. An outbreak of multidrug resistant tuberculosis among hospitalized patients with the acquired immunodeficiency syndrome. *New Engl. J. Med.* 326:1514–21

29. Eisenbach KD, Siffird MD, Cave MD, Bates JH, Crawford JT. 1991. Detection of *Mycobacterium tuberculosis* in sputum samples using a polymerase chain reaction. *Am. Rev. Respir. Dis.* 144:1160–63

30. Elliott AM, Luo N, Tembo G, Halwindi B, Steenbergen G, et al. 1990. Impact of tuberculosis in Zambia: a cross sectional study. *Br. Med. J.* 301:412–15

31. Fischl MA, Uttamchandani RB, Daikos GL, Poblete RB, Moreno JN, et al. 1992. An outbreak of tuberculosis caused by multidrug resistant tubercle bacilli among patients with HIV infection. *Ann. Intern. Med.* 117:177–83

32. Flinn PE, Kenyon AS, Layloff TP. 1992. A simplified TLC system for qualitative and semiquantitative analysis of pharmaceuticals. *J. Liquid Chromatogr.* 15:1639–53

33. Foege W. 1994. Lesson from the past. See Ref. 65, pp. 259–65

34. Frieden TR, Sterling T, Pablo-Mendez A, Kilburn JO, Cauthen GM, Dooley SW. 1993. The emergence of drug resistant tuberculosis in New York City. *New Engl. J. Med.* 328:521–26

35. Gaensler EA. 1982. The surgery for pulmonary tuberculosis. *Am. Rev. Respir. Dis.* 125:73–84

36. Gangadharan PRJ. 1993. Drug resistance in tuberculosis: it's not always the patient's fault. *Tuberc. Lung Dis.* 74:64–67

36a. Godfrey-Fausett P. 1994. The detection of tuberculosis, past, present and future. See Ref. 65, pp. 79–95

37. Gordin FM, Slutkin G, Schecter G, Goodman PC, Hopewell PC. 1989. Presumptive diagnosis and treatment of pulmonary tuberculosis based on radiographic findings. *Am. Rev. Respir. Dis.* 139:1090–93

38. Grigg ERN. 1974. Arcana of tuberculosis. *Am. Rev. Respir. Dis.* 109:636–64

39. Hong Kong Chest Serv./Tuberc. Res. Cent, Madras/Br. Med. Res. Counc. 1984. A controlled trial of 2 month, 3 month, and 12 month regimens of chemotherapy for sputum smear negative pulmonary tuberculosis: results at 60 months. *Am. Rev. Respir. Dis.* 130:23–28

40. Hopewell PC. 1992. Impact of human immunodeficiency virus infection on the epidemiology, clinical features, management and control of tuberculosis. *J. Infect. Dis.* 15:540–47

41. Hopewell PC. 1994. "The Cure": Organization and administration of therapy for tuberculosis. See Ref. 65, pp. 99–120

42. Hopewell PC, Sanchez-Hernandez M, Baron RB, Ganter B. 1984. Operational evalution of treatment for tuberculosis: Results of a "standard" 12 month regimen in Peru. *Am. Rev. Respir. Dis.* 129:439–43

43. Huebner RE, Villarion ME, Snider DE. 1992. Tuberculin skin testing and the HIV epidemic. *J. Am. Med. Assoc.* 267:409–10

44. Kamanfu G, Mlika-Cabanne N, Girard PM, Nimubona B, Mfizi P, et al. 1993. Pulmonary complications of HIV infection in Bjumbuva, Burundi. *Am. Rev. Respir. Dis.* 147:658–63

45. Kassim S, Sassan-Morokro M, Doorly R, Ackah A, Digbev H, et al. 1992. Prospective study of pulmonary tuberculosis and HIV-1 and HIV-2 infections, Abidjan, Côte d'Ivoire. *Int. Conf. AIDS and 3rd STD World Congr., 8th, Amsterdam* (Abstr. PoB. 3086)

46. Kim SJ, Hong YP. 1992. Drugs resistance of *Mycobacterium tuberculosis* in Korea. *Tuberc. Lung Dis.* 73:219–24

47. Kleeberg HH, Oliver MS. 1984. *A world atlas of initial drug resistance.* Tuberc. Res. Inst. S. Afr. Med. Res. Counc. (MRC). Pretoria, South Africa

48. Laing R. 1990. Rational drug use: an unsolved problem. *Trop. Dr.* 20:101–3

49. Laing R. 1994. Antituberculosis drug supply: meeting a global need. See Ref. 65, pp. 166–80

50. Luelmo F. 1982. BCG vaccination. *Am. Rev. Respir. Dis.* 125:70–72

51. Manchester K. 1984. Tuberculosis and leprosy in antiquity: An interpretation. *Med. Hist.* 28:162–73

52. Deleted in proof

53. McKeown T. 1979. *The Role of Medicine. Dream, Mirage or Nemesis?* pp. 45–65, 92–96. Princeton NJ: Princeton Univ. Press

54. McNamee D. 1993. Health costs. *Lancet* 342:63–64

55. Morse D, Brothwell DR, Ucko PJ. 1964. Tuberculosis in Ancient Egypt. *Am. Rev. Respir. Dis.* 90:524–41

56. Murray CJL. 1994. Value for money

in tuberculosis control. See Ref. 65, pp. 193–208

57. Murray CJL, Styblo K, Rouillon A. 1990. Tuberculosis in developing countries: burden, intervention and cost. *Bull. Int. Union Tuberc.* 65:2–20

58. Murray CJL, Styblo K, Rouillon A. 1993. Tuberculosis. In *Disease Control Priorities in Developing Countries,* ed. DT Jamison, WH Mosley. New York: Oxford Univ. Press/World Bank

58a. Narain JP, Raviglione MC, Kochi A. 1992. HIV-associated TB in developing countries. Epidemiology and strategies for prevention. *Tuberc. Lung Dis.* 73: 311–21

59. Nunn P, Brindle R, Carpenter L, Odhiambo J, Wasunna K, et al. 1992. Cohort study of human immunodeficiency virus infection in patients with tuberculosis in Nairobi, Kenya: analysis of early (6 month) mortality. *Am. Rev. Respir. Dis.* 146:849–54

60. Onorato IM, McCray E, Field Serv. Branch. 1992. Prevalence of human immunodeficiency virus infection among patients attending tuberculosis clinics in the United States. *J. Infect. Dis.* 165:87–92

61. Pape J, Jean SS, Ho JL, Hafner A,Johnson WA. 1993. Effect of isoniazid prophylaxis on incidence of active tuberculosis and progression of HIV infection. *Lancet* 342: 268–72

62. Pitchenik AE, Cole C, Russell BW, Fischl MA, Spira TJ, Snider DE. 1984. Tuberculosis, atypical mycobacteriosis, and the acquired immunodeficiency syndrome among Haitians and non-Haitian patients in south Florida. *Ann. Intern. Med.* 101:641–45

63. Pitchenik AE, Rubinson HA. 1985. The radiographic appearance of tuberculosis in patients with the acquired immune deficiency syndrome (AIDS) and pre-AIDS. *Am. Rev. Respir. Dis.* 131:393–96

64. Porter JDH. 1991. Tuberculosis in developing countries. *Commun. Dis. Rep.* 1:R136–39

65. Porter JDH, McAdam KPWJ, eds. 1994. *Tuberculosis—Back to the Future.* London: Wiley.

66. Porter JDH, McAdam KPWJ, Feachem RGA. 1993. Tuberculosis—the challenge is international. *World Health* July/Aug:10–12

67. Prignot J. 1993. Multidrug resistance of tubercle bacilli- facts and implications for National Programmes. *Int. Union TB Lung Dis. Newsl.* June

68. Reichman LB. 1991. The U-shaped curve of concern. *Am. Rev. Respir. Dis.* 144:741–42

69. Riley RL. 1982. Disease transmission and contagion control. *Am. Rev. Respir. Dis.* 125:16–19

70. Rodrigues LC, Smith PG. 1990. Tuberculosis in developing countries and methods for its control. *Trans. R. Soc. Trop. Med. Hygiene* 84:739–44

71. Schatz A, Bugie E, Waksman SA. 1944. Streptomycin, a substance exhibiting antibiotic activity against gram-positive and gram-negative bacteria. *Proc. Soc. Exp. Biol. Med.* 55: 66–69

72. Schulzer M, Fitzgerald JM, Enarson DA, Grzybowski S. 1992. An estimate of the future size of the tuberculosis problem in sub-Saharan Africa resulting from HIV infection. *Tuberc. Lung Dis.* 73:52–58

73. Selwyn PA, Hartel D, Lewis VA, Schoenbaum EE, Vermund SH, et al. 1989. A prospective study of the risk of tuberculosis among intravenous drug users with human immunodeficiency virus infection. *New Engl. J. Med.* 320:545–50

74. Small PM, Schecter GF, Goodman PC, Sande MA, Chaisson RE, et al. 1991. Treatment of tuberculosis in patients with advanced human immunodeficiency virus infection. *New Engl. J. Med.* 324:289–94

75. Snider D. 1991. *Shortages of antituberculosis drugs, outbreaks of multidrug resistant disease and new drug development in the US.* Presented at Meet. Coord. Advis. Rev. Group Tuberc. Progr., 2nd, WHO, Geneva, Switzerland, 22 Nov.

76. Snider D. 1992. The impact of tuberculosis on women, children and minorities in the United States. *World Congr. Tuberc. Bethesda* (Abstr. C1)

77. Snider DE, Roper WL. 1993. The new tuberculosis. *New Engl. J. Med.* 326: 703–5

78. Solorzano Moguel JJ, Alvarez Cuevas ME. 1991. Atención del enfermo tuberculoso a nivel comunitário en el estado de Chiapas, Mexico. *Bol. Of. Sanit. Panam.* 111:432–38

79. Styblo K, Meijer J. 1976. Impact of BCG vaccination programmes in children and young adults on the tuberculosis problem. *Tubercule* 57: 17–43

80. Deleted in proof

81. Sudre P, Dam GT, Kochi A. 1992. La tuberculose aujourd'hui dans le monde. *Bull. WHO* 70:297–308

82. Sunderam G, McDonald RJ, Maniatis T, Oleske J, Kapila R, Reichman LB. 1986. Tuberculosis as a manifestation of the acquired immunodeficiency syndrome (AIDS). *J. Am. Med. Assoc.* 256:362–66

83. Theuer CP, Hopewell PC, Elias D, Schecter GF, Rutherford GW, Chaisson RE. 1990. Human immunodeficiency virus infection and tuberculosis patients. *J. Infect. Dis.* 162:8–12

84. Toman K. 1979. Tuberculosis case finding. In *Tuberculosis Case-Finding and Chemotherapy.* Geneva, WHO pp. 6–8

85. UNICEF. 1992. State of the World's Children. New York: Oxford Univ. Press/UNICEF

86. Wadhavan D, Hira S, Mwansa N, Perine P. 1992. *Preventive tuberculosis chemotherapy with isoniazid among persons infected with HIV.* Presented at Int. Conf. AIDS, 8th, Amsterdam, 19–24 July

87. Weil D. 1994. Anti-tuberculosis drug supply: meeting global need. See Ref. 65, pp. 123–66

88. Weyer K, Kleeberg HH. 1992. Primary and acquired drug resistance in adult black patients with tuberculosis in South Africa: results of a continuous national drug resistance surveillance programme involvement. *Tuberc. Lung Dis.* 73:106–12

89. World Bank. 1993. *World Development Report 1993.* New York: Oxford Univ. Press/World Bank

90. WHO. 1992. Managing tuberculosis at the district level. *WHO Tuberc. Progr. Geneva*

91. Young DB. 1994. Future research needs. See Ref. 65, pp. 218–20

Annu. Rev. Public Health. 1994. 15:325–43

EFFICACY OF LABELING OF FOODS AND PHARMACEUTICALS

W. Kip Viscusi

Department of Economics, Duke University, Durham, North Carolina 27706

KEY WORDS: risk communication, hazard warnings, risk

INTRODUCTION

Over the past several decades, the US Congress and regulatory agencies have developed a complex system of informational regulations for food and drugs that goes far beyond indications such as "USDA Approved." Individual states have also begun to display increasing interest in this issue. California, for instance, has adopted its own warning system for risks of cancer and reproductive toxicity, and many other states are also considering warning measures.

These efforts have diverse objectives. One function is to provide information about beneficial features, such as information about the nutritional value of foods and the medical conditions that pharmaceutical products can address. A second function is to alert the consumers to possible adverse effects of the product, for instance sodium labels for foods, health warnings for cigarettes, and information about adverse reactions to drugs. A third function of warnings is to indicate the particular types of precautions that should be exercised, e.g. cautioning against driving after drinking alcoholic beverages, and against adverse drug interactions.

Examination of food and drug warnings is instructive more generally since these warnings embody all the functions of risk communication mechanisms. Moreover, the presence of the learned intermediary—the physician in the case of prescription medications—provides an interesting variation on the context of risk communication.

325

0163-7525/94/0510-0325$05.00

Instituting an effective warnings program is different from simply disseminating all that is known about a product. The subsequent sections explore the prerequisites for an effective design of a hazard communication system for food, pharmaceutical products, and cigarettes. Cigarettes, with addictive properties similar to many drugs, have served as the model warnings effort for saccharin, alcoholic beverages, and carcinogenic agents.

The discussion of the rationale for hazard warnings provides a benchmark for judging the efficacy of warnings. I introduce the general issues pertaining to the content, structure, and format of the design of warnings. To be effective, warnings must first be processed by consumers. Finally, I address the effect of warnings on risk perceptions and on consumer behavior.

THE RATIONALE FOR HAZARD WARNINGS

There are a variety of policy options on hazardous products at the local, state, or federal level. At the most extreme, these products could be banned altogether. Second, the product characteristics could be regulated to eliminate certain kinds of risks, for example by banning particular food additives. Third, firms could be permitted to market these products along with an accompanying warning. Finally, there could be no action whatsoever. Consequently, hazard warnings can be viewed as an intermediate policy option between no action and either regulation or proscription of a product.

For hazard warnings to be a potentially attractive policy, there must presumably be some reason to believe that the product is on balance beneficial to some consumers who have been appropriately alerted to its characteristics, otherwise more stringent policy options should be pursued. Food and drugs generally are viewed as raising various issues pertaining to individual welfare, and the key issue is whether the benefits derived from these products exceed the associated costs to the consumers.

The task for hazard warnings is to create an awareness such that consumers will make the decisions that they would have made if they were fully informed. For both the purchase decision and the product use decision, the critical issue is whether expected consumer welfare has been enhanced, based on the true risks associated with the product. These probabilities will not necessarily be those perceived by the consumer. Moreover, it may be the case that the consumer's expected welfare has been raised by a product even though the product lowers the consumer's welfare based on the true probabilities. What matters from the policy standpoint is the consumer's expected welfare using the actual risks associated with the product. The fact that consumers might gladly purchase a product while ignorant of the associated risks does not make a purchase worthwhile.

Figure 1 illustrates the context in which decisions about food and drug

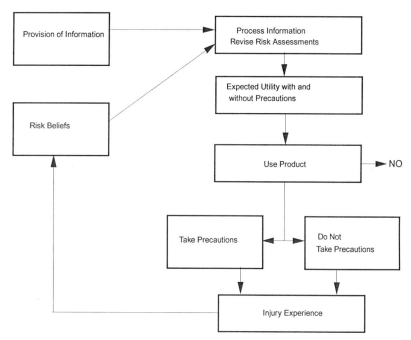

Figure 1   Information processing and economic behavior.

warnings operate. The policy lever in this context is the information provided, which is illustrated at the upper left portion of the diagram. Although the discussion will generally be in terms of hazard warnings, when conceptualizing the role of risk information it is more appropriate to consider the hazard communication system. Prescription drugs, for example, are dispensed by physicians who have access to extensive information compiled in the *Physician's Desk Reference* regarding the properties of the drugs. This compilation of information draws primarily upon the patient package inserts that accompany pharmaceutical products. The physician also has extensive medical training and continually updates this information both through the medical literature and professional seminars that can be drawn upon to brief the patient regarding the consequences of the drug. The pharmacist also may provide information. What is consequential is not necessarily the specific product label or patient package insert but rather the net informational effect of all sources of information provided to the consumer.

For any information to affect individual beliefs, it must first be processed. The intervening link between the provision of information and its influence on risk beliefs is an information-processing stage. Individuals must first receive the information, understand it, and then incorporate it in their memory, and ultimately in their decisions (7). Because of cognitive constraints, individuals are limited to the amount of information that they can process from any particular warning. Moreover, some information, such as detailed medical information pertaining to the consequences of certain prescription drugs, requires medical training to interpret it properly.

A practical consequence of these concerns is that excessive information can lead to two problems that have received close attention in the warnings literature (6, 18): label clutter, where too much information in a particular warning can lead to less effective information processing than a more concise warning message; and information overload, when there is a proliferation of warning labels. If everything in the drugstore and supermarket is labeled hazardous, then in effect hazard warnings convey no relative information. Provision of risk information consequently has an important external effect on the efficacy of other risk messages since overuse of very strong warning messages tends to dilute the attention paid to other warnings.

The net effect of the information provided combines with the person's prior beliefs regarding the risk to determine the posterior risk assessment associated with the product. If individuals have very firm initial beliefs or if the risk information is not as convincing, there will be little effect of the information on risk perceptions.

The two key aspects of the warning message are the risk that is conveyed and the informational content associated with this message. In particular, is this message credible when compared to the individual's existing information about the product? Studies of the effect of hazard warning labels for chemical products (19) indicate that information that simply serves as a reminder and does not convey new knowledge about the risk will not alter prior beliefs. Similarly, information that the recipients of the knowledge do not regard as convincing will not alter consumers' prior beliefs concerning the properties of the product.

Once risk beliefs are formed, the individual then assesses the expected utility conferred by the product. This will be done along a variety of dimensions. As is indicated in the bottom panels of Figure 1, the consumer makes two kinds of dichotomous choices—whether to use the product and whether to take precautions. First, will the purchaser choose to exercise the associated precautions? Given this choice of optimal precautions, how does the expected utility associated with purchasing the product compare with the expected utility derived from expenditures on other goods? If, in the consumer's view, expected utility will be raised through product purchase, the product will be bought, where this judgment will be based on the consumer's own subjective judgments formed after the receipt of risk information.

Purchase of the product will lead to experiences with the product that may involve a product-related injury or signals of the likely risk of injury, such as a traffic ticket for driving while intoxicated. These injury experiences in turn will affect risk beliefs that form the basis for subsequent product decisions and that will be influenced by future risk information.

A noteworthy element of this entire process is that the government cannot monitor the key risk-taking decisions. There can be no governmental mandate that a particular product will be bought or used in a certain manner, nor can these decisions be monitored or controlled, unlike worker safety behavior, which is under the employer's supervision. Thus, whether the consumer heeds the advice of the hazard warnings is discretionary.

CONTENT, STRUCTURE, AND FORMAT

Several aspects of hazard warnings affect how they are ultimately perceived by consumers. The first pertains to the content of the warning. In particular, what message are we conveying to consumers and what is the specific language used to convey this information? Because individuals have cognitive limitations and limited information processing capabilities, warnings must be conveyed in a manner that can be readily understood and processed. For example, it would make little sense to provide consumers with copies of scientific articles relating to prescription drugs for their own judgments as to the implications of this literature. Instead, drafters of warnings attempt to process the pertinent information to make it accessible to the recipient.

The manner of presentation of the information is also consequential. One aspect of the presentation is the placement of the warning. Is the warning on the product included as part of a package insert, or communicated orally by, for example, a physician? The design of the warning label is another key aspect of the presentation. The structure of the warning component of the label is of consequence, as is its relationship to the other information provided on the label. For example, antidote information that appears at the bottom of labels for hazardous chemicals is seldom read by consumers until after an adverse experience with a product has occurred (6). The overall context in which the warning is presented on the label is also important. If the patient package insert or the label gives detailed directions for use of the product, as is the case for drugs, it may be important to integrate the appropriate precautionary information within the context of product use instructions.

More than simple marketing design, the format of the label is essential to conveying the requisite information and ensuring that it is processed.

Thus, print size, color, and graphic design may affect the efficacy of the warning, although there are diminishing returns. Evidence suggests that once labels have attained a sufficient degree of readability, nuances such as greater print size do not enhance the efficacy of the warning label (6).

Another aspect of the label that affects its effectiveness is the presence of other information. Our limited information processing capabilities prevent us from effectively absorbing the warning message if we are inundated with too much information. In such contexts, consumers may know that products are potentially dangerous, but may not be aware of the specific product risks or how to prevent them.

Because consumers are confronted with a variety of different labels for similar products, standardization is generally desirable. If some companies were to use the word "warning" in situations where others would use "caution," then these words would not have a similar meaning across products. To enable consumers to make judgments for different products, it is desirable to have a uniform warnings vocabulary for language and symbols that can be readily interpreted.

Food Labeling

The federal government has two different labeling programs for food. The US Department of Agriculture has authority for grading and inspecting meat as well as food, grains, and nonfood crops. For the most part, the risk-related aspect of this activity consists of prohibiting tainted products from coming to market. The labeling program was designed primarily to indicate differences in character of meat rather than degrees of risk, although the two are not entirely unrelated.

In contrast, the US Food and Drug Administration (FDA) has exercised substantial influence over hazard warnings and nutrition labeling, as well as legal authority over advertising for food. The *Federal Food Drug and Cosmetic Act,* enacted in 1938, gave the FDA authority to determine the amount of food additives that could be present in food, where these additives were to be presumed unsafe unless it could be demonstrated that they were central to the product. In 1958, the act was amended to include carcinogens. Substances shown to cause cancer in either animals or humans were deemed unsafe. This stipulation, known as the Delaney Clause, has turned out to be a quite stringent requirement given the increased ability to identify low-risk carcinogens (5).

In 1973 the FDA issued regulations pertaining to nutrition labeling. These regulations, which became effective in 1975, required that all products for which a nutrition claim was being made had to bear a label providing nutrition information. In addition, the regulation specified that the upper portion of the label must provide information concerning serving size, calories, and nutritional breakdown, whereas the lower portion of the label gave information pertaining to the US Recommended Daily Allowance (USRDA) of various nutrients.

In 1992 this labeling system was amended in several ways: serving sizes were standardized to promote comparability; information pertaining to calories from fat, dietary fiber, saturated fat, and cholesterol was added; and the percent of USRDA was restricted to pertain only to more salient nutrients, such as Vitamin C and calcium. In each case of the FDA food nutrition labels, it is noteworthy that a standardized vocabulary was established by the agency as well as a standard format for presenting the information to facilitate comparisons across products regarding their nutritional value.

One of the more controversial labeling efforts now administered by the FDA pertains to hazard warnings for saccharin. After a Canadian study reported the development of tumors in rats that had been fed saccharin, the FDA attempted to implement the Delaney Clause by banning saccharin as a food additive. This action aroused substantial public debate, particularly since there were competing risks (5, 15). Use of saccharin decreased obesity, and therefore had beneficial effects on heart disease and other health outcomes. The compromise solution is that in 1977 Congress passed the *Saccharin Study and Labeling Act,* which mandated a standard warning label to appear on products containing saccharin: "Use of this product may be hazardous to your health. This product contains saccharin which has been determined to cause cancer in laboratory animals."

Cigarettes and Alcoholic Beverages

Perhaps the best known warning labels mandated by Congress are those for cigarettes. In particular, cigarette packages and cigarette advertising have borne a series of warning labels over the past three decades. The development of these warnings is summarized in Table 1. The cigarette warning effective in 1965 required that consumers be apprised that "smoking may be hazardous to your health." This warning was then strengthened in 1969 to indicate that "smoking is dangerous to your health." In 1984 these warnings were expanded to include a series of four rotating warnings alerting consumers to cigarette-related risks of cancer, health risks generally, pregnancy, and carbon monoxide, among other risks.

Congress has followed a similar approach with respect to alcoholic beverages in mandating an on-product warning. Beginning November 14, 1990, Congress required that alcoholic beverage containers bear the following warning: "GOVERNMENT WARNING: (1) According to the Surgeon General, women should not drink alcoholic beverages during pregnancy because of the risk of birth defects. (2) Consumption of alcoholic beverages

Table 1 Cigarette warning content summaries

Warning period	Warning content[a]
Cigarette warning, 1965	"Caution: Cigarette Smoking May Be Hazardous to Your Health."
Cigarette warning, 1969	"Warning: The Surgeon General Has Determined That Cigarette Smoking Is Dangerous To Your Health."
Cigarette warning, 1984	1. "SURGEON GENERAL'S WARNING: Smoking Causes Lung Cancer, Heart Disease, Emphysema, and May Complicate Pregnancy."
	2. "SURGEON GENERAL'S WARNING: Quitting Smoking Now Greatly Reduces Serious Risks to Your Health."
	3. "SURGEON GENERAL'S WARNING: Smoking by Pregnant Women May Result in Fetal Injury, Premature Birth, and Low Birth Weight."
	4. "SURGEON GENERAL'S WARNING: Cigarette Smoke Contains Carbon Monoxide."

[a] All warnings wording is specified by legislation. See 15 U.S.C. §§ 1331–1341 (1982).

impairs your ability to drive a car or operate machinery, and may cause health problems."

Drug Labeling

Drug labeling regulations began with the enactment of the *Pure Food and Drug Act* in 1906, which specified that drug labels could not make "false or misleading" statements and that all addictive substances (including alcohol) must be indicated on the drug label. These requirements were expanded in 1938 with the passage of the *Federal Food, Drug, and Cosmetic Act,* which required that all drugs include information about how to use the product, how long a product could be used, and warning information about unsafe dosages. In addition, beginning in 1938, a distinction was made between nonprescription drugs, which could be purchased by general consumers, and prescription drugs, for which a physician's prescription was necessary. The introduction of the role of the learned intermediary, the physician, was to ensure that dangerous drugs were not used indiscriminately. After the thalidomide tragedy in Europe in which babies with severe birth defects were born to mothers who had used this drug, the FDA requirements were strengthened with amendments to the *Federal Food, Drug, and*

Cosmetic Act, passed in 1962. Under these amendments, the FDA classified drugs based on both their safety and efficacy, and it required that warning labels include information pertaining to the active ingredients, the indications and directions for use, the mechanism of drug action, as well as potential adverse effects of the drug.

The quantity of information to be conveyed to consumers, however, was too unwieldy to be compressed into a single warning label. Moreover, it was desirable for product manufacturers to convey additional information to physicians to enable them to prescribe drugs more appropriately. To achieve this objective, the FDA developed requirements on patient package inserts (PPIs). These inserts provide more detailed information to product users and are compiled annually in the *Physician's Desk Reference.* The warning information included in the PPI is based on information submitted to the FDA by the manufacturer, where the actual warning language is drafted in house by the FDA, primarily by pharmacologists and physicians. Because of the centralized manner in which the warnings are issued, the pharmaceutical warnings program serves as perhaps the best model of a standardized warnings vocabulary.

PROCESSING WARNING INFORMATION

For hazard warning information to have an effect on risk perceptions and individual decisions, it must first be received and processed by the intended recipient, a requirement that may not always be met in practice. As the examination of the processing of warning information below indicates, exposure to the information is seldom complete, and even labels written for a general audience may not always be fully understood. Thus, how the warning message is conveyed and whether it will reach the intended recipient are of paramount concern.

Nutrition Labeling

The performance of various nutrition labeling programs has been mixed. Here it is useful to distinguish the performance of on-product warnings from that of in-store point-of-purchase displays.

In a study of nutrition labeling for the US Food and Drug Administration, Heimbach (3) assessed the extent to which individuals process the sodium content listings given on food labels. This study found that only one fourth of all respondents recalled a sodium content listing. Moreover, only forty percent of all respondents recalled reading an ingredient listing on food products. In each case, fewer than half of the consumers read the health-related information provided on food products.

These results may not reflect the long-term effect of the nutrition labeling effort. This study, performed in February 1983, may have been undertaken prematurely since the FDA only began encouraging food manufacturers to voluntarily label the sodium contents of their products in 1982. Moreover, salt and sodium content listing is not necessarily of substantial interest to many consumers, since the degree to which these substances pose a health risk varies and only a minority of the population is on a sodium-restricted diet. A recent study of the effect of fiber content in cereals found that this nutritional information, which is of broad concern, did affect consumption patterns (3a).

Even if consumers process the information, there is no assurance that it will be used. The degree to which consumers actually take advantage of this information in making their purchase decisions is sometimes low. Evidence suggests that few consumers comprehend nutrition labels and use the information in making their purchase decisions.

Interestingly, Heimbach (2) found that many consumers had trouble comprehending the nutrition information even after it was processed. For example, consumers had difficulty dealing with the percentage and ratio information and in calculating the number of servings needed to supply 100 percent of the USRDA for a particular nutrient. Moreover, technical terms such as "polyunsaturated fat" and "hydrogenated," and even "carbohydrates" pose difficulties for consumers. Other studies have found similar results, as there is often a confusion between salt and sodium.

Point-of-purchase displays have also been used to convey information about nutrition. The nutrition point-of-purchase displays examined by Russo et al (12) had little impact on the purchasing behavior of consumers of positively valued nutrients. In contrast, information on ingredients that are considered "bad"—in particular, the amount of sugar added to breakfast cereal—was processed by consumers and significantly affected their behavior.

The point-of-sale study by Muller (10) examined the effect of a matrix that gave nutrition information by brand. This study had more favorable findings, as brand-by-nutrient information increased the nutritiousness of the products that consumers purchased.

Drug Information

A study for the Rand Corporation by Kanouse et al (4) assessed the degree to which patients read the drug leaflets accompanying prescription drugs. The structure of the study tended to produce an overstatement of the degree to which individuals read information provided to them about drugs. In particular, when the 2000 volunteer participants received their prescription drugs at the pharmacy, they were given a leaflet concerning the risks posed by the drug and told that they would be called about the information contained in the leaflet.

Notwithstanding these instruction that should have produced more diligent information processing than would normally happen, only 69–74 percent of the subjects claimed to have read the leaflets. Furthermore, only 45–54 percent of the participants in the study kept the leaflet.[1]

Other studies of PPI information processing have surveyed current users of oral contraceptives to ascertain the degree to which they have processed the risk information. The study by Morris, Mazis, & Gordon (8) indicated that 88 percent of current users of oral contraceptives claim to have read the PPI. However, the degree to which subjects could recall specific information provided on the insert was less. Of current users of oral contraceptives, 69 percent could correctly recall information on usage of the drug, and only 50 percent could correctly recall information on common reactions to the drug.

This study did not include analysis of whether the respondents actually read the PPI or the extent to which individuals who did not receive the PPI could have answered the factual questions correctly without the PPI based on what their doctor had told them. Thus, there were no adequate experimental controls.

The study of aspirin warnings by Morris & Klimberg (9) suggests that, overall, roughly half of all consumers of aspirin process the risk information included on the product label. Only 25 percent of all aspirin users surveyed were aware of the Reye's syndrome warnings, 53 percent were aware of the contraindications against flu and aspirin usage, and 40 percent could spontaneously recall Reye's syndrome.

Beer and Cigarette Warnings

Examination of the processing of warnings for beer and cigarettes is useful because these warnings programs are at quite different stages of development. Cigarette warnings are well established, and these warning messages are well understood, although many consumers do not continue to read the warning information in advertising and on the product once they have already seen it repeated several times. Nevertheless, there is striking awareness of the basic content of these messages as, for example, between 99 and 100 percent of all respondents have heard that "cigarette smoking is dangerous to a person's health" and that "cigarette smoking will most likely shorten life."

The experience with the alcoholic beverage warnings program is much shorter, and evidence regarding receipt of that information is more sketchy. Scammon, Mayer, & Smith (13) found that as of July 1990, awareness

---

[1]These ranges in response are attributable to the variation in percentages according to which of the three leaflets used in the study was given to the subjects. The study analyzed three different drugs.

of the alcoholic beverage warning in a survey of Utah consumers had reached 35 percent, but since 73 percent of the respondents indicated that their alcoholic beverage consumption did not exceed one drink per month, and in many cases was zero, it is difficult to generalize upon these results because of the state's high Mormon population. These various studies suggest that conveying the warning message to consumers is a critical link that cannot be ignored in designing an effective risk communication system.

THE EFFECT ON RISK PERCEPTIONS

Although it is clearly important that hazard warnings provide accessible and comprehensible information, the risk perceptions formed must also be accurate. One can view this as posing a more refined question about the processing of risk information. Not surprisingly, this issue has been much less thoroughly examined than the actual receipt of the risk information.

However, information does exist in two different contexts in which risk information has been assessed relatively precisely. The cigarette experience provides a substantial data base on which to make judgments. The trends in the Gallup poll responses on lung cancer risk perceptions reflect the provision of hazard warnings. Before hazard warnings were in place in 1958, 45 percent of all respondents believed that cigarette smoking was one cause of lung cancer. In a 1969 survey, after the first two sets of cigarette warnings had been in place, this awareness figure had risen to 70 percent. By 1977, awareness of lung cancer risks from smoking had gone up to 81 percent (16). However, the effect of hazard warnings per se is difficult to isolate from the extensive public information campaigns about cigarette smoking. Moreover, awareness of these risks does not necessarily imply that risk perceptions are accurate. One could, for example, be aware of the risk of fatality from automobile crashes but believe that these risks are only one chance in a trillion per year.

A more instructive set of information about risk perceptions pertains to the level of the risk assessment. These figures are quite striking. Overall, individuals believe that 43 out of 100 smokers will get lung cancer because they smoke and that 54 out of 100 smokers will die of some smoking-related cause, such as lung cancer or heart disease (16). These figures exceed the "true" estimated risks of smoking, which as of 1991 were 0.06–0.03 for the lung cancer mortality risk and 0.23–0.46 for the total mortality risk of smoking (16). The amount of expected life lost by smokers also exceeds scientific estimates.

The potential mismatch between the warning information and the underlying risk associated with the product is illustrated in the warnings language under California's Proposition 65. This proposition, enacted in 1986, requires that risk information be provided on hazardous exposures that pose a lifetime cancer risk of at least 1/100,000. Products above the cancer-risk threshold are Liquid Paper, mantles for Coleman lanterns, and snuff. There is also a requirement about risks of reproductive toxicity. Coffee and soft drinks with caffeine are among many products above this risk threshold. The full effect of these warnings has yet to become apparent because of a series of legal challenges to Proposition 65. However, examination of the risk perceptions that would be induced by the warning language is of great interest since other states are considering similar measures. In particular, Proposition 65-type measures have been proposed in Hawaii, Illinois, Missouri, New York, Ohio, Oregon, and Tennessee, and a measure is under study in the legislature of Massachusetts (17).

The warning language mandated under Proposition 65 for carcinogens is: "WARNING: The State of California has determined that this product is dangerous to your health." This warning was patterned after the cigarette warning, but cigarettes pose a lifetime cancer risk that is approximately 10,000 times greater than the warnings threshold in Proposition 65. Not surprisingly, given the similarity of the warning language to the 1965 cigarette warning, many consumers believe that the product in question is just as risky as cigarettes. In particular, 21 percent of all Illinois respondents examining products bearing this warning believe the product would have a risk level between zero and that posed by one 12-ounce saccharin cola for which the estimated lifetime risk is 1/2500, 44 percent estimate that the Proposition 65 product poses a risk between one saccharin cola and one pack of cigarettes, and 35 percent of all respondents believe that the risk is between that of one and five packs of cigarettes. Overall, respondents believe that the Proposition 65 warning poses the same average risk as do 0.58 packs of cigarettes, or a lifetime risk in excess of 1/10. This perceived risk is 10,000 times greater than the warnings risk threshold under Proposition 65.

The actual risk perceptions generated by this measure will depend in part upon its implementation. However, the basic message is that conveying warning information does not necessarily ensure accurate probability assessments. When the level of risk perceptions is a potential concern, and not simply awareness of a potential consequence of the product, care must be exercised to ascertain that the risk perceptions generated are accurate. Language appropriate in one context may fail to convey risks of a different character.

BEHAVIORAL RESPONSES TO WARNINGS

Hazard warnings aim to provide information that will alter individual behavior either in respect to the purchase of the product or its use. Although this is the intended outcome, examining changes in behavior does not necessarily provide a perfect indication of the efficacy of the warnings. If individuals were fully informed before receiving the warning information, then no change in behavior would be expected. Similarly, if the warnings provide an excessively adverse portrayal of the product and its risks, then there will be a response, but this response may not necessarily be commensurate with the level of risk.

Tetracycline Warnings

An interesting example of the effect of hazard warnings on the market for drugs is that for tetracycline. Although tetracycline is a beneficial drug, it can cause tooth staining in young children. Although the discoloration of children's permanent teeth is only cosmetic, the drug has been the subject of widespread litigation. Moreover, the FDA mandated warnings for tetracycline to alert physicians and potential consumers to the risk of permanent discoloration, beginning in April 1963.

An instructive test for the efficacy of this warning is the extent of the market response, as measured by prescribing practices that reflect the influence of the warning. Figure 2 gives the trends in physician mentions (i.e. prescriptions and refills of prescriptions) per 1000 population for two groups—age group 0–8, the specific targets of the FDA warning, and age group 9 and above. If the pattern of drug use for those affected by the warning was not influenced by the provision of the warning information, then it would have been expected to follow the same kind of trend as the use of tetracycline for the age group 9 and above. As illustrated in Figure 2, the use of tetracycline continued to increase throughout the 1960s for the older age group. However, for the age 0–8 group, the trend flattened out in 1963 when the warning was first given, and decreased steadily thereafter. Use of tetracycline declined from approximately 400 mentions per 1000 population in 1963 to under 100 mentions per 1000 population in 1975. Use of tetracycline in the younger age group did not decline to zero because tetracycline continues to be an effective drug in treating many diseases, such as Rocky Mountain spotted fever and lyme disease. Thus, physicians must make a tradeoff between the risk of the adverse effect of tooth discoloration and the beneficial effects of the drug. However, the shift in the consumption pattern for the drug is evidence of an effect of the warning on physician behavior.

The analysis of tetracycline and other products considered below rests on common features: the level of consumption of a product observed after the warnings and how this differed from what would have been observed had the warnings not been in place. It is not sufficient to ascertain whether consumption of the product has dropped. It may have been that the warnings were effective in a situation in which consumption was growing, but that the nature of the influence was to decrease the rate of growth, even though

Mentions per 1000 population

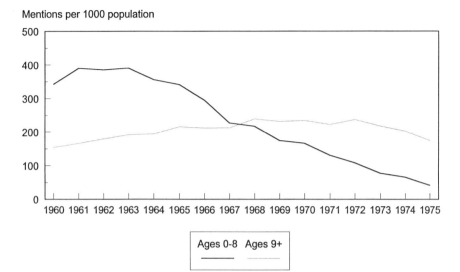

Figure 2   Use of tetracycline, 1960–1975, as measured by mentions (prescriptions and renewals).

it may not have decreased the rate of growth by so much that a decline was observed. Thus, the appropriate test is not whether consumption of the labeled product has decreased but rather whether consumption is less than it would have been in the absence of the warning.

Caution is needed in drawing conclusions about the efficacy of the warning based on such studies. If there is no effect on consumption, this is an indication that warnings did not influence behavior, but it does not necessarily imply that consumers are misinformed. One situation in which warnings would have no effect is when they do not provide any new information that alters consumers' beliefs. If these beliefs were accurate initially, the warnings would serve no useful purpose. In addition, the existence of an effect on consumption is not necessarily an outcome to which one should attach a value judgment. If the goal of the warning was to decrease consumption of the product, an outright ban would be more effective. The existence of some effect of the warning suggests that the warning did play a constructive role in terms of fulfilling its intended purpose, but the magnitude of the effect alone is generally not sufficient to determine whether this effect is too little or too great.

Cigarette Warnings

Figure 3 illustrates trends in cigarette consumption as a function of time and indicates the three different warning eras. The 1965 and 1969 warnings were generally associated with a flattening in the consumption of cigarettes, and the 1984 warning was associated with a decline in consumption. If only the effects of the warnings are examined, the conclusion would be that these warnings were instrumental in dampening cigarette consumption.

However, the situation with cigarettes was not a pure controlled experiment in any sense. Numerous other sources of information also affected the trend in cigarette smoking. The landmark report on smoking issued by the Department of Health, Education, and Welfare in 1964 and the ensuing public debate were undoubtedly influential in driving the tapering-off of cigarette consumption in the mid-1960s. Moreover, the Surgeon General has issued annual reports on cigarette smoking over the past two decades, and there have been many other smoking-related actions. For example, in 1971 cigarette advertising was banned on television and radio.

Numerous econometric studies have attempted to isolate the effect of the hazard warnings from other informational events that may have affected consumption (16). Some evidence is presented in the literature that the warnings had an effect on market purchases of cigarettes, but the contemporaneous nature of the informational events makes it difficult to attribute a specific extent of this decline in smoking to the hazard warnings as distinct from other sources of information.

Saccharin Warnings

A market-based approach has also been used to assess the effect of saccharin warnings on consumption of products containing saccharin. The saccharin

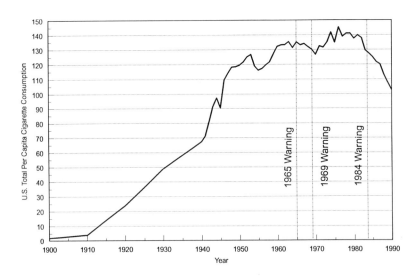

Figure 3 Trends in US per capita cigarette consumption, 1900–1989.

warning label went in place in early 1978, although news coverage of the risks associated with saccharin had begun in early 1977. Although the studies of saccharin have had some difficulty in disentangling the influence of the warning label from the surrounding publicity, overall there does seem to be evidence of an effect of the warning label on consumption of products containing this chemical. Schucker et al (14) found that diet soft drink sales grew faster during the period before the warnings were in place. In particular, the average annual growth rate in diet soft drink sales was 17.2 percent in 1975–1977, as compared to 1.8 percent in 1978. Sales of regular soft drinks continued to grow at an annual rate of 3–6 percent. In a subsequent study with additional data, Orwin, Schucker, & Stokes (11) concluded that to the extent that the effect of the public information in the warning label could be isolated, the evidence suggested that the warning label reduced sales of saccharin soft drinks by 4 percent and media coverage by 17 percent.

Heart Disease Information

A more narrowly focused study of the effect of warnings on behavior examined a program at Stanford University to provide information regarding heart disease (1a). The study aimed to alert consumers to the risks associated with smoking, excessive weight, diets high in saturated fat and cholesterol, and a lack of exercise. The Stanford physicians sought to disseminate information to a large number of consumers through distribution of a booklet on heart-related risks and a cooking guide for low-fat recipes.

The test in this instance focused on the effect of the information on patients' diets, exercise, smoking habits, weight, plasma cholesterol concentrations, egg consumption, and general knowledge. Based on these various criteria, there was evidence of a statistically significant effect of the program in the direction intended by the researchers.

Experimental Evidence

Controlled field experiments using alternative labels have also been used to assess the efficacy of warnings in other contexts. For example, researchers have assessed the effect of hazard warning labels for products such as toilet bowl cleaner, insecticide, workplace chemicals, and bleach by using this approach (6, 18). By undertaking experiments in which different samples were given alternative labels, it is possible to control for different aspects of the information provided and to test for their influence. This research technique is useful in ascertaining the effect of hazard warnings, assuming that the warning information is processed in the same manner as it would be in an experimental study, but it may tend to overstate the degree to which consumers will receive information since, as was noted above, not all warning information is processed by the intended recipients.

CONCLUSION

The role of food and drug warnings is clearly a central concern in the market for these products. Both food and drugs are potentially risky consumer products with both beneficial and possibly adverse effects on individual health. Given the consequences to individual mortality and morbidity that might occur from use of these products, it is not surprising that government has been active in mandating warnings.

Not coincidentally, the first sets of warnings for which the specific language was mandated by Congress were for cigarettes, saccharin, and alcoholic beverages. Moreover, perhaps the most well-developed long-standing federal warnings effort is the warning system for prescription drugs administered by the Food and Drug Administration. This program is in many respects a model of a well-run warning system. The FDA has maintained a standardized warnings vocabulary across labels for different products and producers. As a result, the warning language is comparable, as is the format in which the information is conveyed to the recipient groups. Since consumers benefit not only from the warnings themselves but also from the provision of information to them by the learned intermediary, the physician, this medical context has a well-developed risk communication network.

In contrast, other federal warnings programs are far less structured. In the case of occupational safety and health regulations pertaining to risk communication, there is no specification whatsoever regarding the content and structure of the warnings that must be provided other than that hazardous chemicals must be labeled adequately. Similarly, even in the case of pesticide warnings that must undergo approval by the US Environmental Protection Agency (EPA), there is no effort to standardize the structure and content of warning labels for comparable products manufactured by different companies, as is done for prescription drugs and nutrition labeling.[2]

Notwithstanding the comparative success of the food and drug warnings efforts, there remain open issues, both with respect to policy and research. Consumers do not always process the information provided, and if the information is not received it will not have the intended effect. In addition, even when the information is processed and there is an effect on market behavior, the resulting risk perceptions are not necessarily always accurate

---

[2]For example, comparison of the warning labels for household bleach across different manufacturers reveals stark differences. Some products, such as Clorox, include warning language only at the bottom of the warning label, whereas others, such as the Brite brand made by the Kroger company, integrate the risk information more prominently as part of the directions for use.

nor the decisions well-chosen. The recurring research issue that must continue to be addressed is whether these warnings promote the kinds of choices that consumers would make if they were accurately informed of the risks of the product and made sound decisions based on this information.

Any *Annual Review* chapter, as well as any article cited in an *Annual Review* chapter, may be purchased from the Annual Reviews Preprints and Reprints service. 1-800-347-8007; 415-249-5017; email: arpr@class.org

---

Literature Cited

1. Adler D, Pittle R. 1984. Cajolery or command: Are education campaigns an adequate substitute for regulation? *Yale J. Regul.* 1:159–93.
1a. Farquhar JW, Wood PD, Breitrose H, Haskell WL, Meyer AJ, et al. 1977. Community education for cardiovascular health. *Lancet* 1:1192–95
2. Heimbach JT. 1981. *The Public Understanding of Food Label Information*. Washington, DC: FDA
3. Heimbach JT. 1983. *The Public Responds to Labeling of the Sodium Content of Foods*. Washington, DC: FDA
3a. Ippolito PM, Mathios AD. 1990. Information, advertising and health choices: A study of the cereal market. *Rand J. Econ.* 21:459–56
4. Kanouse D, Berry SH, Hayes-Roth B, Rodgers WH, Winkler JD. 1981. Informing patients about drugs. *Rand Corp. Rep. R-2800-FDA*
5. Lave LB. 1981. *The Strategy of Social Regulation: Decision Frameworks for Policy*. Washington, DC: Brookings Inst.
6. Magat WA, Viscusi WK. 1992. *Informational Approaches to Regulation*. Cambridge: MIT Press
7. Morgan WG, Fischoff B, Bostrom A, Lave L, Atman C. 1992. Communicating risk to the public. *Environ. Sci. Technol.* 26:2049–56
8. Morris LA, Klimberg R. 1986. A survey of aspirin use and Reye's Syndrome awareness among parents. *Am. J. Public Health* 76:1422–24
9. Morris LA, Mazis MB, Gordon E. 1977. A survey of the effects of oral contraceptive patient information. *J. Am. Med. Assoc.* 28:2504–8
10. Muller T. 1985. Structural information factors which stimulate the use of nutrition information: A field experiment. *J. Mark. Res.* 22:143–57
11. Orwin RG, Schucker RE, Stokes RC. 1984. Evaluating the life cycle of a product warning: Saccharin and diet soft drinks. *Eval. Rev.* 8:801–22
12. Russo JE, Staelin R, Nolan CA, Russell GJ, Metcalf BL. 1986. Nutrition information in the supermarket. *J. Consum. Res.* 13:48–70
13. Scammon DL, Mayer RN, Smith KR. 1990. *Alcohol warnings: How do you know when you have had one too many?* Work. Pap., Univ. Utah
14. Schucker RE, Stokes RC, Stewart ML, Henderson DP. 1983. The impact of the saccharin warning label on sales of diet soft drinks in supermarkets. *J. Public Policy Mark.* 2:46–56
15. Travis C, Richter SA, Crouch EAC, Wilson R, Klema ED. 1987. Cancer risk management: A review of 132 federal regulatory decisions. *Environ. Sci. Technol.* 21:415–20
16. Viscusi WK. 1992. *Smoking: Making the Risky Decision*. New York: Oxford Univ. Press.
17. Viscusi WK. 1993. *Product Risk Labeling: A Federal Responsibility*. Washington: AEI Press
18. Viscusi WK, Magat WA. 1987. *Learning About Risk: Consumer and Worker Responses to Hazard Information*. Cambridge: Harvard Univ. Press
19. Viscusi WK, O'Connor C. 1984. Adaptive responses to chemical labeling: Are workers Bayesian decision makers? *Am. Econ. Rev.* 74:942–56

Annu. Rev. Public Health. 1994. 15:345–66

RELAPSE PREVENTION FOR SMOKING CESSATION: Review and Evaluation of Concepts and Interventions

S. J. Curry and C. M. McBride

Center for Health Studies, Group Health Cooperative of Puget Sound and Department of Health Services School of Public Health and Community Medicine, University of Washington, Seattle, Washington 98101

KEY WORDS: smoking cessation, relapse prevention, intervention, behavior

INTRODUCTION

Cigarette smoking continues to be the leading cause of premature morbidity and mortality in the United States (95). Although recent surveys reveal an encouraging decline (71), over 25% percent of the population are still regular smokers, and the prevalence of smoking approaches 50% in certain segments of the population (62, 71).

Efforts to encourage and assist smokers to quit are an important component of the public health campaign against this epidemic (63). Cessation efforts include mass media campaigns, the incorporation of nonsmoking advice and follow-up into health care delivery systems, provision of cessation assistance at the worksite, and the introduction of community-wide programs that promote nonsmoking norms, enforce regulations restricting smoking in public places, and provide an integrative structure for cessation efforts in different modalities.

A major challenge to smoking cessation efforts is relapse prevention. That approximately one out of four adults continues to smoke is in part attributable to the high rates of relapse among smokers who seriously attempt to quit smoking. For example, in the 1986 Adult Use of Tobacco Survey (AUTS; 72) 26% of the respondents who had smoked during the year prior

345

0163-7525/94/0510-0345$05.00

to the survey indicated that they had quit smoking for at least one week during the previous year. Unfortunately, nearly half of these smokers (49%) subsequently relapsed and were smoking at the time of the survey. Relapse rates following more intensive treatment for smoking cessation are even higher. In a seminal paper published in 1971, Hunt and colleagues (43) estimated relapse rates following treatment for smoking cessation at approximately 80%. Although some studies have shown much lower relapse rates (e.g. MRFIT; see 42), between 50% and 75% of smokers who quit following treatment will relapse within one year (31).

It is important to place relapse in the broader context of the smoking cessation process. Smoking cessation is a process that unfolds over time. As captured by Prochaska & DiClemente's stage model of change, smokers progress through multiple stages, beginning with contemplation of quitting, moving to making a firm commitment and preparing to quit, progressing to action for initial cessation, and maintaining abstinence (76). In their most recent presentation, the stage model is depicted as a spiral process that smokers can and do move up and down over time (77). Although not defined as a discrete stage of change, relapse is very much a part of this process. As indicated earlier, the vast majority of smokers make multiple attempts to quit smoking. This means that relapse is not an irrevocable state—the process is cyclical, and smokers can and do "recycle" through the stages. Although we cannot precisely predict how many times a smoker will cycle through the stages before quitting permanently, we do know that successful quitters average at least three serious quit attempts. Work by Prochaska & DiClemente suggests that the cessation process can take up to seven years (76, 77). In our work with self-help interventions for smoking cessation (17), we found that over 20% of smokers who had quit for at least a week and relapsed by a three-month follow-up had successfully quit again by a twelve-month follow-up (i.e. reported at least one week of abstinence that was biochemically verified).

Efforts to decrease relapse rates have been guided by research to identify the factors that cause relapse as well as by randomized evaluations of interventions to prevent relapse. This review has several sections. The first section focuses on defining and assessing relapse rates. The second section reviews conceptual models of relapse and summarizes findings on predictors of relapse. The third section reviews the recent literature on evaluations of interventions to prevent relapse. The paper concludes with discussions of both the public health efforts that could be undertaken based on the currently available research and suggests areas for future research.

Of necessity, this review is selective in the literature it covers; we focus primarily on articles and chapters published since 1986, when the National Heart, Lung and Blood Institute (NHLBI) sponsored a national working conference on relapse prevention (88). We intend to complement reviews of specific smoking cessation interventions, such as mass media (28), worksite programs (24, 27), health care provider interventions (64), self-help interventions (14), community interventions (50), as well as general reviews of the smoking cessation field (2, 49). We also acknowledge and will parallel other recent excellent reviews of the relapse prevention field by Mermelstein et al (55), Shiffman (87), Sutton (93), and Brownell et al (11).

DEFINITIONS AND RATES OF RELAPSE

The concept of smoking cessation as a dynamic process that may involve repeated cycles of abstinence and relapse suggests the need to define several outcomes in the analysis of relapse. Because relapse implies achieving initial cessation, definitions of relapse must be in reference to a defined period of abstinence. Moreover, distinction between sporadic episodes of smoking or lapses, and resumption of regular smoking over an extended period of time or relapse, are also suggested. Finally, outcomes that would evidence recycling following relapse also need to be defined (e.g. repeated quit attempts; a second period of initial cessation).

Definitions

The 1986 National Working Conference on Smoking Relapse recommended standard definitions to promote measurement comparability across studies. Recommended definitions are: a *quit episode* is defined as 24 hr of continuous abstinence; a *lapse* or *slip* is defined as not more than six consecutive days of smoking following at least 24 hr of abstinence, and *relapse* is seven consecutive days of smoking following a quit episode (69). Although relatively few studies published since this conference have used these definitions (7, 29, 72), most make the key conceptual distinction and define relapse in reference to a minimum period of initial abstinence or quit episode. Definitions of quit episodes in the literature have included: seven days of not smoking (3, 15, 44, 46), having smoked less than one cigarette in the previous four days (92) or the previous seven days (100), five consecutive days of not smoking (79), and thirty days of not smoking (90).

Few studies differentiate a lapse from a relapse, and those that do use varying definitions. Lapse has been defined as smoking occasionally but on less than one occasion per week (65, 66), any smoking (7), smoking at least one cigarette in the month after quitting (5), a single episode of smoking followed by a return to abstinence (3, 15). Similarly, definitions of relapse have varied and include: three consecutive days of smoking five or more cigarettes (58), three consecutive days of smoking (7, 13), having smoked more than five cigarettes over a 30-day period (92). Most studies classify relapse simply as smoking any cigarettes since the quit episode (69, 90, 94, 97).

A few recent studies assess "recycling" or renewed efforts to attain abstinence following relapse. Recycling has been defined as at least one week of abstinence following complete relapse (7, 15).

Patterns and Rates of Relapse

Different definitions of cessation, lapse, and relapse can result in significant variability in estimates of their rates. More stringent definitions of initial cessation (e.g. one week vs 24 hr of abstinence) can eliminate a sizeable proportion of smokers from the denominator used to calculate relapse rates, thereby decreasing the estimated prevalence of relapse. For example, Hughes et al (41) estimate a 76% relapse rate at a seven-day follow-up by including all smokers who attempted to quit in the denominator. When relapse is calculated with only those smokers who quit for 48 hr, the relapse rate is 26%.

Although different definitions of outcome make it difficult to provide definitive rates of relapse, common patterns of relapse have been observed. Regardless of whether cessation is self-initiated or the result of participation in a formal treatment program, a large proportion of those who quit smoking will relapse in the first three months after quitting, with estimates varying from 35% to 81% (7, 41, 43). The risk of relapse begins to stabilize at about six months following cessation (7, 41). Hughes et al (41) reported a dramatic decrease in the risk of relapsing over time, with relapse defined as any smoking following a quit attempt. By a six-month follow-up less than 1% of subjects were relapsing per day compared to 34% who were relapsing in the first two days following cessation. However, a recent Surgeon General's Report indicates that among those who sustain abstinence for at least a year, a third or more may eventually relapse (95). A resurgence of risk for relapse in postpartum despite sometimes lengthy sustained prepartum abstinence further supports the ongoing risk of relapse. Postpartum relapse rates have been remarkably consistent, with about 26% of those who maintained abstinence throughout pregnancy relapsing within the first six weeks postpartum (25, 52, 53, 59). There is also fairly consistent evidence that while individual lapses/slips do not necessarily lead to relapse, any smoking following cessation suggests a high probability of return to regular smoking sometime during the follow-up period. As many as 80–90% of those who experience a lapse return to regular smoking (6, 7). Although less is known about patterns of recycling, a few studies have reported from 6% to 38% of those who relapse may regain abstinence (7, 15, 94).

UNDERSTANDING THE RELAPSE PROCESS

Optimally, relapse prevention strategies will derive from conceptually based research on the determinants of relapse. Before reviewing findings from studies of treatment outcome of relapse prevention strategies, we briefly describe key models and concepts that have guided work in understanding relapse and summarize general findings from research on predictors of relapse.

Conceptual Models of Relapse

Understanding of the factors associated with relapse is not simple. In his comprehensive review of conceptual issues in the study of relapse, Shiffman discusses the "entangled gestalt of [relapse] causes", which includes three types of risk factors: enduring personal characteristics, background variables, and precipitants (87). By combining personal characteristics and background variables we can distinguish individual and environmental factors that *predispose* a smoker to a higher risk of relapse (e.g. degree of physical addiction; number of smokers in one's social environment) from factors that *precipitate* a relapse crisis (e.g. interpersonal conflict, coping skills).

Social learning theory is a useful model for identifying the types of predisposing factors (both personal characteristics and background variables) that can increase a person's vulnerability to relapse (4). This model proposes reciprocal associations among characteristics of the person (e.g. beliefs and expectations about maintaining abstinence, degree of physical addiction); behavior (e.g. prior cessation experience, coping skills); and the environment (e.g. degree of psychosocial stress, social networks). Environmental variables can also encompass community characteristics such as perceived norms for smoking, the existence and enforcement of smoking restrictions, although these have not been widely studied as predisposing factors for relapse (16).

Emerging from the same cognitive-behavioral tradition, Marlatt & Gordon's relapse prevention model (51) has been the leading conceptual model of relapse precipitants. The relapse prevention model focuses on proximal situational determinants of relapse (also called high-risk situations). Among the key tenets of this model are: (*a*) There are certain types of situations in which relapse is more likely to occur; (*b*) Whether an individual engages in a coping response when in a high-risk situation is a critical determinant of the situation's outcome (abstinence or relapse). Successfully coping in one situation will increase an individual's self-efficacy or confidence in his or her ability to cope in other high-risk situations; (*c*) Failure to cope (either because of lack of skills or interference with coping due to stress, alcohol consumption, etc) decreases self-efficacy and increases an individual's positive expectancies regarding the effects of smoking; (*d*) The combination of decreased efficacy and heightened positive expectations can lead to a single episode of smoking (aka "lapse" or "slip"); (*e*) The likelihood of a full-blown relapse following a lapse is determined by the individual's cognitive-affective reaction to the slip and this reaction is called the abstinence violation effect (AVE). Based on attribution theory (96), Marlatt & Gordon's model posits that the intensity of the AVE is increased when attributions for a slip focus on internal, stable, and global factors that are seen as uncontrollable (e.g. lack of willpower). Emotional reactions of guilt and self-blame associated with these attributions further increase the likelihood of relapse. Alternatively, the intensity of the AVE is decreased by external, unstable, specific, and controllable attributions (e.g. failure to plan ahead for a specific high-risk situation).

Models of predisposing and precipitating factors can be linked to the extent that they relate to the frequency and intensity of high-risk situations. For example, Niaura and colleagues (61) propose that conditioning-based models of learning can provide a bridge between predispositional physiologic factors and precipitant situational determinants of relapse. They postulate that individuals can differ in their reactions to environmental and affective cues associated with smoking and suggest that higher levels of "cue reactivity" are associated with an increased risk of relapse. Associations among physiological, cognitive, affective, situational and coping-skill constructs form a "dynamic regulatory feedback system". Similar to Shiffman's concepts of synergistic and buffering interactions between relapse determinants (87), this model posits that very intense cue reactions could undermine existing coping skills and intensify internal, stable, uncontrollable attributions. Conversely, strong coping skills and a sense of personal control could dampen reactivity.

Predisposing Factors for Relapse

Compared to a fairly extensive literature on personal characteristics and background variables that predict long-term abstinence, relatively few studies have focused exclusively on these factors as predictors of relapse. Distinguishing between studies of long-term abstinence and relapse is important because smokers who fail to achieve long-term abstinence include both those who quit and relapse and those who fail to achieve initial cessation. To the extent that certain factors are strongly related to achieving initial cessation, they may be less likely to predict relapse because the subgroup of quitters at risk for relapse is more homogeneous. This may be particularly true for demographic characteristics such as age, sex, and education, which have been associated with achieving initial cessation, but generally do not predict relapse (7, 55).

Differences in specific measures, study populations, and timing of assessments result in a somewhat cloudy picture of the key personal characteristics and background variables that increase the risk of relapse following initial cessation. The picture is cloudy not because studies report contradictory associations, but because not all studies find significant differences on the same variables. With regard to *smoking history,* several studies have found that heavier smoking predicts relapse (15, 53, 81, 89), whereas other studies report no significant associations between amount smoked or pack/years of smoking and relapse (7, 29, 94). High levels of post-cessation cravings have predicted early relapse among male and female smokers (46) and late relapse among females (94). With extended follow-up, Killen et al (45) found that post-cessation craving along with high degrees of dependence (assessed on a modified Fagerstrom scale) were associated with a greater risk of relapse one and two years post-cessation.

Findings are mixed with regard to *stress* and relapse. Cohen et al (13) report that increases in perceived stress accompany relapse, but the direction of that association was unclear from their data. Results from other studies suggest that perceived stress is not prospectively associated with relapse (29, 40). However, daily hassles as an indicator of background stress have predicted relapse in a couple of studies (15, 94). There is also some evidence that anxiety, perhaps as a response to stress, is associated with relapse (7, 20).

The collected evidence is stronger for self-confidence and social support as predictors of relapse. Several studies show that post-cessation *confidence* in maintaining abstinence (measured either at the end of treatment for group program participants or shortly after cessation for self-quitters) is lower among quitters who subsequently relapse (7, 8, 29, 53, 98). Haaga & Stewart (36) also report that low confidence in being able to recover from an initial lapse is associated with a higher likelihood of relapsing after a slip. As one indicator of *social support* for nonsmoking, the presence of other smokers in one's immediate social environment has emerged in several studies as a significant predictor of relapse (7, 15, 20, 29, 58).

Although less extensively studied as predictors of relapse, two other variables deserve mention as predisposing factors. Results from two recent studies implicate *patterns of alcohol consumption* as an important risk factor for relapse. Garvey et al (29) found that greater levels of weekly intake of alcohol predicted relapse among self-quitters. A history of alcohol abuse was one of two significant predictors (along with pack/years smoked) in the study by Simon et al (89) of risk factors for relapse following major surgery. *Weight gain* following smoking cessation has received considerable attention (34, 47), and an implicit assumption has been that concerns about weight control and actual weight gain would contribute to relapse. Two studies report no association between baseline weight (expressed as BMI) and relapse (89, 94). Hall et al (39) found that weight gain following cessation was associated with a decreased risk of relapse. Garvey et al (29) reported that, among women, those who smoked for weight control were less likely to relapse. Together these findings suggest that women who smoked for weight control had expected to gain weight following smoking cessation and, therefore, were less likely to relapse if they gained weight. McBride and colleagues report that weight concerns did predict postpartum relapse, with women who expected to return to their prepregnancy weight within six months of delivery more likely to relapse (53). In this instance it was concern about losing weight rather than concern about gaining weight that predisposed the women to relapse.

Precipitants of Relapse

Research on the precipitants of relapse support the main theoretical assumptions that relapse is situation-specific, coping responses in high-risk situations influence the likelihood of initial smoking, and the Abstinence Violation Effect influences the probability of progressing from a lapse to a relapse.

Although smokers' ratings of post-cessation craving predispose smokers to relapse, such cravings are not commonly identified as immediate precipitants (87). The three most common situations or mood states in which relapse occurs are: (a) intrapersonal negative emotional states such as frustration, anger, depression, and boredom; (b) interpersonal conflicts; and (c) social settings in which other smokers are present (5, 6, 51, 53, 65, 84, 86). Some studies also point to the consumption of alcohol or food as important precipitants, perhaps because of their prior association with smoking (29, 66, 86). These situational characteristics reflect several of the predisposing factors discussed above (e.g. the presence of smokers in one's environment, background stress and anxiety, and patterns of alcohol consumption).

There is unequivocal evidence that smokers who engage in one or more coping strategies when confronted with a high-risk situation are less likely to smoke. (3, 5, 18, 85). Most typologies of coping strategies distinguish between cognitive and behavioral coping (e.g. 18, 44, 85). The general consensus is that most strategies are equally effective and that the prognosis for maintaining abstinence in a given situation is highest when using both cognitive and behavioral strategies (i.e. *thinking* and *doing* something when tempted to smoke). Recent research demonstrates associations between cue reactivity (measured as changes in heart rate and skin conductance in response to smoking cues) and skills for coping with high-risk situations (1, 60). In a laboratory study conducted prior to treatment for smoking cessation, Abrams and colleagues presented smokers with high-risk situations and assessed the smokers' cue reactivity and their strategies for avoiding smoking. Smokers who quit and relapsed evidenced greater cue reactivity and were less skillful at coping with the high-risk situations than successful quitters.

Attempts to predict future relapse on the basis of coping reported in a specific high risk have not succeeded (3). However, among pregnant smokers there is evidence that the types of coping strategies used prior to delivery can affect the likelihood of postpartum relapse. McBride and colleagues reported that snacking and avoiding high-risk situations to cope with urges to smoke during pregnancy were the strongest predictors of postpartum relapse (53).

Although the few studies that focus on the Abstinence Violation Effect (AVE) as a predictor of relapse use different measures (3, 19, 66), they provide support for the construct's validity. Both Curry et al (19) and O'Connell et al (66) found that more internal and stable causal attributions predicted failure to recover abstinence following a slip. Baer et al (3) found that feelings of guilt following initial smoking predicted more immediate relapse. As indicated earlier, smokers may recover immediately from a specific lapse, but most smokers (up to 85%) who lapse eventually relapse (3, 7).

RELAPSE PREVENTION INTERVENTIONS

Interventions to prevent relapse include: (a) booster sessions and extended contacts, (i.e. renewed or ongoing contact that continues after conclusion of a formal cessation program); (b) relapse prevention training (i.e. instruction in cognitive and behavioral skills for resisting urges to smoke in high-risk situations); and (c) intervention supplements designed to provide social support or to address common sequelae of smoking cessation (e.g. weight control). While it is useful to distinguish between these three approaches to intervention, studies of relapse prevention interventions do not fall neatly into these categories. Some relapse prevention efforts have been an amalgam of all three approaches and others have tested their relative effectiveness in factorial designs. Although many trials have been conducted in clinical settings, more recent studies have evaluated adjuncts to minimal self-help approaches as relapse prevention strategies. We draw primarily from trials conducted since the National Working Conference on Relapse in 1986 (88) to review evidence for the effectiveness of the three approaches. These studies are summarized in Table 1.

Booster Sessions and Extended Contacts

Booster sessions were a natural outgrowth of early models of smoking cessation interventions based on conditioning theories. Within this paradigm,

Table 1 Summary of relapse prevention interventions trials, 1986–1993

Authors/Year/Reference	N	Number of treatment arms	Type of intervention	Relapse prevention components	Length of follow-up	Definition of relapse	RPT effects	Follow-up abstinence rates
Scott et al, 1986 (83)	29	2	W	Biochemical monitoring	12 mos.	No specific definition	No	@ 12 mos: wait list gp. 0%; tx gp 33%
Brandon et al, 1987 (8)	65	3	GP	RPT	12 mos.	No specific definition	Yes	@ 3 mos: RP 66%; control 37%; @ 6 & 12 mos. no differences
Omenn et al, 1988 (67)	402	6	GP/SH	RPT	12 mos.	No specific definition	No	@ 12 mos: 25% (GP) 20% (SH)
Curry et al, 1988 (15)	139	4	GP/SH	RPT	12 mos.	Any cigarettes in past week	No	@ 12 mos: 17–26% (SH) 25–38% (GP)
Russell et al, 1988 (80)	42	3	GP	Physical activity	18 mos.	No specific definition	No	@ 18 mos: 34%
Rand et al, 1989 (79)	51	3	W	Contingency payments Biochemical monitoring	12 mos.	Breath samples above CO cut point	Yes	@ 1 mos: comparison groups 29%, 31%; tx gp 75%; @ 6, 12 mos. no difference
Stevens, Hollis, 1989 (92)	587	3	GP	RPT	12 mos.	@ 12 mos. any cigarettes in previous 6 mos.	Yes	@ 12 mos: comparison groups 34%, 33%; tx gp: 41%

Study	N		Program	Intervention	Follow-up	Abstinence definition	Verified	Results
Killen et al, 1990 (46)	1218	12	SH	RPT Nicotine replacement	12 mos.	Puff in past 7 days	No	@ 12 mos: no gum 18%; ad lib gum 20%; fixed schedule gum 25%
Ossip-Klein et al, 1991 (70)	1813	2	SH	RPT Hotline	18 mos.	Any cigarettes past 90 days	Yes	@ 18 mos: RPT + hotline 12%; RPT 8%
Minneker-Hugel et al, 1992 (57)	316	5	GP	RPT 3 Booster sessions	12 mos.	No specific definition	No	40% @ 6 mos.
Wynd, 1992 (99)	76	2	GP	Visual imagery	3 mos.	No specific definition	Yes	@ 3 mos: Comparison 51%; tx gp 72%
Prochaska et al, 1992 (77)	756	4	SH	RPT Phone counseling Written feedback	18 mos.	Any cigarettes last 24 hr each follow-up	Yes	@ 18 mos. Interactive feedback 14%; ALA 5%
Hall et al, 1992 (39)	165	3	GP	Weight gain prevention	52 wks.	Any cigarettes prior week each follow-up	No	@52 wks. Comparison gp 35%; wt. conditions combined 21%
Mermelstein et al, 1992 (55)	626	2	SH	Telephone counseling	9 mos.	Any cigarettes past 7 days each follow-up	Yes	@ 9 mos: Standard gp 48%; recycling gp. 58%
Gruder et al, 1993 (35)	793	3	GP	RPT Social support	24 mos.	Any smoking past 3 days each follow-up	No	@ 24 mos: Comparison gp 1.8%; social support 7.7%

GP = Group program; SH = Self-help program; W = Worksite program; RPT = Relapse prevention training; ALA = American Lung Association booklet.

relapse results from a decay of treatment effects. The goal of booster sessions is to provide a new dose of treatment to disrupt the decay curve. Thus, booster sessions occur after formal involvement in a smoking cessation program is completed and there has been some period of no contact. Although early booster sessions typically involved readministration of aversive procedures (e.g. rapid smoking, electric shock therapy), more recent approaches include both refresher information as well as strategies designed to reinforce the individual's efforts to maintain abstinence. Evaluations of the booster session approach in the late 1970s and early 1980s were not encouraging (82). Identifying the appropriate timing for the sessions and getting participants to attend sessions months after the end of treatment are significant barriers.

Since 1986, two trials (8, 57) have evaluated the impact of booster sessions on long-term abstinence. Consistent with earlier studies, Brandon et al (8) reported only short-term benefit to booster sessions occurring 2, 4, 8, and 12 weeks after a formal cessation program. Although abstinence rates in the booster group were higher at a three-month follow-up, there were no differences at six or twelve months, which suggests that boosters merely delayed relapse to smoking. Similarly, Minneker-Hugel et al (57) found no added benefit of booster sessions that occurred six months after the end of a relapse prevention training program (RPT). Attendance at the booster sessions was low despite agreement during treatment to attend. Results of this study also suggest that boosters diluted the impact of relapse prevention training. Those assigned to RPT plus booster sessions had lower long-term abstinence rates than those who received booster sessions after a standard cessation program.

Extended contact approaches involve less frequent, ongoing contact following an initial smoking cessation intervention in such forms as written feedback, telephone counseling, ongoing physiological assessment, and support groups. Evaluations of extended contact approaches have been more promising. Ossip-Klein found significantly higher sustained abstinence rates among quitters who lived in a community with access to a call-in hotline (70). The hotline provided 24-hr prerecorded messages of support, and daytime access to counselors who assisted with coping skills for high-risk situations. Although it is a challenge to persuade smokers to use hotlines for help with initial smoking cessation (30), results from Ossip-Klein et al (70) suggest that such strategies may be of particular interest and use to those who quit smoking.

Proactive telephone counselor calls are also a promising approach to extended contact since call schedules can be tailored to meet the individual needs of the client. When evaluated as an adjunct to written self-help materials, Orleans et al (68) demonstrated that telephone counseling calls significantly increased both initial cessation and continuous abstinence. Computer-generated written personalized feedback, based on smokers responses to periodic assessments, has also significantly increased sustained abstinence (78). The addition of proactive telephone counseling calls to the written feedback did not improve long-term abstinence rates, which suggests a threshold for the benefits of multiple extended contacts. Gruder and colleagues (35) extended a mass-media self-help program with a combination of group support sessions, a buddy system, and follow-up telephone counseling calls. Initial quit rates were significantly higher among smokers receiving the extended contacts compared to a randomized control group of smokers who only participated in the mass-media program. While long-term abstinence rates were higher, extended contacts did not significantly decrease rates of relapse over 24 months of follow-up.

A recent study by Mermelstein and colleagues (54) suggests that the content of extended telephone counseling calls may be important. These investigators compared two approaches to telephone counseling following a group cessation program. Counseling in a "standard" condition involved general encouragement and support for maintaining abstinence or attempting to quit again. Counseling in a "recycling" condition involved debriefing temptation or relapse episodes and discussing specific difficulties and problems areas in maintaining abstinence. Compared to the standard condition, rates of recycling were higher for relapsers in the recycling condition. Unfortunately, the recycling protocol increased relapse rates among abstainers compared to the standard condition. The more intensive extended telephone interventions encouraging abstainers to focus on potential difficulties may undermine their self-confidence by over-emphasizing the difficulties of quitting. In contrast, general support and encouragement may enhance their confidence and, thus, be more helpful in the long run.

Other approaches to extended contact such as ongoing physiological assessment and contingency payments for continued abstinence have been evaluated in work-site settings and demonstrate little effect on reducing relapse rates (79, 83). Overall findings from these studies suggest that such extrinsic incentives delay rather than prevent relapse.

Relapse Prevention Training

Marlatt & Gordon's cognitive-behavioral relapse prevention model (51) is the cornerstone of relapse prevention training (RPT). The main components of RPT are skills training to anticipate and resist relapse in high-risk situations, and cognitive restructuring to deal with self-defeating attributions following isolated episodes of smoking (lapses). Applications of RPT to smoking cessation take two forms. One approach has been to offer relapse prevention interventions after the conclusion of a general smoking cessation program (e.g. ref. 8) and sometimes only to those who have achieved initial cessation (e.g. ref. 92). Alternatively, RPT has been integrated with other smoking cessation intervention components and offered to all smokers attempting to quit (e.g. 15, 38, 67). In the latter case, relapse prevention is delivered as an integral part of the smoking cessation program rather than as an adjunct that begins after the program. To date these two general approaches (integrated vs adjunct) have not been compared in randomized trials.

Evidence in recent studies for the superiority of RPT compared to other intervention approaches is mixed. An early evaluation of skill training for relapse prevention conducted by Hall and colleagues (38) reported significantly higher one-year abstinence rates for the skills training intervention compared to a discussion-only control group. In a more recent study, Stevens & Hollis also found significant effects for RPT delivered in group format to abstainers after a cessation program compared to a discussion group and a no-treatment control (92). In their study, one-year abstinence rates were 21% higher among smokers who received RPT (41% vs 34%). In a 1984 study, Davis et al (21) reported significantly higher long-term abstinence rates among smokers who received a self-help relapse prevention manual (*A Lifetime of Freedom From Smoking*). The maintenance manual increased abstinence rates when combined with either smoking cessation leaflets or with a more detailed smoking cessation manual. Long-term abstinence rates were highest in the combined cessation and maintenance manuals condition.

In contrast to these positive findings, Killen et al (46) reported no effects of written relapse prevention modules in a factorial study of nicotine gum and RPT. Studies by Omenn et al (67) and Curry et al (15) also found no significant effects for relapse prevention training. Both studies evaluated RPT in group and self-help formats. Although the formats were randomly assigned in Curry et al and self-selected in Omenn et al neither study found significant differences in abstinence rates by format. Curry et al (15) also assessed the impact of RPT on the timing of relapse and rates of recycling. They found that RPT participants relapsed sooner than participants in an absolute abstinence program, but were significantly more likely to recycle to other quit attempts. Thus, while RPT may not decrease the risk of relapse, it may encourage repeated cessation attempts among those who do relapse. As previously discussed, Mermelstein and colleagues (54) also found that RPT delivered via telephone counseling encouraged recycling among relapsers (but increased the risk of relapse among abstainers).

There is additional evidence that RPT is more effective with certain subgroups of smokers. Curry et al found significantly higher abstinence rates with RPT among women compared to men (15). Hall et al reported that lighter smokers were more likely than heavier smokers to benefit from skills training (38). Women tend, on average, to be lighter smokers than men.

Several investigators have noted the complexity of RPT and speculate that smokers may have difficulty assimilating the relapse prevention concepts and complying with the components of coping skill training. Compliance with RPT components is a particular challenge with more minimal self-help interventions (46). Ensuring a coherent intervention message may also be important. For example, smokers who are using nicotine replacement therapies such as transdermal patches may find it difficult to combine the more complex skill training approach with a simple medically oriented treatment.

Supplements

In addition to general skill training for coping with high-risk situations, relapse prevention can include supplemental strategies to address common sequelae of smoking cessation such as withdrawal symptoms, weight gain, stress, or depression. Supplement approaches described in the literature include nicotine replacement and other types of pharmacotherapies such as clonidine and triptophan, weight and stress management.

Nicotine replacement therapy (NRT) may prevent early relapse to smoking by minimizing withdrawal symptoms. Results from randomized trials of both nicotine polacrilex and transdermal nicotine patches suggest that these therapies do indeed prevent relapse while being used (26). Unfortunately, relapse rates can be as high following cessation of NRT as they are after cessation of behavioral interventions. Although this suggests that RPT could be a useful adjunct to NRT, results of a recent randomized factorial study of self-help relapse prevention manuals along with nicotine gum are not encouraging. Killen and colleagues (46) reported significantly higher sustained abstinence rates in the NRT-only group than NRT in combination with RPT. Follow-up data indicated low rates of compliance with the relapse prevention modules.

Recent studies have evaluated weight control training as a strategy to prevent relapse. Results of a randomized trial (73) indicated some incremental improvement in sustained abstinence with the addition of a behavioral weight control component to a standard group cessation program. The weight control component included keeping food diaries, instruction in reducing caloric intake, and increasing daily exercise. However, no differences were recorded across intervention groups in weight gain following cessation. Thus, improved abstinence rates were not a result of weight gain prevention. Findings reported by Hall and colleagues (39) have raised some concern about weight management components. Subjects in individualized (assisted by an exercise counselor) and nonspecific (nutritional and exercise information) weight intervention groups had significantly lower abstinence rates compared to a standard smoking cessation control condition. In addition to concern about the added complexity of the weight interventions, the authors raise the possibility that caloric reduction encouraged smoking. This contention challenges the appropriateness of weight management as a supplment to smoking cessation interventions. Clearly more research is needed to assess the potential role for weight management supplements to prevent relapse (47).

Supplemental approaches to reduce stress and negative affect associated with cessation have only been evaluated in very small trials with equivocal results. Russell et al (80) evaluated physical activity (a nine-session walk/jog program) as a relapse prevention strategy. No differences were recorded in the long-term abstinence rates of those in the activity group compared to a discussion control and a no-treatment control group, although the sample size ($n = 42$) may have limited the ability to detect any differences. Of greater concern is that subjects in the physical activity condition reported increased tension-anxiety levels compared to the other two groups. Wynd (99) evaluated relaxation/visual imagery to reduce stress and prevent relapse. Again sample size was small ($n = 76$). Subjects who had participated in a formal smoking cessation program and quit were randomized to an imagery group or a no-treatment control. Subjects in the imagery group were invited to attend three 90-minute booster sessions over a three-month period. Subjects were instructed in deep breathing exercises, progressive muscle relaxation, and imagery practice. Initial results were promising and recorded significantly lower rates of relapse in the imagery group (28%) compared to the control group (49%). Unfortunately, follow-up did not extend beyond the end of treatment, thus long-term compliance and potential impact cannot be evaluated. Both interventions were delivered in a group format and while it is premature to abandon these approaches, issues of compliance and cost-effectiveness of intensive interventions like these must be considered.

CONCLUSIONS AND FUTURE DIRECTIONS

In 1978 researchers identified prevention of relapse following smoking cessation as a major challenge and described as primitive the existing state of knowledge regarding relapse prevention (48, 74). As evidenced in this review, our understanding of the relapse process has increased dramatically during the past 15 years. An extensive body of conceptually based research identified individual and environmental factors that increase the risk of relapse as well as the specific types of situations in which relapse is most likely to occur. Studies of successful quitters have provided detailed descriptions of the types of strategies used to cope successfully with high-risk situations.

Increased understanding of the relapse process allows a core set of intervention components to be devised to prevent relapse. Unfortunately, unequivocal evidence for the effectiveness of such interventions has not emerged from randomized trials. The consensus in the smoking cessation field is that significant advances in the conceptual and empirical understanding of the relapse process have not been matched by major gains in relapse prevention interventions (49, 55). Lack of consistent findings in randomized evaluations of RPT likely result from many factors including different treatment protocols, small sample sizes, and self-selected samples of heavily addicted smokers volunteeering for the studies. Participants may also be overwhelmed by the complexity of relapse prevention training. Virtually all state-of-the-art smoking cessation programs incorporate the basic principles and components of relapse prevention interventions. For example, the National Cancer Institute's manual for physicians, *How to Help Your Patients Stop Smoking* (33), includes sections on debriefing relapses and on special concerns of people who have stopped smoking. Glynn et al (32) include, "specific strategies and exercises for maintenance of nonsmoking, avoiding relapse and recycling in case of initial failure or relapse" as one of three components to be included in any self-help/minimal intervention program. Thus, in recent years it has been difficult to find meaningful comparison programs against which to evaluate relapse prevention programs.

The continued high incidence of relapse following initial smoking cessation suggests the need to shift our attention from relapse *prevention* to relapse *management*. By focusing on smoking cessation as a learning process that involves the acquisition of new skills, the value of relapse prevention interventions may lie in their ability to encourage smokers to recycle through the cessation process more quickly. Our conclusion that relapse is better managed than prevented is not intended to discourage efforts to help smokers quit. It is easy for practitioners and smokers to become overly discouraged in the face of relapse. However, relapse means that a smoker has seriously tried to quit and has had some initial success. Placing relapse in the context of the overall quitting continuum and encouraging smokers to continue their efforts is an important public health goal.

Relapse management fits readily into the public health practice of tobacco control as outlined by Novotny et al (62). Public information campaigns, an integral part of social marketing efforts, could disseminate messages designed to minimize the guilt and discouragement that accompany relapse and to encourage smokers to continue their cessation efforts (see ref. 63). Sustained involvement in quitting smoking will also be facilitated by easy access to smoking cessation resources. Cost-effective minimal interventions can be provided through worksites, healthcare delivery systems, or community groups, and supported by telephone counseling or newsletters (14, 62).

Public health campaigns for tobacco control may also help to prevent relapse. Community-based efforts that strengthen social norms against smoking and legislative restrictions on smoking in public places could reduce relapse by decreasing exposure to high-risk situations and increasing social support for abstinence. Increasing the price of cigarettes through taxation also may discourage ex-smokers from resuming the financial burden of smoking.

Ideally, more intensive efforts to prevent and/or manage relapse will be guided by further research. Additional data on patterns of recycling following relapse and on the timing of long-term relapse are desirable. Much of the currently available data come from relatively small samples of smokers who participated in studies of treatment outcomes. With a shift to population-based evaluations of minimal interventions, such data are available from larger and more representative samples of smokers. The use of standard definitions of cessation and relapse and reporting of relapse and recycling rates as outcomes in future studies of treatment outcomes is recommended. The Behavioral Risk Factor Surveillance System (BRFSS) questionnaire was modified in 1990 to include questions on when, for how long, and how many quit attempts were made during the past year (62). These new data will also provide estimates of relapse and recycling rates. In addition, the BRFSS can be used to test for associations between community-based tobacco control efforts and relapse.

Despite relatively disappointing results to date, we recommend continued development and evaluation of interventions to prevent relapse. Most promising are personalized adjuncts to minimal interventions such as telephone counseling and written personalized feedback. Studies have yet to determine the optimal number and timing of these personalized adjuncts. Population-based data on the timing of relapse and recycling will be helpful. Recent work in the area of motivational interviewing techniques (56) may be particularly useful in developing telephone counseling protocols to encourage recycling after relapse.

Literature Cited

1. Abrams DB, Monti PM, Carey KB, Pinto RP, Jacobus SI. 1988. Reactivity to smoking cues and relapse: Two studies of discriminant validity. *Behav. Res. Ther.* 26(3):223–25

2. Abrams DB, Emmons K, Niaura RD, Goldstein MG, Sherman C. 1991. Tobacco dependence: An integration of individual and public health perspectives. In *The Annual Review of Addic-*

tions Treatment and Research, ed. PE Nathan, JW Langenbucher, BS Mc-Crady, W Frankenstein, 1:391–436. New York, NY: Pergamon

3. Baer JS, Kamarck T, Lichtenstein E, Ransom CC, Jr. 1989. Prediction of smoking relapse: Analyses of temptations and transgressions after initial cessation. *J. Consult. Clin. Psychol.* 57(5):623–27

4. Bandura A. 1986. *Social Foundations of Thoughts and Actions.* Prentice Hall: Englewood Cliff, NJ

5. Bliss RE, Garvey AJ, Heinold JW, Hitchcock JL. 1989. The influence of situation and coping on relapse crisis outcomes after smoking cessation. *J. Consult. Clin. Psychol.* 57(3): 443–49

6. Borland R. 1990. Slip-ups and relapse in attempts to quit smoking. *Addict. Behav.* 15:235–45

7. Brandon TH, Tiffany ST, Obremski KM, Baker TB. 1990. Postcessation cigarette use: The process of relapse. *Addict. Behav.* 15:105–14

8. Brandon TH, Zelman DC, Baker TB. 1987. Effects of maintenance sessions on smoking relapse: Delaying the inevitable? *J. Consult. Clin. Psychol.* 55(5):780–82

9. Deleted in proof

10. Deleted in proof

11. Brownell KD, Marlatt GA, Lichtenstein E, Wilson GT. 1986. Understanding and preventing relapse. *Am. Psychol.* 41(7):765–82

12. Carmody TP. 1992. Preventing relapse in the treatment of nicotine addiction: Current issues and future directions. *J. Psychoact. Drugs* 24(2):131–58

13. Cohen S, Lichtenstein E. 1990. Perceived stress, quitting smoking, and smoking relapse. *Health Psychol.* 9(4): 466–78

14. Curry SJ. 1993. Self-help interventions for smoking cessation. *J. Consult. Clin. Psychol.* 61:790–803

15. Curry SJ, Marlatt GA, Gordon J, Baer JS. 1988. A comparison of alternative theoretical approaches to smoking cessation and relapse. *Health Psychol.* 7(6):545–56

16. Curry SJ, Wagner EH, Cheadle A, Diehr P, Koepsell T, et. al. 1993. Assessment of community-level influences on individuals' attitudes about cigarette smoking, alcohol use and consumption of dietary fat. *Am. J. Prev. Med.* 9:78–84

17. Curry SJ, Wagner EH, Grothaus LC. 1991. Evaluation of intrinsic and extrinsic motivation interventions with a self-help smoking cessation program. *J. Consult. Clin. Psychol.* 59:318–24.

18. Curry S, Marlatt GA. 1985. Unaided quitters' strategies for coping with temptations to smoke. In *Coping and Substance Use,* ed. S Shiffman, TA Wills, 10:243–65. New York, NY: Guilford Press

19. Curry S, Marlatt GA, Gordon JR. 1987. Abstinence violation effect: Validation of an attributional construct with smoking cessation. *J. Consult. Clin. Psychol.* 55:145–49

20. Daughton DM, Roberts D, Patil KD, Rennard SI. 1990. Smoking cessation in the workplace: Evaluation of relapse factors. *Prev. Med.* 19:227–30

21. Davis AL, Faust R, Ordentlich M. 1984. Self-help smoking cessation and maintenance programs: A comparative study with 12-month follow-up by the Am. Lung Association. *Am. J. Public Health* 74:1212–17

22. Deleted in proof

23. Deleted in proof

24. Fielding JE. 1984. Health promotion and disease prevention at the worksite. *Annu. Rev. Public Health.* 5:237–65

25. Fingerhut LA, Kleinman JC, Kendrick JS. 1990. Smoking before during and after pregnancy. *Am. J. Public Health* 80:541–44

26. Fiore MC, Jorenby DE, Baker TB, Kenford SL. 1992. Tobacco dependence and the nicotine patch: Clinical guidelines for effective use. *J. Am. Med. Assoc.* 268:2687–94

27. Fisher KJ, Glasgow RE, Terborg JR. 1989. Worksite smoking cessation: A metaanalysis of long-term quit rates from controlled studies. *J. Occup. Med.* 32:429–39

28. Flay RR. 1987. Mass media and smoking cessation: A critical review. *Am. J. Public Health.* 79:153–60

29. Garvey AJ, Bliss RE, Hitchcock JL, Heinold JW, Rosner B. 1992. Predictors of smoking relapse among self-quitters: A report from the normative aging study. *Addict. Behav.* 17(4):367–77

30. Glasgow RE, Lando H, Hollis J, MCrae SG, La Chance, P-A. 1993. A stop-smoking telephone help line that nobody called. *Am. J. Public Health.* 83(2):252–53

31. Glasgow RE, Lichtenstein E. 1987. Long-term effects of behavioral smoking cessation interventions. *Behav. Ther.* 18:297–324

32. Glynn TJ, Boyd GM, Gruman JC. 1990. Essential elements of self-help minimal intervention strategies for

smoking cessation. *Health Educ. Q.* 17(3):329–45

33. Glynn TJ, Manley MW. 1989. How to help your parents stop smoking. *A National Cancer Institute Manual for Physicians*. NIH Publ. No. 89–3064. Bethesda, MD, US Dep. Health Hum. Serv.

33a. Gossop M, ed. 1989. *Relapse and Addictive Behavior*. New York: Tairstock/Rutledge

34. Gritz ER, St. Jeor ST, Bennett G, Biener L, Blair SN, et al. 1992. National Working Conference on Smoking and Body Weight Task Force 3: Implications with respect to intervention and prevention. *Health Psychol.* 11:17–25 (Suppl.)

35. Gruder CL, Mermelstein RJ, Kirkendol SK, Hedeker D, Wong SC, Schreckengost J, et al. 1993. Effects of social support and relapse prevention training as adjuncts to a televised smoking-cessation intervention. *J. Consult. Clin. Psychol.* 61(1):113–20

36. Haaga DAF, Stewart BL. 1992. Self-efficacy for recovery from a lapse after smoking cessation. *J. Consult. Clin. Psychol.* 60(1):24–28

37. Hall SM, Ginsberg D, Jones RT. 1986. Smoking cessation and weight gain. *J. Consult. Clin. Psychol.* 54:342–46

38. Hall SM, Rugg D, Tunstall C, Jones RT. 1984. Preventing relapse to cigarette smoking by behavioral skill training. *J. Consult. Clin. Psychol.* 52(3): 372–82

39. Hall SM, Tunstall CD, Vila KL, Duffy J. 1992. Weight gain prevention and smoking cessation: Cautionary findings. *Am. J. Public Health* 82(6):799–803

40. Hall SM, Havassy BE, Wasserman D. 1990. Commitment to abstinence and acute stress in relapse to alcohol, opiates and nicotine. *J. Consult. Clin. Psychol.* 58:175–81

41. Hughes JR, Gulliver SB, Fenwick JW, Valliere WA, Cruser K, et al. 1992. Smoking cessation among self-quitters. *Health Psychol.* 11(5):331–34

42. Hughes GH, Hymowitz N, Ockene JN, Simon N, Vogt TM. 1981. The multiple risk factor intervention trial (MRFIT) V. Intervention on smoking. *Prev. Med.* 10:476–500

43. Hunt WA, Barnett LW, Brauch LG. 1971. Relapse rates in addiction programs. *J. Consult. Clin. Psychol.* 27: 455–56

44. Kamarck TW, Lichtenstein E. 1988. Program adherence and coping strategies as predictors of success in a smoking treatment program. *Health Psychol.* 7(6):557–74

45. Killen JD, Fortmann SP, Kraemer HC, Varady A, Newman B. 1992. Who will relapse? Symptoms of nicotine dependence predict long-term relapse after smoking cessation. *J. Consult. Clin. Psychol.* 60(5):797–801

46. Killen JD, Fortmann SP, Newman B, Varady A. 1990. Evaluation of a treatment approach combining nicotine gum with self-guided behavioral treatments for smoking relapse prevention. *J. Consult. Clin. Psychol.* 58(1):85–92

47. Klesges RC, Benowitz NL, Meyers AW. 1991. Behavioral and motivational aspects of smoking and smoking cessation: The problem of post-cessation weight gain. *Behav. Ther.* 22:179–99

48. Lichtenstein E. 1978. Future needs and directions in smoking cessation. In *Progress in Smoking Cessation: Proc. Int. Conf. Smoking Cessation*, June 21–23, ed. J. Schwartz, pp. 386–93. New York: Am. Cancer Soc.

49. Lichtenstein E, Glasgow RE. 1992. Smoking cessation: What have we learned over the past decade. *J. Consult. Clin. Psychol.* 60(4):518–27

50. Lichtenstein E, Wallack L, Pechacek TF. 1990–91. Introduction to the Community Intervention Trial for Smoking Cessation (COMMIT). *Int. Q. Commun. Health Educ.* 11:173–85

51. Marlatt GA, Gordon JR, eds. 1985. *Relapse Prevention: Maintenance Strategies in the Treatment of Addictive Behaviors*. New York: Guilford Press

52. McBride CM, Pirie PL. 1990. Postpartum smoking relapse. *Addict. Behav.* 15:165–68

53. McBride CM, Pirie PL, Curry SJ. 1992. Postpartum relapse to smoking: A prospective study. *Health Educ. Res.* 7(3):381–90

54. Mermelstein RJ, Hedeker D, Wong SC. 1992. *Predictors of recycling in smokers who fail to quit*. Presented at Annu. Conv. Assoc. Adv. Behav. Therapy, 26th, Boston, MA

55. Mermelstein RJ, Karnatz T, Reichmann S. 1992. Smoking. In *Principles and Practice of Relapse Prevention*, ed. PH Wilson, 3:43–68. New York, NY: Guilford Press

56. Miller WR, Rollnick S. 1991. *Motivational Interviewing: Preparing People to Change Addictive Behavior*. New York: Guilford Press

57. Minneker-Hugel E, Unland H, Buchkremer G. 1992. Behavioral relapse

prevention strategies in smoking cessation. *Int. J. Addict.* 27(5):627–34

58. Morgan GD, Ashenberg ZS, Fisher EB, Jr. 1988. Abstinence from smoking and the social environment. *J. Consult. Clin. Psychol.* 56(2):298–301

59. Mullen PD, Quinn VP, Ershoff DH. 1990. Maintenance of nonsmoking postpartum by women who stopped smoking during pregnancy. *Am. J. Public Health* 80:992–94

60. Niaura RS, Abrams DB, DeMuth B, Pinto R, Monti P. 1989. Response to smoking-related stimuli and early relapse to smoking. *Addict. Behav.* 14: 419–28

61. Niaura RS, Rohsenow DJ, Binkoff JA, Monti, PM Pedraza M, Abrams DB. 1988. Relevance of cue reactivity to understanding alcohol and smoking relapse. *J. Abnorm. Psychol.* 97(2):133–52

62. Novotny TE, Fiore MC. 1990. Trends in smoking by age and sex, United States 1974–1987: The implications for disease impact. *Prev. Med.* 19:552–61

63. Novotny TE, Romano RA, Davis RM, Mills SL. 1992. The public health practice of tobacco control: Lessons learned and directions for the states in the 1990s. *Annu. Rev. Public Health* 13:287–318

64. Ockene JK. 1987. Physician delivered interventions for smoking cessation: Strategies for increasing effectiveness. *Prev. Med.* 7:723–37

65. O'Connell KA. 1990. Smoking cessation: Research on relapse crises. *Annu. Rev. Nurs. Res.* 8:83–100

66. O'Connell KA, Martin E.J. 1987. Highly tempting situations associated with abstinence, temporary lapse, and relapse among participants in smoking cessation programs. *J. Consult. Clin. Psychol.* 55(3):367–71

67. Omenn GS, Thompson B, Sexton M, Hessol N, Breitenstein B, et al. 1988. A randomized comparison of worksite-sponsored smoking cessation programs. *Am. J. Prev. Med.* 4(5):261–67

68. Orleans CT, Schoenbach VJ, Wagner EH, Quade D, Salmon MA, et al. 1991. Self-help quit smoking interventions: Effects of self-help materials, social support instructions, and telephone counseling. *J. Consult. Clin. Psychol.* 59(3):439–48

69. Ossip-Klein DJ, Bigelow G, Parker SR, Curry S, Hall S, Kirkland S. 1986. Task Force 1: Classification and assessment of smoking behavior. *Health Psychol.* 5:3–11 (Suppl.)

70. Ossip-Klein DJ, Giovino GA, Megahed N, Black PM, Emont SL, et al. 1991. Effects of a smokers' hotline: Results of a 10-county self-help trial. *J. Consult. Clin. Psychol.* 59(2):325–32

71. Pierce JP, Fiore MC, Novotny TE, Hatziandreu EJ, Davis RM. 1989. Trends in cigarette smoking in the United States. *J. Am. Med. Assoc.* 261:61–65

72. Pierce JP, Hatziandreu E, Flyer P, Hull J, Maklan D, et al. 1990. Tobacco use in 1986: Methods and basic tabulations from the adult use of tobacco services. (NIH Publ. No. 90–2004). Bethesda, MD: US Dep. Health Hum. Serv.

73. Pirie PL, McBride CM, Hellerstedt W, Jeffery RW, Hatsukami D, et al. 1992. Smoking cessation in women concerned about weight. *Am. J. Public Health* 82(9):1238–43

74. Pomerleau OF, Adkins D, Pertschuck M. 1978. Predictors of outcome and recidivism in smoking cessation treatment. *Addict. Behav.* 3:65–70

75. Deleted in proof

76. Prochaska JO, DiClemente CC. 1983. Stages and processes of self-change of smoking. Toward an integrative model of change. *J. Consult. Clin. Psychol.* 51:390–95

77. Prochaska JO, DiClemente CC, Norcross JC. 1992. In search of how people change: Applications to addictive behaviors. *Am. Psycholog.* 47: 1102–14

78. Prochaska JO, DiClemente CC, Velicer WF, Rossi JS. 1993. Standardized, individualized, interactive and personalized: Self-help programs for smoking cessation. *Health Psychol.* 12:399–405

79. Rand CS, Stitzer ML, Bigelow GE, Mead AM. 1989. The effects of contingent payment and frequent workplace monitoring on smoking abstinence. *Addict. Behav.* 14:121–28

80. Russell PO, Epstein LH, Johnston JJ, Block DR, Blair E. 1988. The effects of physical activity as maintenance for smoking cessation. *Addict. Behav.* 13: 215–18

81. Salive ME, Cornoni-Huntley J, La-Croix AZ, Ostfeld AM, Wallace RB, Hennekens CH. 1992. Predictors of smoking cessation and relapse in older adults. *Am. J. Public Health.* 82(9): 1268–71

82. Schwartz JL. 1987. *Review and Evaluation of Smoking Cessation Methods: The United States and Canada, 1978–1985.* (NIH Publ. No. 87–2940). Bethesda, MD, US Dep. Health Hum. Serv.

83. Scott RR, Prue DM, Denier CA, King AC. 1986. Worksite smoking intervention with nursing professionals: Long-term outcome and relapse assessment. *J. Consult. Clin. Psychol.* 54(6):809–13

84. Shiffman S. 1982. Relapse following smoking cessation: A situational analysis. *J. Consult. Clin. Psychol.* 50:71–86

85. Shiffman S. 1984. Coping with temptations to smoke. *J. Consult. Clin. Psychol.* 52:261–267

86. Shiffman S. 1986. A cluster-analytic typology of smoking relapse reports. *Addict. Behav.* 11:295–307

87. Shiffman S. 1989. Conceptual issues in the study of relapse. See Ref. 33a, pp. 149–79

88. Shumaker SA, Grunberg NE, eds. 1986. *Proc. Natl. Work. Conf. Smoking Relapse: Health Psychol.* 5 (Suppl.)

89. Simon JA, Browner WS, Mangano DT. 1992. Predictors of smoking relapse after noncardiac surgery. *Am. J. Public Health* 82(9):1235–37

90. Sloan RP, Dimberg L, Welkowitz LA, Kristiansen MA. 1990. Cessation and relapse in a year-long workplace quit-smoking contest. *Prev. Med.* 19:414–23

91. Deleted in proof

92. Stevens VJ, Hollis JF. 1989. Preventing smoking relapse, using an individually tailored skills-training technique. *J. Consult. Clin. Psychol.* 57(3):420–24

93. Sutton S. 1989. Relapse following smoking cessation: A critical review of current theory and research. See Ref. 33a, pp. 41–72

94. Swan GE, Denk CE, Parker SD, Carmelli D, Furze CT, Rosenman RH. 1988. Risk factors for late relapse in male and female ex-smokers. *Addict. Behav.* 13:253–66

95. US Dep. Health Hum. Serv. 1990. *The Health Benefits of Smoking Cessation.* US Dep. Health Hum. Serv., Public Health Serv., CDC, Cent. Chronic Dis. Prev. Health Promot., Off. Smoking Health. DHHS Publ. No. (CDC) 90–8416

96. Weiner B. 1974. *Achievement Motivation and Attribution Theory.* Morristown, NJ: General Learning Press

97. Wewers ME. 1988. The role of postcessation factors in tobacco abstinence: Stressful events and coping responses. *Addict. Behav.* 13:297–302

98. Wojcik JV. 1988. Social learning predictors of the avoidance of smoking relapse. *Addict. Behav.* 13:177–80

99. Wynd CA. 1992. Relaxation imagery used for stress reduction in the prevention of smoking relapse. *J. Adv. Nurs.* 17:294–302

100. Yates AJ, Thain J. 1985. Self-efficacy as a predictor of relapse following voluntary cessation of smoking. *Addict. Behav.* 10:291–98

Annu. Rev. Public Health. 1994. 15:367–79

CHILD ABUSE

Andrea M. Vandeven and Eli H. Newberger

Children's Hospital, 300 Longwood Ave, Boston, Massachusetts; Department of
Pediatrics, Harvard Medical School, Boston, Massachusetts, 02115

KEY WORDS;   child physical abuse, child sexual abuse,

HISTORICAL CONTEXT

Although child abuse has been documented through human history, it is a
problem that has only intermittently entered public discourse. The publication
in 1962 of an article entitled "The Battered Child Syndrome" by C. Henry
Kempe, a prominent academic pediatrician, and his colleagues (34) provoked
a new era of concern for child abuse victims in the United States and
stimulated the development of county, state, and federal programs to assure
their protection. Kempe and others promoted the notion that child abuse
could be treated effectively if it were systematically diagnosed by physicians
alerted to the outlines of the "syndrome," and if cases were reported to
mandated authorities. Legally requiring physicians to make such reports was
the concept at the core of child abuse reporting laws proposed in the early
1960s. By 1968 such laws were adopted in every state (25).

Experience suggests that this medicalized model of child abuse, which
reformulated a social condition in terms of medical symptoms, diagnosis,
and treatment, has been inadequate to the tasks of identifying cases and
protecting victims (14, 42). Physician response to child abuse and neglect
is variable, with the social status and race of the child and the nature of
the practice setting (public or private) influencing the actions of medical
practice as much as the particular injury to the child (29). Moreover, the
rudimentary comprehension of the etiology of child abuse, driven by overly
simple conceptual models and a paucity of methodologically rigorous research, has served poorly to guide the development of clinical practice and
social policy. Initial theorizing about child abuse placed heavy emphasis on
the posited psychopathology of parents, and a series of uncontrolled clinical

367

0163-7525/94/0510-0367$05.00

studies supported the formulation. Notwithstanding the yield of subsequent controlled studies, which indicate that the prevalence of psychiatric disturbance is no greater than in comparison groups, the orientation of child protection agencies and workers remains toward talking cures and the threat of child placement if the "treatment" is rejected or ineffective. Research, and more tellingly, clinical practice, have demonstrated the great complexity of child abuse, a phenomenon with multiple causes and manifestations that by its nature demands a more fully dimensionalized, public health approach.

EPIDEMIOLOGY

Definitions of child abuse have expanded over the years from an initial focus on physical injuries inflicted by care-givers to today's broader conceptualization, which includes sexual victimization of children, neglect and emotional abuse, and the denial of life support to severely handicapped children, especially newborns. In practice, the decision to call an event abusive is to some extent a judgment call, as there are frequently gray areas where the definition is influenced by the professional's own biases.

Attempts to establish the incidence and prevalence of child abuse and neglect have been hampered by multiple methodologic problems, not least of which are related to the variety and inconsistency of definitions. Very often, the contingencies of the data source determine the operational definition, for example, as when data are collected from child welfare rolls of "confirmed" or substantiated cases of physical abuse. Such cases typically represent the most severe and unequivocal cases of abuse, and counting only such cases may seriously underestimate the actual incidence of abuse, with many cases screened out as "accidents" or as representing artifacts of "excessive discipline." Reports of child abuse are not equivalent to incidents of child abuse. Epidemiologic data on sexual abuse are vulnerable to misinterpretation because case reports are often based on the subjective interpretation of clinical and behavioral data. Unlike physical abuse, seldom in these cases is there a physical symptom or finding such as a bruise or broken bone.

Despite these problems, for the purposes of this discussion it is useful to consider some of the more systematic estimates of prevalence and incidence, most of which are based on survey data and case reports. Gil measured the incidence of physical child abuse in two ways in the late 1960s (26). Based on a survey of a national probability sample, he estimated that there were between 2.5 and 4 million cases per year. He also assembled and analyzed all US case reports in 1967 and 1968. Here, by contrast, the yearly prevalence was only 6 to 7 thousand per year, suggesting substantial under-reporting and biases favoring the reporting of poor people and members of racial and cultural minorities. Because government funding goes principally to support protective social services, and because resources in the child protection field have been so meager relative to the needs, there has been an extremely limited commitment of funding for measurement and research (41).

Straus, Gelles & Steinmetz collaborated on the first nationally representative survey of violence in American families, which used a scale to measure the techniques family members used to resolve conflicts among themselves (49). (Child neglect and sexual victimization were not included in their definition of family violence.) From parents' own reports of violence toward their children they estimated a prevalence of physical abuse in 1975 of 1.5 million children aged 3 to 17 years. Their 1985 re-survey, which employed telephone rather than face-to-face interviews, suggested a 47 percent decline in abuse prevalence, or approximately 800,000 cases in the year (24). The authors note that some of the decline is explained by the exclusion of families without telephones (because families without telephones may be more isolated and economically disadvantaged, both risk factors for abuse). In 1985 there may have been greater sensitivity to talking about violence; this could discourage parents from discussing events in 1985 that would have been disclosed in 1975. Although the authors argue that their data do indeed represent an actual decline in violence directed at children, in the interval 1975–1985, another set of surveys, conducted by Westat, Inc. for the National Center on Child Abuse and Neglect in the Department of Health and Human Services, suggests an increase in the prevalence and incidence of child abuse and neglect (39, 40). These studies, however, also employ different definitions and measure the frequency of events discerned by various professional and institutional observers in an attempt to plumb the depths and dimensions of the metaphorical iceberg of abuse. To illustrate the extent to which the politics of victimization affect the methods of its measurement, it is worth noting that the Reagan administration rejected use of a methodology that would allow comparison of the NCCAN data with the studies by Straus, Gelles & Steinmetz. Also, when the findings of an increase in prevalence were submitted to the sponsoring agency, they were embargoed. It took a lawsuit under the Freedom of Information Act to force D.H.H.S. to release the data (W Howard, personal communication). It was widely believed by experts in the field that the government did not want to measure an increase in abuse that might be attributed to cuts in social welfare spending and which would embarrass the Reagan administration.

With regard to the prevalence of child sexual abuse, the second National Incidence Study, using as a basis official case reports, projected 155,900 new cases of sexual abuse for 1986 (36). As with physical abuse, official case reports always indicate lower prevalence estimates than estimates based on community surveys. The widely divergent estimates of prevalence, of between 6% and 62% for women and 2% to 15% for men (20), derive from variations in definition and sampling methodology similar to those found in the efforts to measure physical family violence and child neglect. The methodological issues have been discerningly reviewed by Finkelhor (20). A narrow definition and rigorous sampling techniques were used by Siegel and coworkers, who derived an overall prevalence of child sexual abuse of 6.8% for women and 3.8% for men using survey data from a community-based population study on mental health (47). The higher prevalence estimates in other reports derive from broader definitions of sexual abuse, including, for example, sexual coercion in dating, and from sampling techniques that may be weighted toward finding victims, such as clinically derived samples. Feldman and colleagues have also recently contributed a critical analysis of published child sexual abuse prevalence studies, and conclude that the apparent increase in prevalence, particularly in the number of case reports, can be attributed to changes in reporting laws and a social climate of increased awareness (18).

RISK FACTORS FOR CHILD ABUSE AND NEGLECT: A Problematic Knowledge Base

Much of the research into the causes of child abuse and neglect is of dubious merit, limited by numerous methodologic inadequacies. Most of the clinical literature is composed of uncontrolled studies drawn from clinical settings. Systematic biases limit the value of many of the more rigorous studies that examine risk factors believed to be associated with abuse. Because of the costs and logistical problems of conducting prospective investigations, many studies rely on case-control or cross-sectional designs, methods that are arguably most susceptible to bias (36). Unfortunately, these types of studies have led to the assignment of a causative role for many putative risk factors, when in fact there is scant rigorous evidence to that effect and only an association can be demonstrated. For example, it is widely assumed that parental substance abuse and alcoholism can "cause" child abuse, with these posited causal variables mediated through "poor parenting." Bays, in a recent critical review of the literature on the association between child abuse and alcohol and substance abuse, noted many studies purporting to show high rates of substance abuse and alcoholism in abusing or neglecting families. However, we are far from being able to discern a causative link, since most of the studies are so confounded by other possible risk factors (4).

More recently, well-designed longitudinal studies have been published which examine putative risk factors more rigorously. Steir and associates studied the contribution of young maternal age to the risk for child abuse

(48). Medical records of a cohort of children born to teenage mothers were reviewed and compared with those of demographically similar children born to older mothers. Artifacts of physical abuse, neglect, and sexual abuse were identified. From the data in this well-controlled study, the authors conclude that children of teen mothers are at greater risk for all forms of maltreatment. Another commonly studied parental factor thought to contribute to child maltreatment is a history of child abuse in the offending parent. In their review, Kaufman & Zigler summarized the available studies considering the intergenerational "transmission" of child abuse, including at least two prospective studies. They estimate that the rate of abuse in families where the parents were themselves abused as children is approximately six times higher than the rate in the general population (33). Notwithstanding the widely persistent belief that abusive parents are mentally ill, there appears to be no convincing evidence for specific personality traits or markers that can be construed as causally related to later child abuse (52).

With regard to causal factors associated with the children themselves, a prospective study of high-risk mothers found no higher rate of child maltreatment among those children born prematurely (15). Children with disabilities have also been thought to be at higher risk for abuse, but in a review, White et al report that there is insufficient evidence to support the notion that physical disability, in and of itself, is a risk factor for abuse (50).

Zigler & Hall provide a clear overview of the evolution in conceptualiztion of the etiology of child abuse (54). There exist many "unitary" theories (psychoanalytic, cognitive-developmental, attachment, and social learning theories, for example), which seek to explain child abuse from a single point of view (41). Although support may be found for any particular theory, it has become clear that no single theory is, in and of itself, sufficient to organize and explain the complex processes of etiology and behavioral and symptom manifestation. Further complicating the attempt to tease out the most salient factors in child maltreatment is the tendency for many of these factors to aggregate, e.g. young maternal age with poor educational attainment and poverty. Without large, population-based studies permitting the statistical controlling of several factors simultaneously, it is often difficult to do more than speculate about the discrete contributions of one or another factor.

Some theorists have proposed that rather than any one particular factor "causing" child maltreatment, it takes a convergence of risks to produce the circumstances propitious to abuse. Antecedents of personal and family stress are of special interest and importance. Among these are large family size (26, 54, 55), single parent status (23, 26), family conflict (28, 30), social isolation (43), and poverty (27, 44), all of which have been clearly shown to be associated with risk of abuse. But it is perhaps overly reductionistic to attribute child abuse to stress on families. Most workers in the field, particularly clinicians, are impressed with the numerous life-contextual factors that appear to contribute to child abuse. Clinicians are uniquely well situated to appreciate the interaction between, say, the stress on a parent and and the special qualities of a particular child who may live in a burdensome and isolating environment. A multifactorial conceptualization of the etiology of child abuse has been described usefully by Belsky (7), building on the "ecological" theory of child development proposed by the psychologist Urie Bronfenbrenner (9).

In this framework, a child (who is posited somehow to be vulnerable or provocative) and parent are seen as embedded in a social environment that may promote child abuse (45). This concept has expanded in the ecological model to include the family's neighborhood as a context for child maltreatment (22, 56). The family's community influences child rearing through its social networks, which provide social and emotional support, and the promotion of group values and behaviors. Thinking of abuse "ecologically" can promote a comprehension of the connections among various factors: for example, the social isolation of an impoverished single mother who may live in a neighborhood beset with high crime, where overt acts of violence are frequent. How can one disentangle these inter-related issues to come to identify the cause of child abuse in this family? While it may seem intuitively right to posit that such factors as poverty, social isolation, spousal abuse, and parental history of child abuse contribute to creating an environment conducive to child abuse, the process—and the abuse—is not inevitable. At this stage, attempts to test the ecological theory are just beginning, and the published studies are often difficult to compare because of the different samples, abuse definitions, and measured variables. As an example of one such study, Zuravin examined economic and social support factors in Baltimore (56) and found that in comparing particular neighborhoods, higher rates of abuse and neglect were independently associated with higher rates of poverty and vacant housing, and with families living in single dwellings. For further discussion of the evidence linking various factors to physical child abuse, the reader is directed to several recent reviews (2, 10, 46).

The sexual abuse of children is understood by workers in the field as primarily an expression of distorted power relationships, as opposed to a symptom of adult psychological disturbance, although sexual deviancy has been found frequently in offenders. Most offenders are male, and many have themselves suffered sexual victimization in childhood (19). Their offending behavior can be understood as an injurious way of coping with residual feeling of powerlessness and personal inadequacy. In many troubled families there may be multiple forms of victimization, e.g. child physical and sexual abuse and spouse abuse: one must have the conceptual and practical tools to understand, measure, and address the interaction of multiple contributing risk factors.

SEQUELAE OF ABUSE

Child homicide is the most dramatic outcome of child abuse. It represents one of the five leading causes of death for children between the ages of 1 and 18 years (12). Infant homicides are not always accurately identified, and are probably underreported (31, 32). Physically abused children are frequently quite seriously injured, and they may suffer permanent disability, affecting every organ system. The financial burden of their subsequent medical care is almost surely immense, especially if they suffer neurologic damage, although to our knowledge such costs have never been systematically measured. Although permanent physical damage after sexual abuse occurs in a minority of cases, sexually transmitted infections, including AIDS, have been documented to result.

Perhaps far greater social significance attaches to the developmental and psychosocial sequelae of child abuse, particularly in cases where abuse remains undetected or ignored, and as a result, unaddressed. Although much of the data have come from uncontrolled or poorly designed studies, it is increasingly evident that very many children who have been the victims of abuse appear to be burdened with social, emotional, and cognitive disabilities. These include a tendency to aggression in adolescence, a propensity to use violence toward intimates, language disorders, and lower performance on standardized tests of intelligence (1, 17, 35, 37, 51). For example, using a longitudinal study design, Widom examined a cohort of children identified as abuse victims from 20 years previously, tracing the subsequent adult criminal arrest records of these individuals (51). Compared with nonabused children, abused and neglected children were at greater risk for arrest as juvenile offenders and as adult offenders, and they were far more likely to be arrested for violent offenses. Although Widom controlled carefully for age, sex, and race, there were few children from the higher socioeconomic groups present in the original child abuse cohort. Results of similar follow-up studies must be viewed critically, however, as the majority of subjects came from impoverished families, and it is difficult to separate the effects of abuse and neglect from the developmental consequences associated with growing up poor (16).

Evidence has begun to accumulate on the pervasive impact of childhood sexual abuse. Beitchman and colleagues reviewed critically the literature regarding both short- and long-term consequences of child sexual abuse (5, 6). In formulating the effects in childhood, they acknowledge that it is almost impossible to separate the specific impacts of sexual abuse from the consequences of living in a home environment characterized by high rates of parental deviancy and family breakdown. In studies focusing on adolescents, the authors noted frequent reports of promiscuity and sexual dissatisfaction, as well as destructive "acting out" behaviors in both boys and girls. Long-term effects in women who report a history of childhood sexual abuse include greater rates of depression and suicidal ideation and behavior, and psychosomatic disturbances. Further, these women appear increasingly vulnerable to revictimization, including rape and spousal abuse. However, the authors believe there is insufficient evidence to discern a consistent relationship between childhood sexual abuse and the later development of such psychiatric disorders as multiple personality disturbance or borderline personality disorder. There is, unfortunately, only a small corpus of data on the long-term effects in men. What students of sexual abuse have characterized as the "second order" effects can be particularly burdensome and costly. Evidence is accumulating that childhood sexual abuse may contribute to adolescent drug use and teen pregnancy (8), and to the high-risk behavior that predisposes the adult to HIV exposure (53).

INTERVENTIONS AND PREVENTION

The discussion of the response to child abuse can most conveniently be divided between those activities called into play when abuse is discovered, and those intended to prevent the occurrence of child abuse in the first place. There has been much effort made to teach those professionals who deal with children how to detect child abuse, and what to do once it is suspected. These endeavors include articles and seminars directed at practicing physicians who may occupy influential positions to intervene in abusive situations. Until relatively recently there has been a reluctance within organized medicine to become involved in the area of family violence, but this attitude has evolved impressively, as can be seen from the proclaimed support by state and local medical societies of more activist stands on behalf of victims.

Once cases of child abuse are recognized, in most instances physicians and professionals who work with children are mandated to report the families to state child protective services. There is a long history of involvement of child welfare personnel in the affairs of so-called troubled families, and it is on this tradition that much of the states' actions rest. Though the intervention should in theory include a balanced mix of counseling and family support services, with removal of the child from the family only as a "last resort," child protective services are seriously overburdened in both the number and complexity of cases they are required to follow. Decisions must often be made quickly and expediently, and there are situations where, for want of services to assist the family, children are removed to foster or institutional care. In addition, many child welfare services have not kept pace with current research into the causes and consequences of child abuse, with the result that protective decisions are at times made on the basis of outmoded stereotypes and assumptions that may in fact be irrelevant to the needs of the child and his or her family. Nuanced evaluations weighing the protection of the child within the context of family preservation are at times beyond the capacity of child welfare workers; instead, a false dichotomy may be created where the child's needs and rights are pitted against those of the parents.

A further complicating factor is the criminalization of child abuse. In the face of diminished resources and a broad pessimism in the Reagan-Bush years toward social welfare programs, the legal system has increasingly served to drive child welfare and medical workers to gather evidence to sustain prosecutions, rather than to assess individual family situations and offer services to promote the child's and family's protection and welfare. Often, the mandate and evidentiary needs of the law enforcement community prosecuting the case do not converge with the needs of the child and family. Even attempts to streamline the assessment of child abuse cases, involving child psychologists, social workers, and prosecutors in simultaneous evaluations, often stumble because of differences in professional approach and institutional purpose.

Published reports of initiatives aimed at the primary prevention of child maltreatment have recently been systematically reviewed by MacMillan and colleagues (38). Screening a population as to risk of future child abuse offers the potential for early detection or perhaps prevention. Efforts to screen families for risk of future child abuse have been hampered by our fundamental inability to define those factors most relevant in the causation of child maltreatment. Further, there is distinct harm associated with the mislabeling of families as potential child abusers. Interventions that aim to prevent child abuse generally fall into one of two categories: perinatal and early childhood support and visitation programs, and education programs for children, parents, and teachers. In summarizing the studies that have looked at home visitation, MacMillan and colleagues report that there is good evidence to support home visitation by specially educated community women or by public health nurses to families characterized by teen or single parenthood. The best programs were flexible enough to allow the workers to respond to family crises and generally support the parent, as well as educating the parent in child-care skills. Adequate medical and social service backup was an added requirement, although intensive contact with a hospital or pediatrician was not necessary. Added research is needed to determine which elements of the program are most effective, and for which populations, as well as defining the duration and frequency of the home visits.

Finally, the authors consider education programs, based primarily in the schools and focused on children, with special attention to prevention of sexual abuse and abduction (38). Although several studies suggest that education programs significantly increase the knowledge base of the targeted children, behavioral outcomes have been less adequately measured. We are only beginning to examine whether such programs actually reduce the prevalence of sexual abuse, although certainly many children have disclosed their previous or current victimizations after being exposed to these programs. In a recent telephone survey of a nationally representative sample of 2000 children aged 10 to 16 and their caretakers, Finkelhor found that children who had participated in the most comprehensive programs were more likely to use the strategies such as saying no or running away when placed in a situation of potential abuse (21). These children were also more likely to report actual or attempted abuse. The best programs embedded sexual abuse prevention into more broad-based efforts emphasizing self-assertiveness and social skills, and included parent participation.

Cost-effectiveness research in the prevention of child maltreatment is only in the earliest stages: we are only now rigorously evaluating the effectiveness of many programs, a necessary first step to cost-effectiveness analysis. What few studies there are tend to be methodologically flawed. In his recent review of the available data, Dubowitz reports that home health visitors, lay group counseling, and family and group therapy appear to be worthwhile interventions (13).

THE PUBLIC HEALTH APPROACH TO CHILD ABUSE

It is becoming increasingly clear that the issues underlying child maltreatment are convergent with many of the most vexing current concerns of public health workers. Community violence, drug and alcohol misuse, HIV transmission, and high-risk behaviors—all appear to play a role in the phenomenon of child abuse and its consequences. If in the effort to improve preventive and therapeutic services to children and their families we can revise our etiological taxonomy and move beyond the simplistic notions of disturbed perpetrator and helpless victim, the child protection field will contribute strategies that will be collaborative and embracive, and efforts to reform current practice will dovetail with other informed public health initiatives (3). With regard to research, much is known about what we need to know and how we should address the task, even in the difficult and ambiguous area of child abuse (36). Among the topics of greatest interest are the impacts of victimization, and the relationship among the personal, family, and community antecedents of abuse. The forthcoming report of the NIH Panel on Research on Anti-Social, Aggressive and Violence-Related Behaviors and Their Consequences contains useful recommendations on a panoply of related issues: research topics and theoretical orientation, methods, ethics, and the application of findings in programs and policies.

Appropriate support and cooperation of the agencies that provide services to victims will also be needed to enable the collection of better data, competently to assess community needs, and to measure the effectiveness of interventions, both those aimed specifically at child abuse and those with implications for abuse prevalence and risk that focus more broadly on other public health risks. We look forward to more prospective longitudinal studies that allow the evaluation of the complex web of interacting risk factors, and, most especially, those studies that attempt to discern influences which promote resiliency in those "at risk" families that seem to avoid child maltreatment. Lastly, there is an urgent need for more systematic appraisal of the financial costs and benefits of alternative approaches to child protection, in order better to allocate resources to this salient, visible, but poorly understood public health problem (11, 13).

Any *Annual Review* chapter, as well as any article cited in an *Annual Review* chapter, may be purchased from the Annual Reviews Preprints and Reprints service. 1-800-347-8007; 415-259-5017; email: arpr@class.org

Literature Cited

1. Aber JL, Allen JP, Carlson V, Cicchetti D. 1989. The effects of maltreatment on development during early childhood: recent studies and their theoretical, clinical, and policy implications. See Ref. 10, pp. 579–619

2. Ammerman RT, Hersen M, eds. 1990. *Children at Risk: An Evaluation of Factors Contributing to Child Abuse and Neglect.* New York: Plenum

3. Barber-Madden R, Cohn AH, Schloesser P. 1988. Prevention of child abuse: a public health agenda. *J. Public Health Policy* 9:167–76

4. Bays J. 1990. Substance abuse and child abuse: impact of addiction on the child. *Pediatr. Clin. North Am.* 37:881–904

5. Beitchman JH, Zucker KJ, Hood JE, DaCosta GA, Akman D. 1991. A review of short-term effects of child sexual abuse. *Child Abuse Negl.* 15: 537–64

6. Beitchman JH, Zucker KJ, Hood JE, DaCosta GA, Akman D, Cassavia E. 1992. A review of the long-term effects of child sexual abuse. *Child Abuse Negl.* 16:101–18

7. Belsky J. 1980. Child maltreatment: an ecological integration. *Am. Psychol.* 35:320–35

8. Boyer D, Fine D. 1992. Sexual abuse as a factor in adolescent pregnancy and child maltreatment. *Fam. Plann. Perspect.* 24:4–11

9. Bronfenbrenner U. 1979. *The Ecology of Human Development.* Cambridge, MA: Harvard Univ. Press

10. Cicchetti D, Carlson V, eds. 1989. *Child Maltreatment: Theory and Research on the Causes and Consequences of Child Abuse and Neglect.* Cambridge/New York: Cambridge Univ. Press

11. Daro D. 1988. *Confronting Child Abuse: Research for Effective Program Design.* New York: Free Press

12. Div. Injury Control, CDC. 1990.

Childhood injuries in the United States. *Am. J. Dis. Child* 144:627–46

13. Dubowitz H. 1990. Costs and effectiveness of interventions in child maltreatment. *Child Abuse Negl.* 14: 177–86

14. Dubowitz H, Newberger EH. 1989. Pediatrics and child abuse. See Ref. 10, pp. 76–94

15. Egeland B, Brunnquell D. 1979. An at-risk approach to the study of child abuse: Some preliminary findings. *J. Am. Acad. Child Psychiatry* 18:219–35

16. Elmer E. 1977. A follow-up study of traumatized children. *Pediatrics* 59: 273–79

17. Erickson MF, Egeland B, Pianta R. 1989. The effects of maltreatment on the development of young children. See Ref 10, pp. 647–84

18. Feldman W, Feldman E, Goodman JT, McGrath PJ, Pless RP, et al. 1991. Is childhood sexual abuse really increasing in prevalence? An analysis of the evidence. *Pediatrics* 88:29–33

19. Finkelhor D. 1987, The sexual abuse of children: current research reviewed. *Pediatr. Ann.* 17:233–41

20. Finkelhor D. 1991. Child sexual abuse. See Ref. 10, pp. 79–94

21. Finkelhor D. 1994. Victimization prevention training in action: A national survey of children's experiences coping with actual threats and assaults. *Am. J. Public Health.* Submitted

22. Garbarino J. 1977. The human ecology of child maltreatment: a conceptual model for research. *J. Marriage Fam.* 39:721–501

23. Gelles RJ. 1989. Child abuse and violence in single-parent families: Parent absence and economic deprivation. *Am. J. Orthopsychiatry* 59: 492–501

24. Gelles RJ, Straus MA. 1988. *Intimate Violence. New York: Simon & Schuster*

25. Gershenson CP. 1979. Child maltreatment and the federal role. In *Child Abuse and Violence*, ed. DG Gil, pp. 18–36

26. Gil DG. 1970. *Violence Against Children: Physical Abuse in the United States*. Cambridge, MA: Harvard Univ. Press

27. Gil DG. 1977. Child Abuse; Levels of manifestation, causal dimension, and primary prevention. *Victimol. Int. J.* 2:186–94

28. Gruber K, Jones R. 1983. Identifying determinants of risk of sexual victimization of youth. *Child Abuse Negl.* 7:17–24

29. Hampton RL, Newberger EH. 1985. Child abuse incidence and reporting by hospitals: significance of severity, class, and race. *Am. J. Public Health* 75:56–60

30. Herrenkohl RC, Herrenkohl EC. 1985. Some antecedents and developmental consequences of child maltreatment. In *New Directions for Child Development: Developmental Perspectives on Child Maltreatment,* ed. R Rizley, D Cicchetti, pp. 57–76. San Francisco: Jossey-Bass

31. Jason J, Carpenter M, Tyler CW. 1983. Under-reporting of infant homicide in the United States. *Am. J. Public Health* 73:195–97

32. Jason J, Gilliand JC, Tyler CW. 1983. Homicide as a cause of pediatric mortality in the United States. *Pediatrics* 72:19111–93

33. Kaufman J, Zigler E. 1989. The intergenerational transmission of child abuse. See Ref. 10, pp. 129–50

34. Kempe CH, Silverman FN, Steele BF, Droegemueller W, Silver HK. 1962. The battered child syndrome. *J. Am. Med. Assoc.* 181:17–24

35. Kinnard EM. 1980. Emotional development in physically abused children. *Am. J. Orthopsychiatry* 50:686–96

36. Leventhal JM. 1982. Research strategies and methodologic standards in studies of risk factors for child abuse. *Child Abuse Negl.* 6:113–23

37. Lynch MA, Roberts R. 1982. *Consequences of Child Abuse.* New York: Academic

38. MacMillan HL, MacMillan JH, Offord DR. 1993. Periodic health examination, 1993 update: 1. Primary prevention of child maltreatment. The Canadian Task Force on the Periodic Health Examination. *Can. Med. Assoc. J.* 148:151–63

39. Natl. Cent. Child Abuse Negl. 1981. *National Study of the Incidence and Severity of Child Abuse and Neglect.* Washington, DC: DHHS

40. Natl. Cent. Child Abuse Negl. 1988. *Study Findings: Study of the National Incidence and Severity of Child Abuse and Neglect.* Washington, DC: DHHS

41. Newberger EH. 1991. Child abuse. See Ref. 46, pp. 51–78

42. Newberger EH, Bourne R. 1978. The medicalization and legalization of child abuse. *Am. J. Orthopsychiatry* 48:593–607

43. Newberger EH, Reed RB, Daniel JH, Hyde JN, Kotelchuck M. 1977. Pediatric social illness: toward an etiologic classification. *Pediatrics* 60:178–85

44. Pelton LH. 1978. Child abuse and

neglect. The myth of classlessness. *Am. J. Orthopsychiatry* 48:608–17

45. Pianta B. 1984. Antecedents of child abuse. Single and multiple factor models. *School Psychol. Int.* 5:151–60

46. Rosenberg ML, Fenley MA, eds. 1991. *Violence in America: A Public Health Approach.* New York/Oxford: Oxford Univ. Press

47. Siegel JM, Sorenson SB, Golding JM, Burnam MA, Stein JA. 1987. The prevalence of childhood sexual assault. The Los Angeles Epidemiologic Catchment Area Project. *Am. J. Epidemiol.* 126:1141–53

48. Steir DM, Leventhal JM, Berg AT, Johnson L, Mezger J. 1993. Are children born to young mothers at increased risk of maltreatment? *Pediatrics* 91: 642–48

49. Straus MA, Gelles RJ, Steinmetz SK. 1980. *Behind Closed Doors: Violence in the American Family.* New York: Doubleday

50. White R, Benedict MI, Wulf L, Kelley M. 1987. Physical disabilities as risk factors for child maltreatment: A selected review. *Am. J. Orthopsychiatry* 57:93–101

51. Widom CS. 1989. The cycle of violence. *Science* 244:160–66

52. Wolfe DA. 1985. Child-abusive parents: An empirical review and analysis. *Psychol. Bull.* 97:462–82

53. Zierler S, Feingold L, Laufer D, Velentgas P, Kantrowitz-Gordon I, Mayer K. 1991. Adult survivors of childhood sexual abuse and subsequent risk of HIV infection. *Am. J. Public Health* 81:572–75

54. Zigler E, Hall NW. 1989. Physical child abuse in America: past, present and future. See Ref. 10, pp. 38–75

55. Zuravin SJ. 1987. Child maltreatment and teenage first births: A relationship mediated by chronic sociodemographic stress. *Am. J. Orthopsychiatry* 58:91–103

56. Zuravin SJ. 1989. The ecology of child abuse and neglect: Review of the literature and presentation of data. *Violence Vict.* 4:101–20

Annu. Rev. Public Health. 1994. 15:381–411

JOB STRAIN AND CARDIOVASCULAR DISEASE

Peter L. Schnall and Paul A. Landsbergis

Cardiovascular and Hypertension Center, New York Hospital-Cornell University Medical College, New York, NY 10021

Dean Baker

Occupational Health Center, University of California Irvine, Irvine, California 92717

KEY WORDS: stress, work, hypertension, heart disease

INTRODUCTION

Cardiovascular disease (CVD) is the leading cause of death in the United States, accounting for 43 percent of all deaths (7). Essential hypertension affects as many as 50 million Americans (85). Cigarette smoking, serum cholesterol, hypertension, physical inactivity, overweight, and diabetes have been identified as risk factors for CVD, but the causes of essential hypertension are still poorly understood.

Several research traditions have implicated psychosocial stress as a potential risk factor for CVD. Various models focus on personal characteristics such as Type A behavior (94) or hostility (22, 24, 120), or environmental stressors such as lower socioeconomic status (SES) (15, 78, 92), unemployment (13), or social isolation (20, 43). The literature on occupational stress has been dominated by two perspectives, the person-environment (P-E) fit model (16) and Karasek's job demands-control or "job strain" model (52, 58). While the P-E fit model "focuses on the interaction between the individual and the environment" (9), the job strain model focuses on objective features of the work environment that can trigger disease. In 1985, Baker evaluated the evidence for these two models and concluded that the job strain model has greater "predictive power" than that of the P-E fit

381

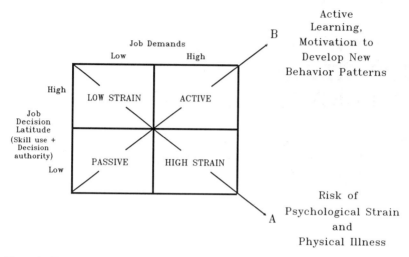

Figure 1   Karasek job strain model.

model (9). Many subsequent studies have tested the job strain model. It is now appropriate to evaluate this decade of research and provide recommendations for future investigations.

Karasek defines job strain (Figure 1) as jobs characterized by high "psychological workload demands" combined with low "decision latitude" (52, 58). Decision latitude is the primary measure of the concept of control and is defined as the combination of job decision-making authority and use of skills on the job. Questionnaire items often used to define job demands and job decision latitude are listed in Table 1. Such work situations are hypothesized to result in biological arousal, mediated by increases in catecholamines and blood pressure, contributing ultimately to the development of CVD. In addition, job strain (also known as "high-strain" jobs) may promote unhealthy coping behaviors, such as smoking, that contribute to CVD.

While significant positive associations have been observed between job strain and CVD, important questions remain. First, can the observed effect of job strain be due to confounding by other CVD risk factors or some forms of bias? Second, if the association is real, what are the underlying biological mechanisms; is there a direct effect, or is the effect mediated via known coronary risk factors? Third, what is the nature of the interaction between the constructs job demands and job decision latitude in the job strain model? Fourth, what refinements of the measurement of these con-

Table 1   Items from the US Quality of Employment Surveys often used to define psychological job demands and job decision latitude (56)

Psychological job demands
  1. My job requires working very fast
  2. My job requires working very hard
  3. I am not asked to do an excessive amount of work*
  4. I have enough time to get the job done*
  5. I am free from conflicting demands that others make*

Job decision latitude (the sum of two equally weighted subscales)
  Decision authority
  1. My job allows me to make a lot of decisions on my own
  2. On my job, I have very little freedom to decide how I do my work*
  3. I have a lot of say about what happens on my job
  Skill utilization
  1. My job requires that I learn new things
  2. My job involves a lot of repetitive work*
  3. My job requires me to be creative
  4. My job requires a high level of skill
  5. I get to do a variety of different things on my job
  6. I have an opportunity to develop my own special abilities

*Reverse scored

structs are needed? Fifth, should the theoretical model be refined or expanded? Finally, what directions are needed for future research?

ASSESSMENT OF THE EVIDENCE

Consistency Across Populations

Between 1981 and 1993, 36 studies were published, most of which found a significant positive relationship between job strain and CVD or all-cause mortality[1] (see Table 2) or job strain and CVD risk factors, such as hypertension (see Table 3). Major early studies had to rely upon available national data bases in Sweden (49, 50, 54) and the U.S. (59) to link job characteristics with CVD. Recent studies have tended to focus on CVD risk factors (primarily elevated blood pressure) in smaller-scale studies in Sweden

[1]The majority of studies of job strain and disease outcome (10 of 15 studies) examined coronary heart disease as outcome, particularly myocardial infarction. However, 3 of the 15 studies examined all-cause mortality. The studies of cardiovascular disease mortality (50, 54) did not include all cardiovascular diseases, rather only those with a putative stress-related etiology—arteriosclerotic heart disease, cerebrovascular disease, and peripheral vascular disease (ICD codes 400–404; 410–414; 427, 430–436; and 440–445, respectively).

Table 2 Studies of job strain and cardiovascular disease

First author, year	Reference	Study participants	Illness outcome	Effect of job strain
		Cross-sectional studies		
LaCroix, 1987	69, 39	519 female North Carolina office workers	Angina pectoris	Lower prevalence of angina for high latitude non-VDT work
Johnson, 1988	49	13,779 employed Swedish men	CVD morbidity	PR = 2.2* for high demand, low support, low latitude vs low demand, high support, high latitude. PR = 7.22* for blue-collar men
Karasek, 1988	59	1960–62 US HES: 2409 men 1971–75 US HANES: 2424 men	MI	SOR = 1.5* for high strain job titles vs other SOR = 1.6*
		Case-control studies		
Karasek, 1981	54	22 cases and 66 matched controls from 1968–77 national sample of 1915 Swedish men	CVD mortality	OR = 4.0* (for personal schedule freedom + high demands); For workers with low education: OR = 14.3*** by unmatched analysis (cells too sparse for matched analysis)
Alfreddson, 1982	4, 6	334 employed men and 882 matched controls in Stockholm aged 40–64	MI	Hectic job + monotony: NS Hectic job + no private visits: OR = 1.3* Hectic job + no influence: OR = 1.4* Hectic job + few possibilities to learn: OR = 1.5*
Theorell, 1987	110	72 male MI survivors < age 45 116 matched controls (Stockholm)	MI (survivors)	Demands divided by low monotony,** and demands divided by personal schedule freedom* were significantly higher in cases

Reference		Population	Outcome	Results
Hammar, 1993	36	9,295 employed men and women and 26,101 matched controls in Sweden aged 30–64	MI	Hectic job: + monotony: RR = 1.2* (men) RR = 1.4* (women) + few possibilities to learn: RR = 1.3* (both) + low influence on planning work: RR = 1.3* (both) + low influence on work tempo: RR = 1.2* (m) RR = 1.1* (w) + low influence on work hours: RR = 1.3* (m) RR = 1.2* (w)

Cohort studies

Reference		Population	Outcome	Results
LaCroix, 1984	68	548 men, 328 women, aged 45–64, in Framingham, MA followed for 10 yrs	CHD	Self-report: All women: RR = 2.9*; Clerical women: RR = 5.2** National job averages: Women***, and men**
Alfredsson, 1985	5	958,096 Stockholm residents aged 20–64 followed for 1 year	MI (hospitalizations)	Hectic job and low influence: NS Hectic job and monotony: Women: SMR = 164*; Men: SMR = 153* Men aged 20–54: SMR = 118* Men aged 20–54: SMR = 157* Hectic job and few possibilities to learn: Women (NS); Men: SMR = 128*; Men aged 20–54: SMR = 157*
Haan, 1988	33	603 male and 299 female Finnish factory workers followed 10 years	CHD	OR = 5.0* for low control, low variety, high physical strain vs other
Johnson, 1989	50	7219 employed Swedish men followed for 9 years	CVD morbidity and mortality	Top quintile of iso-strain (high demands, low latitude, low social support) vs bottom quintile: Morbidity: Men: PR = 1.8**; Blue-collar men: PR = 2.0** Mortality: Men: RR = 1.9*; Blue-collar men: RR = 2.6*

Table 2 (*Continued*)

First author, year	Reference	Study participants	Illness outcome	Effect of job strain
Reed, 1989	93	4737 Hawaiian men, aged 45–65, followed for 18 years	CHD	Non-significant trend for *lower* strain men to have higher CHD
Astrand, 1989	8	391 male Swedish factory employees, aged 35–65, followed for 22 yrs	All-cause mortality	High latitude + high support work = 32% mortality vs other combinations = 42%, 46%, 44% mortality*
Theorell, 1991	115	79 male employed Swedish MI survivors < age 45 followed 6–8 years	Mortality from MI recurrence	RR = 6.2, if demands/discretion dichotomized at median Demands/discretion significant predictor in logistic regression*
Falk, 1992	25	477 retired men, aged 68–69, from Malmo, Sweden, followed for 6 years	All-cause mortality	Adjusted RR = 1.6* for high demands and low personal schedule freedom If low social support: adjusted RR = 2.1–4.6*

Abbreviations: HES, 1960–61 US Health Examination Survey; HANES, 1971–75 US Health and Nutrition Examination Survey; VDT, video display terminals; MI, myocardial infarction; CVD, cardiovascular disease; CHD, coronary heart disease; NS, not significant at $p < 0.05$; RR, risk ratio; SMR, standardized morbidity ratio; SOR, standardized odds ratio; OR, odds ratio; PR, prevalence ratio. *$p < 0.05$; **$p < 0.01$; ***$p < 0.001$.

(e.g. 109, 114) and the U.S. (75, 99–101, 116) in which both individual-level exposure and outcome data were collected.

Estimates of relative risk for men in cohort studies with positive results have ranged from 1.6 for all-cause mortality among 477 retired Swedish men followed for six years (25), to 1.9 for CVD mortality among a representative sample of 7219 Swedish male employees followed for nine years (50), to 6.2 for 79 male Swedish myocardial infarction (MI) survivors followed for 6–8 years (115). A relative risk of 2.9 for coronary heart disease (CHD) among 328 women followed for 10 years was observed in the Framingham Heart Study (68).

Positive associations were reported in both blue-collar (8, 32, 33, 36, 79) and white-collar workers (36, 53, 55), and in both women and men. In eight of the eleven studies where comparisons could be made, effect sizes were similar for men and women (5, 33, 36, 53, 55, 81, 114, 116). However, most of the studies have been conducted with Northern European racial/ethnic groups located in Europe or the U.S. Only three studies were conducted with a predominantly non-Caucasian population (30, 37, 93).

Consistency Across Study Designs

Positive associations were found among cross-sectional, case-control, and cohort studies (Tables 2 and 3). Of eight cohort studies (six of CVD and two of all-cause mortality), seven found significant associations (5, 8, 25, 33, 50, 68, 115). Seventeen of the 36 studies were population-based, which supports the generalizability of the results. In addition, significant associations were found with various formulations of the independent variable (job strain). A strategy to obtain more objective measures of job characteristics, in which average scores for a particular job title are imputed to individuals in that job title (instead of using the individual's own self-reported scores), was used in eleven studies. Seven of these "imputation" studies found significant associations (4, 5, 36, 59, 68, 81, 109), while two provided mixed results (30, 113).

Consistency Across Outcome Measures

Consistent results have been found across types of CVD outcome measures (e.g. CHD, CVD morbidity or mortality, MI, MI recurrence, as well as all-cause mortality) (see Table 2). In addition, 21 studies examined job strain and CVD symptoms or risk factors (see Table 3). Null results were reported for job strain and serum cholesterol (37, 86, 90), while job strain was associated with smoking in two (32, 81) of four studies.

Of eight studies of job strain and blood pressure measured in a clinic setting (3, 19, 37, 75, 79, 86, 90, 116) in which typically only a few casual readings are taken, only one (37) found a significant association.

Table 3 Studies of job strain and cardiovascular disease symptoms and risk factors

First author, year	Reference	Study participants	Illness outcome	Effect of job strain
		Cross-sectional studies		
Karasek, 1987	55	5000 male and 3700 female Swedish white-collar workers	CHD symptoms	Men: Workload SOR = 1.2; Control SOR = 0.92* Women: Workload SOR = 1.1*; Control SOR = 0.82*
Matthews, 1987	79	288 male workers, aged 40–63, in 2 Pittsburgh factories	Casual DBP	Participation: r = −0.15* Promotion: r = −0.13*
Mensch, 1988	81	5335 male and 4874 female employed U.S. youth aged 19–27 in 1984	Smoking	Highest smoking rates in high demand-low latitude jobs*
Harenstam, 1988	38	66 male Swedish prison guards	Ambulatory BP	Skill use assoc with work and leisure SBP** Job demands and decision latitude (NS)
Pieper, 1989	90	12,555 men in 3 US national and 2 regional studies	BP, smoking, cholesterol	Job strain (NS) Job decision latitude associated with lower smoking and lower SBP*
Karasek, 1990	53	Swedish white-collar workers facing major company-initiated job changes	CHD symptoms	Evidence for fewer symptoms if workers participated in change decisions, and had more latitude due to changes
Green, 1990	32	389 male US chemical plant employees aged ≥40	Smoking	Smoking cessation (NS) Smoking amount: SOR = 1.7*; increase in smoking: SOR = 3.7**
Theorell, 1991	109	161 Swedish males aged 35–55 with borderline hypertension	Ambulatory BP	Significantly associated with work, home and sleep DBP** SBP (NS)

Netterstrom, 1991	86	1209 employed male and female residents of Copenhagen	Casual BP, smoking, cholesterol, etc	Most risk factors (NS) Some evidence for higher fibrinogen, glycated hemoglobin
Van Egeren, 1992	116	20 female and 17 male Michigan employees	Ambulatory BP	SBP: Work = +12 mm Hg***; Home = +7 mm Hg*; Sleep = +7 Hg DBP: Work = +4 mm Hg*; Home, Sleep (NS) Effect for both males and females
Albright, 1992	3	1396 San Francisco bus drivers	Hypertension (from casual readings)	NS
Haratani, 1992	37	2672 male Japanese workers in 2 factories	Casual BP, smoking, cholesterol	SBP**; DBP** Smoking (NS); Cholesterol (NS)
Light, 1992	75	Employed North Carolina men (n = 65) and women (n = 64), aged 18–47	Ambulatory BP	Men: Work SBP = +6 mm Hg*; Work DBP = +4 mm Hg* Women: Work SBP = −1 mm Hg; Work DBP = −2.2 mm Hg (NS)
Georges, 1992	30	1377 Mexican-American men aged 18–74 (1982–4 US HHANES)	Skinfold thickness CBFD	Skinfold thickness: F = 4.9* Central body fat distribution (CBFD) (NS)
Theorell, 1993	108	56 female Swedish nurses and nurses aides	Ambulatory BP	Significantly associated with work SBP, DBP; SBP upon waking Leisure SBP, DBP; DBP upon waking (NS)

Table 3 (*Continued*)

First author, year	Reference	Study participants	Illness outcome	Effect of job strain
Case-control studies				
Schnall, 1990, 1992	100, 101	88 cases and 176 controls, males, aged 30–60, from New York City	Hypertension (based on repeated work-site casual readings), LVMI, ambulatory BP	SBP: Work = +6.8 mm Hg**; Home = +6.5 mm Hg**; Sleep = +6.2 mm Hg** DBP: Work = +2.8 mm Hg*; Home = +2.4 mm Hg*; Sleep = +1.7 mm Hg Hypertension: OR = 2.7*; LVMI = 9.7 g/m² higher*
Cohort studies				
Karasek, 1981	54	National sample of 1461 Swedish men interviewed in 1968 and 1974	CHD symptoms	Highest symptom level among high strain workers using prevalence data (but not incidence)
Theorell, 1985	113	71 Stockholm men in 1981–82 followed for 10 yrs since age 18	Ambulatory BP	NS; but significant interaction: hypertensives have higher SBP rise at work if in a high-strain job
Theorell, 1988	114	51 men, 22 women employed in 6 jobs in Stockholm followed for 1 year	Ambulatory BP	Work SBP higher (by 4 mm Hg) during highest vs. lowest job strain periods in 1 year*; Work DBP (NS) Effect for both males and females Leisure SBP, DBP (NS)

| Chapman, 1990 | 19 | 2100 male, 534 female Australian govt employees followed for 5 years | Casual BP | Women: quantitative demands**, poor work support***, job insecurity**, associated with DBP in certain age groups (3 of 24 tests significant at p < 0.01) Men (NS); SBP (NS) |
| Schnall, 1992 | 99 | 197 New York City men followed for 3 years | Ambulatory BP | For those in high strain jobs at both rounds (n = 15) vs those in non-strain jobs at both rounds (n = 138): Work SBP = +6.0 mm Hg*; Work DBP = +4.3 mm Hg* |

Abbreviations: CHD, coronary heart disease; SBP, systolic blood pressure; DBP, diastolic blood pressure; BP, blood pressure; HHANES, Hispanic Health and Nutrition Examination Study; CBFD, Central Body Fat Distribution; LVMI, left ventricular mass index; SOR, standardized odds ratio; OR, odds ratio; NS, not significant at $p < 0.05$.
$*p < 0.05$; $**p < 0.01$; $***p < .001$.

However, ambulatory blood pressure monitors give both a more reliable measure (there is no observer bias and the number of readings is increased) and a more valid measure of average blood pressure (since blood pressure is measured during a person's normal daily activities) than casual measures of blood pressure (89). Of nine job strain studies utilizing ambulatory blood pressure, five yielded significant positive results (99, 101, 108, 109, 116), while the remaining four yielded a mixture of positive and null results (38, 75, 113, 114). Taken as a whole, these results suggest job strain acts, in part, to cause CVD through the mechanism of elevated blood pressure.[2]

Effect Modification

Few of the studies stratified by potential effect modifiers of the job strain-CVD relationship such as age, SES, gender, or social support.

AGE   Higher risk of CHD due to job strain was found among older Framingham women (68) (risk ratio = 5.1 for age 55–64 compared to risk ratio = 2.9 for all participants, aged 45–64), and of CVD among older Swedish white-collar men (50) (standardized risk ratio = 1.7 for age > 44 compared to standardized risk ratio = 0.3 for age ≤ 44). Greater effect sizes also were found for heart disease symptoms among older Swedish white-collar workers (53), and blood pressure among older New York City employees (101). While this evidence suggests that older employees are more susceptible to job strain, other more likely explanations are that age is a proxy variable for cumulative exposure, and that these associations reflect either greater cumulative exposure, or latency where exposure has a greater effect after several years since first exposure.

SOCIOECONOMIC STATUS   Swedish blue-collar men (49, 50) and Swedish men with low education (54) exhibited substantially stronger associations between job strain and CVD than higher SES groups. In the Framingham

---

[2]Many mechanisms play a role in the development of the two distinctly different diseases of arteriosclerosis and atherosclerosis with some risk factors (e.g. hypertension) playing a role in both diseases. While we are not yet certain of the specific mechanism by which job strain contributes to cardiovascular disease, the evidence strongly suggests that job strain leads to increased blood pressure which, in turn, contributes to the burden of hypertension-related sequelae such as arteriosclerotic cerebrovascular disease, stroke, and hypertensive heart disease. In addition, increased blood pressure (often synonymous with hypertension) is itself a risk factor for the development of atherosclerosis (i.e. it damages arteries and accelerates cholesterol deposition in the lining of the arteries) and thus it now appears likely that job strain contributes to CHD morbidity and mortality by this indirect mechanism. Finally, some preliminary research suggests that job strain may contribute directly to coronary heart disease mortality through several mechanisms (e.g. by increasing arrythmias in susceptible individuals with coronary artery disease).

Heart Study (68), such differences were minor for men. However, women in clerical jobs reporting job strain had substantially greater risk of CHD than all women in the sample. Stronger associations in lower status jobs were also reported in a Stockholm blood pressure study (114).

It is possible that interactions exist between job strain and standard coronary risk factors, more limited economic resources or coping strategies, and other environmental physical, chemical, or psychosocial health hazards, such as job insecurity. However, since lower social class appears to be a proxy for these other risk factors (lower status workers are at increased risk of CVD (15, 78, 92) and blood pressure elevation (98)), the heterogeneity of effect may also result from residual confounding by these risk factors.

GENDER   In the Framingham Heart Study, when using self-report job data, significant effects on CHD were observed for women only and, when "imputing" national occupational averages of job strain, stronger significant effects were reported for women than men (68). However, in studies in North Carolina (75) and New York City (72), job strain was not associated with blood pressure for women, while it was for men. On the other hand, a Swedish study did find an effect on blood pressure for women (108), and a US study (116) found significant effects for combined samples of men and women.

An absence of effect on blood pressure for women may be due, in part, to their lower prevalence of hypertension before age 55 (7). A greater effect of job strain on CHD for women, if replicated, may result from interaction with home demands (35), salary and promotion inequities (75), or job segregation.

SOCIAL SUPPORT   Social support was an effect modifier in the Swedish study of retired men (25) (increased job strain-mortality risk ratios for those with low social support), in the Swedish factory worker study (8) (reduced high latitude-mortality risk ratios for those with high workplace social support), and in a Swedish national study (49) (increased high demand–low latitude-CVD prevalence ratios with greater workplace social isolation). However, no studies of the relation between social support, job strain, and blood pressure have been reported.

ALTERNATIVE EXPLANATIONS FOR ASSOCIATIONS

Confounding

STANDARD RISK FACTORS   Of the thirteen positive CVD studies (Table 2), all controlled for age, all but two (36, 50) controlled for cigarette smoking, and six (8, 25, 33, 59, 68, 115) controlled for both serum cholesterol and high blood pressure (HBP). Thus, confounding may still remain in some studies. However, since these variables may be in the causal pathway between job strain and CVD, including these variables in analysis could represent overcontrol of these risk factors. For example, if job strain leads to high blood pressure, controlling for blood pressure would underestimate the association between job strain and CVD.

In the nine studies of ambulatory blood pressure (Table 3), all controlled for age, all but three (109, 113, 114) controlled for body mass index, while some studies also controlled for other potential confounders: physical activity (38, 75, 99, 101, 109), race (75, 99, 101), smoking and alcohol use (38, 99, 101).

SOCIOECONOMIC STATUS   Potential confounding by SES or social class presents a problem (29), since CVD is more prevalent among lower SES groups (15, 78, 92), and it might be assumed that job strain is correlated with lower SES. To address this concern, many of the thirteen positive CVD studies controlled for SES with such measures as education (4, 8, 25, 54, 59, 110, 115) or occupational status (8, 36, 49, 50, 68, 93). Similarly, some of the nine ambulatory blood pressure studies controlled for education (99, 101, 108) or occupational status (38, 75, 114). The San Francisco bus driver study (3) restricted its sample to one occupation, thus controlling for SES. However, one consequence of single occupation studies is that the range of objective demands and latitude is narrower than in a between-occupation study, leading to reduced statistical power.

The Karasek model posits that job strain is not equivalent to low SES. Rather, low-status and low-income jobs exist in the low strain, passive, and high-strain quadrants of the model (Figure 1). In fact, studies demonstrate that conventional social status scales are almost orthogonal to job strain (58). For example, in the New York City blood pressure study (101), education was not correlated with job strain ($r = 0.01$) among men. In the Swedish factory worker study (8), the effect of low job decision latitude on mortality was seen after controlling for occupational status, and status did not show any independent predictive power. Similarly, in a North Carolina study (75), job strain was not associated with occupational status in men ($r = -0.01$); rather, status was positively related to both demands and latitude, i.e. to active jobs.

In the North Carolina study (75), occupational status was associated with low strain work among women ($p < 0.015$) *and* with higher blood pressure ($r = 0.22$). (A null association between job strain and blood pressure for women was observed.) However, in a Danish study, job strain was significantly more prevalent among lower social class groups (84). Thus, there remains a need to examine patterns of association between SES and job strain in various populations, and the necessity to control for SES to determine the independent effect of job strain.

PERSONALITY   Potential confounding by personality also raises important methodological and theoretical issues. Major methodological limitations of research in this area are the failure to examine environmental conditions (e.g. job characteristics) that shape personality measures and psychological attributes, and possible biased reporting of psychological states and traits due to awareness of illness (particularly in cross-sectional studies). Also, with notable exceptions (e.g. 107), there have been inadequate efforts to develop a theory that specifies interactions between environmental stressors and personality characteristics in the development of hypertension and CVD.

A recent meta-analysis, which included several prospective studies, demonstrates a modest association between coronary heart disease and anxiety, depression, anger, and hostility (28). However, the potential influence of job characteristics in shaping these psychological states and traits, as suggested by other research, has rarely been examined. For example, in a US study, the substantive complexity of work (analogous to decision latitude) predicted increased intellectual flexibility, nonauthoritarianism, and intellectually demanding leisure time ten years later (66). In Sweden, workers whose jobs became more "passive" (low demand–low latitude) over six years reported less participation in political and leisure activities. In contrast, workers in jobs that became more "active" participated more in these activities (58).

Type A behavior is primarily associated with higher status, success-oriented, active (high demand–high control) jobs, making it an unlikely confounder of the job strain–CVD association. Recent research suggests that the hostility component, rather than Type A behavior itself, is the cardiovascular risk factor (28, 120). Since hostility is highly correlated with Type A behavior, it is not likely to be correlated with job strain.

The evidence linking personality measures with CVD risk factors (such as HBP) appears even more uncertain. Asymptomatic hypertensives (64), as well as normotensives with a family history of hypertension (107), seem to express fewer emotions, have a noncomplaining attitude, and lack an ability to differentiate feelings, similar to denial (58). Theorell hypothesizes that such personality characteristics might result, in part, from a stressful psychosocial work environment that "enforces a noncomplaining attitude and prevents development of active emotional coping" (107).

Some studies suggest a positive relationship between psychological variables such as suppressed anger and hypertension (22, 24). Others report a negative correlation between anxiety and hypertension (82). Mild hypertensives did not differ from normotensives on anger, anxiety, hostility, Type A behavior, or other psychological measures in the New York City blood pressure study (100). In most of the positive studies, hypertensives have been aware of their blood pressure and therefore these psychological characteristics could result from diagnosis and labeling rather than representing etiological factors (46, 95). For example, one study found that hypertensives who were aware of their status scored higher than normotensives and unaware hypertensives on neuroticism, anxiety, and Type A behavior (46).

The concept of "negative affectivity" or "neuroticism" as a confounder of the stress-psychological strain association has been widely investigated (80). Individuals high on this trait are hypothesized to *report* more dissatisfaction and have low psychological well-being. Controlling for this variable in some studies reduces the stressor-strain association. Some studies have shown an association between neuroticism and development of angina pectoris, but not with MI (21). In the New York City blood pressure study, "trait anxiety", a widely used measure of negative affectivity (118), was not correlated with work systolic ($r = 0.01$), work diastolic blood pressure ($r = 0.00$), or job strain (71, 99).

Therefore, it is unlikely that personality variables account for the association between job strain and hypertension or CVD. However, research is still needed to develop a theory that specifies possible interactions between environmental stressors and personality characteristics, and to improve the methodology of such studies.

WORK ENVIRONMENT   The organization of work and job design can create job strain. In addition, aspects of the work environment may be potential confounders of the job strain-CVD association. For example, physical activity is protective for CVD (87), and was therefore controlled in many of the reviewed studies (4, 5, 8, 32, 49, 59, 75, 93, 101, 109, 110). Confounding by job insecurity, or chemical and physical work hazards, however, has rarely been assessed. Carbon monoxide (105), solvents (119), other chemicals, and shiftwork (2) have been associated with CVD (18, 67). Job insecurity (61, 98), noise (106), and lead (91) have been associated with modest elevations of blood pressure.[3] However, the relatively weak

[3]Continuing economic recession and government budget cuts may be expected to create greater job insecurity and lowered staffing levels (and resulting higher job demands). In addition, many newly created jobs are predominantly clerical and or in the service sector, which are more likely to be high strain (23, 58). Such employment trends, the social context of job strain, and the work environment will be important future research areas.

association of these hazards with CVD make it unlikely that they are responsible for the job strain-CVD association.

Bias

SELECTION BIAS   Selection bias can be a threat to the validity of studies where: (*a*) low participation rates exist (43, 69, 114, 116); (*b*) selection in and out of certain jobs might occur as a result of disease (4); or (*c*) selection into jobs might occur as a result of personality characteristics (individuals vulnerable to CVD might select into high strain jobs (e.g. 81, 100, 109)). Studies suggest that selection out of high strain jobs does occur with advancing age. For example, US data show relatively *fewer* occupants of high strain jobs among older age groups (59). In Sweden, among individuals whose job characteristics did *not* change over six years, prospective job strain/heart disease associations were stronger than in the full population (54). If individuals leaving high strain jobs (i.e. example (*b*) above) are also leaving the labor force due to illness, then this "healthy worker effect" will lead to an underestimate of effect sizes. (See Karasek et al (59) for a more detailed discussion of selection factors.)

INFORMATION BIAS   Self-report bias is a potential problem in many job strain studies since exposure has often been assessed through questionnaires completed by study participants. Self-reports may be inaccurate descriptions of job characteristics, or may be biased by personality traits such as negative affectivity. More objective measures of job strain are needed in intervention studies.

In eleven job strain studies, researchers employed an analytic technique to overcome self-report bias and obtain more objective measures of job characteristics—the imputation of average scores for a particular job title to individuals in that job title. This average job title score, free of the individual's subjective assessment, then predicts outcome for the individual. Large within-occupation variance exists in job characteristics (55% of reliable variance for latitude, and 93% for demands), since job titles such as nurse, machinist, secretary or teacher are somewhat heterogeneous in skill levels, autonomy, or demands (102). As a result, in the US studies, mean scores of job characteristics are adjusted for demographic covariates when imputed to an individual participant (102). Despite this adjustment, the imputation strategy introduces (nondifferential) misclassification and a bias towards the null. Thus, positive findings using the imputation method (4, 5, 36, 59, 68, 81, 109) provide strong support for the model, while negative studies may result, in part, from loss of power. More individual-level job data and health data are clearly needed in future research.

BIOLOGICAL MECHANISMS

Although the biological mechanisms by which job strain acts to influence the development of CVD remain unclear, three possible pathways have been suggested:

1. Known risk factors for CVD, such as blood pressure, cholesterol, or smoking, may increase.
2. The coronary atherosclerosis process may be accelerated via mechanisms outside the known risk factors, for instance, coagulation processes.
3. In the final stages of CHD, MIs or arrhythmias may be precipitated among vulnerable persons with underlying coronary artery disease, for instance, through increased sympathoadrenal activity.

Via Known Risk Factors

Job strain has been linked to elevation of blood pressure when measured using an ambulatory device. In addition, there is some evidence relating job strain to cigarette smoking. To date, however, job strain has not been associated with serum cholesterol.

Job strain might elevate blood pressure through increases in left ventricular mass (101) or chronic physiological arousal (38, 63, 111). Frankenhauser and colleagues in Sweden have confirmed the involvement of two neuro-endocrine systems in the stress response—the sympathoadrenal medullary system (which secretes the catecholamines, adrenalin and noradrenalin), and the pituitary-adrenal cortical system (which secretes corticosteroids such as cortisol). Building on the work of Henry & Stephens (41), Frankenhauser showed that under demanding conditions where the organism can exert control in the face of controllable and predictable stressors (analogous to active work in the Karasek model), adrenalin levels increase, but cortisol decreases. Effort without distress is experienced. However, in demanding low control situations (analogous to Karasek's high strain jobs), both adrenalin and cortisol are elevated and effort with distress is experienced (26, 27, 57). Elevated levels of both catecholamines and cortisol appear to have severe consequences for myocardial pathology (104). In Franken-hauser's model, low demand–low control situations, analogous to Karasek's passive jobs or Seligman's concept of "learned helplessness" (1), create feelings of depression and helplessness and elevated cortisol, although only mild elevations in catecholamines (26).

These models are unlikely to capture the full complexity of the actual stress response. Short-term cortisol elevation has been associated with healthier coping in stressful situations (58, 114). Similarly, adrenalin secretion that quickly returns to baseline levels may reflect a healthy active behavior pattern.

Personal control may exert a positive effect by reducing the duration of the stress response (26). Repetitive and machine-paced jobs, as well as excessive overtime, tend to prolong unwinding, the return of neuroendocrine levels to baseline (26, 27). Of six ambulatory blood pressure studies that provided such data, four (38, 101, 109, 116) indicated a carryover effect in which the work *and home* blood pressure of high strain workers was elevated above levels of other workers. Four studies even indicated elevated *sleep* blood pressures among high strain workers (101, 108, 109, 116), providing strong support for the job strain model. Another obstacle to unwinding may be the dual role, with the additional responsibility for household and children, of many women (35).

Atherosclerosis

The possible influence of job strain on the progression of coronary athero-sclerosis is an important research area. One study of men who had suffered an MI before age 40 indicated by coronary angiograms more progression of coronary atherosclerosis over five years in those with low job decision latitude than in others (74). However, another study of men who had suffered an MI before age 45, did not support this hypothesis (88).

Some evidence was provided by an association between low decision latitude and high plasma fibrinogen concentration, suggesting a link with coagulation and, accordingly, atherosclerosis (77). However, job strain was not associated with fibrinogen in another study (83). This pathway is consistent with the association between adrenalin levels and coagulation (31, 34, 58), e.g. the stimulation of thrombocyte adhesiveness by adrenalin.

Precipitation of Myocardial Infarctions or Arrhythmias in Vulnerable Persons

Only one directly relevant study has been published regarding this third pathway (115). Indirect evidence is provided by two studies (62, 86) that show an association between job strain and glycated hemoglobin, a possible index of long-lasting sympathoadrenal activity. Low decision latitude was associated with elevated plasma adrenalin concentration at rest (65), and with increased urine catecholamine output (38). Job strain was also associated with workday elevations in catecholamines (but not blood pressure) among urban bus drivers (17).

The influence of sympathoadrenal activity on physiological processes relevant to the precipitation of illness in vulnerable persons is well-known, via increased oxygen demand, increased risk of clot formation, and decreased thresholds for arrhythmias. Another possibility is that job strain may inhibit anabolic (regenerative) processes and thereby increase the vulnerability of the heart (57). A recent longitudinal study (112) showed that plasma testosterone concentrations tend to decrease when job strain increases. Relevance of this index of anabolic activity to acute coronary disease is speculative at this stage.

THE NATURE OF THE JOB STRAIN MODEL

The job strain model was not designed to replace the earlier, more complex person-environment fit model of occupational stress originating from the University of Michigan (16, 42) or the recent refinement of the Michigan model by the National Institute for Occupational Safety and Health (NIOSH) (44). The Michigan model incorporates the following features: both perceived and objective stressors; the potential moderating effects of social support, personality factors, nonwork factors, and demographic measures; feedback loops; and a wide variety of outcome measures. Issues of self-reported vs objective job characteristics and effect modification are, of course, also important issues for the job strain model. However, in contrast to the Michigan model, the job strain model emphasizes the need to distinguish features of the work environment that can be categorized as demands or control (and does not simply list all job factors as potential stressors), examines the interaction between demands and control, and emphasizes the stress-producing properties of these objective factors, and not solely individual perceptions, or person-environment fit.

Originally, job strain was defined as resulting "when job demands are high and job decision latitude is low" (52). In later research, various mathematical forms of job strain have been reported with significant results suggesting a certain robustness to the job strain concept. However, this robustness may be, in part, an artifact of the selection process of reporting positive associations and ignoring negative ones. Therefore, research needs to continue on the appropriate form of the risk factor. The following forms have been reported:

Main effects model   Seventeen (4, 8, 19, 30, 36–38, 49, 53–55, 59, 68, 69, 81, 90, 110) of 25 studies that examined main effects found some significant associations between job decision latitude and outcome. However, associations between job demands and outcome were significant in only eight (6, 30, 37, 49, 54, 55, 59) of 23 studies.

Components of job decision latitude   Job decision latitude has been defined as the combination of skill utilization and decision-making authority. While the two components are often highly correlated (52, 102)), intellectual discretion and personal schedule freedom were not highly correlated in a Swedish study (54) (r = .29). In studies where the components were examined separately (4–6, 30, 36, 38, 54, 79, 81, 110, 115), there was no indication that one of the components was a better predictor of CVD risk. Eight of 12 measures of authority and 10 of 15 measures of skill were significantly associated with outcome.

Social support   Workplace social support has been added to the job strain model as a third major job characteristic in several studies of CVD (8, 25, 49, 50), as well as psychological strain outcomes (e.g. 60, 71). Evidence was provided for both a social support main effect (25, 49), and a buffering of the effects of job strain (8, 25, 49). Because of the extensive literature on the beneficial effects of social support on cardiovascular and psychological health (20, 42), future job strain research should incorporate this variable.

Interaction models   Although the procedure in the reviewed studies most commonly has defined as high strain participants above the median on demands and below the median on latitude, a newer approach (32, 114, 108–110, 115, all with positive results) creates a quotient term (demands divided by latitude) and a single continuous independent variable. Both methods, while congruent with theory, should also examine the main effects of demands and decision latitude to determine whether significant associations are due to the joint effect of the job variables or primarily to the effect of only one variable. Only two (37, 49) of five studies (19, 37, 49, 90, 93) found a significant interaction effect using the traditional partialled product interaction term for latitude × demands, after controlling for the main effects of latitude and demands.

   The quotient model has the advantage of allowing investigators to explore the effect of choosing arbitrary cutpoints to categorize the continuous variable and examine resulting effect estimates. In case-control studies, for example, a continuous job strain variable could be dichotomized at various points, resulting in varying proportions of exposed vs unexposed. The resulting odds ratios could be plotted as a tool to explore nonlinear or nonmonotonic dose-response curves (117). An alternative approach is to trichotomize demands and latitude and construct a nine-cell exposure variable (49, 99), or use quartiles and construct a 16-cell variable (54) and examine the pattern of effects. Such exploratory techniques might reveal thresholds (nonlinear effects) beyond which the effect of job strain is evident.

Thresholds   If population thresholds exist, the proportion of participants in any given study sample experiencing job strain sufficient to significantly increase CVD risk may vary. For example, if only 10 percent of a given sample are experiencing high job strain, yet 25 percent of the sample is classified as high strain due to dichotomizing demands and latitude at the sample's median, misclassification and a dilution of the effect estimate occurs.

For example, the San Francisco bus driver study (3) reported an average level of decision latitude of 30.8, 0.44 standard deviations below the national US QES mean for males of 33.0 (56). If the national average had been applied, many of these bus drivers would have been classified as high strain or passive workers, rather than being equally distributed across the four quadrants of the model. Another study (75) used different classification cutpoints for men (latitude < 40) and women (latitude < 37) in the sample. Although this procedure resulted in similar proportions of participants being classified as high strain (23% and 29%, respectively), unless different effect thresholds actually exist for men and women corresponding to these values misclassification was introduced.

Although the strategy of using national averages of demands and latitude might provide more valid classification cutpoints in a particular study, it does not resolve the issue of the possible existence of a threshold of effect or provide the best way to identify it.

REFINEMENTS NEEDED IN MEASUREMENT OF EXPOSURE

Scale Development

Scales used to measure job strain were originally derived from secondary analysis of existing US and Swedish surveys and were therefore created post hoc; they were empirically and not entirely theoretically derived. In addition, several studies relied on measures of task-level demands and latitude that varied from the original construct. For example, in the Framingham Heart Study (68), a combination of self-reported job demands above the median and low scores on a two-item "supervision clarity" scale were used. The Finnish factory worker study (33) combined measures of latitude with physical rather than psychological strain. However, many US studies have used the same 14 US QES items to measure latitude and demands (3, 30, 32, 59, 68, 75, 81, 90, 93, 99, 101, 116).

The need to employ items general enough to be used across occupations or populations causes some constraint in instrument development. Such items may not capture the subtleties or specifics of demands and control within a particular job title or workplace. To achieve statistical power through an adequate range of job characteristics and number of subjects, some specificity is sacrificed and misclassification results, with a dilution of effect size. In addition, general items are more open to misinterpretation. For example, the psychological demands scale items "work fast" and "work hard" (Table 1) might be confused with physical demands. Therefore, in addition to including both general and specific job characteristics items in workplace assessment instruments, we suggest more psychometric research to improve the internal validity of the general job strain scale items.

Subjective Reporting of Exposure

The job strain model posits the critical role played by objective job characteristics in producing ill health, but there is a potential lack of correspondence between subjective reporting and objective job characteristics. However, in one of the few studies where expert ratings were available (of education "expected of a particular occupation"), those ratings *were* highly correlated ($r = 0.64$–0.69) with self-report of "intellectual discretion" (54). On the other hand, the rating of psychological demands has a much greater within-occupation variance than decision latitude (102), and therefore likely has a greater subjective component.

Questions remain about which factors may influence subjective perception, and mediate, moderate, or confound the health effects of objective job strain. Such factors could potentially include worksite-specific factors such as organizational climate (99, 101) (e.g. recognition, participation, support), demographic measures, cognitive processes (e.g. denial), or personality characteristics. Also, the integration of perceived high demands and low decision latitude with objective job features (machine-paced work, shiftwork, piece-rate work, involuntary overtime, short-cycle time, electronic surveillance (96)) into a more complex exposure model might reduce information bias and misclassification of exposure to biologically relevant occupational stressors.

Duration of Exposure

In all but two studies (99, 114), job strain was assessed at only one point in time; therefore, the duration of exposure to job strain cannot be assessed. Use of current exposure as a proxy for past exposure may be inaccurate, in part because people often gain skills with time and age, may be promoted, may select out of high strain jobs, or their job characteristics may change even within the same job title. For example, in the New York City blood pressure study (99), 22% of the cohort changed job strain status over three years. The consequence of not measuring past exposure is misclassification and a dilution of effect size. The effect of different profiles of duration and intensity, or peak exposures (such as threat of job loss (98)) also need to be properly specified.

One remedy to this problem is a new Swedish job-exposure matrix (51) that allows the imputation of job characteristics scores to study participants based on age, gender and length of employment in a particular job title. Another solution is the collection of individual-level job history information to help determine cumulative exposure, as in the current New York City blood pressure cohort study (70).

EXPANDING THE JOB STRAIN MODEL

The job demands scale derived from the US QES (56) primarily contains measures of workload demands, along with one item on role conflict. However, the Job Content Questionnaire (JCQ) developed by Karasek and colleagues (56) and the NIOSH generic job stress instrument (44) also contain items on cognitive demands that may contribute to stress, such as long periods of intense concentration. The NIOSH instrument contains additional items on demands such as role conflict, role ambiguity, responsibility for people, and threat of violence or injury.

Job decision latitude has traditionally been limited to task-level characteristics (Table 1). Researchers have suggested that control not only over task characteristics but also over aspects of work group, departmental, or organizational functioning (47), either individually or collectively (45, 48), may be important in reducing the impact of job demands. The JCQ and NIOSH instruments, for example, contain items on influence over work group policies and procedures. Some researchers have conceived of such higher level influence and participation (along with support and recognition) as characteristics of organizations, rather than occupations, and labeled it organizational climate (76).

The JCQ and NIOSH instruments also contain questions on other features of the work environment such as physical exertion, job insecurity, hazardous physical or chemical exposures, and alternative employment opportunities. The association of these other job and labor force characteristics with job strain has rarely been examined, and may confound or modify the effect of job strain on CVD risk. A study of German factory workers provided some evidence that job insecurity, work pressure, status inconsistency, and a combined high effort-low reward variable were prospectively associated with heart disease (103).

Since hypertension is prevalent in all industrialized societies and since blood pressure does *not* typically rise with age in unacculturated (40) or primitive hunting and gathering societies (97), we need to consider what aspects of industrial society (such as social class differences or job strain) may account for this effect. The job strain paradigm (high demands + low control + low support) may provide a useful working model for more general social stress. For example, home and family demands and lack of control may affect health (35). Unemployment, with its resulting health effects (13), can be conceived of as an extreme case of loss of control. Lower SES also presents increased CVD and other health risks (78), possibly due to limited influence, resources, and opportunities, as well as a poor physical environment.

CONCLUSIONS AND RECOMMENDATIONS

Fifteen years after Karasek provided the theory and impetus for job strain research, a body of literature has accumulated that strongly suggests a causal association between job strain and CVD. Several biological mechanisms for this association have been proposed and have received some empirical support, especially elevated blood pressure. Therefore, intervention studies to evaluate the effect of reducing job strain are timely and necessary. However, conceptual limitations of the model, and limitations in the current measurement of job strain need to be addressed to effectively undertake the next stage of research. Therefore, we propose that:

1. Other aspects of job demands aside from workload, e.g. cognitive demands, should be added to the construct. Workplace social support should be added as a third major job characteristic in the job strain model. Domains of demands, latitude and support, other than task-level need to be included in the model. These could include latitude or influence over work group, departmental and organizational functioning, promotion opportunities, and a supportive workplace climate.

2. The job strain survey instrument needs to be refined to reflect this expanded model and to enable it to be used in workplace assessment and intervention studies. Therefore, the original questions in Table 1 should be evaluated further for their construct validity and alternative wording considered. Questions reflecting new domains in the model should be added. In addition, measures of other relevant work conditions (physical exertion, job insecurity, shiftwork, physical work hazards, new technology), employment opportunities, and nonwork (e.g. family) demands, latitude and support need to be standardized and included in the questionnaire. Finally, workplace-specific questions are needed for assessment and intervention.

3. Additional physiological measures (e.g. blood pressure, left ventricular mass index, catecholamines, cortisol, testosterone, platelet aggregation) and health behaviors (e.g. alcohol, smoking cessation) should be included

in studies to develop a better understanding of the mechanisms by which job strain leads to CVD.

4. Population-based prospective epidemiological studies of CVD are needed, which use an expanded Job Content Questionnaire, including subjective and objective measures of job characteristics, work histories, social support, and other work environment variables, so that valid assessments of the health impacts of occupational stress can be made.

5. Periodic detailed Quality of Employment Surveys are needed to determine job characteristics, time trends, current national occupational averages, and proportion of employees facing high strain work.

6. To enhance its external validity, the job strain model should be tested in different populations, particularly women and non-Northern European racial/ethnic groups.

7. Job strain assessment instruments should be included in workplace health surveillance programs.

8. Primary prevention efforts to reduce job strain should be implemented while initiating more definitive intervention studies. Effective programs to reduce job stress in general (although not specifically job strain) have been reviewed (45, 73).

9. Epidemiologists and other public health practitioners can play an important part in interdisciplinary teams who would design and implement intervention studies to assess the effect of reducing or preventing job strain on these outcome measures.

Job strain is associated with a range of adverse health outcomes, including psychological strain such as exhaustion or depression (52, 96), hypertension, various forms of CVD, and other outcomes (11, 12, 14). Therefore, further understanding of the nature of this risk factor, as well as better specification of the construct, holds promise for both epidemiologic research and primary prevention of psychological distress, hypertension, and CVD.

ACKNOWLEDGMENTS

This work was supported in part by grants HL 18232 and HL 30605, from the National Heart, Lung and Blood Institute, an NRSA fellowship (HL 08578) to PAL, and grant ES 00928 from the National Institute of Environmental Health Sciences.

We thank Drs. T. Theorell and B. Israel for advice and suggestions on an earlier draft of this paper. We are also indebted to Dr. R. Karasek for his pioneering work in this field, and for his insight, advice, and support. Earlier versions of this paper were prepared for discussion for the Heart at Work program of the American Heart Association, and for presentation at the APA/NIOSH Conference on Occupational Stress, Washington, DC, November, 1992.

Literature Cited

1. Abramson LY, Seligman MEP, Teasdale JD. 1978. Learned helplessness in humans: Critique and reformulation. *J. Abnormal Psychol.* 87:49–74

2. Akerstedt T, Knutsson A, Alfredsson L, Theorell T. 1984. Shift work and cardiovascular disease. *Scand. J. Work Environ. Health* 10:409–14

3. Albright CL, Winkleby MA, Ragland DR, Fisher J, Syme SL. 1992. Job strain and prevalence of hypertension in a biracial population or urban bus drivers. *Am. J. Public Health* 82:984–89

4. Alfredsson L, Karasek RA, Theorell T. 1982. Myocardial infarction risk and psychosocial work environment: An analysis of the male Swedish working force. *Soc. Sci. Med.* 16:463–67

5. Alfredsson L, Spetz CL, Theorell T. 1985. Type of occupation and near-future hospitalization for myocardial infarction and some other diagnoses. *Int. J. Epidemiol.* 14:378–88

6. Alfredsson L, Theorell T. 1983. Job characteristics of occupations and myocardial infarction risk: Effect of possible confounding factors. *Soc. Sci. Med.* 17:1497–503

7. American Heart Association. 1992. *1993 Heart and Stroke Facts.* Dallas, TX: Am. Heart Assoc.

8. Astrand NE, Hanson BS, Isacson SO. 1989. Job demands, job decision latitude, job support, and social network factors as predictors of mortality in a Swedish pulp and paper company. *Br. J. Ind. Med.* 46:334–40

9. Baker DB. 1985. The study of stress at work. *Annu. Rev. Public Health* 6:367–81

10. Deleted in proof

11. Bongers PM, deWinter CR, Kompier MAJ, Hildebrandt, VH. 1993 Psychosocial factors at work and musculoskeletal disease. *Scand. J. Work Environ. Health.* 19:297–312

12. Brandt LPA, Nielson CV. 1992. Job stress and adverse outcome of pregnancy: A causal link or recall bias? *Am. J. Epidemiol.* 135:302–11

13. Brenner MH. 1987. Economic change, alcohol consumption and heart disease mortality in nine industrialized countries. *Soc. Sci. Med.* 25:119–32

14. Brett K, Strogatz D, Savitz D. 1991. Occupational stress and low birth weight delivery. Presented at Ann. Meet. Soc. Epidemiol. Res. 24th, Buffalo, NY. *Am. J. Epidemiol.* 134:722–23

15. Buring JE, Evans DA, Fiore M, Rosner B, Hennekens CH. 1987. Occupations and risks of death from coronary heart disease. *J. Am. Med. Assoc.* 258:791–92

16. Caplan RD, Cobb S, French JRP Jr, Van Harrison R, Pinneau SR Jr. 1975. *Job Demands and Worker Health.* Cincinnati, OH: Natl. Inst. Occup. Saf. Health. Publ. No. 75–168

17. Carrere S, Evans GW, Palsane MN, Rivas M. 1991. Job strain and occupational stress among urban public transit operators. *J. Occup. Psychol.* 64:305–16

18. Cent. Dis. Control Prevent. Cardiovascular diseases. 1985. *Morbid. Mortal. Wkly. Rep.* 34

19. Chapman A, Mandryk JA, Frommer MS, Edye BV, Ferguson DA. 1990. Chronic perceived work stress and blood pressure among Australian government employees. *Scand. J. Work Environ. Health* 16:258–69

20. Cohen S. 1988. Psychosocial models of the role of social support in the etiology of physical disease. *Health Psychol.* 7:269–97

21. Costa PT, McCrae RR. 1985. Hypochondriasis, neuroticism, and aging: When are somatic complaints unfounded? *Am. Psychol.* 40:19–28

22. Cottington EM, Matthews KA,

Talbott E, Kuller LH. 1986. Occupational stress, suppressed anger, and hypertension. *Psychosom. Med.* 48: 249–60

23. Dep. Labor, State of New Jersey. 1988. *Employment projections. Vol. II: Occupational outlook for New Jersey and selected areas 1986–2000.* Trenton, NJ: Dep. Labor

24. Diamond EL. 1982. The role of anger and hostility in essential hypertension and coronary heart disease. *Psychol. Bull.* 92:410–33

25. Falk A, Hanson BS, Isacsson S-O, Ostergren P-O. 1992. Job strain and mortality in elderly men: Social network, support, and influence as buffers. *Am. J. Public Health* 82: 1136–39

26. Frankenhauser M. 1989. A biopsychosocial approach to work life issues. *Int. J. Health Serv.* 19:747–58

27. Frankenhauser M, Johansson G. 1986. Stress at work: Psychobiological and psychosocial aspects. *Int. Rev. Appl. Psychol.* 35:287–99

28. Friedman HS, Booth-Kewley S. 1987. The 'disease-prone personality'. *Am. Psychol.* 42:539–55

29. Ganster DC. 1989. Worker control and well-being: A review of research in the workplace. In *Job Control and Worker Health,* ed. SL Sauter, JJ Hurrell, CL Cooper, pp. 3–23. New York: Wiley

30. Georges E, Wear ML, Mueller WH. 1992. Body fat distribution and job stress in Mexican-American men of the Hispanic Health and Nutrition Examination Survey. *Am. J. Hum. Biol.* 4:657–67

31. Gertler MM, White PD. 1976. *Coagulation Factors and Coronary Heart Disease: A 25-year Study in Retrospect.* Oradell, NJ: Med. Econ.

32. Green KL, Johnson JV. 1990. The effects of psychosocial work organization on patterns of cigarette smoking among male chemical plant employees. *Am. J. Public Health* 80: 1368–71

33. Haan MN. 1988. Job strain and ischaemic heart disease: An epidemiological study of metal workers. *Ann. Clin. Res.* 20:143–45

34. Haft JJ. 1974. Cardiovascular injury induced by sympathetic catecholamines. *Prog. Cardiovasc. Dis.* 17:73–86

35. Hall EM. 1992. Double exposure: The combined impact of the home and work environments on psychosomatic strain in Swedish men and women. *Int. J. Health Serv.* 22:239–60

36. Hammar N, Alfreddson L, Theorell T. 1993. Job characteristics and incidence of myocardial infarction: A study of men and women in Sweden, with particular reference to job strain. *Int. J. Epidemiol.* In press

37. Haratani T, Kawakami N, Araki S. 1992. *Job stress and cardiovascular risk factors in a Japanese working population.* Presented at Int. Symp. Epidemiol. Occup. Health, 9th., Cincinnati, OH

38. Harenstam A, Theorell T. 1988. Work conditions and urinary excretion of catecholamines: A study of prison staff in Sweden. *Scand. J. Work Environ. Health* 14:257–64

39. Haynes SG, LaCroix AZ, Lippin T. 1987. The effect of high job demands and low control on the health of employed women. In *Work Stress: Health Care Systems in the Workplace,* ed. JC Quick, RS Bhagat, JE Dalton, JD Quick, pp. 93–110. New York: Praeger Sci.

40. He J, Klag MJ, Whelton PK, Chen JY, Mo JP, et al. 1991. Migration, blood pressure pattern, and hypertension: The Yi Migrant Study. *Am. J. Epidemiol.* 134:1085–91

41. Henry JP, Stephens PM. 1977. *Stress, Health and the Social Environment: A Sociobiologic Approach to Medicine.* New York: Springer-Verlag

42. House JM. 1981. *Work Stress and Social Support.* Reading, MA: Addison-Wesley

43. House JS, Landis KR, Umberson D. 1988. Social relationships and health. *Science* 241:540–45

44. Hurrell JJ, McLaney MA. 1988. Exposure to job stress—A new psychometric instrument. *Scand. J. Work Environ. Health* 14(Suppl. 1):27–28

45. Int. Labor Off. 1992. *Conditions of Work Digest: Preventing Stress at Work.* Geneva, Switzerland: ILO

46. Irvine MJ, Garner DM, Olmsted MP, Logan AG. 1989. Personality differences between hypertensive and normotensive individuals: Influence of knowledge of hypertenion status. *Psychosom. Med.* 51:537–41

47. Israel BA, Schurman SJ, House JS. 1989. Action research on occupational stress: Involving workers as researchers. *Int. J. Health Serv.* 19:135–55

48. Johnson JV. 1989. Collective control: Strategies for survival in the workplace. *Int. J. Health Serv.* 19:469–80

49. Johnson JV, Hall EM. 1988. Job strain, work place social support, and cardiovascular disease: A cross-sectional study of a random sample of the Swedish working population. *Am. J. Public Health* 78:1336–42

50. Johnson JV, Hall EM, Theorell T. 1989. Combined effects of job strain and social isolation on cardiovascular disease morbidity and mortality in a random sample of the Swedish male working population. *Scand. J. Work Environ. Health* 15:271–79

51. Johnson JV, Stewart W. 1993. Measuring work organization exposure over the life course with a job-exposure matrix. *Scand. J. Work Environ. Health* 19:21–28

52. Karasek RA. 1979. Job demands, job decision latitude, and mental strain: Implications for job redesign. *Adm. Sci. Q.* 24:285–308

53. Karasek RA. 1990. Lower health risk with increased job control among white collar workers. *J. Organ. Behav.* 11:171–85

54. Karasek RA, Baker D, Marxer F, Ahlbom A, Theorell T. 1981. Job decision latitude, job demands, and cardiovascular disease: A prospective study of Swedish men. *Am. J. Public Health* 71:694–705

55. Karasek RA, Gardell B, Lindell J. 1987. Work and non-work correlates of illness and behaviour in male and female Swedish white collar workers. *J. Occup. Behav.* 8:187–207

56. Karasek RA, Gordon G, Pietrokovsky C, Frese M, Pieper C, et al. 1985. *Job Content Instrument: Questionnaire and User's Guide.* Los Angeles, CA: Univ. South. Calif.

57. Karasek RA, Russell RS, Theorell T. 1982. Physiology of stress and regeneration in job related cardiovascular illness. *J. Hum. Stress* 8:29–42

58. Karasek RA, Theorell T. 1990. *Healthy Work.* New York: Basic

59. Karasek RA, Theorell T, Schwartz JE, Schnall PL, Pieper CF, Michela JL. 1988. Job characteristics in relation to the prevalence of myocardial infarction in the US Health Examination Survey (HES) and the Health and Nutrition Survey (HANES). *Am. J. Public Health* 78:910–18

60. Karasek RA, Triantis KP, Chaudry SS. 1982. Coworker and supervisor support as moderators of associations between task characteristics and mental strain. *J. Occup. Behav.* 3:181–200

61. Kasl SV, Cobb S. 1983. Variability of stress effects among men experiencing job loss. In *Handbook of Stress,* ed. L Goldberger, S Breznitz, pp. 445–65. New York: The Free Press

62. Kawakami HS, Hyashi T, Matsumoto T. 1989. Relationship between perceived job stress and glycosylated hemoglobin in white-collar workers. *Ind. Health* 27:149–54

63. Kjeldsen SE, Eide I, Aakesson I, Leren P. 1983. Increased arterial catecholamine concentrations in 50-year-old men with essential hypertension. *Scand. J. Clin. Lab. Invest.* 43:343–49

64. Knox S, Svensson J, Waller D, Theorell T. 1988. Emotional coping and the psychophysiological substrates of elevated blood pressure. *Behav. Med.* 2:52–58

65. Knox S, Theorell T, Svensson J, Waller D. 1988. The relation of social support and working environment to medical variables associated with elevated blood pressure in young males: A structural model. *Soc. Sci. Med.* 21:525–31

66. Kohn ML, Schooler C. 1982. Job conditions and personality: A longitudinal assessment of their reciprocal effects. *Am. J. Sociol.* 87:1257–86

67. Kristensen TS. 1989. Cardiovascular diseases and the work environment. A critical review of the epidemiologic literature on chemical factors. *Scand. J. Work Environ. Health* 15:245–64

68. LaCroix AZ. 1984. *High demand/low control work and the incidence of CHD in the Framingham Cohort.* PhD thesis. Univ. North Carolina, Chapel Hill, NC

69. LaCroix AZ, Haynes SG. 1987. Chest pain in users of video display terminals (letter). *J. Am. Med. Assoc.* 257:627–28

70. Landsbergis PA. 1991. *Occupational stress and hypertension.* Individ. Natl. Res. Serv. Award. Bethesda, MD: Natl. Heart Lung Blood Inst.

71. Landsbergis PA, Schnall PL, Dietz D, Friedman R, Pickering TG. 1992. The patterning of psychological attributes and distress by job strain and social support in a sample of working men. *J. Behav. Med.* 15:379–405

72. Landsbergis PA, Schnall PL, Schwartz JE, Warren K, Pickering TG. 1993. Job strain, hypertension and cardiovascular disease: A review of the empirical evidence and suggestions for further research. In *Job Stress 2000: Emerging Issues,* ed. S. Sauter, GP Keita. Washington, DC: Am. Psychol. Assoc. In press

73. Landsbergis PA, Schurman S, Israel B, Schnall PL, Hugentobler M, et al.

1993. Job stress and heart disease: Evidence and strategies for prevention. *New Solut.* 3:42–58

74. Langosch W, Brodner B, Borcherding M. 1983. Psychosocial and vocational longterm outcomes of cardiac rehabilitation with postinfarction patients under the age of forty. *Psychosom. Med.* 40:115–28

75. Light KC, Turner JR, Hinderliter AL. 1992. Job strain and ambulatory work blood pressure in healthy young men and women. *Hypertension* 20: 214–18

76. Litwin GH, Stringer RA. 1968. *Motivation and Organizational Climate.* Cambridge, MA: Harvard Univ.

77. Markowe HL, Marmot MG, Shipley MJ, Bulpitt CJ, Meade TW, et al. 1985. Fibrinogen: A possible link between social class and coronary heart disease. *Br. Med. J.* 9:291–96

78. Marmot M, Theorell T. 1991. Social class and cardiovascular disease: The contribution of work. In *The Psychosocial Work Environment: Work Organization, Democratization and Health,* ed. JV Johnson, G Johansson, pp. 33–48. Amityville, NY: Baywood Publ.

79. Matthews KA, Cottington EM, Talbott E, Kuller LH, Siegel JM. 1987. Stressful work conditions and diastolic blood pressure among blue collar factory workers. *Am. J. Epidemiol.* 126:280–91

80. McCrae RR. 1990. Controlling neuroticism in the measurement of stress. *Stress Med.* 6:237–41

81. Mensch BS, Kandel DB. 1988. Do job conditions influence the use of drugs. *J. Health Soc. Behav.* 29:169–84

82. Meyer E, Derogatis LR, Miller M, Reading A. 1978. Hypertension and psychological distress. *Psychosomatics* 19:160–68

83. Moller L, Kristensen TS. 1991. Plasma fibrinogen and ischaemic heart disease risk factors. *Arterioscler. Thromb.* 11: 344–50

84. Moller L, Kristensen TS, Hollnagel H. 1991. Social class and cardiovascular risk factors in Danish men. *Scand. J. Soc. Med.* 19:116–26

85. Natl. Heart Lung Blood Inst. 1993. *Rep. Joint Natl. Comm. Detect. Eval. Treat. High Blood Pressure, 5th.* Bethesda, MD: Natl. Heart Lung Blood Inst. NIH Publ. No. 93–1088

86. Netterstrom B, Kristensen TS, Damsgaard MT, Olsen O, Sjol A. 1991. Job strain and cardiovascular risk factors: A cross sectional study of employed Danish men and women. *Br. J. Ind. Med.* 48:684–89

87. Paffenberger RS, Hyde RT, Wing A, Hsieh C. 1986. Physical activity, allcause mortality, and longevity of college alumni. *New England J. Med.* 314:605–13

88. Perski A, Olsson G, Landou C, deFaire U, Theorell T, Hamsten A. 1992. Minimum heart rate and coronary atherosclerosis: Independent relations to global severity and rate of progression of angiographic lesions in men with myocardial infarction at a young age. *Am. Heart J.* 123:609–16

89. Pickering TG. 1991. *Ambulatory Monitoring and Blood Presure Variability.* London: Science Press

90. Pieper C, LaCroix AZ, Karasek RA. 1989. The relation of psychosocial dimensions of work with coronary heart disease risk factors: A meta-analysis of five United States data bases. *Am. J. Epidemiol.* 129:483–94

91. Pirkle JL, Schwartz J, Landis JR, Harlan WR. 1985. The relationship between blood lead levels and blood pressure and its cardiovascular risk implications. *Am. J. Epidemiol.* 121: 246–58

92. Pocock SJ, Shaper AG, Cook DG, Phillips AN, Walker M. 1987. Social class differences in ischaemic heart disease in British men. *Lancet* II:197–201

93. Reed DM, LaCroix AZ, Karasek RA, Miller FD, MacClean CA. 1989. Occupational strain and the incidence of coronary heart disease. *Am. J. Epidemiol.* 129:495–502

94. Rosenman RH, Brand RJ, Sholtz RI, Friedman M. 1976. Multivariate prediction of coronary heart disease during 8.5 year follow-up in the Western Collaborative Group Study. *Am. J. Cardiol.* 37:903–10

95. Rostrup M, Ekeberg O. 1992. Awareness of high blood pressure influences on psychological and sympathetic responses. *J. Psychosom. Res.* 36:117–23

96. Sauter SL, Murphy LR, Hurrell JJ. 1990. Prevention of work related psychological disorders. *Am. Psychol.* 45: 1146–58

97. Schnall PL, Kern R. 1981. Hypertension in American society: An introduction to historical materialist epidemiology. In *The Sociology of Health and Illness,* ed. P. Conrad, R Kern, pp. 97–122. New York: St. Martin's Press

98. Schnall PL, Landsbergis PA, Pieper

CF, Schwartz J, Dietz D, et al. 1992. The impact of anticipation of job loss on worksite blood pressure. *Am. J. Ind. Med.* 21:417–32

99. Schnall PL, Landsbergis PA, Schwartz JE, Warren K, Pickering TG. 1992. *The relationship between job strain, ambulatory blood pressure and hypertension.* Presented at Int. Symp. Epidemiol. Occup. Health, 9th., Cincinnati, OH

100. Schnall PL, Pieper C, Schwartz JE, Karasek RA, Schlussel Y, et al. 1990. The relationship between 'job strain,' workplace diastolic blood pressure, and left ventricular mass index: Results of a case-control study. *J. Am. Med. Assoc.* 263:1929–35. Also, letter to the editor. *J. Am. Med. Assoc.* 1992. 267:1209

101. Schnall PL, Schwartz JE, Landsbergis PA, Warren K, Pickering TG. 1992. The relationship between job strain, alcohol and ambulatory blood pressure. *Hypertension* 19:488–94

102. Schwartz JE, Pieper CF, Karasek RA. 1988. A procedure for linking psychosocial job characteristics data to health surveys. *Am. J. Public Health* 78:904–9

103. Siegrist J, Peter R, Junge A, Cremer P, Seidel D. 1990. Low status control, high effort at work and ischemic heart disease: Prospective evidence from blue-collar men. *Soc. Sci. Med.* 31: 1127–34

104. Steptoe A. 1981. *Psychological Factors in Cardiovascular Disorders.* London: Academic

105. Stern FB, Halperin WE, Hornung RW, Ringenburg VL, McCammon CS. 1988. Heart disease mortality among bridge and tunnel officers exposed to carbon monoxide. *Am. J. Epidemiol.* 128:1276–88

106. Talbott E, Helkamp J, Matthews K, Kuller L, Cottington E, Redmond G. 1985. Occupational noise exposure, noise-induced hearing loss, and the epidemiology of high blood pressure. *Am. J. Epidemiol.* 121:501–14

107. Theorell T. 1990. Family history of hypertension—an individual trait interacting with spontaneously occurring job stressors. *Scand. J. Work Environ. Health* 16(Suppl. 1):74–79

108. Theorell TG, Ahlberg-Hulten G, Jodko M, Sigala F, Soderholm M, de la Torre B. 1993. Influence of job strain and emotion on blood pressure in female hospital personnel during work hours. *Scand. J. Work Environ. Health.* 19:313–18

109. Theorell T, deFaire U, Johnson J, Hall EM, Perski A, Stewart W. 1991. Job strain and ambulatory blood pressure profiles. *Scand. J. Work Environ. Health* 17:380–85

110. Theorell T, Hamsten A, de Faire U, Orth-Gomer K, Perski A. 1987. Psychosocial work conditions before myocardial infarction in young men. *Int. J. Cardiol* 15:33–46

111. Theorell T, Hjemdahl P, Ericsson F, Kallner A, Knox S, et al. 1985. Psychosocial and physiological factors in relation to blood pressure at rest—A study of Swedish men in the upper twenties. *J. Hypertens.* 3:591–600

112. Theorell T, Karasek RA, Eneroth P. 1990. Job strain variations in relation to plasma testosterone fluctuations in working men—a longitudinal study. *J. Intern. Med.* 227:31–36

113. Theorell T, Knox S, Svensson J, Waller D. 1985. Blood pressure variations during a working day at age 28: Effects of different types of work and blood pressure level at age 18. *J. Hum. Stress* 11:36–41

114. Theorell T, Perski A, Akerstedt T, Sigala F, Ahlberg-Hulten G, et al. 1988. Changes in job strain in relation to changes in physiological states. *Scand. J. Work Environ. Health* 14: 189–96

115. Theorell T, Perski A, Orth-Gomer K, Hamsten A, deFaire U. 1991. The effect of returning to job strain on cardiac death risk after a first myocardial infarction before age 45. *Int. J. Cardiol.* 30:61–67

116. Van Egeren LF. 1992. The relationship between job strain and blood pressure at work, at home, and during sleep. *Psychosom. Med.* 54:337–43

117. Wartenberg D, Northridge M. 1991. Defining exposure in case-control studies: A new approach. *Am. J. Epidemiol.* 133:1058–71

118. Watson D, Pennebaker JW. 1989. Health complaints, stress and distress: Exploring the central role of negative affectivity. *Psychol. Rev.* 96:234–54

119. Wilcosky TC, Simonsen NR. 1991. Solvent exposure and cardiovascular disease. *Am. J. Ind. Med.* 19:569–86

120. Williams R. 1989. *The Trusting Heart.* New York: Times Books

Annu. Rev. Public Health. 1994. 15:413–36
Copyright © 1994 by Annual Reviews Inc. All rights reserved

RATIONING ALTERNATIVES FOR MEDICAL CARE

Charles E. Phelps

Department of Community and Preventive Medicine, Departments of Political Science and Economics, University of Rochester, Rochester, New York 14642

KEY WORDS: medical care, rationing, health insurance, medical care supply, medical care demand

INTRODUCTION

All societies can and must ration medical care, as they can and must ration all other goods and services that require any resources to produce. In some societies, markets accomplish this task: in others, waiting in line (or other barriers to receiving the good or service) performs the rationing function. In still others, informal or formal rules specify who may receive which services, and when. To some people, the word "rationing" implies only such activities as lines and queues or rules of access, but a wider vision of rationing incorporates all activities that perform the same function. Rather than viewing rationing as an undesirable activity, I will demonstrate that appropriate rationing of services provides an important and useful societal function, e.g. with regard to medical care. No society, not even the wealthiest in the world, can provide all conceivable amounts and quality of medical care to every citizen. If managed properly, rationing activities direct the use of services to those who will benefit most, and lead to the correct total amount of medical care being produced and used.

Understanding that all societies ration care in some way is an important first step in this discussion. A brief comparison of international data on health care spending provides insight into how this works. Figure 1 shows the annual per capita medical care spending for major industrialized countries in the world, all converted to $US. The bubbles represent the size of each country (population); the United States is the largest bubble at the upper right end (highest income, highest spending). The predictive power of per capita income in explaining per capita medical care spending among these

413

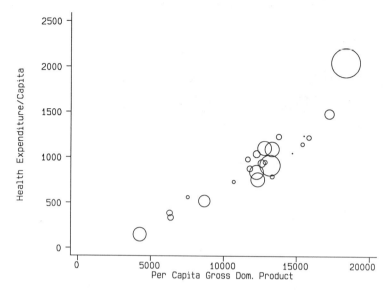

Figure 1   Annual per capita spending on medical care as a function of annual per capita income in 24 industrialized OECD member nations, denoted in 1987 US$.

countries is remarkable. Despite wide differences in the political economies of these countries, as well as disparities in the organization and delivery of health care, the amount of money spent on health care moves directly with income. The relationship between per capita income and per capita medical spending shows that—at the societal level—medical care is a "luxury," since a 1% change in per capita income produces about a 1.4% to 1.8% increase in medical care use, based on regression estimates using data shown in Figure 1. In Figure 1, the US lies well above the best-fit regression line, i.e. has higher spending than would be predicted by it per capita income. However, the points in Figure 1 reveal a slight U-shaped curvature that may make a straight line the wrong choice. The same graph as Figure 1, but using logarithms of per capita spending and per capita income, would show a nearly perfect straight line relationship, with the US lying directly on the best-fit line. There is no conceptual basis for picking either natural units of measurement or logarithms, and in this case, the data seem to suggest that the logarithmic formulation fits the data slightly better. If so, one should not view the US as an abnormal "outlier". (For a more comprehensive discussion see Ref. 33). The *level* at which care is rationed (i.e. per capita spending level) increases predictably with higher per capita income, and the *methods* that each country uses to accomplish the desired rationing differ greatly across countries, but these data irrefutably show that each country does have some effective method for limiting total expenditure on medical care. The mechanisms range from quasi-market methods in the US to controlled market methods in Japan, Germany, and Canada, to socialized (government-owned and operated) systems in the United Kingdom and Sweden. Yet, almost independently of the method chosen to ration care, per capita income predicts very well the resultant per capita medical care spending.

Spending in these societies is not limited because they cannot afford more: in each case, spending on medical care has grown systematically through time. In the United States, for example, the proportion of Gross Domestic Product (GDP) spent on medical care has increased through the past four decades from 5% to over 13%. When spending reached 10% of GDP, many observers opined that our society could not afford more, yet we have chosen to buy more and more through time. Similarly, the rate of increase in medical care spending has been as large or even larger in other modern industrialized societies. Annual real (inflation-corrected) medical care spending per capita has increased by ~5% per year over the past 40 years in countries as diverse as the United States, United Kingdom, Canada, and Germany; Japan's rate of increase has been almost twice as high. Clearly, the choices at any fixed point in time do not represent an upper limit of what these societies can afford. Rather, they ration care through various means, and choose to ration at a higher total level of spending as income increases, and through time.

Methods of rationing care fall into several categories: (*a*) those affecting patient (consumer) behavior, such as copayments, deductibles, limits to the scope of benefits of an insurance plan, waiting in lines, delays to appointments, and other similar instruments; (*b*) those affecting providers' behavior, including administrative rules (guidelines, protocols), provider payment systems, and similar instruments; and (*c*) system-wide limits on accessibility of care, which in turn often generate rationing instruments in categories (*a*) or (*b*).

This paper discusses the major approaches to rationing care in each category, and provides, where possible, evidence on the effects of employing such instruments.

CONSUMER-BASED RATIONING INSTRUMENTS

Rationing by Price—Insurance Benefit Provisions

The leading determinant by far of individuals' use of medical services is health status—whether or not the individual is sick, and if so, how sick.

However, price—and its close companion, health insurance—systematically alter people's use of medical care. In any population, it is easy to find well-insured individuals who use little or no medical care within a given time period (e.g. one year), and others with no insurance who consume large amounts of medical care. However, higher prices systematically alter people's choices about using medical care. Higher prices (less insurance coverage) lead to lower use of medical care. Thus, any instrument that raises price serves to ration care, on average.

For covered services, the most important insurance features include the magnitudes of coinsurance, copayments, deductibles, and other traditional features of insurance coverage. Here, evidence is clearest on the consequences of these instruments on use of medical care. A large investigation conducted for the Federal government in the 1970s and 1980s by the RAND Corporation (The RAND Health Insurance Experiment—RAND HIE for short) used the classic randomized controlled trial format to measure the effects of different insurance plans on medical care use. The experimental plans varied the proportion of expenses paid by the patient, in each case capped by a catastrophic coverage provision limited to the smaller of $1000 or a fraction of family income (either 5%, 10%, or 15%). At one extreme, the free care plan provided 100% coverage for all services. At the other extreme, the plan paid only 5% (95% copayment) until the catastrophic cap had been met, at which point it paid for all subsequent services. Intermediate plans paid 50% and 75% of all services, again with the same out-of-pocket limits on spending as the 95% coinsurance plan had. The 95% coinsurance plan resembles a classic "catastrophic coverage only" plan. The 25% coinsurance plan comes closest to the most common coinsurance features in private health insurance in the USA, although existing plans differ widely along these and other dimensions. A separate plan had a $150 per person deductible (limited to $450 per family), and 100% coverage for all expenses above the deductible; the deductible applied only to out of hospital care. These results, reported in detail elsewhere (19, 20, 26–28, 30), are summarized next.

Table 1 shows both the actual data from the RAND HIE and adjusted estimates that correct for outliers in specific insurance plans, all given in 1984 $US. Total spending was highest for the most generous plan (zero coinsurance), and lowest for the least generous catastrophic insurance plan. On average, people on the least generous plan used about two thirds of the medical care compared to those with complete coverage. Intermediate coverage plans produced intermediate levels of medical care use. The largest drop in medical care use occurs in the transition from full coverage to some copayment. Both the 25% coinsurance plan and the $150 per person deductible (the most generous of the plans that required some copayments)

Table 1   Effects of health insurance coverage on annual medical care use (All expense data in 1984 dollars)*

Insurance plan	Visits	Outpatient expense	Annual probability of admission	Inpatient expense	Total expense (Adjusted)
Free care (0% coinsurance)	4.56	$340	.128	$409	$750
25% Coinsurance	3.33	260	.105	373	617
50% Coinsurance	3.03	224	.092	450	573
95% Coinsurance (catastrophic)	2.73	203	.099	315	540
$150 Individual deductible (ambulatory only)	3.02	235	.115	373	630

Source: Ref. 28

*For rough comparisons, inflation in the decade from 1984–1994 is estimated at 40% for the consumer price index and 120% for the medical care sector

had spending about 15 to 20% lower than the full coverage plan. Shifting all the way to a catastrophic-coverage-only plan yielded about the same additional reduction in spending. The largest shifts in using medical care occurred for ambulatory treatment, and the smallest for hospital care.

In an innovative analysis of the HIE data to understand better the roles of deductibles on demand, one RAND study (19) simulated the effects of various deductibles on medical care use for different types of illnesses (acute, chronic, well-care, and care requiring hospitalization), including plans not specifically used in the actual study. Figure 2 summarizes their results. As noted before, the initial effect of paying *something* (moving from a deductible of zero to $50 per year) creates a considerable change in medical care use for all except hospital care, where *something* occurs between deductibles of $500 and $1000. For all types of ambulatory care they studied, increasing the size of the deductible has diminishing but still important effects on medical care use. Recall that these data reflect 1984 prices; equivalent 1993 deductibles would be about 40% greater, to reflect changes in the Consumer Price Index (CPI). Other studies show an even more dramatic effect of deductibles (and small copayments) on use of dental services (26).

These results clearly show that coinsurance and deductible provision of health insurance have important rationing effects. As standard economic theory predicts, more generous insurance benefits, by lowering the price of

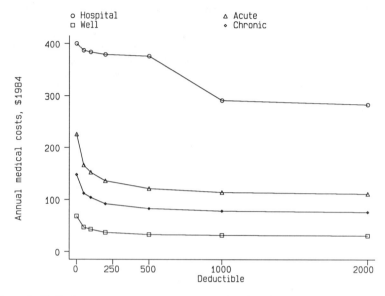

Figure 2 Medical care use per person per year as a function of size of annual deductible in health insurance plan.

care at the time people receive treatment, lead to more use of care. The magnitude of these effects is important both statistically and for policy purposes.

Does "Free for All" Make Sense?

Among all possible rationing devices, *price* makes the most sense in one important way: to the extent that prices correspond to costs of providing care (an important leap of faith in many health care systems, to be sure), using prices to ration care makes individuals' private financial "ouch" correspond to the costs that society must bear to provide the medical care itself. Providing full coverage insurance (free care for all) completely breaks down any connection between the costs of providing medical care and its value to patients. This disconnection is the most important reason to charge some price to patients for receiving medical care. Without it, patients and their providers have every incentive to use too much medical care, ignoring as they do the costs of producing that care.

All societies, as noted above, have achieved some mechanism for rationing care, either through price or by societal limits on the total amount of care provided. When something other than price provides the rationing mechanism, such as waiting in queues or rules about who receives what care (and when), two perverse results can emerge. First, deterrents like waiting time simply create deadweight losses to the society, since they represent costs without benefit. Second, unlike higher prices, they do not spur production of more goods and services. In a well-functioning market, prices higher than the costs of producing a good or service signal to entrepreneurs the desirability of entering to produce more.

However, for several important reasons, it makes sense to have mechanisms that at least partly divorce costs of producing medical care from the decisions to use that care. Health insurance breaks that link by making care less costly to patients (as they use it) than it costs to produce. Why is this desirable? Perhaps most important, health insurance reduces financial risk that individuals confront. The better the coverage, the less financial risk people face. People who dislike risk gain psychological benefits from reducing risk. Good health insurance balances off the reduction of risk with increasing the perverse incentives associated with overuse of free care.

Models of the *best* health insurance plans (19, 48) to make this balance correctly point towards plans that contain modest deductibles ($100 to $300) and coinsurance rates of about 25%, remarkably similar to the traditional major medical insurance plans commonly marketed in the United States. These plans ration the use of care to about 75% of what fully covered people would use, but also provide good financial protection against major financial risk.

PROVIDER-BASED RATIONING

In the use of medical care, patients do not freely choose much of the medical care they consume. Legal rules prohibit, for example, the use of prescription drugs or hospitals without the action of a licensed physician. Doctors and patients can be considered as a decision-making team for much medical treatment. Doctors act both as advisors to patients about the proper course of treatment and also as treaters. In this dual role, they face conflicting financial pressures. The presence of third party insurance makes the distinction between patient and provider somewhat irrelevant, since these third parties (insurance plans, government) pay much (if not all) of the charges for medical care chosen jointly by the doctor and the patient. Whichever way one views the doctor (either as advisor or seller), it is clear that many approaches exist to ration the use of medical care by either constraining the decisions made by providers or by altering the incentives they face.

Altered Incentives

The most widely studied and understood approach to altering incentives for providers centers on the question of the unit of payment for services rendered.

In the traditional payment of doctors, hospitals, dentists, pharmacists, and other providers, reimbursement comes on a fee-for-service basis. At the other extreme, payment in some settings comes on a capitation basis, whereby the provider is responsible for providing all care for a given set of patients for a fixed period of time (e.g. one year) no matter what illness befalls the patients. Pure staff-model HMOs, for example, provide care under such arrangements. In between, payments can be based on a scheme intermediary between fee for service and capitation. Payment based on an episode of illness offers one such approach, most prominently featured in the Prospective Payment System of Medicare, which pays for hospital services on a flat amount per hospitalization, the specific amount depending on the patient's diagnosis.

Within capitation payment systems, the incentives to providers directly lead to cautious use of medical interventions, analogous to rationing. By contrast, a high-paying fee-for-service system offers incentives to providers to treat more, since each unit of care provided increases the profits of the provider. (This literally holds true any time the added revenue exceeds the added variable costs of providing the treatment.) A conceptual model of this process has been developed by Woodward & Warren-Boulton (47). They show how providers would recommend more treatment under the fee-for-service system, and less under the capitation system.

Fortunately, a randomized controlled trial has been conducted that not only demonstrates this phenomenon, but also compares the treatment rates actually observed with a gold standard of professional recommendations for care from a specialist medical association. In this study (17), pediatric residents in a continuity care clinic at Vanderbilt University were randomized to receive either a flat salary (capitation payment) or a fee-for-service payment for each service rendered. The payment rates were established so that, on average, doctors would earn about the same amount per day no matter which payment system they were on. However, the marginal incentives differ greatly in the two payment systems, corresponding exactly to those discussed by Woodward & Warren-Boulton, which in turn correspond closely to the two standard methods of paying doctors (salary or fee-for-service). Patients attending the hospital clinic were randomized to doctors, so there were no effects of either doctor or patient self-selection to one system or the other. Finally, the researchers used the standard recommendations for well care promulgated by the American Academy of Pediatrics as a basis for judging the appropriate amounts of care, at least for routine well-care visits.

The results of this study were remarkable. Not only did the doctors on fee-for-service recommend (and achieve patient compliance for) more treatment than did those doctors on flat salary, but the comparison with the

Table 2 Effects of fee for service vs salary payment incentives on doctors' use of medical care

	Fee for Service	Salary
Total visits scheduled	4.9	3.8
Actual total visits	3.6	2.9
Well care visits	1.9	1.3
Percent of AAP well care visits missed	4%	9%
Percent of patients with well care visits beyond AAP standard	22%	4%

Note: All differences statistically significant
Source: Ref. 17

AAP standard was also exactly as predicted: doctors on fee-for-service recommended more well-care visits than the AAP standard, and salary-paid doctors recommended fewer. Almost all extra visits came in the area of well care (Table 2).

The phenomena studied in this randomized trial are also commonly observed on a larger scale and in real-world insurance plans. The most widespread evidence on the role of provider incentives comes through the observed differences in the cost of providing equivalent amounts of health insurance coverage (e.g. full insurance) under fee-for-service arrangements vs those of traditional prepaid plans, now commonly called Health Maintenance Organizations (HMOs). These plans have grown through the years, but only in a few geographic regions to the point where they dominate the health insurance market.

In these prepaid groups, typically (*a*) patients pay a fixed sum per year for all of their medical care (as they would with a health insurance premium); (*b*) they receive all of their medical treatment from a closed panel of doctors affiliated with the plan; and (*c*) the doctors—usually in a separate group practice that contracts with the health plan—are paid on a flat salary per year. Other *open-panel* arrangements exist where patients can receive their treatment from a wider set of doctors, most of whom conduct a traditional fee-for-service practice, and treat the prepaid patients on a negotiated fee-for-service basis. These plans, known as Independent Practice Associations (IPAs), stand part way between the traditional fee-for-service system and the pure prepaid HMO practice plan.

The most comprehensive study of these prepaid practice plans was undertaken by Luft (24). Careful review of the costs of care for many prepaid groups and (as best possible) corresponding comparison groups using fee-for-service medical care reveals systematic differences in the costs of providing care. The prepaid group practices cost less for comparable populations and benefits provided, with the difference typically in the 1/4 to 1/3 range. However, these comparisons have been questioned as to whether the populations were truly comparable. If favorable self-selection for the prepaid groups had been taking place (e.g. they enrolled relatively healthy people into their plans), then they might look less costly just because of the health of the people they treat, not the way they provide care.

On this issue, several studies have shown that people who enroll into HMOs when offered the opportunity were relatively low users of medical care in the year before they enrolled into the HMO (5, 11, 18). However, one randomized controlled trial (27) showed significantly lower health care costs among persons randomly assigned to an HMO compared with those in the same community receiving fee-for-service treatment with full coverage. The randomized study results show in general that most savings in health care costs arise from reduced use of the hospital, a finding common in Luft's studies as well. The difference between the randomized study (27) and the other studies may well relate to the role of chronic disease. People with chronic disease may be more reluctant to change doctors, as a requirement to enroll into a closed panel group practice, than those without chronic care underway. People with chronic illnesses will more likely have higher past-year costs than those without such conditions. Not surprisingly, therefore, those voluntarily enrolling into HMOs have lower previous-year costs than those who remained in their previous insurance plan and with their previous providers. The RAND experimental study bypassed such issues by confirming agreement to participate in the study *before* people knew which plan they would join. (Fortunately, there was also no differential dropping out among those actually assigned to the HMO plan in that study.) The RAND study results (27) probably predict better what would happen with widespread enrollment into HMO-like plans.

Proponents of the prepaid practice system often argue that a key feature of their success in restraining medical costs is their use of preventive services. Indeed, the catch-phrase "health maintenance organization" emphasizes this idea, based on the Franklinesque adage that an ounce of prevention is worth a pound of cure. Rhetoric aside, however, corroborating evidence has proven elusive. First, few HMOs have record systems that allow careful comparison of the use of preventive services with comparable fee-for-service plans. (There is no incentive to do so since they do not bill by the visit.) This factor alone has made it difficult to determine if HMOs actually do use more preventive services than their fee-for-service counterparts. Second, evidence is now growing that, while many preventive services work in the sense that they improve health, they do so only at added total expense. (A later section reviews this evidence in more detail.) To the extent that this is true, HMOs cannot literally save money by using preventive services, no matter how fervent the wish to the contrary. Third, people commonly move from one insurance plan to another, and from region to region, thereby blunting the economic incentives for HMOs to employ even those preventive services that do save money on net. Fourth, as discussed previously, the salary payment system for doctors encourages them to reduce the amount of care, even (as the experiment among pediatric doctors showed) preventive care. Indeed, in that study, this incentive seems to work strongest *especially* for preventive care. Finally, when people enroll into prepaid group plans, their medical care use almost immediately falls in comparison to what one would find in the fee-for-service system for the same people, as in the RAND study (27). Most preventive interventions have years passing before the expected payoff emerges.

A more likely explanation for the overall prepaid group vs fee-for-service difference arises from the differential financial incentives to use hospital care and referrals to specialists. This particularly holds true for surgical procedures, which historically have a relatively high unit return per hour of effort.

A different and important example of the effects of incentives on providers arose from the introduction in 1983 of the Prospective Payment System (PPS) to pay for Medicare patients' hospital care under Part A of the Medicare program. (This system does not apply to physician fees associated with hospital care.) From its inception in 1965 until the 1983 PPS revisions, Medicare, like most private health insurance, had essentially paid hospitals on a fee-for-service basis. Medicare used a complicated system to adjust for differences between costs and charges (known as the Ratio of Costs to Charges Applied to Charges, or RCCAC), but in its essence, the system paid for each element of care delivered by the hospital. The PPS system changed all that. Under PPS, each patient admitted to hospital becomes assigned to one of nearly 500 Diagnostically Related Groups (DRGs), for which the hospital receives a flat per-case payment (8). (There are additional payments for extremely long stays, outliers.)

As with doctors' financial incentives under capitation payment, the PPS system makes the marginal revenue to the hospital zero for extra days in the hospital, extra lab tests, extra services provided, etc. In general, this system should provide strong incentives for providers to reduce length of stay, and also to eliminate those tests and therapies that do not directly contribute to lower overall costs of treating the patient during the episode/hospitalization. An important issue appears here, of course: doctors on hospital medical staffs, not the hospital's employees, direct the flow of activity around the patients. If anything, this practice would weaken the ability of the hospital to control such variables as length of stay and test use, relative to a hypothetical setting where doctors were employees of the hospital. However, despite this odd organizational arrangement between doctors and hospitals common in the United States (doctors work independent of the hospital and are paid more for more care given, but direct the hospital's resource use), the Medicare PPS system produced a dramatic change in hospital length of stay.

Technological change had been producing a slow downward drift in average length of stay (ALOS) in hospitals for decades, as revealed in these data. However, the declines in ALOS accelerated remarkably in 1984 and 1985, as the rules came into effect. No comparable decline in ALOS took place for non-Medicare patients, effectively ruling out unusually large technological change in the hospital as the primary cause. Almost all analysts of the US health care system attribute the lower length of stay to the financial incentives of the PPS system.

GUIDELINES AND RULES

Guidelines and rules fall into several categories worth considering separately: (a) Limiting the number of persons eligible for a program (as in Medicaid programs, maternal and child health programs, Veterans' Administration programs, etc); (b) Limiting the treatments for which payment will be made under a program for those eligible; (c) Reviewing individual cases for appropriateness of treatment, either retroactively (and denying payment) or concurrently (and altering treatment patterns of providers as treatment is underway); (d) Reviewing providers to assess whether *rates* of use of an intervention are too high, and warning or punishing doctors who are out of compliance; (e) Establishing in advance sets of conditions that must exist in the patient's health history before treatment is deemed desirable; these can be either quite general (as in the AMA's practice parameters or in many guidelines now being promulgated) or quite specific (protocols, or pejoratively, cookbook medicine); (f) Considering new types of rules specifying general characteristics that treatments must satisfy before they become eligible for funding. Most common among these would be cost-effectiveness criteria, partially embedded in the new and controversial Oregon Medicaid program (32).

Most of these types of rules limit expansion of treatment along some dimension (or margin) of decision making. Economists identify such margins as either intensive (the rate of treatment of those being treated) or extensive (the number of people being treated). Guidelines and rules can operate along both margins. The following sections review each of these ideas separately.

LIMITING PROGRAM ELIGIBILITY   One method of rationing services simply limits the number of persons eligible to receive them. Private insurance does this in a very simple way: those who pay the insurance premium are eligible to receive treatment through the program; others are excluded. Public insurance programs such as Medicare, Medicaid, Maternal and Child Health, Veteran's Administration, and other programs limit eligibility by defining parts of the US population who may participate in the program (e.g. Medicare covers the elderly, those with end-stage renal disease, and those classified as having permanent disabilities; Medicaid rules, although they vary by state, always specify income cutoffs above which people may not participate). Every eligible person typically may receive all benefits provided to any person within the program.

Understanding the fiscal consequences of expanding along the extensive margin (adding more people) is often difficult. To understand well, for example, the consequences of raising the income limits for a Medicaid program, or loosening the definitions of permanently disabled in the Medicare program, requires knowing the relative health status of those currently enrolled vs those who would become newly enrolled. In Medicare, for example, relaxing the rules for permanent-disability coverage could readily include large numbers of persons with AIDS, a relatively expensive group for whom to provide coverage. In attempting to predict the cost consequences of moving to a universal health insurance plan in the United States, recent government estimates from diverse federal agencies have differed by a factor of two, mostly on a basis of making different assumptions about the relative healthiness (and, inversely, costliness) of current Medicaid enrollees vs the group of persons currently lacking any form of public or private insurance.

LIMITING THE SCOPE OF TREATMENTS FOR WHICH PAYMENT IS MADE   All health care or health insurance programs make an intrinsic choice: How many people to include (the extensive margin) vs how much to provide to each of them (the intensive margin). For a given budget, one can adjust up on one margin at the expense of the other going down. Precisely this conflict led the State of Oregon to propose their now famous (or infamous) rules that would limit the scope of treatments covered (the intensive margin) to expand coverage to more citizens (the extensive margin). Currently, many health insurance plans cover essentially any service prescribed by a licensed physician; others include only those activities undertaken within the hospital inpatient setting; others include all prescribed treatments except for a predetermined set of exclusions (e.g. cosmetic surgery). Below I discuss in more detail a specific mechanism by which such choices could rationally be made. However chosen, such limitations have historically formed an important part of the rationing control of health insurers.

INDIVIDUAL CASE REVIEW   Some approaches to reducing use of medical care involve case-by-case review of medical activities, either retrospectively, concurrently, or prospectively. Such activities are often quite labor-intensive, and hence have had little impact on the ongoing practice of medicine. Typically these activities take place within the hospital, with a few counter-examples.

Retrospective review sometimes involves denial of payment for procedures later classified as unwarranted. In a classic study of the effect of such an intervention, Lohr et al (23) analyzed the effects of a program for retrospective denial of antibiotic injections in the New Mexico Medicaid program whenever the injection was not supported by a positive test for the presence of bacterial organisms that would be susceptible to the antibiotic. The results showed a two thirds reduction in the rate of injections as doctors realized the consequences of continuing their previous pattern of behavior.

Concurrent review of medical activity almost invariably takes place within the hospital, and usually (at least at present) involves length of stay decisions for inpatients. Currently, for example, most hospitals review the stays of Medicare patients, partly as a way of achieving compliance with the DRG-based prospective payment system discussed previously. A review committee within the hospital can provide an anonymous backstop for individual physicians to discharge a patient earlier than the patient or family might prefer, as well as actually altering a physician's choices about the proper length of stay. Medicaid and some private insurance programs also have concurrent review of length of stay for some patients, usually involving requests for permission to extend the stay of a patient beyond a predetermined number of days, given the patient's diagnosis. Available evidence shows some effect of utilization review on inpatient hospital use, but the effect on total cost is indeterminate (15).

Prospective review can involve a variety of activities, all of which (by the nature of the event) must be relatively "elective" at least in terms of their timing. Many dental insurance plans have prior review programs to authorize (or deny) treatment protocols planned by dentists for a wide variety of procedures, including orthodontia and endodontia. X-rays of the patient's mouth provide much of the needed evidence on the potential value of the treatment. For medical interventions, some programs have instituted a process either of prior review before certain surgical interventions, or of suggesting (sometimes requiring) that the patient receive a second opinion before proceeding to surgery. Available evidence is mixed regarding the potential cost savings from either approach (21). Some commercial software systems are available to assist in pre-operative screening for "appropriateness" of treatment, but these cover only a limited set of conditions. Most second opinion programs only make the option available to the patient. In one case, the Massachusetts Medicaid program actually requires that patients obtain a second opinion before undergoing certain elective surgical procedures, low back surgery, hysterectomy, and gall bladder surgery (13). The program reduced the frequency of these surgical procedures by about 10 percent, most notably for low back surgery, but it has not been widely adopted in private insurance as a presurgical requirement.

REVIEW OF PROVIDERS' RATES OF CARRYING OUT INTERVENTIONS (PROFILING) An alternative approach to analyzing providers' behavior considers not the choices made on a case-by-case basis, but rather the *rates* at which providers undertake various activities. These retrospective reviews can often be accomplished by use of computer analysis of claims and hospital discharge data, rather than using case-by-case chart reviews, making costs much lower. The disadvantage is that such analyses produce more limited information on each case than a chart review can provide. The general notion is to identify and then "home in on" for further review those doctors carrying out abnormally high (or low) rates of specific activities. Many of these approaches are supported by commercially developed software, but little testing or comparison of them has been made in the scientific literature. Many insurers now have an active interest in reviews of this kind, and their use will likely increase through time.

PROVIDING GUIDELINES AND PROTOCOLS   Perhaps one of the most puzzling phenomena in modern health services research has been the repeated demonstrations of large and systematic variability in the use of specific interventions for populations of apparently similar age, gender, and other relevant composition (see Refs. 34–36, 45, 46 for a selective sample of the huge relevant literature and references cited therein). The commonest approach uses population rates of treatment, and measures variability as the (weighted) coefficient of variation (COV) in rates of use across regions, normally weighted by the population size within each region, using epidemiologic methods of indirect standardization or regression analysis to control for age and gender differences across populations.

For some procedures where the reasons for medical intervention seem quite clear (e.g. hip fracture, acute myocardial infarction), cross-regional variations are always quite low, with COVs ranging from 0.1 to 0.15, or even lower. Other interventions routinely show high variability across regions (e.g. hospitalization for back injury, back surgery, diabetes, high blood pressure, gastroenteritis, otitis media, and several psychiatric admission categories), with COVs in the range of 0.4 to 0.6, or larger. Variations appear larger for nonsurgical than for most surgical hospital admissions. Cardiac and mental illness conditions predominate in lists of hospital admissions with high variability. Similar patterns of variability arise in health care systems completely different from that in the US, including in Canada (social insurance) and Britain (socialized medical care).

These well-documented variations in treatment patterns suggest widespread disagreement among providers of care about the correct ways to use various interventions. It cannot be the case that all observed regions have the "right" rate, by either a medical-professional or an economic standard (e.g. one where marginal benefits and marginal costs were equated). Some (perhaps all) regions must be using too much of an intervention; some (perhaps all) must be using too little. The observation of widespread variations does not tell us what the "right" rate might be, but it does signal serious disagreement about the right rate.

More than any other phenomenon, this variability underlies the concept that guidelines for providing care would provide an alternative basis for reducing the costs of medical care use without rationing in the traditional sense. In a sense, guidelines seek to affect patterns of use of medical care by rationalizing the use of existing resources, rather than rationing them. The concept has merit if the existing variations really are due to disagreement about proper ways to use medical interventions, since information made available to providers in the form of guidelines, practice parameters, or more specific protocols could both reduce total rates of use and improve health outcomes of the patients treated. Introduction of guidelines and profiles frequently has reduced aggregate rates of use, sometimes quite substantially; sometimes, introduction of guidelines has produced no discernible change in behavior (16).

The literature on the consequences of using guidelines is only now emerging, since serious interest in guidelines is recent. In Maine, for example, a collaborative project with the state medical society demonstrated considerable reduction in "high" rates of use of several interventions, such as low back surgery and caesarean section (7). In another study, guidelines promulgated by professional societies on the use of preoperative tests (chest x-ray, routine EKG, and such) not only reduced unwarranted tests, but also (disturbingly) produced a parallel decline in the use of these tests even in cases for which they continued to be recommended (25). Thus, the proper use of guidelines, together with their construction and dissemination, needs research (3). The use of guidelines in determining the package of covered services is central to the plan for universal insurance in the United States recently proposed by the American College of Physicians (ACP) (39).

COST-EFFECTIVENESS CRITERIA   One can consider general criteria for including or excluding interventions from a set of those approved for coverage on predetermined criteria. It would make most sense economically to rank medical care interventions on the basis of their cost-effectiveness, and use this ranking to determine the set of covered services (scope of benefits). The meaning of "cost effectiveness" must be accurately defined. Some people incorrectly interpret the phrase to mean that the intervention actually saves money as well as improving health outcomes. This overly stringent construction ignores the value to patients of health produced by the intervention. Unfortunately, this standard is often confused with a correct definition of cost effectiveness, and has been applied—usually for preventive interventions—as a standard for determining whether a new intervention should be included in coverage packages. (This approach was specifically mandated in the consideration of free influenza vaccinations for the elderly in Medicare.)

A more careful definition of cost effectiveness (CE) measures the added medical care costs from an intervention relative to the added health outcomes. This ratio of incremental costs divided by incremental effectiveness forms the basis for modern CE analysis. It requires two things: (a) Methods to provide specific ways to measure health care outcomes using the same yardstick no matter what the medical intervention; and (b) a rule to decide how much is too much to pay for added benefits. The most popular yardstick—called Quality Adjusted Life Years (QALY, pronounced "kwa-lee")—combines gains both in length of life and in the quality of life (43, 44). With this yardstick in hand, we can estimate the cost-effectiveness of virtually any medical intervention, measured as added dollars spent per added QALYs obtained.

The incremental cost per QALY varies enormously across medical interventions used in the USA. A few interventions actually save money as well as improving health, whereas most, including most preventive care, add costs while adding QALYs. Breast cancer screening (mammography) and cervical cancer screening (Pap smear) provide QALYs at cost between about $10,000 and $30,000 per QALY, depending on the intervention and the target population. Some medical care interventions add QALYS for several hundred or several thousand dollars each. However, many others add QALYs at costs of hundreds of thousands and sometimes millions of dollars per QALY. How we use these types of interventions will **and should** come under increasing scrutiny in the new cost-conscious environment. This scrutiny works in both directions: we should expand the use of interventions that produce QALYs cheaply, and reduce the extent of use of those with extremely high incremental costs per QALY produced. The problems come from trying to identify which is which, and in finding ways to change how we use resources in the health care system at present.

The issue seldom hinges on *whether* an intervention is good, but rather *for whom* it is good (Table 3). For most interventions described in Table 3, the CE ratio rises sharply as the "extensive margin" is expanded. For example, low-dose lovastatin, a cholesterol-lowering drug, has a low CE ratio for high-risk populations, but a cost per QALY almost 1000 times higher for low-risk patients. It also has lower cost-effective alternatives. Order-of-magnitude differences in the CE ratio appear for coronary artery bypass surgery, depending on the criteria for patient selection.

Where should we stop? As in each example, for almost every medical intervention, there exists *some* set of patients for whom the intervention produces health improvements at relatively low cost per QALY. As the intervention spreads to a wider group, the "bang for the buck" invariably declines. Unfortunately, we do not currently have either a good understanding of the costs per QALY for many interventions (and groups receiving those interventions) or—more importantly—a mechanism to decide when "enough is enough" and behave accordingly.

The typical approach to determining "where to stop" on the cost per QALY scale looks at medical care interventions in widespread use and says "if the $/QALY approaches those of commonly used interventions, it will be acceptable to add this new intervention," or asks "Is this treatment in the same league as those being used now?" This approach begs the question, however: If the current health care system has produced badly skewed results, by using most medical care interventions excessively, then comparison with current practice will merely expand the range of decisions made poorly. We could readily expect this, if for no other reason than the distorting effects of health insurance on decisions to use medical interventions, as discussed above.

Garber & Phelps (12) have devised an alternative strategy from outside of the health care system to determine people's valuation of medical interventions. They developed an economic model that derives the optimal CE cutoff, the maximum $/QALY that a utility-maximizing consumer would select, if given the choice. They derive key parameters for this model from other observed decisions that people make outside of the health care system, revealing their fundamental preferences regarding risk-avoiding behavior (called the "relative risk aversion measure," commonly labeled as "r^*").

Figure 3 shows the key results (Figure 3). The optimal cutoff declines slowly with age, simply on the grounds that fewer years remain for a person to reap the benefit of improved health outcomes. The optimal CE cutoff is slightly lower for males than females at any age (a more stringent criterion) because women live longer on average. The economic literature centers the key risk-avoiding measure at about $r^* = 2$, ranging from 1 to 4 for most studies (hence the display of this range in Figure 3). The optimal CE ratio

Table 3 Estimated cost-effectiveness of commonly used medical interventions

Intervention	Cost/life-year ($1989)
Low-dose lovastatin for high cholesterol[a]	
Male heart attack survivors, age 55–64, cholesterol level ≥250	1,600
Male heart attack survivors, age 55–64, cholesterol level <250	1,700
Female hypertensive nonsmokers, age 35–44	710,000
Female nonsmokers, age 35–44	1,500,000
Exercise electrocardiogram as screening test[b]	
40 year-old males	92,200
40 year-old females	248,500
Hypertension screening[c]	
40 year-old males	20,400
40 year-old females	31,300
Breast cancer screening[d]	
Annual breast examination, females age 55–65	11,300
Annual breast examination and mammography, females age 55–65	30,400
Physician advice about smoking cessation[e]	
1% quit rate, males age 45–50	2,800
Pap smear every 3 years[f]	
Females, starting at age 20, continuing to 74	17,800
Coronary Artery Bypass Graft[g]	
Left main coronary artery disease	6,500
Single vessel disease with moderate angina	65,300
Neonatal Intensive Care Units[h]	
Infants 1000–1500 grams	8,100
Infants 500–999 grams	57,200

Refs. 4, 6, 9, 10, 14, 22, 42, 44

varies considerably with this measure, so a more precise measurement would have immense value to the health care community. It also varies broadly within income. At the central risk-aversion measure of $r^* = 2$, a simple rule of thumb emerges from this work: Set the optimal CE ratio at about two to three times annual income. This rule is not hard and fast, of course,

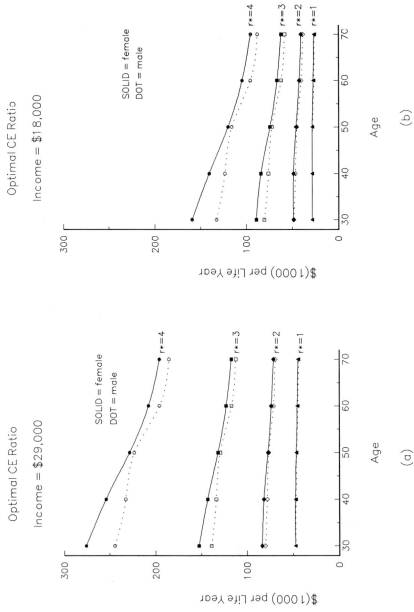

Figure 3 Optimal cost effective cutoffs for choosing medical care by income, gender, age, and degree of aversion to risk.

but it does provide some guidance for implementing CE ratios independent of the standard approach that relies on the CE ratios of other commonly used medical interventions.

This approach suggest that individuals, if freely allowed to choose, would select very different amounts of medical care depending on their income. When we look across choices made at the aggregate (national) levels, as shown in Figure 1, this is precisely what occurs. Within specific countries, however, one often finds much more homogeneity in the amount of service received by different income classes. In part because of the effects of health insurance, one finds relatively little difference in per capita spending across income groups (28, 30). Many social programs deliberately seek to reduce differences in access to medical care across income groups. Ultimately, social policy choices on this issue will necessarily shift towards a more egalitarian policy providing equal care across income groups or a policy that allows individual distinctions by income group. As harsh as this may seem to some, the available evidence suggests that lower income people may well prefer more income to more medical care, other things being equal, in which case the egalitarian approach does not serve them as well as other public policies that would require the same public expenditure on their behalf.

RATIONING AT THE SYSTEM LEVEL (CENTRAL PLANNING)

Another method of implementing rationing focuses on the overall capacity to provide health care within a system, rather than at the doctor or provider level. In many modern industrialized societies, health care is rationed at a national or state level through top-down budgeting both for capital expansion and for annual operating costs. Great Britain and Canada are two prominent examples.

In the United States, system planning has been in place since the 1950s in varying forms and over differing geographic regions, although less so now than in the 1970s. The usual means of implemention has been to alter the rate of entry into the hospital and nursing home industries through certificate of need (CON) and similar requirements. It has been difficult to measure the efficacy of such planning overall in reducing capital investment, although in "mature" plans some effect on lowering of investment has been noted. In some cases, however, total costs have apparently been driven up by CON laws (37, 41), despite the attempt to limit system capacity.

System-wide rationing can produce different results, some formal and clear, others informal and indistinct. First, and probably most obvious to outside observers, capacity-level rationing may of necessity trigger the use of other lower level rationing devices such as discussed previously. How treatment is rationed within the British National Health Service, for example, was documented in a fascinating study by Aaron & Schwartz (1). For example, patients over 50 years old in that system rarely receive kidney dialysis. Doctors have evolved a practice whereby older patients are never referred "up the line" from primary care doctors to specialists, a rationale justified by the assertion that the patients are "too fragile" to sustain the procedures, or that "for persons with such advanced disease, the best thing that we can do is to make their remaining life comfortable."

The repercussions of system-wide rationing may be subtle enough to render them almost indistinguishable from informal rationing: the availability of resources in a community may actually affect the style of doctors' practice, and hence their recommendations to patients. The widespread variability in the use of medical resources across regions (see discussion above) indicates that no clear consensus exists on the use of medical interventions. Attempts to link the rates of use of various interventions with the availability of medical care resources within a particular region have met with limited or no success, although positive correlations have been noted between rates of use of an intervention and the number of relevant specialists per capita in the region. Causation is difficult to determine in these types of studies; supply (availability) may effectively be following demand. Furthermore, supply may determine demand in the sense that availability sets a style for doctors, which in turn affects their recommendations to patients. This is clearly an area needing further study.

CONCLUDING REMARKS

Rationing, broadly taken, encompasses methods by which societies limit access to health care resources, and presumably also thereby limit health care spending. Methods extend from pure rationing rules to markets. Rationing of medical care must involve both patients and providers, since both parties are involved in decisions about using medical care. Effective rationing serves numerous valuable functions, including limiting expenditure on medical care appropriately (thereby releasing resources for other economically valuable goods and services) and guiding the delivery of services to those for whom the services have maximal value. Obviously, many procedures exist to ration care that serve neither of these desirable allocative functions well. The pervasive role of health insurance disrupts the effective functioning of the market in rationing health care activities. Other nonmarket mechanisms, such as incentives and rules affecting both providers and patients, are now in place to implement this rationing function.

New methods to ration health care, involving cost-effectiveness analysis and similar techniques, offer an alternative to maximize existing medical care resources. However, to sustain the effectiveness of such new methods, our society would need to underwrite the research needed to ascertain cost-effective ways to deliver health care, an investment that has only now begun.

Literature Cited

1. Aaron HJ, Schwartz WB. 1984. *The Painful Prescription: Rationing Hospital Care.* Washington, DC: The Brookings Inst.

2. Acton JP. 1975. Nonmonetary factors in the demand for medical services: Some empirical evidence. *J. Pol. Econ.* 83:595–614

3. Audet A, Greenfield S, Field M. 1990. Medical practice guidelines: current activities and future directions. *Ann. Int. Med.* 113:709–14

4. Boyle MH, Torrance GW, Sinclair JC, Horwood SP. 1983. Economic evaluation of neonatal intensive case of very-low-birth-weight infants. *N. England J. Med.* 308:1330–37

5. Buchanan J, Cretin S. 1986. Fee-for-service health care expenditures: Evidence of selection effects among subscribers who choose HMOs. *Med. Care* 24:39–51

6. Cummings Sr, Rubin SM, Oster G. 1989. The cost effectiveness of counseling smokers to quit. *J. Am. Med. Assoc.* 261:75–79

7. Dep. Health Care Rev., Div. Health Policy Progr. Eval. 1986. *Confronting Regional Variations: The Maine Approach.* Chicago: Am. Med. Assoc.

8. Dep. Health Hum. Serv., Health Care Financ. Admin., Medicare Progr. 1984. *Prospective payment for Medicare Inpatient Hospital Services, final rule.*

9. Eddy DM. 1989. Screening for breast cancer. *Ann. Int. Med.* 111:389–99

10. Eddy DM. 1990. Screening for cervical cancer. *Ann. Int. Med.* 113:214–26

11. Eggers P, Prihoda R. 1982. Pre-enrollment reimbursement patterns of medicare beneficiaries enrolled in 'At Risk' HMOs. *Health Care Financ. Rev.* 4:155–73

12. Garber AM, Phelps CE. 1992. *Eco-nomic foundations of cost-effectiveness analysis.* Cambridge, MA: Natl. Bur. Econ. Res. Work. Pap. 4164

13. Gertman PM, Stackpole DA, Levenson DK, Manuel BM, Brennan RJ, Janko GM. 1980. Second opinions for elective surgery. *N. England J. Med.* 302:1169–74

14. Goldman L, Weinstein MC, Goldman PA, Williams LW. 1991. Cost-effectiveness of HMG-CoA reductase inhibition or primary and secondary prevention of coronary heart disease. *J. Am. Med. Assoc.* 265:1145–51

15. Gray BH, Field MJ, eds. 1989. *Controlling Costs and Changing Patient Care? The Role of Utilization Management.* Washington, DC: Natl. Acad. Press

16. Greco PJ, Eisenberg JM. 1993. Changing physicians' practices. *N. England J. Med.* 329:1271–74

17. Hickson GB, Altmeier WA, Perrin JM. 1987. Physician reimbursement by salary or fee-for-service: Effect on physician practice behavior in a randomized prospective study. *Pediatrics* 80:344–50

18. Jackson-Beeck M, Kleinman JH. 1983. Evidence for self-selection among health maintenance organization enrollees. *J. Am. Med. Assoc.* 250:2826–29

19. Keeler EB, Buchanan JL, Rolph JE, Hanley J, Reboussin D. 1988. *The demand for episodes of treatment in the health insurance experiment.* Santa Monica, CA: RAND Corp. Rep. R-3454-HHS

20. Leibowitz A, Manning WG, Keeler EB, Duan N, Lohr KN, Newhouse JP. 1985. The effect of cost sharing on the use of medical services by children. *Pediatrics* 75:942–51

21. Lindsay PA, Newhouse JP. 1990. The

cost and value of second surgical opinion programs: a critical review of the literature. *J. Health Polit. Policy Law* 15:543–70

22. Littenberg B, Garber AM, Sox HC Jr. 1990. Screening for hypertension. *Ann. Int. Med.* 112:192–202

23. Lohr K, Brook RH, Kaufman MA. 1980. Quality of care in the new Mexico medicaid program: The effect of the New Mexico experimental medical care review organization on the use of antibiotics for infectious diseases. *Med. Care* 18 (Suppl.)

24. Luft HS. 1981. *Health Maintenance Organizations: Dimensions of Performance*. New York: Wiley

25. Macario A, Roizen MF, Thisted RA, Kim S, Orkin FK, Phelps CE. 1992. Reassessment of preoperative laboratory testing has changed the test-ordering patterns of physicians. *Surg. Gynecol. Obstet.* 175:539–47

26. Manning WG, Benjamin B, Bailit HL, Newhouse JP. 1985. The demand for dental care: Evidence from a randomized trial in health insurance. *J. Am. Dent. Assoc.* 110:895–902

27. Manning WG, Leibowitz A, Goldberg GA, et al. 1984. A controlled trial of the effect of a prepaid group practice on the use of services. *N. England J. Med.* 310:1505–14

28. Manning WG, Newhouse JP, Duan N, et al. 1987. Health insurance and the demand for medical care: Evidence from a randomized experiment. *Am. Econ. Rev.* 77:251–73

29. Newhouse JP. 1974. A design for a health insurance experiment. *Inquiry* 11:5–27

30. Newhouse JP. 1993. *Free for All? Lessons from the RAND Health Insurance Experiment, and the RAND Health Insurance Experiment Group*. Cambridge, MA: Harvard Univ. Press

31. Newhouse JP, Williams AP, Bennett BW, Schwartz WB. 1982. Where have all the doctors gone? *J. Am. Med. Assoc.* 247:2392–96

32. Oregon Health Serv. Comm. 1991. *Prioritization of health services: a report to the governor and legislature*. Salem, OR

33. Phelps CE. 1992. *Health Economics*, pp. 495–500. New York: Harper Collins

34. Phelps CE, Mooney C. 1992. Correction and update on priority setting in

medical technology assessment in medical care. *Med. Care.* 31:744–51

35. Phelps CE, Parente ST. 1990. Priority setting for medical technology and medical practice assessment. *Med. Care.* 28:703–23

36. Roos NP, Wennberg JE, McPherson K. 1988. Using diagnosis-related groups for studying variations in hospital admissions. *Health Care Financ. Rev.* 9:53–62

37. Salkever DS, Bice TW. 1976. The impact of certificate of need controls on hospital investment. *Milbank Mem. Fund Q.* 54:185–214

38. Scitovsky AA, Snyder NM. 1972. Effect of coinsurance on the demand for physician services. *Soc. Secur. Bull.* 35:3–19

39. Scott HD, Shapiro HB. 1992. Universal insurance for American health care. *Ann. Int. Med.* 117:511–19

40. Simon JL, Smith DB. 1973. Change in location of a student health service: A quasi-experimental evaluation of the effects of distance on utilization. *Med. Care.* 11:59–67

41. Sloan FA, Steinwald B. 1980. Effects of regulation on hospital costs and input use. *J. Law Econ.* 23:81–110

42. Sox HC Jr, Littenberg B, Garber AM. 1989. The role of exercise testing in screening for coronary artery disease. *Ann. Int. Med.* 110:456–59

43. Torrance GW. 1987. Utility approach to measuring health-related quality of life. *J. Chronic Dis.* 40:593–600

44. Weinstein MC. 1981. Economic assessment of medical practices and technologies. *Med. Decision Making* 1:309–330

45. Wennberg JE, Freeman JL, Culp WJ. 1987. Are hospital services rationed in New Haven or over-utilised in Boston? *Lancet* 1:1185–88

46. Wennberg JE, McPherson K, Caper P. 1984. Will payment based on diagnosis-related groups control hospital costs? *N. England J. Med.* 311:295–330

47. Woodward RS, Warren-Boulton F. 1984. Considering the effect of financial incentives and professional ethics on 'appropriate' medical care. *J. Health Econ.* 3: 223–37

48. Zeckhauser R. 1970. Medical insurance: A case study of the trade-off between risk spreading and appropriate incentives. *J. Econ. Theory* 2:10–26

Annu. Rev. Public Health. 1994. 15:437–59

MANAGED CARE PLANS:
Characteristics, Growth, and Premium Performance

Robert H. Miller

Institute for Health and Aging, University of California, San Francisco, California 94109

Harold S. Luft

Institute for Health Policy Studies, University of California, San Francisco, California 94109

KEY WORDS: managed care, health maintenance organizations, preferred provider organizations, health insurance, premiums

INTRODUCTION

Managed care is a key feature of most health care reform proposals. The policy debate over health care reform has tended to focus on issues of health care financing and purchasing, such as the scope and level of benefits, the amount of subsidies to small businesses, and the size of purchasing coalitions. Much less attention has been focused on the organizations that pay providers and deliver health care services. Here we describe major types of managed care plans, outline relationships between purchasers, intermediaries, and providers of managed care plans, and provide a brief overview of their growth and transformation.

We are not proposing a definitive classification scheme for managed care organizations and plans. Rather, we point out limitations in the categorizations of existing plans and the difficulties in creating new ones. Our goal is to provide the reader with background and context to better understand the performance of managed care plans over the past dozen years. We conclude with a discussion of the limitations of what is known about the

437

0163-7525/94/0510-0437$05.00

levels and rates of growth of health care premiums, a crucial indicator of the performance of managed care plans.

KEY ORGANIZATIONS IN MANAGED CARE

Several types of organizations are central to managed care. On the demand side, purchasing organizations such as employers, employer coalitions, Medicare, Medicaid, other government agencies, and some labor unions contract with health benefit intermediaries in order to offer health plan coverage to enrollees or beneficiaries. In the policy debate over health care reform, there has been much discussion about increasing the power of purchasing organizations through the formation of large purchasing coalitions or alliances, the creation of incentives for enrollees to choose fewer and lower cost health plans, and the development of uniform standards for data collection and reporting that would permit purchasers and their enrollees to compare utilization, cost, quality, and satisfaction performance among competing health plans and therefore make more cost-effective choices.

On the supply side, key organizations in managed care include health benefit intermediaries, physician networks, large medical groups, hospitals, and integrated delivery systems.

1. Health benefit intermediaries can perform various functions. For example, they can contract with purchasers to offer their health care plans to potential enrollees; determine enrollee eligibility; create and manage provider networks; and pay providers for services delivered to enrollees. Arrangements between purchasers and health benefit intermediaries vary. For example, an employer may self-insure and determine enrollee availability while one health benefit intermediary manages the provider network and another pays claims. Alternatively, one health benefit intermediary may insure the employer, determine eligibility, manage the network, and pay claims. Major intermediaries of managed care health benefits perform a full range of functions, and some offer multiple plans, including health maintenance organization (HMO), preferred provider organization (PPO), and other managed care plans. Major intermediaries often are owned by commercial or Blue Cross/Blue Shield carriers, large national PPO or HMO managed care chains, or larger regional managed care organizations.
2. Physician networks consist of solo and small group physicians who serve Individual Practice Association (IPA) HMO, PPO, Point-of-Service (POS), and other enrollees in managed care plans. Such physicians have nonexclusive relationships with the intermediary—they can continue to see indemnity insurance and Medicare patients, and often contract with

multiple organizations. We focus on networks of physicians, since physicians are responsible for generating about 75 percent of all expenditures on patient care (11).

3. Large medical groups provide physician services to prepaid group practice (PGP) and network model HMOs, as well as some services to other types of plans. After steadily increasing over time (14), large medical groups have recently surged in importance, especially with the creation of new, mostly capitated groups—based on primary care physicians—that contract nonexclusively with HMOs. Note that although medical staffs in staff model HMOs are not medical groups in a legal sense, they can be so similar to the latter that the terms staff and group model HMO are sometimes used interchangeably. In such plans, the medical group relies on the HMO for all or nearly all of its patients, and the HMO likewise relies on the medical group to manage its physician services.

4. Hospitals usually contract nonexclusively with health benefit intermediaries, but sometimes contract directly with purchasers. In markets with substantial managed care penetration, individual hospitals often belong to hospital chains or alliances that in turn are increasingly part of larger integrated delivery systems.

5. Integrated delivery systems (IDSs) include at least one physician organization and one hospital in a local market area, and may include other health care provider organizations. One form of the IDS is the "physician-hospital organization," which consists of a hospital that either owns, controls, or is closely tied to at least one medical group or IPA (or vice versa).

KEY CHARACTERISTICS OF MANAGED CARE PLANS

The provider network is the single most important feature distinguishing a managed care from an indemnity (fee-for-service (FFS)) plan. The characteristics of coverage in a managed care health plan underscore the importance of the network: an enrollee in a managed care health plan who goes out of network for service has worse coverage, or maybe no coverage at all, for that service. As used here, managed care plans exclude indemnity plans with utilization review (UR), where no network is involved. While increasingly common, our definition is not universally accepted; that is, some analysts define indemnity plans with UR as managed care plans (31).

Table 1 summarizes the four characteristics typically associated with different types of managed care plans: risk-bearing physician organizations and network physicians; physician organization type; exclusivity of the relationship between health benefit intermediary and medical group; and out-of-network coverage.

Table 1 Characteristics of common types of health plans

Type of health plan	Risk-bearing	Physician Organization Type					Benefits Coverage out-of-network
		Staff MDs	Large group(s)	Network solo/small group MDs	Exclusive relationship with		
					Intermediary	MDs	
HMO	Often	Varies	Varies	Varies	Varies	Varies	No
PGP	Yes	No	Yes	No	Yes	Yes	No
Staff	No	Yes	No	No	Yes	Yes	No
Network	Yes	No	Yes	No	No	No	No
IPA	Yes	No	No	Yes	Varies	No	No
Mixed	Often	Varies	Varies	Varies	Varies	Varies	No
PPO	No	No	Varies	Often	Varies	No	Yes
(EPO)	No	No	Varies	Often	Varies	No	No
POS	Varies	Varies	Varies	Varies	Varies	Varies	Yes
(Open-ended HMO)	Often	Varies	Varies	Varies	Varies	Varies	Yes

Major Types of Managed Care Plans

PPO plans have three defining characteristics. First, they do not capitate or put at risk their network physician members. PPOs pay physicians FFS, sometimes as a discount from usual, customary, and reasonable (UCR) charges, and sometimes with a fee schedule. Second, enrollees in a PPO plan usually receive services from a network of solo/small group physicians and a network of hospitals that have nonexclusive relationships with the PPO, although some PPO enrollees receive services from large group practices. The absence of risk sharing by providers in a PPO and the nonexclusive relationship means that there is little "organizational linkage" between the physician and the PPO—it is not unlike any of a broad range of third party payers, except for the agreed-upon fees. Third, enrollees in a PPO plan receive some benefit coverage if they obtain health care services from a non-network provider. Under some currently used definitions, exclusive provider organization (EPO) plans are similar to PPO plans, except that enrollees do not receive benefit coverage for services from a non-network provider. Although some EPOs are capitated, individual EPO providers usually are not. In general, PPO plans offer enrollees the broadest provider choice of all managed care plans.

HMO plans typically have two defining characteristics: providers are at direct or indirect financial risk for providing services, and enrollees usually have no coverage for out-of-network service use (see POS plans below). The five commonly identified types of HMO plans are distinguished from each other by the type of organization of physicians that delivers the services, and the exclusivity of the relationship between the health benefit intermediary and large medical groups (see Table 1). A staff model HMO has an exclusive relationship with the physician staff who are employees of the HMO; a PGP model HMO has exclusive relationships with large, capitated medical groups that contract exclusively with the HMO; a network model HMO contracts nonexclusively with large medical groups; an IPA model HMO contracts (exclusively or nonexclusively) with an IPA that contracts non-exclusively with solo and small group physicians, or else the HMO contracts directly with solo and small group physicians; and mixed model HMO plans contract with more than one type of provider organization or network.

POS plans have only one typical characteristic. When service is needed (the "point-of-service"), enrollees can choose to obtain services out-of-net-work and still obtain some coverage for those services. Otherwise, as Table 1 shows, POS plan characteristics vary so much that the term has multiple meanings. In some definitions, the POS plan is an HMO plan with an out-of-network coverage option, also known as the open-ended HMO plan. In other definitions, the POS plan is a PPO plan with the added feature of a gatekeeper to monitor "in network" services. In still other definitions, the POS plan is a relabeled PPO plan.

A key distinction among plans is whether or not plan physicians orient their practice styles towards capitation and risk. We distinguish between large risk-bearing organizations that account for most or all of a physician's income, and risk-bearing networks that only provide a part (sometimes small) of the physician's income. In a staff model HMO or in a PGP contracting with an HMO, the organization is capitated and bears risk, whereas the individual physician may be part of a large risk pool and may bear little or no direct risk. (Members of a risk pool are at least partially "at risk" for expenditures that are higher than a budgeted amount for a certain set of services). Nevertheless, because the staff HMO or capitated medical group pays virtually all of a physician's salary, the organizations have enough formal and informal administrative, utilization management, financial and group norm levers at their disposal so that they can select and retain those physicians who adhere to conservative practice styles consistent with capitation and risk-bearing. Individual physicians are at risk of losing their full-time jobs if their practice patterns are in marked conflict with those of the group as a whole. However, the economic costs or savings associated with a specific treatment decision will have little identifiable impact on the physician's income. For a medical group that serves both HMO and FFS patients, the importance of risk-bearing to the organization and the impact of risk-bearing on the individual physician depends heavily on the proportion of services that are capitated.

Capitated, risk-bearing IPA networks provide only a portion of the income of their network physicians and generally have fewer implicit or informal organizational levers than medical or staff groups to obtain patterns of physician practice consistent with the risk borne by the IPA. As a result, capitated IPAs rely more on their remaining financial and utilization management levers, including physician-specific capitation payments, greater risk-sharing with individual physicians (16), and greater emphasis on prospective and concurrent review of decisions on individual patient care. Because PPOs do not subject network physicians to risk-bearing, they have to focus on fee reductions and case-by-case utilization management to contain health care expenditures. When IPAs and PPOs have large enough enrollee volume per network provider, they can engage in physician profiling. In such cases, they can examine a provider's overall utilization patterns, and offer feedback to that provider, rather than just engage in case-by-case utilization management. We focus on risk-bearing by providers, rather than by the health benefit intermediary, because it can be argued that a carrier providing insurance for a set PPO plan premium is as much at risk as an HMO providing insurance for a set HMO plan premium.

Limitations of Managed Care Plan Categories

The set of categories outlined is both complicated and not entirely consistent with existing terminology, reflecting the complicated, rapidly changing medical care environment and the fact that the common terminology has been designed more for marketing than for research. Thus labels are often used in conflicting and confusing ways. Two specific limitations are worth underscoring.

First, some classifications do not convey much information or are not robust in the face of a rapidly changing marketplace. As HMO health benefit intermediaries expand geographically or merge, they contract with more than one type of physician organization, making the generic category of "mixed model" HMO plan increasingly common. As medical groups or IPAs expand geographically or merge, they become more complex organizationally, especially in areas where managed care market penetration is relatively large. For example, large primarily capitated medical groups that are based on primary care physicians (PCPs) sometimes contract with health benefit intermediaries to accept most of the risk for providing *all* physician services and, in turn, contract with IPAs consisting of specialists. As another example, HMO health benefit intermediaries increasingly contract with integrated delivery systems that may have multiple types of relationships with physician organizations. In each case, the resulting HMO plans would either end up in the generic "mixed model HMO" classification, or in some additional classification. More generally, because the dozens of local area medical marketplaces are so diverse and dynamic, the number and complexity of different relationships and characteristics among health benefit intermediaries and providers is increasing rapidly, turning the activity of classifying plans into an ongoing game of "catch-up" with the marketplace.

Second, for a given type of physician organization, exceptionally wide variation in financial and organizational characteristics can have an important impact on health plan performance. For example, some IPAs capitate and share substantial financial risk with providers, and have acquired several organizational characteristics of large capitated medical groups, thereby adding to the methods they can use to control utilization of health care service. Such IPAs have obtained sufficient leverage from their enrollee volume to "capture the attention" of the provider who is more likely to carefully consider both the financial impact of service use and the IPA's information feedback. Moreover, this increased enrollee volume gives the IPA a better understanding of the utilization patterns of each physician in the network, enabling the IPA to identify and drop chronically overutilizing, overreferring physicians. In contrast, some IPAs pay physicians FFS and put physicians at small financial risk, do not engage in sophisticated utilization management, provide minimal profiling and information feedback on physicians, and have few or no criteria on physician selection or retention. Although we would expect very different performances from the two types of IPAs, their enrollees are grouped together under the same "IPA HMO plan" classification. Medical groups in network model HMOs are similarly diverse.

CHANGING RELATIONSHIPS BETWEEN HEALTH BENEFIT PURCHASERS, INTERMEDIARIES, AND PROVIDERS

Prior to 1980, the two major types of private health benefit intermediaries had distinctly different relationships with providers. Commercial and Blue Cross/Blue Shield carriers that contracted with employers to offer or administer indemnity insurance plans were the major health benefit intermediaries in the FFS sector. Carriers had distant, nonexclusive relationships with virtually any provider. On the other hand, prepaid group practice (PGP) or staff model HMOs, such as Kaiser, Group Health Cooperative of Puget Sound, or Harvard Community Health Plan, were the predominant health benefit intermediaries in the capitated sector. In contrast to the carriers, they had close, exclusive relationships with a select panel of providers. In a staff model HMO, it often has been impossible to distinguish between the health benefit intermediary and the integrated delivery system that provides services, because the HMO pays physicians whom it employs and hospitals that it usually owns. In a prepaid group practice HMO, the health benefit intermediary (such as Kaiser Foundation Health Plan, Inc.) and the medical groups (such as The Permanente Medical Groups) usually have worked so closely together that they often are considered two sides of the same coin, even though they are separate entities.

With the rise of newer forms of managed care plans, relationships between intermediaries and managed care providers have become far more diverse. (The legal arrangements are even more complex; here we focus on the content of the relationships). Because large commercial and Blue Cross/Blue Shield carriers now offer employers managed care plan products, they have transformed themselves into major health benefit intermediaries in the managed care sector. However, unlike previous intermediary/provider managed care relationships, many carriers and other managed care health benefit intermediaries have nonexclusive, "arms-length" relationships with network providers, medical groups, hospitals, and integrated delivery systems. For example, network model HMOs have "arms-length" relationships with large medical groups that the HMOs do not own, control, or contract with exclusively.

The extent to which PPO, IPA HMO, or network HMO health benefit intermediaries are directly involved in the actual delivery of health care services varies. For example, an IPA HMO may contract with, and capitate, an independent IPA, and only monitor quality of care (sometimes not very rigorously). In that case, the IPA HMO is simply a broker between health plan purchaser and the IPA. Alternatively, an IPA model HMO may directly organize solo and small group physicians into networks, conduct extensive utilization management and profiling, offer a stream of information feedback to physicians, and even convene meetings of network physicians to discuss results. Some health benefit intermediaries who want even more control over the health care delivery system purchase or manage medical groups and hospitals, and so move towards fully integrating the roles of offering health plans and owning and managing the delivery system. Again, there are many other possible relationships.

Some HMOs that previously never paid for nonemergency, out-of-network health care use by enrollees, now offer a POS product (the open-ended HMO) in which the HMO provides reduced enrollee coverage for out-of-network health care use, therefore becoming a health benefit intermediary for FFS providers. In another major shift, some health benefit intermediaries are actually reducing their utilization management of health care services as they increasingly capitate and pass more of the financial risk to independent IPAs, large medical groups, and integrated delivery systems. Some of the latter organizations, as the primary risk-takers, want to manage their risk by taking full control over utilization management, thereby relegating the health benefit intermediary to quality assurance monitor. Such provider organizations may not even share their utilization and quality data with the health benefit intermediary.

In some markets, health benefit intermediaries are capitating physician/hospital organizations or integrated delivery systems to provide *all* health care services, and are placing most of the financial risk for providing services onto the latter organizations. Some of these provider organizations have challenged the standard triad of health plan purchaser, health benefit intermediary, and health care provider by engaging in "direct contracting" with employers and other health plan purchasers, and thus are bypassing health benefit intermediaries. Such organizations are attempting to capture and share with purchasers some of the 15 to 20 percent share of the premium dollar that typically goes to health benefit intermediaries. However, in many markets, this move entails several risks. The provider organization may lack underwriting expertise, although some large integrated delivery systems have the capital to buy local health benefit intermediaries and thus gain the required underwriting expertise. Also, the provider organization may jeopardize service delivery contracts with existing health benefit intermediaries, who may not want to contract with a competitor. Nevertheless, these arrangements will likely become increasingly important in some local market areas as provider organizations grow in size and increase their local market share.

MANAGED CARE PLANS BEFORE 1980

Although managed care plans became widespread only during the 1980s, "managed care" has a relatively long history. As documented by Starr in *The Social Transformation of American Medicine* (33), professional medical organizations adamantly opposed all forms of "managed care". They fought ceaselessly and successfully for decades to keep a direct, FFS relationship between physician and patient and preclude intermediaries between the two (33). At the turn of century, professional medical associations confronted markets in which some companies directly hired physicians as employees, or engaged in competitive, capitated "managed care" contracts with groups of physicians, as they would with any other type of supplier of goods and services. By the 1920s the medical profession had virtually stopped corporations and government from hiring physicians and seeking competitive bids for medical care contracts, eliminated other forms of cost containment, taken over medical education and training, gained authority to monitor its own performance, and above all, established the dominant model of practice as solo practitioners who received FFS payment (23, 33). In part, the professional associations succeeded in wresting control over the market for their skills from corporate and governmental buyers by threatening to expel from the association any physicians who broke ranks. Over time, these actions were increasingly effective as more hospitals were willing to deny blacklisted physicians access to their beds. Although the professional associations eventually accepted the intermediary of the insurance company, they did so because the latter left FFS payment intact, did not interfere with medical practice, and increased physician incomes (33).

Because physician professional associations created an environment hostile to any type of managed care, HMOs that developed in the 1930s and 1940s—such as Kaiser Permanente in California, Group Health Cooperative in Seattle, or the Health Insurance Plan of New York—required some exceptional advantage that allowed them to survive. Such HMOs tended to be either well-financed (so that they could control their own hospitals), politically protected, and/or organized and run by large consumer cooperatives who believed strongly in the value of prepaid medical care (33). Although other factors also slowed the growth of HMOs, the medical professional associations certainly helped relegate managed care plans— mostly group and staff HMO models—to a small niche in a world where health care services were dominated by FFS payment and indemnity insurance.

As late as 1970, there were just 3 million HMO enrollees. Moreover, despite rapid percentage growth in the 1970s, as late as 1980 there were still only 9 million HMO enrollees, even though many business and government leaders increasingly recognized that health care expenditures were climbing much more rapidly than many other expenditures and even though the federal government undertook some limited initiatives to speed the creation of new HMOs (13, 20).

THE GROWTH OF MANAGED CARE SINCE 1980

Reacting to high rates of increase in health care premium costs, employers have been the driving force propelling the growth of managed care since 1980. Between 1970 and 1980, spending for health services and supplies by business rose from 3.1 to 4.9 percent of total compensation, and from 36.1 to 42.6 percent of after-tax profits. These trends accelerated between 1980 and 1990, as such spending rose from 4.9 to 7.1 percent of total compensation, and from 42.6 to 107.9 percent of after-tax corporate profits (22). Between 1984 and 1992, health benefit costs to the employer per active employee rose 141% (5), or four times the 35% increase in the consumer price index (36)

The very large increase in enrollment in newer types of managed care plans began in the first half of the 1980s, fueled by particularly high increases in indemnity insurance premiums—between 20 and 30 percent per year for Blue Cross and Blue Shield plans in 1982–84 (7). Increasing numbers of employers attempted to move their employees into managed care plans to contain rising medical claims costs in the face of recession-diminished profits and in the absence of any federal government initiative. Large employers, often with operations in multiple local markets in multiple states, usually took the lead. To maintain their market share, indemnity insurance carriers serving these large employers began offering managed care plans as quickly as they could. Meanwhile, new entrepreneurial organizations, offering mostly PPO and IPA HMO plans, competed strongly with the carriers in many local market areas.

We use with some trepidation estimates of the growth of different types of managed care plans. Organizations producing the estimates have somewhat different definitions of managed care plans, and some of these organizations have changed their own definitions of plans, at times without adjusting previous statistics. Moreover, the "mixed model" HMO plan category actually contains members in the other four types of HMO plans, the PPO plan category contains EPO plan enrollees, and the POS category is only vaguely defined. Nevertheless, there are unmistakable trends in the development of each major type of plan.

The PPO category offered the easiest and quickest move to managed care for employers, enrollees, carriers, and providers, because it was most similar to the FFS system. One industry source estimated that there were only four PPOs in the US in 1982, whereas there were over 1000 separate plans and hundreds of separate PPO entities by 1992 (25). By 1993, 22 percent of all workers with employer-based insurance in firms with more than 200 workers were enrolled in PPOs (19).

Both the PPO plan network and characteristics of benefit coverage reflect its FFS roots. PPO plans attracted employers and enrollees by establishing broad networks of providers that reduced the need for enrollees to switch physicians when moving to a PPO plan, and allowed their continued use of non-network, FFS providers, although at a reduced benefit level. To attract enrollment to early PPO plans, some employers even offered their enrollees in-network coverage superior to that of the employer's indemnity plan, whereas out-of-network coverage was similar to that of the indemnity plan. In fact, many employers merely switched their indemnity plans to PPO plans, arguing that it meant no reduction in coverage or benefits. To attract often reluctant physicians into their networks, PPOs continued to pay physicians FFS, did not put them at financial risk, and enabled them to continue to stay in their individual offices and see FFS patients. At the same time, PPO plans did offer some new managed care elements, including the network, discounts from usual, customary and reasonable (UCR) charges, or set fees in return for greater enrollee volume (at least in theory), and some form of utilization management.

Individual Practice Association HMO plan membership grew approximately tenfold from 1980 to 1992, rising from approximately 1.5 million enrollees in 1980 (20)—less than 20% of all HMO enrollees—to over 14.7 million members (41 percent of all HMO enrollees) by 1992 (29). Not included are some unknown share of IPA HMO plan members in "mixed model" HMOs. Growth in the number of new IPA HMOs was especially rapid in 1983–86 (2) and in IPA HMO plan enrollment in 1983–88 (20)).

The IPA developed as a hybrid of the FFS system and the HMO. Many newly created IPAs reflected their FFS roots in that, with their wide networks, they allowed some enrollees to keep their same physicians when they changed plans, and allowed physicians to practice independently in their offices, see FFS patients, and have the freedom to contract with other managed care organizations. At the same time, the IPA reflected HMO roots: sharing financial performance risk with the health benefit intermediary, an IPA in turn shares (passes off) some of its risk to its physician members, who usually are organized into risk pools. Like medical groups in the PGP HMO plans, IPAs also engage in utilization management.

Although staff, PGP, and network models also grew, enrollment gains were less dramatic. Between 1980 and 1992, enrollment in staff model HMO plans grew from 1.7 million to 2.9 million members, in PGP HMO plans from 5.7 million to 9.7 million members, and in network plans from less than 1 million to 4 million members (20, 29). By 1992, HMOs had over 38 million enrollees (30).

Point-of-service plans began to grow in the late 1980s. POS plans also reflected the legacy of FFS payment system, offering some health benefit coverage for out-of-network, usually FFS, health care service use. At the same time, some POS plans are essentially HMO plans with out-of-network coverage.

By 1993, all types of HMO plans accounted for 26 percent of all enrollees from mid- and large-size employers offering health insurance, PPO plans accounted for 22 percent, and POS plans accounted for 10 percent, whereas indemnity insurance plans accounted for 42 percent of all enrollees. Most of the latter plans include at least some utilization management (19).

We emphasize that movement from indemnity towards managed care plans by employers, enrollees, carriers, and providers varied greatly among local market areas, and within any one market area. For example, even for employers committed to a managed care strategy to contain health care costs, the shift of enrollees into managed care plans was often very slow, for several reasons. First, many employer benefits departments had little expertise in health benefits or managed care (3). Second, initially there were few PPO, and even fewer HMO, plans available. Third, employers had to consider the impact of the move to managed care on their employee relations, especially where changes in health benefits required renegotiation of existing union contracts (26).

One of the most dramatic shifts during the period was the transformation of major carriers—Blue Cross/Blue Shield and large commercial carriers—from processors of claims and payers of bills in the old, unmanaged FFS system into organizers and managers of networks, and, in some cases, into owners and managers of complicated health care delivery systems. According to one estimate, commercial carriers derived about 1 percent of their premium income from managed care in 1984. This figure had risen to over 25 percent by 1990 (17) and has continued to increase rapidly.

For many health benefit intermediaries, the transition from indemnity to managed care plans was difficult. Given the rapid shift in employer demand for managed care plans, carriers and other health benefit intermediaries had to create, buy, and/or contract with PPO and IPA networks in a very short period of time. In many cases, health benefit intermediaries had to manage those networks in dozens of local market areas, even though they had minimal expertise in managed care or in managing delivery systems. Their methodology for network provider selection and review often was quite primitive because they usually had little information on the network physicians whom they selected. Although large carriers could use their indemnity databases to look at the comparative performance of physician providers, even those carriers did not have enough local market share to obtain sufficient data on individual physicians to make informed selection decisions in many local markets. Some selection methods were too expensive (for example, use of actual medical records), whereas others had inherent limitations (for example, word-of-mouth from other providers in the area and a review of credentials). Because many physicians were initially reluctant to join networks, health benefit intermediaries often took whoever wanted to sign up. Many PPOs and IPAs were unable to obtain enough leverage from enrollee volume to have an impact on provider behavior, or enough data to identify providers with conservative practice styles and good outcomes.

Several other factors also made the transformation to managed care difficult. To induce employees to switch to managed care plans, "first generation" PPO plans increased benefits compared to the existing indemnity insurance plans, making it harder to contain utilization increases. Thus, one study of an early plan showed large utilization *increases* for a PPO plan compared to an indemnity plan (10). As mentioned previously, employers often provided enrollees with little incentive to enroll in the lowest cost plans or to use network providers because employers paid most of the premium for all plans, and created only a small differential in coverage between in- and out-of-network use. Moreover, provider self-selection into managed care often was reactive rather than pro-active, and grudging rather than eager. Because of the arms-length nature of their relationship to providers, networks had to emphasize purely financial arrangements (such as small risk pools) or "arms-length" arrangements governing utilization management (such as the infamous 800 telephone numbers for prior authorization). Many of these physicians saw managed care as encroaching on their professional and economic autonomy and increasing their costs, in terms of time, money, and aggravation, especially when they contracted with several or numerous plans.

MANAGED CARE LEARNING CURVES

Since 1980, purchasers, health benefit intermediaries, provider organizations and physicians have been ascending their respective managed care learning curves.

Among employers, benefits departments acquired more health care expertise and learned how to leverage their purchasing power. For example, employers steered enrollees along a continuum of managed care plans—from looser to tighter forms of managed care—by reducing health plan choices, increasing employee premium payments for higher cost plans, and increasing coverage differentials between in- and out-of-plan coverage. Some employers joined health care business coalitions, demanded more information from health benefit intermediaries about utilization, cost, outcome, and satisfaction, and obtained more guarantees about health plan performance. Others contracted directly with provider organizations and delivery systems.

More enrollees loosened established bonds to their physicians, either because they saved money by doing so, or because they had no choice. Many enrollees who moved to managed care first enrolled in PPOs, became acquainted with restrictions on out-of-plan use, the more limited panel of providers, and procedures to access specialists and to enter hospitals, and then moved to tighter managed care plans.

Health benefit intermediaries and provider organizations became familiar with managed care. In particular IPAs and PPOs changed over time. As enrollee volume per physician grew in more successful PPOs and IPAs, the latter could adopt more sophisticated methods of management, physician profiling, information feedback to physicians, and re-selection of physicians based on their utilization patterns. Some PPOs adopted fee schedules for physicians and fixed daily charges for hospitals instead of discounts from billed charges, and began to use primary care physician gatekeepers (thereby creating some of the POS plans). Similarly, more IPAs began to pay providers capitation rather than FFS. Many multispecialty group practices that were not part of PGP HMOs had to change their internal management and incentive structure as they reoriented from FFS to capitation, while more large primary care physician-based medical groups were created and grew rapidly. Meanwhile, more hospitals merged or became part of regional delivery systems that were more oriented to capitation and risk-sharing. The latter have purchased or created close partnerships with medical groups and IPAs, enabling them to contract with health benefit intermediaries to provide both hospital and physician services.

More physicians were drawn into organized networks and medical groups. For many solo and small group physicians this was a radical change. They had to familiarize themselves about which organizations were better than others, in terms of remuneration, risk, and the "hassle factor".

In general, the 1980s saw increased corporatization of medicine, whereby large organizations gained greater control over the practice of medicine.

MANAGED CARE AND INDEMNITY PLAN PERFORMANCE: PREMIUM LEVELS AND RATES OF GROWTH

Overview of evidence on managed care plan performance

In comparing health plans, key dimensions of performance include health care utilization and expenditures (for example, hospital admission rates, ambulatory care visits, use of expensive tests or procedures, and expenditures for each type of health services utilization); use of preventive tests, exams, and procedures; quality of care, including health outcomes; enrollee satisfaction; enrollee out-of-pocket expenditures; and the level and rate of growth of health care expenditures and premiums.

In another study, we analyzed the research literature on the performance of managed care plans relative to indemnity plans (27). We selected studies that met the following criteria: data from 1980 forward, private insurance or Medicare plan enrollees, a comparison group, a reasonable attempt at statistical adjustment for noncomparable HMO and indemnity plan enrollees, and peer-reviewed findings (with two specific exceptions). Only a handful of studies on the performance of PPO plans met the criteria for inclusion into that study.

Compared to indemnity plans, HMO plans had the following characteristics: lower hospital utilization, including a somewhat lower hospital admission rate and consistently shorter length of stay; greater use of less costly alternatives to expensive procedures or tests; greater use of preventive examinations, procedures and tests; roughly comparable quality of care; and somewhat lower enrollee satisfaction with the care provided, but much greater satisfaction with costs. The evidence did not support the hypothesis that prepaid group practice/staff HMO plans were necessarily more effective than IPA and network HMO plans, although substantially more research is needed on this issue. In general, evidence on managed care plans by dimension of performance was scant. As a result, we urged caution in generalizing from the results of the studies we analyzed because of such factors as unmeasured selection bias, the diversity of health plans and local market conditions, the rapidity of change in the marketplace, and the small number of research results.

For several dimensions of managed care plan performance, peer-reviewed research evidence is particularly weak. Only one study, albeit strong methodologically, indicated that HMO plans have had an impact on the rate of growth of system-wide hospital costs (32). Only two studies on the level of total health care expenditures per enrollee met our criteria for inclusion in our analysis, and no peer-reviewed study provided estimates of the rate of growth of total expenditure per enrollee, by type of health plan.

In one crucial area—purchaser premiums—there is only one peer-reviewed study (4). Although valuable, the study examined only one aspect of premium performance (the impact of offering HMO plans on the level of employer premiums), for just one market (Minnesota) and one year (1986). After adjusting indemnity plan deductibles, premiums, and out-of-pocket maximums to equal those in HMO plans, that study found that offering an HMO plan *raised* family coverage premiums by over $25 per month because HMO plans had higher premiums than indemnity plans and because indemnity plan premiums were 15 percent higher than they would have been without offering an HMO, due to adverse selection. The increased cost was less in the more mature Minneapolis market, suggesting that the impact of adverse selection on premium costs may diminish over time and with increased competition.

The absence of peer-reviewed evidence on health plan premium differences is remarkable. From the perspective of employer and government purchasers, premium cost per enrollee and its increase over time is *the* most important dimension of health plan performance. Premium performance indicators should be particularly useful to policy makers because they provide "bottom-line" summaries of financial performance from the purchaser's perspective. Note, however, that differences in benefits, coverage, and out-of-pocket costs mean that premiums may give little indication of patterns in overall social costs or the costs as perceived by the enrollee.

Here we summarize published survey data on levels and rates of growth in per enrollee health care premiums. Although some of these data are widely disseminated, especially in corporate and government circles, we emphasize that these data should be used only with great caution. Note that for employer self-insured plans, we use the term "premium" to equal the amount of employer expenditures for employee health plan insurance (including administrative expenditures), plus the amount of employee "ex ante" contributions towards the insurance cost (but not copayments and other out-of-pocket costs).

Premium Levels

Survey data from 1991 to 1993 indicate that HMO plans have between 1 percent higher and 20 percent lower premiums for family coverage than other health plans, and between 7 and 15 percent lower premiums for single coverage (Table 2). As discussed below, these figures are not adjusted for differences in characteristics among enrollees and plans.

1. *For family coverage,* three employer surveys indicate that premiums for HMO plans were from 1 percent higher to 7 percent lower compared to indemnity plans, from 0 to 7 percent lower compared to PPO plans, and from 7 to 20 percent lower compared to POS plans (15, 19, 34). Because the share of the premium paid by the employer can differ by type of health plan and by single vs family coverage, HMO plans can produce very different savings or costs, relative to indemnity plans, for the employer and employee.

2. *For single coverage,* premiums for HMO plans were from 7 to 13 percent lower compared to indemnity plans, 10 to 13 percent lower compared to PPO plans, and 9 to 15 percent lower compared to POS plans.

For policy making purposes, these premium data must be used cautiously.

1. The data are not adjusted for differences among plans in age, gender, health status, number of dependents, location, coverage, or other differences in enrollee or plan characteristics. Some of the needed adjustments could have an important impact on the premium comparisons. For example, because HMO plans have a pattern of favorable risk selection

Table 2 HMO premium levels: percent difference from other plans (employer-based insurance)

Data source	Family coverage: HMO difference from			Single coverage: HMO difference from		
	Indemnity	PPO	POS	Indemnity	PPO	POS
HIAA (1991)	0.6	0.0	−9.5	−12.8	−11.6	−12.2
Hay Huggins (1992)	−6.5	−5.1	−7.2	−9.7	−10.5	−8.8
KPMG Peat Marwick (1993)	−4.3	−7.1	−20.4	−7.0	−12.7	−15.1

(27), adjusting for differences in enrollee characteristics would raise HMO premiums relative to indemnity plans. Purchaser opinion survey data are consistent with the evidence on selection bias in the peer-reviewed literature. In 1992, 60 percent of employers thought that HMOs attracted favorable risks, compared to only 16 percent who thought that was not the case (5). More important, only 36 percent of employers thought that their HMO plan premium fairly reflected the risks the HMO plan attracted, compared to 29 percent who thought that was not the case. On the other hand, because HMOs provide more comprehensive coverage for most services (34), adjusting for coverage differences would lower the combined levels of premiums plus out-of-pocket expenditures for HMO plans relative to indemnity plans.

2. The data compare premium costs by type of plan for all employers, rather than only for those employers who offered all types of plans. For example, for all employers in the KPMG Peat Marwick survey, family and single coverage HMO plan premiums were 4 and 7 percent lower, respectively, than indemnity plans. However, for only those employers who offered both HMO and indemnity plans, HMO family and single coverage cost 16 and 19 percent less, respectively, than indemnity plans. Moreover, the latter statistics compare plans offered in the same location, which helps adjust for substantial differences in the level of total health expenditures among local market areas.

We did not use data from the A. Foster Higgins Survey (5) even though data from that survey are widely cited. Note that their premium level by health plan is the sum of premiums paid for active employees *and* retirees for each type of health plan, divided by the number of *active* employees enrolled in each type of health plan. Since market penetration by at-risk HMO and PPO plans is less in the Medicare than in the employer-based health insurance market, a disproportionately large share of retirees is enrolled in supplementary Medicare indemnity plans. Therefore, even if premiums paid for active employees, per active employee, were the same for each type of health plan, indemnity plan premiums calculated by A. Foster Higgins would still be greater than managed care plan premiums.

Rate of Growth of Premiums

Over time the rate of growth of premiums—and better yet, the rate of growth of premiums and out-of-pocket expenditures—is a crucial indicator of health plan performance. Even small differences in annual rates of growth over an extended period of time can mean relatively large differences in cumulative expenditures.

Some limited evidence indicates that HMO plans may recently have had

Table 3 Compounded annual real rate of growth of HMO and indemnity plan premiums, employer-based insurance, 1986–93, 1987–92

Data source	1986–93			1987–92		
	HMO	Indemnity	PPO	HMO	Indemnity	PPO
HIAA/KPMG Peat Marwick	6.5	7.5	7.6	7.6	9.1	9.1

a slightly lower rate of growth of premiums than other types of plans. Survey data for the 1986–93 time period (6, 8, 17–19, 34) show that HMO premiums grew by a compounded annual rate of 10.7 percent, or slightly lower than the 11.7 and 11.9 percent per year increase for indemnity and PPO plans, respectively. In real terms (premiums divided by the consumer price index), HMO plan premiums grew by 6.5 percent per year compared to 7.5 percent for indemnity and 7.6 percent for PPO plans, a difference of about 1 percent per year (Table 3). On the other hand, the real rate of increase in premiums was high for all plans.

Two much-cited previous studies on the rate of growth of enrollee premiums used data from 1976 to 1981 (28) and from 1962–74 (24), or for a period prior to the beginning of the widespread growth of managed care plans. The former study found little difference in the rate of growth of HMO and indemnity plan premiums, whereas the latter study found mixed evidence.

Once again, data limitations require that the more recent figures be used with caution:

1. *Few years of data* We do not have enough years of reasonably consistent employer survey data to firmly establish differences in premium trends by type of health plan. Because increases in health care premiums have been cyclical (7, 9), altering the specific start and end dates of the data could have a major impact on estimates of trends in premium growth rate over time. Moreover, if the premium cycle differs between HMO plans and conventional insurance plans, then the observed differences among plans could either narrow or widen.
2. *Risk adjustment* If HMO plans have a pattern of increasingly or decreasingly favorable risk selection, adjusting for that fact would narrow or widen the differences in premium growth rates. Ideally, researchers would want to follow stable groups of enrollees who maintained membership in their indemnity or managed care plans for years. However, substantial shifts from indemnity to managed care plans have occurred, both at the level of the local and national market, and often at the level

of the individual employer. None of the surveys has attempted to adjust for changes in differences in risk selection over time.

3. *Location adjustment* As indicated above, different local markets have different average levels of health care expenditure and different rates of growth of managed care plans. HMO plan growth in areas with lower average levels of health care expenditure would automatically lower HMO premium rates of growth and might raise rates of growth for indemnity plans unless HMO growth slows increases in local area premium.

4. *Coverage changes* Indemnity plan benefits may have declined relative to HMO plans over the recent period. Adjusting for this factor might increase the difference among plans in premium growth rates.

5. *Survey methodology* Estimates of premium growth rates are sensitive to the specific survey methodologies used. For example, using HIAA survey data between 1988 and 1991, indemnity plan premiums increased by 70 percent when survey analysts calculated the rate of growth of premiums from the employer's yearly estimates of premium levels, compared to an increase of 60 percent when analysts used the employer's estimate of the rate of growth of premiums in the previous year (8, 34). Although the two methods had little impact on the relative difference of rate of growth of premiums between indemnity and HMO plans, the PPO rate of premium growth was substantially lower than that for HMO plans (52 percent v 64 percent) using the first method, but about the same (52 percent v 53 percent) using the second method.

6. *Estimate variation among surveys* Even though estimates of the rate of growth of premiums by health plan type are similar over a period of several years among surveys, estimates of the rate of growth of premiums for a type of plan for any one year are sometimes substantially dissimilar.

We emphasize that although it is important to compare the rate of growth of premiums of managed care to indemnity plans, it is even more important to determine the impact of managed care plans on the overall rate of growth of premiums. For example, even if HMO premiums grew at the same rate as other health plan premiums, HMO plans could still have a major impact if they substantially lowered the overall rate of growth of premiums. Alternatively, if HMOs select either low-risk enrollees or conservative practitioners, or if FFS providers increase utilization in response to a declining market share, then the rates of growth could diverge without an impact on the overall rate of growth. Once again, we do not have any evidence on this dimension of health plan performance.

SUMMARY AND CONCLUSIONS

Over the past dozen years, network-based managed care plans have under-gone a remarkable transformation. At the beginning of the 1980s, managed care plans occupied a niche in a marketplace dominated by indemnity insurance plans. By 1993, managed care plans accounted for a growing majority of health plan enrollees. Moreover, enrollment in newer forms of managed care quickly surpassed that of the older group and staff model HMOs. Beginning as hybrids of elements of group and staff model HMO plans and of the old FFS system, these newer types of network-based plans have evolved as they have grown. Reacting to rapidly rising health care premium costs, employers wanted to move their employees and dependents relatively quickly into managed care plans. However, employers and en-rollees were not prepared to make a rapid, wholesale shift from indemnity insurance and FFS towards the older, more restrictive type of group and staff model HMO plans. Moreover, intermediaries and providers were not prepared to accommodate such a shift, even if employers and employees wanted it to take place. Indeed, many of the major actors—employers, enrollees, health benefit intermediaries, physician networks, medical groups, hospitals and integrated delivery systems—have had to ascend very sub-stantial managed care "learning curves". Although we have witnessed the overall movement of many enrollees from managed care plans that closely resembled the indemnity insurance plans toward plans with more similarities to the group and staff model HMOs, the extent of the changes has varied markedly among the dozens of local market areas, and even within local market areas.

As the health care system evolves, the number and complexity of different types of contractual managed care relationships are increasing almost expo-nentially. The resulting difficulty in classifying managed care plans has implications for health services researchers. Increasingly, it is important to compare performance among health plans not at the level of the entire health plan, but at the level of the provider organizations or networks that actually provide health care services to enrollees. The Medical Outcomes Study adopted this approach (12, 21, 35), providing useful insights into the dual effects of risk-sharing and provider organization on health care utilization, quality of care, and enrollee satisfaction. As well, if managed care plan classifications are to be meaningful, it is important to clearly specify the characteristics of the provider organization and the rest of the delivery system in whatever research is undertaken.

The performance of managed care plans since 1980, especially the relatively high rate of growth of their premiums, has to be understood in an historical context. The past period has been one of dynamic change in both the markets for health insurance and health care services. The question is whether the health care premium growth rate record of the past dozen years reflects the growing pains of a newer, more efficient type of health care system, or whether it reflects chronic problems that remain endemic to the US health care system. Major differences in health care reform policies in part depend on different appraisals of answers to this critical question.

ACKNOWLEDGMENTS

This study was supported by a subcontract to the George Washington University, Center for Health Policy Research, as part of the latter's Delivery Order #4, Contract #282-92-0040 with the Office of the Assistant Secretary for Health, Department of Health and Human Services. Sections of this chapter are derived from our final subcontract report (27).

Any *Annual Review* chapter, as well as any article cited in an *Annual Review* chapter, may be purchased from the Annual Reviews Preprints and Reprints service. 1-800-347-8007; 415-259-5017; email: arpr@class.org

---

Literature Cited

1. Deleted in proof
2. Christianson JB, Sanchez SM, Wholey DR, Shadle M. 1991. The HMO industry: Evolution in population demographics and market structures. *Med. Care Rev.* 48:3–46
3. Darling H. 1991. Employers and managed care: What are the early returns? *Health Affairs* 10(4):147–60
4. Feldman R, Dowd B, Gifford G. 1993. The effect of HMOs on premiums in employment-based health plans. *Health Serv. Res.* 27:779–812
5. Foster Higgins. 1992. *Foster Higgins Health Care Benefits Survey. Report 1: Medical Plans.* Princeton, NJ: Foster Higgins
6. Gabel J, DiCarlo S, Sullivan C, Rice T. 1990. Employer-sponsored health insurance, 1989. *Health Affairs* 9(3):161–75
7. Gabel J, Formisano R, Lohr B, DiCarlo S. 1991. Tracing the cycle of health insurance. *Health Affairs* 10(4):48–61
8. Gabel J, Jajich-Toth C, Lissovoy G, Rice T, Cohen H. 1988. The changing world of group health insurance. *Health Affairs* 7(3):48–65

9. Gabel JR. 1992. Perspective: A look at insurance data. *Health Affairs* 11(4):186–90
10. Garnick DW, Luft HS, Gardner LB, Morrison EM, Barrett M, Harvey B. 1990. Services and charges by PPO physicians for PPO and indemnity patients. An episode of care comparison. *Med. Care* 28:894–906
11. Ginzberg E. 1992. Physician supply policies and health reform. *New Engl. J. Med.* 268:3115–18
12. Greenfield S, Nelson EC, Zubkoff M, Manning W, Rogers W, et al. 1992. Variations in resource utilization among medical specialties and systems of care. *J. Am. Med. Assoc.* 267:1624–30
13. Gruber LR, Shadle M, Polich CL. 1988. From movement to industry: The growth of HMOs. *Health Affairs* 7(2):197–208
14. Havlicek PL, Eiler MA, Neblett OT. 1992. *Medical groups in the U.S. A survey of practice characteristics. 1993 edition.* Chicago, IL: AMA
15. Hay/Huggins Company. 1993. *1992 Hay/Huggins Benefits Report. Execu-*

tive Summary. Philadelphia, PA: Hay/
Huggins Co. Inc.

16. Hillman AL. 1987. Financial incentives
for physicians in HMOs: Is there a
conflict of interest? New Engl. J. Med.
317:1743–48

17. Hoy EW, Curtis RE, Rice T. 1991.
Change and growth in managed care.
Health Affairs 10(4):18–36

18. KPMG Peat Marwick. 1992. Health
Benefits in 1992. Newark, NJ: KPMG
Peat Marwick

19. KPMG Peat Marwick. 1993. Health
Benefits in 1993. Newark, NJ: KPMG
Peat Marwick

20. Kraus N, Porter M, Ball P. 1991.
Managed Care: A decade in review,
The Interstudy Competitive Edge. Ex-
celsior, MN: Interstudy

21. Kravitz RL, Greenfield S, Rogers W,
Manning WG, Zubkoff M, et al. 1992.
Differences in the mix of patients
among medical specialties and among
systems of care: Results from the
Medical Outcomes Study. J. Am. Med.
Assoc. 267:1617–23

22. Levit KR, Cowan CA. 1991. Business,
households, and governments: Health
care costs, 1990. Health Care Fin.
Rev. 13:83–93

23. Light D, Levine S. 1988. The changing
character of the medical profession:
A theoretical overview. Milbank Q.
66(Suppl. 2):10–32

24. Luft HS. 1980. Trends in medical care
costs: Do HMOs lower the rate of
growth? Med. Care 18:1–16

25. Marion Merrell Dow. 1993. Managed
Care Digest. PPO Edition 1993. Kansas City, MO: Marion Merrell Dow

26. Miller RH, Luft HS. 1991. Diversity

and transition in health insurance plans.
Health Affairs 10(4):37–47

27. Miller RH, Luft HS. 1994. Research
on the cost-effectiveness of Managed
Care Health Plans: A literature anal-
ysis. Rep. Off. Assist. Sec. Health,
Dep. Health Hum. Serv. San Francisco,
CA: Univ. Calif., San Francisco

28. Newhouse JP, Schwartz WB, Williams
AP, Witsberger C. 1985. Are fee-for-
service costs increasing faster than
HMO costs? Med. Care 23:960–66

29. Porter MJ, Ball PA. 1992. Interstudy
Competitive Edge 2(1). Excelsior, MN:
Interstudy

30. Porter MJ, Ball PA, Kraus N. 1992.
Interstudy Competitive Edge 1(2). Excelsior, MN: Interstudy

31. Relman AS. 1993. Controlling costs
by "managed competition"—would it
work? New Engl. J. Med. 328:133–35

32. Robinson JC. 1991. HMO market penetration and hospital cost inflation in
California. J. Am. Med. Assoc. 266:
2719–23

33. Starr P. 1982. The Social Transformation of American Medicine. New York:
Basic

34. Sullivan CB, Miller M, Feldman R,
Dowd B. 1992. Employer-sponsored
health insurance in 1991. Health Affairs
11(4):172–185

35. Tarlov AR, Ware JE, Greenfield S,
Nelson EC, Perrin E, Zubkoff M.
1989. The Medical Outcomes Study:
an applications of methods for monitoring the results of medical care. J.
Am. Med. Assoc. 262:925–30

36. US Bur. Census. 1991. Statistical Abstract of the United States 1991, (111th
edition). Washington, DC: US GPO

Annu. Rev. Public Health. 1994. 15:461–85

UNDERINSURED AMERICANS: A Review

Alan C. Monheit[1]

Agency for Health Care Policy and Research, 2101 East Jefferson Street, Suite 500, Rockville, Maryland 20852

KEY WORDS: uninsured, health insurance, access to care

INTRODUCTION

Health insurance plays a critical role in assuring timely access to medical care and protection against the risk of costly and unanticipated medical events. Consequently, many underinsured Americans—those uninsured or with inadequate coverage—may face difficulty obtaining and paying for medical care and their plight has become a primary reason for national health care reform. Whether lack of insurance reflects a failure of the private market to supply affordable coverage or a conscious choice made by those who undervalue health insurance, there is a strong belief that the benefits derived from health insurance should be more widely distributed.

Underlying this belief is the perception that expanded health insurance coverage (designed to minimize inappropriate use due to reduced out-of-pocket costs) will have a favorable effect on efficiency and equity, and hence, upon social welfare. (By efficiency I refer to a situation in which no person can be made better off without making at least one person worse off.) As is well known from the theory of insurance, risk-averse individuals

---

[1]The author is Senior Research Manager, Center for General Health Services Intramural Research, Agency for Health Care Policy and Research (AHCPR). The views expressed in this paper are those of the author and no official endorsement by AHCPR or the Department of Health and Human Services is intended or should be inferred.

can be made better off if their risks can be pooled with those of others with similar risk profiles and transferred, at an actuarially fair price, to an entity with comparative advantage in risk bearing (i.e. an insurance company) (4). Since all parties have freely agreed to this transfer, overall efficiency and social welfare are enhanced.

Mediating the financial consequences of health-related risks is, however, only one aspect of the benefits from coverage. Health insurance also improves access to medical care and these services confer benefits to the underinsured as well as to others (e.g. through the control of contagious diseases, satisfaction from knowing that those in ill health are obtaining care, etc). Consequently, those without health insurance or with inadequate coverage may fail to obtain a socially appropriate level of care and this also represents a loss in social welfare (36). In addition, Menzel (26) cites a "pre-commitment" to care as a benefit of health insurance. Such insurance not only provides financial security and spreads costs among the well and ill, "but assures that we will use needed health services." Finally, even if individuals "choose" to be underinsured because coverage is "unaffordable" even at an actuarially fair price, our sense of equity and fairness may be compromised. All these reasons have played a role in shaping public opinion toward expanded coverage.

Informed public policy initiatives to expand health insurance coverage and estimates of their costs require knowledge of the size, demographic composition, and economic circumstances of the underinsured, and, therefore, an understanding of how such estimates are derived. Although empirical research has provided a finely etched portrait of the *uninsured,* far less is known about those with inadequate coverage, and the appropriate interpretation of these estimates remains a subject of debate.

In this review, I examine several issues related to estimates of the underinsured population, their characteristics, and their access to medical care. Since most research is based upon the *uninsured* population, I focus primarily on these findings. I begin by reviewing how estimates of the underinsured population are obtained and identify the sources of controversy regarding their interpretation; next, I describe characteristics of the underinsured, emphasizing the relationship between employment and health insurance status; I also review studies of health insurance "dynamics" and their relationship to static or point-in-time estimates of the uninsured; I conclude by assessing the effect of being uninsured on medical care use.

COUNTING UNDERINSURED AMERICANS

THE UNINSURED POPULATION   National estimates of the uninsured population have been derived from a variety of household survey data. Some have been explicitly designed to obtain information on health insurance status in the context of collecting data on medical care use and expenditures. In contrast, other surveys obtain information on health insurance as part of data collection efforts seeking information on labor force activity, wages, and employment.

Some of the earliest estimates of the size of the uninsured population can be derived from household surveys by the Center for Health Administration Studies and the National Opinion Research Center (CHAS/NORC) of the University of Chicago (3). The CHAS/NORC data indicate that a substantial proportion of families and individuals lacked health insurance in the 1950s and that this proportion declined markedly by 1970. For example, 37% of all families were without health insurance in 1953, 31% in 1958, 26% in 1963, and 17% in 1970. Estimates of individuals lacking hospital coverage are of a similar magnitude: 43% of all individuals in 1953, 35% in 1958, 32% in 1963, and 23% in 1970.

Given the importance of the uninsured population in the ongoing debate over health care reform, it may be surprising to learn that these estimates are computed as a *residual*. In particular, a survey respondent is determined to be uninsured if he/she fails to respond affirmatively to questions regarding coverage obtained through private health insurance plans or public programs. How such questions are asked and the interpretation of responses have been a source of confusion and disagreement among analysts and have led to varying estimates of size of the uninsured population. In this section, I review estimates from three widely used household surveys: the Current Population Survey (CPS), the Survey of Income and Program Participation (SIPP), and the National Medical Expenditure Survey (NMES).

To put these estimation issues in perspective, Table I provides national estimates of the uninsured population for selected years and time periods and reveals the following:

1. A consistent, long-term series of estimates is not available
2. Analysts using the same data obtain varying estimates for specific time periods
3. Estimates across alternative data vary, both for given points in time and for trends over several years
4. Estimates of the uninsured vary depending upon whether they are for a point in time, for all of the year, or for part of the year.

Several examples illustrate these points: (*a*) CPS data reveal a sharp decline in the percent of the nonelderly population uninsured after 1986 or 1987. However, as discussed below, this decline reflects changes in the

Table 1 Alternative estimates of the nonelderly population without health insurance, selected years

Year	Population (Thousands)	CPS[1] CRS	CPS[1] SWARTZ	CPS[1] HCFA	NMCES/NMES[2] First quarter	NMCES/NMES[2] Fourth quarter	NMCES/NMES[2] All-year	SIPP[3] First quarter
				Percent of population				
1977	189.8				13.8	13.0	9.2	
1979	194.5	14.6						
1980	199.0		14.6	14.9				
1981	200.6			NA				
1982	202.1		15.2	15.2				
1983	203.8	16.9	16.1	16.0				
1984	205.6	17.7	17.1	17.0				15.4
1985	207.2	17.6		17.8				15.0
1986	209.4	17.5	17.5	17.6				16.3
1987	210.8	14.4	17.5	17.6	17.2	16.1	11.4	15.8
1988*	212.7	15.1	15.2	14.4 (16.2)[4]				15.7
1989	214.7	15.3		15.1 (17.0)				14.5
1990	216.6	15.7		15.3 (17.4)				15.5
1991	218.8			15.7 (18.0)				15.7

*Change in CPS Health Insurance Questions
NA: not available
Population estimates for 1980 and subsequent years are from ref. 21; for 1977 from ref. 52, for 1979 from ref. 50
[1] CPS estimates are from refs. 42, 50 and Swartz (personal communication); HCFA estimates are from ref. 21
[2] 1977 estimates are from ref. 52; 1987 NMES estimates are from ref. 37
[3] SIPP estimates are from unpublished data, courtesy of Jack McNeil, US Bureau of the Census
[4] Estimates in parenthesis exclude cover sheet responses for children's health insurance coverage

CPS questionnaire rather than a sharp reversal of a consistently estimated time series;[2] (b) CPS data reveal a continuing upward trend in the percent of the population uninsured between 1987 and 1990, while SIPP suggests a period of decline followed by a sharp increase; (c) Estimates for 1987, when all three surveys are represented, differ widely; (d) While the CPS is supposed to yield estimates of persons uninsured all year, the estimates resemble point-in-time estimates from the first quarter of the 1977 National Medical Expenditure Care Survey (NMCES) and 1987 NMES; (e) Point-in-time estimates of the uninsured exceed estimates of the all-year uninsured

[2]Levit et al (21) assert that elimination of the so-called "cover sheet" questions introduced in the 1988 CPS to verify children's health insurance status can "remove some but not all of the inconsistencies" between 1987 and 1988 and thus provide a "broad indication of the cumulative growth [of the uninsured population] from 1980 to 1991 (see Table 2 estimates in ref. 21). However, this adjustment still yields a marked decline in the uninsured population after 1987 and does not produce a reliable and consistent trend in health insurance coverage.

since the former include the all-year uninsured as well some of the part-year uninsured.[3]

The reason for these differences is that each survey has a different purpose, has different recall periods, and analysts apply different editing rules to produce estimates.

Insurance Estimates from Alternative Household Surveys

THE CURRENT POPULATION SURVEY   The CPS is designed to provide national estimates of employment, unemployment, and characteristics of the civilian labor force as well as information on the economic status and the personal characteristics of the US population. Since the March income supplement to CPS' Annual Demographic File includes questions about health insurance, analysts seeking yearly estimates of the uninsured during the 1980s have relied upon this data source. The size of CPS (some 158,000 individuals from 57,000 households in 1991) has also enabled analysts to provide state estimates of health insurance coverage (8).

Since the CPS health insurance questions are designed to ascertain an individual's health insurance status *in the year prior to the March supplement,* CPS should yield *annual* estimates of health insurance status. However, interpretation of CPS estimates has been a major source of controversy and has led to revised insurance questions after 1987.

Questions regarding interpretation of CPS estimates emerged in the early 1980s when comparisons were made with estimates from the 1977 NMCES and 1980 National Medical Care Utilization and Expenditure Survey (NMCUES). As Table 1 illustrates, CPS estimates bore little resemblance to all-year uninsured estimates from NMCES; they were much higher than expected and closer to NMCES first-quarter estimates. Swartz (43) sought to resolve these disparities by reviewing differences in data collection and estimation procedures (sampling frame, weights construction, imputation procedures, degree of nonresponse bias, and location and wording of insurance questions) among CPS, NMCES, the Health Interview Survey, and NMCUES. Swartz concluded that recall problems dominated CPS estimates: respondents appeared to report their insurance status *as of the March interview date rather than the previous year.* The yearlong recall period and similarity of CPS estimates to point-in-time estimates made this a reasonable hypothesis.

The confusion in interpreting CPS estimates is illustrated in Table 1. The Congressional Research Service (CRS) treats these as all-year estimates

---

[3]Short (37) reports that 11.4% of the nonelderly population were uninsured all year in 1987 and that 10.9% were insured part of the year so that a fifth of all nonelderly Americans were without health insurance for all or part of 1987.

(they are from the March supplement of the year following that stated in the table). Note that Swartz's 1980, 1984, and 1987 estimates, considered to be point-in-time estimates for March of each year, are almost identical to CRS' 1979, 1983, and 1986 annual estimates. Estimates from the Health Care Financing Administration also differ from CRS estimates and are nearly identical to those of Swartz.

In an alternative explanation, Kronick (18) noted that the wording of CPS insurance questions prior to the 1988 revision could lead to an overestimate of the uninsured population. First, the CPS questionnaire did not directly inquire about the health insurance status of each person in the household. Instead, CPS insurance questions asked about coverage (defined as having a plan in one's own name) of persons age 15 or older who worked during the prior year. Respondents were then asked to identify who else in the household was included in the plan. Consequently, arbitrary editing rules were used to assign insurance status to certain individuals. For example, unmarried children 21 years of age or younger living with a policyholder were assumed to be covered while older children were considered uninsured. As Kronick noted, this could understate the number of covered dependents since some policies cover dependent children who are full-time students up to age 23 and some even allow coverage of married children up to age 21. Second, dependents on a health insurance plan were assigned coverage only if the policyholder resided in the household. This critical problem in questionnaire design meant that insured dependents covered by persons outside the household (such as children of divorce, those in foster care, or residing with relatives) were considered uninsured. Finally, since the health insurance questions were asked of all persons age 15 or over, children less than 15 with policies *in their own name* were not coded as insured. The cumulative effect of these procedures was to overstate estimates of the uninsured.

Kronick also recognized that recall error (as hypothesized by Swartz) could lead to inflated CPS estimates of the uninsured but argued that its contribution might be "overstated." He noted that reported insurance status was more consistent with changes in employment status over the past year than with respondents' March employment status so that many respondents appeared to report their prior year's health insurance status. Next, 1988 CPS estimates of the uninsured from the revised questionnaire (34), which addressed many of the shortcomings cited above, were 6 million persons lower than preliminary NMES estimates for the first quarter 1987 (38). The lower estimate suggests that CPS "at least for some people" is measuring insurance status during the prior year. Finally, Kronick argued that it was unlikely that most respondents uninsured at the March interview would forget to report coverage held in the prior year.

The revised CPS health insurance questions now directly ask whether each person 15 or older is covered by a health insurance plan and whether the plan is in his/her name. As a result, persons insured by a policyholder outside the household are now counted as insured. A set of questions on the cover sheet now asks whether any children under age 15 were covered in the past year. These revisions yield lower estimates of the uninsured population after 1987 (Table 1). Kronick (18) noted that the revised CPS questions were associated with a dramatic decline in the percentage of persons 15–18 years of age who were uninsured while the percentage of uninsured adults hardly changed. He attributed the difference in uninsured estimates after revision to changes in children's health insurance status.

Estimates from the revised CPS questionnaire remain a source of debate, especially with regard to children's health insurance status. As Swartz & Purcell (48) noted in their critique of Moyer's 1988 estimate of 31.1 million uninsured, the revised questionnaire yielded inconsistent health insurance responses for 13% of children 15 to 17 years of age and 14% of children less than 15, thereby affecting the status of some 4.3 million children. These inconsistencies can be attributed to new questions asking whether anyone age 15 or older (not just those who worked in the prior year) was covered by private insurance and to the cover sheet questions that directly queried whether children under 15 had Medicare or Medicaid, or private health insurance. The former questions yielded discrepant responses for children aged 15–17 reported as having private insurance but whose parents did not have private insurance that covered the children; the latter yielded discrepancies with the main CPS health insurance questions. (Moyer did not address the latter problem and treated all children with contradictory responses as insured). Swartz & Purcell's editing of these inconsistent response patterns yielded an estimate closer to 33.5 million uninsured persons, about 8% higher than that of Moyer.

Briefly, issues regarding estimates from SIPP and NMES include the following:

The Survey of Income and Program Participation (SIPP)   The introduction of SIPP in the mid-1980s provided alternative data on health insurance. In contrast to the other surveys, SIPP is a longitudinal household panel survey (conducted over 36 months) designed to provide detailed monthly information on the economic circumstances of the civilian, noninstitutionalized US population. Its purpose is to enable analysts to monitor the economic well-being of the population, to predict participation in public programs, to estimate program costs, and to gauge how changes in program regulations would affect the population at risk. Health insurance status was included among questions related to nonwage benefits and SIPP data yielded monthly, quarterly, and annual estimates of coverage. Monthly data have enabled researchers to examine health insurance dynamics and to compute the length of spells without coverage.

Point-in-time estimates of the uninsured from the 1984 SIPP (Table 1) were lower than those from other surveys and reflected a number of problems with the SIPP questionnaire. First, the wording and structure of the insurance questions allowed all persons residing in the household, regardless of their relationship to the policyholder, to be assigned coverage as dependents. Specifically, if the respondent identified as the policyholder reported that everyone in the household was covered, all other persons were considered insured even if they were unlikely to qualify as a dependent under typical health insurance rules. The Bureau of the Census reported an overestimate of 1.4 million insured persons as a result of this procedure (J McNeil, personal communication). In addition, respondents were not asked about CHAMPUS coverage (the Civilian Health and Medical Program of the Uniformed Services). Subsequent changes in the SIPP questionnaire resolved these problems so that SIPP estimates after 1987 are comparable to those from the CPS.

1987 National Medical Expenditure Survey Estimates of the uninsured from NMES have been subject to less controversy than other surveys. In part, this reflects the fact that NMES is designed to obtain information on health insurance along with other data directly related to an individual's health insurance status: health care use and expenditures, sources of payment, and employment circumstances. Moreover, the NMES health insurance section is the most extensive of any of the surveys under review.

The NMES health insurance instrument queries the respondent not only with regard to coverage by a specific kind of private plan (indemnity, HMO, or extra cash/dread disease plans) or public coverage (Medicare, Medicaid, other public programs, and CHAMPUS), but also tries to corroborate the source of coverage (by requesting policy numbers and identification cards). Persons holding private insurance are also asked to identify its source (employer, union, insurance company, or other group) and the respondents are asked whether coverage was obtained from any employer identified in the NMES employment section. Editing of NMES insurance data makes use of a variety of information to resolve inconsistencies and to impute missing values. Besides information on employment circumstances and components of income (such as AFDC payments) common to other surveys, NMES is in the unique position to use information on sources of payment for medical care to help edit insurance responses.

Despite these efforts, NMES uninsured estimates for the nonaged population in the first quarter of 1987 (36.1 million or 17.2%) may be subject to recall error: quarterly estimates decline so that by the fourth quarter of 1987, estimates (34.3 million or 16.1%) are comparable to those from the revised March 1988 CPS (34.5 million or 16.2% assuming the CPS estimate is point-in-time) and to SIPP estimates (33.2 million or 15.8%). This may reflect the fact that respondents may be reluctant to provide information until they are more familiar with survey procedures or are confident that the information will be used appropriately.

Persons with inadequate health insurance coverage   In contrast to the uninsured, estimates of the population with inadequate health insurance have been uncommon. In part, this reflects difficulties in obtaining data to produce such an estimate and in defining what is meant by inadequate coverage. As regards the former, essential data include total and out-of-pocket medical expenditures, the mix of services used, characteristics of health insurance plans, and family income. The entire set of elements are unavailable in most household data.

Difficulties in defining inadequate coverage arise because value judgments are required regarding the socially acceptable level of risk that an individual should bear. As a result, definitions of inadequate coverage directly confront alternative views of the purpose of health insurance: should coverage be structured to protect individuals from low-probability/high-cost medical events or should insurance finance predictable kinds of medical care or care that society wishes to encourage (e.g. preventive health services).

Farley (12) provided the only systematic attempt to estimate the population with inadequate health insurance. To identify this group, she used data from the 1977 NMCES to construct the distribution of medical expenditures and to compute expenditures associated with alternative levels of risk (i.e. the probability that an individual with specific demographic characteristics will fall into the 90th, 95th, or 99th percentile of the expenditure distribution and thus have a 10%, 5%, or 1% risk of high medical expenses) and expenditures associated with such risk by type of service. She applied NMCES health insurance data to determine out-of-pocket expenditures and constructed the distribution of such expenditures as a percent of income. To define the inadequately insured, she emphasized a conceptual approach consistent with the economic theory of insurance: that rational, risk-averse individuals desire protection from low-probability, high-cost events. Using one definition, persons with inadequate coverage are defined as those having a 1% chance of spending 10% of family income on medical care. In 1977, such individuals comprised 12.6% of the privately insured under age 65 and 8.3% of all nonelderly persons. Combining the inadequately insured with persons uninsured all or part year, Farley estimated that 26.7% of the nonelderly are underinsured.

To conclude, efforts to obtain timely estimates of the uninsured population during the 1980s have questioned the consistency of alternative survey estimates. As a result of changes in survey design and in interpretation of data, recent point-in-time estimates from alternative surveys are in sufficiently close agreement. NMES uninsured estimates for the fourth quarter of 1987 (34.3 million or 16.1%) are close to CPS estimates for the first quarter of 1988 (34.5 million or 16.2%). By the end of the 1980s, CPS and SIPP estimates were also quite close. As of this writing, updated estimates of persons with inadequate coverage have not been available.

WHO ARE THE UNDERINSURED?

Despite disagreement over the size of the uninsured population, a general consensus exists regarding their characteristics. Estimates from all the surveys discussed above yield roughly the same description of the uninsured as that from NMES (Table 2). In presenting these data, I first identify those groups most at risk to be uninsured based upon a general set of characteristics; next, I examine the composition of the uninsured according to these characteristics. These two perspectives yield different conclusions only insofar as the size of specific population groups outweighs the greater likelihood that others will be uninsured.

As Table 2 reveals, persons most at risk to be uninsured include young adults aged 18 to 24, members of minority groups, unmarried persons, those at or near poverty or with low incomes, and persons residing in the South or West.[4] Persons with these characteristics do not necessarily dominate the uninsured: because of their relative population size, persons aged between 25–54, whites, those married or single, and those with middle incomes are more numerous among the uninsured. Although persons in families with a working adult are less likely to be uninsured, the uninsured are dominated by workers and their dependents.

Farley (12) also described the population with inadequate coverage. Persons with nongroup coverage were far more likely to be inadequately insured than those with group insurance, as were women and children compared to men; persons not employed, self-employed, or working part-time compared to full-time workers; those living in poverty; persons aged 19 to 24 as well as those aged 55 to 64; and those in fair or poor health.

These characteristics have raised issues regarding gaps in insurance coverage and the appropriate role for public policy in expanding coverage. One puzzling issue is the contradiction that while employment greatly reduces

---

[4]Markowitz et al (24) emphasized the employment circumstances of young adults as a primary reason for their lack of coverage.

Table 2 Selected characteristics of the nonaged population without health insurance: First quarter, 1987

Characteristic	Total population (thousands)	Percent uninsured	Percent of all uninsured
TOTAL	209,981	17.4	100.0
Age in years			
Less than 6	21,631	16.7	9.9
6–18	45,475	16.9	21.1
19–24	22,675	30.2	18.8
25–54	98,155	15.7	42.2
55–64	22,046	13.4	8.1
Race/Ethnicity[a]			
White	158,656	14.2	61.6
Black	26,028	23.8	17.0
Hispanic	17,888	32.9	16.1
Sex			
Male	103,607	18.4	52.1
Female	106,374	16.6	47.9
Family Income[b]			
Poor	29,163	38.8	30.9
Near poor	8,724	37.4	8.9
Low	27,749	29.1	22.1
Middle	74,258	13.0	26.4
High	72,978	5.9	11.8
Census Region			
Northeast	43,637	12.8	15.3
Midwest	52,461	12.6	18.1
South	71,163	21.3	41.4
West	42,720	21.5	25.2
Employment Status of Adult Persons in families with:			
Working adult	180,523	15.6	76.9
No working adult	29,457	28.7	23.1

[a] Other racial/ethnic groups not shown

[b] Where near poor refers to persons with income between the poverty line and 125% of the poverty line; low income, over 125% to 200% of the poverty line; middle income, over 200% to 400% of the poverty line; and high income, over 400% of the poverty line

Sources: refs. 37, 38

the risk of being uninsured, the uninsured are comprised primarily of workers and their families.

EMPLOYMENT AND HEALTH INSURANCE STATUS   Since the workplace is the source of most private health insurance in the United States (38), employment is the strongest correlate of private coverage. However, research on the uninsured has demonstrated that employment does not necessarily lead to health insurance. Data for at least a decade indicate that employed persons are roughly half of the uninsured (32). Together with their dependents such persons comprise roughly three quarters of the uninsured. This finding has been a critical factor in focusing public attention on the uninsured, in shaping the debate over appropriate policy responses, and in pointing to the failure of the private market to provide affordable coverage to employees of small firms, to those in poor health, and to workers in seasonal or transitory employment.

Gaps in insurance coverage among the employed were a derivative finding from research examining unemployment and health insurance loss during the 1982–83 recession. Using data from the 1977 NMCES, Monheit et al (29) found that 8% of the unemployed (520,000 persons) lost health insurance, and 11% of the unemployed were never insured. Applying a predictive model of health insurance loss to the March 1982 CPS, the authors estimated that 13% of the unemployed (1.4 million persons) lost coverage in early 1982. These estimates were considered small compared to other studies that were not nationally representative (See refs. 6, 13). Monheit et al (29) also found that a considerable number of employed persons lacked health insurance throughout 1977—9% of all workers employed throughout 1977 (7.6 million workers)—which exceeded the most pessimistic estimates of health insurance loss among the unemployed. The authors questioned the equity implications of targeting the unemployed for special consideration "when many employed-uninsured workers may also face difficulties in obtaining medical care."

In a second study, Monheit et al (28) sought "to redirect the policy debate on the uninsured" by refining their earlier estimates of the employed uninsured. The authors estimated that the employed uninsured and their dependents represented some three quarters of the uninsured: the employed uninsured comprised more than half of all persons uninsured throughout 1977, and their nonworking uninsured dependents were over one fifth of all uninsured persons. These results have persisted in more recent estimates of the uninsured using NMES and CPS (32, 43, 44).

The characteristics of the employed uninsured portray a group generally at a disadvantage in the labor market: young adults, those in poor economic circumstances (low wages and family incomes at or near poverty), those poorly educated, and in industries and occupations characterized by seasonal or transitory employment and less technical skills (28, 43). However, the employed uninsured also consist of substantial numbers of prime age, full-time wage earners: about half were over 30 years of age, 60% worked 35 or more hours per week, and half resided in middle- or high-income households.

Research has also revealed that uninsured workers generally do not decline offers of health insurance made by employers. Instead, such workers are typically employed by firms that *fail to offer coverage*. Monheit et al (28) disclosed that 89% of uninsured workers did not receive an offer of coverage so that only 11% of uninsured workers declined an offer of coverage. Recent work by Long & Marquis (22) implies that only about 13.9% of uninsured workers decline offers of coverage.[5]

One cannot, however, infer that the lack of coverage among employed persons is strictly a failure by suppliers of employment-related insurance. Certain workers may prefer wage income to health insurance, either because they expect to use few health services or because of their economic circumstances. Such workers may seek employment in firms that offer compensation entirely in wage income. Typically, such firms tend to be small and are among the least likely to offer coverage. Recent empirical evidence is consistent with such behavior: Monheit & Short (33) observed that employees of small firms tend to be young adults, low-wage earners, and part-time workers; Long & Marquis (22) also found such workers in firms that do not offer coverage. The characteristics of these workers raises the issue of whether they would enroll if coverage were offered. Long & Marquis (22) noted that workers who decline offered coverage are similar to those employed by firms that do not offer coverage (in terms of wage rates, hours of work, and turnover) and concluded that "lack of demand for insurance by their workers may be a factor in the employer's decision not to offer health benefits."

As noted, the focus on uninsured workers and their employment circumstances has drawn attention to the small firm, as employer surveys have shown health insurance offers to decline markedly as firm size diminishes. Data from the Health Insurance Association of America reveal that in 1989 only 26% of firms with fewer than 5 employees and 54% with 5 to 9 employees offered health insurance, compared to 99% of firms with over 100 employees (41). Small employers report the cost of coverage and low profitability as "very important" reasons for not providing coverage (40).

---

[5]Long & Marquis estimated that 2% of the 99 million workers aged 16–64 (1.98 million workers) declined insurance offers and remained uninsured. These workers represent 13.9% of the 14.3 million uninsured workers in 1988 (44).

The differential income taxation of health insurance premiums paid by owners of small unincorporated firms for their coverage also contributes to their unwillingness to provide coverage to themselves and their workers (30). In contrast to employees and owner-operators of incorporated businesses who can fully deduct employer contributions to health insurance, self-employed owners of unincorporated (typically small) businesses can only deduct 25% of their health insurance premiums.

Whether motivated by demand or supply considerations, the failure of small firms to provide coverage has led to a concentration of the uninsured in such enterprises. Monheit & Short (33) indicated that one third of uninsured employees and dependents are associated with establishments of less than 10 employees and one half are with establishments of 25 or fewer employees. This concentration has drawn attention to the costs and availability of coverage in the small group market and to underwriting practices alleged to segment that market according to favorable risks. Such practices include denying coverage to certain occupations and industries, denial of coverage because of preexisting medical conditions, and durational rating, which can make yearly premium increases quite volatile (15, 53). Small firms also face higher premiums because of the greater administrative load associated with marketing costs and claims administration for a small and unstable employee base, and because of the greater variability in their health care expenditures due to their size. However, there has been increasing concern over whether the behavior of insurers can be really justified on the basis of the health care experience of small groups or are largely exclusionary practices designed to limit access to coverage through excessive premiums.

Increased penetration of the small group market has become a critical element in extending health insurance coverage to the general population. The choices available to the policymaker appear to be either mandated employer coverage or voluntary approaches via tax credits or subsidies. Monheit & Short (32) estimate that failure to include establishments of 25 or fewer in an employer mandate would only extend coverage to a fifth of the uninsured. Approaches using tax incentives and subsidies to small firms have yet to demonstrate that these incentives will elicit a significant response (25, 49).

THE DECLINE IN EMPLOYMENT-RELATED HEALTH INSURANCE COVERAGE
Structural changes in the US economy—the shift of employment from manufacturing to services, the rise in part-time employment, and the decline in union membership—have been cited as explanations for why employed persons will continue to be disproportionately represented among the uninsured (7). Indeed, between 1980 and 1986, the percent of the nonelderly population with employment-based coverage declined by 2.6 percentage points and the percent uninsured increased from 15.1% to 17.6% (23).

Several studies discount the structural shift hypothesis. Analyses by the US Congressional Research Service (50) assert that the "dramatic decline" in work-related coverage from 1979 to 1986 resulted from "something other than a shift of jobs into the service-producing sector". CRS attributed the decline to (a) a reduction in rates of coverage of spouses and children under 18, and (b) a shift in demographics from children under 18 (a typically high-coverage group) to others living in the household (a low-coverage group). These shifts are also consistent with a deterioration in the ability of employees to pay for family coverage during this period: the cost of family coverage increased 66% during the 1980s (50; see also 16, 27).

Long & Rodgers (23) also used CPS data between 1980 and 1987 to assess whether the shift in employment to low insurance industries (i.e. construction, trade, and services) or the decline in rates of coverage within all industries was the primary reason for the reduction in coverage among workers. They constructed a Laspeyres' Index of health insurance and a similar index of industry employment. A comparison of these indices for employees and dependents revealed that the decline in insurance across industries far outweighed the shift of employment toward low insurance industries. They suggested that the decline in health insurance coverage was much more uniformly distributed among the workforce than previously thought and could not be resolved by targeting several declining sectors of the economy.

Kronick (19) examined "the frayed connection between employment and insurance" between 1979 and 1989 that led to a 3.8 percentage point increase in the uninsured population. He also discounted the impact of structural changes in employment on the growth in the uninsured population and emphasized a decline in workers' ability to pay for coverage. Using CPS data, Kronick found that coverage losses were largely confined to low-wage workers (annual earnings of $15,000 or less) and argued that increases in medical care costs and in the price of coverage to small businesses were the most likely causes for the declining rates of coverage.

In sum, research on the characteristics of the uninsured has identified important gaps in the relationship between employment and health insurance status and raised a number of hypotheses regarding the preferences of the uninsured and the behavior of employers in decisions to offer health insurance. In addition, attention has also focused on allegations that the health insurance market has segmented risks among employee groups rather than provided coverage on the same basis to employees of all types of firms. This in turn has stimulated new research suggesting that health insurance benefits are an impediment to employment changes (9). Finally, research suggests that the decline in employment-related coverage during the 1980s was attributable more to declining rates of coverage across all industries, demographic shifts from high- to low-coverage groups, and rising costs of coverage than to changes in the distribution of employment.

HEALTH INSURANCE DYNAMICS

Thus far our discussion has focused upon a rather static picture of the uninsured, derived from point-in-time estimates or "snapshots" of their size and characteristics. These estimates are, however, unable to measure several factors crucial to establishing effective policy initiatives. These include the length of time a person is without coverage, the extent to which the uninsured acquire coverage and the type of coverage obtained, whether multiple spells health insurance loss are common, and the reasons for transitions between insured and uninsured states. Such *dynamic* aspects of health insurance status are essential for understanding whether lack of coverage is largely a transitory or long-term phenomenon and for the design of policy initiatives that would "provide coverage for appropriate periods of time and target persons who truly have difficulty acquiring or retaining health insurance coverage" (31).

Walden et al (52) provided the first hint that an individual's health insurance status could fluctuate over a year. They noted that the insured population included persons covered for only part of the year so that "estimates [of insurance coverage] for periods shorter than a year will yield different counts than annual estimates. " Their analysis also suggested that a considerable number of Americans might be "chronically" uninsured, lacking any coverage for at least a year.

Using 1977 NMCES data, Walden et al (52) estimated that 7.6% of the US population were insured part of the year, with young children, young adults, members of minority groups, and those at or near poverty particularly vulnerable to discontinuities in insurance coverage. Part-year coverage was more likely among the Medicaid population than among persons with private insurance (42.6% of the former compared to only 7.1% of the latter) and a majority of both groups remained uninsured after losing their coverage. A comparable proportion of Americans (8.7%), were uninsured throughout calender year 1977, with young adults, minority groups, those in poor economic circumstances, those with part-year or no employment experience, and those in rural areas or in the South and West most at risk.

These early estimates of changes in health insurance status lacked precision because they compared health insurance status at a particular household interview date to that at an earlier interview. Monthly insurance status between interviews was unavailable. Consequently, persons uninsured between interviews could be counted as insured all year if they had health insurance at the time of each interview. Conversely, some of the all-year uninsured may have had months of coverage that went undetected.

Further interest in the dynamics of health insurance was stimulated by monthly data from SIPP and by studies of spells of poverty and welfare (5, 10, 35). These studies revealed that point-in-time estimates of the poverty and AFDC populations obscured movements in and out of such states: that most poverty or welfare spells were of short duration but that point-in-time estimates captured persons in the midst of fairly long spells. Analyses of unemployment found that ignoring multiple spells could seriously understate annual unemployment experience (2).

Monheit & Schur (31) used SIPP data to examine the variety of dynamic aspects of health insurance status: transitions in health insurance status over a 32-month period, the type of coverage gained or lost, the length of uninsured spells, and the extent to which point-in-time estimates were based upon the long-term uninsured. Recognizing that point-in-time estimates of the uninsured population "may mask a high degree of instability and turnover among persons without health insurance, " they examined two cohorts: (a) persons with private insurance during their first SIPP reference month, and (b) persons uninsured at the onset of SIPP. The former group provided the opportunity to observe the process of health insurance loss and its resolution; the latter group permitted consideration of the dynamics underlying commonly used point-in-time estimates of the uninsured. A comparison of these cohorts also revealed considerable heterogeneity in their characteristics and in their health insurance experience.

Pairwise monthly comparisons of the health insurance status of individuals in each cohort revealed the coverage of the privately insured cohort to be far more stable than that of the uninsured cohort: 78% of the former had no change in insurance status and remained privately insured compared to only 27.4% of the latter who were uninsured for the entire 32-month period. These chronically uninsured persons were in poor economic circumstances (45% were poor and 20% near-poor) and the majority were not employed (15.5% were unemployed and 37.2% were not in the labor force). The health insurance experience of the uninsured cohort was far more volatile than the privately insured cohort: 44.5% of the former had more than one change in their health insurance status compared to only 17.2% of the latter. Finally, over a quarter of the privately insured cohort who lost coverage had multiple spells of health insurance loss. Of those in the uninsured cohort who acquired coverage, over one third had additional periods without insurance.

Monheit & Schur also examined the process of health insurance loss and acquisition. Two thirds (64.4%) of privately insured persons with a one-time loss of coverage reacquired insurance compared to one half of the uninsured cohort. The greater ability of losers of private insurance to reacquire such coverage and remain insured compared to the uninsured cohort reflects striking differences in their economic status and labor force attachment. Persons in the uninsured cohort were three times as likely to be in poverty as were losers of private coverage; 50% of all persons and 77% of policyholders losing employment-related coverage worked full-time compared to only 36% of the uninsured cohort. Finally, the authors found that losers of employment-related coverage experienced a decline in their economic status (monthly income declined from an average of $2340 before the loss to $2083 in the month after the loss and the percent in poverty increased from 12% to 22%). This suggests that public policy to encourage continuation of coverage (such as COBRA or state mandates) may require subsidies to help defray the out-of-pocket costs of continuing coverage.

Monheit & Schur considered the type of coverage lost and acquired by the privately insured cohort. Persons with privately purchased plans lost coverage at almost twice the rate of those with employment-based coverage. Since loss of nonemployment-related coverage is associated with default of premiums or a decision not to renew coverage, this difference reflects disparities in the economic status of the groups. For example, 36.4% of persons with nonemployment-related coverage and 45% of those losing such coverage had incomes less than 1.5 times the poverty line compared to only 10.5% of those with work-related coverage. Finally, most (84%) of those losing employment-related coverage subsequently reacquired such coverage. Half of those losing privately purchased coverage were able to obtain new coverage through the workplace. The overwhelming majority of those who lost coverage as policyholders or dependents retained their status when new insurance was acquired.

Monheit & Schur also found striking differences between the cohorts regarding length of time without health insurance. On average, the majority of privately insured losers completed their uninsured spells in 4.9 months and those with multiple spells completed each spell in 4.3 months. Those with spells in progress (whose endpoints were not observed) were without coverage for a year and those with multiple spells whose last spell was incomplete averaged almost 7 months per uninsured spell. Since persons in the uninsured cohort were without coverage at the onset of SIPP, the authors computed total months without coverage. On average, the uninsured cohort lacked coverage for 20 of the 32-month SIPP panel compared to only 8 months for losers of private coverage. Two thirds of the uninsured cohort lacked coverage for more than a year compared to only one fifth of the privately insured cohort. Consequently, point-in-time estimates of the uninsured reflect the experience of long-term uninsured and mask transitions in coverage among the privately insured.

Swartz & McBride (47) also used the 1984 SIPP to characterize spells without health insurance, using the first spell of health insurance loss and considering complete and incomplete spells (i.e. those whose beginning is observed but whose completion is unobserved). They dealt directly with the latter by applying hazard functions to estimate the duration of spells in progress. Their estimate of the distribution of uninsured spells yielded results similar to Monheit & Schur: uninsured spells observed from their onset are considerably shorter than spells in progress. The latter, which are the basis for point-in-time estimates of the uninsured, can be a misleading indicator of the duration of time without health insurance. They found that half of all uninsured spells observed from their onset are completed within four months whereas only 15% are beyond 24 months; 60% of those in progress last longer than 24 months and 13% end within four months

Swartz & McBride also examined the relationship between spell length and individual characteristics. They found young adults and persons aged 55 to 64 are somewhat more likely to have spells in excess of 24 months than individuals aged 25 to 54. They also found that the majority of spells in each income group last less than five months. Persons in the lowest income category (below $400 per month) were most likely to have uninsured spells exceeding 24 months, while those in the highest income class ($2400 per month) were least likely (23% and 8%, respectively). Employed persons were more likely to have spells of less than 5 months than those unemployed or outside the labor force, and the latter were most likely to have spells exceeding 24 months. Similar to Monheit & Schur, they also found that losers of employment-related insurance had spells of short duration.

Swartz, Marcotte & McBride (46) revised their initial estimates of the distribution of uninsured spells, which was based on observed beginnings. Their new estimate includes spells whose onset is not directly observed: spells with unobserved beginning dates and those with beginning dates obtained from retrospective information on the last time coverage was held. Since such spells are likely to be longer than those with observed beginning dates, Schwartz and colleagues were concerned that their earlier estimates of the distribution of uninsured spells were biased toward short spell lengths. Although spell lengths with retrospectively reported beginning dates greatly exceed those with observed beginnings (mean of 29 months and median of 30 months for the former compared to 7 and 4 months for the latter), their new estimate of the uninsured spell distribution closely resembles their earlier work: they found that 48% of uninsured spells end within 5 months, 19% are more than two years, and the median spell is almost 7 months. The similarity of these findings reflects the fact that the long spells whose beginning dates are not directly observed are a small proportion (less than one fifth) of all spells. Based on these findings, the authors conclude that most uninsured spells are of short duration but that a nontrivial proportion (over one sixth) of all spells last more than two years.

The heterogeneity of the uninsured population and the variation in their spell lengths have also led Swartz, Marcotte & McBride (45) to examine how demographic and economic characteristics affect the probability that an uninsured spell will end. Using characteristics at the onset of a spell, they found that exit probabilities increase and spell lengths decline for persons with higher educational attainment (the most important impact), with family incomes in excess of $2460 per month, for those employed in sectors with high rates of coverage, for those not unemployed, for full-time rather than part-time workers, for persons currently or previously married, and for persons 18–24 years of age. The authors suggest that higher exit probabilities for full-time workers indicate that many may face waiting periods of several months before obtaining coverage as new employees. The authors also speculated that since low education, low wages, and part-time employment reduce exit rates, the effectiveness of an employer mandate may be limited since such workers are likely to be in firms exempt from the legislation.

In sum, studies of health insurance dynamics reveal a heterogeneity among the uninsured population and their health insurance experience. The commonly used point-in-time estimates of the uninsured are not representative of all persons experiencing uninsured spells since lengthy spells may be over-represented. This has important policy implications, in terms of targeting groups at risk and assessing the extent to which lack of coverage can be resolved via market forces or through direct policy intervention. These analyses also suggest that a comprehensive approach to expanding health insurance is required, given the number of persons with transitions between insured and uninsured states and the poor employment characteristics of the long-term uninsured.

CONCLUDING COMMENTS: THE UNINSURED AND THEIR USE OF HEALTH SERVICES

Public sentiment toward expanded health insurance coverage reflects a concern that the uninsured may fail to obtain a socially appropriate level of health care. Although health care use by the uninsured is frequently compared to that by insured persons, use by the latter cannot define the social optimum since it may reflect inefficiencies due to moral hazard. However, from an equity perspective, it is still instructive to compare access to and use of health services by insured and uninsured persons since use by the former may reflect a social norm. In virtually any such comparison, the uninsured are at a disadvantage.

Having a usual source of medical care is a frequently used measure of access since it is strongly correlated with the ability to obtain services, the level of service use, and the quality and satisfaction of care received (1). Various data indicate that the uninsured are less likely to have a usual source of care than their insured counterparts. Using NMES, Cornelius et al (11) found that two thirds of the uninsured had a usual source of care compared to 82% of persons with private insurance. Similar disparities have been reported by Aday et al (1) using the 1982 and 1976 CHAS/NORC surveys and by Kasper & Barrish (17) using the 1977 NMCES.

The 1987 NMES reveals broad disparities in medical care use between the insured and uninsured. Lefkowitz & Monheit (20) found that only 64% of nonelderly persons uninsured all year used health services in 1987 compared to 84% of the privately insured and 83% of those with public coverage. On average, the uninsured who used services had lower expenditures ($915) than those with private insurance ($1316) and public coverage ($2619), but paid over three quarters of expenditures out of pocket compared to only half by the privately insured and less than one fifth by persons with public coverage. Such differences remained even when family income, ethnic/racial background, and health status were considered separately. Hahn & Lefkowitz (14) showed similar disparities between insured and uninsured nonelderly populations for a variety of health services. For example, 71% of privately or publicly insured persons used ambulatory physician care compared to only 48% of the uninsured; one quarter of privately insured persons and one fifth of those with public coverage used ambulatory nonphysician services compared to only 13% of the uninsured; and 56% of persons with private or public coverage obtained prescription drugs compared to 36% of the uninsured. A review of studies regarding use of health services by insurance status has led the Office of Technology Assessment (51) to conclude that "existing research supports common sense notions and anecdotal evidence that availability of third party payment for health care can be important, in particular to gaining access to care and to the way care is delivered".

These comparisons are consistent with the fact that uninsured and insured persons face different out-of-pocket prices for medical care. However, because these estimates do not control for various other factors that affect medical care demand, the observed differences may not be solely attributable to health insurance. Spillman (39) has isolated the effect of insurance on the use of health services by applying a two-part econometric model of medical care demand using the 1980 NMCUES. She compared differentials in use between the all-year insured and uninsured populations for nonemergency ambulatory care, emergency care, and inpatient hospital care. The two-part model yields estimates of the likelihood of service use (via a probit equation) and the level of use among users (estimated by ordinary least squares). Combining these estimates yields expected annual use of health services.

Spillman's multivariate analysis indicates substantial utilization differences between the all-year uninsured and insured. Uninsured men and women were 71% and 79% as likely as their insured counterparts to have at least one nonemergency ambulatory visit in 1980, and had two thirds the number of visits of insured users and half the expected number of visits of the all-year insured. Although differentials between insured and uninsured children were the smallest, the latter had only 71% of the expected number of visits of the insured. Uninsured adults were also found to use only 60% of the expected number of emergency services of insured adults. The largest differences were for impatient hospital use, with uninsured men and women only 26% and 30% as likely as the insured to have a hospital admission and only half to two thirds of the average number of inpatient days of insured users of hospital care. Estimates of hospital use revealed that uninsured men used only 12% as many days as insured men while uninsured women use only one fifth of the days predicted for insured women. Finally, uninsured children were 25% less likely to have a hospital admission than were insured children.

These disparities raise the question of whether expanded coverage will make a difference in the health status of the uninsured or in their health outcomes once care is received. A review of empirical evidence (51) concludes that "a number of studies have found that adverse outcomes appear to be related to the lack of health insurance coverage", with the uninsured more likely than the privately insured to have (a) avoidable hospitalizations; (b) diagnoses indicating "later stages of life-threatening diseases"; (c) emergency/urgent hospitalizations; and (d) higher inpatient mortality even after controlling for health status at admission. However, the review concludes that "the evidence on differences in health outcomes between uninsured and privately insured individuals is less consistent and compelling than the evidence on utilization and process".

In sum, research on the underinsured has made important progress in measuring the size of the population at risk, identifying their characteristics, and describing their experience without health insurance coverage, both in terms of the length of time without coverage and with regard to the implications for access to medical care. Such research has also helped to identify the shortcomings of private health insurance in the United States. These findings should continue to help shape the debate over appropriate ways to expand coverage to the underinsured.

Literature Cited

1. Aday LA, Fleming GV, Andersen R. 1984. *Access to Medical Care in the US: Who Has It and Who Doesn't.* Chicago: Plurbis Press/Univ. Chicago

2. Akerlof GA, Main BG. 1980. Unemployment spells and unemployment experience. *Am. Econ. Rev.* 70:241–48

3. Andersen OW, Lyons J, Anderson R. 1976. *Two Decades of Health Services: Social Survey Trends in Use and Expenditures.* Cambridge, MA: Ballinger Publ.

4. Arrow KJ. 1963. Uncertainty and the welfare economics of medical care. *Am. Econ. Rev.* 53:941–73

5. Bane MJ, Ellwood DT. 1986. Slipping into and out of poverty: The dynamics of welfare spells. *J. Hum. Res.* 21:1–23

6. Berki SE, Wyszewianski L, Lichtenstein R, Gimotty PA, Bowlyow JE, et al. 1985. Health insurance coverage of the unemployed. *Med. Care* 23:847–54

7. Black JT. 1986. Comment on the employed uninsured and the role of public policy. *Inquiry* 23:209–12

8. Chollet D. 1988. *Uninsured in the United States: The Nonelderly Population without Health Insurance, 1986.* Washington, DC: Employee Benefits Res. Inst.

9. Cooper P, Monheit A. 1993. Does employment-related health insurance inhibit job mobility? *Inquiry* 30: In press

10. Corcoran M, Duncan GJ, Gurin G, Gurin P. 1985. Myth and reality: The causes and persistence of poverty. *J. Policy Anal. Manage.* 4:516–36

11. Cornelius L, Beauregard K, Cohen J. 1991. Usual sources of medical care and their characteristics. *AHCPR Publ. No 91-0042. Natl. Med. Expend. Res. Find. 11.* Agency Health Care Pol. Res. Rockville, MD: Public Health Serv.

12. Farley PJ. 1985. Who are the underinsured? *Milbank Mem. Fund Q. Health Soc.* 63:476–503

13. Gold M, McEachern Y, Santoni T. 1987. Health insurance loss among the unemployed: Extent of the problem

and policy options. *J. Public Health Policy* 8:44

14. Hahn B, Lefkowitz DC. 1992. *Annual expenditures and sources of payment for health care services.* AHCPR Publ. No. 93–0007. Natl. Med. Expend. Surv. Res. Find. 14. Agency Health Care Policy Res. Rockville, MD: Public Health Serv.

15. Hall MA. 1992. The political economics of health insurance market reform. *Health Aff.* 11:108–24

16. Jensen GA, Morrisey MA, Marcus JW. 1987. Cost-sharing and the changing pattern of employer-sponsored health benefits. *Milbank Fund Q.* 65:521–50

17. Kasper JA, Barrish G. 1982. *Usual Sources of Medical Care and their Characteristics.* Natl. Health Care Expend. Study Data Prev. 12, Natl. Cent. Health Serv. Res. Hyattsville, MD: Public Health Serv.

18. Kronick R. 1989. *Adolescent Health Insurance Status.* Washington, DC: US Congr. Off. Technol. Assess.

19. Kronick R. 1991. Health insurance, 1979–1989: The frayed connection between employment and insurance. *Inquiry* 28:318–32

20. Lefkowitz DC, Monheit AC. 1991. *Health Insurance, Use of Health Services, and Health Care Expenditures.* AHCPR Publ. No. 92–0017. Natl. Med. Expend. Res. Find. 12. Agency Health Care Policy Res. Rockville, MD: Public Health Serv.

21. Levit KR, Olin GL, Letsch SW. 1992. Americans' health insurance coverage, 1980–91. *Health Care Financ. Rev.* 14:31–57

22. Long SH, Marquis MS. 1992. Gaps in employment-based health insurance: Lack of supply or Lack of demand? In *Health Benefits and the Workforce,* pp. 37–42. US Dep. Labor, Pension Welfare Benefits Admin., Washington, DC

23. Long SH, Rodgers J. 1992. *Did changes in the composition of jobs explain increases in the number of uninsured? Evidence from the CPS,*

1980–1987. Presented at Annu. Meet. Am. Econ. Assoc.

24. Markowitz MA, Gold M, Rice T. 1991. Determinants of health insurance status among young adults. *Med. Care* 29:6–19

25. McLaughlin CG, Zellers WK. 1992. The shortcomings of voluntarism in the small-group insurance market. *Health Aff.* 11:28–40

26. Menzel PT. 1983. *Medical Cost, Moral Choices: A Philosophy of Health Care Economics in America*. New Haven: Yale Univ. Press

27. Monheit AC, Cunningham PJ. 1992. Children without health insurance. *Future Child*. 2:154–70

28. Monheit AC, Hagan MM, Berk ML, Farley PJ. 1985. The employed uninsured and the role of public policy. *Inquiry* 22:348–64

29. Monheit AC, Hagan MM, Berk ML, Wilensky GR. 1984. Health insurance for the uninsured: Is federal legislation needed? *Health Aff.* 3:1

30. Monheit AC, Harvey PH. 1993. Sources of health insurance for the self employed: Does differential taxation make a difference? *Inquiry* 30: 293–305

31. Monheit AC, Schur CL. 1988. The dynamics of health insurance loss: A tale of two cohorts. *Inquiry* 25:315–27

32. Monheit AC, Short P. 1989. Mandating health care for working Americans. *Health Aff.* 8:22–38

33. Monheit AC, Short P. 1989. *The economics of health insurance offerings in small firms*. Presented at Annu. Meet. Am. Public Health Assoc., Chicago, IL

34. Moyer E. 1989. A revised look at the number of uninsured Americans. *Health Aff.* 8:102–10

35. O'Neil JA, Bassi L, Wolf DA. 1987. The duration of welfare spells. *Rev. Econ. Stat.* 69:241–48

36. Pauly MV. 1971. *Medical Care at Public Expense: A Study in Applied Welfare Economics*. New York: Praeger

37. Short P. 1990. *Estimates of the Uninsured Population, Calendar Year 1987*. DHHS Publ. No. (PHS) 90–3469. Natl. Med. Expend. Surv. Data Summary 2. Agency Health Care Policy Res. Rockville, MD: Public Health Serv.

38. Short P, Monheit A, Beauregard K. 1989. *A Profile of Uninsured Americans*. DHHS Publ. No. (PHS) 89–3443. Natl. Cent. Health Serv. Res.

Health Care Technol. Assess. Rockville, MD: Public Health Serv.

39. Spillman BC. 1992. The impact of being uninsured on utilization of basic health care services. *Inquiry* 29:457–66

40. Sullivan C. 1990. Why employers do not offer coverage. In *Providing Employee Health Benefits: How Firms Differ*. Washington, DC: Health Insur. Assoc. Am.

41. Sullivan C, DiCarlo S, Lippert C. 1990. Characteristics of firms that do and do not offer health insurance. In *Providing Employee Health Benefits: How Firms Differ*. Washington, DC: Health Insur. Assoc. America

42. Sulvetta MB, Swartz K. 1986. *The Uninsured and Uncompensated Care: A Chartbook*. George Washington Natl. Health Policy Forum, Washington, DC

43. Swartz K. 1986. Interpreting the estimates from four national surveys of the number of people without health insurance. *J. Econ. Soc. Measure*. 14:233–56

44. Swartz K. 1992. A research note on the characteristics of workers without employer-group health insurance based on the March 1988 current population survey. In *Health Benefits and the Workforce*, pp. 13–20. US Dep. Labor, Pension Welfare Benefits Admin., Washington, DC

45. Swartz K, Marcotte J, McBride T. 1993. Personal characteristics and spells without health insurance. *Inquiry* 30:64–76

46. Swartz K, Marcotte J, McBride T. Spells without health insurance: The distribution of durations when left-censored spells are included. *Inquiry* 30: 77–83

47. Swartz K, McBride TD. 1990. Spells without health insurance: Distributions of durations and their link to point-in-time estimates of the uninsured. *Inquiry* 27:281–88

48. Swartz K, Purcell PJ. 1989. Counting uninsured Americans. *Health Aff.* 8: 193–97

49. Thorpe KE, Hendricks A, Garnick D, Donelan K, Newhouse JP, et al. 1992. Reducing the number of uninsured by subsidizing employment-based health insurance. *J. Am. Med. Assoc.* 267: 945–48

50. US Congress. Res. Serv. 1988. *Health Insurance and the Uninsured: Background Data and Analysis*. Washington, DC: Library of Congress

51. US Congress, Off. Technol. Assess. 1992. *Does Health Insurance Make a*

Difference? Background Pap., OTA-BP-H-99 Washington, DC: US GPO

52. Walden DC, Wilensky GR, Kasper JA. 1985. *Changes in Health Insurance Status: Full-Year and Part-Year Coverage.* Data Preview 21, Natl. Health Care Expend. Study, Natl.

Cent. Health Serv. Res. Health Care Technol. Assess. DHHS Publ. No. (PHS)85–337

53. Zellers WK, McLaughlin CG, Frick KD. 1992. Small business health insurance: Only the healthy need apply. *Health Aff.* 11:174–180

Annu. Rev. Public Health. 1994. 15:487–509

HEALTH STATUS OF VULNERABLE POPULATIONS

Lu Ann Aday

Behavioral Sciences and Management and Policy Sciences, University of Texas
School of Public Health, Houston, Texas 77225

KEY WORDS: health status, relative risk, social status, social capital, human capital

WHO ARE THE VULNERABLE?

Relative Risk

Vulnerable populations are *at risk* of poor physical, psychological, and/or social health. Underlying this definition of vulnerability is the epidemiological concept of risk, in that there is a *probability* that an individual could become ill within a given period of time. The word "vulnerable" is derived from the Latin root vulnus (wound). A framework for studying the origin and consequences of vulnerability to poor health is summarized in Figure 1 (1).

Community and associated individual characteristics are *risk factors* predictive of the incidence of poor physical, psychological, and/or social health. Risk factors encompass those attributes or exposures (smoking, drug use, and lead paint poisoning, for example) that are related or lead to increases in the probability of occurrence of health-related outcomes.

Relative risk refers to the ratio of the risk of poor health among groups exposed to the risk factors versus those who are not so exposed (22). Relative risk reflects the differential vulnerability of different groups to poor health.

The concept of risk assumes that there is always a chance that an adverse health-related event will occur. Correspondingly, *everyone* is potentially at risk of poor physical, psychological, and/or social health. Some may, however, be more or less at risk of poor health at different times in their

487

0163-7525/94/0510-0487$05.00

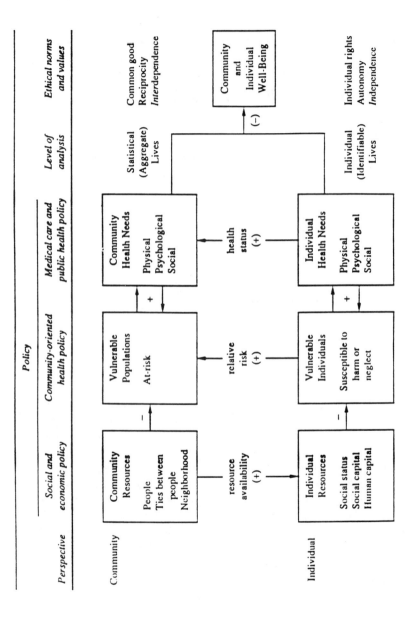

Note: (+) indicates direct relationship (**likelihood** of outcome *increases* **as** predictor **increases**); (–) indicates inverse relationship (likelihood of outcome *decreases* **as** predictor **increases**).

Figure 1 Framework for studying vulnerable populations.

lives, while certain individuals and groups are more apt to be at risk than others at any given point in time.

Having poor physical health (such as a debilitating chronic illness) may also make one more vulnerable to (at risk) poor psychological (depression) or social health (few supportive social contacts). The risk of harm or neglect would be multiplied for those who are in poor health and have few material (economic) and nonmaterial (psychological or social) resources to assist in coping with illness.

Health Status

Health is a complex and multidimensional concept. An array of definitions and indicators of health have been developed and applied to measure it (24). The World Health Organization (WHO) defines health as a "state of complete physical, mental, and social well-being and not merely the absence of disease or infirmity" (59). Comprehensive efforts to conceptualize and measure health have tended to distinguish the physical, mental, and social dimensions reflected in the WHO definition (56, 57).

Health can be measured in either positive or negative terms, that is, in terms of positive indicators of health status (such as age- and sex-specific norms of height or weight or a scale of positive mental health) or the total absence of health, reflected in disease-specific mortality (death) rates (51). Concepts of morbidity define the middle range of a continuum defined by theoretical positive and negative end points that mark the total presence or absence of health. The higher risk (or likelihood) of poor health is reflected toward the negative end of this underlying, multidimensional health status continuum.

Though a variety of indicators of the WHO dimensions of health (physical, mental, and social) have been developed, generally physical refers to "the physiologic and physical status of the body," and mental or psychological health as "the state of mind, including basic intellectual functions such as memory and feelings". Physical and mental indicators tend to "end at the skin", while indicators of social health extend beyond the individual to encompass the quantity and quality of social contacts with others (56).

The magnitude of individual or community needs along each of these dimensions differs depending on how they are defined and measured (6, 13, 24, 40, 51, 57). Assessments of community health needs generally focus on aggregate, statistical indicators of the rates of prevalence or incidence of morbidity or mortality (such as infant mortality rates, HIV-seroprevalence, percent of the elderly with limitations in activities of daily living, and so on). Individual health needs assessments measure the health status of identifiable people or patients (based on symptoms or diagnoses of illness, for example). The former has principally been the focus of public health policy and programs and the latter of personal medical care service delivery and practice.

Vulnerable Populations

The vulnerable populations that are the primary focus of this review are those for whom poor physical, psychological, or social health has or is likely to become a reality: high-risk mothers and infants; chronically ill and disabled; persons with AIDS; mentally ill and disabled; alcohol or substance abusers; suicide- or homicide-prone; abusing families; the homeless; and immigrants and refugees.

The major reasons for focusing on these groups in examining the health and health care needs of vulnerable populations are as follows: (*a*) the needs of affected individuals are in many cases debilitating or life-threatening; (*b*) they require an extensive set of medical and nonmedical services; (*c*) the growth in their number and magnitude of needs are placing greater demands on the medical care, public health, and related social and human services service delivery sectors; (*d*) their multi-faceted needs are, however, not adequately met through existing financing or service delivery arrangements; and (*e*) federal, state, and local policymakers are increasingly concerned about how to deal with the prospect of a growing number of Americans at risk of serious physical, psychological, and/or social health problems.

WHY ARE THEY VULNERABLE?

Ethical Norms and Values

An individual perspective on the origins of poor physical, psychological, or social health views health to be primarily a function of personal lifestyle choices, and poor health outcomes the result of failure by individuals to assume adequate personal responsibility for their health and well-being (21). This perspective highlights personal autonomy, independence, and associated individual rights as the principal ethical norms and values for guiding decision-making regarding the amelioration of risk. The individual is the primary focus of efforts to diminish risk.

A community perspective on the origins of health needs focuses on the differential risks that exist for different groups as a function of the availability of opportunities and resources for maximizing their health. Poor health results because communities fail to invest in and assume responsibility for the collective well-being of their members (50). Norms of reciprocity, trust, and social obligation acknowledge the webs of interdependence and mutual support and caring that are essential for minimizing the risks of poor physical, psychological, or social health. The community and associated social and environmental risk factors are the focus of interventions motivated by this perspective.

Resource Availability

The beginning point for understanding the factors that increase the risk of poor health originates in a macro-level look at the availability and distribution of community resources (Figure 1). Individuals' risks vary as a function of the opportunities and material and nonmaterial resources associated with (*a*) the personal characteristics (age, sex, and race/ethnicity) of the individuals themselves; (*b*) the nature of the ties between them (family members, friends, and neighbors, for example); and (*c*) the schools, jobs, incomes, and housing and associated factors (such as violence or crime) that characterize the neighborhoods in which they live. The corresponding rewards and resources available to individuals as a function of these social arrangements include (*a*) social status (prestige and power); (*b*) social capital (social support); and (*c*) human capital (productive potential) (See Table 1).

SOCIAL STATUS   As seen in Table 1, social status refers here to ascribed (or biologic) characteristics (age, sex, race, and ethnicity), reflecting the roles people play in society and the corollary socially defined opportunities and rewards, such as prestige and power, they may have as a result. Minorities often have poorer health and fewer material and nonmaterial resources to meet their needs than do majority race individuals. The prevalence of certain types of illness and the need to depend on others for assistance due to poor health differs at different stages of life (infancy, adolescence, adulthood, and old age). Women report higher rates of many types of illness than men, which has been variously attributed to their differing health needs, the stress associated with the complex of deferential and demanding roles women play, as well as to its being more socially acceptable for women to admit their vulnerability. However, men may also be placed at greater risk of poor health outcomes as a function of working in hazardous jobs, or being influenced by societal sex role expectations regarding heavy drinking or the use of violence to settle arguments. Those individuals with a combination of statuses (poor, minority elderly women or young males) that put them at a high risk of having both poor health and few material and nonmaterial resources are in a highly vulnerable position (19).

SOCIAL CAPITAL   Social capital resides in the quantity and quality of interpersonal ties between people. Families provide social capital to members in the form of social networks and support and associated feelings of belonging, psychological well-being, and self-esteem. The value of social

Table 1 Comparisons of relative risk*

Community and Individual Resources	Relative Risk	
	Higher risk	Lower risk
The people: social status		
Age	Infants Children Adolescents Elderly	Working-age adults
Sex	Females	Males
Race and ethnicity	African Americans Hispanics Native Americans Asian Americans	Whites
The ties between people: social capital		
Family structure	Living alone Female-headed families	Extended families Two-parent families
Marital status	Single Separated Divorced Widowed	Married/mingles
Voluntary organizations	Nonmember	Member
Social networks	Weak	Strong
The neighborhood: human capital		
Schools	Less than high school	High school +
Jobs	Unemployed Blue collar	White collar
Income	Poor Near poor	Nonpoor
Housing	Substandard	Adequate +

Note: The terms to designate the race and ethnicity categories in this table are used in talking about these groups in general. When presenting specific data in the text on these groups, the designation (such as black or Asian) in the original source from which the data were derived are generally used. *Mingles* are individuals who are not married but are living with a sexual partner. Voluntary organizations include churches, volunteer interest groups, and civic or neighborhood organizations.

*Reprinted with permission: Aday, Lu Ann. *At Risk in America: The Health and Health Care Needs of Vulnerable Populations in the United States*, Table 1.1, p. 9. Copyright 1993 by Jossey-Bass Inc. Publishers (1).

capital to individuals (single mothers) is that it provides resources (such as having someone to count on for child care) they can use to achieve other interests (going to school or working). Social support is an important resource for individuals in coping with and minimizing the impact of negative life events or adversity on their physical and mental health. Physical, psychological, and social well-being are directly enhanced for people who have supportive social networks (15, 19). People likely to have the least social capital (or the fewest social ties to count on) are those living alone or in female-headed families, those who are not married or in an otherwise committed intimate relationship, those who do not belong to any voluntary organizations (such as churches or volunteer interest groups), or have weak or nonexistent social networks of family or friends (12, 15).

HUMAN CAPITAL   Human capital refers to investments in people's skills and capabilities (such as vocational or public education) that enable them to act in new ways (master a trade) or enhance their contributions to society (enter the labor force). Social capital can also enhance the generation of human capital through, for example, family and community support for encouraging students to stay in school. Neighborhoods that have poor schools, high rates of unemployment, and substandard housing may reflect low levels of investments in the human capital (or productive potential) of the people who live there (12, 58).

The assumption underlying the framework introduced here (Figure 1) is that social and economic, as well as medical care and public health, programs and policies are needed to (directly or indirectly) address the health and health care needs of vulnerable populations and the availability of community and individual resources to meet them.

HOW DO WE MEASURE THEIR HEALTH STATUS?

Two major methodological problems in accurately identifying the prevalence and health status of vulnerable populations are (*a*) ambiguities in the definitions and the lack of comprehensive, comparable, and (*b*) timely data on subgroups of the vulnerable (1).

Definitions

As indicated earlier, vulnerable populations are defined to be at risk of poor physical, psychological, and/or social health. Vulnerability to (or risk of) poor health will be examined at a number of different points along the underlying health status continuum defining the presence or absence of health—that is, groups who are identified on the basis of having a current health problem (chronically ill and disabled, persons with acquired immune deficiency syndrome), as well as those who are at a higher than average risk of having serious health problems either now or in the future (persons who are HIV-positive, high-risk mothers and infants, homeless, immigrants and refugees).

Prevalence or incidence data will be primarily used to identify the health needs of vulnerable populations. The major categories of vulnerable populations that are the focus of this review, based on their principal current or likely physical, psychological, or social health needs, include:

physical: high-risk mothers and infants, chronically ill and disabled, persons with AIDS;
psychological: mentally ill and disabled, abusers of alcohol or other substances, suicide- or homicide-prone; and
social: abusing families, the homeless, and immigrants and refugees.

This classification is intended to reflect the primary types of health problems experienced in each group. Their needs are, however, quite likely to be multidimensional and overlapping, in that poor health along one dimension (physical) is quite likely to be compounded with poor health along another (psychological or social, for example) (1).

In addition, the relative (or comparative) risk of the prevalence or incidence of illness will be reviewed for different demographic subgroups (e.g. age, sex, race and ethnic, education, income, etc) of these populations, to examine the impact of the relative availability of social status, social capital, and human capital resources on vulnerability to poor physical, psychological, or social health.

High-risk mothers and infants have been identified using a variety of predictors and indicators of both morbidity and mortality (such as low or very low birthweight infants and maternal and infant deaths). The chronically ill and disabled have been defined based on diagnoses, disability, and functional status, as well as quality-of-life measures. The case definition of AIDS has been revised three times since it was first published in 1982. At least four generations of studies in the mental health field can be identified in this century, all of which used either different approaches or instruments (record sources and key informants, psychiatric clinical judgments, standardized surveys, and measures of social functioning), for defining cases of mental illness.

The measurement of alcohol and other substance abuse is made more difficult by the fact that there are different stages in the development of the addictive behaviors: nonaddictive use; excessive use (abuse); addictive dependency; and recovery or relapse. Accurate reports of homicides and suicides depend on accurately classifying the intent of the perpetrators of the acts resulting in these deaths. Maltreatment can include both acts of commission (abuse) and omission (neglect), as well as a variety of types of harm or endangerment (physical, sexual, or emotional). The condition of homelessness can be assessed with respect to time (temporarily, episodically, or chronically homeless) or location (living on the streets, in temporary housing, or doubled up with relatives). Immigrants and refugees encompass those who are in the U.S. legally as well as those who are not, and among the latter, settlers, sojourners, and commuters (permanent residents, temporary visitors, and those who regularly cross the Mexican or Canadian borders to work, respectively) are all included.

Data Sources

Another important problem in estimating the number (or prevalence) and health status of people who are vulnerable is that the quality and completeness of the data for identifying them are limited. The data sources used here include clinical diagnoses of disease, patient self-reports of illness, vital statistics inventories on births and deaths, and health and social service agency records on clients.

These different sources tend to yield variant estimates of those in need *within* a particular group, which also make direct comparisons of the magnitude of need *across* groups difficult. Different universes (or groups) of individuals are used as the basis for different estimates. Further, estimates based on survey data (such as the prevalence of alcohol or other substance abuse or family violence) may also have systematic biases resulting from only selected groups or individuals being included in or responding to the survey, as well as variable (sampling) errors associated with the size and complexity of the sample design.

Trend data that document increases in certain types of problems (such as child abuse and neglect) are also confounded with the increased visibility and likelihood of reporting these types of events. Often data are not available in a timely fashion or vary in quality and completeness across studies and sources. Cutbacks in funding, as well as changes in definitions of cases over time (which may be warranted to capture the changing dynamics of the problem, such as AIDS), can nonetheless jeopardize the availability of longitudinal data to trace changes in the incidence or prevalence of these problems.

The lack of demographic identifiers or detail (by race and ethnicity, for example) can also limit analyses of differences between groups for whom the risk or magnitude of problems are most likely to vary.

Many people have more than one type of health problem. Low birthweight babies may have congenital defects or other adverse outcomes associated with prematurity that result in long-term physical or mental impairment. Particularly high-risk categories of mothers and infants include those in which the mother or her sex partner(s) used drugs or were HIV-positive. Pregnant women with abusive partners or those who are homeless or fleeing political persecution are particularly at risk of poor outcomes for themselves and their unborn children. Accurate national estimates on the number of these and other groups with a multiplicity of cross-cutting needs are not readily available. Examination of data for discrete subgroups should not, however, obscure the *mosaic* of physical, psychological, and social needs that characterize the lives of many of the vulnerable.

In the section that follows the health status and relative risks of selected subgroups of vulnerable populations are examined. Many of the groups described here (high-risk mothers and infants, chronically ill and disabled, and persons with AIDS, among others) are the focus of the Year 2000 Public Health Service Objectives for improving the nation's health (41). When available, the health objectives for these groups, and the extent they have been or are likely to be achieved, will be discussed. It should be recognized, however, that the Year 2000 Objectives for the Nation are largely based on expert opinions and reasonable standard-setting derived from extrapolating recent trends. They should then be principally viewed as a point of reference or benchmark for comparisons with current estimates, and not a normative *ideal* for the future of the nation's health.

WHAT DO WE KNOW ABOUT THEIR HEALTH STATUS?

High-Risk Mothers and Infants

LOW BIRTHWEIGHT   The Year 2000 Objectives for the Nation provide for an incidence of no more than 5% of all live births being a low birthweight infant and no more than 1% very low birthweight (41). The 1990 rates of 7.0% and 1.3% are then higher than the national objectives, and appear to be increasing, rather than declining (32).

INFANT MORTALITY   Though infant death rates have declined substantially over the past twenty years, they continue to exceed the Year 2000 Objectives target of no more than 7.0 total infant deaths, 4.5 neonatal deaths, and 2.5 postneonatal deaths per 1000 live births (41). In 1990 the rates were 9.2, 5.8, and 3.4, respectively (31). The US infant mortality rate is higher than many other major industrial nations. The rates for selected countries, based on 1988 data were, for example: Japan (4.8), Sweden (5.8), Finland (6.1), Netherlands (6.8). In that year (1988), the US infant mortality rate of 10.0 ranked it 23rd among other countries (30).

PRENATAL CARE   The Year 2000 Objectives provide for a goal of 90% of women seeking care in the first trimester of their pregnancy (41). However, the actual rate has remained stable at around 76% since 1979 (32).

MATERNAL MORTALITY   The 1990 rate of 8.2 maternal deaths per 100,000 live births remained more than twice the Year 2000 Objectives target maximum of 3.3 (31, 41).

RELATIVE RISKS   Very young, minority, and poorly educated mothers are much less likely to have adequate prenatal care and more likely to bear low birthweight or very low birthweight infants. The rates of low birthweight babies, inadequate prenatal care, and infant and maternal mortality are two to three times higher among African-American women than white women. This racial disparity shows no signs of diminishing, and may, in fact, be widening (31, 32). Substantial evidence exists that both the contemporary and historical effects of poverty and related risks (sanitation, crowding, nutrition, injury, smoking, and substance abuse) and resource disparities (income, insurance coverage) have played a major role in contributing to low-birthweight and infant mortality differentials for African Americans compared to whites (1).

Chronically Ill and Disabled

DEATH RATES FOR CHRONIC DISEASES   Heart disease has been the leading cause of death over the past twenty years, followed by cancer and stroke. The number of age-adjusted deaths due to heart disease declined 40% from 253.6 per 100,000 in 1970 to 152.0 per 100,000 in 1990. The rate for strokes has declined by more than half to 27.7 in 1990, compared to 66.3 in 1970, though it is still short of the Year 2000 Objective's goal of 20.0. Further, the death rate for cancer (135 deaths per 100,000) remains higher than the Year 2000 Objective of 130 (31, 41).

Based on 1988 data, the life expectancy at birth for males in the United States (71.5) ranked 22nd among other countries and for females (78.4) the U.S. ranked 18th (30).

PREVALENCE OF CHRONIC CONDITIONS   Hypertension and arthritis are the most frequently reported chronic conditions among the noninstitutionalized population, though the prevalence of these conditions has declined slightly over the past decade. The rates for arthritis were 125.2 per 1000 persons in 1991, compared to 133.0 in 1982. For hypertension the corresponding rates were 111.8 and 116.9 (27, 29).

LIMITATION IN MAJOR ACTIVITY DUE TO CHRONIC CONDITIONS   The percent of the U.S. noninstitutionalized population having to limit their activities due to chronic illness has remained around 13% to 14% since the 1970s (or 35 million Americans in 1991). Approximately twenty-four million people were limited in or unable to carry out their *major* daily activity (29, 30).

LIMITATION IN ACTIVITIES OF DAILY LIVING (ADL) AND INSTRUMENTAL AC-TIVITIES OF DAILY LIVING (IADL)   According to the 1987 National Medical Expenditure Survey, about 1 in 10 (11.4%) of the noninstitutionalized elderly (those living in private residences) had limitations in personal care activities (ADLs or activities of daily living), and 17.5% had limitations in home-management activities (IADLs or instrumental activities of daily living) (23). The prevalence of activity limitation is much higher among the institution-alized nursing home population. Based on the 1985 National Nursing Home Survey, around 90% had at least one ADL and 85% had one or more IADLs (28).

RELATIVE RISKS   The prevalence and the magnitude of limitation in daily activities, as well as deaths, due to chronic disease increase steadily with age. At every age, men are more likely to die from major chronic illnesses such as heart disease, stroke, and cancer than women, though among those living with these, elderly women have more problems in being able to carry out their normal daily routines. African Americans—particularly African American men—are more likely to experience serious disabilities as well as die from chronic illness than are either white men or women (23, 27–31).

Persons with AIDS

AIDS CASES   From the beginning of the AIDS epidemic in 1981, through March 1993, a cumulative total of 284,840 cases had been reported in the United States. In January 1993, the AIDS case definition was expanded beyond an earlier (1987) definition to include all persons with severe immunosuppression, based on CD4-T cell counts, as well as an expanded set of HIV-associated illnesses. Based on the pre-1993 definition, the number of cases in the first quarter of 1993 (14,197) was 21% higher than in the first quarter of 1992 (10).

AIDS DEATHS   Around two thirds of those contacting AIDS have died of the disease since the beginning of the epidemic. In 1990, it ranked as the tenth leading cause of death overall in the United States and for whites, and was the seventh leading cause of death among blacks. Most deaths have occurred among homosexual/bisexual men and among women and heterosexual men who are intravenous drug users (31).

HIV PREVALENCE   Approximately one million people in the United States are estimated to have the HIV virus (8). CDC has conducted seroprevalence studies in a number of different institutional sites. Average prevalence rates among individuals seen at these sites varied from 5.9% to patients in tuberculosis clinics to 0.0051% among blood donors (9). Based on current prevalence estimates and annual incidence of AIDS cases, it is estimated that there will be at least 61,000–98,000 new cases in 1993 (8), which means that the number in this and successive years may well exceed the Year 2000 Objectives ceiling of no more than 98,000 new cases annually (41).

RELATIVE RISKS   Early in the AIDS epidemic, homosexual or bisexual males were most likely to be affected. In recent years, more and more mothers and children are at risk due to women or their sex partners using intravenous drugs. Higher proportions of African Americans and Hispanics, compared to whites, are likely to be HIV-positive, to develop and die of AIDS, and to have contracted the disease through drug use or sexual contact with drug users (8–10, 30, 31). Identifying vulnerable populations with respect to AIDS must acknowledge those at different points along the continuum of risk (those who have or have died of full-blown AIDS, those with human immune deficiency syndrome who are certain to contract it, as well as groups that have a particularly high likelihood of experiencing HIV/AIDS due to their sexual or behavioral practices).

Mentally Ill and Disabled

COMMUNITY PREVALENCE RATES   The Epidemiological Catchment Area (ECA) surveys were conducted during the early 1980s in five US cities (New Haven, CT; Baltimore, MD; St. Louis, MO; Durham, NC; and Los Angeles, CA), using the Diagnostic Interview Schedule (DIS) to screen for mental illness. Based on combined data for all five ECA communities, around fifteen percent (15.4%) of the population were estimated to have experienced at least one mental disorder during the past month. The overall rates increased from 15.4% having experienced a mental disorder within the past month, to 19.1% having had a problem within the past six months (six month prevalence), and to 32.2% *ever* having experienced a mental health problem (lifetime prevalence) (42).

TREATED RATES—INPATIENT PSYCHIATRIC SERVICES   There were 1.6 million inpatient psychiatric admissions in 1986. Affective disorders were the most frequent reasons for admission (30.8%), followed by schizophrenia (23.1%) and alcohol-related disorders (14.8%) (44).

TREATED RATES—OUTPATIENT PSYCHIATRIC SERVICES   There were 2.1 million admissions to outpatient psychiatric facilities in 1986. Adjustment disorders were the most frequent reason for admission (23.1%), followed by affective disorders (14.4%). The VA had the highest admission rates for alcohol-related disorders (18.6%) (44).

TREATED RATES—NURSING HOMES   Findings from the 1985 National Nursing Home Survey revealed that nearly two thirds (65.3%) of nursing home residents had at least one mental disorder. The most prevalent disorder (experienced by 46.7% of residents) was organic brain syndrome (OBS), including Alzheimer's disease (47).

RELATIVE RISKS   The prevalence of different types of mental disorders, as well as where people get treatment for them, vary for age, sex, and race groups. Children are more likely to have developmental or behavioral problems. Compared to children or the elderly, substance abuse, schizophrenia, affective disorders, and anxiety disorders are more prevalent among adults under 65 years of age. Relative to younger adults, the noninstitutionalized elderly are much more apt to experience severe cognitive impairment. Though the prevalence of mental illness in general is greater for women, substance abuse and antisocial personality disorders are much more prevalent among men. Nonwhites are more likely to receive inpatient and outpatient psychiatric care in state and county mental hospitals than are whites, while private psychiatric hospitals are more likely to see whites rather than blacks on an outpatient basis (20, 39, 42–44, 47).

Alcohol or Substance Abusers

HOUSEHOLD POPULATION, 12+ YEARS   Based on the National Household Survey on Drug Abuse, which covers the population age 12 and older living in households in the contiguous United States, the prevalence rates for use of any illicit drug (the percent who used it at least once within the 30 days prior to the survey) decreased steadily from 1985 to 1991—from 23 million (12.1%) in 1985 to 14.5 million (7.3%) in 1988 to around 13 million (6.2%) in 1991.

Marijuana remains the most commonly used illicit drug. Approximately 67.7 million Americans (33.4%) have tried marijuana at least once. The prevalence of cocaine use increased steadily from the early 1970s to mid-1980s. During the three-year period from 1988 to 1991, however, the number of current cocaine users decreased substantially from 2.9 million (1.5%) to 1.8 million (0.9%), but among those who used cocaine in the past year, 855,000 used it once a week or more in 1991 compared to 662,000 in 1990. The rates of cigarette and alcohol use declined from 1985 to 1991. Current cigarette use (in the past month) dropped from 32% in 1985 to 27% in 1991. The current alcohol use (in the past month) rates also declined from 1985 to 1991 from 59% in 1985 to 51% in 1991 (33–37).

HIGH SCHOOL SENIORS   In 1992, 14.4% of all high school seniors said they had used an illicit drug at least once during the previous month—down from a high of 38.9% in 1978 and 1979. Marijuana was and continues to be the most frequently used drug. The percent of students who used cocaine in the past month increased sharply from 1.9% in 1975 to 5.2% in 1980, and peaked at 6.7% in 1985. The rates of reported use of cocaine have declined since 1985, however, to a low of 1.3% in 1992 (55).

The prevalence of current cigarette smoking among high school seniors (27.8%) is similar to that for the US household population twelve years of age and older. The percent of high school seniors reporting having drunk an alcoholic beverage in the past month was lowest in 1992 (51.3%)—down from a high of 72.1% in 1978 (55).

ALCOHOL-RELATED MORTALITY RATES   The 1990 rate of death attributable to alcohol-related causes was 7.2 per 100,000 (31). The average annual per capita consumption of pure alcohol declined from a high of 2.76 gallons in 1980–81 to 2.54 gallons in 1987—principally due to the decline in the consumption of hard liquor (2).

EMERGENCY ROOM DRUG ABUSE REPORTS   Reports of drug-related visits to an emergency room (ER) in participating cities through the Drug Abuse Warning Network (DAWN) showed that the number of drug-related ER visits increased from 1988 to 1989, followed by a sharp decrease in 1990. A similar pattern was observed for cocaine-related visits. However, from 1990 to 1991, and continuing into 1992, the number of drug-related, as well as cocaine-related, visits to hospital emergency rooms began to increase, a trend attributed to the serious health consequences that were starting to be experienced by hard-core drug users (38).

RELATIVE RISKS   Young adults in their late teens and early twenties, particularly men, are more likely to smoke, drink, and use illicit drugs than their younger or older counterparts. Native American youth are much more apt to use alcohol, drugs, and cigarettes than are either white or other minority (Hispanic and Asian) youth. Minority users are also more likely to develop life-threatening patterns of abuse, as evidenced by higher rates of addiction related deaths. Death rates for cirrhosis or other alcohol related causes are greater among Native Americans compared to either whites or African Americans. Minorities (particularly African Americans) constitute a disproportionate share of medical emergencies and deaths due to cocaine abuse (4, 33–38, 55).

Suicide- or Homicide-Prone

SUICIDE   Suicide is the eighth leading cause of death in the United States. The Year 2C~0 Objectives for the Nation are to reduce suicides to no more than 10.5 per 100,000 people (41). In 1990 the age-adjusted rate was 11.5. Though the overall rates of suicide have changed little since 1950, the rates for teenage and elderly white males have increased substantially over that period, which may be due to an increase in associated social and economic stressors (such as marital disruption and divorce or unemployment, for example).

HOMICIDE AND LEGAL INTERVENTION   Homicide is the eleventh leading cause of death in the United States. The Year 2000 Objectives are to reduce homicides to no more than 7.2 per 100,000 (41). The age-adjusted rate in 1990, including those due to legal intervention, was 10.2. Since 1950 these rates have ranged from a low of 5.2 (1960) to a high of 10.8 (1980) (30, 31).

RELATIVE RISKS   Of those who die from intentional acts of violence, elderly white men and young Native American men are most likely to kill themselves, and young African-American, Native American, and Hispanic men are most likely to be killed at the hand of others. The violence-related death rates for these groups have increased dramatically in recent years, primarily due to the greater use of deadly weapons, particularly firearms, in these encounters (30, 31, 41).

Abusing Families

CHILD ABUSE AND NEGLECT REPORTS   Since 1976, the National Study on Child Neglect and Abuse Reporting has collected annual data on official reports of child maltreatment from state level Child Protective Service (CPS) programs. In 1987, an estimated 2,178,000 reports were filed for child abuse and neglect in 1,404,000 families. The rate of reporting was estimated at 34.0 children per 1000 US children. This is substantially higher than the number (669,000) and rates (10.1) reported in 1976 (3).

CHILD ABUSE AND NEGLECT INCIDENCE RATES   The Study of the National Incidence and Prevalence of Child Abuse and Neglect is based on a national probability sample of community professionals in 29 US counties regarding cases their agencies had handled. Data are based on unduplicated counts of individual children collected at only two points in time (1980 and 1986).

Based on the 1980 Study of the National Incidence and Prevalence of Child Abuse and Neglect, 625,100 (or 9.8 per 1000) children were reported to professionals in that year as having been abused or neglected. In 1986, there was a 49% increase from 1980 in the number of children to 931,000 (14.8 per 1000). The largest increase between 1980 and 1986 by type of abuse (based on similar definitions) was in the category of sexual abuse, for which rates almost tripled (from 0.7 to 1.9).

The Year 2000 Objectives provide that the rates of maltreatment overall and for each specific type of maltreatment fall below the rates in the 1986 Study of the National Incidence and Prevalence of Child Abuse and Neglect. The incidence rates of abuse and neglect in that study, using a more inclusive definition than that used in comparisons of the 1980 and 1986 data (whether they had actually been harmed or were deemed to be in danger of harm), are 9.4 (abuse) and 14.6 (neglect) per 1000 children (26, 41, 46).

DOMESTIC ELDER ABUSE   A Survey of States on the Incidence of Elder Abuse was conducted in 1988, based on a structured survey form sent to state Adult Protective Service (APS) and State Units on Aging (SUA) in 54 jurisdictions. The estimated unduplicated number of reports of elder abuse, neglect, or exploitation in domestic (home or noninstitutionalized) settings identified for the 1986–88 fiscal years (FY) were as follows: 117,000 (FY 1986); 128,000 (FY 1987); 140,000 (FY 1988). Somewhat over half of these reports were substantiated. Based on an estimate by the National Aging Resource Center on Elder Abuse that only 1 in 14 incidents of elder abuse are actually reported, the number of "reportable" cases was estimated to be much greater than the actual number of reports—1.6 million (FY 1986); 1.8 million (FY 1987); and 2.0 million (FY 1988) (49).

FAMILY VIOLENCE   The National Surveys of Family Violence, conducted in 1976 and 1986, attempted to identify incidents of intrafamily violence that may not have been reported to CPS, APS, or other agencies. A range of methodological and societal changes makes interpretations of comparisons between the 1976 and 1986 studies problematic, though both suggest that the incidents of family violence actually reported to authorities are far less than the number that actually occur. The rates of very severe parent-to-child violence (parent kicked, bit, or hit child with fist; beat up the child; or used a gun or knife), based on that study, were 19 per 1000 children aged 3 to 17 in 1985. The corresponding rates of severe violence between spouses were as follows: husband-to-wife—30 per 1000 wives; wife-to-husband—44 per 1000 husbands. The rate of very severe family violence estimated for children in 1985 (19.0 per 1000 children), based on this survey, is twice the rate of abuse (9.4 per 1000 children) actually reported to agencies in 1986, according to the Study of the National Incidence and Prevalence of Child Abuse and Neglect (14, 26, 48).

RELATIVE RISKS   Unemployment and associated economic hardship contribute to maltreatment, and particularly neglect, within families, as well as to a number of the other health risks reviewed previously (such as high-risk pregnancies or mental illness). Though minority children are disproportionately reported to authorities as being victims of abuse or neglect, it is not apparent that maltreatment is in general more prevalent in minority families, once socioeconomic differences between families are taken into account (3, 14, 26, 41, 46, 48).

The Homeless

Based on a variety of data sources, it appears that around one million men, women, and children may be homeless on any given night, and up to twice that number may be homeless at some time during the year. Though estimates of the numbers of homeless from different data sources and years do not permit accurate profiles of the trends in the growth of the homeless population, several studies have documented steady increases of around twenty percent per year on average in the demands for emergency and associated homeless shelters and services in many US cities since the early 1980s (7, 17, 18, 25, 54).

Respiratory ailments, tuberculosis, skin conditions, venereal, and other infectious diseases are more prevalent among homeless adults, relative to the general population, as are dental and mental health problems. Homeless children are much more likely to experience physical, mental, emotional, educational, developmental, and behavioral problems, and they are less likely to have obtained preventive health care services, such as routine immunizations, compared to children who are not homeless. The prevalence of mental illness appears to be greater among homeless women, while alcohol and substance abuse are more prevalent among homeless men—as is the case in the general population. Homeless women are, on the other hand, uniquely vulnerable to unwanted pregnancies, adverse birth outcomes, and sexual and physical assault (1).

RELATIVE RISKS   A survey conducted in 28 cities 1991 by the US Conference of Mayors showed the following characteristics of the homeless population in the cities studied: single men (50%); families with children (35%); single women (12%); unaccompanied youth (3%). Around a fourth (24%) of the homeless were children. Minorities are overrepresented among the homeless in most cities. The racial/ethnic composition of the homeless was 48% black, 34% white, 15% Hispanic, 3% Native American, and 1% Asian. The US Conference of Mayors study also documented that only 18% of the homeless were employed in full- or part-time jobs, 23% were veterans, 29% mentally ill, 40% alcohol or substance abusers, and 7% had AIDS (53).

Immigrants and Refugees

IMMIGRANTS   The number of immigrants to the United States has increased steadily over the last three decades: 1961–70: 3,321,700; 1971–80: 4,493,300; 1981–90: 7,338,100 (52). Immigrants have an official legal (documented) status—that of aliens who are admitted for the purpose of obtaining permanent residence. During the 1960s, the largest number of immigrants came from Europe and North America—particularly Mexico. In the 1980s, most came from Asia, reflecting the out-migration subsequent to the Viet Nam war. There are, in addition, an imprecise number of illegal (undocumented) aliens. Some estimates have put the number of undocumented aliens at two to four times the number of legal immigrants (5, 45).

REFUGEES   A series of statutes have specified the provisions (the length of time in residence, for example) required to permit certain groups of refugees to seek permanent residence (immigrant) status. The Refugee Act of 1980, effective April 1, 1980, provided for a uniform admission procedures for all countries, based on the United Nation's definition: "a wellfounded fear of persecution". The number of refugees, as well as the proportion they represent of the total immigrant population, has increased steadily over the past three decades: 1961–70: 212,843; 1971–80: 539,447; 1981–90: 1,013,620. The proportions they represented of the total immigrant population for the respective time periods were 6%, 12%, and 14%. Refugees were a particularly substantial proportion (27%) of the Asian immigrants during the 1980s (52).

RELATIVE RISKS   The demographic and socioeconomic profiles of different immigrant and refugee groups vary a great deal. In some groups of immigrants, such as Southeast Asians, bipolar groupings often occur that reflect more socially and economically advantaged versus disadvantaged statuses, based on socioeconomic level, migration cohort, and/or refugee status. The most disadvantaged subgroups are least likely to have had routine preventive care (such as childhood immunizations and dental and prenatal care) and are likely to have the most numerous and most serious health problems, such as gastrointestinal disorders, parasitic infections, respiratory disease, flu, pneumonia, tuberculosis, injuries, or, in the instance of Asian immigrants in particular, sudden unexplained death syndrome (SUDS) and hepatitis. The prevalence of depression and posttraumatic stress syndrome is widespread among refugee populations, and particularly refugee women and children (1, 11, 16, 45).

SUMMARY

The notion of risk underlying the concept of vulnerability implies that *everyone* is potentially vulnerable (or at risk), that is, there is always a chance of developing health problems. The risk is, however, greater for those with the least social status, social capital, and human capital resources to either prevent or ameliorate the origins and consequences of poor physical, psychological, or social health.

The completeness and accuracy of information on the health status of the vulnerable populations examined here varies substantially across groups. Methodological work is needed to derive standardized definitions of terms, specify the content and timing for collecting information for minimum basic data sets, and develop uniform standards for evaluating and reporting data quality on the health status of vulnerable populations.

The variety of indicators of vulnerable populations examined indicates that during the decade of the 1980s the incidence of serious physical, psychological, and/or social needs increased (at worst) and was uname-liorated (at best) for millions of Americans.

AIDS emerged as a new and deadly threat from a handful of cases classified as Gay-Related Immune Deficiency in the early part of the 1980s to what now may be over a million Americans who are HIV-positive. The number of homeless has increased an average of 20% a year to estimates now ranging up to one million men, women, or children homeless on any given night to twice that number who may be homeless sometime during the year. Over seven million people immigrated to the United States during the period from 1981 to 1990—an increasing proportion of whom are refugees carrying with them the physical, psychological, and social wounds of war. The number of children abused by family members or other intimates has burgeoned to an estimated 1.6 to 1.7 million per year, and with the greater use of firearms, intentional acts of violence toward oneself or others are becoming increasingly deadly in their consequences.

Though fewer Americans smoke, drink, and use illicit drugs in general than was the case earlier in the decade of the 1980s, the use of cocaine (and particularly crack) among hard-core addicts has resulted in increases in the numbers of drug-related deaths. Previously favorable trends in reducing the numbers or rates of high-risk mothers and newborns slowed or reversed during the past decade, and the dependency needs of the chronically physically and mentally ill are becoming more, not less visible, as families and communities increasingly face the challenge of health and mental health policy-motivated deinstitutionalization decisions, and a growing number of elderly Americans.

The framework introduced here provides a conceptual, empirical, and normative point of reference for understanding the origins and consequences of poor health that can guide the development of research and policy agendas to address the health and health care needs of what appear to be a growing number of vulnerable Americans.

ACKNOWLEDGMENTS

The author acknowledges the granting of copyright permission by Jossey-Bass Inc. Publishers for the use of the following from: Aday, Lu Ann. *At Risk in America: The Health and Health Care Needs of Vulnerable Populations in the United States,* Chapters 1, 2, 3 and 10 [selected excerpts]; Figure 1.1 (p. 3); Table 1.1 (p. 9).

Literature Cited

1. Aday LA. 1993. *At Risk in America: The Health and Health Care Needs of Vulnerable Populations in the United States.* San Francisco: Jossey-Bass
2. Alcohol, Drug Abuse, and Mental Health Admin. 1990. *Alcohol and health: 7th spec. rep. US Congr. Sec. Health Hum. Serv.* DHHS Publ. No. ADM 90-1656. Washington, DC: US GPO
3. Am. Humane Assoc. 1989. *Highlights of Official Aggregate Child Neglect and Abuse Reporting, 1987.* Denver, CO: Am. Humane Assoc.
4. Bachman JG, Wallace JM Jr, Kurth CL, Johnston LD, O'Malley PM. 1991. *Drug use among black, white, Hispanic, Native American and Asian Amer-*
ican high school seniors (1976-1989): Prevalence, trends, and correlates. Monitoring the Future Occas. Pap. No. 30. Inst. Soc. Res. Ann Arbor, MI: Univ. Mich.
5. Bean FD, Edmonston B, Passel JS, eds. 1990. *Undocumented Migration to the United States: IRCA and the Experience of the 1980s.* Santa Monica, CA: RAND Corp.
6. Bergner M. 1989. Quality of life, health status, and clinical research. *Med. Care* 27:S148–56
7. Burt MR, Cohen BE. 1989. *America's homeless: Numbers, characteristics, and programs that serve them.* Urban Inst. Rep. 89-3. Washington, DC: Urban Inst. Press

8. Centers for Disease Control. 1990. HIV prevalence estimates and AIDS case projections for the United States: Report based upon a workshop. *Morbid. Mortal. Wkly. Rep.* 39 (No. RR-16), 1–31

9. Centers for Disease Control. 1992. *National HIV, serosurveillance summary: Results through 1990, HIV-NCID-11-91-011.* Atlanta, GA: CDC

10. Centers for Disease Control and Prevention. 1993. Current, trends: Impact of the expanded AIDS surveillance case, definition on AIDS case reporting—United States, first, quarter, 1993. *Morbid. Mortal. Wkly. Rep.* 42 (No. 16):308–10

11. Chavez LR, Cornelius WA, Jones OW. 1985. Mexican immigrants and the utilization of U.S. health services: The case of San Diego. *Soc. Sci. Med.* 21:93–102

12. Coleman JS. 1990. *Foundations of Social Theory.* Cambridge, MA: Harvard Univ. Press

13. Freeman HE, Levine S, eds. 1989. *Handbook of Medical Sociology.* Englewood Cliffs, NJ: Prentice Hall. 4th ed.

14. Gelles RJ, Straus MA. 1988. *Intimate Violence: Causes and Consequences of Abuse in the American Family.* New York: Simon & Schuster

15. Gore S. 1989. Social networks and social supports in health care. See Ref. 13, pp. 306–31

16. Haines DW, ed. 1989. *Refugees as Immigrants:, Cambodians, Laotians, and Vietnamese in America.* Totowa, NJ: Rowman & Littlefield

17. Hombs ME, Snyder M. 1982. *Homelessness in America: Forced March to Nowhere.* Washington, DC: Commun. Creat. Non-Violence

18. Hombs ME, Snyder M. 1983. *Homelessness in America: Forced March to Nowhere.* Washington, DC: Commun. Creat. Non-Violence. 2nd ed.

19. Kaplan HB. 1989. Health, disease, and the social, structure. See Ref. 13, pp. 46–68

20. Karno M, Hough RL, Burnam MA, Escobar JI, Timbers DM, et al. 1987. Lifetime prevalence of specific psychiatric disorders, among Mexican Americans and non-Hispanic whites in Los Angeles. *Arch. Gen. Psychiatry* 44:695–701

21. Knowles J. 1977. Doing better and feeling worse: Health in the United States. *Daedalus* 106:1–278

22. Last JM, ed. 1983. *A Dictionary of Epidemiology.* New York: Oxford Univ. Press

23. Leon J, Lair T. 1990. *Functional status of the noninstitutionized elderly: Estimates of ADI. and IADL, difficulties.* DHHS Publ. No. PHS 90-3462. Natl. Med. Expend. Surv. Res. Findings 4, Agency Health Care Policy Res. Washington, DC: US GPO

23a. Manderscheid RW, Sonnenschein MA, eds. 1990. *Mental Health, United States 1990.* DHHS Publ. No. ADM, 90-1708. NIMH. Washington, DC: US GPO

24. McDowell I, Newell C. 1987. *Measuring Health: A Guide to Rating Scales and Questionnaires.* New York: Oxford Univ. Press

25. Natl. Alliance to End Homelessness. 1988. *Housing and Homelessness.* Washington, DC: Natl. Alliance End Homelessness

26. Natl. Cent. Child Abuse Negl. 1988. *Study findings: Study of national incidence and prevalence of child abuse and neglect: 1988.* Washington, DC: US GPO

27. Natl. Cent. Health Stat. 1985. *Current estimates from the national health interview survey: United States, 1982.* DHHS Publ. No. PHS 85-1578. Vital Health Stat. Ser. 10, No. 150. Washington, DC: US GPO

28. Natl. Cent. Health Stat. 1989. *The national nursing home survey: 1985 summary for the United States.* DHHS Publ. No. PHS 89-1758. Vital Health Stat. Ser. 13, No. 97. Washington, DC: US GPO

29. Natl. Cent. Health Stat. 1992. *Current estimates from the national health interview survey, 1991.* DHHS Publ. No. PHS 93-1512. Vital Health Stat. Ser. 10, No. 184. Washington, DC: US GPO

30. Natl. Cent. Health Stat. 1992. *Health, United States, 1991.* DHHS Publ. No. PHS 92-1232. Washington, DC: US GPO

31. Natl. Cent. Health Stat. 1993. *Advance report of mortality final statistics, 1990.* Mon. Vital Stat. Rep. Vol. 41, No. 7, Suppl. Washington, DC: US GPO

32. Natl. Cent. Health Stat. 1993. *Advance report of final natality statistics, 1990.* Mon. Vital Stat. Rep. Vol. 41, No. 9, Suppl. Washington, DC: US GPO

33. Natl. Inst. Drug Abuse. 1991. *National household survey on drug abuse: Highlights 1990.* DHHS Publ. No. ADM 91-1789. Washington, DC: US GPO

34. Natl. Inst. Drug Abuse. 1991. *National*

household survey on drug abuse: Main findings 1990. DHHS Publ. No. ADM 91-1788. Washington, DC: US GPO

35. Natl. Inst. Drug Abuse. 1991. National household survey on drug abuse: Population estimates, 1990. DHHS Publ. No. ADM 91-1732. Washington, DC: US GPO

36. Natl. Inst. Drug Abuse. 1991. Overview of the 1991 national household survey on drug abuse. C-83-1-a. NIDA Capsules. Washington, DC: US GPO

37. Natl. Inst. Drug Abuse. 1991. Summary of findings from the 1991 national household survey on drug abuse. C-86-13. NIDA Capsules. Washington, DC: US GPO

38. Natl. Inst. Drug Abuse. 1993. Preliminary estimates from the Drug Abuse Warning Network: third quarter 1992 estimates of drug-related emergency room episodes. Adv. Rep. No. 2. Washington, DC: US GPO

39. Off. Technol. Assess. 1986. Children's mental health: Problems and services—A background paper. OTA-BP-H-33. Washington, DC: US GPO

40. Patrick DL, Bergner M. 1990. Measurement of health status in the 1990s. Annu. Rev. Public Health 11:165–83

41. Public Health Serv. 1990. Healthy people 2000: National health promotion and disease prevention objectives: Full report, with commentary. DHHS Publ. No. PHS, 91-50212. Washington, DC: US GPO

42. Regier DA, Boyd JH, Burke JD Jr, Rae DS, Myers JK, et al. 1988. One-month prevalence of mental disorders in the United States. Arch. Gen. Psychiatry 45:977–86

43. Robins LN, Helzer JE, Weissman MM, Orvaschel H, Gruenberg E, et al. 1984. Lifetime prevalence of specific psychiatric, disorders in three sites. Arch. Gen. Psychiatry 41:949–58

44. Rosenstein MJ, Milazzo-Sayre LJ, Manderscheid RW. 1990. Characteristics of persons using specialty inpatient, outpatient, and partial care programs in 1986. See Ref. 23a, pp. 139–72

45. Rumbaut RG, Chavez LR, Moser RJ, Pickwell SM, Wishik SM. 1988. The politics of migrant health care: A comparative study of Mexican immigrants and Indochinese refugees. Res. Sociol. Health Care 7:143–202

46. Sedlak AJ. 1991. National incidence and prevalence of child abuse and neglect: 1988. Revised rep. Rockville, MD: Westat Inc.

47. Strahan GW. 1990. Prevalence of selected mental disorders in nursing and related care homes. See Ref. 23a, pp. 227–40

48. Straus MA, Gelles RJ, Steinmetz SK. 1981. Behind Closed Doors: Violence in the American Family. Newbury Park, CA: Sage Publ.

49. Tatara T. 1990. Summaries of national elder abuse data: An exploratory study of state statistics: Based on a survey of state adult protective service and aging agencies. Washington, DC: Natl. Aging Resour. Cent. Elder Abuse

50. Tesh SN. 1988. Hidden Arguments: Political Ideology and, Disease Prevention Policy. New Brunswick, NJ: Rutgers Univ. Press

51. Twaddle AC, Hessler RM. 1977. A Sociology of Health. St. Louis: Mosby

52. US Bur. Census. 1992. Statistical abstract of the United States: 1992. Washington, DC: US GPO. 112th ed.

53. US Conf. Mayors. 1991. A status report on hunger and homelessness in America's cities: 1991. Washington, DC: US Conf. Mayors

54. US Dep. Hous. Urban Dev. 1984. A report to the Secretary on the homeless and emergency shelters. Off. Policy Dev. Res., Washington, DC: US Dep. Hous. Urban Dev.

55. Univ. Michigan. 1993. 1992 national high school senior drug abuse survey: Monitoring the future survey. News Inf. Serv. Release, April 9, 1993. Ann Arbor, MI: Univ. Mich.

56. Ware JE Jr. 1986. The assessment of health status. In Applications of Social Science to Clinical Medicine and Health Policy, ed. LA Aiken, D Mechanic. New Brunswick, NJ: Rutgers Univ. Press

57. Ware JE Jr. 1987. Standards for validating health measures: Definition and content. J. Chronic Dis. 40:473–80

58. Warner KE, Luce BR. 1982. Cost-benefit and Cost-effectiveness Analysis in Health Care: Principles, Practice, and Potential. Ann Arbor, MI: Health Admin. Press

59. WHO. 1948. Constitution of the World Health Organization. In Handbook of Basic Documents. Geneva: WHO

Annu. Rev. Public Health. 1994. 15:511–34
Copyright © 1994 by Annual Reviews. All rights reserved

HEALTH SERVICES IN HEAD START

E. Zigler

Department of Psychology, Yale University, New Haven, Connecticut 06520

C. S. Piotrkowski

NCJW Center for the Child, National Council of Jewish Women, New York, New York 10010

R. Collins

Collins Management Consulting, Inc., Vienna, Virginia 22180

KEY WORDS: poverty, children, immunization, disabilities, screening

INTRODUCTION

Head Start is a comprehensive federal program for preschool children and families living in poverty that has four key components: education, social services, parent involvement, and health. Initiated in the summer of 1965, it was part of the "War on Poverty" that aimed to ameliorate the inequalities in housing, education, employment, and living conditions of 35 million poor Americans. Although many other programs developed during the War on Poverty did not survive, Head Start did. It represents "one of the major social experiments in the second half of the twentieth century" in the United States (9).

In general, Head Start has tended to enjoy bipartisan support at the federal, state, and local levels. During Fiscal Year 1993, Head Start served an estimated 721,000 children and their families in approximately 2000 communities nationwide, with a commitment by the current administration to provide full funding during this decade for all eligible three-year-old and four-year-olds in families living in poverty. In Fiscal Year 1993 the Head

511

0163-7525/94/0510-0511$05.00

Start budget stood at $2.8 billion; the proposed expansion would more than double this budget.

The prospect of dramatic increases in program funding for Head Start triggered a sharp debate in the Congress and the media over Head Start's effectiveness. The ensuing controversy centered on whether or not Head Start produced tangible benefits that justified the investment of substantial additional Federal funds. Particular attention was focused on the delivery of health services, because of the premature release of a "working draft" report from the Office of Inspector General (OIG) of the US Department of Health and Human Services (25). The preexisting consensus around the program's effectiveness thus was subjected to its most serious challenge in nearly two decades.

The overarching goals of this chapter are to make more widely known the important role Head Start has played in improving the health of our nation's economically disadvantaged young children, to dispel some misconceptions about the role of health in Head Start, and to provide a data-based portrayal of the health services Head Start provides. We rely on published reports and unpublished data, including our own analyses of Head Start program information.

The chapter is divided into several sections: (a) the historical context of health services in Head Start; (b) documentation of the well-known adverse effects of poverty on children's health and the extent to which Head Start, in fact, serves poor children; (c) a description of the goals, objectives, and requirements of the health services component of Head Start, including services for children with disabilities; (d) assessments of the extent to which Head Start enhances the delivery of health services to poor children; meets its stated performance standards for the delivery of health services; and improves health outcomes for poor children; and (e) policy and program recommendations to improve the Head Start health services structure, as Head Start prepares to expand.

THE HISTORICAL CONTEXT

Early Head Start was based on a belief that education served as the route out of poverty. Coupled with the strong environmentalism of the social sciences of the 1960s that emphasized the primary role of the social environment in the formation of intelligence, this belief suggested that environmental "enrichment" could make poor children smarter and therefore more successful at school. Such naive environmentalism helped contribute to the mistaken notion that Head Start primarily was a program designed to raise children's IQ, with consequent positive effects on educational attainment (40). Although this mistaken emphasis on IQ has given way to a broader notion of Head Start's contribution to the developing child's social competence, the idea that Head Start was a "silver bullet" to raise children's IQ has had several negative consequences.

First are periodic assaults on the efficacy of Head Start that are based on misunderstanding of the comprehensive nature of the Head Start vision and the Head Start program itself. For example, neglected in discussions of Head Start's effectiveness are the provision of social services to Head Start families and the mandated inclusion of Head Start parents in all aspects of programming, including decision-making (26). Equally obscured in debates about the efficacy of Head Start is the leadership Head Start has taken as a provider of comprehensive health services for preschool children living in poverty.

Because the public debate over Head Start's effectiveness arose when this chapter was being prepared, we became concerned that consideration of the health services component of Head Start was shaped more by myth than fact. Therefore, we believed it important to address common misconceptions about the historical role of health in Head Start.

Misconceptions Regarding the Role of Health in Head Start

The first misconception is that Head Start has became concerned with health services only in recent years, shifting from an emphasis on the program's primary educational goal. In fact, the overall goal of Head Start, as spelled out in Head Start regulations, is to promote the child's *social competence*. This term is used by Head Start to encompass a holistic view of the child that includes his/her cognitive, linguistic, social, emotional, and physical development. Consequently, Head Start's four program components are education, parent involvement, social services, *and* health.

This holistic view—which extended to a recognition of the importance of the child's family—was explicit from the beginning. Health services have *always* been an integral part of Head Start's comprehensive services strategy. The original planning committee for Head Start was headed by Dr. Robert Cooke, the pediatrician-in-chief at Johns Hopkins Hospital, who recruited two other pediatricians and a professor of nursing to serve as members (8). The committee recognized that "environmental enrichment would not be of much benefit to children who were ill or hungry" (38) and placed "improving the child's physical health" first in a list of seven program objectives (39). It urged the Office of Economic Opportunity to consider the whole child in Head Start's programmatic development, and a health and nutrition component was built into Head Start from its inception. Another pediatrician, Dr. Julius Richmond, served as the first national director of Head Start.

The second misconception is that Head Start's health objectives and requirements are less clear or of lower priority than for other program components. On the contrary, from the beginning, children were to receive pediatric and neurologic physical measurements; an assessment of nutrition, vision, hearing, and speech; and selected tests for tuberculosis, anemia, and kidney disease (39). The Head Start Program Performance Standards, developed from 1972 to 1975 and first published as regulations in 1975 (29), include detailed requirements regarding health services. These Head Start standards, described below, are comprehensive, operationally specific, and enforceable.

The third misconception is that there is little objective evidence concerning Head Start health services. Ironically, more systematic data have been collected concerning the delivery of health services than for any other of Head Start's program components. There are also some data concerning health outcomes. Although, like researchers and policy analysts everywhere, we always would prefer more documentation to less, the fact remains that there is ample evidence to draw responsible conclusions regarding the delivery of health services to poor children in Head Start.

Support for Health Services in Head Start

In the summer of 1965, when Head Start opened its doors to more than one-half million children, pediatricians were among those volunteering their time and services. Over the course of one summer, many children who had never been to a doctor before received physical and dental exams and inoculations (24). Mental health services also were viewed as important, and psychological services were included in early Head Start guidelines. In the 1960s mental health professionals also volunteered their services to local Head Start programs (5).

Throughout most of the 1970s, the Head Start Bureau had a Health Services Branch headed by a pediatrician that included a nurse, nutritionist, and—at least for part of that time—a psychologist. In addition, the Head Start Bureau also had a special educator with responsibility for children with disabilities. Staff at the Health Services Branch were supplemented by an extensive training and technical assistance (T/TA) network and numerous demonstration projects. Through an interagency agreement, the US Public Health Service Division of Dentistry provided T/TA in the monitoring of Head Start grantees, virtually without interruption, until October 1992. Additionally, from 1968 to 1982, Head Start entered into contracts, first with the American Academy of Pediatrics (24) and then with Westinghouse Health Systems, to provide medical support to every Head Start program.

From 1982 through 1986, the national Head Start medical, nutrition, and mental health training and technical assistance support networks were discontinued. Instead, a variety of different methods were attempted to provide support through statewide and regional networks, resulting in considerable variation in the quality of support (32). In 1987, the Head Start Health Services Branch was abolished, thereby further weakening the administrative infrastructure that supported health services from within Head Start.

From 1987 until October of 1992, oversight of training and technical assistance in the medical, nutrition, mental health, and dental services areas was placed in the Division of Maternal, Child and Infant Health under interagency agreements (e.g. 15). In addition, separate T/TA support arrangements were made for Head Start American Indian grantees, generally in collaboration with the Indian Health Service. The Maternal and Child Health Bureau was responsible for providing a part-time physician to supervise a small part-time staff in the areas of dental, nutrition, mental health, and public health nursing. There was also some support for Head Start in the Public Health Service Regional Offices. At its peak, each PHS Regional Office consisted of one full-time generalist coordinator and varying numbers of part-time specialists and/or consultants covering medical, dental, mental health, and nutrition services. The Public Health Service maintained a consultant pool with names of over 500 consultants who could be called upon for on-site monitoring or T/TA support to Head Start grantees. In 1992, the Administration on Children Youth and Families initiated a program with the American Psychological Association to provide volunteer psychologists to local Head Start programs. As of this writing, 525 psychologists had signed on as volunteers (10).

Despite attempts to strengthen the health services T/TA and monitoring efforts, numerous problems resulted from placing responsibility for training and technical assistance for health services *outside* the Head Start Bureau (1, 33). For example, Public Health Service and Head Start Regional Offices had wide latitude in setting goals for the number of grantees to site visit for training and technical assistance, with most choosing the lower end of the 20% to 33% range permitted. Some Head Start grantees were unaware of the free health support services available to them.

The last interagency agreement expired in late 1992 and the central T/TA support for Head Start within the Division of Maternal, Child and Infant Health ceased operations. Informal liaison and support arrangements continued at the regional level, but no documentation of these activities nor the levels of funding or effort were available to us. At the time this chapter was written, the Head Start Bureau had a Health and Disability Services Branch with an acting chief. No information was available concerning plans for future staffing or the provision of health training and technical assistance.

POVERTY AND CHILDREN'S HEALTH

The ill effects of poverty on children's health are well-recognized. Conditions to which poor children are particularly vulnerable include inadequate prenatal care; maternal substance abuse; infant mortality; low birthweight; lead poisoning; AIDS/HIV; poor nutrition; inadequate immunizations; and lack of access to adequate health care.

Children's health is inextricably linked to maternal health, and poverty is associated with a host of poor health outcomes and adverse health conditions for childbearing women. Over 4.5 million of the nearly 59.2 million women in the childbearing years of 15–44 had used an illicit drug in the previous month, according to the 1991 National Household Survey on Drug Abuse. Of these women, more than 600,000 had used cocaine and 3.3 million had used marijuana. The highest percentages of crack and other hard-core drug abuse were among African Americans, the unemployed, high school dropouts, and inner-city residents (22). Of the 3432 children under five years of age with Acquired Immune Deficiency Syndrome, 88% of the diagnosed exposure was traced to a mother with/at risk for HIV (human immunodeficiency virus) infection, according to data compiled in December 1992 by the Centers for Disease Control and Prevention. The majority of mothers who transmit HIV to their infants were infected through intravenous drug use or heterosexual contact with injecting drug users (3).

Poor women are less likely to receive adequate prenatal care and are more likely to have low-birthweight babies (2500 grams or less). In 1989, one out of four women in the United States received no prenatal care during their first trimester. Among African American women, over 40% received no first trimester prenatal care (35). In addition to poverty and inadequate prenatal care, factors related to low birthweight include low levels of maternal education, teenage parenthood, poor nutrition, smoking, and substance abuse. Most of these factors represent preventable social conditions associated with poverty (37). These problems are compounded by alcohol consumption. Alcohol consumption during pregnancy, especially heavy drinking, is associated with miscarriage, mental retardation, low birthweight, and congenital defects, including Fetal Alcohol Syndrome (FAS) and Fetal Alcohol Effects (FAE) (35).

The number of low-birthweight babies increased in 1989 to 7% of births, the highest level observed in more than a decade. Rates for African American babies (13.2 children per 100) were roughly double the percentage of white babies (35). Low-birthweight children suffer two to three times as much from such disabilities as blindness, deafness, mental retardation, learning disorders, and hyperactivity as normal-weight children. Extremely low-birthweight children (less than 3.5 pounds) need special education at four times the rate of children born at normal weight (19, 37).

Low birthweight is the leading cause of infant death. The infant mortality rate in 1991 was 8.9 deaths before age 1, per 1000 births (2). While this represents an improvement over the rate in the previous decade, largely as a result of advances in medical technology (30), the United States still compares poorly with other developed countries on this indicator of child health. The risk of being one of the thousands of babies who died in 1991 was substantially greater for minority children and children living in poverty, with the mortality rate for African American babies being substantially higher than that of white babies (17, 30).

Children living in poor families also are at risk for insufficient dietary intake, inadequate diet, and limited access to dietary supplements. Pediatric anemia, which in the majority of cases is iron-deficiency anemia, is one of the most common nutritional problems in the United States. The child with iron-deficiency anemia may suffer from listlessness, fatigue, headaches, or dizziness. Chronic anemia can lead to poor growth and weight gain, mental, and physical sluggishness, heart problems, impaired immune responses, and inadequate school performance. Infants from poor families are three times more likely than nonpoor children to be iron-deficient (19).

Poor children also are more likely to live in deteriorated housing; lead poisoning is one of the greatest environmental health hazards facing them. The prevalence of lead poisoning is highest among African American children living in poor, inner-city areas (12, 20). Lead poisoning has serious neurotoxic effects on young children. In severe cases, it can cause death or permanent brain damage (17).

Not only does poverty place children at greater risk for health problems, but children living in poverty also have less access to health services. National survey data reveal major differences in the use of health services by children in poor families. More than one in five of the nation's poorest children (family incomes under $10,000 annually) had no physician contact in 1990, compared with one in seven high-income children (family incomes over $35,000). Low-income children are more than three times as likely as affluent children never to have received a preventive health examination (4). During the 1980s, immunization rates for young children eroded, particularly for polio, measles, rubella, mumps, and DPT (diphtheria, pertussis, and tetanus). In 1992, the percentage of 24-month-olds appropriately immunized ranged from 30% in Texas to 84% in Vermont, with the majority of states reporting vaccination coverage below 60% (4).

Moreover, the changing face of poverty means that today's poor children are faced with new challenges that may compromise their mental health. Increased violence, homelessness, AIDS, and parental substance abuse affect not only a child's physical health, but also his or her socioemotional development.

Some notion of the magnitude of the problem for Head Start children is available from an exploratory examination of the records of 290 Head Start children from five agencies in Maine, conducted in 1991–92 (15a). In this sample of children (representing 12% of all enrolled children), 72% had at least one serious health problem that required follow-up by their families and by Head Start staff. Two programs had sufficient data regarding emotional and family problems for analysis. In one program, more than one out of five children in the sample were being followed by state agencies, such as protective services, or were living in foster homes. Many children in both programs were experiencing serious emotional stress due to family losses or dysfunction. Most of these children also had chronic health problems.

Families Served by Head Start

It is clear from the foregoing discussion that children living in poverty are at-risk for serious health problems. In assessing Head Start's effectiveness in improving access to health services for economically disadvantaged children, it is important to determine if, in fact, Head Start reaches its targeted population.

Information is available from two principal sources. One source of data comes from Head Start programs themselves. Each year, local Head Start programs submit a Program Information Report (PIR) that includes aggregate program data, periodically including selected information on characteristics of children and families participating during that operating year.

Based on recent PIR data, Head Start participants can be described as follows: The median family income of two thirds of the participants is less than $9000, and 84% of the families have yearly incomes of less than $12,000. Two thirds of children served are minorities. Single parents head 55% of the families. Roughly one half of Head Start families receive Aid to Families with Dependent Children (AFDC) and therefore are eligible for other child and family services. Over 63% of Head Start children are enrolled in Medicaid. Approximately 13.4% of Head Start children have diagnosed disabilities.

Reliable national estimates of children who participated in Head Start during the years 1976 through 1988 also are available from the National Health Interview Survey (NHIS) administered by the National Center for Health Statistics. One of the survey questions asks if any child in the family was ever enrolled in Head Start. The NHIS was administered in 1988 to a nationally representative sample of 17,110 households. An analysis of the 1988 Child Health Supplement to the NHIS (10a) on children aged five to seventeen indicated that there were 1449 Head Start children and 9978 non-Head Start children in that age range in the survey. After weighting, these NHIS data reflect a representative sample of the children served by Head Start during the years 1976 to 1988.

The NHIS-CH data indicate that, compared to children who had not been in Head Start, children who had been in Head Start were: three times as likely to live in families with incomes below the poverty level (Head Start, 40%; others, 12%); half as likely to live in families earning over $20,000 (Head Start, 35%; others, 71%); half as likely to live in households with both biological parents present (Head Start 34%; others, 61.5%); twice as likely to live in one-parent households, generally with their mother (Head Start, 42%; others 21%); more than twice as likely to have parents with less than a high school degree (Head Start, 27%; others, 12%); half as likely to have parents with some college education or training beyond high school (Head Start, 25%; others, 51%); three times more likely to live in households where no adult was currently employed (Head Start, 29%; others, 9%); and less likely to live in families where two adults were both employed (Head Start, 30%; others, 49%).

Both the data from Head Start programs themselves and the NHIS-CH are consistent in indicating that the Head Start program serves the population targeted by legislation, with virtually all families having low incomes and substantial numbers being single parents and families on AFDC. Thus, the families and children served by Head Start are at-risk for the health problems associated with poverty described above.

HEAD START HEALTH SERVICES: GOALS, OBJECTIVES, AND REQUIREMENTS

In pursuit of the overarching goal of facilitating the development of children's social competence, the objectives for Head Start health services as set forth in the Head Start Program Performance Standards (29) are to improve a child's health and physical abilities, correct physical and mental problems, enhance access to a nutritional diet and improve a family's attitude towards health care. According to Head Start regulations, the health services component of the program include the following objectives:

To provide a comprehensive health services program that encompasses a broad range of medical, dental, nutrition, and mental health services, including handicapped children;

To promote preventive health services and early intervention;

To attempt to link the child's family to an ongoing health care system to insure that the child continues to receive comprehensive health care even after leaving the Head Start program.

By focusing on health promotion, prevention, and early intervention, these goals represent good medical and public health practices. The specific health services requirements are detailed and comprehensive, as well. Health services standards and related guidance account for over half of the content of the 1992 Head Start Performance Standards.

Health promotion activities include health education for parents, children, and staff. Parents are to be provided with information about available health resources and are encouraged to become involved in their children's health care. Head Start programs encourage, and sometimes require, parents to accompany their children to medical and dental examinations and appointments.

Head Start centers are required to serve breakfast to children who have not had it at home. Each child in a part-day program must receive meals and snacks which provide at least one third of daily nutritional needs. In a full-day program, the child must receive one half to two thirds of daily nutritional needs. Parents are to receive nutrition education and are to be advised about food assistance programs. Head Start nutrition services are closely coordinated with the Food and Nutrition Service of the US Department of Agriculture (USDA). The standards also require that nutrition services be based upon identified nutritional needs and problems of the target population, taking into account nutrition assessment data (height, weight, hemoglobin/hematocrit) obtained for each child; special dietary needs and feeding problems, especially of children with disabilities; family eating habits; and major community nutrition problems. Virtually all Head Start programs qualify for reimbursement under USDA's child nutrition programs.

Specific provisions focusing on prevention and intervention include requirements to obtain a complete medical, dental, and developmental history of the child and to obtain a thorough medical and dental screening and examination, conducted by a physician and dentist, respectively. These health screenings must include growth assessment (weight, height, and age); vision testing; audiometric and other hearing testing; speech screening; hemoglobin or hematocrit determination; tuberculin testing; assessment of current immunization status; and, where indicated, urinalysis and assessments for sickle cell anemia, lead poisoning, and intestinal parasites. In addition, screenings must include a focus on the special needs of children with actual or suspected disabilities. Children with identified medical and dental problems are required to receive treatment for those problems; children with professionally diagnosed disabilities must receive appropriate special services (34).

Mental health standards require that a mental health professional be available, at least on a consultation basis, to Head Start programs. Activities of the mental health professional should include periodically observing children; consulting with and training teachers and other staff; assisting in developmental screening and assessment; assisting in providing special help for children with atypical behavior or development, including speech;

orienting parents and working with them to achieve mental health objectives; and advising in the use of other community resources and referrals.

Regulations focused on children with disabilities were issued in 1993 (10b), although the legislative requirement that at least 10 per cent of Head Start enrollment consist of children with professionally diagnosed disabilities was enacted in 1972. Otherwise, the health services standards described above have been in effect, with only minor changes, since 1975. Prior to that time, similar health services were called for, but did not have the force of regulations.

In addition to these regulatory provisions, Migrant Head Start serves children from birth to age six, as do the Comprehensive Child Development Program demonstrations. A major future shift toward an even more comprehensive, family-centered health services strategy for Head Start was foreshadowed in the Head Start Improvement Act of 1992. This legislation authorized Head Start to arrange for younger siblings to obtain health services. At the time this chapter was written, regulations to implement these provisions had not yet been promulgated.

Funding of Health Services

Head Start grant funds may be used to fund health services, but only as a "dollar of last resort." Medicaid, including the Early and Periodic Screening, Diagnosis, and Treatment (EPSDT) Program, has been the principal public program that pays for health services for low-income families and their children (for a more complete discussion of Medicaid programs, see (14, 28)). Today every state must provide Medicaid to all pregnant women and children under age six with family incomes at 133% or below the Federal poverty level. Also mandated are coverage for preventive and primary care services—including well-child care—and a portion of outreach activities to enroll families also are covered. States have some flexibility in determining which optional services to cover and to set payment rates for providers, so there is considerable variability among states in their Medicaid programs. Under the EPSDT Program states also must provide early and periodic screening for illness and physical and mental conditions; diagnosis and treatment; and follow-up care and case management to eligible children. New policy also requires all eligible children aged 6 months to 72 months to be screened for lead poisoning (12). Since the early 1980s, an interagency agreement between the Health Care Financing Administration and Head Start has facilitated reimbursements for certain medical services for Head Start participants (28).

Despite improvements in Medicaid, not all low-income children and their families who are potentially eligible are actually enrolled. Neither eligibility for Medicaid nor having a Medicaid card guarantees access to health care, for the nonfinancial barriers can be numerous and daunting (e.g. 16, 30). The complex Medicaid system itself can pose significant barriers. Families may be denied coverage because of failure to comply with the complex procedural requirements, such as filling in forms properly and not missing appointments. States have had particular problems in reaching out and enrolling eligible children in EPSDT programs and in finding adequate supplies of pediatricians willing to participate. There is wide variation in enrollment among states; on average only 39% of eligible children in a state are enrolled (14). Thus, states are still finding it difficult to fully implement EPSDT programs.

ASSESSING HEALTH SERVICES IN HEAD START

In 1993, Head Start grantees and delegate agencies included community action agencies, city and county government agencies, nonprofit organizations, single-purpose agencies, school systems, Indian Tribes, and other organizations. Health services typically are provided in coordination with a diverse system of local health providers, including hospitals, neighborhood health centers, private physicians and dentists, and community mental health centers. Indian and Migrant Head Start grantees face special health challenges and tend to collaborate with the Indian Health Service and the Migrant Health Service.

Above we described the goals and requirements of health services in Head Start. Those provisions delineate *what should be happening,* according to Head Start regulations. This section examines what actually is happening by focusing on three related questions: Does Head Start improve the delivery of health services to children living in poverty? Do the health services delivered meet the Head Start Performance Standards? What is the health impact of Head Start health services?

Does Head Start Improve the Delivery of Health Services to Children Living in Poverty?

Available data indicate that Head Start increases access to preventive health services and treatment for children living in poverty. An early evaluation of Head Start's health services was conducted by Abt Associates, Inc. (11). This study examined Head Start's medical, dental, and nutritional sub-components (not mental health), using a longitudinal experimental design. The study was conducted at four sites, selected nonrandomly from counties identified by the US Public Health Service as "underserved" in terms of medical and dental services. Within each of the four sites, 200 to 300 children eligible to enter Head Start in the fall of 1980 were recruited for the evaluation. Groups of children, matched by age and sex, were randomly assigned to a Head Start experimental or non-Head Start control group.

Although the methodology was generally sound in concept, the researchers experienced serious operational problems, including differential attrition in the experimental and comparison groups. There were apparent diffusion effects, resulting in the comparison group receiving health services they normally might not have obtained. Nonetheless, the report concluded that non-Head Start children were less likely to receive preventive services and treatment for diagnosed or known medical problems than children in Head Start.

More specifically, Head Start children were more likely to receive medical examinations and screenings than non-Head Start children. Head Start children also were more likely to receive treatment for pediatric health problems, and there were likely to be fewer problems at the post-test. Compared to children in the control group, Head Start children also were more likely to receive dental examinations, to receive more dental services, to visit the dentist with their families and to make such visits regularly.

The nutritional intake evaluation showed Head Start children who regularly attended the centers consumed appreciably more calories and protein than non-Head Start children or children who were frequently absent from the centers. Head Start families served meals that were richer in nutrient quality than non-Head Start families.

The Head Start Synthesis Project, which reviewed over 1600 published and unpublished research documents related to Head Start, was one of the most comprehensive assessments of Head Start's impact (7, 18). Thirty-four research reports in the area of health care met the criteria for inclusion in the review. The reviewers concluded that Head Start children received better dental care and that they were, "considerably more likely than non-Head Start children to receive medical and dental examinations; speech, language, and developmental assessments; nutritional evaluations; and biochemical, vision and hearing screenings." Head Start children with disabilities also were successfully "mainstreamed" into the programs (36).

Almost no Head Start research was supported by the Federal government during the 1980s. However, one small study stands out as particularly noteworthy. Hale et al (13) examined the medical records of 40 children enrolled in Head Start, 18 low-income children on a Head Start waiting list, and 20 children in a nursery school serving middle-class families. These groups of children were compared with regard to health screenings and dental examinations. Moreover, medical records were examined for immunizations and pediatric check-ups since birth. Although the sample was not large, the methodology was sound and the inclusion of a middle-class comparison group (primarily white) is noteworthy.

Findings are consistent with those described above. During the time they were in Head Start, the Head Start children were more likely than low-income waiting-list children to receive dental examinations (95% versus 39%) and age-appropriate health screenings. Head Start children were significantly more likely than waiting-list children to be screened for lead, hematocrit, tuberculin, blood pressure, hearing, and vision. Parental motivation as an explanatory factor for these group differences was ruled out by the fact that the children of highly involved Head Start parents did not differ from those of parents with low involvement. Moreover, prior to Head Start, the groups did not differ in the number of well-child check-ups to age 3. In fact, prior to Head Start, children of highly involved Head Start parents received fewer immunizations than the waiting-list low-income children to 18 months of age. Thus, it appears that, for these low-income children, the formal Head Start health services delivery system made an important difference in their access to preventive care.

What is even more striking about the findings is that children in Head Start fared as well or better than the middle-class children on a number of indicators! While in Head Start, Head Start children were significantly more likely than the middle-class comparison children to receive dental examinations (95% versus 75%). Head Start children also were more likely to receive tuberculin, blood pressure, hearing, and vision screenings than the middle-class children. Again, the impact of the Head Start program itself is reflected in the fact that *prior* to Head Start, the middle-class children had more well-child physicals by age 3 than the Head Start children and more immunizations than the Head Start children of highly involved parents. Along with earlier research, this study also clearly indicates that Head Start effectively improves access to preventive health services for low-income children. Although one cannot readily generalize from one study, the findings also suggest that children in Head Start may be receiving some health services comparable to those received by middle-class children, at least while they are enrolled in the program.

Do Health Services Meet the Head Start Performance Standards?

To address this question, two principal sources of information were used. The first is the Program Information Report (PIR), completed by all Head Start programs in June of each year. Categories of the PIR are based on the Head Start Program Performance Standards, although some subsets of questions vary annually. One potential drawback of the PIR is that it is based on program self-report (L Brush, A Gaidurgis, & C Best, unpublished data). However, these data have been relied upon for many years for such purposes as internal Federal Head Start management and for reports to

Congress. Although PIR reports reveal dramatic improvements over the past two decades in health indicators, the national pattern for the past five years is remarkably stable. We therefore have focused our presentation on selected performance indicators for operating year 1991–92, which reflect reports from Head Start grantees and delegate agencies as of June 1992. When data from previous years must be used, it is noted in the text.

The second source of information comes from the Self Assessment Validation Instrument (SAVI) or, in its most recent version, the Head Start On-Site Program Review Instrument (OSPRI).[1] The OSPRI is based on an annual self-assessment to be conducted by the Head Start program, supplemented once every three years by an on-site multidisciplinary team that visits the program for approximately a week. The on-site team relies on multiple methodologies, including interviews with staff and parents and a review of a sample of child and family records, as well as other written documents. The OSPRI also parallels the Performance Standards and leads to a judgment of whether or not the grantee is in compliance with a particular requirement. If found out of compliance, the Head Start grantee must take corrective action or risk defunding.

Data[2] available for Fiscal Years 1991 and 1992 summarize the major areas of noncompliance with Performance Standards that resulted from on-site multidisciplinary team visits using the OSPRI (or SAVI). In 1991, 355 grantees were monitored; in 1992, 410 grantees were monitored. Below we note the major areas of *noncompliance* for Fiscal Year 1992 and provide the 1991 data for comparison purposes.

It should be noted that the national summary indicates the percentage of Head Start grantees not in compliance with a particular requirement at the time of the site visit. This is a very conservative estimate because a grantee with many Head Start delegate agencies may be found out of compliance if one delegate agency is.

NUTRITION   Data from the 1988–89 PIR indicate that 91% of Head Start children received complete nutrition screenings. These included growth, hemoglobin/hematocrit, eating habit, and dietary needs assessment. About one in six of these children had nutritional problems; two thirds of them were referred for professional evaluations (about 5% of them were anemic); and almost three quarters received treatment. On-site evaluations indicated

---

[1]Of the 57 pages of program checklists, 22 pages relate to the health component and 5 pages relate to disabilities.

[2]These data are reported in an unpublished document, made available by the US Department of Health and Human Services as an attachment to a Request for Proposal for contractor support for Head Start training and technical assistance in March, 1993 (*Major Areas of Noncompliance: Head Start Monitoring Tracking System, National Summary*).

the following percentages of grantees who were out of compliance with the nutrition guidelines in Fiscal Year 1992: 21.5% were not supervised by a qualified nutritionist; 16% lacked an organized nutrition education program; 23% did not adequately involve parents in nutrition services; 20% were out of compliance in assessing nutritional needs and identifying problems using child assessment data; and 17% were out of compliance with regard to discussing the nutritional status of children with parents. (The comparable figures for Fiscal Year 1991 were: 24%; 13%; 17%; 13%; 11.5%.)

MEDICAL SCREENINGS AND TREATMENT   According to the PIR data, 98% of children in Head Start were medically screened. One out of five children (22.5%) screened was identified as needing medical treatment. Most children (96%) who needed medical treatment received it, and eight out of ten (81%) completed treatment. Data from the on-site monitoring teams indicated that in Fiscal Year 1992, 23% were out of compliance with keeping medical records; 25% were out of compliance with health screenings; 23% were out of compliance with regard to the treatment of all health problems detected; 18% were out of compliance in their plans for medical and dental emergencies; and 25% were out of compliance with having a functioning Health Services Advisory Committee. (Comparable figures for Fiscal Year 1991 were: 18%; 25%; 17.5%; 13%; 25%.)

DENTAL EXAMINATIONS AND TREATMENT   According to the PIR data, more than nine out of ten (95.5%) children received dental exams. Almost one third (32%) of the children examined needed dental treatment, and most (96.5%) of them received it. Eight out of ten (82%) completed treatment. In Fiscal Year 1992, 24% of grantees were not in compliance with regard to dental records. (The comparable figure for Fiscal Year 1991 was 26%).

CHILDREN WITH DISABILITIES   The PIR data indicate that over one out of eight children (13%) enrolled in Head Start had been diagnosed as having a disability. (These include mental retardation, health impairments, visual handicaps, hearing impairments, emotional disturbance, speech and language impairments, orthopedic handicaps, and learning disabilities). This is over the 10% required by the Performance Standards. On-site monitoring teams found the following levels of noncompliance with Performance Standards in Fiscal Year 1992: 18% of grantees did not include at least 10% of children with disabilities; in 22%, parents were not adequately involved in the diagnostic process and in planning an individualized program to meet the special needs of their child; 18% did not meet requirements for staff and volunteer training; in 15%, disability conditions were not confirmed by licensed/certified professionals; and in 17%, individualized services for defined conditions were not provided according to individual child plans. (Comparable figures for 1991 were 15.5%; 19%, 13%, 17%; 17%.)

IMMUNIZATIONS   The PIR data indicate that almost nine out of ten (88%) Head Start children were fully immunized and an additional 8% were *up-to-date* on their immunizations. Immunization was not indicated as a major area of noncompliance cited by the on-site review teams. These data are not seriously inconsistent with those reported recently by the Office of Inspector General (26), whose report was based on information gathered from on-site visits or telephone interviews with a sample of 80 Head Start grantees and delegate agencies. The OIG found that "84% of children are fully immunized" (25), using the Head Start Program Information Report criteria for immunization. However, using the definitions of the Centers for Disease Control and Prevention and the American Academy of Pediatrics, the OIG report concluded that only 43.5% were fully immunized.

MENTAL HEALTH   According to the PIR data, 2% of children enrolled in Head Start were referred for mental health treatment, with 77% of them receiving treatment. On-site monitoring teams indicate that in Fiscal Year 1992, 19.5% of grantees did not have a mental health professional available; and 21% did not have regular group meetings of parents and staff. (Comparable figures for 1991 are 15% and 17.5%.)

FUNDING   According to PIR data, children enrolled in Medicaid/EPSDT accounted for 63% of total actual Head Start enrollment in 1991–92. Head Start programs did succeed in improving their showing on this performance indicator, rising from 52% in 1987–88 to 66% in 1990–91, and then declining slightly. Nine out of ten Head Start children enrolled in Medicaid/EPSDT received at least some medical services paid for by Medicaid/EPSDT. All told, four out of ten Head Start children (42%) received medical services at low or no cost to Head Start. This represents an increase from 30% in the proportion of children benefiting from services paid for largely by non-Head Start sources in 1987–88.

COMMENTS ON HEALTH SERVICES   Despite the problems associated with changes in the health services training and technical support infrastructure at the federal level (see above), these analyses confirm the important role Head Start continues to play in providing health services to three- and four-year-old children in low-income families. Most Head Start children are brought up-to-date on their immunizations, participate in comprehensive health screenings, and eight or more out of ten complete the needed medical and dental treatments, conclusions that are consistent with a recent report prepared for the Administration on Children, Youth and Families (L Brush, A Gaidurgis, & C Best, unpublished).

As indicated by the on-site monitoring teams and the PIR data, the vast majority of programs appear to comply with Performance Standards with regard to required health services. The noncompliance reports are deliberately conservative yardsticks of performance and represent worst-case scenarios. Because the requirements generally call for 100% compliance, a finding of noncompliance of a grantee does *not* mean that no children are receiving the mandated service. It means only that not all children are receiving the requisite level of care. It is not uncommon for a grantee to be found out of compliance because one of the delegate agencies to whom it subcontracts services for some children might be operating below standard, while other grantee activities or other delegate agencies are in full compliance.

At the same time, improvements can be made. For example, the early Abt study (11) conducted in the 1980s found that record-keeping was a particular problem. Similarly, the Office of Inspector General's report (25) underscored preexisting concerns about health record-keeping in Head Start programs and the need for corrective action. Consistent with the on-site monitoring data reported above, a review of two studies of 15 Head Start programs indicated that inadequate record-keeping was the major form of noncompliance with regard to dental services (L VandeWiele, unpublished).

Problems of record-keeping have been known to those involved with Head Start for some time. The Head Start Health Coordinators, in a Task Force Report dated July 1990, flagged concerns about the quality of health record-keeping among Head Start programs and made specific recommendations to improve the monitoring system, including the PIR and the SAVI/OSPRI (31). The Task Force further recommended that a system of computerized child health records be developed. The Head Start Bureau is currently testing a Head Start Family Information System (HSFIS) that would include computerized child health records, with the objective of using the grantee's HSFIS data base, in lieu of the PIR, for reporting child health data at the national level.

The Abt study (11) found considerable variability in the quality of management of health services among the four Head Start sites examined. But many problems were due, not to the Head Start programs, but rather to the broader context in which Head Start programs are embedded. Particular problem areas identified were shortage of follow-up treatment, the inadequacy of community health delivery systems for low-income children and their families, the lack of ready availability of Head Start direct funding for services, and difficulty in obtaining Medicaid funding for services, even when children were eligible. In other words, while the comprehensive health services program as outlined in the Head Start requirements represents good practices, Head Start programs face practical problems in meeting them. A recent study of health needs in Head Start programs in Maine identified similar problems (15a).

Although the researchers in the Abt study deliberately selected medically underserved communities for the study sample, they still exemplify health delivery issues that persist. Funding is one example. There have been important improvements in Medicaid since the Abt study was done, and current data indicate that six out of ten Head Start children are enrolled in Medicaid/EPSDT, with most of those children receiving medical services paid for by Medicaid. Although new opportunities exist under the EPSDT Program and Public Law 99-457 to fund some of the health services Head Start provides—such as outreach, case management, transportation, screening and "medical day care"—caseloads for health coordinators can be excessive and Head Start grantees are not always able to adequately use new regulations to fund services (28). For example, a recent survey of states by the Alliance to End Childhood Lead Poisoning (12) found that Head Start programs in only seven states were reimbursed by Medicaid for lead screening.[3] As another example, a review of two recent studies of 15 Head Start programs indicated that, while the dental services received were generally of high quality—programs provided age-appropriate dental education, fluoridation, and followed appropriate oral hygiene practices—inadequate funding was the reason given for being unable to meet every child's needs (L VandeWiele, unpublished).

What is the Health Impact of Head Start Health Services?

Available data are most sparse here, as evaluations of Head Start have tended to focus on cognitive, rather than on socioemotional and physical outcomes (6; E Zigler, unpublished data). Nonetheless, the data that do exist are promising. Immunization against childhood infectious diseases is the single most effective intervention to reduce illness and mortality in children (27). Given what appear to be high rates of immunization of Head Start children (according to Head Start PIR reporting criteria), on its face, Head Start is effectively promoting positive health outcomes.

The ABT study (11) found that children in Head Start had less dental plaque and were more likely to have fillings than control children and that Head Start children's diets had higher levels of vitamins A, B12, and C, calcium, magnesium, phosphorus, and riboflavin than those of non-Head Start children. At post-test, Head Start children were more likely than

---

[3]Hale et al (13) found that fewer than one third of the Head Start children in their small study were screened for lead.

children in the control group to have no problems identified by a battery of developmental measures, and Head Start children were less likely to have speech and language deficiencies. It should be recalled that the study had some problems with differential attrition from the control and experimental groups.

The Head Start Evaluation, Synthesis and Utilization Project's review of early research on health and Head Start also found that Head Start produced meaningful improvements in physical health, motor coordination, and development (18). Head Start children experienced a lower incidence of pediatric problems and a level of health comparable to more advantaged children. Head Start children tended to have higher protein, calorie, and essential nutrient intake and tended to be healthier according to biochemical indices. Head Start children received better dental care, had fewer cavities and practiced better dental hygiene. The largest gains in motor development were for children with physical handicaps and those with developmental delays. Vogel et al (36) found that speech-impaired Head Start children showed communication gains of six months over those of nonserved comparison children.

Head Start can promote mental health in at least two ways: indirectly, through the program itself as it enhances the social competence of children, and directly, through the management and treatment of children with identified psychological problems. Unfortunately, mental health services remain a neglected area of evaluation. The Head Start Evaluation, Synthesis and Utilization Project located no evaluations of the Head Start mental health services component (18). A recent review (L. VandeWiele, unpublished, 1992) shows similar gaps, although some innovative programs to improve mental health services delivery in Head Start do exist and warrant closer examination. Similarly, health outcomes for Head Start children with disabilities has been a neglected area of research. A 1985 study by Roy Littlejohn Associates identified by VandeWiele reported that six years following Head Start, mainstream environments generally were not available to Head Start children with disabilities.

CONCLUSIONS AND RECOMMENDATIONS

As the program expands to serve all eligible children, with over 27 years of experience Head Start has immense potential to provide a comprehensive, integrated health services delivery system for young children living in poverty. Our analysis of available data leads to the conclusion that children in Head Start receive more and better preventive health services and treatment than low-income children not in Head Start. Nutrition, medical and dental screenings, and the integration of children with disabilities are especially strong components of the program.

Head Start not only provides some services directly, but it also helps link children and families to a community network of health services and to a "medical home" that may lead to ongoing participation in preventive and remedial health activities (28). This "brokering" function of Head Start is especially important because of the barriers poor families face in gaining access to health care. Moreover, Head Start plays an invaluable role in helping to educate parents about the importance of health promotion and prevention.

Despite these positive conclusions, the benefits of Head Start still are not available to the majority of children eligible for the program, as Head Start currently does not serve most eligible children. Moreover, the record of Head Start's health services is not uniformly successful, as not all enrolled children receive the full complement of medical and dental services. These difficulties have been recognized by the Head Start community for some time (21). Although the available data lead us to conclude that Head Start is effective in ensuring that most enrolled children are immunized, given the importance of immunizations, further research would be especially welcome to confirm this. The effectiveness of mental health services remains unknown, and more data are needed on lead screenings and treatment. In part, what Head Start can deliver is constrained by local health resources. There is variation in what services states pay for, and there are communities in which Head Start is unable to effectively gain access to the health delivery system, sometimes because public health agencies may be nonexistent or underfunded and because insufficient providers are available.

With an eye to improving quality, we make the following recommendations that focus on strengthening the infrastructure that supports health services in Head Start and evaluating health services and health outcomes.

1. The management of the health services component should be strengthened at the federal, regional, and local levels with:

   (a) A full-time Director of Health within the Head Start Bureau, with additional qualified staff in the areas of nutrition, mental health, disabilities, and health promotion.

   (b) A qualified health coordinator in each Head Start Region, with lines of reporting and accountability carefully and clearly delineated. Each Regional federal health coordinator should be supported by expert consultants in the medical, dental, mental health, nutrition, and disabilities fields.

   (c) A qualified nurse or health assistant to serve as a health coordinator for each Head Start program, with full-time coordinators in Head Start centers serving 100 or more children, in accordance with the recommendations of the Head Start Health Coordinators Task Force (31). This person should function as part of a multidisciplinary program team that includes qualified staff from the parent involvement, social services, and education components. The team should focus services on children and families based upon assessed needs.

2. The Head Start Bureau should establish a Health Services Task Force to develop a plan for improving the health services component. The Task Force should concentrate on several areas:

(*a*) The effects of changes in national health care policy on Head Start. Currently, Medicaid EPSDT supports an array of preventive services, including outreach and case management. How will changes in national health care policy affect these important services?

(*b*) Technical assistance to Head Start programs to take full advantage of Medicaid and other public funding sources. This would include a state-by-state knowledge base of variations in Medicaid outreach and supplemental programs and other public health services. Such technical assistance will be extremely important with any changes in national health care policy.

(*c*) A systematic plan for improving the health services component to accompany expansion that would emphasize continuity and integration of services. This plan should be based on all available monitoring and performance data and data from Head Start demonstrations and special programs. Currently, there are 32 demonstrations on the transition from Head Start to school. There also are over 100 Head Start programs that begin at birth. These should be examined for what can be learned about how best to provide for early, comprehensive, family-based continuity of health services within Head Start.

(*d*) Review policies with regard to immunizations. Given the importance of immunization and the concerns raised by the Office of Inspector General's report (25), criteria proposed by the CDC and American Academy of Pediatrics for immunization should be reviewed to determine if they are appropriate for Head Start.

(*e*) An improved record-keeping and monitoring system that would provide a systematic "report card" on health services. Such an improved system would include computerizing child and family health records, including immunizations and health services tracking, preferably as part of an overall child and family information system. The on-site monitoring system to determine compliance with the Performance Standards should be strengthened through the improvement of health monitoring tools and training of site visitors that increase reliability of judgments about the quality of health services.

(*f*) A plan for systematic, planned research on health delivery and on health outcomes to produce information for policy and program planning. Priority areas should be Medicaid participation and barriers to it; immunizations, screenings, and treatment for lead poisoning; and mental health. In the area of mental health, for example, it is important to know how effective different types of mental health services are (e.g. case consultation, education of staff, identification of children with problems, outcomes of treatment or referrals for treatment).

Head Start has an excellent record overall in helping to deliver health services to economically disadvantaged children. The proposed expansion of Head Start provides a unique opportunity to build on this history to further improve health services for children living in poverty.

Literature Cited

1. *Annual Report of the Public Health Service—Head Start health services network, Fiscal Year 1991.* 1991. Maternal and Child Health Bur. US Dep. Health Hum. Serv., Washington, DC

2. Cent. Future Child. Staff. 1992. Recommendation. In *The Future of Children,* 2:6–7. Cent. Future Child. David Lucile Packard Found.

3. Cent. Dis. Control Prevent. 1993. US AIDS cases reported through December 1992. *HIV/AIDS Surveillance.* Public Health Serv. US Dep. Health Hum. Serv. Washington, DC

4. Children's Defense Fund. 1992. *Maternal and Child Health Data Book: The Health of America's Children 1992.* Washington, DC

5. Cohen DJ, Solnit AJ, Wohlford P. 1979. Mental health services in Head Start. In *Project Head Start: A Legacy of the War on Poverty,* ed E Zigler, J Valentine, pp. 259–82. New York: Free Press

6. Collins RC. 1990. *Head Start research and evaluation: A blueprint for the future.* Recommend. Advis. Panel Head Start Eval. Design Project. Vienna, VA: Collins Manage. Consult. Inc.

7. Collins RC, Kinney PF. 1989. *Head Start research and evaluation: Background and overview.* Tech. Pap. Prepared for Head Start Eval. Design Proj. Vienna, VA: Collins Manage. Consult., Inc.

8. Cooke R. 1965. Reprinted 1972. *Recommendations for a Head Start program by panel of experts.* Off. Child Dev., Dep. Health, Educ. Welfare. Washington, DC

9. Cooke RE. 1979. Introduction. See Ref. 5, pp. xxiii–xxvi

10. DeAngelis T. 1993. Psychologists have tradition of helping kids get Head Start. *APA Monit.* 24:8–9

10a. Deloria D, Thouvenelle S. 1993. *Who does Head Start serve?* Presented at 2nd Natl. Head Start Res. Conf., Washington, DC

10b. Federal Register. Jan. 21. 1993. *Head Start Program: Final Rule.* (45 CFR Part 1304, 1305, & 1308). Washington, DC: US GPO

11. Fosburg LB. 1984. *The Effects of Head Start Health Services: Executive Summary of the Head Start Health Evaluation.* Cambridge, MA: Abt Assoc., Inc.

12. Guthrie AM, McNulty M. 1993. *Making the most of Medicaid: State progress in childhood lead poisoning prevention.* Washington, DC: Alliance End Child. Lead Poisoning

13. Hale BA, Seitz V, Zigler E. 1990. Health services and Head Start: A forgotten formula. *J. Appl. Dev. Psychol.* 11:447–58

14. Hill IT. 1992. The role of Medicaid and other government programs in providing medical care for children and pregnant women. See Ref. 2, pp. 134–53

15. Interagency Agree. Admin. Child. Families, Admin. Child. Youth Families, Head Start Bur. Public Health Serv., Health Res. Serv. Admin., Maternal Child Health Bur. Fiscal Year 1992

15a. Keith AB, Leeman CA. 1993. *The health needs assessment project for Maine's Head Start program.* Presented at 2nd Natl. Head Start Res. Conf., Washington, DC

16. Klerman LV. 1992. Nonfinancial barriers to the receipt of medical care. See Ref. 2, pp. 171–85

17. Klerman LV. 1991. *Alive and Well? A Research and Policy Review of Health Programs for Poor Young Children.* New York: Natl. Cent. Child. Poverty

18. McKey RH, Candelli L, Ganson H, Barrett BJ, McCankey C, et al. 1985. *The impact of Head Start on children, families, and communities: Final report of the Head Start Evaluation, Synthesis and Utilization Project.* Admin. Child. Youth Families Contract No. 105-81-C-026

19. Miller CA, Fine A, Adams-Taylor S. 1989. *Monitoring Children's Health: Key Indicators.* Washington, DC: Am. Public Health Assoc.

20. Natl. Cent. Child. Poverty. 1990. *Five million children: A statistical profile of our poorest young citizens.* School of Public Health. Columbia Univ., New York

21. Natl. Head Start Assoc. 1990. *Report of the Silver Ribbon Panel, Head Start: The nation's pride, a nation's challenge, recommendations for Head Start in the 1990's.* Alexandria, VA

22. Natl. Inst. Drug Abuse. 1991. *National household survey on drug abuse: Population estimates 1991.* Revised Nov. 20, 1992. US Dep. Health Hum. Serv., Washington, DC

23. Deleted in proof

24. North AF Jr. 1979. Health services in Head Start. See Ref. 5, pp. 231–57

25. Off. Insp. Gen. 1993. *Evaluating Head Start Through Performance Indicators.* US Dep. Health Hum. Serv., Washington, DC

26. Parker FL, Piotrkowski CS, Peay L. 1987. Head Start as a social support for mothers: The psychological benefits of involvement. *Am. J. Orthopsychiat.* 57:220–23

27. Perrin J, Guyer B, Lawrence JM. 1992. Health care services for children and adolescents. See Ref. 2, pp. 58–77

28. Pizzo PD, Chavkin D. 1991. Head Start and Medicaid: A new marriage for the 1990's. *Natl. Head Start Assoc. J.* 9:53

29. *Program Performance Standards for Operation of Head Start Programs by Grantees and Delegate Agencies.* Reprinted 1992. 45 CFR Part 1304

30. Racine AD, Joyce TJ, Grossman M. 1992. Effectiveness of health care services for pregnant women and infants. See Ref. 2, pp. 40–57

31. Stubbs PE. 1990. *Head Start Health Coordinators' Task Force Report.* US Dep. Health Hum. Serv., Washington, DC

32. Stubbs PE. 1988. Head Start. In *Maternal and Child Health Practices,* ed. H Wallace, G Ryan, A Oglesby. Oakland, CA: Third Party Publ. Comp.

33. *Summ. Head Start Health Conf.* 1992. Maternal and Child Health Bureau. US Dep. Health Hum. Serv., Washington, DC

34. *The status of handicapped children in Head Start programs: 1991.* Annu. Rep. US Dep. Health Hum. Serv. Congr. US Serv. Provided Child. Disabil. Head Start Progr. Head Start Bur. Admin. Child., Youth Families. Admin. Child. Families. US Dep. Health Hum. Serv. Washington, DC

35. US Dep. Health Human Serv., Public Health Serv., 1992. *Fact Sheet*

36. Vogel RJ, Brandis MR, Barnhouse WP. 1978. *Evaluation of the process of mainstreaming handicapped children into project Head Start, Phase I Final Report, May 1978 and Phase II Final Report.* Appl. Manage. Sci. Admin. Child., Youth Families Contract No. HEW 105-76-1113

37. Wilson AL, Neidich G. 1991. *Infant Mortality and Public Policy,* Vol. 2. Soc. Policy Rep., Soc. Res. Child Dev. pp. 1–21

38. Zigler E, Anderson K. 1979. An Idea whose time had come: The intellectual and political climate. See Ref. 5, pp. 3–19

39. Zigler E, Muenchow S. 1992. *Head Start: The Inside Story of America's Most Successful Educational Experiment.* New York: Basic

40. Zigler E, Trickett PK. 1978. IQ, social competence, and evaluation of early childhood intervention programs. *Am. Psychol.* 33:789–98

Annu. Rev. Public Health. 1994. 15:535–59

METHODS FOR QUALITY-OF-LIFE STUDIES[1]

Marcia A. Testa

Department of Biostatistics, Harvard School of Public Health, Boston, Massachusetts 02115

Johanna F. Nackley

Phase V Technologies, Inc., Wellesley Hills, Massachusetts 02181

KEY-WORDS: quality-of-life methods, patient outcomes, clinical trials, statistics

INTRODUCTION

The interpretation of quality-of-life data for therapeutic decision making and policy planning requires a comprehensive understanding of the methodologies employed in the design, data collection, and analysis phases of the research. The assumptions and limitations of the quality-of-life measures and the associated methods of study design and data analysis should be carefully reviewed prior to using quality-of-life outcomes as dependent variables of interest. To date, the primary focus of quality-of-life, methodologic research has been on defining the construct of "quality of life" (3, 57, 69, 93), deliberating its role in outcomes research (71, 78, 87), and choosing the appropriate measurement instruments (4, 40, 70). Much less attention has focused on the design and statistical methodology used to substantively evaluate and interpret quality-of-life treatment effects and differences. And yet, rigorous evaluation of therapeutic interventions such as pharmacologic treatment, surgery, and preventive programs depends almost entirely upon the adequacy and appropriateness of the methodologies employed and the manner in which analytical models are used to interpret the results. Without adequately defining and applying the methodologic assumptions, analytical

[1]Publication of this article does not necessarily represent approval, concurrence, or official endorsement of the statements and opinions herein by the AHCPR, the Public Health Service of the US Department of Health and Human Services.

0163-7525/94/0510-0535$05.00

models, and statistical techniques, valid conclusions regarding treatment effects and the relative risks, benefits, and costs of alternative therapies are difficult to achieve, if not untenable.

Analytical and statistical methodology in quality-of-life research is fragmented and lacks careful integration among the diverse but related fields of health, behavioral, social, therapeutic, and quantitative research methods. Techniques to measure quality of life are drawn from evaluation, health survey, nursing, clinical, psychometric, and sociometric research. Study designs are adapted from survey, observational, and interventional methodologies. Statistical methods are often based upon simple linear models and treatment contrasts, but more sophisticated techniques include multivariate linear models, tests of global hypotheses, longitudinal methods of data analysis, nonparametric rank statistics, failure time and survival methods, and health-state Markov processes. The objective of this report is to evaluate current measurement, design, and statistical methodology used in quality-of-life outcomes research by critically reviewing the published literature in the field. Because quality-of-life research spans many diverse disciplines, this review focuses on methodologies related primarily to medical and public health interventional and observational studies, with an emphasis on therapeutic clinical trials.

Quality of life is widely perceived to have substantial potential as an endpoint in medical and health-outcomes research. Health-related quality-of-life endpoints are being used increasingly to evaluate pharmacologic agents in clinical trials of cancer (50, 64), HIV (81, 91), arthritis (5, 59), heart failure (11, 92), and hypertension (10, 17, 47, 83, 85). They are also being employed to adjust measures of effectiveness for therapeutic decision making and to plan allocation of resources (24, 29, 32, 34). In addition to the primary statistical methods used in estimating the quality-of-life parameters, major methodologic issues arise in secondary analyses that attempt to incorporate the quality-of-life estimates into adjusted measures of "effectiveness".

The relevant methodologies used in quality-of-life outcomes research must address the design, measurement, analysis, and interpretation of the quality-of-life measures and the corresponding effects of treatments. With regard to these issues, Guyatt et al (39) asked two relevant and practical questions: (a) how should health-related quality-of-life measures be compared, and (b) how can we make health-related quality-of-life results from controlled trials meaningful to the intended audience? To address some of the specific issues of design, measurement, and analyses, the methodologic areas involving quality-of-life measurement, estimation, hypothesis testing, and use of summary indices in effectiveness models will be reviewed from both a qualitative and quantitative perspective.

MEASUREMENT OF QUALITY-OF-LIFE OUTCOMES

The measurement properties of the quality-of-life indices and scales used in therapeutic trials affect their ability to detect meaningful treatment differences. These properties are a function of both the theoretical framework from which the quality-of-life constructs are derived, and how well the scales perform in measuring those constructs. A scale can be evaluated by several indices that measure performance, including reliability, validity, responsiveness, and sensitivity. A scale's level of performance can have a profound impact on the conclusions for a particular clinical trial or case-control study. In addition, the appropriate use of summary quality-of-life estimates in subsequent models of cost-effectiveness and cost-utility of alternative drug, interventions, and treatments (84) requires an understanding of how performance levels can influence secondary analyses of overall treatment effectiveness.

Conceptualizing Quality of Life

Our ability to measure quality of life depends to a great extent upon how it is conceptualized (7, 68). In medical and health survey research, the term quality of life is an organizing concept that brings together a set of domains related to the physical, functional, psychological, and social health of the individual. When used in this context it is often referred to as "health-related quality of life" to differentiate it from its use in other contexts, including references to the level of crime, adequacy of housing, fairness of taxes, and cultural environment. An extremely comprehensive and thorough review of the field of quality-of-life research as it pertains to the development of health policy is given by Patrick & Erickson (72). Table 1 depicts the process of translating the concept of quality of life into more measurable constructs.

According to the representation in Table 1, health-related quality of life involves the five broad dimensions of opportunity, health perceptions, functional status, morbidity or impairment, and mortality. Depending upon the specific target population and the purposes of the study, it may not always be necessary to measure all dimensions to fully evaluate quality of life, if certain assumptions hold. For example, in a multicenter, randomized, double-blind clinical trial comparing the effects of antihypertensive medications (captopril, methyldopa, and propranolol) on quality of life, the primary focus was on the domains of general health perceptions, functional status, and self-reports of symptoms (17) because the other dimensions were assumed to be relatively constant. Randomization was used to ensure equal balance for opportunity, the disease was asymptomatic, and all patients were titrated to produce similar effects for efficacy and safety, with the assumption

Table 1   A multidimensional conceptualization of quality of life[1]

Dimensions	Domains	Indicators (Indices, Scales, Subscales)
Opportunity	Social or cultural	Access to care, societal stigma, support
	Coping	Ability to withstand stress, psychological or physical
Health Perceptions	General health perceptions	Self-rating, worry, concern
	Expectations/satisfaction	Satisfaction with functioning
Functional	Social	Work and daily role
	Psychological	Distress (anxiety, depression, loss of behavioral and emotional control)
		Well-being (positive affect, emotional ties, life satisfaction)
	Cognitive	Memory, alertness, reasoning
	Physical	Activity restrictions, fitness
Morbidity	Signs	Objective clinical findings directly observable
	Symptoms	Subjective evidence indirectly observable
	Self-reports	Patient self-reports of symptoms and conditions
	Physiologic	Laboratory measures, pathology
	Diagnosis and severity	
Mortality	Death	Survival, years of life lost
	Duration of life	

[1]Adapted from a model proposed by Patrick & Erickson (72)

that length of life and mortality would be comparable in all groups. However, in other studies, equal efficacy among therapies might not be a reasonable assumption and therefore morbidity and mortality would have to be factored into the evaluation model. The range of dimensions and the added requirements for disease-specific evaluation should always be considered.

The range of responses and extent of coverage of domains will influence the accuracy of the measures, especially as they reflect changes in quality of life during intervention studies. For example, a generic health survey instrument might be sensitive to picking up distinctions between individuals who differ by clinical status; however, a more disease-specific questionnaire might be needed to detect changes within individuals in a specific clinical class. Turner approached the issue of measurement using a three-dimensional model to evaluate patient outcomes in rehabilitation (89). The first dimension includes the *areas* of assessment such as impairment, disability, and handicap. The second dimension included the *domains* of assessment that are generally accepted as relevant for rehabilitation outcomes (physical, mental, emotional, and social), and the third dimension, the *type* of measure classified according to its applications as evaluative, predictive, and discriminate (54). The model is important because it relates the measure's purpose, structure, and application.

For example, a functional health status measure commonly used in cancer clinical trials such as the Karnofsky Performance Status Scale (52), covers a very broad range of functioning from death (0 points) to full health (100 points indicating normal: no complaints: no evidence of disease). The average asymptomatic patient with hypertension or who is HIV-positive might only be able to function daily to his or her satisfaction between a score of 90 (able to carry on normal activity, minor signs, or symptoms of disease) and 100. Changes of 10 points might have a very large impact on the ability of the asymptomatic patient to function and might reduce his or her usual day-to-day functional capacity by more than 50%, even though 10 points only represents 10% of the total Karnofsky scale. Hence a seemingly "small effect" under one set of assumptions of 10 percent can translate into a very large effect of 50 percent based upon individual expectations. Small differences between individuals on the overall scale can translate into relatively large differences within individuals because they are calibrated against the patient's own internalized expectations of quality of life.

Three properties of quality-of-life measures influence how and how well the constructs are measured and analyzed. As depicted in Table 1, the hypothetical constructs and corresponding measurement scales are *multidimensional* and *multilayered*. Thirdly, they are most often measured *indirectly*. To address the multidimensional property of the measures one must address the multivariate nature of the data and the multiple and global hypotheses that they will generate. Alternatively, one must find ways to combine the various constructs and domains through the use of summary parameters or utility weighting procedures that make it possible to incorporate quality of life into general models of risk-benefit and cost-effectiveness.

In addition, the measures are multilayered and nested. That is, we measure constructs by forming single questions or items; these are grouped into sub-scales, which, in turn, form broader scales that may themselves be part of even broader composites jointly reflecting overall quality of life. Hence, sub-scales are nested within scales, which are nested within composites, which are nested within domains, which are nested within the major dimensions. What level does one use for the primary analysis? Certainly the layers and dimensions are not independent, with inner layers being subsets of outer layers. Summary parameters from factor analysis or other linear functions of the individual layers attempt to deal with both the multilayering and multidimensionality.

The third property of quality-of-life scales involves the indirect nature by which one must measure the quality-of-life constructs. In addition to the random variability between individuals associated with most biomedical variables which can be measured directly, indirect measures contain other random effects associated with the inherent variability within question-naires/forms, between forms, within-subject, between interviewers, and over time.

The Validities of Health-related Quality-of-life Measures

Validity is defined as the capacity of the instrument to measure what it intends to measure. Kirshner & Guyatt (54) recognized that the performance indices or the "validities" of a scale have different implications across the three types of quality-of-life measures, namely, evaluative, predictive, or discriminant. While discriminative indices should demonstrate large and stable between-subject variation so that groupings of similar patients can be contrasted to other groupings, evaluative indices must possess high test-retest reliability and responsiveness to true changes in quality of life. Much of the current debate surrounding the interpretation of the meaning of quality-of-life data is due to applying the same performance standards appropriate for discriminate measures to evaluative measures for which such standards are inappropriate.

Nonintervention-Based Validities

The validities of a scale tell us how well our measure quantifies the true response (62). We assess validity according to the degree of relationship of a test or scale with another variable of interest. The validity coefficient of a measurement Y with respect to a second measurement X is defined as the absolute value of the correlation coefficient

$$\rho_{yx} = \frac{\sigma_{yx}}{\sigma_y \sigma_x}$$

where σ_y, σ_x and σ_{yx} are the corresponding standard deviations and covariance. As seen here, the validity coefficient of a measurement can only be stated in relation to a second measure. Thus, although claims are often made concerning the fact that a quality-of-life scale has been "vali-dated", one cannot speak meaningfully about a "valid quality-of-life scale" or a "valid quality-of-life instrument" without first defining the measure X against which the scale Y is being correlated or compared.

Nonintervention-based validities tell us how well the measures are func-tioning at a single point in time. For example, reliability, including measures of within-form homogeneity of items (internal consistency) and between-forms stability (test-retest), are indications of how precise and stable the measures are. Construct validity, including convergent, trait, and discrimi-nant validity, assess how well the scales relate to other measures that purport to measure the same construct. A thorough review of measurement theory can be found in a number of texts (63, 80).

Intervention-Based Validities

The accurate measurement of change in quality-of-life scales is paramount in interventional studies of health (37, 38, 41). To this end, researchers are interested in measuring both the overall effects of treatments as well as in examining the individual differences in treatment response. In interventional and observational studies quality of life is usually measured longitudinally and involves multidimensional scales describing the physical, emotional, and social health status of the patient. While the reliability of the scales is established by evaluating internal consistency (6, 16) and test-retest repro-ducibility as cited above, the ability to detect meaningful treatment effects is more difficult to define and evaluate.

The instrument's responsiveness (37) to true change and its sensitivity to treatment effects are being used increasingly for validation of evaluative measures such as those used to assess changes due to intervention. Knowl-edge of a scale's responsiveness and sensitivity are essential in determining both the power of the statistical analyses and the interpretation of the findings.

A demonstration of responsiveness is necessary in a therapeutic interven-tion study because it helps to discriminate between scales that are likely to change and those that are not. This knowledge is especially important when designing "equivalence trials" or when attempting to prove the null hypoth-esis of no treatment effect. One could easily be unaware of a large Type II error (assuming no difference, when a true difference actually exists) because the error could be due to low responsiveness rather than small sample size. Recently, Guyatt (38) and Tuley (88) proposed a *responsiveness index* using the change from baseline to the final evaluable double-blind visit. The index is a scaled measure of this change and is defined as the ratio between the *mean change* from baseline to endpoint after treatment and the *standard deviation of change* within untreated, stable subjects.

Low responsiveness, lack of sensitivity, and significant confounding are often not taken into account when designing a clinical trial. When these omissions occur, conclusions based upon acceptance of the null hypothesis of "no effect" can be extremely misleading. Alternatively, even highly statistically significant treatment effects have been criticized because it is difficult to relate the quality-of-life change units employed into a known or measurable health or social consequence. Do the statistically significant changes reflect a substantial change in quality of life, or one that is minimal? In a cost-effectiveness analysis conducted by Edelson (24) comparing anti-hypertensive medications, the incremental cost effectiveness (per quality-adjusted life year gained using the more expensive therapy) varied by as much as $1.4 m based upon reductions in quality of life as small as 1 percent. What was so striking about this quality-adjusted, cost-effectiveness analysis was the very narrow range of quality-of-life changes that caused a reversal in the final conclusions (84). It is certainly possible that the estimates of incremental costs suffer from high error when they attempt to distinguish between such small quality-of-life effects.

How responsive the quality-of-life scale is to therapeutic effects is a function of the validity and precision of the scale and the magnitude of the actual drug effect. Using Guyatt's responsiveness index, Testa et al (85) computed the quality-of-life change from baseline to the final evaluable double-blind visit to represent the response of the patient to treatment. Most importantly, the investigators then went on to evaluate the *sensitivity* of their measures to detect differences in treatment response by analyzing the longitudinal changes between drug treatments in relationship to the scale's responsiveness to changes in stressful life events as reported by patients during the course of the study. As shown in Figure 1, changes in General Perceived Health could be calibrated to stressful life events. Pooled data from two clinical trials of antihypertensive therapies in elderly men found that a 0.1 responsiveness unit change (approximately .06 between-individual standard deviation units) on the General Perceived Health scale corresponded to 32 Life Change Units (LCUs) on the Holmes and Rahe Social Readjustment Scale (48; MA Testa, unpublished observations). Therefore, a quality-of-life change of this magnitude could be translated into an effect size comparable to changing to a different line of work (36 LCUs) or major change in arguments with spouse (35 LCUs).

While the published research supporting a negative relationship between stressful life events, disease, and mental health was abundant (8, 9, 43, 44, 53, 60, 86, 94), using this relationship to estimate the responsiveness and sensitivity of the quality-of-life measures represents new ground for intervention-based validation for comparative clinical trials. However, the methods had been established and used much earlier in observational studies of medical outcomes (7, 101). In the HIS study by Brook et al, investigators found that for the subscales of general health and vitality (two of the three subscales used in the General Perceived Health in the study by Testa et al (85) cited above), a 31-point LCU change resulted for every .08 between-individual standard deviation change in those subscales. Despite the differences in the study design, and length of follow-up, the calibrations were remarkably similar to the study by Testa et al (85), indicating the stability of the relationships between stressful life events and functional health. Such findings make objective stressful life events an excellent criterion variable for assessment of the responsiveness of a quality-of-life scale. Other studies have assessed the responsiveness of health status measures to change using relative efficiency statistics (a ratio of paired t statistics) (58), and receiver-

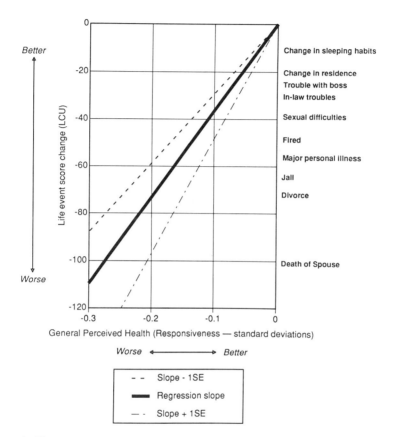

Figure 1   Linear trend in General Perceived Health (responsiveness units change since last visit) as a function of stressful life events (LCU score change reported since last visit). Note that changes in the range of 0.10 to 0.20 responsiveness index units reflect the influence on quality of life of important life events such as loss of a job. (Reprinted from Testa et al (85) with permission.)

operating characteristic curves that describe the ability of a scale to detect improvement using an external, dichotomous criterion (21, 22).

Respondent Variability

The question of validity brings up a related issue of intra- and interrespondent variability. Jachuck first noted that patients, relatives, and physicians all had different perceptions of what constituted improvement in the patient's quality of life during antihypertensive therapy (49). Physicians consistently rated patients as having improved, whereas relatives uniformly agreed that they had worsened. The sources of variability associated with such factors as who is reporting, how reports are obtained, and where assessments are conducted all contribute to respondent variability.

In a study comparing nifedipine GITS and atenolol on aspects of the patient's quality of life, three respondents, patient, clinician, and spouse, were used to assess between-form interrater variability (83). The spouse was a more sensitive discriminator of treatment differentials in two areas, predicting withdrawal from the study and sexual dysfunction. For the physician, the correlation between the frequency of each symptom reported by the patient and the frequency reported by the physician was fairly high ($r = .81$). However, the physician had a much higher threshold for reporting side effects, related to their severity, specificity, and medical implications (1). The percent of symptoms present by usual safety reporting (spontaneous reports by physicians) was less than 10 percent of that reported by patients, and physician checklists still only provided 25–33% of the levels reported by patients. These results indicate that even clinically straightforward measures such as adverse events and symptoms contain a large portion of subjectivity, which is an important component of the patient's quality of life.

Parallel forms developed for the patient to complete in the clinic (using a long-form version) and at home (using a shorter-form version) were used to study intra-individual, between-form variability (82). The take-home short forms were nearly identical in reliability to those administered in the clinic, as measured by Cronbach's standardized alpha coefficient; but the clinic-based assessments proved to be the more sensitive discriminator for the quality-of-life treatment differentials overall.

HYPOTHESIS TESTING

One of the weakest areas in quality-of-life research is hypothesis testing and the subsequent interpretation of the results. Conflicting reports and claims are made due to a lack of understanding of design and analysis methodologies, including (*a*) the role of measurement error on subsequent statistical tests; (*b*) inadequate power; (*c*) failure to deal with confounding effects such as age, sex and severity of illness; (*d*) length of study bias; (*e*) early withdrawal from the study; and (*f*) problems with missing data.

What Constitutes a Meaningful Quality-of-Life Treatment Effect?

When making medical decisions or when designing and adopting summary parameters for cost-effectiveness and cost-utility analysis studies, it is often difficult to determine what constitutes a *meaningful quality-of-life treatment effect*. Even relatively small changes can have a fairly large impact on the incremental cost-effectiveness of different therapeutic alternatives. Similarly, claims of improved quality of life, stable quality of life, or a relatively better quality of life imply knowledge concerning how great the impact will be for an effect of a predetermined magnitude. How do clinicians, policy planners, and health economists decide what is a "small" or a "large" effect? This question bears directly on very practical and important design and statistical issues. How do we set appropriate effect sizes for alternative hypotheses such that our hypotheses test what we want them to test? What is the magnitude of a quality-of-life decrement that has a dispositive effect on the individual and subsequently on society? These questions must be answered before valid interpretation of quality-of-life data can be made.

Estimating the Power of a Quality-of-Life Study

As cited previously, Brook et al conducted extensive research on health status measures in the Health Insurance Study (HIS) involving 3924 individuals (7). When studying the power of quality-of-life measures they recommended that external criteria be reported along with the usual measures of effect sizes (standard deviations and percent change in the mean). Brook and colleagues determined that the HIS study should be powerful enough to detect differences for all physical health measures in terms of the effects of five years of aging, and for all mental health measures, differences equal to the amount of stress associated with a small debt [17 (LCU) on the Holmes-Rahe scale]. Thus they defined the associated changes in quality of life that would accompany these events as being clinically meaningful and important.

Table 2 summarizes the results of the HIS power analysis and the calibration with external criteria for a number of scales. The data indicated that the HIS study had the prerequisite power to detect fairly small between-individual standard deviation effect sizes of between .07–.08 units. For a discriminant measure used to classify patients, tests powered to detect effects of .07–.08 between-individual standard deviations would seem to be very powerful. Cohen's guidelines for cross-sectional data for the relative magnitude of effect sizes for behavioral measures (15) recommend .2 between-individual standard deviations as a small effect, .5 as a medium effect, and .8 as a large effect. In contrast to these recommended values, the effect sizes in Table 2 between .07 and .08 do appear relatively very small. However, as also pointed out by Cohen, the relative magnitude of longitudinal effect sizes required for detection by evaluative measures should be based upon within-individual standard deviations and will vary from those required by descriptive measures.

In the HIS study the minimally clinically significant effect of 17 LCUs

Table 2 Summary of the statistical power and calibration between longitudinal effects (between-individual standard deviations units) and external criteria (years of aging and the Holmes and Rahe Life Change Units (LCU) scale) in the Rand Health Insurance Study[1]

Scale	Effect sizes	
	SD units	External criteria
Physical Limitations	.073	3.6 years
Self-Care	.075	10.1 years
Function Status Index	.071	3.5 years
Positive Well-Being	.080	30.7 LCUs
General Health	.081	30.9 LCUs
Vitality	.081	30.4 LCUs
Depression	.087	19.9 LCUs
HIS-GWB	.081	20.4 LCUs
Mental Health Index	.080	19.9 LCUs

The HIS Health status measures had the power to detect effect sizes of this magnitude as computed with alpha = .05, beta = .10, assuming pretests and covariates and a sample of 3924 adults.
[1]Source: Brook et al (7)

would correspond to between .04–.08 between-individual standard deviations depending upon the particular scale. Note that even if the .2 "small effect" guidelines for the estimation of power had been applied, the HIS study would have missed changes in general health corresponding to 75 LCUs, which is approximately equivalent to the impact of divorce (73 LCUs) on general health.

Simultaneous Test Procedures

Three types of questions might be asked with respect to multivariate quality-of-life data: (a) multiple univariate; (b) structured multivariate; and (c) intrinsically multivariate. As described by Hand & Taylor (42), "the last case is addressing the question of whether or not a comparison is significant on a group of variables simultaneously, and the individual identities of the variables is regarded as irrelevant to the basic question". Such is the case when answering the question of whether a "quality-of-life" difference exists. Because it is the "construct" quality of life that is under investigation and not whether each of its subcomponents is different, primary attention should focus on the intrinsically multivariate question. However, should the intrinsically multivariate question show significance, then further questions would be appropriate: on which variables or combinations of variables is the comparison significant? Since by design, each of the measures that make up quality of life is correlated with all other measures, standard ways of controlling for error inflation, such as Bonferroni, are inappropriate and would only provide the absolute maximum overall error rate leading to overly conservative testing and inflated Type II error.

Many psychometric measures such as the Mental Health Index (12, 90) contain several scales. If one wishes to promote a specific scale or subscale as important in its own right and apart from the overall concept of quality of life, then Gabriel's simultaneous test procedures could be used (31). However, it may not be the primary intent of a quality-of-life study to promote or examine a particular scale such as sleep disturbance, anxiety, or vitality separate and apart from its contribution to overall quality of life. Therefore, one might choose to concentrate on univariate summary measures derived from factor analysis or prespecified weighting procedures and the corresponding multivariate profiles. Factor analysis identifies weights based upon statistical correlations and variances among the measures and reduces the total set of measures to linear functions that contain the essence of the information. Individual examination of multivariate subscales or computation of summary measures might be desired to examine the relative strength of the treatment effects across the scales, as well as between treatments. At the higher levels, how one combines the functional domains of psychological, social, general perceived, and physical health is still a matter of debate. At this level, the conceptualization regards domains within levels as being of relatively equal importance.

Global Hypotheses Tests for Multidimensional Responses

To define a "change" in quality of life, either positive or negative, one must contend simultaneously with issues of the multiplicity of responses, the multivariate nature of the variables, and the longitudinal nature of the data. Several analytic techniques have been proposed for analyzing clinical trials with multiple endpoints (65, 75, 96). In clinical trials of quality of life, multivariate test statistics such as Hotelling's T^2 are often used to determine treatment effects (76). However, this statistic is intended to detect any departure from the null hypothesis and therefore might lack the power to detect specific types of departure (e.g. therapeutically favorable, not favorable). For a set of p quality-of-life endpoints without prespecified priorities, the question of how can significance testing be used while preserving Type I error and allowing correlated endpoints has been addressed in different ways (74).

Pocock addressed several issues of *hypothesis testing* in quality-of-life clinical trials including the repeated use of significance tests comparing multiple outcomes (74). He proposed that a "directional" global test such as that proposed by O'Brien (65) would be most suitable for combining measures related to the same aspect of quality of life. He also cited the need to calibrate a change in quality of life to a "minimally clinically important mean difference". A series of articles recently reported various opinions on the types of analytical and statistical analyses that should accompany quality-of-life multiple endpoints research (27, 28, 33, 66, 77).

However, quality-of-life measures are not strictly "multiple endpoints" in the sense that they are supposed to measure a more global construct through subsets of interrelated constructs. While the multiple endpoints procedures may be suitable for combining variables for which no single syndrome or pathologic process has been defined (e.g. weight, reductions in blood pressure, increases in insulin sensitivity, changes in creatinine level, and lipid levels), quality-of-life endpoints that are linked through a careful conceptualization of dimensions, domains, and indicators deserve to be treated as interrelated constructs rather than unrelated entities. This has led investigators to rely on more sophisticated methods of longitudinal modeling, as reviewed briefly in the following sections.

Longitudinal Models of Quality of Life

The most relevant method for dealing with intervention and observational studies involve models that take into account the longitudinal nature of the data. Quality-of-life studies involve problems and sources of bias found in most longitudinal designs including selection bias, heterogeneity, directionality, and confounding. Repeated measures over time on the same individuals are not independent. In addition to the problem of withdrawals and persons lost to follow-up, the conceptual problem of choosing the appropriate model characterizing the changes over time is complex.

Longitudinal assessments of quality of life involve repeated sampling, especially in assessing cognitive functioning, depression, and anxiety where the cyclic trends are important. In addition, long-term surveillance involves prospective repeated evaluations of several domains over time. Ekstrom et al reviewed the statistical methods applied to psychiatric research studies that used parallel groups and multivariate repeated measures designs (25) and recommended increased use of multivariate analysis of variance.

Even when the autocorrelation structure of a times series is not of direct interest in longitudinal studies of quality of life, it has an indirect bearing on the estimation of the parameters that are subsequently calculated. Failure to account for the autocorrelation function in relevant cases results in potential bias when estimating test statistics for quality-of-life studies (14).

A thorough and comprehensive review of statistical models for longitudinal studies of health was compiled by Dwyer et al (23). Waternaux & Ware (95) reviewed linear models for analysis of longitudinal data and cited several methodologies including longitudinal random-effect models that take into account two corresponding sources of error, including within- and between-subject variance components. Appropriate estimation methods for these types of models include the restricted maximum likelihood estimation (REML) methods (45). Laird (55) and Laird & Ware (56) used the EM algorithm proposed by Dempster, Laird & Rubin (20) to obtain REML estimates.

Other investigators use a more global longitudinal approach based upon the stochastic processes describing the various transitions between health states (2, 67). Those models that use continuous observations depicting health states at discrete points in time can be considered autoregressive processes if the current state depends only on the previous state. Discrete observations can be modeled by a Markov chain. Such models have been used to model disease processes such as HIV infection in other contexts (61).

Still other investigators rely upon an approach using structural equation models to model the complex interrelationships among biopsychosocial variables (51). These models allow estimation of stochastic models with continuous state space and the incorporation of latent variables and error terms. Latent variables are essentially "indirect measures" and thus the model might be fitting for the analysis of quality of life. The modeling of these indirect constructs by a set of indicator variables reduces the error from measuring the construct only through single variables. These methods also have the advantage of allowing for the modeling of explicit assumptions about the measurement error. Zwinderman modeled the measurement of change in quality of life using a latent logistic regression model that allowed for the inclusion of parameters for the time process, the effects of clinical treatments, and the interaction parameters (102).

Effect of Missing Data, Early Withdrawal, Length Bias and other Confounders

The problems associated with early withdrawal from a quality-of-life study are particularly troublesome because of the high degree of association between decreases in quality of life and missing data and early withdrawal from the study. This is particularly true in therapeutic trials comparing agents that cause side-effects. In this case, one cannot adopt the assumption of noninformative loss to follow-up. Patients might miss a visit because of some event unrelated to the treatment or disease. Here the missing data is assumed to be random and noninformative. However, if patients miss a visit because they are too sick (physically or emotionally) due to either side-effects of therapy or disease progression, the missingness is informative. Informative missingness occurs when the probability of response depends on the outcome or other covariates. When patients withdraw permanently from the study and no further quality-of-life follow-up information is available, the problem is even more serious and complex.

Choi & Stablein reviewed the mechanisms by which missing data occur (13) and identified three different mechanisms: (*a*) the treatment or the group to which the subject is assigned; (*b*) the outcome; and (*c*) both the treatment and the outcome. In a study comparing two antihypertensive agents, nifedipine GITS and atenolol, the change in quality of life from baseline to last-available visit showed a much larger deterioration for those who withdrew early from the trial as compared to those who completed the study protocol (83). When treatment differences were calculated based upon all cases (last observation carried forward (LOCF)) or 24-week completers, the conclusions were quite different. The LOCF analysis showed no treatment differences whereas the completer analysis showed a more favorable effect for nifedipine GITS, as shown in Figure 2. What is the correct conclusion concerning the treatment differences? One could insist upon maintaining the clinical trial model and the "intent to treat" principle using the LOCF method or other forms of missing value imputation. Or one could adopt the pharmacoepidemiologic or pharmacoeconomic model that would strive to estimate quality of life in those individuals who would practically continue on medication and whose collective experiences with loss of work, side-effects and the positive effects of therapy would contribute to future functioning in society. Heyting et al (46) reviewed statistical complexities that arise

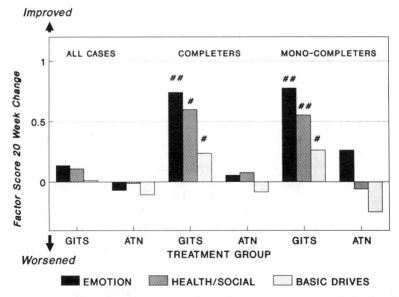

Figure 2 Factor score 20-week changes from baseline for patients receiving nifedipine GITS and atenolol. Statistical contrasts: nifedipine statistically different from atenolol, p <.01, #p <.05. Reprinted from Testa et al (83) with permission.

from outcome-related drop-outs in longitudinal clinical trials. The authors proposed methods derived from sample surveys with nonresponse and for observational studies. In a comparison of five different methods for dealing with early withdrawal, they concluded that methods from sample surveys and observational studies were the most advantageous. However, they cautioned that the ability to answer explanatory, rather than pragmatic, questions, arising from a comparative trial with drop-outs is still a complex issue.

Several studies have been designed with too short a follow-up period to make valid conclusions concerning the steady-state functional health of the patients under study. For example, a study by Steiner et al (79) with four groups and 360 male patients made conclusions after only four weeks of stable treatment with antihypertensive therapy. Another study by Dahlof & Dimenas drew conclusions after only two weeks about 77 hypertensive patients who were treated in two groups (18). Length bias is a particularly relevant issue in studies of this type, whether due to early withdrawal or study design, because changes in quality of life are not instantaneous and might emerge only after several months.

Another issue that affects the sensitivity of the measurement instruments deals with the ceiling/floor effects experienced by quality-of-life scales, which is dependent upon baseline quality of life. This is related to the issue of responsiveness. That is, patients cannot improve if they are already at the top of the scale, or deteriorate when they are already at the bottom of the scale. Responsiveness, and therefore sensitivity to treatment effects, is dependent upon the mean values of the scale itself. If patients fall outside of the range for which the scales have meaning where estimation of the true score is not possible, the scale will have both low responsiveness and sensitivity. If the effects of treatment are dependent upon the values of covariates that characterize those groups of individuals, then the ability to detect treatment effects may be seriously confounded. The study by Testa et al recommended controlling for baseline scores in the longitudinal analysis as a way of controlling for differences in responsivity within groups (85).

Other confounders are more obvious. Conclusions based upon single group open-label post-marketing trials claiming absolute "improvement" or "worsening" are unfounded because the studies lack both a randomized control design and the blinding required to rule out a placebo effect. One study, which assessed the effect of enalapril on hypertension and quality of life in a single-arm, open-label study of 4988 patients, made the claim that "Quality of life, determined by mean of the Nottingham Health Profile questionnaire, was favourably influenced in patients participating in this study" (19) even though it was neither unblinded nor contained a control group. Statements of absolute change in terms of worsening or improvement in uncontrolled studies should always be viewed cautiously.

QOL SUMMARY INDICES FOR USE IN EFFECTIVENESS MODELS

Several types of economic analyses can be used in the evaluation of new medical technologies, including pharmacologic agents (30, 99, 100). Effectiveness measures convey the overall benefit that the agent has on the treated population. When a drug is more effective and more costly than a comparative agent, cost-effectiveness analysis estimates the incremental gain in the therapeutic benefit per unit cost. Quality of life can affect the value of the effectiveness measure, such as survival or time to a clinically defining event, thereby readjusting incremental cost-effectiveness. In a comprehensive review, Weinstein (97) cites several examples that reinforce the need for incorporation of quality of life in cost-effectiveness analyses.

Quality-Adjusted Measures of Effectiveness

Several methods of analysis have been proposed to quality-adjust measures of efficacy for use in therapeutic decision making and economic evaluation. These techniques are commonly referred to as cost-utility analyses because of the utility weights placed on the outcomes of treatment. Pliskin (73) considered five health states in a study of hemodialysis versus kidney transplantation in the treatment of end-stage renal disease with corresponding utilities 1, .88, .7, .55, and 0, with utility = 1 describing a patient carrying a functioning transplant, working full time and returning to preuremic levels of activity, and utility = 0 describing a patient who is chronically ill and almost totally disabled (on dialysis or carrying a transplant).

Another model for evaluating coronary artery bypass surgery made utilities dependent on both the current health state as well as the baseline life-style of the patient (98). That is, individuals who were active had a greater reduction in life quality when experiencing pain with strenuous activity, than those patients who were sedentary. Such models are important because they account for the very real differences in health perceptions among patients with the same illness in common.

Both models have been applied to *descriptive* simulations using data on efficacy and quality of life from prior studies and evaluations. However, a recent model called *Quality-Adjusted Time Without Symptoms and Toxicity* (Q-TWIST), which relies on utility-weighted partitions of survival, has been used for *estimation* purposes in the evaluation of treatments for breast cancer (35, 36). The approach is similar to that of Pliskin (73) and divides survival time into three health states: time spent during periods of toxicity; time spent during the periods following progression of disease; and time spent free from both toxicity and progression. Survival time is quality-adjusted according to the utilities assigned to the two health states of toxicity, μ_{tox}, and progression, μ_{prog}, assuming a utility of 1 for *Time Without Symptoms and Toxicity* (TWIST).

Recently, the Q-TWIST model was applied to data from a clinical trial (26) comparing the use of zidovudine (AZT) versus placebo in patients with AIDS-related complex (34). The study illustrated that the decision to treat can be affected by the relative values the patient assigns to μ_{ae} and μ_{prog}. While the original analysis determined that zidovudine resulted in delay of the progression to an AIDS-defining clinical event and incurred "minimal" side effects (26), the Q-TWIST risk-benefit analysis concluded that the decision to treat should be dependent upon the value of utility (ranging from 1 = no toxicity or disease symptoms to 0 = worst health state) that the patient or physician gives to the quality of life experienced during toxicity, μ_{tox}, when compared to the utility given to the time after an AIDS-defining disease progression, μ_{prog}. Depending upon patient preference, zidovudine could be "effectively" better than placebo or "effectively" worse than placebo. The estimation of suitable indices or global measures appropriate for use in pharmacoeconomic models is necessary if such models are to be used in health-policy planning.

Health State Transition and Utility Models

Most quality-of-life trials are designed to measure quality of life at specific points in time rather than allowing time to vary randomly. In the fixed-time model, given a large enough patient population, it is possible to estimate the rate of transitions between health states by Markov models typically employed in compartmental analysis using the number of patients in each health state at fixed timepoints. In these models, $n(tj)$, the number of individuals in health state j at time t is the random variable, rather than the amount of time as required for the Q-TWIST model.

Rate parameters $L(i,j)$, representing the rate at which individuals transit from health state j to health state i, can be estimated along with treatment effects using population-parameter random effects estimation techniques. The estimated time spent in each compartment or health state can be obtained from a function of the rate parameters. Since it is possible to estimate the amount of time spent in each health state from the estimated transition rates and since it is possible to obtain utility weights using a rating scale, a global summary parameter GQOL is estimable from the linear combination of utilities and times given by

$$GQOL = \sum_{j=1}^{p} \mu_j \, \tau_j$$

where μ is the utility associated with health state j (j = 1, 2, 3,...p) and τ is the amount of time spent in health state j as estimated from the rate parameters.

SUMMARY

Methodologies involving the use of quality-of-life patient outcomes in observational and interventional studies of health are drawn from a large and diverse field of research methods. The multidimensional way in which quality of life is conceptualized will affect the way it is measured and the complexity of the measurement. At the earliest stages of research, one must rely on methods common to the fields of tests and measurement, survey research, psychometrics and sociometrics to measure constructs that are not directly observable. Indices measuring performance can either focus on the scale's ability to perform in noninterventional, cross-sectional studies or interventional, longitudinal studies. Indices of stability, internal consistency, responsiveness with respect to true changes in quality of life, and sensitivity to treatment effects can be used to assess the scale's adequacy as a dependent variable of interest. Respondent variability can occur due to factors such as different reporters (patient, spouse, physician), the manner and form of administration (long form vs short form; self-administration vs interview) and the assessment environment (clinic, home).

Finally, since quality-of-life research often involves inferential statistics and hypothesis testing, the statistical and epidemiologic principles of good study design should be followed. In addition, one should account for the reliability, responsiveness, and the sensitivity of the scale when designing the scientific hypotheses, and should specifically address the meaning of quality-of-life effect sizes by interventional-based validation. Design considerations must address the statistical issues of power, the determination of effect sizes through validation by external criteria, longitudinal data, effects of withdrawal and early termination, ceiling and floor effects, and heterogeneity of responsiveness and sensitivity among individuals.

The problem of estimating quality-of-life summary parameters for use in pharmacoeconomic models is receiving increasing attention in this era of health-care reform and fiscal restraint. While medical decision theory has used cost-effectiveness models and quality-adjusted life years since the early 1970s, estimation of population parameters to differentiate among different medical interventions is relatively new. The assessment of the patient outcomes associated with medical interventions in terms of the risks, benefits and costs will clearly be a major focus of health-care reform. Development of new methodologies in quality-of-life research should build upon the strong foundation already established in the areas of clinical research, epidemiology, biostatistics, economics and behavioral science. The purpose of quality-of-life research is ultimately to change the way we deliver and intervene in health care. Improvement in the health-related quality of life is a major objective in public health research. Research findings in this area have the potential to alleviate human suffering, minimize discomfort and morbidity, and positively affect health and well-being.

ACKNOWLEDGMENTS

We thank Dr. Donald C. Simonson, Brigham and Women's Hospital and the Joslin Diabetes Center, and Harvard Medical School, Boston, who served as the physician consultant and medical reviewer for this report.

Support for this research was provided by a grant from the Agency for Health Care Policy and Research (AHCPR), No. R01 HS07767-01, and NIAID Contract No. NO-A1- 95030.

Literature Cited

1. Anderson RB, Testa MA. 1994. Symptom distress checklists as a component of quality of life measurement: Comparing prompted reports by patient and physician with concurrent adverse event reports via the physician. *J. Drug Inf.* 28: In press

2. Beck JR, Pauker SG. 1983. The Markov model of medical prognosis. *Med. Decis. Mak.* 3:419–58

3. Bergner M. 1985. Measurement of health status. *Med. Care* 23(5):696–704

4. Bergner M, Rothman ML. 1987. Health status measures: An overview and guide for selection. *Annu. Rev. Public Health*. 8:191–210

5. Bombardier C, Ware J, Russell IJ, Larson M, Chalmers A, et al. 1986. Auranofin therapy and quality of life in patients with rheumatoid arthritis: Results of a multicenter trial. *Am. J. Med.* 81:565–78

6. Bravo G, Potvin L. 1991. Estimating the reliability of continuous measures with Cronbach's alpha or the intraclass correlation coefficient: toward the integration of two traditions. *J. Clin. Epidemiol.* 44:381–90

7. Brook RH, Ware JE, Davies-Avery A, Stewart AL, Donald CA, Rogers WH.

1979. Conceptualization and measurement of health for adults in the health insurance study: Vol. 8, Overview. *Rand Corp. R-1987/3 HEW.* Santa Monica, Calif. 55 pp.

8. Brown GW, Birley JLT. 1968. Crises and life changes in the onset of schizophrenia. *J. Health Soc. Behav.* 9:203–14

9. Brown GW, Harris TO, eds. 1989. *Life Events and Illness.* New York: Guilford Press. 496 pp.

10. Bulpitt CJ, Fletcher AE. 1992. Quality of life evaluation of antihypertensive drugs. *PharmacoEconomics* 1:95–102

11. Bulpitt CJ, Fletcher AE. 1992. Measurement of the quality of life in congestive heart failure—influence of drug therapy. *Cardiovasc. Drugs Ther.* 2:419–24

12. Cassileth BR, Lusk EJ, Strouse TB, Miller DS, Brown LL, et al. 1984. Psychosocial status in chronic illness: a comparative analysis of six diagnostic groups. *N. Engl. J. Med.* 311:506–11

13. Choi SC, Stablein DM. 1988. Comparing incomplete paired binomial data under random mechanisms. *Stat. Med.* 7:929–39

14. Chow SC, Ki F. 1994. On statistical

characteristics of quality of life assessment. *J. Biopharmaceut. Stat.* In press

15. Cohen JC. 1977. *Statistical Power Analysis for the Behavioral Sciences*, pp. 24–27. New York: Academic. 474 pp.

16. Cronbach LJ. 1951. Coefficient and alpha and the internal structure of tests. *Psychometrika* 16:297–334

17. Croog SH, Levine S, Testa MA, Brown B, Bulpitt CJ, et al. 1986. The effects of antihypertensive therapy on the quality of life. *N. Engl. J. Med.* 314:1657–64

18. Dahlof C, Dimenas E. 1992. General well-being during treatment with different ACE inhibitors: two double-blind placebo-controlled cross-over studies in health volunteers. *Eur. J. Clin. Pharmacol.* 43:375–79

19. de Lame PA, Droussin AM, Thomson M, Verhaest L, Wallace S. 1989. The effects of enalapril on hypertension and quality of life: A large multicenter study in Belgium. *Acta Cardiol.* 44(4): 289–302

20. Dempster AP, Laird NM, Rubin DB. 1977. Maximum likelihood from incomplete data via the EM algorithm. *J. R. Stat. Soc. Ser. B* 39:1–38

21. Deyo RA, Centor RM. 1986. Assessing the responsiveness of functional scales to clinical change: an analogy to diagnostic test performance. *J. Chronic Dis.* 39:897–906

22. Deyo RA, Diehr P, Patrick DL. 1991. Reproducibility and responsiveness of health status measures: Statistics and strategies for evaluation. *Controlled Clin. Trials* 12:142s–58s

23. Dwyer JH, Feinleib M, Lippert P, Hoffmeister H. 1992. *Statistical Models for Longitudinal Studies of Health.* New York: Oxford Univ. Press. 385 pp.

24. Edelson JT, Weinstein MC, Tosteson ANA, Williams L, Lee TH, Goldman L. 1990. Long-term cost-effectiveness of various initial monotherapies for mild to moderate hypertension. *J. Am. Med. Assoc.* 263:407–13

25. Elstrom D, Quade D, Golden RN. 1990. Statistical analysis of repeated measures in psychiatric research. *Arch. Gen. Psychiatry* 47:770–72

26. Fischl MA, Richman DD, Hansen N, Collier AC, Carey JT, et al. 1990. The safety and efficacy of zidovudine (ZDV) in the treatment of subjects with mildly symptomatic human immunodeficiency virus type 1 (HIV) infection; a double-blind, placebo-controlled trial. *Ann. Intern. Med.* 112: 727–37

27. Follman D, Wittes J, Cutler J. 1992 Rejoinder. *Stat. Med.* 11:453–54

28. Follman D, Wittes J, Cutler J. 1992. The use of subjective rankings in clinical trials with an application to cardiovascular disease. *Stat. Med.* 11: 427–37

29. Freedberg KA, Tosteson ANA, Cohen CJ, Cotton DJ. 1991. Primary prophylaxis for *Pneumocystis carinii* pneumonia in HIV-infected people with CD4 counts below $200/mm^3$: a cost-effectiveness analysis. *J. Acquir. Immune Defic. Syndr.* 4:521–31

30. Freund DA, Dittus RA. 1992. Principles of pharmacoeconomic analysis of drug therapy. *PharmacoEconomics* 1: 20–32

31. Gabriel KR. 1968. Simultaneous test procedures in multivariate analysis of variance. *Biometrika* 55:489–504

32. Gelber RD, Goldhirsch A. 1986. A new endpoint for the assessment of adjuvant therapy in post menopausal women with operable breast cancer. *J. Clin. Oncol.* 4:1772–79

33. Gelber RD, Goldhirsch A. 1992. Comment. *Stat. Med.* 11:439–41

34. Gelber RD, Lenderking WR, Cotton DJ, Cole BF, Fischl MA, et al. 1992. Quality-of-life evaluation in clinical trials of zidovudine therapy for patients with mildly symptomatic human immunodeficiency virus type 1 (HIV) infection. *Ann. Intern. Med.* 116:961–66

35. Glasziou PP, Simes RJ, Gelber RD. 1990. Quality adjusted survival analysis. *Stat. Med.* 9:1259–76

36. Goldhirsch A, Gelber RD, Simes RJ, Glasziou P, Coates AS. 1989. Costs and benefits of adjuvant therapy in breast cancer: a quality-adjusted survival analysis. *J. Clin. Oncol.* 7:36–44

37. Guyatt G, Walter S, Norman G. 1987. Measuring change over time: Assessing the usefulness of evaluative instruments. *J. Chron. Dis* 40:171–78

38. Guyatt GH, Deyo RA, Charlson M, Levine MN, Mitchell A. 1989. Responsiveness and validity in health status measurement: A clarification. *J. Clin. Epidemiol.* 42:403–8

39. Guyatt G, Feeny DF, Patrick D. 1991. Issues in quality-of life measurement in clinical trials. *Controlled Clin. Trials* 12:81S–90S

40. Guyatt GH, Feeny DH, Patrick DL. 1993. Measuring Health-related Quality of Life. *Ann. Intern. Med.* 118:622–29

41. Guyatt GH, Veldhuyzen Van Zanten

SJO, Feeny DH, Patrick DL. 1989 Measuring quality of life in clinical trials: a taxonomy and review. *Can. Med. Assoc. J.* 140:1441–48

42. Hand DJ, Taylor CC. 1991. *Multivariate Analysis of Variance and Repeated Measures: A Practical Approach for Behavioural Scientists,* pp 81–93. New York: Chapman & Hall. 262 pp.

43. Haney CA. 1980. Life events as precursors of coronary heart disease. *Soc. Sci. Med.* 14A:119–26

44. Harris T, Brown GW, Bifulco A. 1986. Loss of parent in childhood and adult psychiatric disorder: the role of lack of adequate parental care. *Psychol. Med.* 16:641–59

45. Harville DA. 1977. Maximum likelihood approaches to variance component estimation and to related problems. *J. Am. Stat. Assoc.* 72:320–40

46. Heyting A, Tolboom JTBM, Essers JGA. 1992. Statistical handling of drop-outs in longitudinal clinical trials. *Stat. Med.* 11:2043–61

47. Hollenberg NK, Testa MA, Williams. 1991. Quality of life as a therapeutic endpoint: An analysis of therapeutic trials in hypertension. *Drug Saf.* 6:83–93

48. Holmes TH, Rahe RH. 1967. The social readjustment rating scale. *J. Psychosom. Res.* 11:213–18

49. Jachuck SJ, Brierley H, Jachuck S, Willcox PM. 1982. The effects of hypotensive drugs on the quality of life. *J. Coll. Gen. Pract. (Occas. Pap.)* 32:103–5

50. Johnson JR, Temple R. 1985. Food and Drug Administration requirements for approval of new anticancer drugs. *Cancer Treat. Res.* 69:1155–57

51. Joreskog KG. 1979. Statistical estimation of structural models in longitudinal-developmental investigations. In *Longitudinal Research in the Study of Behavior and Development,* ed. JR Nesselroade, PB Bates, 11:303–74. New York/London: Academic. 386 pp.

52. Karnofsky DA, Burchenal JH. 1949. The clinical evaluation of chemotherapeutic agents in cancer. In *Evaluation of Chemotherapeutic Agents,* ed. CM MacLeod, pp 201–5. New York: Columbia Univ. Press

53. Kiecolt-Glaser JK, Garner W, Speicher C, Penn GM, Holliday J, Glaser R. 1984. Psychosocial modifiers of immunocompetence in medical students. *Psychosom. Med.* 46:7–14

54. Kirshner B, Guyatt G. 1985, A methodologic framework for assessing health indices. *J. Chron. Dis.* 38:27–36

55. Laird N. 1982. Computation of variance components using the EM algorithm. *J. Stat. Comput. Simulat.* 14:295–303

56. Laird NM, Ware JH. 1982. Random-effects models for longitudinal data. *Biometrics* 38:963–74

57. Levine S, Croog S. 1984. What constitutes quality of life? A conceptualization of the dimensions of life quality in healthy populations and patients with cardiovascular disease. In *Assessment of Quality of Life in Clinical Trials of Cardiovascular Therapies,* ed. N Wenger, ME Mattson, CD Furberg, J Elinson, pp. 46–58. New York: Le Jacq Publ. Inc. 374 pp.

58. Liang MH, Larson MG, Cullen KE, Schwartz JA. 1985. Comparative measurement efficiency and sensitivity of five health status instruments for arthritis research. *Arth. Rheum.* 28:542–47

59. Liang MH, Katz JN. 1992. Measurement of outcome in rheumatoid arthritis. *Bailliere's Clin. Rheumatol.* 6:23–37

60. Locke SE, Kraus L, Lesserman J, Hurst MW, Heisel JOS, Williams RM. 1984. Life change stress, psychiatric symptoms, and natural killer cell activity. *Psychosom. Med.* 46:441–53

61. Longini IM, Byers RH, Hessol NA, Tan WY. 1991. Estimating the state-specific numbers of HIV infection using a Markov model and back calculation. *Stat. Med.* 11:831–43

62. Lord FM, Novic MR. 1968. Basic equations of the classical model for tests of fixed length. See Ref. 63, pp. 61–63

63. Lord FM, Novick MR. 1968. *Statistical Theories of Mental Test Scores.* Reading, MA: Addison-Wesley. 568 pp.

64. McMillem C, Fiegl P, Metch B, Hayden KA, Meyskens FL Crowley J. 1989. Quality of life end points in cancer clinical trials: review and recommendations. *J. Natl. Cancer Inst.* 81:485–95

65. O'Brien, P. 1984. Procedures for comparing samples with multiple endpoints. *Biometrics* 40:1079–87

66. O'Brien P. 1992. Comment. *Stat. Med.* 11:447–49

67. Olshewski M, Schumacher M. 1990. Statistical analysis of quality of life data in cancer clinical trials. *Stat. Med.* 9:749–63

68. Patrick DL, Bush JW, Chen MM. 1973. Toward an operational definition of health. *J. Health Soc. Behav.* 14:6–23

69. Patrick DL, Erickson P. 1988. What constitutes quality of life? Concepts and dimensions. *Qual. Life Cardiovasc. Care* 4(3):103–27

70. Patrick DL, Deyo RA. 1989. Generic and disease-specific measures in assessing health status and quality of life. *Med. Care* 27:S217–32

71. Patrick DL, Bergner M. 1990. Measurement of health status in the 1990s. *Annu. Rev. Public Health* 11:165–83

72. Patrick D, Erickson P. 1992. *Health Status and Health Policy. Quality of Life in Health Care Evaluation and Resource Allocation.* New York: Oxford Univ. Press. 478 pp.

73. Pliskin JS. 1974. *The management of patients with end-stage renal failure: A decision theoretic approach.* PhD thesis. Harvard Univ. Cambridge

74. Pocock SJ. 1991. A perspective on the role of quality-of-life assessment in clinical trials. *Controlled Clin. Trials* 12:257S–65S

75. Pocock SJ, Geller NL, Tsiatis A. 1991. The analysis of multiple endpoints in clinical trials. *Biometrics* 43:487–98

76. Press SJ. 1972. *Applied Multivariate Analysis.* New York: Holt, Rinehart & Winston

77. Remington RD. 1992. Comment. *Stat. Med.* 11:451–52

78. Spitzer BH. 1987. State of science 1986: Quality of life and functional status as target variables for research. *J. Chronic Dis.* 40(6):465–71

79. Steiner SS, Friedhoff AJ, Wilson BL, Wecker JR, Santo JP. 1990. Antihypertensive therapy and quality of life: a comparison of atenolol, captopril, enalapril and propranolol. *J. Hum. Hyperten.* 4:217–25

80. Streiner DL, Norman GR. 1992. *Health Measurement Scales.* New York: Oxford Univ. Press. 175 pp.

81. Tarlov AR. 1992. Outcomes assessment and quality of life in patients with human immunodeficiency virus infection. *Ann. Intern. Med.* 116:166–67

82. Testa MA. 1993. Parallel perspectives on quality of life during antihypertensive therapy: impact of responder, survey environment and questionnaire structure. *J. Cardiovasc. Pharmacol.* 21(Supple.2):S18–25

83. Testa MA, Hollenberg NK, Anderson RB, Williams GH. 1991. Assessment of quality of life by patient and spouse during antihypertensive therapy with atenolol and nifedipine gastrointestinal therapeutic system. *Am. J. Hypertens.* 4:363–73

84. Testa MA, Lenderking W. 1992. The role of quality-of-life and cost-effectiveness research in therapeutics and drug development. *PharmacoEconomics* 2:107–17

85. Testa MA, Anderson RB, Nackley JF, Hollenberg NK, Quality-of-Life Hypertension Study Group. 1993. Quality of life and antihypertensive therapy in men. A comparison of captopril and enalapril. *N. Engl. J. Med.* 328:907–13

86. Theorell T, Lind E, Floderus B. 1975. The relationship of disturbing life changes and emotions to the early development of myocardial infarction and other serious illnesses. *Int. J. Epidemiol.* 4:281–93

87. Thier SO. 1992. Forces motivating the use of health status assessment measures in clinical settings and related clinical research. *Med. Care* 30:MS15–22

88. Tuley MR, Mulrow CD, McMahon CA. 1991. Estimating and testing an index of responsiveness and the relationship of the index to power. *J. Clin. Epidemiol.* 44:417–21

89. Turner RR. 1990. Rehabilitation. In *Quality of Life Assessments in Clinical Trials,* ed. B Spilker, pp. 247–67. New York: Raven

90. Veit CT, Ware JE. 1983. The structure of psychological distress and well-being in general populations. *J. Consult. Clin. Psychol.* 51:730–42

91. Wachtel T, Piette J, Mor V, Stein M, Fleishman, Carpenter C. 1992. Quality of life in persons with human immunodeficiency virus infection: Measurement by the medical outcomes study instrument. *Ann. Intern Med.* 116:129–37

92. Waller DG. 1991. Effect of drug treatment on quality of life in mild to moderate heart failure. *Drug Saf.* 6(4):241–46

93. Ware JE. 1984. Conceptualizing disease impact and treatment outcomes. *Cancer* 53(10):2316–23

94. Warren S, Greenhill S, Warren KG. 1982. Emotional stress and the development of multiple sclerosis: Case-control evidence of a relationship. *J. Chron. Dis.* 35:821–31

95. Waternaux C, Ware J. 1992. Unconditional linear models for analysis of longitudinal data. See Ref. 23, pp. 99–114

96. Wei LJ, Johnson WE. 1985. Combining dependent tests with incomplete repeated measurements. *Biometrika* 72:359–64

97. Weinstein MC. 1981. Economic as-

sessment of medical practices and technologies. *Med. Decis. Mak.* 4:309–30

98. Weinstein MC, Pliskin JS, Stason WB. 1977. Coronary artery bypass surgery, decision and policy analysis. In *Costs, Risks and Benefits of Surgery,* ed. JP Bunker, BA Barnes, F Mosteller, pp. 342–371. New York: Oxford Univ. Press. 401 pp.

99. Weinstein MC, Stason WB. 1985. Cost-effectiveness of interventions to prevent or treat coronary heart disease. *Annu. Rev. Public Health* 6:41–63

100. Weinstein MC, Stason WB. 1988. Foundations of cost-effectiveness analysis for health and medical practices. *N. Engl. J. Med.* 296:716–21

101. Williams AW, Ware JE, Donald CA. 1981. A model of mental health, life events and social supports applicable to general populations. *J. Health Soc. Behav.* 22:324–36

102. Zwinderman AH. 1990. The measures of change of quality of life in clinical trials. *Stat. Med.* 9:931–42

Annu. Rev. Public Health. 1994. 15:561–79

TECHNOLOGY ASSESSMENT AND PUBLIC HEALTH[1] [2]

Elaine J. Power, Sean R. Tunis, and Judith L. Wagner

Office of Technology Assessment, U.S. Congress, Washington, DC 20510

KEY WORDS: technology assessment, medical technology, cost, effectiveness, guidelines

INTRODUCTION

In the 17 years since the publication of the first report about medical technology assessment (111), the idea that health care technologies merit scrutiny has become widely accepted. This is especially true in the public health arena, where decisions about technologies such as HIV-screening and tuberculosis treatment are often controversial, occasionally agonizing, and always have a broad array of potential repercussions on the well-being of society.

That health technology assessment can be valuable is no longer seriously questioned. The concern now is that technology assessment and related techniques are being cast as one of the "magic bullets" for certain ills of the American health care system. These techniques are in danger of being viewed as either a painless solution to the country's ever-increasing health care costs, or the mechanism by which we can make painful choices impartially and apart from the messy arena of politics.

THE CONCEPT OF HEALTH TECHNOLOGY ASSESSMENT

Technology assessment has its roots in the political and social debates of the 1960s, when the environmental and social consequences of technologies

---

[1] The US Government has the right to retain a nonexclusive, royalty-free license in and to any copyright covering this paper.

[2] The opinions expressed in this article are those of the authors and do not necessarily reflect the views of the Office of Technology Assessment.

such as the pesticide DDT and the supersonic transport plane were prime topics for political discussion at every level. Early uses of the term specifically required that technology assessments should identify indirect effects of technological innovations and assess these effects for the purpose of improving decisions regarding the social use of the technology (110). The term "technology" was clearly intended to be broadly defined; an early report to identify candidate technologies for assessment included such items as acupuncture for pain relief, prenatal tests for fetal deformities, and clinics for compulsory heroin treatment (83).

Technology assessment has gained considerable acceptance in the health field over the past decade, but its acceptance has come at a cost to its identity (39). The phrase "technology assessment" is now sometimes applied to such diverse activities as hospital purchasing decisions (69), randomized clinical trials (22), and cost-effectiveness evaluations of public health programs (50).

To bring some order to the current state of confusion, in this paper we define "health care technology" to comprise drugs, devices, procedures, and the organizational and supportive systems within which health care is delivered. The inclusion of "organizational and supportive systems" is an acknowledgment that the implications of a health intervention depend on its context, and that clusters of individual technologies organized in a specific way can themselves become a more complex technology—e.g. an intensive care unit.

"Health technology assessment," as used here, is a structured analysis of a health care technology that is performed to provide input to a policy decision. Requisite components of a health technology assessment include the collection or generation of information about a technology, a synthesis and critical analysis of that information in the context of the policy decision to be made, and presentation of the result in language relevant to the decision.

Medicare coverage of immunizations and screening tests exemplifies the utility of technology assessments for policy decisions. The original Medicare statute excluded from coverage all primary preventive services. Over time, however, vaccines for pneumococcal pneumonia, influenza, and hepatitis B; screening mammography; and Pap smears have all been shown to be beneficial to elderly persons for relatively low cost (82a, 113, 115, 118, 120). Each has been added to the Medicare statute as a covered benefit, and in at least some cases (e.g. pneumococcal vaccine coverage), the addition was directly influenced by the technology assessment (30). Most recently, Medicare began covering therapeutic shoes for diabetic patients upon completion of a study of the costs and effects of this preventive technology (125a).

Although as originally conceived, technology assessments were to be aids to public policymakers (20), they are used by many private-sector decision-makers as well. The perspective and breadth of a given technology assessment is determined by the policy decision to be made. If the decision relates to insurance coverage, for example, the technology assessment might address issues of effectiveness, utilization, costs to the insurer, effects on the costs and use of other services, and potential for legal liability in the case of noncoverage. The assessment thus might draw upon such tools as randomized clinical trials, epidemiological studies of disease prevalence, cost studies, and legal analyses. In contrast, an assessment of the same technology as part of a national research and development policy might place much more emphasis on factors that influenced the technology's development, and on the broad social consequences of its application.

CONTRIBUTIONS OF HEALTH TECHNOLOGY ASSESSMENT

Perhaps the single most important contribution of health technology assessment as a field has been its emphasis on the need for valid scientific evidence to improve medical and public health decisions.

Early reports on the assessment of medical technologies acknowledged that data to answer even the most fundamental questions about a technology—is it safe, and does it work?—were often lacking (51, 78, 111, 116, 117). Although all new drugs must meet Food and Drug Administration (FDA) standards for safety and efficacy before being marketed (21 U.S. Code 355 (i)), drugs are widely prescribed for medical conditions other than those for which the FDA has examined efficacy data (for example, see ref. 109). Only the most novel medical devices undergo similar levels of FDA scrutiny, and medical procedures and practices undergo no prospective regulatory scrutiny at all (37, 97). Consequently, most technology assessments are forced to confront either an absence of valid and reliable data on the effectiveness of the technology in question, or a morass of conflicting and often suspect data.

The scarcity of data on health effects of many technologies has stimulated two different kinds of efforts. The first has been a continued emphasis on methods that result in reliable and valid data, particularly randomized clinical trials. Although for ethical, logistical, and financial reasons such trials are not always possible, they are nonetheless well-established as the method of choice where feasible (9, 16a, 117). Multiple examples exist of new, high-cost technologies becoming widely disseminated after introduction, without clear evidence of their clinical value or consideration of their broader implications (for example, see refs. 49, 53, 93, 112). And many new interventions that were initially met with enthusiasm later have been shown, through careful studies, to be worthless or even dangerous (31).

A second major contribution has been to emphasize the need not just for information on the efficacy of a technology in a specific population, but also on the overall effectiveness of that technology across the breadth of settings and patients to which it is applied. That many medical technologies are applied without knowledge of or agreement on their actual effectiveness is apparent from the repeated documentation of great variation across geographic areas in the rate of procedures such as hysterectomy (15, 90, 95, 136); and from the finding that a substantial number of major procedures, such as coronary artery bypass surgery, are performed without appropriate clinical indications (8, 139, 140).

The importance of good evidence on effectiveness for appropriate decision-making is well-illustrated by the recent interest and debate on the role of vitamins in preventing birth defects. Case-control studies performed in the 1980s found suggestive evidence that the ingestion of folic acid supplements before and during pregnancy was associated with a lower incidence of neural tube defects (75, 82). But some studies showed ambiguous rather than positive effects (74), and researchers acknowledged that other factors, such as healthier overall diets of women taking folic acid supplements, might explain the apparent relationship (82). A randomized trial of high-risk women in the United Kingdom provided evidence of a benefit of supplementation in this group (80). Not until the results of a randomized controlled trial of average-risk women and a careful case-control study became available in 1992 (19, 137), however, was the evidence sufficiently convincing to prompt an unambiguous US recommendation that all women should increase their periconceptional intake of folic acid (77). It has been estimated that full implementation of this recommendation could reduce by 60% the number of cases of spina bifida and anencephaly in the United States (85).

Efforts to assess medical technologies have also increased attention to the measurement of costs and cost-effectiveness (35, 114, 132). Although it is not clear that technology assessment can lay direct claim to the greater willingness to consider cost-effectiveness in decision-making that seems to be developing, the focus that technology assessment has placed on valid cost and cost-effectiveness measurement has almost certainly been an enabling factor.

Cost-effectiveness analysis has been a particularly useful tool for assessing preventive interventions in which a prime question is not only whether to screen, but whom, how, when, and how often. Pap smear screening for cervical cancer, for example, is well-established as an effective clinical preventive service (129). The optimal frequency of screening women of different age groups, however, has been a source of disagreement among screening recommendations (32, 102, 129, 133). This disagreement confounds decision-making not only by physicians and patients but by insurers, managed care providers, and public health screening programs.

Furthermore, the policy implications of different screening schedules are considerable. Eddy, in a cost-effectiveness study of Pap smear screening, estimated that routine screening every four years from the age of 20 through 75 would cost about $10,000 per year of life added to the population of women entering the program. Screening more frequently would add more years of life, but at a very high cost—over $1 million for each year of life added to the population of women in an annual screening proram (26). Similarly, Muller and colleagues examined the cost-effectiveness of Pap smear screening in elderly women and calculated that the incremental costs (compared with a five-year screening schedule) of screening every three years or annually were $6,000 and $40,000 per life-year saved, respectively (82a). Moreover, screening high-risk women (e.g. those who smoke or who have a history of frequent sexual encounters) was especially cost-effective; even annual screening would have an estimated incremental cost per life-year saved of only $6,500 for this group. This finding would justify significant resources aimed at increasing the proportion of high-risk elderly women who receive screening (121).

The field of medical technology assessment can also take credit for highlighting the fact that the effects of existing as well as new technologies deserve scrutiny. For example, of the first ten case studies of individual medical technologies published by the congressional Office of Technology Assessment (in 1981–82), at least four were studies of well-established technologies that had been in use for years (cervical cancer screening, kidney dialysis, colon cancer screening, and neonatal intensive care) (119). The need to reassess technologies that have been previously examined, as new information becomes available, also has been stressed (6, 51).

In many ways, technology assessment applied to public health decisions is closer to the original vision of technology assessment as a public policy tool than almost any other application currently in use. In the public health context, technology assessment demonstrates not only the need to focus on good information but also the importance of economics, law, and ethics to the formation of good public health policies. Any consideration of a policy to encourage the development of single-use needles as an intervention to combat AIDS, for example, must consider not only the effectiveness of such a program in reducing the incidence of HIV infection, and the feasibility and economic costs of carrying out such a program, but the ethical, legal, and highly political issues involved (124). Similarly, cost-effectiveness analyses are important in considering policy decisions for compulsory and supervised administration of antituberculosis drugs, but issues of personal autonomy and the legal rights of society to compel treatment for the public good are equally important (40, 108).

Insufficient breadth of an assessment can result in suboptimal policies. The National Heart, Lung, and Blood Institute's 1988 recommendations regarding cholesterol screening, for instance, were behind a forceful public health initiative aimed at convincing all American adults to undergo repeated cholesterol screening (126), yet they did not consider the social and economic consequences of this activity. A later assessment of the effects of following NHLBI's recommendation for persons over age 65 found that full compliance would increase annual health care expenditures by between $2.9 billion and $14.3 billion (in 1988 dollars), with no demonstrable benefit to the health of this population (122).

ENHANCING THE INFORMATION BASE

Current efforts to improve the information available on health care technologies focus particularly on new and improved methods of evaluating the effectiveness of technologies already in use. For some technologies, clinical trials have previously been conducted, and current efforts focus on how to strengthen their results and make them more meaningful to the general population of patients and health care settings. For many other technologies, attempting to improve available information means trying to establish whether they work at all, and how effective they are compared with alternative technologies also in use.

NHLBI's cholesterol screening recommendations, for example, relied on data primarily from nonelderly men, raising questions about their generalizability to women and elderly populations (36, 138). In addition, other studies raised questions about whether screening and treatment for this condition actually reduced overall mortality, as opposed to just heart disease-related mortality (81).

These kinds of questions have led to a search for new techniques, or new ways of applying existing techniques, for evaluating effectiveness. Some techniques are new ways of evaluating health outcomes; others are new methods of comparing technologies, or advances in using existing information to make new or more powerful statements. Examples of these new developments are described below.

Improving the measurement of health outcomes   An important theme in health research over the past five years has been the growing emphasis on measuring outcomes that most matter to patients (e.g. protecting vision), rather than only clinical surrogate markers (e.g. reducing intraocular pressure). Research in the areas of both disease-specific and more general measures of self-assessed health has flourished (for example, see ref. 64). Uses of such information include better ways by which to assess a patient's improvement after treatment; better outcome measures with which to compare health care interventions; and better measures of the state of the public's health. Particular attention has been given recently to the use of brief, generic measures of health status that are relatively general and simple to perform (e.g. the SF-36, a 36-item questionnaire) (87).

New uses of randomized trials   Confidence in existing clinical trial results is often limited by small sample sizes and difficulty generalizing from the highly selective trial population to the population at large. One successful technique to overcome some of these limitations is the large simple randomized trial. These trials enroll many thousands of patients, so patient comorbidities "wash out" in the randomization process, avoiding the need for artificially strict patient selection. Additionally, the trials are very simple in design and require data collection on only one or two significant endpoints, making it practical for busy physicians in community settings to participate (143). These characteristics enable health care interventions to be tested and compared in ordinary settings while keeping the costs of such a large trial relatively low. The main methodological limitation of such trials is that they require the use of a very few endpoints, such as mortality, that can be easily and reliably measured. Despite their advantages for a number of uses, and their track record in the area of treatments for heart disease (42, 55, 56), they have rarely been used in the United States.

A second intriguing application of the randomized trial design is the "firms" trial, in which patients are randomized among entire clinics or other institutional settings (14, 79, 84, 127). This application permits the investigators to test not only changes in specific therapies, but changes in the processes through which care is delivered. Diverse applications to date have included research on colorectal screening performed by nurse clinicians (13), counseling patients to quit smoking (18), and the effects of computerized reminders to clinicians on practice change (47, 63).

Enhanced use of existing databases   In the 1970s, Wennberg and others pioneered the use of insurance claims and other administrative data to document and explore great variations in medical practice over relatively small geographic areas (94, 136). Building upon this work, researchers have used information on practice variation documented in administrative data to generate discussions among physicians regarding the most appropriate practices (59), to identify discrepancies in the rates with which different groups (i.e. women or minorities) receive treatments (5), and to identify areas where actual outcomes are substantially worse than physicians may perceive them to be (57). The potential to use administrative databases to compare the effectiveness of different technologies directly is suspect, since such databases contain limited information and cannot be stripped of unknown biases (e.g. in patient selection for interventions). Thus, most intriguing findings will need to be confirmed with more valid prospective methods (105), but support for such trials may be difficult to find (M. Barry, *Chronology of the American Urological Association's Benign Prostatic Hyperplasia Treatment Outcomes Study Proposal,* unpublished document, 1992).

Several efforts are ongoing to combine and augment existing databases to produce much richer sources of information. The Health Care Financing Administration and the National Cancer Institute, for example, are collaborating to merge Medicare claims data with cancer registry data (E Sondick, personal communication). These enhanced databases might find a variety of epidemiological uses.

Synthesizing information through meta-analysis   The technique of meta-analysis—a structured, quantitative review—has existed formally since the 1970s (38) and has been widely applied to medical and public health topics (23, 27, 98, 106). With the broader use of meta-analysis has come increased recognition that making explicit the criteria for selecting and evaluating studies increases the value of any literature review. Equally important, meta-analysis involves the statistical pooling of study results to increase their power, enabling a degree of certainty regarding the conclusions that is greater than that from the individual studies, particularly when those studies were too small to detect results reliably.

Although there is considerable controversy about the kinds of situations in which statistical pooling of results is valid (for example, see refs. 11, 23), the sheer volume of studies on many topics makes meta-analysis, or at least a highly structured review, a critical component of informed decision-making for many health care topics (2, 130). Published meta-analyses have shown, for example, that vitamin A supplements decrease child mortality from measles (29), that the case-management strategy proposed by the World Health Organization can reduce early-childhood mortality from pneumonia (99), and that there is a dose-response relationship between alcohol intake and risk of breast cancer (67).[3]

Integrating information on costs and outcomes   Cost-effectiveness analysis is a structured, comparative evaluation of the relative costs and effects

---

[3]The meta-analysis of alcohol intake and breast cancer could not determine whether this relationship is causal, but more recent evidence continues to support the relationship (M. Longnecker, personal communication.)

of two or more health care interventions (24, 114). Costs are measured in dollars; effects are typically measured in units of mortality (e.g. number of deaths averted), morbidity (e.g. cases of cancer detected), or a weighted integration of both, such as quality-adjusted life years. In some cases the results of a cost-effectiveness analysis are unambiguous; one alternative is both cheaper and more effective than the other (e.g. measles vaccination vs no vaccination) (96). More commonly, however, one technology is more effective but also more costly than the other, and a conclusion regarding the relative cost-effectiveness of the competing technologies requires value judgments on whether the additional costs are worthwhile.

Comparing the results of different cost-effectiveness analyses also requires close attention to the methods and assumptions behind them, which can radically affect the cost-effectiveness ratios reported (71, 114, 134). Recent research into the measurement of patient preferences, for example, has been accompanied by a proliferation of ways in which quality-adjusted life years are measured (43, 58, 107). Also, cost-effectiveness methods do not themselves address such vital social issues as distributive justice.

INCORPORATING EVIDENCE INTO CLINICAL PRACTICE

A major question that remains is whether technology assessments, or even more specific evidence, such as the findings of clinical trials, ultimately affect the health care that people receive.

In fact, substantial information suggests that in the area of clinical medicine, as well as in public health practice, there are major gaps between existing evidence and useful practice. For example, use of intravenous lidocaine, which has not been shown to have any benefit following heart attack, continues to be recommended by experts as standard therapy, while post-attack clot-dissolving therapy was not mentioned in most major textbooks for many years after its effects on mortality had been clearly documented (2). Similarly, use of cortico-steroids in the management of lung complications related to premature birth is inconsistent, in spite of substantial evidence accumulated over many years demonstrating the effectiveness of this therapy (68).

As the lack of evidence for many common clinical practices has become increasingly apparent, policymakers have sought to improve the efficiency of the health system. One strategy gaining considerable attention over the past several years is the development of consensus statements or practice guidelines (3, 60, 142). The Agency for Health Care Policy and Research is sponsoring guideline development that seeks to synthesize available studies and expert opinion on selected technologies or conditions, to derive evidence-based strategies that will change practices accordingly (54).

Changes in provider behavior traceable to dissemination of practice guidelines have, however, been difficult to document (41, 66, 76). Lomas and colleagues studied the effects of a national guideline on Caesarean section which, if fully implemented, would have decreased rates of this procedure. Despite widespread knowledge of and agreement with the guideline, clinical practices were unaffected (65). Similarly, NIH guidelines developed through consensus conferences have generally not been associated with changes in clinical practice (62). Even intensive implementation efforts, involving direct contact with physicians, frequent reinforcement, or specific recommendations on individual patient charts, have in many cases resulted in few changes in practice (21, 45, 89).

Thus in health care, as in other fields, simple dissemination of information is often not enough to effect change. Rather, a large array of forces, policies, and pressures all blend to determine what practices are followed, and what factors are likely to change them (28, 33).

Even recommendations based on compelling evidence from clinical trials do not always prevail in the face of conflicting forces. For example, the decision to perform Caesarean section may not be affected by a simple recommendation that generally favors vaginal delivery after a previous C-section, if the primary reason for doing a C-section is fear of catastrophic injury to newborns, and consequent physician exposure to a malpractice suit (65). In addition, the relative convenience of C-section from the physicians' perspective may discourage vaginal deliveries.

While changes in practice are often slow to occur, many new technologies are adopted rapidly despite lack of evidence that they are effective, and often with considerable reason to believe that they are not. A recent case in point is the rapid increase in use of an antigen test to detect prostate cancer. There is as yet no evidence that testing improves outcomes, and a good chance that it results in considerable needless diagnostic testing and therapeutic interventions with high rates of expected complications. The increased use in this test has come after widespread press coverage and a corresponding consumer demand (104). The promotional efforts of parties likely to profit by increased detection and treatment of prostate cancer—such as test manufacturers and urology centers—have probably contributed as well.

The frequent failure of passive educational strategies to affect behavior has sparked a strong interest in identifying more effective approaches to modifying clinical practice. One method with some reported success is "academic detailing", in which effective practices are promoted using the techniques of persuasive communication developed by pharmaceutical companies (100). Researchers have used this technique successfully to modify drug prescribing behavior and the use of blood transfusions by surgeons (4, 101). Several health plans and hospitals have incorporated guidelines into formal quality improvement programs, which involve feedback of practice information to clinicians along with benchmark information derived from guidelines or average practices (12). In use of preventive services, a number of studies have demonstrated significant improvement using computer-generated reminders, suggesting considerable potential for computer applications to strengthen the link between evidence and practice (34, 44, 72).

Methods such as utilization review and the application of financial rewards and penalties have in some situations been potent means of changing practice patterns. Few studies, however, have been able to demonstrate that the quality of care improves under these circumstances (48, 52). One health maintenance organization offers financial premiums to clinicians based on their rates of preventive practices, and has seen increased use of Pap smears, childhood vaccinations, and mammography (S Zatz, personal communication). Such strategies may be particularly useful for preventive services where appropriate clinical strategies are well documented and do not differ widely based on patient circumstances.

APPLICATIONS OF HEALTH TECHNOLOGY ASSESSMENT

Despite examples of technology assessment's contribution to Federal health policymaking, such as the influence of assessments of preventive services on Medicare policy, the Federal government's efforts at health technology assessment have often lacked financial support. The only continuing executive-branch effort at some level of health technology assessment began existence in 1978 as the National Center for Health Care Technology (Public Law 95-623). After the political demise of that organization in 1981, a vestige of it became the Office of Health Technology Assessment in the National Center for Health Services Research. The duties of this small office were reduced to advising the Medicare program regarding the safety and effectiveness of medical technologies being considered for coverage.

The Agency for Health Care Policy and Research (AHCPR), created out of the National Center for Health Services Research in 1989, inherited many of the Center's functions, including the Office of Health Technology Assessment. In addition, AHCPR was charged with undertaking a new initiative aimed at establishing the effectiveness of medical interventions and developing guidelines for practitioners based on evidence of effectiveness. The government's current interest in technology assessment, effectiveness research, and guidelines development is readily apparent from the budget of AHCPR, which rose from $50 million in fiscal year 1990 to $128 million in fiscal year 1993 (128). Some of its activities are geared towards improving the general output of health care (e.g. through promoting guidelines on effective care), while other activities are aimed at helping Medicare and other government programs run more efficiently (e.g. through translating guidelines into review criteria).

In the private sector, health technology assessment activities have largely abandoned the focus on broad social impacts and focused instead on more specific needs. Early efforts were carried out primarily by a few large insurers (e.g. the Blue Cross and Blue Shield Association) and medical societies (e.g. the American Medical Association and the American College of Physicians) to help guide clinical and coverage policies. Lately, however, there has been an explosion of private sector technology assessors, which include a wide variety of managed care providers, university departments, consulting firms, and business and health provider coalitions. Even State governments have created their own dedicated technology assessment bodies, such as Minnesota's Health Technology Advisory Committee. The rapid growth of these activities attests to the increasing importance given to knowledge of the costs and health effects of specific health care technologies in private sector decision-making.

Activity in the private sector is especially interesting in light of the fact that it was opposition by manufacturers and health care providers that helped bring about the death of the National Center for Health Care Technology in 1981 (7, 88). Ten years later, physicians' organizations are actively involved in the guidelines activities of AHCPR (17); the Health Industry Manufacturers' Association has established its own Health Care Technology Institute (46, 91, 92); and a collaborative group of manufacturers, payers, and providers in Minnesota has published a consensus document advocating technology assessment that is being used in State health reform efforts (73; D Haugen, personal communication).

Insurers, hospitals, and managed care providers are now entrenched consumers of technology assessment. The American Hospital Association, for example, issues a periodical, the *Hospital Technology Scanner,* which offers in-depth commentary on new technologies. The Hospital Association of New York State recently produced a detailed manual on how to do and use technology assessments for hospital decision-making (16). Even more recently, the Blue Cross and Blue Shield Association and Kaiser Permanente announced a collaborative technology assessment effort, an undertaking that expands considerably the Association's previous health technology assessment activity.

Technology assessment performed by, or sponsored by, manufacturers has also become a major activity. Pharmaceutical manufacturers, prompted by such activities as consideration of cost in providers' drug formularies, and consideration of cost-effectiveness in drug approvals in other countries (25, 86), are investing in their own cost-effectiveness and quality-of-life studies to market their drugs effectively and affect the decisions of purchasers (B. Luce, personal communication).

Perhaps the most ambitious use of health technology assessment to date has been Oregon's attempt to use cost and effectiveness information as a foundation for creating an entire health benefits program. The state's attempt to rank all primary and acute care services offered under Medicaid according to their importance and effectiveness gained national attention and spawned a furious debate over the ethics of the process (103). The ultimate reliance of Oregon on the opinions and judgments of its appointed commissioners to value services, and the lack of solid data to assist them in making their decisions (125), was a blunt reminder that health technology assessment has limitations.

EXPECTATIONS AND REALITIES

Health technology assessment is a relatively recent technique that fills a very real need for integrated, critical evaluation of technology-related issues important to both public- and private-sector policy decisions. Nevertheless, except when applied to the most straightforward and narrow decision, health technology assessment helps to clarify choices and their consequences, rather than solving problems. It would be unfortunate if disillusionment with technology assessment's inability to be a panacea for cost containment or quality assurance led us to discard its very real contributions.

Some of those contributions are eminently clear. Technology assessment's thirst for reliable, valid information has encouraged investigation of better ways to measure both costs and health effects of medical and public health interventions. The disparity between knowledge of a technology's effectiveness and its diffusion into the health care community has gained increasing attention, and research findings indicating that certain medical procedures are inappropriate or dubious have gained widespread coverage in the popular media (1, 10, 141).

Nonetheless, better information and analyses of health care technologies will not themselves resolve the central dilemma of the American health reform debate: how to extend health care coverage to all citizens without compromising the quality of care or significantly increasing the cost of care experienced by individuals. Although research on the effectiveness of health care interventions can help identify circumstances where those interventions are of very small benefit, it cannot decide for us whether to eliminate them from our care. No amount of effectiveness research will enable us to make vast expansions in the covered population without fiscal or social pain. No amount of technology assessment will enable us to define a unique set of health care benefits that society will greet with unchallenged consensus. Done well, however, these research and assessment activities can ensure that when we must make painful decisions, we make them out of knowledge rather than ignorance.

ACKNOWLEDGMENTS

The authors are grateful to Cheryl Liechty for her invaluable help in preparing this manuscript.

Any *Annual Review* chapter, as well as any article cited in an *Annual Review* chapter, may be obtained through the Annual Reviews Preprints and Reprints service.
1-800-347-8007; 415-259-5017; email: arpr@class.org

Literature Cited

1. Angier N. 1993. Wait-and-see policy backed for prostate. *New York Times.* May 26
2. Antman E, Lau J, Kupelnick B, Mosteller F, Chalmers TC. 1992. A comparison of results of meta-analyses of randomized control trials and recommendations of clinical experts. *J. Am. Med. Assoc.* 268:240–48
3. Audet AM, Greenfield S, Field M. 1990. Medical practice guidelines: current activities and future directions. *Ann. Intern. Med.* 113:709–14
4. Avorn JL, Soumerai SB. 1983. Improving drug therapy decisions through educational outreach: a randomized controlled trial of academically-based "detailing." *N. England J. Med.* 308: 1457–63
5. Ayanian JZ, Udvarhelyi IS, Gatsonis CA, Pashos CL, Epstein AM. 1993. Racial differences in the use of revascularization after coronary angiography. *J. Am. Med. Assoc.* 269: 2642–46
6. Banta H, Thacker S. 1990. The case for reassessment of health care technology. *J. Am. Med. Assoc.* 264:235–40
7. Blumenthal D. 1983. Federal policy toward health care technology: the case of the National Center. *Milbank Mem. Fund Q. Health Soc.* 61:584–613
8. Brook RH, Kamberg, C, Mayer-Oakes A, Beers MH, Raube K, et al. 1990. Appropriateness of acute

medical care for the elderly: an analysis of the literature. *Health Policy* 14:225–42
9. Brown BW. 1984. The randomized clinical trial. *Stat. Med.* 3:307–11
10. Brown D. 1993. Little benefit seen in prostate surgery. *Washington Post,* May 26
11. Bulpitt C. 1988. Meta-analysis. *Lancet* 2:93–94
12. Burns LR, Denton M, Goldfein S, Warrick L, Morentz B, Sales B. 1992. The use of continuous quality improvement methods in the development and dissemination of medical practice guidelines. *Q. Rev. Biol.* 18:434–39
13. Cargill V, Conti M, Neuhauser D, McClish D. 1991. Improving the effectiveness of screening colorectal cancer by involving nurse clinicians. *Med. Care* 29:1–5
14. Cebul R. 1991. Randomized, controlled trials using the metro firm system. *Med. Care* 29:SJ9–18 (Suppl.)
15. Chassin MR, Brook RH, Park RE, Keesey J, Fink A, et al. 1986. Variations in the use of medical and surgical services by the medicare population. *N. England J. Med.* 314:285–90
16. Ciccone KR, Chesnut TJ. 1992. *Medical Technology Assessment: A Model for Decision Making.* Rockville, MD: Hospital Assoc. New York State and Bader & Assoc. 1st ed.
16a. Clark PI, Leaverton PE. 1994. Scientific and ethical issues in the use of

placebo controls in clinical trials. *Annu. Rev. Public Health* 15:19–38

17. Clinton JJ. 1991. From the Agency for Health Care Policy and Research. *J. Am. Med. Assoc.* 265:1508

18. Cohen SJ, Stookey GK, Katz BP, Drook CA, Smith DM. 1989. Encouraging primary care physicians to help smokers quit: a randomized controlled trial. *Ann. Intern. Med.* 110:648–52

19. Czeizel AE, Dudas I. 1992. Prevention of the first occurence of neural-tube defects by periconceptional vitamin supplementation. *N. England J. Med.* 327:1832–35

20. Daddario EQ, quoted in Hetman F. 1973. *Society and the Assessment of Technology,* pp. 54–55. Paris: OECD

21. Davis DA, Thomson MA, Oxman AD, Haynes RB. 1992. Evidence for the effectiveness of CME: a review of 50 randomized controlled trials. *J. Am. Med. Assoc.* 268:1111–17

22. Diamond G, Denton T. 1993. Alternative perspectives on the biased foundations of medical technology assessment. *Ann. Intern. Med.* 118:455–64

23. Dickerson K, Berlin J. 1992. Meta-analysis: state-of-the-science. *Epidemiol. Rev.* 14:154–76

24. Doubilet P, Weinstein MC, McNeil BJ. 1986. Use and misuse of the term 'cost effective' in medicine. *N. England J. Med.* 314:253–56

25. Drummond M. 1992. Basing the prescription drug payment on economic analysis: the case of Australia. *Health Aff.* Winter:191–206

26. Eddy DM. 1990. Screening for cervical cancer. *Ann. Intern. Med.* 113:214–26

27. Eddy DM, Hasselblad V, Shachter R. 1990. An introduction to a Bayesian method for meta-analysis: the confidence profile method. In *Medical Innovation at the Crossroads,* Vol. I: *Modern Methods of Clinical Investigation,* ed. A Gelijns, pp. 101–16. Washington, DC: Natl. Acad. Press

28. Eisenberg JM. 1986. *Doctor's Decisions and the Cost of Medical Care: The Reasons for Doctor's Practice Patterns and Ways to Change Them,* pp. 1–25. Ann Arbor: Health Admin. Press

29. Fawzi W, Chalmers C, Herrera M, Mosteller F. 1993. Vitamin A supplementation and child mortality: a meta-analysis. *J. Am. Med. Assoc.* 269: 898–99

30. Deleted in proof

31. Fineberg HV, Hiatt HH. 1979. Evaluation of medical practices: the case for technology assessment. *N. England J. Med.* 301:1086–91

32. Fink DJ. 1988. Change in American Cancer Society checkup guidelines for detection of cervical cancer. *CA Cancer J. Clin.* 38:127–28

33. Fox RD, Mazmanian PE, Putnam RW, eds. 1989. *Changing and Learning in the Lives of Physicians.* New York: Praeger

34. Frame PS. 1990. Can computerized reminder systems have an impact on preventive services in practice? *J. Gen. Intern. Med.* 5S:S112–15

35. Fuchs V, Garber A. 1990. The new technology assessment. *N. England J. Med.* 323:673–77

36. Garber AM, Wagner JL. 1991. Practice guidelines and cholesterol policy. *Health Aff.* Summer:52–66

37. Gelijns AC. 1989. *Technology Innovation: Comparing Development of Drugs, Devices, and Procedures in Medicine.* Washington, DC: Natl. Acad. Press

38. Glass GV. 1976. Primary, secondary, and meta-analysis of research. *Educ. Res.* 5:3–8

39. Goodman C. 1992. It's time to rethink health care technology assessment. *Int. J. Technol. Assess. Health Care* 8:335–58

40. Gostin M. 1991. Public health powers: the imminence of radical change. *Milbank Mem. Fund Q. Health Soc.* 69(Suppl. 1–2):268–90

41. Grilli R, Apolone G, Marsoni S, Nicolucci A, Zola P, Liberati A. 1991. The impact of patient management guidelines on the care of breast, colorectal, and ovarian cancer in patients in Italy. *Med. Care* 29:50–63

42. Gruppo Italiano por lo Studio della Streptochinasi nell'infarto miocardio (GISSI). 1986. Effectiveness of intravenous thrombolytic treatment in acute myocardial infarction. *Lancet* 1:397–402

43. Guyatt GH, Feeny DH, Patrick DL. 1993. Measuring health-related quality of life. *Ann. Intern. Med.* 118:622–29

44. Harris RP, O'Malley MS, Fletcher SW, Knight BP. 1990. Prompting physicians for preventive procedures: a five year study of manual and computer reminders. *Am. J. Prev. Med.* 6:145–52

45. Headrick LA, Speroff T, Pelecanos HI, Cebul RD. 1992. Efforts to improve compliance with the National Cholesterol Education Program Guidelines. *Arch. Intern. Med.* 152:2490–96

46. Health Policy Altern. Inc. 1993. *Policy Brief: Managed Competition and Other*

Health Reform Proposals: An Overview. Health Care Technol. Inst., Alexandria, Va.

47. Hershey CO, Goldberg HI, Cohen DI. 1988. The effect of computerized feedback coupled with a newsletter upon outpatient prescribing charges. *Med. Care* 26:88–93

48. Hillman AL, Pauly MV, Kerstein JJ. 1989. How do financial incentives affect physicians' clinical decisions and the financial performance of health maintenance organizations? *N. England J. Med.* 321:86–92

49. Hillman AL, Schwartz JS. 1985. The adoption of CT and MRI in the United States. *Med. Care* 23:1283–94

50. Hishashige A. 1992. Technology assessment of periodic health examinations for school children in Japan. *Int. J. Technol. Assess. Health Care* 8:219–33

51. Inst. Med. 1985. *Assessing Medical Technologies.* Washington, DC: Natl. Acad. Press

52. Inst. Med. 1989. *Controlling Costs and Changing Patient Care: The Role of Utilization Management.* Washington, DC: Natl. Acad. Press

53. Inst. Med. 1989. *Medical Professional Liability and the Delivery of Obstetrical Care,* Vol. 2. Washington, DC: Natl. Acad. Press

54. Inst. Med. 1992. *Guidelines for Clinical Practice: From Development to Use.* Washington, DC: Natl. Acad. Press

55. ISIS-1 Collaborative Group. 1986. Randomised trial of intravenous atenolol among 16,027 cases of suspected acute myocardial infarction: ISIS-1. *Lancet* 2:57–66

56. ISIS-2 Collaborative Group. 1988. Randomised trial of intravenous streptokinase, oral aspirin, both, or neither among 17,187 cases of suspected acute myocardial infarction: ISIS-2 *Lancet* 2:349–60

57. Javitt JC, Tielsch JM, Canner JK, Kolb MM, Sommer A, Steinberg, EP. 1992. National outcomes of cataract extraction: increased risk of retinal complications associated with Nd:YAG laser capsulotomy. *Opthamology* 99:1487–98

58. Kamlet MS, Carnegie Mellon Univ., Pittsburgh, PA. 1992. *A Framework for Cost-utility Analysis of Government Health Care Programs.* Prepared Off. Dis. Prev. Health Promot., Public Health Serv., US DHHS, in coop. Found. Health Serv. Res., Washington, DC

59. Keller RB, Soule DN, Wennberg JE, Hanley DF. 1990. Dealing with geographic variations in hospital use: the experience of the Maine Medical Assessment Foundation's Orthopaedic Study Group. *J. Bone Joint Surg.* 72A:1286–93

60. Kelly JT, Swartwout JE. 1990. Development of practice parameters by physician organizations. *Q. Rev. Biol.* 2:54–57

61. Kiefer DM. 1973. Technology assessment: a layman's overview. In *Technology Assessment in a Dynamic Environment,* ed. MJ Cetron, B Bartocha, pp. 3–34. New York: Gordon & Breach

62. Kosecoff J, Kanouse DE, Rogers WH, McCloskey L, Winslow CM, Brook RH. 1987. Effects of the National Institutes of Health Consensus Development Program on physician practice. *J. Am. Med. Assoc.* 258:2708–13

63. Landefeld C, Rosenthal G, Aucott J, Whalen CC, Wright JT, et al. 1992. The Cleveland Veterans Affairs Medical Center Firm System. *Int. J. Technol. Assess. Health Care* 8:325–34

64. Lohr KN. 1992. Applications in health status measures in clinical practice. Overview of Third Conference on Advances in Health Status Assessment. *Med. Care* 30:MS1–14

65. Lomas J, Anderson GM, Domnick-Pierre K, Vayda E, Enkin MW, Hannah WJ. 1989. Do practice guidelines guide practice? The effect of a consensus statement on the practice of physicians. *N. England J. Med.* 321:1306–11

66. Lomas J, Haynes RB. 1988. A taxonomy and critical review of tested strategies for the application of clinical practice recommendations: from "official" to "individual" clinical policy. *Am. J. Prev. Med.* 4:77–94

67. Longnecker MP, Berlin JA, Orza MJ, Chalmers TC. 1988. A meta-analysis of alcohol consumption in relation to risk of breast cancer. *J. Am. Med. Assoc.* 260:652–56

68. Lumley J. 1991. Preventing and managing prematurity. *Int. J. Technol. Assess. Health Care* 7:460–77

69. Lumsdon K. 1992. Beyond tech assessment: balancing needs, strategy. *Hospitals* Aug. 5, pp. 20–26

70. Deleted in proof

71. Mason J, Drummond M, Torrance G. 1993. Some guidelines on the use of cost effectivenes league tables. *Br. Med. J.* 306:570–72

72. McPhee SJ, Bird JA. 1990. Imple-

mentation of cancer prevention guidelines in clinical practice. *J. Gen. Intern. Med.* 5S:S116–22

73. Medical Alley. 1992. *Technology Task Force Report.* Medical Alley

74. Mills JL, Rhoads GG, Simpson, JL, Cunningham GC, Conley MR, et al. 1989. The absence of a relation between periconceptional use of vitamins and neural-tube defects. *N. England J. Med.* 321:430–35

75. Milunsky A, Jick H, Jick SS, Bruell CL, MacLaughlin DS, et al. 1989. Multivitamin/folic acid supplementation in early pregnancy reduces the prevalence of neural tube defects. *J. Am. Med. Assoc.* 262:2847–52

76. Mittman BS, Siu AL. 1992. Changing provider behavior: applying research on outcomes and effectiveness in health care. In *Improving Health Policy and Management: Nine Critical Research Issues for the 1990's,* ed. SM Shortell, UE Reinhardt, pp. 195–226. Ann Arbor: Health Admin. Press

77. Morbid. Mortal. Wkly. Rep. Use of folic acid for prevention of spina bifida and other neural tube defects—1983–1991. *Morbid. Mortal. Wkly. Rep.* 40:513–16

78. Moses LE, Brown BW Jr. 1984. Experiences with evaluating the safety and efficacy of medical technologies. *Annu. Rev. Public Health* 5:267–92

79. Mosteller F. 1991. The contribution of firms: A fresh movement in medicine. *Med. Care* 29:JS3–4

80. MRC Vitamin Res. Study Group. 1991. Prevention of neural tube defects: results of the medical research council vitamin study. *Lancet* 338: 131–37

81. Muldoon MF, Manuck SB, Matthews KA. 1990. Lowering cholesterol concentrations and mortality: a quantitative review of primary prevention trials. *Br. Med. J.* 301:309–14

82. Mulinare J, Cordero JF, Erickson JD, Berry RJ. 1988. Periconceptional use of multivitamins and the occurence of neural tube defects. *J. Am. Med. Assoc.* 260:3141–45

82a. Muller C, Mandelblatt J, Schechter CB, Power EJ, Duffy BM, et al. 1990. *Costs and Effectiveness of Cervical Cancer Screening in Elderly Women.* OTA-BP-H-65. Washington, DC: US Congr. Off. Technol. Assess.

83. Natl. Sci. Found., Off. Explor. Res. Problem Assess., Res. Appl. Dir. 1973. *Candidates and Priorities for Assessments, Vol. IV: An Approach to Priorities,* prepared by R Ayres, A Shapanka, K Humes, IRT-310-R, Washington, DC: US GPO

84. Neuhauser D. 1992. Progress in firms research. *Int. J. Technol. Assess. Health Care* 8:321–24

85. Oakley G Jr. 1993. Folic acid-preventable spina bifida and anencephaly. *J. Am. Med. Assoc.* 269:1292–93

86. Ontario Min. Health.1992. Cost Effectiveness of Drugs. Ont. Min. Health, Ont., Canada

87. Patrick DL, Deyo RA. 1989. Generic and disease-specific measures in assessing health status and quality of life. *Med. Care* 27:S217–32

88. Perry S. 1982. Special report: the brief life of the National Center for Health Care Technology. *N. England J. Med.* 307:1095

89. Pilote L, Thomas RJ, Dennis C, Goins P, et al. 1992. Return to work after uncomplicated myocardial infarction: a trial of practice guidelines in the community. *Ann. Int. Med.* 117:383–89

90. Polednak AP. 1993. Geographic variation in the treatment of prostate cancer in Connecticut. *Int. J. Technol. Assess. Health Care* 9:304–10

91. Popkin J & Co. 1993. *Policy Brief: The Comparison of Medical Equipment Price Trends to Overall Inflation.* Health Care Technol. Inst., Alexandria, VA

92. Popkin J & Co. 1993. *Policy Brief: The Role of Medical Equipment and Supplies in the Prices of Inputs and Outputs of Medical Care.* Health Care Technol. Inst., Alexandria, VA

93. Power EJ. 1987. The adoption and use of extracorporeal shock wave lithotripsy by hospitals in the United States. *Int. J. Technol. Assess. Health Care* 3:397–404

94. Roos LL, Roos NP. 1983. Assessing existing technologies: The Manitoba Study of Common Surgical Procedures. *Med. Care* 21:454–62

95. Roos NP. 1984. Hysterectomy: variations in rates across small areas and across physicians' practices. *Am. J. Public Health* 74:327–35

96. Russell LB. 1986. *Is Prevention Better Than Cure?* Washington, DC: Brookings Inst.

97. Russell LB, Sisk JE. 1988. Medical technology in the United States. *Int. J. Technol. Assess. Health Care* 4:269–86

98. Sacks HS, Berrier J, Reitman D, Ancona-Berk VA, Chalmers TC. 1987. Meta-analyses of randomized controlled trials. *N. England J. Med.* 316:450–55

99. Sazawal S, Black R. 1992. Meta-anal-

ysis of intervention trials on case-management of pneumonia in community settings. *Lancet* 340:528–33

100. Soumerai SB, Avorn J. 1990. Principles of educational outreach ('academic detailing') to improve clinical decision making. *J. Am. Med. Assoc.* 263:549–56

101. Soumerai SB, Salem-Schatz S, Avorn J, Casteris CS, Popovsky MA. 1993. A controlled trial of educational outreach to improve blood transfusion practice. *J. Am. Med. Assoc.* 270:961–66

102. South. Med. J. 1981. NIH Consensus Development Panel summary—cervical cancer screening: the Pap smear. *South. Med. J.* 74:87–89

103. Strosberg MA, Wiener JM, Baker R, Fein IA. 1992. *Rationing America's Medical Care: The Oregon Plan and Beyond.* Washington, DC: Brookings Inst.

104. Stuart ME, Handley MA, Thompson RS, Conger M, Timlin D. 1993. Clinical practice and new technology: prostate-specific antigen (PSA). *HMO Pract.* 6:5–11

105. Temple R. 1990. Problems in the uses of large data sets to assess effectiveness. *Int. J. Technol. Assess. Health Care* 6:211–19

106. Thacker S. 1988. Meta-analysis: a quantitative approach to research integration. *J. Am. Med. Assoc.* 259:1685–89

107. Torrance GW. 1986. Measurement of health state utilities for economic appraisal: a review. *J. Health Econ.* 5:1–30

108. United Hospital Fund. 1992. *The Tuberculosis Revival: Individual Rights and Societal Obligations in a Time of AIDS.* New York: United Hosp. Fund

109. US Congr., Gen. Account. Off. 1991. *Off-Label Drugs: Initial Results of a National Survey.* GAO/PEMD-91–12BR. Washington, DC: US GPO

110. US Congr., House Represent., Comm. Sci. Astronaut. 1973. *Off. Technol. Assess: Background and Status,* prepared Congr. Res. Serv., Comm. Print No. 99–672 O. Washington, DC: US GPO

111. US Congr. Off. Technol. Assess. 1976. *Development of Medical Technology: Opportunities for Assessment.* Washington, DC: US GPO

112. US Congr. Off. Technol. Assess. 1978. *Assessing the Efficacy and Safety of Medical Technologies.* 052–003–00593–0. Washington, DC: US GPO

113. US Congr. Off. Technol. Assess. 1979.

A Review of Selected Vaccine and Immunization Policies: Based on Case Studies of Pneumoccocal Vaccine. 052–003–00701–1. Washington, DC: US GPO

114. US Congr. Off. Technol. Assess. 1980. *The Implications of Cost-effectiveness Analysis of Medical Technology.* 052–003–00765–7. Washington, DC: US GPO

115. US Congr. Off. Technol. Assess. 1981. *Effectiveness of Influenza Vaccination.* Washington, DC: US GPO

116. US Congr. Off. Technol. Assess. 1982. *Strategies for Medical Technology Assessment.* Washington, DC: US GPO

117. US Congr. Off. Technol. Assess. 1983. *The Impact of Randomized Clinical Trials on Health Policy and Medical Practice.* Washington, DC: US GPO

118. US Congr. Off. Technol. Assess. 1984. *Update of Federal Activities Regarding the Use of Pneumoccocal Vaccine: A Technical Memorandum.* 84–601069. Washington, DC: US GPO

119. US Congr. Off. Technol. Assess. 1986. *Abstracts of Case Studies in the Health Technology Series.* OTA-P-2225(Revised). Washington, DC: US GPO

120. US Congr. Off. Technol. Assess. 1987. *Breast Cancer Screening for Medicare Beneficiaries: Effectiveness, Costs to Medicare and Medical Resources Resources Required.* Washington, DC: US GPO

121. US Congr. Off. Technol. Assess. 1989. *The Use of Preventive Services By the Elderly.* Washington, DC: US GPO

122. US Congr. Off. Technol. Assess. 1989. *Costs and Effectiveness of Cholesterol Screening in the Elderly.* 052–003–01151–4. Washington, DC: US GPO

123. Deleted in proof

124. US Congr. Off. Technol. Assess. 1992. *Difficult-to-Reuse Needles for the Prevention of HIV Infection Among Injecting Drug Users.* OTA-BP-H-103. Washington, DC: US GPO

125. US Congr. Off. Technol. Assess. 1992. *Evaluation of the Oregon Medicaid Proposal.* OTA-H-531. Washington, DC: US GPO

125a. US Dep. Health Hum. Serv., Health Care Finan. Admin. 1993. *Program Memorandum to Carriers* (July 1993)

126. US Dep. Health Hum. Serv., Natl. Inst. Health, Natl. Heart, Lung, Blood Inst., Natl. Cholesterol Program, Adult Treatment Panel. 1988. Report of the National Cholesterol Education Program Expert Panel on Detection, Evaluation, and Treatment of High Blood

Cholesterol in Adults. *Arch. Intern. Med.* 148:36–39

127. US Dep. Health Hum. Serv., Natl. Inst. Health, Off. Med. Appl. Res. 1991. *Health care delivery research using hospital firms, Workshop Summary, April 30–May 1, 1990.* Bethesda,Md: USPHS, NIH, OMAR

128. US Exec. Off. President, Off. Manage. Budget. 1991. *Budget of the US Government.* 041–001–00357–6. Washington, DC: US GPO

129. US Dep. Health Hum. Serv., Prevent. Serv. Task Force. 1989. *Guide to Clinical Preventive Services.* Baltimore, MD: William & Wilkins

130. US Dep. Health Hum. Serv., Public Health Serv. Agency Health Care Policy Res. 1992. *AHCPR-Commissioned Clinical Practice Guidelines.* Rockville, MD

131. US Dep. Health Hum. Serv., Public Health Serv., Agency Health Care Policy Res. 1993. *Fiscal Year 1994, Vol. 9: Justification of Estimates for Appropriations Committees.* US Dep. Health Hum. Serv., Washington, DC

132. Warner KE, Luce BR. 1982. *Cost-Benefit and Cost-Effectiveness Analysis in Health Care: Principles, Practice, and Potential.* Ann Arbor: Univ. Michigan Press

133. Washington Report. 1988. Organizations speak out on Pap smear frequency. *Washington Rep.* 6:1

134. Weinstein MC. 1990. Principals of cost-effective resource allocation in health care organizations. *Int. J. Technol. Assess. Health Care* 6:93–103

135. Deleted in proof

136. Wennberg JE, Gittlesohn A. 1982. Variations in medical care among small areas. *Sci. Am.* 246:120–26, 129, 132, 134

137. Werler M, Shapiro S, Mitchell A. 1993. Periconceptional folic acid exposure and risk of occurent neural tube defects. *J. Am. Med. Assoc.* 269:1257–61

138. Wilson PW, Christiansen JC, Anderson KM, Kannel WB. 1989. Impact of national guidelines for cholesterol risk factor screening: the Framingham Offspring Study. *J. Am. Med. Assoc.* 262:41–44

139. Winslow CM, Kosecoff JB, Chassin MR, Kanouse DE, Brook RH. 1988. The appropriateness of performing coronary artery bypass surgery. *J. Am. Med. Assoc.* 260:505–9

140. Winslow CM, Solomon DH, Chassin MR, Kosecoff J, Merrick NJ, Brook RH. 1988. The appropriateness of carotid endarterectomy. *N. England J. Med.* 318:721–27

141. Winslow R. 1993. Prostate surgery is increasing sharply even though benefits are questioned. *Wall St. J.* May 26

142. Woolf SH. 1990. Practice guidelines: a new reality in medicine. I. Recent developments. *Arch. Intern. Med.* 150: 1811–18

143. Yusuf S, Collins R, Peto R. 1984. Why do we need some large, simple, randomized trials? *Stat. Med.* 3:409–20

SUBJECT INDEX

CUMULATIVE INDEXES

CONTRIBUTING AUTHORS, VOLUMES, 6-15

591

CHAPTER TITLES, VOLUMES 6–15

Symposium on Nutrition

Symposium on Selected Clinical Syndromes Associated with Aging

PREFATORY CHAPTER